THE
EUROPEANS
IN AUSTRALIA

A HISTORY

volume one

The Beginning

ALAN ATKINSON

Melbourne

OXFORD UNIVERSITY PRESS

Oxford   Auckland   New York

For my Father, who died in 1991.
A mere paper return for many gifts in deed.

OXFORD UNIVERSITY PRESS AUSTRALIA
Oxford New York
Athens Auckland Bangkok Bogota Bombay
Buenos Aires Calcutta Cape Town Dar es Salaam
Delhi Florence Hong Kong Istanbul Karachi
Kuala Lumpur Madras Madrid Melbourne
Mexico City Nairobi Paris Port Moresby
Singapore Taipei Tokyo Toronto Warsaw
and associated companies in
Berlin Ibadan

OXFORD is a trade mark of Oxford University Press

National Library of Australia
Cataloguing-in-Publication data:

Atkinson, Alan Thomas.
The Europeans in Australia: a history.
Bibliography.
Includes index.
ISBN 0 19 550708 8 (v. 1).
1. Australia – History. I. Title.
994

Edited by Janet Mackenzie
Indexed by the author
Text design by Heather Jones
Cover design by Anitra Blackford
Typeset by Superskill Graphics Pte Ltd
Printed through Bookpac Production Services, Singapore.
Published by Oxford University Press
253 Normanby Road, South Melbourne, Australia

Contents

Illustrations

Maps

Plates

Acknowledgments

Except for some early parts of Chapter 1, this volume was written between January 1993 and April 1996. Most of Part 1 was completed during study leave in Oxford – that is, by April 1993 – and the remainder in Armidale, New South Wales. However, the research goes back much further and some of the debts which I have thus incurred are very old.

Much of the English material was collected during the northern winter of 1973–74. For access to private papers during that period I am grateful to Lady Mairi Bury (Castlereagh Papers, Mountstewart, Co. Down), the late Sir John Carew Pole (Pole Carew Papers, Cornwall Record Office), Mrs H. Coatalen (Hook Papers, Bucklebury, Berkshire), the tenth Duke of Northumberland (Percy Family Letters and Papers, Alnwick Castle), and Mr C. E. Wrangham (Wilberforce Papers, Rosemary House, Catterick, Yorkshire). Mr Roland Thorne, of the History of Parliament Trust, gave me detailed help. I am grateful also to the staff of the Natural History Museum, London (then the British Museum [Natural History]), (Sir Joseph Banks Papers); Bedfordshire Record Office (Whitbread Papers); the British Library of Political and Economic Science (Horner Collection); Buckinghamshire Record Office (Hobart Papers); Dr Williams's Library, London (Robert Millar Papers); Essex Record Office (Sperling Correspondence); the India Office; the Linnaean Society; the Manx Museum (Atholl Papers and Heywood Family Papers); the National Library of Scotland (Sir Robert Liston Papers and Minto Papers); Manchester College, Oxford (Shepherd and Ridyard Papers); the Public Record Office of Northern Ireland (Huey Journal and help with the Castlereagh Papers); the Scottish Record Office (Melville Castle Muniments and Seafield Muniments); and University College Library, London (Bentham Papers).

During three subsequent visits to Britain, in 1980, 1988 and 1992–93, I saw the papers of Cox and Kings, army agents, at Lloyds Bank, Pall Mall, the Granville Sharpe Papers at Gloucestershire Record Office and a number of eighteenth-century publications at the Cambridge University Library and at the Guildhall Library, London. Over the entire period of research I have accumulated material too diverse to list, and debts of kindness, at the Bodleian Library, Oxford (especially Rhodes House); the British Library (formerly the British Museum); the National Register of Archives in London and its Scottish equivalent in Edinburgh; and (most of all) the Public Record Office, both at Kew and Chancery Lane. My visit in 1980 was funded by a research fellowship from the Research School of Social Sciences at the Australian National University and that of 1988 by a visiting fellowship at Clare Hall, Cambridge, by the Henry Charles Chapman Visiting Fellowship at the Institute of Commonwealth Studies, University of London, and by a grant from the Australian War Memorial.

Similar debts date from visits to the United States in 1989 and 1991, the first supported partly by the Australian Department of Foreign Affairs and Trade and by the Institute of Early American History and Culture, and the second by the Australian-American Educational Foundation (as a Fulbright Short-Term Scholar). I am grateful to staff at the Huntington Library, Los Angeles; the Institute of Early American History and Culture, Williamsburg; the State Library, Richmond, Virginia; the Maryland Hall of Records, Annapolis; the Maryland Historical Society, Baltimore; and the William Clements Library, University of Michigan.

I owe a great deal indeed for kindness during the second American trip to Lois Green Carr and Jack Ladd Carr, in Annapolis, to my Annapolis landlady, Mrs Lillian Fisher, and to Roger Thompson, Pamela Ross and John C. Dann at Ann Arbor. The six months in Oxford, 1992–93, when I began writing in earnest, were made both more pleasant and more useful by Joanna Innes at Somerville College and Paul Langford at Lincoln.

My Australian debts have been more miscellaneous, large and continuous. Much has been done for me over many years by staff at the Mitchell Library and the State Archives in Sydney and at the Dixson Library, University of New England. Substantial annual grants for research have come from my university. My History colleagues at Armidale and, in earlier years, at the Australian National University and the University of Western Australia, have been part of the long preparation for this book. The ideas which have come up in discussions with students in my undergraduate course at the University of New England, 'Botany Bay' (1987–92), helped in the same way, more perhaps than they thought at the time. Several recent research students – Jan Barkley, Dan Byrnes, Philip Gregory, Marie McInnes, Kate Thomas, Gloria Thompson and Shirley Tuff – have together done a great deal in sharpening my understanding of the very first years of European stettlement in Australia.

The entire text was read in draft by Marian Quartly and Miriam Dixson and I am extremely grateful to them for the trouble they have taken with it, and for saving me from errors and ineptitudes. Chris Bayly, Jenny Bridge, Rhys Isaac, Stuart Macintyre and Allan Martin read large parts, and I am likewise grateful to them for the effort involved. I have not employed a research assistant except for odd jobs, but I greatly appreciate the work of those who have helped along the way, especially Lisa Coppe, Gillian Hughes, Perry McIntyre and Trin Truscett. Bob Broughton, archivist at the University of Tasmania, was extremely helpful in supplying a copy of the James Belbin diary, and Marty Barringer, of the Lauinger Library, Georgetown University, Washington, DC, went far beyond the call of duty in securing the picture of the hanging of the pirate, Stede Bonnet, which appears in Chapter 2. Mrs Barbara Brockbank and Mrs Colleen Read gave me useful material relating to their respective ancestors, Richard Atkins and Fane Edge, which I would not have found otherwise, and Dr Geoffrey Buckwell and Mr Terry Wills Cook did the same with the Wills family. I am more grateful than I can say to Mollie Gillen, who has given me access to the great collection of material on late-eighteenth-century convict transportation to Australia which she has gathered over many years. Her influence on the writing has been considerable.

Peter Rose, at Oxford University Press, has been patient and helpful over a long period, and I am grateful also to my editor, Janet Mackenzie, and to my cartographer at the University of New England, Rudi Boskovic. For permission to use copyright material I am indebted to Penguin Australia (the Aboriginal narratives which introduce each of the three parts of the volume) and to Random House UK Limited (the lines from Derek Walcott's poem, 'The Sea is History', on page 197).

A history such as this – a social history which frequently focuses on the lives of obscure individuals – is necessarily built on a broad foundation: not only on the interpretative ideas, written and unwritten, of other scholars but also on the compilation and publication of documents and of mere historical detail from the period, now a major industry in Australia and, for many of those who do it, a labour of love. The book could not have been written without my having to hand, for instance, Carol Baxter's *Musters and Lists, New South Wales and Norfolk Island* (1988) and *Musters of New South Wales and Norfolk Island, 1805–1806* (1989); R. J. Ryan's *Land Grants, 1788–1809* (1981), and the various journals (of Ralph Clark, Arthur Bowes Smyth and Philip Gidley King) which R. J. Ryan has edited with Paul Fidlon. Biographical dictionaries have been essential in the same way, especially Mollie Gillen's path-breaking work, *The Founders of Australia: A Biographical Dictionary of the First Fleet* (1989), and its successor, Michael Flynn's biographical dictionary of the Second Fleet (1993).

Because of Sydney's importance for so much of my writing, I have relied for years, and in many ways, on Sydney friends and relations: Barbara Austin, who died in 1990 and who belonged profoundly to Sydney, and Phyl and Alan Coates most of all. At the centre of what I say in this book (and elsewhere) is the idea of inheritance, the nexus of generations. Its writing has been overshadowed in a pervasive way by the deaths of both my parents and so by the hard and homely facts of inheritance, material and moral. The moral ideas which are central to the following chapters appear there deliberately as items of inheritance, my own inheritance and that of the first Europeans in Australia being, I am afraid, much intermingled. The work therefore owes a vast deal to the good and exacting lives, and something even to the deaths, of both my father and my mother.

Finally, the argument (especially in the later chapters) is deeply coloured with the influence of my wife, Catherine Pound, who has led me to think more carefully about the connection between history and literature and about the power of imagination among both men and women during the years around 1800. I am grateful to her for that, and for much more.

Foreword

I

When Manning Clark set out forty years ago to write his *History of Australia*, he said that it was to be about the coming of civilisation to Australia. The story which I want to tell in this and the two volumes which, I hope, will follow might be described in much the same terms. Needless to say, it is not the same story, nor is it likely to reach the same pitch of greatness. This is a history of common imagination in Australia, and by 'common' I mean both ordinary and shared. It is an attempt to describe the day-to-day intellectual notions associated with life as an Australian among Australians, one of the conquerors of a new world, the denizen of a certain space, a subject and a social being. It is about the tension and marriage between government and people – individual people and numbers of people together – a relationship which in this country has been highly distinctive from the very first weeks of European settlement in 1788.

This story is about Europeans in Australia. I have chosen the word 'Europeans', not because I want to add anything very significant to the growing literature which concentrates on the diversity of white immigration, apart from the British, which shows what has been done by Greeks in Australia, Germans in Australia, Croatians in Australia, and so forth. My concern is mainly with the British and Irish and their descendants in this country, that combination of national cultures which for many generations made up the vast majority of Australian Europeans. The English play a particularly important part. I use the word 'Europeans' because 'British' and 'English' are both words which, in the Australian context, have too many associations with authority alone, with invasion and the machinery of power, and while I am greatly concerned with these things they are not the beginning and end of the story. 'Europeans' seems to catch something of the deep cultural foundation on which white settlement was built. Its use also points the reader to the epoch with which I am most concerned, the two centuries which fill the interval between the purely Aboriginal past, before 1788, and the future as we understand it in the 1990s, a period of radical adjustments with Asia, with Australians from Asia, and with the rest of the world. This history is an attempt to show what the Europeans did with Australia when they had the field more or less to themselves, and in particular during the first four or five generations, up to the period of the Great War, 1914–18.

My arguments are shaped by a belief that, from the very beginning, Australian political culture (by which I mean methods of thinking about self and authority at all levels) was remarkably original, especially when we take into account the remoteness and smallness of early European settlement. To some extent the first colonisers did what British colonisers had done in other parts of the world during the previous two hundred years. But white settlement began here during the 1780s, a decade of extraordinary creativity, the climax of the European Enlightenment. The purpose of settlement – the disposal of criminals – might seem uninspiring. But the very fact that this was to be a community of convicts and ex-convicts raised, almost by accident, profound questions about the common rights of the subject, the responsibilities of power and the possibility of imaginative attachment to a land of exile.

During the eighteenth century, government in Britain had become much more ambitious and bureaucratised, much more the product of a literate and polite culture and much more dependent on extensive paperwork, than any government had ever been before. In New South Wales this government confronted at short range a people, the convicts, who were, in general, no more than semi-literate and much less than semi-polite. This history is about voices and language. The convicts and the class from which they came in Britain took their ideas about society and government from a culture shaped by the living voice, and in England and its colonies the living voice was privileged far beyond any other country in the world. The idea of freedom of speech had very deep roots in English life. However, government in that period, and especially the Enlightenment approach to government which Arthur Phillip, the first Governor, brought with him, placed a peculiar emphasis, not only on the new duties of authority, but on the silence of the people. Much of what I want to say, especially in the present volume, is an account of negotiations between different forms of conversation: the weighty, broad and permanent conversations of pen and paper, which men like Phillip were so good at and which shaped the understanding also of educated women, and (on the other hand) the narrow and ephemeral conversations, the living, burning, sharp-edged exchanges of individuals face to face.

This may sound like an account of insubstantial things. My argument is inspired by a belief that in any civilisation words are fundamental to everything else. William Paley, the eighteenth-century philosopher, thought in much the same way. 'Men act from expectation', he said, and 'expectation is, in most cases, determined by the assurances and engagements we receive from others'. Of course, there must be confidence in such assurances and engagements. The words we exchange must be a reliable currency, and the forms of exchange must be shaped by common understanding.

> I am now writing at my ease [said Paley], not doubting (or rather never distrusting, and therefore never thinking about it) but that the butcher will send in the joint of meat, which I ordered; that his servant will bring it; that my cook will dress it; that my footman will serve it up; and that I shall find it upon the table at one o'clock.

And yet, he went on, 'I have nothing for all this, but the promise of the butcher, and the implied promise of his servant and mine. And the same holds of the most important, as well as the most familiar occurrences of social life.'[1] These promises were the work of language, the machinery at the bottom of everything.

This book can also be said to be about promises. It looks especially at the difference between promises which are merely spoken, or implicit in speech, and those which are written down. I dwell, for instance, on the statement of William Bligh, made while he was Governor of New South Wales (1806–08), with reference to leases certified on paper within the town of Sydney: 'his verbal permission to occupy land', he said, 'was better than a lease, for that [a lease] he could take away'.[2]

The men and women of the Enlightenment were puzzled and delighted by language, and especially by the difference between language which springs from the impulse of the moment and that which is endowed with authority beyond time. The gentlemen of the First Fleet took enormous trouble to write down the hitherto unwritten language of the Aborigines, words which seemed at first like unencoded deeds and which thus presented a magnificent challenge, similar to the first mapping of the continent. The reason for their curiosity was the fiery and cryptic relationship which seemed to exist between these two kinds of communication. Oratory was a favourite art, in which artifice was heightened by passion, and vice versa. Similarly, authors who could write for the wide world just as if they were dealing informally with a few friends, from the new novelists like Fielding to revolutionaries like Thomas Paine, were a sensational success. At the very end of the century, the young Wordsworth boasted of his attempts to avoid the normal formalities of written verse and to use the crude but powerful forms of common language, including repetition and tautology.[3] In such ways language became part of the project of revolution, the radical renewal of order. For order of some kind, old or new, could not be avoided. The liberty of sending thoughts abroad must be sweetened by restraint, and vividness conveyed by the discipline of pen and ink. Wordsworth also occasionally bound himself to that rigorous art-form, the sonnet, so as to make music with his linguistic chains:

> In truth the prison, unto which we doom
> Ourselves, no prison is: and hence for me,
> In sundry moods, 'twas pastime to be bound
> Within the Sonnet's scanty plot of ground.[4]

One of the larger questions for this book is whether Australia represented, for its first Europeans, liberty or restraint. As for Wordsworth, the answer was: both at once.

II

European settlement in Australia was the last great initiative of what is called the first British empire, an empire previously restricted to the Atlantic Ocean and to India. Certainly New South Wales can be understood as the beginning of a remarkable project in penology, which ended only with the cessation of convict transportation to Western Australia in 1868. That is an important part of my argument. But it can also be seen as one of a series of experiments in the founding of new and remote communities, a series beginning with Virginia (if we count only successful cases) and including a number of eighteenth-century efforts – Georgia, Nova Scotia, the Floridas, Upper Canada, Sierra Leone – as well as New South Wales. Even more than these transatlantic projects, the establishment of British power in India, also during the eighteenth century, focused British minds on new problems of distance, on the long drawn-out movement of people and orders. The transportation of troops to India was used as a model for the First Fleet to Botany Bay.

Thomas Jefferson, at the time of the American Revolution, declared that the American colonies had their origin in independence. He argued mainly from the fact that most of the original colonists had been voluntary emigrants who had cut themselves off from Britain in order to make new communities on the other side of the ocean. It followed that, by attempting to bring them to heel, the British government was corrupting the essence of an ancient relationship.[5] Assertions of independence have often been backed up by such stories. The sixteenth-century independence of the Church of England from the Church of Rome was partly justified by the notion that English Christianity did not spring from any pope. I write in the 1990s, when Australia's residual links with Britain are an important public issue, and when it is particularly useful to ask exactly how much Australian civilisation owes to what was once called 'the mother country'. For those who want to measure the extent and progress of Australian independence, there are two alternative avenues to follow.

In the first place, it is possible to tell the story of Australia as a march towards the light, as a gradual emancipation from British power, whether constitutional, economic, cultural or spiritual. The British, even the European, connection thus appears as a form of bondage, the antithesis of current or future freedom. There is truth in this perspective, partly, but only partly, because many leading actors in the Australian story (including prime ministers) have used it themselves to script events. But it is also possible to argue, somewhat as Jefferson did in America, that there has been independence of a kind – or of various kinds – in Australia since European settlement began. This makes sense particularly if we think of settlement in the way I have outlined above, as part of the pattern which Jefferson himself was concerned with; in other words, as integral to old methods of empire, evident throughout the Atlantic during the seventeenth and eighteenth centuries. The story of the Europeans in Australia, during the first two hundred years, must remain partly a story of expanding independence, but the historian has to insist that elements of independence have been here from the beginning, and the deeper theme is to be found in the redefinition of independence from generation to generation.

There are other implications. A history of Australia whose leading theme is the story of emancipation from authority almost inevitably makes authority into a black thread in a relatively bright tapestry. The deliberate and far-sighted use of power becomes something foreign to the Australian experience, exercised by Australians themselves mostly as agents and often by default. Indeed, Australians can appear so entirely anti-authoritarian as to be incapable of thinking about the creative use of power, except in a superficial and instrumental way. This is the central problem of late twentieth-century Australian republicanism. 'Australia was born in chains,' so says a distinguished advocate of the republic, 'and is not yet fully free.'[6] We are then, at bottom, not makers of authority but breakers of chains. A history of Australia which looks for evidence of independence from the beginning must take a different view. Central to what I say here is the idea that the weight of empire in European Australia has always been peculiarly abstract, its local agents were very powerful, but its centre was so remote as to be almost metaphysical. This explains why the resentment of empire, even an empire as great as the British, has always been so slight on this continent. But I also want to argue that the use of power in Australia itself has in fact been complex and spacious.

III

I have said that this history has a lot to say about generations of British settlement before 1788. I offer such detail as something relatively new in writing about the Australian past. For a long time the understanding of Australian history was shaped by a lack of detailed interest in the eighteenth century. In their biography of Governor Phillip, first published in 1938, Marjorie Barnard and Flora Eldershaw wrote of the eighteenth century as 'a trough between two crests'. The foregoing age could boast, they said, 'the fruits of Elizabethan adventure, spiritual and material, . . . the ferment of the Puritan Revolution and a new conception of liberty'. And, on the near side, the nineteenth century was a time of 'energy and expansion, of new philosophies and new markets, of questioning and seeking and doing'. Nothing, however, happened in the eighteenth century: it was 'a static time'.[7] This was the common view even for some time after the 1930s, in Britain as well as in Australia. Our understanding of the eighteenth century followed that of our predecessors in the nineteenth, who were naturally pleased with their own achievements and who were inclined to think with contempt about the *ancien régime*, the age which had gone before.

Since World War II, in Britain and the United States and more recently in Australia, a better knowledge of the eighteenth century has emerged. A century whose climax was marked by great political revolutions in North America and France, and by vast and unprecedented demographic and industrial change, especially in Britain, was not 'a static time'. The work of E. P. Thompson and his followers in the 1960s and 1970s, and the writing of the current generation of historians, have opened our eyes to the vigour and complexity of eighteenth-century life. It is no longer good enough to say, as Keith Hancock said in 1930, that 'The whole of Australian history lies within the period which succeeded the French Revolution and the Industrial Revolution.'[8] Even leaving aside the question of Aboriginal history, the history of Europeans in Australia begins much earlier than that. It lies deep in the rich eighteenth century.

The late twentieth century has certain things in common with the eighteenth. The idea of 'progress' is problematic now as it was then. The three-way relationship of ethnicity, politics and social feeling troubles us as much as it troubled men and women two hundred years ago, though ethnicity now is less complicated by questions of rank. Theirs was an age – especially the period from the 1760s to the 1780s – which ended in cataclysmic revolution, affecting everything from forms of government to sense of self. The same could be said of ours, from the 1960s to the 1980s. Thanks to recent revolutions we are now said to be passing beyond the 'modern' era which was their creation.

Hancock also thought that the period of white settlement in Australia had been 'a period filled with a deafening clamour for rights and a few shrill protests about duties'.[9] Like other historians of his generation, he was listening mainly to public voices. He was preoccupied with rights and duties of the more newsworthy kind, those likely to be discussed in official correspondence, parliamentary speeches, newspapers and public meetings. Today Australian historians are equipped to go beyond even their greatest predecessors, such as Hancock, and to listen to other voices. This book aims to show that rights and duties – Paley's promises – were many-layered, multifarious and pervasive. Their birth and death are to be traced within living conversation, inarticulate and unselfconscious talk, and within peculiar communities such as that which gathered about the shores of Port Jackson, on Norfolk Island and Van Diemen's Land from 1788. In the sources used by Hancock and his contemporaries, rights were divorced from duties and both tended to be airy and abstract. Today we, like Paley, tend to see rights and duties as two sides of a single equation, embedded within conversation and pungent with circumstance.

The historian who makes use of ephemeral and private voices, especially those which lived two hundred years ago, has to resurrect the notion of the soul. The word 'soul' has been drained of its original meaning through intervening generations, but I have used it in crucial parts of the argument which follows, and have also taken account of contemporary ideas of the sacred, sacredness being married here to words in the mouth more than to writing. For similar reasons I sometimes use the word 'Christendom'. To a few readers it may seem out of place for the period, but it reflects a set of ideas which were still important, particularly among the inarticulate: a parcel of bigotry, a parcel of faith. I am interested not only in the still, small voice of the God of Christendom but in other still, small voices too: those with which intimate mysteries of place and person might be drawn together.

IV

In setting out my argument in this book, I take whatever position I favour without making explicit references to other writers (except, of course, in the notes). Also, some of my own arguments are new and I make no effort to distinguish these from the rest. They will be obvious to many readers, but I use what remains of this Foreword to summarise where I stand from a historiographical point of view.

Historians disagree as to why, in 1786, the British government chose New South Wales as a site for convict settlement. The names of Dallas, Blainey and Frost are associated with the post-World War II argument which says that there were more profound motives than the need to dispose of convicts.[10] I take the opposite and traditional point of view, restated in recent publications by such authors as Gillen and Mackay.[11] However, I have provided that approach with a new gloss by moving the figure of Thomas Townshend, Lord Sydney, Secretary of State at the Home Office, into the centre of the picture. Sydney's name, indeed, runs through the whole volume. The traditional view has sometimes included the idea that the government wanted to 'dump' convicts condemned to transportation. While I believe that the motivation did indeed centre on the need to dispose of convicts, I here set out a more sophisticated agenda than the word 'dump' suggests. (See Chapters 3, 4 and 10.)

This involves distinguishing the motives for foundation of settlement at Port Jackson from the motives for the foundation of settlement in Van Diemen's Land. There is no explicit debate among historians on the second issue. The most recent authority, Lloyd Robson, seems to echo part at least of the classic statement by John West.[12] Robson's analysis is less clear and more sweeping than West's, but he agrees with West in suggesting that Van Diemen's Land was designed from the beginning to take recalcitrant convicts from New South Wales. I have not been able to find any evidence, to support this idea, and I have followed Margaret Steven in arguing instead for an economic motive, as Blainey and Frost would like to do for Port Jackson.[13] (See Chapter 10.)

I have laid a good deal of stress on the work of the first governor, Arthur Phillip. I have followed up some of my own earlier publications by suggesting that Phillip had priorities of his own, sometimes at odds with those of

Whitehall, especially in his management of the convicts, and in pointing to the importance (from an intellectual point of view) of Major Ross as an alternative focus of ideas for the direction of settlement.[14] Partly by comparison with Ross's approach, I aim to show that Phillip's greatness lay not only in his courage and his powers of leadership but also in his intellectual authority. Conclusions which I have reached elsewhere are central as well to my treatment of the legal status of the convicts, an issue also dealt with in the writings of John Hirst and David Neal.[15]

Questions of gender underlie much of the argument because they affect the relationship of the written with the spoken voice, but in Chapter 7 I have tried to deal in detail with the place which I understand women to have occupied, at least in principle, within the original masculine structure of authority. I have used the insights of Marian Quartly in outlining the gendered visions of society demonstrated by senior officials and officers, and I have tried to argue as well that the presence of women, and their perceived importance as subjects of government, was central to the way authority unfolded.[16] This point recurs in later chapters so as to emerge at the end as one of the central conclusions of the volume. The humane sensibility of the time (sometimes screwed up to a pitch of self-consciousness) had significant results. It meant, among other things, that the treatment of women by men in power was considered a hallmark of good government. Women's reaction was a necessary part of the project, and on the whole they reacted as they were meant to do in European Australia. The process of subjection to such power, and the difficulties and advantages of being subject, are two of my main concerns. I hope this book says something useful about the subjectivity of subjects.

The attitudes which men adopted, as subjects, towards humane authoritarianism are also important. In Chapter 6 I show how the settlement was a product of maritime life and therefore shaped very much by the sensibilities of seamen. This is a new idea, inspired partly by the work of the American maritime historian, Marcus Rediker, and partly by Mollie Gillen's discovery, in her great work, *The Founders of Australia*, that former seamen made up a very large minority of the first male convicts.[17] Most of Chapter 12 explores the notion of brotherhood among Freemasons, the Irish and admirers of the British constitution, and its links with the ideal of fraternity which was part of the agenda of the French Revolution. Here I go further than most authorities have been prepared to do, except for Miriam Dixson. I have drawn a good deal on Dixson's discussion of the Irish in Australia, and on her broader understanding of gender relations.[18]

I have expanded the received understanding of relations between Black and White in the first years, particularly in Chapers 8 and 9. I have followed Ann McGrath in focusing on the importance of gender in shaping racial understanding, and I have tried to apply some of the insights of Marshall Sahlins and Greg Dening, as presented in their work on the eighteenth-century Pacific, in outlining the spirit of mutuality and reciprocity which characterised early dealings between Aborigines and Europeans. Tony Swain's work has powerfully shaped my understanding of the transitional (rather than traditional) aspects of Aboriginal spirituality.[19] Bennelong and Phillip are the central figures here, and I have ventured further than previous historians have done in describing the significance of Phillip's Government House for Bennelong and for those Aborigines who fell in with his view of the invaders.

In Chapter 9 I have explored the spiritual attitude of Europeans themselves in Australia and suggested ways in which it might have been affected by their removal to the wrong side of the globe. Here some of the detail overlaps a little with the work of Philip Gregory, a recent doctoral student at the University of New England, from which I have learnt a great deal.[20]

I have agreed with D. R. Hainsworth and Brian Fletcher on the significance of the officers of the New South Wales Corps, or rather on the way in which their significance dwindled after their very first years in the colony. I have therefore said little about the officers as monopolists and I have tried to build on the argument, explicit in Hainsworth's work and a little less obvious in Fletcher's, that leading ex-convicts were central to the management of the economy from an early stage. I put their rise to power at the mid-1790s. This is an insight which has the potential, long unrealised, to provide altogether a new understanding of the period, especially when it is used in coordination with the 'new social history' approach of writers such as Paula Byrne.[21] I have done what I can with it in that respect, and it is in a sense fundamental to the whole volume in so far as ex-convicts, men and women with small capital, are seen making a distinctive impact on ideas about public faith and legal process.[22]

This approach has led me to my own interpretation of the deposition of Governor Bligh, in January 1808 (Chapters 13 and 14). I say very little about the usual explanation, Bligh's prohibition of the barter of spirits and his attempts to suppress trading monopolies. These were suggested as causes at the time, though few observers of the event made as much of them as historians have done. For instance, one of the greatest of Bligh scholars, George Mackaness, said in 1931, 'it is now quite certain that the primary cause of the great insurrectionary conflagration . . . was Bligh's determination to suppress the rum trade and to settle the currency question'. He offers no discussion as to what 'primary' might mean, he does not show what real impact these policies had and he does not explain why they figure so little in the long inquiry which followed the rebellion, George Johnston's court martial.[23] Few have thought to question the orthodoxy thus established, although Ross Fitzgerald and Mark Hearn have recently said, as I do, that in fact it was not rum which triggered the so-called Rum Rebellion. I argue around the issue of legitimacy and its connection with behaviour. I stress the way in which Bligh undermined his own legitimacy (and even Mackaness says that in his regard for truth and in making promises the Governor was 'certainly not over-burdened with moral scruples').[24] I also deal, in Chapter 13, with Bligh's impact on popular feeling within Sydney, the opinion of propertied ex-convicts, and this I see as essential to his downfall.

Bligh's methods of government affected the safety of homes and enterprise, especially in the town, which means that they affected the livelihood and authority of both men and women in colonial society. Here it is possible to place colonial events within the context of questions being asked in Britain at that time about women, their sense of hierarchy, security and place. In the final chapter (15) these latter questions are pursued in what I say about Elizabeth Henrietta Macquarie, the first woman whose social and aesthetic imagination was harnessed to the use of power in Australia, and about other women who lived in Sydney. Sydney, indeed, emerges towards the end of the volume as the most powerful creation of the Europeans in this part of the world during the first twenty-five years.

I have followed up earlier arguments of my own, published elsewhere, in exploring the extent to which the settlement was run by a process of consultation, and have therefore departed, perhaps as far as it is possible to do, from the view of early New South Wales as a rigid autocracy.[25] This idea runs through large parts of the volume, surfacing particularly in Chapter 11. It links Lord Sydney and the commonwealth tradition of English social and political thought with the shaping of authority in Australia, and it also, I hope, casts new light on the original shape of settlement. Consistently with this approach, I have followed up Brian Fitzpatrick's suggestion (made in 1939 and frequently condemned by historians thereafter) of the original British plan for a 'community of peasant proprietors' in the Antipodes.[26] The type of community envisaged made all the difference to the type of constitution devised at Whitehall.

This book is written with the belief that the past still lives. The past is, however, not only a foreign country but a region thick with competing voices – 'full of noises, / Sounds and sweet airs' – and those of us who hunt among them are like half-deaf people at parties. We have to decide whom to listen to, and to shut out everything else in order to give ourselves room to understand. If my own selection of voices seems sometimes perverse, it is made with the belief that whole-hearted perversity is the best gift of the Europeans to Australia.

PART 1
Original Differences

Stemming the Flood Waters

As told by 'Sugar Billy' Rindjana, Andingari language, Jimmy Moore, Win-gari, Andingari language, and Tommy Nedabi, Wiranggu-Kokatato language affiliations, to Ronald Berndt in 1941.[1]

Marlgaru and Yaul were two brothers, Yaul being the younger. Marlgaru had a kangaroo skin bag full of water and two fire-sticks. They travelled toward the south coast from the northern desert. Yaul was thirsty, but Marlgaru refused his repeated requests for water. They came to Biranbura, west of Fowler's Bay. Yaul had become thin and his throat was parched. Marlgaru left his waterbag hidden under some rocks [over which the sea now swells].

Yaul grew very angry, and when his brother returned, the two quarrelled. Marlgaru went out hunting again. When he was out of sight, Yaul went in search of the bag. Finding it, he jabbed at it with a club, breaking the skin. The water poured out. Marlgaru ran back and tried to save his bag, but the water continued to flow and spread and eventually drowned them both. It also formed the sea.

The water was spreading inland too, but the country was saved from inundation by the action of various Bird Women. When they learnt what had happened, they all came down from the north- and south-east. Minma Ngeni (a small red-breasted bird) came running. Minma Wada-wada (a species of laughing jackass), hearing the noise of water, left the kurrajong roots from which she was collecting water, and slept at six waterholes before reaching Biranbura. Minma Bulin (like a *wada-wada*), Minma Djinda-djinda (willy wagtail), Minma Didarara (a yellow bird with the cry *dira-ter*), Minma Idji-didjidi (bird like a wagtail), Minma Djinbun (a small brown bird), Minma Djil-djil (a red-breasted black or blue bird), Minma Balbal (a parrot), Minma Badal-badal (another kind of parrot), Minma Gil-gilga (a red parrot), Minma Ban-ban (blue and red bell bird), and Dudu (a large blue bird), all flew down to Biranbura, bringing with them the roots of the *ngalda* kurrajong tree. They placed these all along the coast, making a barrier, restraining the oncoming waters that threatened to cover (what became) the mainland. . . .

After making this barrier, all the Dreaming women flew away to their home territory.

Chapter 1

Talk

I

On 19 January 1788 eleven sailing vessels, carrying a little more than a thousand Europeans for the purpose of settling the eastern half of Australia, drew near their destination. On this day the coast about Botany Bay was sighted. One of the officers of the intended garrison recalled the cheerfulness all about him, 'the spirits visible in every eye'. According to another,

> The wind was now fair, the sky serene, though a little hazy, and the temperature of the air delightfully pleasant: joy sparkled in every countenance, and congratulations issued from every mouth. Ithaca itself was scarcely more longed for by Ulysses, than Botany Bay by the adventurers who had traversed so many thousand miles to take possession of it.[1]

This is a kind and degree of happiness shared only by individuals who go from one world to found another. It embodied relief after a long voyage, but it was much more. It was also the pleasure of possession and creation, and as such it lingered for months, even for years, beyond the moment at which the invaders first set foot on Australian soil.

It was not a feeling which depended on any certain prospect of comfort, riches or liberty. Nor did it involve any thought that the current inhabitants of Australia would welcome conquest, though a few of the travellers had convinced themselves that in their future dealings with the Aborigines justice and humanity would prevail. There were poor men and women on the ships who had ideas of their own as to what might be in store, and some had hopes of making an easy life for themselves. But anyone who understood the mind of their Commodore and intended Governor, Captain Arthur Phillip – a mind to be explored in the pages which follow – must have known better.

Liberty was especially doubtful. It is true that in many parts of Europe and North America the last years of the eighteenth century were a time when liberty flourished and rights for men, if not for women, were enlarged as never before. Already for generations Britain and its colonies had been the home of liberty, but the current age promised, or threatened, to carry liberty to new extremes. Britons, and the English in particular, delighted in raising their voices in public, and what they understood to be a manly oratory – demand, protest, declamation, consent – was their meat and drink. Good government, they had long thought, should be full of the sweet to-and-fro of conversation. And the most important conversation, passing backwards and forwards down the generations, a conversation by which the nation as a whole was embroidered with liberty, was between those who had power and those who lacked it. This understanding was summed up in the word 'commonwealth'. All had voices. However, in New South Wales, a British settlement founded in an age of revolution, the future of such conversation was uncertain.

Talking and the freedom of speech were the essence of the English idea of liberty. As the seventeenth-century pamphleteer John Warr put it, 'the minds of men are the great wheels of things: thence come changes and alterations in the world; teeming freedom exerts and puts forth itself'.[2] The rights attached to property were important too, especially landed property. Place, and the type of attachment to place which was defensible in law, refined the idea of being English and thereby underwrote the membership of commonwealth. But talking was pervasive, fluid, protean. Like smoke, it filled the spaces left for it. Like fire, it made its own spaces. It was perfectly consistent with a society of rank and degree, as long as all were sure of their status and of the rights attached to status, so that even violent demands could pose no fundamental danger to the whole. Propertied Englishmen raised their voices in order to send their representatives to parliament, and their representatives raised their voices in parliament (a word which means 'talking') in conversation with each other and the government. In theory all Englishmen, and up to a point Englishwomen, had a right to address the sovereign, officers of state, parliament and magistrates, and a right to expect a response. The duty to hear and the right to be heard both encompassed the right to say 'no'. In short, government from day to day was supposed to depend on the subjects' consent.

There was no necessary connection between commonwealth and democracy, whether democracy in the form advocated at the end of the eighteenth century or that which was to be practised in due course during the nineteenth. Commonwealth did not involve the whole population, listed without discrimination on electoral rolls, speaking on great issues, and in such a way as to deliver a single verdict. It did not involve the sovereignty of the people because neither the people nor anyone else controlled the final word. The idea of national sovereignty itself was not yet fully worked out. It was conversation about particular things, and the voices of individuals and groups were raised in particular ways. The people spoke with a babble of voices. The law courts, with their infinite arguments, summed up the

English system best of all. They therefore occupied a sacred place within the common imagination:

> What whispering is there [in the courts] . . . What swearing is there: yea, what swaggering, what facing and out-facing? What shuffling, what shouldering, what Justling, what leering, what byting of Thumbs to beget quarrels, what holding uppe of fingers to remember drunken meetings, what braving with Feathers, what bearding with Mustachoes.[3]

Swaggering, 'facing and out-facing', were perfected in the courts, by judges in full regalia as much as by witnesses and petty lawyers. But these habits carried through to other forums and arenas.

The people were no part of government. But they might speak to government, might face and out-face, at least according to popular doctrine. Trial by jury was highly prized as a classic method of giving power to common voices. The principle of 'no taxation without representation', on which the power of parliament depended, was equally precious. It meant that people with property could not be taxed by government without the consent of their elected representatives. The Act of Habeas Corpus, 1679, was another statement of principle central to the English and British constitution. It stopped imprisonment without trial. Through being tried the accused acquired a voice, a means of being heard against the Crown itself, a right which in fact grew more substantial within the courts during the eighteenth century, thanks to the increased activity of the lawyers.[4]

The Act of Habeas Corpus also had something to say about the transportation of convicts. According to the Act, no English man or woman might 'be sent Prisoner' out of England except under two conditions. Either he or she 'shall by Contract in Writing agree' to go; or else, having been convicted of a felony and sentenced to death, he or she 'shall in open Court pray to be transported'. There was to be a question asked from the bench and an answer given from the dock.[5] Throughout the eighteenth century, and even into the nineteenth, consent had a part to play in the business of convict transportation. However, in this case the voice of the criminal became increasingly ritualised and feeble. So much so that, fifteen years after settlement began in New South Wales, Jeremy Bentham argued that the transportation system was entirely at odds with this celebrated Act, and so with the constitution itself.[6]

The British attitude to talking was linked with religion and with the obvious glories of Protestantism. The Protestant faith had no institution like the Catholic confessional, in which Christians opened their mouths merely in order to lay themselves open to the judgment of their priests. In Catholic countries this was the main link between the common man and woman and the system of power which meant most to them.[7] In England, after the Reformation, the Church had no such dealings with the mass of the people. During the turmoil of the 1640s, indeed, talk came mainly from the other side, for 'the people in Christ's kingdom' claimed, as they put it, a right 'of consultation, of debating, counselling, prophesying, voting'; even 'swearing i' th' light, gloriously'.[8] This was living conversation, quite distinct from scholarship and writing, which was understood to be the instrument of a mortifying power: 'The dead letter is not the Word, but Christ is the Word.'[9]

In principle, voices were stilled only by proper ceremony. But the means were effective. Most punishments inflicted by the courts were physical ones, designed to incapacitate the criminal, temporarily and permanently, as a thinking, speaking being. The courts were a stage on which men and women of all kinds might raise their voices, but there were other, smaller arenas which punctuated the flow of language. The pillories, or stocks, which occupied a central place in most towns of any significance, were little platforms on which the victims of the law were forced to suffer in silence. This was not quite true of that more celebrated stage, the gallows, because individuals condemned to be hanged were usually allowed to make a speech to the assembled crowd, but their words must have served to underline the ensuing silence. Capital punishment was very common. In cases of treason it was accompanied by a preliminary maiming which drove home beyond doubt the residual power of the state.

Within the circle drawn by these ritual interruptions there flourished a perpetual conversation between the people and their secular governors, a continuous rearrangement of right and wrong across familiar boundaries. One side might often speak from the bench, in splendour and at length, and the other from the dock, briefly and in squalor, but both had their turn. The talking itself was shaped by a need for justification and redemption, in this life or the next. Taking the system as a whole, this added up to a longing, frequently unsatisfied but never lost, for equity.

Such habits and expectations were well established in civil life during the seventeenth century: by the revolutions against Charles I and James II; by legislation, especially Habeas Corpus and the Bill of Rights (1689); and by the courts administering the common law. They thus became part of a peculiar tradition, one which was closely tied to English Protestantism and the integrity of Britain's island boundaries. The great Dr Johnson spoke of 'the *garrulosity* of the people', especially when their rights were at issue. England, in the minds of Englishmen, was a citadel of liberty, a nation, in Milton's words, 'not slow and dull, but of a quick, ingenious, and piercing spirit, acute to invent, subtle and sinewy to discourse'.[10] To its critics and enemies, it was a political Tower of Babel. Its great opponents were the two powers which dominated the European continent, the Catholic monarchies of France and Spain. Geography affirmed that Britain was a world to itself, and no part of any single-voiced empire, such as the Catholic states seemed (to Britons) to be.

Ideas about rights can be undermined in two ways. They can be submerged by new thinking, or they can be worn away by neglect and administrative routine. The eighteenth century – the Age of Enlightenment

– was, above all, a period of invention. It was also a time when educated men and women in Britain talked less about the virtues of Protestantism, and became more interested in ideas which could be shared with the European mainland. Britain itself was a fertile field for novelty (the Scottish Enlightenment was especially remarkable), but the breaking down of old boundaries suggested to many a less self-sufficient culture, and a threat to ancient liberties. Every day, according to one old-fashioned member of the House of Commons, '[they] patiently listen, not only to the schemes, but [to] the jargon of France'.[11] Lord Sydney, who was to be the minister responsible for first sending convicts to New South Wales, was of the same disgruntled point of view.

The French Revolution of 1789 was to disrupt and complicate the progress of enlightenment. It hurried the evolution of new ideas about civil order and the relationship of government and people and in some minds, both revolutionary and counter-revolutionary, it sharpened an insistence that discipline should be met with silence. Precedents might be found in royal policy during the time of Charles I, but the new movement was more pervasive, more ambitious and more successful. 'The Poor', though central to public debate, found their voices, at least in principle, consigned to irrelevance. English tradition was curtailed as a result, but in some places the resulting tension led to profoundly new experiments in public order. One of those places was Australia, which was settled by Europeans during the period of the high Enlightenment. Methods of order in the new community were partly English, in the old sense, but there was much about them that was new and more broadly European. The First Fleet sailed from England two years before the outbreak of revolution in Europe, and for many years in this remote corner of the globe the eighteenth century stood still. For an entire generation, European order was worked out in Australia as if all the exquisite promises of the Enlightenment might still come true.

II

There was another reason why – although the sky near Botany Bay might be 'serene' and the air 'delightfully pleasant' – English liberty shone with uncertain prospects in New South Wales for some years after 1788. Australia's very remoteness made the demands of authority much more urgent than they might otherwise have been. English ideas about talking, and especially about consent, were to be found throughout the English (and later British) empire from its beginnings in the seventeenth century. But peculiar circumstances sometimes called for silence. In some out-of-the-way parts of empire, survival seemed to depend on passive cooperation. For these the English devised an alternative type of order, called military government, a method going back to the time of Elizabeth I and to the first long-term military expeditions to the Netherlands and Ireland. It was found to be useful wherever English settlements were new and fragile or where they were in danger of attack. When Englishmen planned new settlements, they had to reconcile the right of consent with the need for survival. The problem was particularly obvious when the settlement was small and remote from any dependable source of protection and supply.

The earliest colonies of England's Atlantic empire and, much later, the first settlement in Australia, were all cases of this kind. The very first projects, such as Virginia, Bermuda and New South Wales, were uncertain and hazardous, and the resulting similarities among them were more important than the presence or absence of convicts. For the historian, they illuminate each other. In Virginia and in New South Wales the vast distance from anything familiar seems to have caused a kind of paralysis among many of the very first arrivals. In Virginia the people were 'no more sensible than beasts, [and] would rather starve in ideleness . . . then [sic] feast in labour'.[12] In New South Wales the transported men and women ceased for a while to be 'thinking beings'.[13] Such a population needed something like military government. Later settlements, formed when the territories were better known, with neighbours near at hand and often with larger capital, required less of the military style.

The settlement in Virginia in 1607 and its off-shoot at Bermuda in 1612 were the first permanent English communities beyond Britain and Ireland. They were both the work of the Virginia Company of London, a joint-stock enterprise mainly concerned to make money for its shareholders. To begin with, the company was sole proprietor on the North American coast and on the island of Bermuda, an absentee employer and landlord with unrivalled authority on the spot. Most of the men and women who arrived in Virginia in 1607, like the first convicts in New South Wales, were not free agents in the new land. They were labouring people bound to serve the company for seven years, and even the freemen, so called, did not take up land of their own: 'our people', wrote their Governor in 1614, 'were fedde out of the common store and laboured jointly in the manuring of the ground, and planting corne'.[14] The fruit of their labour belonged to the company.

The early government of Virginia passed through several stages. To begin with the commander of the small fleet which had brought them across the Atlantic, Captain Christopher Newport, was in charge. He organised the vessels and he also saw to the choice and stowing of provisions, as Captain Phillip was to do with the First Fleet to New South Wales, 1786–87. On arrival, he found a suitable place for settlement, carried out initial exploration along the coastline, and negotiated with the local people. He was not in charge thereafter because the Virginia Company had arranged for government by council. The people, though bound to serve the company, were otherwise to share in 'all liberties, franchises and immunities' commonly enjoyed in England.[15] By 1610 arguments had led this strange mixture of military and civil rule to be replaced by a more thoroughly military system, with 'one *able* and *absolute Governor*' possessed of the power to dispense with customary rights. The successive governors were all military men, with experience in the Netherlands and Ireland. They applied a civil and criminal code, *Lawes Divine, Morall and Martiall*, which forced the settlers to work in gangs under overseers or 'captains', with drumbeats marking the beginning and end of each day's labour. The death penalty was prescribed for numerous crimes, including the smallest theft of the common stock, such as grain or grapes from a garden.

The sense of emergency in Virginia prefigured that in New South Wales under Phillip, but the Virginian rulers were more extreme. In 1614 the first arrivals in Virginia completed their seven-year terms and were given small allotments of land: three acres each for unmarried men and twelve for families. But even these 'free' men, until 1617–18, had no absolute title either to the soil or to their own time. They were expected to supply the common enterprise with grain, and to work for the company one month in twelve. The stress on corporate or collective interest was very marked. All affairs were concentrated at one point; there was 'neither taverne, beere-house, nor place of relief, but the common kettell'.[16] Similarly, in New South Wales all depended on the government store. 'From the peculiarity of our situation,' wrote the Governor's secretary at Sydney Cove, 'there was a sort of sacredness about our store.'[17] On this last continent, as in America, no freehold was granted to begin with. No-one worked their own land, beyond a small garden patch. All convict labour belonged in principle to the government, and the produce was 'a public stock'.[18]

In Bermuda the first Governor was a ship's carpenter named Richard Moore. Although the Virginia Company had just set up a military regime in Virginia itself, it was more gentle with its people in Bermuda. They too were servants bonded to the company, and their crops were grown in common. Here, however, there was more room for commonwealth. There were half- or quarter-acre gardens, and instead of laying down a draconian code Moore ruled by force of character. At a meeting on their arrival, the settlers agreed among each other 'to use all diligence for the good of the Plantation, and not to purloine or imbesell any of the prohibited Comodities out of the generall estate'. Moore also seems to have been able to persuade them to work extremely hard, building forts as well as growing grain. When he left in 1615, most of the land was divided up. But the landless were still reserved 'for the generall imployment', under orders from the Governor.[19]

Habits of commonwealth were sinewy and fit for all seasons. They suddenly recurred when other sources of authority failed, but they could also coexist with dictatorial methods. At Newfoundland, New England and the West Indies the very first settlements were all tightly organised, but they also operated as common concerns. At New Plymouth, in what was later Massachusetts, thanks to the English backers (and in spite of the settlers themselves) there was no private interest in land or labour for three years after foundation in 1620. Even wives were obliged to wash and cook as directed by the Governor, and the men worked in gangs. But the obligation was strongly coloured with acquiescence. As in Bermuda the settlers agreed among themselves to submit to a rigorous discipline, forming 'a Civil Body Politic' by means of the famous Mayflower Compact.[20] Religion could help the process by which social discipline grew from discipline of self. In the little (and short-lived) community at Portsmouth, Massachusetts, the people agreed not only to 'incorporat our selves into a Bodie Politick' but also to make the New Testament, 'those perfect and most absolute lawes', their sole constitution.[21]

In all these American settlements consent underlay restraint, at least in so far as the settlers were voluntary immigrants from across the Atlantic. They all submitted with something like agreement to the hardship of the early regimes. This was the one great difference from the convicts in New South Wales. But even among the convicts, once landed, and in spite of the cruelty with which they were surrounded, the rules handed down from above became part of daily argument, a means, once again, of justification and redemption. Commonwealth made sense, especially to convicts who accumulated money.

The original settlement in Newfoundland, in 1610, was more like a single household, or a brotherhood of adventurers, than a colony. The feeling of common enterprise can be caught in the reports of the first Governor, John Guy:

> We have spent the time since our arrivall much in landing our victualls, and provision, and making safe places for it and our selves to shroud us untill our house coulde [be] builte. . . . we have digged a saw-pitt hard by the sea side, and put a timber house over it [co]vered with pine bordes.

All the original people seem to have been men (women arrived only in 1612), and all were bound to the Newfoundland Company in London. Their hardihood was cheerfully directed towards a single point, the joint invasion of a new continent.[22] Shared conquest encouraged other forms of sharing, and a consensuality of voices, among a conquering brotherhood.

The pooling of resources was characteristic of every stage of the very early Atlantic settlements. The people themselves mingled their labour and bent to a common discipline. In every case their sponsors in England acted together as well: the Virginia Company in the case of Virginia and Bermuda (Bermuda soon had a company of its own); the Newfoundland Company for Newfoundland; and so on. And the commercial idea of joint-stock was translated to the more down-to-earth idea of a 'generall estate' within the settlements themselves. In New South Wales the 'public stock' reflected instead the corporate interest of the Crown, which bore the cost of the enterprise as the companies had done in earlier times. But for those who were bound to companies or Crown – the men and women who came as indentured servants or convicts, bringing with them their English ideas about argument – there was sometimes little difference when it came to daily labour, rights and liberties.

III

The first English settlers across the Atlantic gave themselves as much room as they could for talking. In the later American settlements, where the people felt much safer than hitherto, this amounted to a good deal. It was customary in such places for all the 'freemen' – men only – of the community to have a voice in government. Freedom was manifest in speaking out, and some had more freedom than others. Bondsmen, for instance, indentured servants bound for a term of years, spoke only within household and workplace. Their rights were merely passive, like the rights of women (for the most part), and were to be enjoyed in partial silence. 'Rogues and vagabonds' were another special case, being men and women who seemed to place themselves, as if by their own free will, beyond the rules.

In Puritan New England the voices of freemen were raised equally in church, freely witnessing to the Lord, and in secular assembly. The habits of one type of meeting reinforced the habits of the other: each was a living commonwealth and corporation.[23] In many places throughout America, wherever public debate opened the way for conflict, strict rules were worked out, so that rhetoric might be developed as an art whose modulated patterns echoed politeness, truth, discipline, duty, those virtues which belonged to the essence of civilisation. Considered as a territory, a continent of power, conversation was carefully mapped and subdivided. Maryland, for instance, was formed from part of the territory of Virginia in 1634. Its charter gave its Lord Proprietor, the second Lord Baltimore, an almost regal authority within the province, but he was bound to pass laws only with 'the advice, assent and approbation of the freemen'. In this multiform sanction – 'advice, assent and approbation' – we hear a little echo of the English Babel transferred to America. The freemen of Maryland themselves, at a very early stage, laid down the rules by which they were to join in debate:

> every one that is to speake to any matter, shall stand up, and be uncovered and direct his speech to the . . . President of the Assembly [the Governor], and if two or more stand up to speak together, the . . . [Governor] shall appoint wh[ich] shall speake.

Also, 'no man shall stand up to speake to any matter untill the partie that spake last before, have sate downe'. No-one was to 'refute the speech of any other with any uncivill or contentious terms', nor (as in Parliament in England) was any to refer to another by his personal name, 'but by some circumloquution [sic]'. Any offender against these rules the Governor might 'command . . . to silence'.[24] Otherwise, the freemen of Maryland, like freemen elsewhere in the colonies, claimed the right to raise their voices even when the Governor found it painful to listen.[25]

Rules such as these were copied from English custom. In other ways settlers did not always pay close obedience to English authority. The liberties of Englishmen abroad might well reach to extremes, even embracing perfect independence from England itself. Colonists were inward-looking and they clung to whatever was useful among themselves: the rights of Englishmen most of all, and also protection against the shared enemies of Englishmen. They discarded whatever might be inconvenient about empire. During the seventeenth century the distance between England and the colonies seemed enormous, traffic was scarce, and the voice of authority, conveyed by mere pen and ink, resounded very feebly across such vast waters.

Some small parties of individuals wandered beyond reach. The system of indentured labour was the means of transporting many thousands of men and women to the mainland colonies of North America and to the West Indies, and afterwards to Australia. In the 1620s some indentured servants in New England set up a new community at a place they called Merry Mount. According to William Bradford, the Governor at New Plymouth, they were told by Thomas Morton, their leader, an educated man, that if they stayed with their masters they would be 'carried away and sould for slaves'. Morton promised that at Merry Mount they would be his 'partners and consociats'; 'we will', he said, 'converse, trad, plante, and live togeather as equalls, and supporte and protecte one another'. He was as good as his word and, according to the Governor,

> he became lord of misrule, and maintained (as it were) a schoole of Athisme.
> . . . They . . . set up a May-pole, drinking and dancing about it many days
> togeather, inviting the Indean women, for their consorts, dancing and frisking
> togither, (like so many fairies, or furies rather,) and worse practises.

For Bradford all this was blasphemy, in both word and deed: not only the atheism, so-called, and the wild conversation, but the 'inviting' of pagan women and the 'frisking' like fairies. The Separatist Puritan forms of Bradford's own language would have sounded strange enough, say, to the inhabitants of Whitehall and Hampton Court, but the babble at Merry Mount was something else again. It was condemned as 'a nest of pirates' and eventually suppressed.[26]

In this conversing and living together at the edge of the empire there sprang up, like new species along a garden fence, some striking examples of Englishness: for 'men like flowers or roots being transplanted take after the soyl wherein they grow'.[27] The people at Merry Mount seem to have lived by hunting and by trading with the Indians. Morton much admired what he understood of Indian society, and he applied himself to finding out about American wildlife. He later wrote a book called *New English Canaan*, which described his discoveries. Nearly three hundred years later we find similar examples of spirited independence among the gangs of bushrangers who lived in the mountains of Van Diemen's Land (now Tasmania). Michael Howe, an English highwayman who had escaped from bondage as a convict, led a party which at one time numbered twenty-nine, convicts like himself, runaway soldiers and his Aboriginal wife, Mary. Howe liked to call himself 'Lieutenant-Governor of the Woods', and when he addressed himself to the Lieutenant-Governor at Hobart he wrote with the politeness due to a fellow head of state. In one letter, signed by himself and ten of his people, he assured His Honour that God 'who Preserved Us from Your Plots in Publick will Likewise Preserve Us from them In Secret'. He asked him to deal with the people of the Woods more openly in future.[28]

Among his kangaroo-skin clothes Michael Howe kept a notebook, also made of kangaroo-skin, in which he wrote down, as he remembered them, the names of the flowers of his native Yorkshire. Independence from empire has never been a good reason for giving up the civilities of Englishness. Howe himself was a candid man. At night-time in September 1816 he and some of his men visited a farm belonging to the Lieutenant-Governor. The overseer exchanged pleasantries with them: 'well, my lads, what do you want . . . I suppose you want something to eat'. They declined some fresh pork, and asked for ham;

> Michael Howe went in search of Eggs . . . and then [as the overseer later recalled] asked me for some Spirits, which I gave him; they took some Cream and beat up the Eggs, Cream and Spirits; they ordered me to make Tea, which I did; they asked me for my Wife's Thread. I brought out my wife's work basket.

They collected a number of other things and then departed, 'bidding us all a good night'. As an afterthought, apparently, 'Michael Howe asked me for my dictionary. I gave it to him, observing to him that it was mine and, as soon as he had done with it, to return it to me; he promised he would'.[29]

Over three centuries of empire, within an infinitude of living conversation, including little exchanges such as this, there were many degrees of independence. Even extreme talk, meant mainly for local listeners, was not always acted on in extreme ways. The Civil Wars in England during the 1640s and 1650s upset established habits and encouraged truculence. 'Our allegiance binds us not to the laws of England [other] than while we live in England', declared the Massachusetts Assembly in 1646, 'for the laws of the Parliament of England reach no further, nor do the King's writs under the great seal go any further.' With the King's execution, the people of Barbados went so far as to make plans 'to model this little limbe of the Commonwealth into a free state'.[30]

The soil might nourish even stranger permutations. Dissident language might be strengthened by the idea that settlers in remote places were tied more tightly to the indigenous people, the original owners, than they were to their fellow Englishmen at home. In England all important rights were conveyed by inheritance, by delegation from above, and by the weight of officialdom. In the New World, during the very first years of English settlement, they might depend instead on the consensus of living voices and immediate conversation. At Merry Mount there was communion of all kinds with the Indians. In Maryland dissident settlers asked among themselves 'what Right the King of England had to grant any thing there' to their pretended overlord, Lord Baltimore. They had themselves made their way within the new land by a process of local treaty and, they thought, they surely owed their fertile acres not to his lordship but to 'their . . . Right from the Natives'.[31] In Central America, on the Gulf of Honduras and the Mosquito Shore, British settlers gathered together on land which they were quite confident was theirs. Like the people of Barbados, they too spoke of belonging to a free state. They and the Indians, they said, were 'one and the same people', and as the Indians had always been free it followed that they too were independent of Whitehall.[32] From Massachusetts to the Mosquito Shore, this was bold language. It was also a form of 'facing and out-facing', a testing of muscle and a wrestling of voices. There was often less independence, and less desire for it, than might appear.

Other understandings counted for more in the end. Within the English empire – the empire of English – there were two overarching qualifications for raising one's voice, for trying to make one's larynx a medium of authority. These were manhood and Christianity. Speech is highly coloured by maleness and femaleness, and within oral cultures truth itself can have its boundaries fixed by gendered sound. When women were condemned for pushing themselves forward, it was their talking which made them most offensive. The voices of women belonged to the consensus of domestic life. They could not conform to the rules which men had made for the shaping of public ideas and the management of public battles. Much could be done by women in limited conversation and they might sometimes exert themselves in a measured way by writing. But their speaking in public was wrong. John Winthrop, Governor of Massachusetts Bay, wrote of his countrywoman, the religious leader Anne Hutchinson, that she was 'a woman of . . . nimble wit and active spirit, and a very voluble tongue, more bold than a man, though in understanding and judgment, inferiour to many women'. She had stepped out of the natural docility of womanhood by making herself 'rather . . . a preacher than a Hearer'.[33] Her contemporary, Margaret Brent, was a Marylander, sister-in-law of Governor Calvert, local agent for the Lord Proprietor, and owner herself of more than a thousand acres. She was allowed to argue in court at St Mary's, and except for being a woman she had all the qualifications of a freeman. In 1648, while the members of the Maryland Assembly were discussing their standing orders, she appeared before them and demanded 'to have [a] vote in the howse for her selfe[,] and voyce also . . . as his L[ordshi]p's Attorney'.[34] This was refused. Given the assumptions of the time, it would have altered the whole character of debate. The members did not even think it necessary, under such provocation, to add to their standing orders a ban on the voices of women. Silence was imposed by silence.

Speakers of English thought that their language was a peculiarly masculine one. It was shaped to the habits of men. 'Its virtues', according to one authority, 'are those of a man.' The manly eloquence of the English, like the great River Nile, 'preserves a majesty even in its abundance; its waters roll rapidly, notwithstanding their depth, it never roars but when its banks are too narrow, nor overflows without enriching the soil'. It was, they happily admitted, 'somewhat courser' than the Latin tongues (French, Italian and Spanish), less subtle and polite, but at the same time it was more truly masculine because it was 'more open, honest, and undesigning'.[35] Like a river its power depended on its restrictions, the bounds which men made for themselves in dealing truthfully with other men. Men's voices were expressions of the public faith, the conscience of the Christian, and especially the English, state. The voices of women, on the other hand, were a little like those of such Catholic peoples. Because they were beings who lived for consensus, and because they were dependent on men, women were not always open about their opinions. They did not understand the rules which, throughout the empire, governed candid disagreement. It was widely believed that dissimulation was a vice characteristic of women: 'a few drops of women's rheum [or tears]', says Shakespeare, ' . . . are / As cheap as lies'. In one of his more conceited remarks, Mr Darcy, in Jane Austen's *Pride and Prejudice* (1813), compared such dissimulation with cunning. It was a vice which a woman might most easily avoid among her family and kin, within the consensus – the silent implications wholly understood, the spontaneity, the habitual words and accents, the shared prejudice – of home.[36]

From an English point of view, Christianity was less exclusive than gender, but it was also more difficult to define. Speech was one of the principal manifestations of the soul, of the created and social self, and to be called 'pagan' was to be placed beyond a boundary, not only of religion, but also of language, culture and race. Pagans were incapable of reflecting the image of God and therefore had no rights under Christian law. A settler who murdered an Indian in Maryland in 1643 argued that he could not be guilty. The offence, he said, was not committed 'ag[ain]st his Lo[rdshi]ps peace or the kings, because the party was a pagan'. In Montserrat, one of the islands of the West Indies, an Act of Council made 'the unchristian like association of white people with Negroes' into a criminal offence.[37] Both Blacks and Indians could be baptised, and there was a common belief, especially among Black slaves, that baptism cancelled skin-colour and might be a means of freedom. One might afterwards make one's way, without let or hindrance, in the world of the English. In 1667 the General Assembly of Virginia legislated to the contrary, but the belief persisted among Blacks even into the late eighteenth century.[38]

Flax spinning in eighteenth-century Ulster: women's labour often allowed for talking, and for the turning over of topics public and private.

Source: Ulster Folk and Transport Museum

In general, men and women were taken to be Christians if they looked like Christians. Timbre was a consideration here as well. Graham Greene captured the European view of things, going back many generations, when he wrote in 1955, 'voices have colour too, yellow voices sing and black voices gargle, while ours just speak'. The conversation of the Hottentots, according to one seventeenth-century Englishman, was 'like the clucking of hens or gabbling of turkeys'.[39] Such mere noises could not stand as echoes of the Word of God, and inhabitants of empire, whether baptised or not, were beyond the bounds of Christendom if their faces, forms and intonations were not English, or at least not European. Even more than Christian women – much more so, indeed – their voices lacked truth. In Virginia they were bundled together as people who could not give evidence in court (except against each other): 'negroes, mulattos, and Indians, [who] are commonly of such base and corrupt principles, that their testimony cannot be depended upon'.[40] In Australia the same ban was to apply to Aborigines. They were forbidden to give evidence on the grounds that they could have no understanding of the Christian oath, which made their testimony worthless. But even beyond that, their language represented disorder. Imagine, said a mid-nineteenth-century European, the anomaly of an Aborigine putting his evidence on record, 'the wild savage of the woods standing amid the hum and press of civilised men'. Aborigines were not part of the conversation of the English, nor of Christendom, and as a result their words could not convey any significant truth. They added up, said another settler, to nothing more than 'the chatterings of the ourang-outang'.[41]

Such ideas about the significance of being Christian survived very long in common memory in Australia. In 1901, the first year of Federation, Henry Lawson gave to the world one of his best characters, Mrs Spicer, whose language embraced this ancient notion: '"I must really git some more knives and forks next time I'm in Cobborah," she'd say. "The children break an' lose 'em till I'm ashamed ter ask Christians ter sit down ter the table."'[42]

The membership of Christendom (generally proven by skin-colour) gave men, and women in some circumstances, the right to think for themselves, the right to argue and the right to refuse. The English wove such assumptions into the theory of commonwealth. They can be glimpsed as well behind arguments about convict labour in Maryland and Virginia during the 1720s: 'disputes between the persons entitled to the service of the felons and the felons themselves concerning their term of servitude'.[43] Technically, convicts should have served for the full period of their sentence, even when it amounted to fourteen years or the whole of their natural life. But this must have looked like involuntary and perpetual slavery, which was unseemly for men and women who were born Christian. Their condition therefore changed when they reached dry land, a custom being established whereby, whatever the term of banishment, no convict was bound to servitude in America for more than seven years.[44]

No English settlement of any complexity (especially one with commercial ambitions) could avoid the use of written records, because the keeping of registers and the documentation of title played an essential part in establishing individual rights to the soil and other property. The consensus of habit, memory and living voices was necessarily supplemented by contract, in which individual rights were defined on paper. English forms of authority were thus replicated beyond England. Nevertheless, talking continued as the main day-to-day means of order within the scattered communities of the English empire during most of the seventeenth century, and talking is an artifice which makes its own boundaries in time and place. It is hard to talk without facing and speaking inwards, to a circumscribed audience large or small, and it is hard for listeners to ignore the way in which the words are said and the way the speaker looks. Speech creates an island of understanding, high and dry, and the habits of speech lead to a sense of place and of particularity. There is power in utterance, in filling a silence, and listeners are easily made into subjects, at least for the moment. None of this is true when talk is crystallised by writing. It then takes on a more fluid currency and a more ambiguous power, timeless but also impermeable. Words on a page, as distinct from words in the air, lose some of the sharper resonance of locality, gender and race. They may enrich local imagination, extending, as it were, the range of the living voice and thus the bounds of community. But at the same time they inevitably shed a little, at least, of the smell and passion of circumstance, the easy subjection, the familiar contingencies of soil and accent.

Writing was shaped by speech. Speech was shaped by writing. This mutuality had been a fact for generations, or even centuries, but there were numerous turning points in the relationship of literate and oral culture. A new sense of common literacy is obvious in the age which produced Shakespeare's plays, the King James Bible, *The Pilgim's Progress*, and the innumerable pamphlets of the English Civil Wars (1641–60). But the written word became self-sufficient, as a means of art and authority, only during the generations which followed. The process was slow. During the eighteenth century even the most sophisticated English novelists – Defoe, Richardson, Fielding – wrote their stories almost as if they were telling them out loud. They used the rambling form common to story tellers from the beginning (obvious in the *Iliad* and the *Odyssey*), the loosely connected episodes, the continual shifting of scenes, even the expectation that early episodes would have passed from memory by the end. However, within the first generation of European settlement in Australia (the period of this volume) writers began to draw at last on the limitless and distinctive virtuosity of pen and ink. Jane Austen's first published novel, *Sense and Sensibility*, appeared in 1811, five months after the court-martial which followed the deposition of Governor Bligh and during Lachlan Macquarie's second year in New South Wales. The tightness of plot, the unchanging or gradually moving scenery and the incisive language signalled a new means of power for the written word.[45] For her characters – the educated and up-to-date among them – writing letters and talking were two aspects of a single sublime art, and the second took much of its form from the first. Simultaneously the methods of empire began to rely much more on written correspondence and on resulting habits of thought. Austen's skills were a world away from many of the events of this book. Early New South Wales was like the shadowy, largely undescribed background world of her novels, the world of the poor, a place in which words and sentences were formed and felt in mouths before they were put on paper, if they were put on paper at all. And yet she and European New South Wales were part of the same phenomenon, an apotheosis for writing.

The circle defined by Christendom and manhood lived on, but during the eighteenth century it was complicated by a multiplicity of other circles, a shuffled pack of conversations, including written ones, cross-cutting, eclipsing, overlapping, undermining. The very notion of the human soul was transformed through being examined within papered layers of self-consciousness. Central to what I say below are the unsettling echoes which occur when parts of a population first become addicted to writing things out.

Chapter 2

Writing

I

Every age has its media, and the media, especially the regularity and completeness of communication, shape people's view of the world. Over the course of the twentieth century, the effects of telephone, telegraph, sound recordings, the cinema and other forms of photography have been compounded by the coming of television, facsimile transfer and computer networks. All have been compounded over again by the more and more rapid movement of people. As the living voice, the actual utterance of the moment, is duplicated and overlaid by other kinds of media, the very understanding of human identity is transformed. Words pass from warm breath into cold storage. Talking is freed altogether from circumstance, and the image of self slips apart from the sense of place.

This process began with the use of writing and it gathered pace as writing became more common and efficient. Within the long march of literacy, as I say in Chapter 1, there were some sudden leaps forward. Take, for instance, the spread of cursive, or running writing, among the literate few in Europe in the twelfth century. This invention allowed pens to keep pace when ideas were on the run. It meant the blossoming of momentary schemes, suggestions, directives and speculations. Unlike other forms (the books of the Bible, the Fathers and so on), cursive was not fixed on the page, ripe only for resurrection by the living voice, for chanting or some other kind of recitation. It was silent and fugitive, but even when it was little more than scribbling it had a liquid currency. In due course it won its own authority.[1] For many generations it was still the preserve of a few but, at last, during the seventeenth century the literate began to multiply. In due course all men and women of the upper and middling ranks were able to write. They could also add up efficiently, thanks to the common replacement of Roman with Arabic numbers. It was a dynamic, ramifying, overwhelming process, comparable with the growth of computer literacy in the 1990s (though that was much more rapid).

The Atlantic Ocean, showing places mentioned in the text

The resulting changes in society were dramatic, and they gave a peculiar distinction to the decades on either side of 1700. Such changes may seem slight compared with those of later centuries, but they were enough to give rise to new attitudes in all sorts of areas: geography, the limits of community, government and common rights, and, once again, the sense of self. Within the English empire they transformed the use of power, especially as it was exercised from the centre. The way was open for extraordinary expeditions beyond the seas, including, eventually, the expedition which first brought Europeans to Australia.

For two hundred years, since the invention of printing in the mid-1400s, there had been a steady increase in the number of books published in Britain, and with it a growing acquaintance with the idea of talking on paper, of making words into ubiquitous monuments of thought. The frenzy of debate which caused and accompanied the civil wars, in the 1640s and 1650s, added to the richness of public conversation. The following generation, though more peaceable, sprang even more eagerly into print, judging from the number of books and pamphlets which date from the 1660s to 1680s. It has been estimated that in 1679–81, for instance, between five and ten million printed items were in circulation. Also the number of people who could read and write had grown – an extensive new class had taken shape within national society – although there is evidence of levelling-off, or consolidation, by the last part of the century.[2]

There was considerably more day-to-day use of pen and ink, a fact clear enough from the new quantities of paper in use, and from the quantities surviving from the period. Coarse brown paper, used for wrapping, had been made in England since the fifteenth century, while the fine white paper used for writing and printing was imported, the necessary skills being mainly French and Italian. In the first years of the seventeenth century English consumption of white paper was very roughly 0.12 kilograms per head each year (no more than a few sheets), and a large part of the population would have been ignorant of its existence. A hundred years later the average consumption had grown six times, and paper was much more widely distributed. The main period of change was, once again, the 1670s and 1680s, when growing demand opened the way for the successful manufacture of white paper in Britain. In 1686 a White Paper Makers Company was formed in London to protect the trade and in the same year parliament banned the export of rags, from which paper was made. Local production grew very quickly, but imports were also well sustained. The finest white paper, in particular, still came from France.[3]

There is no reliable evidence for the changing price of paper, but what we have suggests that growing demand kept pace with new supplies.[4] There was an expanding familiarity with the written record and a willingness to use it in various ways. Ledgers became a more common instrument of power. Writing can create and sustain a useable reality. Also, writing reduces risk. The implementation of credit – paper money – began on a grand scale, as the *modus operandi* of the Bank of England (founded 1694), and from now on the national debt was to be central to the management of the British state.[5] Without a ready resource to the quill there would have been no 'last dying words', those sad memoirs which carried the thoughts of condemned men and women from Newgate and the gallows to a scattered and lasting audience. Even the murmurings of lovers now became immortal on paper, so that love letters (another means of exchanging credit) became for the first time a part of common courtship. 'Why, you old bitch,' says Captain Brazen in Farquhar's *The Recruiting Officer* (1706), 'did you ever hear of love-letters dated with the year and day o' th' month? Do you think *billets doux* are like bank bills?'[6]

The transporting of paper, and also of people thanks to the improvement of roads, became more frequent, and information and answers moved backwards and forwards with increasing speed. There was more efficiency in the way letters, pamphlets and books, and passengers with news, covered long distances. An effective postal service had begun in England in 1653, and it was extended to most North American colonies during the following decades. An intercolonial service began among the mainland colonies themselves in 1692.[7] Partly for commercial reasons, traffic across the Atlantic and from colony to colony both multiplied, which meant that communications within the English empire were regular and reliable beyond anything known before. A system of packet boats, working under government contract, began to carry mail across the ocean in 1702.[8]

Every administrator, businessman and scholar knows that spoken language has to be reshaped when it is written down. Codes, idioms and dialects which work well within closed circumstances can be confusing, and therefore unreliable, in other times and places. Intonation and gesture, the whimsy of breath and lips, have to be replaced by bloodless formalities, and words and symbols have to be found which pass current beyond local boundaries. There was now, in the late seventeenth century, a new effort to standardise weights and measures, to reconcile the places in England, for instance, where a stone weight equalled eight pounds with other places where it equalled eighteen. This reforming generation also took trouble to establish a method of renaming and reclassifying animals and plants, suppressing old local names and replacing them with Latin. But Latin too had its limitations. The first attempts were therefore made to create a new international language, or written code, based on the belief that the understanding of 'things' was common to humanity, and that words might be made to match them with perfect clarity.[9]

Personal letters were increasingly familiar, extending a universal code of politeness. In North America during the first years of the inter-colonial postal service, only nine items were delivered annually for every one hundred people, increasing to fifteen by 1704.[10] But certain recipients – highly educated people and those who could pay postage – monopolised the service from year to year. Getting letters and sending letters was something to boast about, for not everyone could join in this new and electrifying type of conversation: 'O ay, letters – I had letters – I am persecuted with letters – I hate letters – nobody knows how to write letters: and yet one has 'em, one does not know why – they serve one to pin up one's hair.' So says Mrs Millamant, in Congreve's *The Way of the World* (1700).[11] Later the superfluity of paper was to be used in different ways, to light the fire or wrap up the rubbish.

The parcels which travelled by post included learned periodicals, a type of publication which had begun in English in the 1680s and which created a self-conscious and highly conversational 'republic of letters'.[12] This explains the need for new botanical and zoological terms. Regular newspapers began, very gradually, to appear in some of the bigger towns on either side of the Atlantic. They also circulated from one town to another. The stories in newspapers travelled beyond even those people who could read, because the papers were stuck up and read aloud in public places. In the first years of the eighteenth century, London papers were (on average) more than five months old by the time they reached American ports. Nevertheless, they carried a continuous stream of information which emptied itself in the main ports and trickled away among the highroads and footpaths of the new world.[13] In this way remote events became part of a connected narrative, and, before the mind's eye, remote people performed in a single, long-running drama. Remote ideas were absorbed within the conversation of day-to-day.

Money was another face of language, and it too was a code which had its first meaning within local circumstances. From the earliest times, English settlements abroad had made their own arrangements about the way in which money values were to be understood. This was now too awkward for merchants corresponding from colony to colony. In 1704 English ministers tried to set up standard values for coins in use throughout the empire.[14] The same period saw the establishment of Greenwich as the fixed point of the prime meridian of longitude. Atlases, in ever-increasing numbers, were among the new publications of the time, so that anyone who could read a map (and map-reading is a special form of literacy) could find out just where they were in the vast imaginary – virtually real – scheme of things. Travel books multiplied, giving readers vivid accounts of other lands, so that, as Daniel Defoe declared, the 'Compleat English Gentleman' could 'make the tour of the world in books'.[15]

The visionary world and the tangible world thus began to permeate each other. Adventures came to be valued for their capacity to be turned into writing, and by an upside-down sensibility journeys were narratives, to men and women of literary inclination, even before they ceased to be journeys. Towards the end of the eighteenth century, Anna Josepha King sailed from England to Norfolk Island, where her husband was to be lieutenant-governor. She approached, simultaneously, her first childbirth and the treacherous shores of the island, where there was no harbour. One of the gentlemen who was with her remarked how 'she seems to dread that part of the story'.[16] In fact, events embodied in paper and ink could tell you *who* you were. 'I am Sir Wilfull Witwoud,' says one of Congreve's characters, and he added, 'so I write myself', as if that settled the matter.[17] The artifice and affectation of writing thus became a means of certifying life itself: a commodity which otherwise needs no certificate.

During most of the seventeenth century, the settlements of the empire had been a very mixed bag; they were distinguished one from the other especially by their management of various types of enterprise, whether religious, military or commercial. The eighteenth-century empire was bigger, but at the same time it was more straightforward. There was one great line of distinction. In the first place, there were settlements which lived within the single, centralised conversation of pen-and-paper, their dimensions kept in ledgers and their people enlightened by traffic with the centre. In contrast, there were settlements and parts of settlements which existed outside, mostly beyond the marbled waves which carried the packet boats. These were two kinds of European society. It was only towards the end of the century, as we will see, with projects like New South Wales, that the two halves began to be fitted together, the spoken and the written word, in what can be seen as one of the great schemes of the Enlightenment.

II

There was a new form of energy unfolding within the thickening mass of paper and ink. It was partly a new liberty. In 1695 the Licensing Act, passed by Parliament in 1662, expired, bringing to an end the censorship of English works in print. With more and more people sending their ideas into the world, the English government, of necessity, adapted itself to a freedom of speech consistent with English custom and unknown anywhere else in Europe. It adapted with good reason, because the new efficiency of communication helped authority as much as hindering it. Statesmen with imagination could see that all this easy publicity meant not only liberty but a new means of order. As the lines of traffic between different parts of the empire became broader and smoother, the network as a whole could be drawn more tightly together.

During the seventeenth century, England, Scotland and Ireland were ruled by the House of Stuart, and most of the Stuart kings and queens were inspired, more or less, by this vision. James II was the most telling example. His reign was very brief (1685–88), but even as Duke of York, before he became King, James was an eager authoritarian. He was a keen administrator, and he saw ocean traffic, reinforced by a strong navy, as the means of uniting the scattered parts of the empire. He was rigidly unimaginative in many things, but he understood how subjects might be bent and driven by the energetic use of pen and paper. While Duke of York he had imposed a

stern government on his namesake, New York, after its capture from the
Dutch, and as Lord Admiral of England he had overhauled the management
of the Royal Navy. As King he formed the seven colonies of New England
into a single dominion under the firm hand of a governor-general. Had the
1688 Revolution (the Glorious Revolution) not intervened, he might have
incorporated five more and, perhaps, in due course brought all the mainland
colonies under a single regime. His successors, especially William III and
Queen Anne, worked for the same general result but more carefully. During
1685–1713 there were eight years of peace and twenty years of war.
Wartime emergency seemed to justify the careful mustering of resources and
the obedience of subjects empire-wide.[19] The arena which idealists of this
period thus made for their imagination, through the use of pen and paper,
was something like the dominion which belongs to the gaze of a twentieth-
century air traveller. They enjoyed the same sense of participating in magic,
of artifice skating the surface of risk. The eye moves in company with the
sun, picking up patterns and sudden cavities of light, none of which are visible to the subject people who might look upward. From such a perspective
the ocean works as a reflection of power, dividing islands and continents
like items in a ledger, all swiftly scanned by the arrogant, aggregating eye.

During the wars of William and of Anne the thoughts of the government
in London were very much engaged with the Atlantic, and ministers began
to look to the colonies on the other side of the water as a systematic source
of military and naval supply. Naval commanders had always made a practice of recruiting spare seamen in colonial ports, by the use of press-gangs.
During these wars their demands multiplied, and to cope with local complaints impressment was put on a more businesslike foundation, at least in
theory. For a while governors alone, under instructions from the Admiralty,
were entrusted with filling ships. But nothing, not even an Act of Parliament
in 1708, could settle arguments in the public houses and back lanes where
the press-gangs operated. Doubts were cleared up only after two or three
generations, with another revolution and the independence of the United
States.[20]

Naval stores were available in the colonies, as well as sailors. Pine-trees
grew in millions among the forests of the northern mainland, fit for ships'
masts. The trees were also of a kind which might be tapped for the pitch and
tar used in waterproofing wooden vessels. After the 1688 Revolution James
II's dominion of New England was dissolved and some of the old colonies
were resurrected. But in the new charter for Massachusetts the government
took care to include a clause which forbade the colonists from cutting down
and thereby wasting pine-trees belonging to the Crown. The empire already
had its Navigation Acts, passed in 1660–73, which aimed to regulate sea-
going trade. This new attempt to reach across the ocean into ordinary
dry-land lives, to regulate day-to-day behaviour within colonial boundaries,
was something more bold. It was reinforced by an Order-in-Council in
1699, by an Act of Parliament in 1704, and in 1705 by the appointment of

a 'Surveyor-General of Her Majesty's Woods and Forests in America'. All this activity was meant to refer only to trees on public land, but officials pushed forward so vigorously that local landowners had to fight (and were still fighting in the 1770s) to protect their own forests. This evidence of 'tyranny' was another sore point in the dealings between heart and perimeter.[21]

The chief enemy throughout the wars was Louis XIV of France, and the British hero was John Churchill, first Duke of Marlborough, a figure of enormous influence in the reign of Anne. Under Marlborough, the size of the army more than doubled, and henceforth, during the successive wars of the eighteenth century, the British government prepared for battle as many as 100,000 men. Large numbers were released at every declaration of peace, but even so from now on Britain had a standing army of about 35,000, much of it stationed in Ireland ready for sudden movement elsewhere. Naval operations were also enormous compared with anything known hitherto. Some 40,000 men were in the fleets marshalled against France. The dockyards in London and at Portsmouth were expanded and a new one begun at Plymouth. The yards employed many hundreds, and large numbers were needed on top of this simply to keep the forces supplied with food and clothing. The administration at Whitehall grew by 40 per cent, and the number of clerks and others employed throughout Britain in taxing the people, in order to fund the whole enterprise, more than doubled.[22]

Marlborough's victories in battle were partly a result of tactical genius. But they were due also to his skill with logistics: his efficiency with pen and ink. The Duke (like James II) belonged to a new type of military and civil administrator, for whom the infinitely detailed management of people was something like a science and, as such, a source of delight. This new energy, centred at Whitehall, was felt throughout the empire, though sometimes as yet with equivocal results. Colonel Daniel Parke had been Marlborough's aide-de-camp and had carried the news of his great victory at Blenheim from the scene of the battle post-haste to England and Queen Anne. The Queen had rewarded him with a thousand guineas, her portrait set in diamonds, and the governorship of the Leeward Islands. At Antigua, and with his apprenticeship to Marlborough behind him, Parke behaved as one of a new breed of governors. It was his opinion that the islands had hitherto been governed 'under no manner of method' and too much according to their own half-spoken customs. He wanted a new body of officials, outsiders like himself, who would show what could be done in such colonies, and he wanted to see some of the worst local laws altered by legislation from Westminster: 'it must be the Parliament must do it,' he said, 'for they [the islanders] have such laws [as] putt it out of the power of a Governor'. He was anxious to limit slavery and to promote the interests of the poor white settlers, and to this end he made vigorous use of the local Court of Chancery, in which he sat as judge, circumventing the island magistrates.[23]

Parke's ambitions were symptomatic of an empire tied by paper – instructions, reports, legislation – to its metropolitan heart. His failure was not long in coming; it showed that, however promising these links might be, they were no match, as yet, for local rights enshrined within the citadel of local conversation. Distinctive understandings operated through a distinctive accent. He had intervened on behalf of the soldiers of the garrison against their commanding officer, who was keeping back wages for his own profit, and during a confrontation with the Assembly at Antigua the soldiers rallied to him. Excitement mounted, the Governor's opponents marched in a body on Government House, broke in and shot him.[24] The power of mere innuendo – the living sounds of men and women, never transferred to the official record – is evident in the way the murderers dealt with his body. Parke had tried to set aside the customs of a self-sufficient people, but he had apparently made his way further than that. His enemies called him 'voluptuous' and among his papers were found (so it was said) several letters from Antiguan wives. By one account, therefore, the Governor's private parts were cut off at his death and held up as a trophy by 'some, whose Marriage-Bed, 'tis thought, he had defiled'.[25] Among the Antiguans, and no doubt in other places, the empire of politeness was still a thin veneer.

During this generation officials learnt very quickly how to feed, clothe, maintain and move about hundreds and even thousands of men all at once. Piecemeal migration from Britain and Ireland – men, women and children – had increased enormously during the last decades of the seventeenth century. Between 100,000 and 150,000 people departed, took to 'the liquid high-way of the waves', and at the same time the transatlantic slave trade began in a substantial way.[26] With these examples before them, imaginative officials dreamed of moving large numbers of their fellow subjects in a systematic and well-directed way across the ocean. From an administrative point of view, this was to be the supreme challenge of the new empire of paper. It frequently involved force but it also meant working on the common will, a project whose immeasurable complications were as yet only dimly understood. There were several projects, designed to satisfy various purposes. They included one put forward by the Governor of the Leeward Islands (Parke's predecessor) which involved his taking delivery of 10,000 Scots, 'with [he said] enough otemeal to keep them for 3 or 4 months'. These he thought would be useful in strengthening his hand for battle against neighbouring French.[27]

In 1708–09 hundreds of families began to arrive in London, without warning, from Germany, most of them from the area of the Rhenish Palatinate, around Frankfurt. Their native countryside had been devastated by war, and their pockets emptied by their governments to pay for it.[28] The prestige of England currently stood very high in Europe. The English could boast peace within their own coastline and great victories abroad, and this may explain why the Palatines had decided, in such numbers, to rely on

English generosity. They were allowed to camp on the common at Blackheath, just outside London, where they became one of the sights of the city. (They, or a later part of the same migration, included Jacob Phillip, who was to be father of Arthur Phillip, founding Governor of New South Wales.) Some were moved on to settlements in Ireland, and others were sent to various parts of North America. The largest body was transported to New York with the idea that they should be employed among the pine forests, as 'servants of the Crown'. The New York project was the biggest of its kind so far, involving nearly three thousand emigrants. It was crucial to the whole operation that the means be found 'to over-see and keep them at their work', and a hierarchy of officers was appointed remotely similar (for there was no other English precedent) to the administration of the naval dockyards. The Palatines were promised small farms, but they were first expected to work off the cost of their passage from England, and there was no way of knowing how long that would take.[29]

The Palatines were three months at sea, in a fleet of ten vessels. They sailed under naval convoy, and with the Governor of New York on board, but the Governor had no maritime command and it was a loosely managed venture. The people arrived, as he reported, 'in a deplorable sickly condition'. Sixteen per cent had died on the way; one ship was wrecked and two others limped in very late.[30] The whole enterprise was the earliest blueprint, and an inexact one, for the voyage of the First Fleet to Botany Bay. It epitomised the new style of empire more than anything else in this period. Because it was a pioneering effort it is not surprising that it should have been inexpertly organised, especially compared with Phillip's much longer but much more successful expedition to the other side of the world.

The same imperial attitudes were behind the decision, soon after the wars with France ended (1714), to use the North American colonies as a place of large-scale settlement for English convicts. The government was provoked by the troubles which had, as usual, followed demobilisation. Tens of thousands of men were brought back from foreign battlefields and set free in southern ports, with no provision beyond their final pay. The larger armies and navies of this period meant larger numbers thrown into poverty by peace, busier criminal courts and more crowded gaols. In order to cope in this emergency, and also with the idea of placing the whole system of criminal punishment on a better foundation, the Solicitor-General drew up new legislation, the Transportation Act of January 1718.

Convicted criminals had been transported to the North American colonies throughout most of the previous century, but they had been sent in a piecemeal fashion, and much depended on a ship-owner being found willing to carry them and a colony to receive them. Frequently convicts slipped through the net and, as the 1718 Act put it, 'returned to their former wickedness'. Hardly any had gone since the 1670s, when the two main convict colonies, Virginia and Maryland, had announced that they would take no more. The 1718 Act greatly increased the number who were liable, in law, to be transported, it overrode colonial objections, and it ensured that convicts were handed directly to the contractors responsible for their transportation. Most convicts left from London, and the government offered a subsidy of £3 (later £5) a head to London contractors who would agree to take every felon the courts of south-east England could provide. This made for a fairly foolproof system. It also meant that henceforth, on average, eight or nine hundred convicts took to the Atlantic every year, several shiploads, in a steady stream of forced migration.[31] As a result the convict ships became a distinct category of ocean-going transport, like the slave traders now crossing the water from Africa.

The government took no official interest in the conditions of transportation. It was all done by contract, and the contractors made most of their profit by selling the convicts, as seven-year bonded servants, on arrival in America. But the overall structure was endorsed by government, and by the judges and magistrates throughout the counties who took advantage of it in the sentences they handed down in court. When the system came to an end in 1775, with the outbreak of the American Revolution, hundreds of criminals, newly sentenced and ripe for transportation, were left without a destination. It was this emergency which led to the European settlement in New South Wales.

III

These massive movements of people were a result of an increasing aptitude with pen and paper. Amplified administrative skill and, with it, a better sense of geography appeared within England itself in the new attention paid by magistrates to the parish settlement laws, by which individuals were moved about the face of the country so to make sure that they passed their indigent years in the parish of their birth.[32] But within wider horizons such habits also helped to increase the great split I have mentioned above, the division between men and women who belonged to the empire of good order, the conversation of paper, and those who made their lives beyond it. In due course the new administrative techniques inadvertently threw many English-speaking individuals beyond the reach of authority, so that enlightenment increased disorder at the edge of empire. The elegant skills of a juggler may keep a dozen balls in the air, but they still fall higgledy-piggledy when he stops. Moving hundreds or thousands of people about was an interesting exercise in itself and a game of skill. But how were administrators to cope with these masses once they had finished moving them? How were pen and paper to ensure, in a new world, both the seasonal reaping and mowing and the replanting and renewal of humanity?

It was easy for men and women to escape the limits of literate power, which were not well designed as yet for confinement in the long-term. The business of setting thousands of men free from the army and navy at the end

A runaway convict: the standard image as it appeared beside newspaper advertisements in the North American colonies.

Source: The Library Company of Philadelphia

of each war caused major difficulties throughout the entire eighteenth century. Some became beggars on the highways. Others stole, were caught and became convicts. When convicts were transported to America a certain amount of paperwork went with them, enough for county clerks (if they liked) to draw up lists of men and women arriving. But the lists served little purpose, and the convicts tended to melt into the colonial population.[33] Many escaped from their new masters. The *Gazettes* of Virginia and Maryland carried, almost every week, notices of runaways, little paragraphs which vividly captured the image of the escapee even where they failed to capture the man himself (women convicts were rarely mentioned):

> Ran away from the subscriber, living in Prince-George's county, near Mr Richard Snowden's Ironworks, on Sunday last, a convict servant man named WILLIAM SHEPPARD, by trade a shoemaker, about 5 feet 4 or 5 inches high, has short brown hair, is of a swarthy complexion, and has an ugly down look. He has been hurt in his right leg, which causes him to limp and to walk on [the] end of his toes on that side.[34]

The implications of capture were very serious. Print in black and white had its reverberations in flesh and blood. Besides the beatings and the iron collars and chains which masters were entitled to inflict on recaptured servants, their terms of bondage might be altered. In Virginia local legislation stated that the time of absence was to be served twice over and in Maryland it was multiplied ten times.[35]

Some successful runaways made their way down to the sea and home-wards, and others disappeared into the wilds of America. The 'back parts' of North Carolina, as one Maryland governor reported to his English super-ior, were 'long the receptacles of Fugitives for Debt and Felony from the Adjoining Provinces, and Runaway Convicts'. And, he added, 'It is difficult, my Lord, very difficult, to bind people of that Kind by any Laws.' That other body of transportees, the Palatines, also proved troublesome on arrival in New York. Within two or three years they had all been released from bondage and afterwards made their own lives on the frontier.[36]

Such slippery movement might make it hard to know who people were. An age which did much, through writing, to reduce personal risk also made a game of individual identity. Men and women might lose themselves in two or three continents, from ocean to ocean, one sea-change after the other, mingling their dialects, their accents, their images of self, their God-given rank in life among a limitless spectrum of others.[37] Current circumstances might have nothing to do with roots. The same confusion affected all ranks, and from the west end of London to the back parts of Carolina. Attitudes (the post-modern term) struggled with authenticity, and 'humours' and 'character' might be assumed for a month or for a moment: 'Why, I'll swear, Belinda,' says Lady Brute, in Vanbrugh's *The Provok'd Wife* (1697), 'some people do give strange agreeable airs to their faces in speaking. Tell me true: did you never practice in the glass?'[38] The most celebrated performers, in the theatre and in life, were those who rolled many parts into one, and who were at the same time, as one such character in a play of Farquhar's put it, 'men of intrinsic value who can strike our fortunes out of ourselves'.[39] Daniel Defoe's book *Moll Flanders*, a best-seller in its time, was advertised as the story of a woman who was 'twelve Years a Whore, five times a Wife, (whereof once to her own Brother) twelve Years a Thief, eight Years trans-ported Felon to Verginia [sic], at last grew Rich, lived Honest, and died a Penitent'. Defoe himself loved disguises. He once worked as an English secret agent in Scotland, where, he boasted, 'I am all to everyone that I may gain some.'[40]

Another man, John Meffe, or Merth, was English-born, to French Protestant parents who afterwards settled in Holland. He served as appren-tice to a London weaver, but was condemned to transportation for house-breaking in about 1715. Near the American coast, as he recalled late in life, the ship on which he sailed was taken by pirates:

as he refused to Sign a Paper, in order to his becoming a Pirate among them, they set him with eight others a-shore in a Desart Island wholly without Inhabitants. . . . an Indian Cannoe arriving by Accident there, prevented their perishing with Hunger, as they all expected; for getting into the Vessel, when the Indians were gone up the Island, they sailed from one small Isle to another, till they reached the Coast of America.

He got employment as a sailor, 'and lived upon the Ocean a considerable Time, carrying Merchandize from Virginia, South-Carolina, &c. to Barbados, Jamaica, and other British Islands'. He then returned to England. However, he was still under sentence of transportation, and the punishment for coming home before one's time was up was death. He was in daily fear of being caught but, to his own surprise, he found himself unable to run to safety. As he put it, 'he had a sort of illusion upon him', 'some Ill Spirit or Genius', which made him prefer danger in his native land to an aimless liberty abroad. He could no longer live by his 'intrinsic value'. He told his story, and it was written down for the record on the eve of his hanging.[41]

Numbers of demobilised men, especially sailors, took to the sea in their own ships, legally or illegally acquired. Some must have been among the pirates who tried to enlist John Meffe. Pirates figured largely within the empire at this time, and more than any others they represented the spirit of free movement and resistance which was the underside of the new order. Water shaped the British empire, and the implicit laws of sea life were pearls drawn from the plum-coloured depths. The memories and hopes of piracy, or at least the moral economy which helped to shape the pirates' existence (as a later chapter shows), inspired much of the early evolution of European settlement in New South Wales. The story of the pirates demonstrates the shape of empire because it uncovers its alternative, the element of self-sufficiency and the world of living voices. Like all ocean sailors, pirates had their own language, an unwritten argot drawn not only from English, in all its varieties, but from French, Dutch and the tongues of west Africa. ('Bugger', or 'bougre', was a French and then a Dutch word which came to England in the mouths of sailors, and so to the Antipodes.)[42] Such vigour notwithstanding, maritime language was framed by the sublime voice of the sea itself:

> Now what avails it to be brave,
>   On liquid precipices hung?
> Suspended on a breaking wave,
> Beneath us yawn'd a sea-green grave,
>   And silenc'd ev'ry tongue.[43]

Pirates escaped this dilemma by creating their own mini-states on dry land, of which the first, as far as we know, and the most famous, was at Madagascar. The Madagascar settlement seems to have begun in the 1680s, when several pirates retired to the island and set themselves up among the local people, 'each living [wrote Defoe, an authority on pirates] with his own Wives, Slaves, and Dependants, like a separate Prince'.[44]

Britain became a maritime power in a substantial sense during the eighteenth century. Naval bases abroad, staffed by Englishmen, made it possible for fleets to stay away the whole year round, and as a result fleets with their own commodores were appointed for particular parts of the Atlantic and Indian oceans. The Marines were permanently embodied in 1755, as a force of soldiers especially adapted to movements by sea.[45] The waters of the Atlantic, in particular, thus acquired their own long-term population, British and otherwise, which spread eastward into the Indian and even the Pacific oceans during the second half of the century. Similarly, the numbers of pirates multiplied enormously with the declaration of peace and the disbanding of part of the Royal Navy in 1713. For a few years there were as many as 2400, or thirty 'companies', active especially in the Carribean. The Atlantic coast of Africa was also an important rendezvous, especially the mouth of the Sierra Leone River, where the leading man, 'formerly a noted Buccaneer', had 'two or three Guns before his Door, with which he salutes his friends, the Pyrates'.[46]

The Caribbean was a cockpit for the English authorities, even when war was ended, and their attention in those parts was equally divided between the Spanish (who had several Caribbean colonies) and the pirates. The pirates made their headquarters on the island of New Providence, one of the Bahamas. By 1716 there were already fifty men on the island under one Thomas Barrow who called himself 'Governor of Providence', and who said he would make the place 'a Second Madagascar'.[47] Even after his extirpation there were said to be two thousand pirates in those seas. Among the right-minded, piracy was a disease which spread easily among poor men, and a very serious threat to the efficiency of the system embodied, from the centre, in paper and ink. As one observer put it, the pirates 'esteem themselves a Community, and to have one common interest'.[48] They were created by empire and they lived by opposition to empire.

Two mainland settlements in the Caribbean, one on the Gulf of Honduras and the other a little further south on the Mosquito Shore, lived halfway between 'the roguish Common-Wealth' and the more enlightened scheme of things. These settlements had been formed by buccaneers in the middle years of the seventeenth century. In due course the adventurers turned from plundering the Spanish to cutting the valuable timber to be found inland, especially mahogany, fit for English furniture, and the logwood from which cloth dyes were made.[49]

The entire coast belonged in theory to Spain and therefore the government in London took no steps to settle it in a regular way. The people were under the nominal control of the Governor of Jamaica, but they looked after themselves. Pirates and buccaneers ruled themselves by common consent and they were entirely masculine in their methods. As John Meffe discovered, pirates enlisted by contract (though marooning might be the alternative). They had meticulous rules for the management of their ships, the dividing of spoils, the punishment of wrongdoers (including a jury

The port-side hanging of an eighteenth-century pirate, with tall masts in the background.

Source: Lauinger Library, Georgetown University

system) and the election of captains and quartermasters.[50] William Dampier, who lived among the logwood cutters for a month, found a similar spirit of easy-going order. They worked in small gangs and, when it came to transporting the timber, he said, 'every Man is left to his choice to carry what he pleaseth, and commonly they agree very well about it: For they are contented to labour very hard'. They had cattle and killed every Saturday for the succeeding week. Each beast they cut into quarters, 'and taking out all the Bones, each Man makes a hole in the middle of his Quarter, just big enough for his Head to go thro'; then puts it on like a Frock, and trudgeth home; and if he chanceth to tire, he cuts off some of it, and flings it away'. Easy-going and hard-working, the logwood cutters seem to have been the spiritual ancestors of the Australian bushmen, many generations later. They drank hard too, with no sense of securing property for the future. According to Dampier, 'when Ships come from Jamaica with Rum and Sugar, they are too apt to mispend both their Time and Money'. A later traveller found that the Australians 'earn their money like horses and spend it like asses'.[51]

As on the pirate ships, a distinctive type of commonwealth was worked out at Honduras and the Mosquito Shore, and it was deeply entrenched by the passage of time. Magistrates were elected and laws were made by full meetings of 'the people', apparently the heads of households. There was an indigenous system of land-ownership, but there was also little family life because of the scarcity of women.[52] By mid-century some of the communities had been there – their people living and dying, asking and answering, planning and deciding – 'above an hundred years, [and] no Power . . . [had] yet attempted to disturb them'.[53]

This was a community governed very little by pen and ink and very much by living voices, men's voices, as if on board ship. For example, in any regular English colony officials were sworn in with oaths prescribed by parliament. They stood up before the people and recited a form of words devised at Westminster. In these logwood settlements the magistrates had their own oaths, worked out on the spot, and, they said, 'they cared no more for an Act of Parliament than for a piece of broun paper'.[54] All paper from England was equally contemptible. Indeed, thanks to painful air-borne insects, writing itself was a battle on the Mosquito Shore:

> This letter My Lord would require a thousand apologies both for its blots and blunders [wrote an imperial officer from that coast, presumably hitting right and left as he did so]; but if your Lordship could conceive any idea of the persecution and the pain I have suffered from flies [that is, mosquitoes] whilst I was writing it I am sure your goodness would readily forgive them all.[55]

In spite of mosquitoes, he made the effort. By similar efforts, multiplied many times, the power of writing gradually made its mark on such communities, drawing them within the circle of enlightened authority.

The First Fleet left England three months after this letter was written. By now the power of the pirates had been thoroughly broken in the Atlantic and they were never to make any mark on the operations of empire in the western Pacific. (European pirates, that is; Asian ones were very active in the East Indies.) But the customs which had shaped piracy, the power of living voices, the energies and attitudes of seamen, including seamen ashore, were not so easily curtailed.

Chapter 3

Towards Botany Bay

I

Arthur Phillip was Governor of New South Wales for nearly five years, from 26 January 1788 to 11 December 1792.[1] Like most rulers he was both praised and blamed. When complaints were made about him by his people on the spot it was usually to the effect that he never talked, except to give orders; 'Never . . . communicates any part of his plan for establishing the Colony or carrying on his work, to any one – much less, consult them.' 'Our austere Governor', as one officer called him, wrote very fine reports back to England, but he was not an easy man to engage in conversation. His sense of humour was dry, gentle and infrequent. For instance, on an expedition inland, in April 1791, Phillip climbed a hill with his party in order to survey the country. This 'pile of desolation', from which they could see nothing but tedious scrub, the Governor named 'Tench's Prospect Mount', in honour of one of the bubbling and eternally curious young officers who was with him.[2]

Captain Tench saw the joke, but for some of the other gentlemen in the colony Phillip was an opaque, impenetrable despot. Major Robert Ross, who ranked next to the Governor, complained that he 'communicates nothing to any person here but his secretary'. Phillip never asked for advice, except as a last resort, and he saw no need to tell even his officers, in anything but the most general terms, what the Secretary of State expected of them. Ross was entirely in the dark as to 'the intentions of Government'. Even six months after their arrival he had, he said, no inkling of Phillip's opinions about the country: 'he has never done me the honor of informing me of his or asking me for mine'.[3]

Phillip's style was more than a matter of personality. He was a naval officer among soldiers, a man of the sea on dry land, a fish out of water, and that continually jarring fact must have encouraged him to keep to himself. He was a polite and literate version of those maritime captains who made themselves petty princes on Madagascar. As Governor, indeed, he was a symptom of his times. However enigmatic his own character might seem, he was led by the current style of advanced administration to penetrate every aspect of daily life about him, to digest from a distance.

It is difficult to draw a picture big enough to show the significance of Phillip's arrival in Australia, embodying as he did new principles of life and death in Europe's Antipodes. The peoples who had already lived, for thousands of years, on the islands of the western Pacific, in Torres Strait and along the northern edge of Australia, had a story about sharks who left the sea and came ashore. Among some Aborigines in eastern Arnhem Land the Shark was their Ancestor, who had been washed inland and whose great spirit lived among those reedy islands of water, the brown lagoons. Considered in this way the Shark was a source of ceremony and order, a seed of humanity. In Hawaii, the chiefs who ruled the people were called 'sharks that walk on the land'. All Polynesian chiefs were understood, in a ritual sense at least, to be strangers and usurpers. Having crossed the sandy perimeters of each homeland, 'Clothed with the green and crowned with the foam', they lived in a peculiar relationship with the people, for whom their authority was something apart, a fearful symmetry cutting into daily life.[4] Supreme order, with its shining bulk, its blood, justice, sweetness, art and ceremony – and, after all, more blood – came from the sea, from the dangerous depths and from beyond the horizon. It was to be the same with the Europeans in Australia, and considered in this way Phillip was to be distinctly shark-like.

New South Wales was the last of a little family of settlements, the offspring of empire in the age of Enlightenment. These were planned communities, and each was designed to meet various purposes within the framework of imperial and domestic politics. But in each the central idea was the remodelling, renewing and commodifying of lives, and this was to be achieved by the dislodging of people and their movement from one land across vast and gaping oceans to another. Souls were to be trimmed of their sense of place. An earlier generation had begun to experiment with the movement of hundreds, and even thousands abroad. They had polished their skills with the administration of enormous armies. But movement by itself was not enough, nor the mere health and survival of bodies. Imaginative Englishmen now began to think in more elaborate terms, to let their minds move among schemes which would bind families (women began to seem more and more significant) to the soil on the other side of the sea, endowing them with a second birth and a new life, planning not for a voyage but for generations, for the empire's good and even, as far as possible, for the good of the people themselves.

Such schemes were the product of a pen-and-paper culture. They were part of a new science of human nature, so that, although humane, they were also abstract and speculative. They were experimental, especially in their theories about the use of authority, and wherever they could be put into practice they never worked exactly as intended. Ideas blossoming among

Arthur Phillip, first Governor of New South Wales, a man of the sea on dry land: a portrait painted to commemorate his appointment in 1786.

Source: National Portrait Gallery, London

educated people, simply as ideas, did not translate automatically into living order beyond the ocean. When it came to settlement, sometimes the voice of local authority was a feeble whisper, sometimes an all-pervasive roar.

Pen and paper greatly expanded the range of European imagination. The eighteenth century saw the rise of the novel as a newly popular species of literature, mixing up reality and fiction by a process marvellous to its first consumers. This was an old achievement of theatre, but the effect of novels was more pervasive and absolute. When we read, as Thomas Jefferson remarked in 1771, 'We never reflect whether the story . . . be truth or fiction. If the painting be lively, and a tolerable picture of nature, we are thrown into a reverie, from which if we awaken it is the fault of the writer.'[5] The first novels made a deep and echoing impact on the collective imagination, and on common belief about the way in which human beings might respond to new circumstances. Among the very first and most successful was a novel by Daniel Defoe, entitled *The Life and Strange Surprizing Adventures of Robinson Crusoe of York, Mariner: Who lived Eight and Twenty Years, all alone in an un-inhabited Island on the Coast of America, near the Mouth of the Great River of Oroonoque; Having been cast on Shore by Shipwreck, wherein all the Men perished but himself. With an Account how he was at last as strangely deliver'd by Pyrates*. This book and its sequel, *The Farther Adventures*, first appeared in 1719. The story of Robinson Crusoe was extraordinarily popular throughout the eighteenth century. In terms of numbers of volumes sold, it was rivalled only by the Bible and *Pilgrim's Progress*. It was one of the few books of the period which almost everyone knew, whether rich or poor, English or otherwise, and it is still one of the most engaging stories ever written. Jean-Jacques Rousseau described it as the one book every enlightened child must read.[6] It showed the connection between virtue and resourcefulness, common humanity and common sense, all displayed within the unfolding of one man's conscience.

Robinson Crusoe was not only marooned and rescued. He afterwards formed on his island a colony of his own. Some of his settlers were Spaniards, but others were seamen, the 'pyrates' of the title, who had mutinied against their captain and who faced hanging if they went back to England. This part of the story is a description of order without any kind of imposed government (the hero visited but no longer lived on his island). It was order punctuated by fighting, jealousy and negotiation, but order all the same. As Crusoe explained,

> the People [were] under no discipline or Government but my own; who tho' I had influence over them as Father [metaphorically speaking] and Benefactor, had no Authority or Power, to Act or Command one way or other, farther than voluntary Consent mov'd them to comply.[7]

And yet it worked. In the book human nature was tested in remote and desperate circumstances and gradually turned to good, and the spring which gave motion to the whole system – it really created the system – was the moral sensibility of one man, Crusoe himself, who tells us about it.

Thanks to this book, and the ideas which gathered on its subject matter, the European settlement in Australia was to live in the common imagination long before it was given a name and a real dwelling place. It was to be pinned to the map in 1786–88, and the movement from imagination to fact was betrayed by the way in which the first settlers occasionally referred to their new home as an 'island'. In Australia, Crusoe's little universe, overlaid in the telling and re-imagining, was to be shifted from paper to fact. 'I had read Robinson Crusoe many times over and longed to be at sea', wrote John Nicol of his childhood. Born in 1755, New South Wales was to be for him an early destination, though not the last (as his autobiography testifies).[8] Such story-telling and speculation fed, and fed on, a readier sense of geography, a better understanding of the places in which people might be settled, and a traffic in news which was progressively more swift and complete.

A surgeon who had come on the First Fleet tried to explain the distance between Australia and England by writing back to his brother:

> Were I to write as much as would fill up 100 Reams of Paper and every Word to sett off for your country as soon as it dropped from my Pen, and to Scour & Scamper away Helter-Skelter through Southern and Northern Latitudes, by the time the last set off . . . [t]he First Word will not have reached one quarter over the Seas that divides Us.

It was the same gentleman (George Worgan) who wrote jauntily of himself as a new Crusoe, walking with his servant above the cliff at the entrance to Sydney Harbour in April 1788, the blue ocean beneath and the limitless winds coming in. 'I & my Man Friday were rambling about,' he said, 'to shoot a few birds.'[9]

New South Wales was thus built, at the end of the eighteenth century, on a deep basis of imagination. But among the planners imagination was stiffened by experience of various projects of settlement. The Palatine projects in 1709–10 were the first in which government had filled numerous emigrant ships for a destination beyond the blue. Then, for some time after the end of the wars with France (1714) plans had circulated in England for an entirely new colony in North America, inspired not by a wish for private profit, the usual motive, but by a desire to do good. This colony was to be called Georgia. Although it was planned in the public interest and was named for the King, it was to be privately organised. There was to be a society, or board of trustees, who would raise enough money for the emigration of poor English and of foreign Protestants, such as Palatines, who might wish to go. The scheme was first proposed for the unsettled parts between New England and Nova Scotia, but during the 1720s interest shifted southwards to the region beyond the Carolinas. For a while it was thought that a number of young male convicts (not, it was stressed, 'our common Run of Old-Baily Transports') might be sent to this place as bonded servants, to be formed into good men, for Georgia was to be not only a 'land of Liberty and Plenty' but of law and order as well.[10] As it turned out, all the emigrants were free men and women, who sailed with the immediate prospect of becoming independent small farmers.

The emigrants were to enter into contracts with the trustees. They were to receive tools for labour and cooking, and a 'watch coat', musket and bayonet for part-time military duty. (Part of the charm and usefulness of *Robinson Crusoe* was the meticulous attention which the author had paid to the business of supplies and sustenance, the material foundation of settlement.) They were to be gathered in towns or villages and were to receive 50 acres each, which they were not allowed to sell, so as to prevent speculation in land. They were to be rationed for one year according to a strict but plentiful allowance, while they laboured on their own farms, on fortifications and on 'other Works for the common Good and publick Weal'. The Trustees were to fund public buildings, there was to be a public grindstone for every village, and at the capital there was to be a public midwife, who was promised a crown (5s.) 'for every woman she lays'. In return, the people were expected not only to work hard but to behave themselves: 'no Drunkards, or other notoriously vicious Persons' would be taken, and in Georgia itself the drinking and sale of rum was to be prohibited.[11]

The settlement of Georgia came to pass in 1732. It depended on large parliamentary grants, totalling £108,000 over the first ten years (four times the private contributions), but the trustees were left to work out all the details of government. They wrestled with the way in which the day-to-day life of the people might be organised. They were determined not to have a governor, because of 'the pride that name might instil'. Theirs was to be a small community, in which there was to be neither pride nor oppression: a settlement, as it were, of brothers. To begin with it was thought that government might be vested in 'an overseer and council of honest and discreet men'. In the event, there was no council, but a few were chosen from among the emigrants to act as rather humble and half-hearted magistrates.[12]

The result was a vacuum of authority to be filled by others, whose power expanded like so many balloons. James Edward Oglethorpe was a trustee who went out with the first party at his own expense. He was also a general in the British army, and in Georgia he spent time with the troops watching the frontier. From a civilian point of view he was simply a gentleman of high principle who had volunteered to lead the emigrants, and 'to settle them'.[13] To begin with, as one visitor put it, he was 'extreamly well beloved by all his People: The general Title they give him, is FATHER: If any of them is sick, he immediately visits them, and takes a great deal of Care of them: If any Difference arises, he's the Person that decides it.'[14] This was an ideal authority, the sustaining and enlivening power of a Robinson Crusoe. Crusoe never had to contemplate handing out death as well as life, but this was not true of Oglethorpe's more palpable experience in Georgia. There, his eye wandered unrestrained into every aspect of daily affairs. For instance, he once had occasion to interfere in the alteration of two adjoining houses, one of which belonged to his ally, Dr Hawkins. While building was in progress, the general climbed up on Hawkins's window-sill, 'put his Head up betwixt the Joice [joists] of the . . . [other] House', and called up to the builder 'to build the said Joice six inches lower'. He wanted them clear of Hawkins's window. The builder explained that there was no room. Then, said Oglethorpe, the whole house must come down and be built again at the right level. That could not be done, said the builder, without it ending up leaky, but the 'Father' of Georgia had the final word: 'you might have thought of that before'. And, he said, 'if you touch a Shingle of . . . [Hawkins's house] I'LL SHOOT YOU'.[15]

Oglethorpe agreed with the trustees' ban on 'High titles'. He said they spoilt the mind.[16] He was one of the pioneers of a new kind of civilian authority within the British empire, and within Britain itself.[17] He and later figures of the same kind carried forward the transformation of the empire, and the fashioning of a new kind of power, the attractive but ill-defined power of a good father, creator and ruler in one, a figure managing alone at the edge of the vast ocean. Others like him, in other new settlements, were in fact given titles, but often very vague ones such as 'agent', 'conductor' or 'superintendent'. In some cases (like early Georgia) the title of 'governor', with its formal dignity, seemed out of place, but that inhibition was soon lost, while at the same time governors of a traditional type were given some of the more pervasive powers enjoyed by men like Oglethorpe. New wine was put into old bottles, with unpredictable results. This was to happen in New South Wales.

The planning of Georgia had begun with the peace of 1714. About that time there was also a proposal to settle Nova Scotia with men released from the Queen's armies.[18] Nothing was done. However, when a very similar proposal was made in 1749, at the end of another great war and to a new generation of ministers, it was taken up with remarkable speed. An elaborate plan was devised at the Board of Trade, and within two months a fleet of twelve vessels carrying nearly 3000 people, including surgeons, clergy and schoolmasters, had departed for the new land. The Palatine settlement in New York had been a failure from the government point of view. By 1749 it was also a matter of official belief that the first Georgian settlers had been wrongly chosen and wrongly organised. Nova Scotia was to be different. Here there was to be more precision in the exercise of power. The bulk of the men to be settled had been lately discharged from the army and navy. They were ideal for the task, said Lord Halifax, President of the Board and author of the scheme, since they were 'familiariz'd to Subordination and Command and . . . equally willing to obey and active to execute such Orders as shall be given them'.[19]

This system of subordination and command, activity and execution, was to be combined with the liberties of Englishmen. Certainly, the Governor was to have great power in allocating land, and liberty was to be coloured with restraint. But all the first settlers were to be freeholders, and with land they would receive the right to vote. They were to be seen as 'brave unfortunate Men, who have risqued their Lives in His Majesty's Service', and they would be repaid by the paternal devotion of the government, its 'Generosity, Compassion and Gratitude'.[20] They would respond as settlers and subjects, in a spirit of humble good order. As with the Palatine and Georgian projects, the authorities felt sure of the life-giving results of their own generosity. But in their plans for Nova Scotia ministers took on a much more detailed responsibility than they had ever done before. At the same time, by a tighter choice of settler, they were increasing the chances of success. At first sight the Governor of Nova Scotia looked like any other governor. In fact, ministers had collected for His Excellency what they hoped would be a new and malleable people. This made him into a new kind of governor, more isolated and more eminent than usual, a ruler and creator – in Robinson Crusoe's words, a 'Father and Benefactor' – rolled into one.

The men who planned British settlements were learning slowly, and at the same time they were expanding their ambitions. Trial and error does work, even when new errors spring up with every trial.

II

The 1780s were the climactic decade of the eighteenth century, and one of the most exciting periods in the history of the world, or at least the western part of it. They saw the triumph of the American Revolution and the beginning of the French Revolution. According to Wordsworth, 'Europe at that time was thrilled with joy, / France standing at the top of golden hours, / And human nature seeming born again'.[21] In Britain, with the end of the American Revolution, two great issues dominated the conversation of polite and ambitious men and women. These were, first, the status of Blacks throughout the empire and, secondly, penal discipline. Slaves and convicts both challenged the imagination of reformers. Both seemed to live within a restricted, oppressive and exotic culture of their own, beyond the sweetness and light of an improving civilisation. Both might be touched by the humanity of educated men and women and their lives enlarged.

The British empire was changed in a fundamental way by the new attention paid to Blacks within its borders. Reformers were fired by the challenge of considering Blacks and Whites within the empire, even Blacks and Englishmen, on equal terms. For the time being it was mainly a challenge to the imagination because most of the practical implications were, as yet, beyond the horizon. Nevertheless, the old view of the empire, as a system of authority depending on Englishness, on conversation rooted in English dialect, shaped by English mouths for English ears, was now gradually supplanted, at least within some circles. Living voices, whether Black or White, were to be silenced by the new type of authority. The 'Blackness' of voices, obvious still to Blacks and Whites living and listening, as it were, at ground level, began (but only began) to be irrelevant within the new empire of pen and paper. Two questions worried philanthropists. Blackness was usually, but not always, associated with spiritual and physical bondage. How were Black slaves to be changed into free, Christian men and women? Also, how might free Blacks be vested with the sacred rights of property, and especially landed property, the ultimate criterion of liberty? The first question is fundamental to any history of race and racism in the West. But the second question bears more directly on our understanding of early New South Wales. Ideas about free Blacks overlapped with ideas about convicts during the 1780s, and (see Chapter 8) they overlapped in due course with ideas about Blacks in Australia itself.

American independence in 1783 opened up opportunities for change. The arrangements for peace led to a massive rearrangement of population. Propertied Loyalists were resettled in other parts of North America, both north and south of the United States, and fishing families likewise moved from Nantucket, in Massachusetts, to Britain and to Nova Scotia. Spain had been allied with the American colonies against Britain and as a result in Central America more than two and a half thousand people, British subjects Black and White, were now evacuated from Spanish territory on the Mosquito Shore, to be carried across the water to various places about the Caribbean. Most went northwards to the Gulf of Honduras. The management of this last exercise was entrusted to the Superintendent at Honduras, Colonel Edward Despard.

Despard, and other officers like him, were commissioned by the King under the title of 'Superintendant, Agent and Commander in Chief'. In Central America the responsibilities of the Superintendent had always included, in a vague way, the good order and prosperity of the people, but much more important to begin with was the management of British relations with the Spaniards and the indigenous people. In principle the post was like that of the Superintendents of Indian Affairs appointed during the eighteenth century for large parts of mainland North America. The Superintendent was a go-between, a broker appointed by the King to deal with outsiders.[22] At Honduras and on the Mosquito Shore the logwood cutters described this officer merely as 'the Superintendant of His Majesty's Affairs'. He had very little to do with *their* affairs, and he was not in any sense a governor. He was 'His Majesty's Representative,' they said, but they insisted that, 'whether under the description of Superintendant, Consul, or Agent', he had no regular authority over British subjects.[23]

The powers of the Superintendent at Honduras germinated and blossomed during the 1780s. In 1786 most of the settlers on the Mosquito Shore, 2214 in all, were transferred to a strictly limited supply of land at Honduras. As the representative of the King on the spot (but with no constitutional precedents to guide him) Despard took control of the entire business of movement, the comfort of the Mosquito Shore people, their passage from one place to another, the distribution of rations allowed by the British government during the period of transition, and their fair treatment at Honduras. The people already at Honduras had to make room and – since there was no regular system of freehold, the territory being Spanish – it was up to the Superintendent to decide who was entitled to what. The sacredness of property and of all settled rights was a matter for his judgment alone. These were the classic powers, both autocratic and benevolent, of the new type of political administrator.

The task was complicated by the fact that the Mosquito Shore people varied in race and status. The logwood cutters were slave-owners, but they observed a very fine line between slavery and freedom. The slaves had gardens of their own and, because there was no centrally organised system of land-ownership, their title to land was not conditional on that of anyone else. It was 'as sacred', according to one authority, 'as any possessed by a Free born subject'. There were also a number of Blacks, men and women, who were moved from one place to another as free subjects, though dignified by no more than Christian names: 'Bob', 'Judy', 'Nancy', 'Quashy', 'Maria'.[24] In Despard's view all the free people (though apparently not the slaves) were shaken down by the process of movement into one homogeneous mass, equal under his own eye.

The Superintendent gave all settlers a similar right to land, not only rich and poor, new and old, but even Black and White, male and female. The leading men wrote home at length about his 'leveling principles . . . [and] his passion for despotic authority'.[25] Despard's understanding of equity amounted to a fundamental rearrangement of society, and in his radical proposals he was, to all appearances, responsible to no-one but himself. Within the newly enlarged settlement those who had hitherto been the least powerful, 'the lower class of white Men and People of Colour', soon responded to the new dispensation by shifting allegiance from their elected magistrates to the Superintendent. They declared 'in meetings both Public and Private' that former regulations had lapsed, that society had dissolved, and 'that all Men at this time were, or ought to be, on an equal footing'.[26] The epitome of this little revolution, worked by imperial authority at Honduras, was the indignant sketch, drawn by the old leadership, of the 'Croud of Mulattoes &ca' who hung on the coat-tails of Despard and his surveyor, as they redrew the limits of property in that part of the world.[27]

Could Blacks really aspire, on equal terms with Whites, to be landholders within the British empire? Despard thought so, but he was corrected on this point by his minister at Whitehall, the Home Secretary, Lord Sydney. Sydney (formerly Thomas Townshend) was an anomaly within the British Cabinet, and his ideas were in some ways old-fashioned. As Home Secretary, from 1783 to 1789, he was responsible for the colonies. He had long been interested in the way in which the empire might be a medium for

British liberties, traditionally understood. Twenty years before, as a member of what was called 'the Minority' in the House of Commons, he had played a small part in yet another settlement of Palatines, this time in South Carolina. The Minority were interested in the expansion of the empire, but they wanted to push out its boundaries with free people rather than by conquest.[28] The Palatines were nearly as good as Englishmen: they were Protestant, they were European, and their experience at home gave them a wholesome fear of tyranny. It was to be hoped that in North America they would form self-sufficient bodies of yeomen, which would duplicate the humble, sinewy aspects of Englishness.

In general, Sydney approved of Despard's program, but he asked him to show more regard for settled local thinking. Common Englishness included a reverence for living conversation and for entrenched ideas, especially when they affected the rights of property. He pointed out to the Superintendent that in the colonies 'people of Colour, or Free Negroes . . . [were not] considered upon an equal footing with People of a different Complexion'. Such 'natural Prejudices' were the stuff of liberty, and it followed that in the distribution of land Blacks were not to be treated like Europeans, especially the more affluent Europeans.[29]

Sydney was also concerned at this time with the settlement of Blacks on the opposite edge of the ocean, at Sierra Leone on west coast of Africa, once the haunt of pirates. As with the scheme for Georgia, more than fifty years before, this was begun as a private philanthropic enterprise. But its supporters (who included the aged General Oglethorpe) won the approval of the King through Sydney, as Secretary of State, and the government took some responsibility for its success.[30] For the philanthropists themselves it was part of a larger scheme for the emancipation of Blacks throughout the empire, and for the abolition of race as a point of distinction among the subjects of the King. Lord Sydney was not prepared to think in such broad terms. No government, in his view, should try to change the form of society, because in doing so it must break into the settled rights of the people. He had no time for those up-to-date humanitarians who wanted to add to the power of government to meddle in daily life. The Sierra Leone project was approved, not for large-minded humanitarian reasons, but because the Blacks included men who had deserted their owners in America during the revolution and had been recruited into the British forces.[31] The scheme was in that way reminiscent of Nova Scotia in 1749. Former servants of the Crown (Black or White) were entitled to look to the King when they found themselves helpless in the world, as old servants might look to any good master.

The expedition to Sierra Leone was under a joint command. Three privately-owned ships, or transports, carried 'the Black Poor' and their 'Superintendant' or 'Agent Conductor', Joseph Irwin. They went in convoy with a naval vessel under Captain Thomas Boulden Thompson. Thompson had no legal authority over the Blacks themselves, and in this way he was like Oglethorpe in Georgia. He was instructed only to see them safely to Africa, to find a spot at Sierra Leone which might be acquired by negotiation with the local people, and in other ways 'to give every possible assistance' to Irwin during the first period of settlement. On arrival the Blacks were to meet and elect their own 'Chief in Command', who was to take over when the Englishmen departed.[32]

Even before they left England, Thompson decided that the former slaves were beyond Irwin's powers of management. They reached Sierra Leone without mishap, on 10 May 1787, but no progress seemed possible from that point without the captain himself taking a strong hand. In July, he had two Blacks flogged for what he called 'insolence and misbehaviour'. He was then preparing to leave. He was not optimistic about the future happiness of the people, mainly because of their 'obstinacy and laziness', which, he said, 'neither remonstrance, persuasion or punishment have . . . been able to subdue'. It is not surprising that the Blacks should have felt lost between their old bondage and their peculiar new liberty. Thompson even persuaded himself that they would have been happy to go back to slavery.[33] Their Chief was to face the same problems, and within a few years men with more regular authority were sent out to take charge.

At the same time (during the mid-1780s) the British government was confronted with yet another great matter of population disposal which was a direct result of recent war. Since the outbreak of the American Revolution in April 1775, there had been no satisfactory place to send convicts. Ministers considered three possible answers. There had always been a market for convict labour in Virginia and Maryland, and so there was some reason to hope that, even with war – even, perhaps, with American independence – transportation might proceed as it had always done. If not, there were two other options to be followed up. New sites might be found, or else the penal system might be reformed so that convicts stayed in England. At home, it was suggested, convict men might labour for the public good under a discipline carefully designed to lead them into habits of obedience and virtue. The women were understood to be a much less significant problem, if only because they were fewer. They hardly figured in these discussions.

The government turned first to the most radical of these possibilities. In April 1776 the Prime Minister, Lord North, laid before parliament a 'felon's bill', designed to create penal establishments on the spot. The bill seemed (for reasons set out below) to impinge dangerously on questions of liberty under the law, on issues enshrined in Habeas Corpus and on the Christian dignity of Englishmen, and as a result the response in parliament was 'very warm'. Among its opponents, Lord Irnham said that it would establish in England a form of white slavery. But supporters of the bill saw this as old-fashioned nonsense. They drew on the newer attitudes of professional men, humanitarians (a few of them landed gentlemen) and wide-awake career officers of the army and navy. Edward Despard was a classic example of the last type. So was Arthur Phillip. They were individuals with an interest in the efficiency of government, and in the blossoming of a new style of empire. On the streets of London 'a stretch of power' was frequently called for. As one writer in a city newspaper remarked, 'the peace and safety of the community at large, is of much more consequence, than the right of freedom to a set of wretches, who will make no other use of their liberty, than to murder and rob inoffensive and industrious people, who are going about their business'.[34]

The argument between old and new – between customary rights and amplified power – went far beyond parliament. It was to be ground to a sharp point during the 1780s, in many areas of public life, and it can be traced, not only through several great revolutions, but through the early history of European settlement in Australia.

William Eden, a proponent of new ideas, under-secretary of state and the man responsible for the details of the 1776 bill, wanted a more finely articulated penal system, one in which convicts would be punished in a scientific way, strictly according to the seriousness of their crimes. 'Some', he said, 'might be sent to garrison places situated in unwholesome climates; others might be made to work, and confined in houses of correction; others again be employed in preserving the navigation of rivers [that is, by dredging the banks]'. He was not in favour of wholesale transportation, especially as it had been carried on hitherto. He had indeed written a pamphlet against the system several years before, demonstrating thereby a knowledge of the new and peculiarly precise penal theory associated with the Italian, Cesare Beccaria, whose work, *Of Crimes and Punishments*, had appeared in English in 1767. Eden wanted much tighter control, an administrative hierarchy under the eye of government, and the meticulous categorisation of convicts by overseers and clerks. He wanted to encourage reform by the precise and permanent identification of individual convicts, by recording behaviour during punishment, and by shortening or extending terms to match response.[35]

The bill passed in spite of keen opposition, and it became the Hulks Act. It allowed for male convicts to be housed in ships moored in rivers (the Thames in particular) under the management of overseers, who were to control their labour along the river banks and watch their moral progress. Never before had convicts been so closely observed after sentence. Never before in England had Englishmen who were neither soldiers nor seamen been so entirely marshalled under the discipline of the state, and this within reach of all the essential institutions and the finest monuments of British civilisation. They became a tourist attraction. According to one member of parliament, 'people went in thousands and gave them money, particularly ladies of the town, who, as they got their money easily, were known to be generous'.[36] Public interest and public doubts led to an inquiry by a House of Commons select committee in 1779, which offered a second opportunity for gentlemen who disliked the new ideas and who thought that transportation ought to be resumed. One witness suggested to the committee that there might be a market in Florida, which was not affected by the revolution, and even in Georgia, which was. Another, a former governor on the west coast of Africa, suggested a site on the River Gambia, an idea which the committee considered in detail. A third spoke of sending convicts to work on the fortifications at Gibraltar.[37]

The most imaginative suggestion came from the gentleman-botanist Joseph Banks. Banks had been with Captain James Cook on the *Endeavour* in 1768–71, the voyage which had finally proved the non-existence of *Terra Australis Incognita*, the fabled continent which had been thought to embrace the Pacific to the south. His place on that expedition made him one of the very few living Europeans who had seen New Holland (Australia), and he had vivid, though not always accurate, memories of the country around Botany Bay, on the east coast of New South Wales. He suggested that the gaols might be much relieved if two or three hundred convicts were sent to settle in that place. They should be supplied, he said, with provisions for a year, with livestock, seed, equipment for fishing, and arms and ammunition. They might otherwise be left on their own, and he thought that in a very short space of time, if they worked hard, 'they might, undoubtedly, maintain themselves without any Assistance from England'. This scheme appealed to the committee, especially as a means of disposing of those men and women currently imprisoned who were still young and who might make a new life for themselves. But, as they pointed out in their report to the House of Commons, any such project would need a new Act of parliament.[38]

Banks's scheme was also designed to appeal to old-fashioned supporters of the constitution, those like Lord Irnham (mentioned above) who disliked the Hulks Act as an invasion of the liberties of Englishmen. Banks clearly had in mind a settlement in which the convicts would be self-governing. There was to be little official contact with England after the first landing. He made no mention of regular supplies of new convicts: the settlement was to grow by other means. In particular, he thought, 'If the People formed among themselves a Civil Government, they would necessarily increase', a good thing because Botany Bay would then ultimately become a market for British produce.[39] Banks's proposal was shaped to fit the fact that the laws on transportation had never included any reference to bondage or forced labour. Transported men and women had been bound to labour in America for generations, but not as part of their sentence in the English courts. It was still widely (but inaccurately) understood that transportation operated by consent, as it had done in the seventeenth century, so that force could not be justified in law, however necessary it might be in fact. Convicts volunteered to go abroad so as to escape hanging, and they paid for their passage on their arrival in America, either in cash, if they had it, or else through being sold into bondage. Technically – and it was a very important fiction for gentlemen who loved the constitution – they went as free men and women.[40]

The new theorists had to make their way against such principles. They had elaborate ideas about disciplining convicts, but from a legal point of view the addition of any extra penalty such as forced labour, as a member of parliament put it in 1784, was 'a severity that nothing could justify'.[41] It would also have jarred with the great Act of Habeas Corpus (see Chapter 1), which was especially designed to prevent the bondage of Englishmen in any form unaccountable to the courts. Reformers might suggest that government should bind the convicts to itself, whether in England, as with the hulks system, or in some place abroad. But other gentlemen, including Lord Sydney, were convinced that this would be entirely at odds with the constitution. Sydney was one of those 'silly people' (as one advocate of efficiency remarked) who kept on saying, parrot-fashion, that 'The English are free, and should never be slaves.' By their logic, convicts must go to some new country where there was no-one to buy their labour, and they must live there unrestrained. The government might exert itself only in stopping them from getting back. (Escape from Botany Bay, said Banks, 'would be very difficult as the Country was far distant from any part of the Globe inhabited by Europeans'.)[42] As one bluff and laconic member of the House of Commons put it, they should be sent to an island, and then 'give every man a woman' and let them get on with it: 'they might establish a useful colony'.[43]

Under this rubric, it was not the people who needed restraint, but a too eager government. Here was one of the guiding principles of political debate in eighteenth-century England and its empire, part of the doctrine of commonwealth. It led logically in some minds to republicanism and it was one of the guiding ideals of the American Revolution. One oracle for such ideas (but there were many) was the book entitled *Discourses concerning Government*, by Algernon Sidney, Lord Sydney's republican and martyred ancestor. By 1783, the centenary of Sidney's execution, this book had been republished five times, and the name 'Sidney' or 'Sydney' had become one of the current synonyms for patriotism and constitutional liberty: 'Repel the Foe, that desperate, dares invade / The Land protected by great Sydney's shade'. In the same year the former Thomas Townshend had happily chosen as his peerage title, 'Baron Sydney of Chislehurst'. Under the Sidney doctrine, true liberty and order came from the people themselves. And the people need not be numerous. According to the *Discourses*, 'ten may as justly resolve to live together, frame a Civil Society, and oblige themselves to Laws, as the greatest number of Men that ever met together in the World'.[44] Here was a blueprint for colonisers who loved freedom.

The publication of Jean-Jacques Rousseau's even more famous work, *The Social Contract* (1762) had gone further, answering the interest manifest among educated men and women in the process of constitution, in that sweet moment when agreement gave birth to 'a state of society'. Rousseau agreed that liberty did not depend on the majesty of government. On the contrary, he thought that it could best prosper in a place so small that the living voices of men (each ruling his own domestic commonwealth) might reach from one side to the other.[45] Rousseau's influence on English political thought was small for the time being, but such arguments were in the air. In the 1780s, a decade of enormous promise, radical gentlemen were keen to press them on every English peasant, reminding him for instance of his own freely organised village club or benefit society: 'Did it never occur to you, that every state or nation was only a great *club*?'[46]

III

The chemistry which created social order was a subject of endless fascination during the eighteenth century, and popular literature showed that it could operate almost anywhere. Through common conversation men, at least, might organise themselves in spite of, or even in defiance of, parliament, the magistrates and all the other ancient appurtances of the state. Pirates, that 'roguish Common-Wealth', were a famous case, and land-based thieves showed the same *ésprit de corps*. In the 1750s London was headquarters to 'a great Gang of Rogues [as Henry Fielding testified], who are incorporated in one Body, [and] have officers and a Treasury'.[47] In Newgate Gaol the felons had rules for the management of funds, including garnish (the fees taken from prisoners on entry). They elected from among themselves a 'steward', who was the supreme authority, a 'committee of audit' and 'captains of wards'. We cannot know how far principle was matched by practice, and the evidence from Newgate was ambiguous, to say the least. At the Giltspur Street Compter, a smaller London prison, on the other hand, the ruling committee was very fair about garnish, according to the keeper: 'if a person was poor, they never pressed it'. There were no complaints, he said, and 'I never interfere.'[48]

It was another question whether commonwealth methods could flourish among convicts deposited in a remote land, facing fatal disease and exotic dangers. In December 1784 a former African governor set out an elaborate scheme for a settlement of convicts in Africa. He argued that convicts were beyond any normal system of order or discipline. Even as soldiers, he said (and he spoke from experience), they were worse than useless. When two companies of them had been landed in Africa in 1782, 'their whole thoughts were turn'd upon Rapine and Plunder'. So wild and aimless were they that four-fifths were dead within a year. He suggested a cotton plantation on which such people might be employed, near Cape Coast Castle: with barracks of stout timber, triple-locked, gangs of ten managed by 'drivers' with whips, and a special court possessing 'a power to hang all such as desert, or otherwise deserve it'.[49]

The more generous approach was favoured at the Home Office (which administered not only colonies but law and order in Britain itself). Lord Sydney was ardent and honest. True to his Sidney ancestry, his intellectual

Thomas Townshend, Lord Sydney: the portrait of a plain, straightforward and determined man.

Source: Dixson Galleries, State Library of New South Wales

passions focused on the liberty of the subject: 'attachment to the constitution', he very justly said, 'was a consideration superior to every other in his mind'.[50] He worried about the way liberty might be threatened by the Crown. Only the courts, as constituted under the law, might curtail the common rights of Englishmen. Convicts, he thought, were sentenced once and for all by the courts, and any punishment must follow from that sentence alone. 'He did not at all approve', he told parliament in 1776, 'of departing [from] or altering that fundamental principle in our criminal law, that the King may pardon crimes, but not alter punishments when once incurred.'[51] He was less passionate during the 1780s, when he had moved from opposition to government, but by then he was too old to alter his deep devotion to the principles of commonwealth. He would not consider the kind of regime suggested for Cape Coast Castle. He knew that transported convicts might die abroad in large numbers if they were left to themselves, but he was unmoved.[52] They must go, all the same, as free men and women.

Where were they to go? Maryland and Virginia were no longer available, and Sydney, unlike his predecessors, was not prepared to force convicts on remaining parts of the empire. (Even the logwood cutters at Honduras successfully excused themselves.)[53] Early in 1785 his under-secretary, Evan Nepean, inquired about landing them on Turks Islands, among the Bahamas, but it was obvious that from there they would soon scatter to more civilised places.[54] Remoteness seemed absolutely necessary. Cabinet therefore decided on an African destination, namely the island of Lemane many miles up the River Gambia.

The plan for Lemane involved the appointment of a single superintending officer, 'His Majesty's Agent', who was to deal with the neighbouring people just as Despard did with Spaniards in Central America. His duties were mainly maritime. He was to be 'a Mediator . . . between the Natives and the Colony'. But he would also 'take upon him[self] the Command of . . . an arm'd Ship for the Security of the Convicts and the Protection of the Trade there'. He would go out in the first fleet of transports and he would organise matters for the first six months or more. He would then live on board, in 'a more convenient Part of the River', leaving the convicts under a Chief and council elected by the men from among themselves. The Chief was to be guided, when necessary, by the Agent, but he was to choose his own subordinate officers, including magistrates 'to try and punish any of them for Crimes'.[55]

The question of convict transportation during the 1780s was thus to be resolved in the imagination of Lord Sydney by his faith in the ability of convict men to organise themselves, even in the most exotic circumstances, as a community of brothers. The principles which were understood to sustain the British constitution were, it seemed, fundamental principles of human behaviour, at least where Englishmen were concerned. They were fibres capable of holding tightly any parcel of English humanity, from the palace of Westminster to the island of Lemane.

The only detailed evidence that such a scheme would succeed was to be found in the story of Robinson Crusoe. On Crusoe's island the 'pyrates' worked out their own 'Government and Laws', making houses and finding wives, each man for himself, and submitting all in the end to Crusoe for his imprimatur. He was their ruler, and yet at the same time they were 'a Kind of Common-Wealth among themselves'. The program for Lemane also followed the blueprint devised by Rousseau for the founding of a free people, set out in *The Social Contract*. Rousseau's 'legislator' was described as a type of Solon, a 'mechanical genius' who was to lay the foundation of society. He must be distinct from the community, but he could not use force to subordinate it. All must depend on consent, though the legislator might be expected to use the name of some higher authority (divine or otherwise) to embellish his power. The people themselves were, in Rousseau's view, 'an ignorant multitude'. The women were subject to the men, and although the men themselves should enjoy a general sovereignty (a vital fact), they were incapable of planning far beyond their immediate needs. They might choose their own 'chiefs', form households and manage from day to day, but little more. The basis of good order in the long term was to come from a single supreme conscience.[56]

Among forward-thinking men and women of the period this was the ideal model of authority. It had the dazzling and puzzling advantage of reconciling monarchy and commonwealth, authority and freedom, and it was a model applied in a striking range of circumstances, from empires to families. It was a scheme for survival in an age when the flood of pen-and-paper had complicated the understanding of self and undermined certainties about common behaviour. All the leading novels of the age, in some form or other, tackled the resulting sense of danger. Writers took a God-given authority for granted – men above men and men above women – assuming that there must always be some masculine personage who could say, like the God of Moses, 'I am that I am.' But they invited the imagination to play upon the manner in which freedom might thus be simultaneously nurtured and limited by authority. In Samuel Richardson's novel *Clarissa* (1747–48), a virtuous daughter is seduced into rebellion against an overbearing father and dies as a result. Each had rights because authority mattered as much as liberty – that was theoretically certain – but what must be the result in practice? A happier story was to be found in the case of John Adams, the American revolutionary leader, who self-consciously told his own daughter that she might please herself in answering a proposal of marriage. He remained her loving father nevertheless, a point of reference for the exercise of her own judgment and giving or withholding his consent in other matters.[57] Just such an authority, detached but immovable, was to be duplicated at Lemane.

The new method of transportation was founded on the experience of earlier decades. It owed a good deal also to Lord Sydney's reverence for the law and for the consent of the subject. He had been a leading sympathiser with the American Revolution and for similar reasons he was determined that convicts would not be bound to servitude under some agent of the Crown, in England or elsewhere. But it also owed much to the sensibilities of the period. Rousseau's writing was as symptomatic as that of any novelist in this regard, and especially his attempt to marry the One and the Many – inscrutable authority on the one hand and the liberty of the people on the other, the prescription on paper and the wilful, living voices. Happily, perhaps, the plan was never tried at Lemane. In spring 1785 a select committee of the House of Commons, chaired by Lord Beauchamp, gathered enough evidence to condemn the island as a place of fatal diseases in which the convicts would all die within months.[58]

Beauchamp's inquiry was partly a counter-attack by gentlemen in parliament who wanted to see transported convicts under a strict discipline. In his report Beauchamp had little to say about penal theory, but he did declare very strongly against a colony entirely of convicts, 'without any other Government or Controul but what they may from Necessity be led to establish for themselves'. He stated with great confidence that 'such an Experiment has never been made in the History of Mankind' and, he said, there was no good reason for making it now.[59] Whatever the truth on this point, the Home Office was forced to give up Lemane and look for somewhere better. Beauchamp himself had suggested in his report that Das Voltas Bay, on the south-east African coast (in what is now Namibia), might be an ideal site. Lord Sydney and his under-secretary were already aware of it, and a naval vessel was sent straight away to explore.[60] There had been glowing reports – herds of wild sheep, horses, and cattle, luxuriant grape vines, abundant corn, precious stones, iron ore – but as it turned out nothing of the kind could be found. The expedition reported back in July 1786.[61] Sydney then turned, reluctantly, to Botany Bay.

New South Wales had been part of Home Office thinking since Banks had suggested it in 1779. It had already been discussed in Cabinet as a place where younger felons might be sent.[62] It had since been held in reserve, as a last resort in case Das Voltas should prove unsuitable. Early in 1786 Evan Nepean had made inquiries about the cost of sending there 270 convicts, all men. They were to be clothed and rationed for a year but would otherwise be entirely on their own.[63] Beauchamp had been scathing in his comments about the ability of convicts to look after themselves, but Sydney would not budge on this point. He recognised only, as the Lemane scheme shows, that some guidance might be needed to begin with. At Das Voltas, too, the convicts were to manage 'in the same way as was proposed for the Island Le Main'. A naval vessel was to conduct the fleet of transports. Its captain was to land the convicts and to stay with them as long as he saw fit, and he was to leave a guard ship, if necessary, when he departed. From that point the men would be their own masters, and the women subject only to the men.[64]

In August 1786 the first detailed plans were drawn up for New South Wales. The Home Office built partly on the untried foundation of Lemane, Das Voltas and the scheme, mentioned above for the 270 convict men. They also had the advice of individuals who had been thinking about a settlement in New South Wales for some years. The most useful was the American Loyalist, James Mario Matra. Matra, like Banks, had been with Cook on the *Endeavour*. He had given detailed evidence to Lord Beauchamp's committee in 1785 and this had found its way into Home Office files. The blueprint resulting from such advice was for a fairly tight system of government and several years of tutelage. Otherwise the settlement at Botany Bay was to follow the now familiar model.

Two naval vessels were requisitioned which were to remain on the coast of New South Wales for two or three years, under a single command. Sydney was also persuaded of the need for a substantial garrison, at least for the time being. Three companies of Marines were to be sent, for three years, and they were to be accompanied by a chaplain, a commissary, a surgeon and two surgeon's mates.[65] At least, so it seems. The records for the first weeks of decision-making are vague and contradictory. It is only certain that detailed thinking extended to a very limited future, as Nepean was happy to admit: merely 'while the Settlement is in an Infant State'.[66] A newspaper report of 20 September probably sums up official thinking at that time:

> The colony is to be furnished with provisions for two years, and each person or couple are to have a proper quantity of materials for building, and for the purposes of agriculture. Under proper direction they will be enabled to plough, sow, plant, and provide themselves by their industry, with the means of a comfortable subsistence.[67]

When all was properly settled, the convicts were to be left under a government of their own. There was scornful talk of England setting up 'a nest of pirates' in the Antipodes – of reviving the pirate commonwealth which was now dead in fact but very much alive in memory – and there was indeed good reason to fear such an eventuality.[68]

Sailors, let loose at English ports, frequently became convicts, especially in London, where they came up from the docks to the pubs and brothels. They were also the natural inhabitants of an oceanic empire. They were used to the vast distances which were to divide the new community from Britain and would naturally lay the foundation of Lord Sydney's vision. Under some such happy impression in October a sailor stole a pair of silver-mounted spectacles from a shop in Piccadilly. On being arrested, 'with every mark of joy in his countenance, and twirling his hat over his head, [he] hollowed out "*Botany Bay* a hoy!"' His was the motive of all potential pirates, the escape from order. Likewise in November a soldier deliberately stole some clothes (as he told the judge at his trial) because he was 'tired of military life and discipline', and because he hoped for an easier existence on the other side of the world.[69] There is no way of knowing how much these pleasant notions thrived in the foetid gaols and prison hulks as the convicts awaited transportation. However, at Port Jackson itself soon after landing in January 1788, a story took hold among the people that somewhere within walking distance was the home they were entitled to. To begin with this wonderland was described as 'a new settlement where labour would not be imposed on them, and where the inhabitants were civil and peaceable'. In due course imagination added as well the open-ended prospect of 'sweets hitherto unknown'. Convicts frequently went off looking for it, returning exhausted and starved, or never returning at all, even as late as 1803. Consequently European skeletons littered the bush: more than fifty were seen by one individual.[70]

At the Home Office it was understood, at least to begin with, that while the fleet should sail under a commodore, the officer in charge of the garrison was to be the main authority on the ground. Lord Sydney referred to him, in August, as the 'Superintendent'. Robert Ross, a major of Marines, was chosen within a few weeks, and his commission ordered him 'to take the said settlement into your care and charge'. For a while the garrison commander and the commodore were distinguished by the titles 'Deputy Superintendent' and 'Superintendent-General'. The former was to remain on shore, like the Superintendent at Honduras (who also had a garrison command), while the latter was to have a general oversight, like that planned for the maritime commanders at Sierra Leone, Lemane and Das Voltas.[71] Technically, this meant a military government but, if Honduras is any guide, there was a good deal of room for a freely organised community quite apart from the military. British India offered a similar pattern of fortress-and-bazaar. There was talk, for instance, of the garrison settling in behind an entrenchment, from which they might defend themselves in case of disputes with either natives or convicts.[72] Meanwhile, in October, Phillip got his commission, but his duties were not spelt out.

During the months to come before the ships sailed, these arrangements were to undergo a good deal of embroidery, and in the process Lord Sydney's ideal was partly undermined. Nevertheless, the idea of a free settlement in the Pacific, a Lemane next door to Tahiti, a soft, sunshiny republic, was to haunt English – including convict – imaginations for years to come. It was the original Australian utopia, and is hardly dead yet.

It is sometimes said that the founders of European settlement in Australia meant it as a place where convicts would serve out their time in hard labour. Botany Bay, it has been argued, was meant as a Gulag before Gulag. Or else it was to be a place where men would expiate their crimes by building a naval base, or by producing the raw material for sails and masts.[73] Nothing could be further from the truth. In autumn 1786, if not later, New South Wales was envisaged as a land of Englishmen where the rights inherent in living conversation, the rights admired by the more old-fashioned advocates of liberty, would prevail. This remote continent, besides its many disadvantages, had two great virtues in the minds of the Home Office, for as long as Sydney was Secretary of State. It was so far from Europe that transported men and women would find it hard to get back. Also, it was useless. Because it was useless the people who were sent here would work for nothing but their own survival.

At Botany Bay, so it was thought, the convicts would be peasants in a country of their own. Their labour would serve no great imperial purpose. To men like Sydney that seemed a fair guarantee that they would never find themselves in bondage to an authoritarian governor. New South Wales was to be an addition to the old empire, a configuration of old masculine liberties, a ragged but real commonwealth. It was not meant to be a field for any new and unaccountable authority, enlightened by European thinking but hidden from Europe by many miles of water. It was not, so Sydney hoped, to be a place where the Crown might tighten its hold on humble, helpless Englishmen. So Sydney hoped.

Chapter 4

Arthur Phillip and Robert Ross

I

To gentlemen in Downing Street it seemed likely to begin with that the First Fleet (the name we now give it) would also be the last to New South Wales. There was no certain vision of a Second Fleet, a Third Fleet and so on indefinitely. This point is hard to grasp from where we stand, in *their* distant future, especially when we think of the hundreds of convict ships which did in fact follow, in an almost continuous stream, for more than fifty years. But the evidence is clear enough. In 1779, for instance, when Joseph Banks made his original proposal for settlement to a committee of the House of Commons he, certainly, did not think of New South Wales serving the same long-term purpose as Maryland and Virginia had done before the American Revolution. He spoke of a single expedition, which would solve a passing problem by emptying the gaols for the time being. James Matra offered his ideas to Lord Beauchamp's committee in 1785 in just the same terms.[1]

The alternative, which we now take for granted, would have involved the British state committing itself to a complex and unpredictable enterprise, reactivated year by year for the indefinite future. Nothing of that kind had ever been done before. Besides, in 1786–87 it was very hard for most of those involved to imagine that such a remote place, visited so far only once by a British vessel, the *Endeavour*, and in one of the most remarkable sea-voyages ever made, could become a point in any regular traffic. During the months of planning even Captain Phillip once seemed doubtful whether, as he put it, 'Ships may arrive in Botany Bay in future.'[2] For a while, at least, it promised to be a very lonely spot.

There is other evidence of this short-term vision. The King announced the decision to settle New South Wales in his speech at the opening of Parliament on 23 January 1787. He spoke only of 'A Plan . . . for transporting *a number of convicts*' (my emphasis). The plan had been justified, he said (and it was the only reason he gave), by 'the inconvenience which arose from the crowded state of the gaols'.[3] By the time this speech was

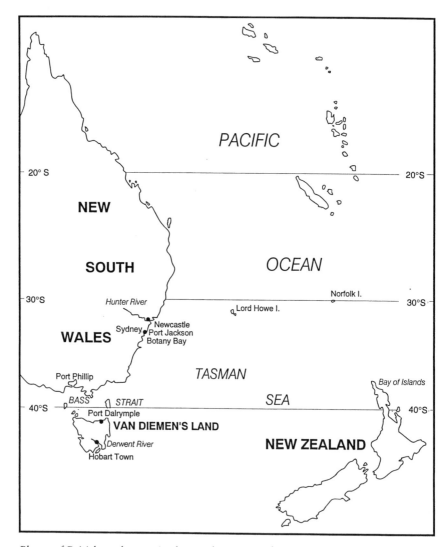

Places of British settlement in the south-west Pacific, 1788–1813

made most of the convicts were embarked, which explains why 'arose' was past tense. All other official statements from 1786–87 used the same limited language. Nowhere was there any boasting about a permanent answer to the problem which had vexed the government and its critics for the last ten years. This was because there were no certainty at all that Botany Bay would be a permanent answer. Though expensive, it was a simple scheme with no clear future.

In its immediacy it echoed, if slightly, a long-forgotten example of Dutch justice. In 1629 the Dutch East India Company ship, *Batavia*, was wrecked at the Abrolhos Islands, off the coast of what is now Western Australia. A few survivors reached Java in an open boat but the rest stayed on the islands where an under-officer, Jeronimus Cornelisz, inspired by a radical religious faith which allowed any wickedness among God's elect, set up a regime of wholesale murder. Help came back from Java three months later and by that time 125 men, women and children had been killed. Jeronimus and seven others were hanged on the spot, but two murderers, Wouter Loos and Jan Pelgrom de Bye, were reprieved so that they might be sent to live on the mainland, with orders to make themselves acquainted with the inhabitants and with possible items of trade. 'Man's luck', they were told, 'is found in strange places; if God guards you, [you] will not suffer any damage from them, but on the contrary because they have never seen any white men, they will offer all friendship.'[4] Neither was seen again by fellow Europeans.

What parallel advice was given to Englishmen setting out for Botany Bay? Major Ross had no instructions at all. Those on record for Phillip, though lengthy enough, looked very little into the future. They directed the Governor's attention wholly to 'the convicts now under sentence or order of transportation', otherwise referred to as those 'which accompany you'.[5] A few lines about 'a further number . . . which you may expect will shortly follow' (and even here there was no hint of continuous traffic) can probably be attributed to a short-lived notion, dating from around Christmas 1786, that the original party should go in two instalments.[6] As it turned out, of course, the hopeful inhabitants of this peculiar settlement all left England together, in May 1787.

There was much confusion about these matters at the time. It was well understood at the Home Office that there would be no more convicts sent at least until Phillip reported back, especially with regard to problems he might have with the Aborigines and with keeping the first party fed.[7] However, the officers, including Phillip, seem to have taken away with them an idea that a supplementary convoy, another ship or ships, might not be far behind.[8] By late 1788, when the English gaols began filling up again, Lord Sydney had such a possibility clearly in mind, but at that point it was equally likely that the government would turn to Newfoundland, Nova Scotia or Quebec.[9]

These contemporary ideas help to explain the way things were managed, especially at the Home Office. Even in 1786, no doubt, Sydney and others were bold enough to imagine that New South Wales might conceivably turn out to be more than a temporary solution. Lemane, its predecessor in official thinking – a much closer and more convenient site – had been spoken of as 'a Place for Annual Transportation'. The first shipment of people to be sent to that island were to be given time to settle: 'in a few years', it was hoped, 'they would become Planters, and take those who might be sent out hereafter into their Service'.[10] Even here, the term was 'might be'. But in the case of New South Wales the original plan was certainly made on a temporary and open-ended basis. One event above all others seems to have turned the project towards permanence, and towards a higher form of order. One event dammed and diverted the gentle meanderings of Home Office policy. That was the appointment of Arthur Phillip as naval commander.

I have already matched Arthur Phillip, living as he has done in the memory of European Australia, with the ancestral Shark. The epitome (it seems) of unselfish authority, strangely blank and unknowable against an intimately known landscape, he stalks the horizon of the past. A mere shadow sometimes, he shines nevertheless as one of a generation struggling to rise, by violence if necessary, above local prejudice, to move on the wings of science and high principle beyond the bounds of living, and dying, conversation: 'We few equals, indifferent of lands, indifferent of times, / We, enclosers of all continents, all castes, allowers of all theologies'.[11] He was not only the starting point of settlement but also the first judge.

What were the fixed points for his judgment? As we see in Chapter 6, Phillip was a humanitarian. For instance, he was interested in Black slavery, that great issue of the 1780s. Some of his ideas on this question in relation to Australia survive among the Home Office files:

> The laws of this country will, of course, be introduced in [New] South Wales, and there is one that I would wish to take place from the moment his Majesty's forces take possession of the country: That there can be no slavery in a free land, and consequently no slaves.[12]

It was an almost gratuitous statement in the circumstances, because there were no plans for slavery. But Phillip's dealings with the Aborigines were to show the same eagerness on questions of race. His patrons in England included Lord Lansdowne, a former Prime Minister, and the Governor may have known something of Lansdowne's famous coterie of intellectuals which met at Bowood House, in Wiltshire.[13] These were very advanced thinkers, and although slavery was not their main interest they were certainly against it. Lansdowne's circle included Jeremy Bentham, which may explain Phillip's other up-to-date notions, on penal discipline. Australia's first European ruler was a man of many virtues.

Phillip wanted New South Wales to be a place of continuous transportation. By ensuring the survival of settlement and by establishing government so securely in the Antipodes, by transporting the power of Whitehall over an extraordinary distance, he, more than anyone else, gave Australia the purpose it was to have within the British empire over the next three generations.

Major Ross complained that Phillip never spelled out to him 'the intentions of Government' for New South Wales, and he had his own reasons for resenting Phillip's silence. A major of Marines was little inferior to a post captain in the navy. There had been some idea at the beginning that these two, Ross and Phillip, should manage in partnership (see the previous chapter). As naval commander, Phillip was to be wholly in charge during the voyage out, he was to decide on a landing place, and he was to see the people properly settled. But with that done, Ross (it seems) was to take charge on dry land, while Phillip attended to his further duties at sea (exploration of the coast, for instance, and management of the guard ship). Phillip was to have the superior commission, but Ross was to have distinct responsibilities of his own.

There was no precedent for any other arrangement. There was no naval officer in the empire who served as a full-time governor on shore. Newfoundland was the only other colony which had a naval governor at all, and there the Governor spent nearly all his time at sea.[14] Besides, Phillip's instructions were not only short on detail about continued transportation. They said little or nothing about day-to-day events at the settlement after the pioneering phase. The Home Office was confident that that phase would be very short.

Had this first arrangement prevailed, Robert Ross would have been a much more obvious and influential figure in the settlement process than he in fact became. He would not have been silenced by Phillip and submerged by the written record. Australians who know their history think of Phillip and Ross as the two original archetypes of the national story. But Ross is important only as the negative to Phillip's positive. Phillip is *pater patriae*, the great original of government, and Ross the first selfish rebel. Ross has an image like Trotsky in Soviet demonology or Snowball in Orwell's *Animal Farm*, as the anti-type who falls in the first stage of the new order. While Phillip saw his colony as the germ of an empire, Ross believed (at least to begin with) that 'this country will never answer to settle in'.[15] While Phillip suffered for his people, Ross spoke without avail about his own difficulties. And yet there was more to Ross than meets the eye. He had his own ideas, and like many who argue fruitlessly with power his ideas represented an undercurrent of thought which was to rise to the surface in due course. He was a lesser man than Phillip, but his vision of the settlement was the first alternative vision during the long conversation of European settlement in Australia. The management of men and women brought by the First Fleet involved their responding to the crisis of choice, exercising the sinews of the soul, and it was Ross who first considered how choice might be negotiated among the subject people. There were some fundamental problems of settlement, first dealt with in this chapter but important for the whole book, which Ross thought about more carefully than Phillip.

Beyond what I have said already, it is hard to know exactly what was envisaged for New South Wales at the Home Office during the first weeks of detailed planning, from August to November 1786, the period in which both Ross and Phillip were appointed. However, Lord Sydney had long been interested in constitutional arrangements at Honduras and the Mosquito Shore.[16] They seem his most likely model in adjusting the relationship of people and Crown at Botany Bay.

It thus appears that in New South Wales power was to come, simultaneously, from above and below. At Honduras, in Sydney's view, it was the duty of the Superintendent to see that all shared in 'the advantages to be derived from the Settlement', and to protect any who might be aggrieved. The people chose their own magistrates. But these individuals were under the Superintendent, who was, in the end, Sydney believed, 'answerable to His Majesty for . . . the impartial administration of Justice'. A system of basic laws had been devised on the spot in 1765, and there was an elected committee entrusted with drawing up supplementary laws for the approval of the people. However, according to Sydney, all local legislation touching 'the Property or Interests of any Description of the Settlers' also needed the consent of the Superintendent.[17] These principles fit with what we know of the proposal for Lemane. They were also in keeping with the ideas which men like Sydney had used in arguing against government policy in America, during the revolution. It seems likely that to begin with they were meant to apply in New South Wales.

There were, however, two main periods of planning for settlement at the Antipodes before the Fleet departed, and changes were made from one period to the other. Captain Phillip received two commissions. The first, dated 12 October 1786, described him simply as 'Governor of our territory called New South Wales'. It was a peculiar document, which made him look more like the governor of a fort than the governor of a colony. It was a product of the first stage of planning, and it looked back, in a narrow sense, to the Honduran model. Only in April 1787, with his second commission (which superseded the first), was Phillip named 'Captain-General and Governor-in-Chief'. This was a much more splendid document. While the first commission had been merely signed by the King, the second, like most colonial governors' commissions, was issued under the Great Seal. Like other proper governors Phillip also become Vice-Admiral within his government, and his salary was increased, from £500 (the sum allowed to the Superintendent at Honduras) to £1000 (half-way between the Governor of St Vincent and the Governor of Bermuda). The increase was made retrospective, from the date of the first commission. During these months the Governor-elect began to be talked of as a man of whom great things were expected.[18]

In short, thanks to a very fluid period of planning, Phillip had advanced his fortunes in a spectacular way. Major Ross had not advanced his at all, except in so far as the salary set aside for him as lieutenant-governor, £250 per annum, now had no work attached to it. (His military pay and duties were another matter.) All was entrusted to Phillip. The new arrangements are partly to be explained by the fact that Ross, who seems to have been brought into the enterprise by Evan Nepean, the Under-Secretary, had failed to impress Lord Sydney. The major's complaints about hearing nothing useful from Phillip were a roundabout way of saying that he had had no information from anyone else either. 'I came out without any orders or instructions from your office', he told Nepean, and this was obviously the main reason for his ignorance as to 'the intentions of Government'. In saying so, he referred to the Secretary of State in terms which were very close to insolence.[19] Phillip, on the other hand, had the entire confidence of his minister. He had been introduced to Lady Sydney, and he was on close terms with His Lordship's son and private secretary, John Thomas Townshend. He was anxious, as he told Sydney, to 'merit the friendship you honor me with'.[20] Although he and Sydney were very different personalities, with different ideas about the new settlement, the Secretary of State had done a great deal for him.

When Lord Sydney had first written to the Admiralty about the Botany Bay expedition, in August 1786, he had asked that arrangements be made 'with all possible expedition'.[21] The fleet carryinig the military settlers to Nova Scotia in 1749 had been ordered in March and had sailed in May. The distance to Australia was much greater but, except for the last stretch, the way there was not entirely unfamiliar. Transports had been carrying soldiers to India for some time, and there seemed to be no reason why preparations for Botany Bay should take much more than two months. During a good part of October 1786, when most of the commissions were issued, Sydney and Nepean were confident of departure by the end of that month. Even then, for several weeks, it seemed to be only a fortnight away.[22] The short-term delays were mainly a result of problems with getting the ships ready. Also, early in December it was decided to send more women, which meant finding another vessel.[23]

By that time, however, the whole enterprise had begun to ferment and complicate itself. The first stage of planning had given way to the second. It was now agreed that Phillip would command from day to day on shore, and as a result the Admiralty was obliged to appoint a second captain (John Hunter) for his ship, the *Sirius*.[24] Phillip himself made pressing demands about equipment and stores, which had to be satisfied, and which took time. Also, there were worries about the constitution, or lack of it, in New South Wales. There were gathering signs that government there might be, as one newspaper put it, 'to every intent and purpose, of the most arbitrary nature'.[25] The call for more women may well have been part of the Home Office response to these worries. The winter certainly seems to have given birth to new ambitions for the settlement, new notions apparently entertained by Lord Sydney himself. He and his subordinates now began to prepare for a colony which would be more conventional and more expensive, with households formed in a regular way. The men of the place were to be managed as subjects, but they were also to be nourished by government, as proprietors, masters and husbands. Outdoors, among London opinion, there was now a settled understanding that Botany Bay was to be a place of 'military tyranny'.[26] But Sydney, having taken some slight precautions, still had reason to think that the English going to that part of the world would enjoy some of the intricate pleasures and, more important, the positive rights of the English in England.

II

There could be no households worthy of the name without secure individual possession of the soil. The original scheme, the ideas of August 1786, came unstuck partly with questions about public justice (see Chapter 5), but also with questions about land rights. The land rights of the Aborigines were not thought to be an important issue, at least in the Home Office. It is true that Sydney was not completely uninterested in the rights of indigenous peoples. For instance, he disliked the word 'savages', and he was probably responsible for its being replaced by 'natives' in Phillip's instructions (a word with richer connotations than it has today).[27] But much more important for him were the land rights of Englishmen.

At Haulover, the Honduran 'capital', property boundaries were marked by 'boards' stuck in the mud. The fact that they stayed there undisturbed suggests that there was general agreement about matters of title. At the Mosquito Shore, according to a local account, methods were more sophisticated: land sales were 'entered on the public Records, kept at the Capital Seat of Government at Black River'.[28] But in neither place was there any freehold title. In other words, landholders had no legal protection against a Superintendent who wanted their land for 'reasons of state'. Only among themselves, in ordinary circumstances, did the system work well. At Sierra Leone the people were likewise expected to agree on questions of title. Here the principles were laid down in theory before they were tried in fact: 'Each person will be allowed, by *common consent*, to possess as much land as it may be judged he or she can cultivate, to which they will always be at liberty to add as much more as their necessity, or convenience may require.'[29] It was thought that boundaries would be safe from government because that too was to work 'by common consent'. Such theories were well understood at the Home Office, which handled government dealings with the Sierra Leone settlement. They grew out of a broad debate, a favourite debate of that generation, about the relationship of land rights and political responsibility. Two of the leading writers on the general question were William Paley, an archdeacon in the Church of England, and Granville Sharp, a gentleman philanthropist and the main voice behind the Sierra

Leone project. But there were many others including, on the Continent, Rousseau.

Paley argued for the importance of property as a social good, over and above what it might do for the individual owner: 'It is the intention of God, that the produce of the earth be applied to the use of man; this intention cannot be fulfilled without establishing property.' At the same time, the right to live by that produce was one of the 'General Rights of Mankind'.[30] Sharp maintained that the best community was one in which land rights were determined, not by private interest, but by common trust. His theories were coloured by a keen sense of history, and by a belief that over recent centuries private interest had stifled community in England. Paley was principally a scholar, but Sharp was an eager activist, and he made it his duty to spread his ideas wherever he could. He had a very complicated program. His arguments about land ownership were linked with arguments about civil defence: men should organise and train together at the local level to defend their land. He also had a good deal to say about common justice. He wanted to revive the Ango-Saxon system of frankpledge, by which communities were made responsible, and were fined, for the crimes of their members.

Lord Sydney was not a radical, but in 1780 he was a member, with Sharp, of the radical Society for Constitutional Information, and he had a fundamental sympathy with the tendency, if not the details, of ideas like Sharp's. In January 1785, when the project for Lemane was being worked out at the Home Office, he received from Sharp his latest book (printed but not yet published). This was mainly an argument about frankpledge, but it included a couple of appendices on colonisation. They stressed the importance of common land in new colonies, and the need to make the commons secure against private enclosure. There were also arguments against letting anyone get too rich, so as to monopolise landed property.[31] Indeed, a general equality in land ownership was essential to old English ideas of commonwealth. It was stressed as well by Rousseau: 'no one citizen should be rich enough to buy another, and . . . none should be so poor as to be obliged to sell himself'. If such evils were possible, citizenship must fail.[32]

Ideas of this kind, or at least the moral assumptions behind them, shaped conversation in the Home Office about the right way to settle convicts abroad. Outcasts from England who had their own land beyond the seas would, it was thought, be better men. They might not have much sense of community to begin with, but it would follow from their equal attachment to the soil. There would be no risk then of their becoming 'a nest of pirates'. At Lemane they were to be left alone under certain regulations and they would take up the land themselves. Numbers would become 'planters', and, it was thought, 'As they grow rich they [will] naturally grow honest.' After all, this is what had happened on Robinson Crusoe's island. The 'pyrates' had been settled for some time before Crusoe asked their chief, now 'a most sober, grave, managing Fellow', to give out individual allotments:

> He divided Things so justly, and so much to every one's Satisfaction, that they only desired one general Writing under my Hand for the whole, which I caused to be drawn up and sign'd and seal'd to them, setting out the Bounds and Situation of every Man's Plantation.

In his ideas for New South Wales, Matra had spoken in just the same terms: 'Give them a few acres of ground as soon as they arrive . . . with what assistance they may want to till them.' In due course, so he argued, 'it is very probable they will be moral subjects of society'. Here was a simple rendition of sophisticated theory. The botanist Johann Reinhold Forster, who had been with Cook on his second voyage, predicted the same again: 'it is sufficiently proved by ancient and modern history that [even thieves] . . . cease to be enemies to society whenever they regain their full human rights and become proprietors and cultivators of land'.[33]

A picture entitled 'The Village Politicians', by David Wilkie (1806): the meetings of men in such places were the reality on which contemporary ideas about commonwealth were built.

Source: The Rt. Hon. the Earl of Mansfield, Scone Palace, Scotland

Ideas about commonwealth were thus reinforced by an Enlightenment understanding of the perfectability of humankind. For men and women of optimistic temperament, wickedness no longer seemed to have any powerful connection with original sin. It could be more usefully attributed to faults of environment and therefore, as a late seventeenth-century authority maintained, might easily be corrected:

> the wisest observers of man's nature have pronounced him to be a creature gentle and sociable, inclined to and fit for conversation, apt to keep good order, to observe rules of justice, to embrace any sort of vertue, if well managed; if instructed by good discipline, if guided by good example, if living under the influence of wise laws and virtuous governors.[34]

Lord Sydney was apparently anxious to forward such a process in the Antipodes, by doing what he could for the moral fabric of the settlement. He tried unsuccessfully to prevent wine or spirits from being added to the common provisions sent with the First Fleet, even for the garrison. No money was embarked at all. Robinson Crusoe had had money with him on his island, but his situation rendered it 'nasty sorry useless stuff'. Granville Sharp had banned it from Sierra Leone, hoping that the people would work out a system of exchange based on what they could do for each other.[35] It may be that Sydney deliberately followed Sharp's example, and certainly money must have seemed a more likely cause of corruption among felons than among former slaves.

Generally speaking, the instructions which Sydney devised for Governor Phillip bear the mark of this blueprint. Some parts might suggest otherwise. The labour of the convicts was assigned to the Governor, just as it had been assigned, in former times, to planters in Maryland and Virginia. In principle this made him master of the entire labour force in the Antipodes, and on his arrival he was to set everyone to work immediately. His people were to 'proceed to the cultivation of the land', and in doing so they were to labour, as the instructions put it, 'under such inspectors or overseers, and under such regulations as may appear to you to be necessary'. Whatever they produced was to be 'a publick stock', to be used as Phillip himself thought best.[36]

But this was to be a short-term arrangement. Nearly all the convicts (94 per cent) had only seven-year sentences, and, as we have seen, it was doubtful whether any more might follow. All would have served at least a year by the time they landed in New South Wales, and some three or four years, and they could not be kept in bondage once their time was up. This fact alone means that their dependence on Phillip would be brief. It is significant then, that although so many people would soon be free, the Governor's instructions, with all their detail, make no reference to the fact. And this was only part of the story. The Governor's responsibilities, it seems, did not extend even to the end of each term of transportation. Before that happened most of the convict men – 'any' said the instructions, 'who shall, from their good conduct and a disposition to industry, be deserving of favour' – were to be released from public labour. They were then, 'with all convenient speed', to be made into peasant farmers.[37] The women would become wives. The rest of the men would presumably (as Matra had suggested) be attached to the little enterprises thus established.

In other words, the Home Office made no plans for long-term public labour. Phillip was to find his own 'inspectors or overseers' (presumably from among the convicts themselves) for the interim period, and none were sent out with him. He was also to make his own regulations, and this is in spite of the fact that Britain had a Penitentiaries Act (1779), which included voluminous detail on hard labour for convicts. Instead of this model, it seems that he was expected to follow the advice of James Matra. Once the people were landed, their crimes should be forgotten: 'they are not, by any means,' said Matra, 'to be reproached for their former conduct', for men and women were more likely to reform themselves if they were not reminded every day of 'the hideous and mortifying deformity of their own vices'.[38] Such logic was in line with the priorities of the minister, Lord Sydney, and especially with Sydney's thoughts about the rights of Englishmen. Force might be used to make the convicts work, but only for a year or two, until the future of the settlement was guaranteed.

It was hoped that the people would begin to be self-supporting after the first, or at most the second grain harvest. 'It is presumed', wrote Nepean in August 1786, 'that after the First year, one half of the Expence of Victualling the Convicts and Marines may be saved.' This was partly wishful thinking, and partly a conclusion drawn from the testimony of Joseph Banks, whose memories of the *Endeavour* expedition led him to think that the soil at Botany Bay was very fertile. Grain would undoubtedly thrive there.[39] Nepean made no attempt to budget beyond the third year. By that time, so he and Sydney believed, the new land would have been taught to yield up its bounty to its new masters.

This was the financial agenda. Since the original method of government was justified by the need to ensure survival, two or three years must also have been the time-scale for unfolding the common liberties of the people at Botany Bay. A settlement which could support itself economically could look after itself in other ways as well. Or so it appeared in Whitehall.

Matra thought that the convicts should hold their land as 'absolute property', but it is not clear what he meant by that.[40] Lord Sydney's other projects all involved settlement in territories beyond the empire. Even at Honduras and the Mosquito Shore there could be no freehold title, guaranteed by the Crown, because the whole coast was acknowledged to belong to Spain. At Sierra Leone, Lemane, and probably Das Voltas, all the land required for settlement was to be 'purchased' by the Crown from whatever local prince seemed to be in control. But 'purchase' meant possession under an annual tribute. There was to be no permanent acquisition of territory, and thus there could be no freehold title in those places either.

What about Botany Bay? In 1770 Captain Cook had claimed the coastline of New South Wales, from Cape York to South Cape, Van Diemen's Land, in the name of King George III. But few in London in the 1780s knew quite what this meant. Lord Beauchamp's committee asked Sir Joseph Banks, in 1785, whether he thought land for settlement might be acquired from the Aborigines 'by Cession or Purchase'. Banks said he thought not, because there was nothing the Aborigines would take in return for their soil (unlike the Africans at Lemane). He assured the committee that it hardly mattered anyway, as the Blacks were of wandering habits and would 'speedily abandon' whatever territory was needed.[41] This advice seems to have carried the day. Indeed, by October 1786 the government had decided to push its claims of sovereignty far beyond even Cook's discoveries. Phillip's first commission embraced, as 'our territory called New South Wales', a vast area, extending over nearly half of what we now know to be the Australian land mass. Here alone was a fundamental point of distinction between New South Wales and the projects it otherwise resembled, one which opened the way for freehold title by British subjects, sanctioned under normal process of law. According to international convention, the current inhabitants might have claimed such title themselves, under the Crown, by right of prior occupation, but it seems to have been agreed at Whitehall that they should be ignored and the land thrown open entirely to Europeans. The Aborigines were said to be mere wanderers. New South Wales was *terra nullius*, a land hitherto free, not only of sovereignty but of ownership by anyone; a blank page ready for the pen of empire.[42]

The land at Botany Bay was to be distributed under the direction of the Governor himself. It was first thought that Phillip would find someone from among the officers or convicts who would settle boundary lines and other details, and probably the Governor's secretary might have been expected to certify land grants. However, the measuring was entrusted at the last minute to a Surveyor of Lands, who was appointed from England and who went out with the fleet.[43]

It was remarkable, on the face of it, that freehold title should have been so carefully regulated in what was meant to be a settlement of reprobate peasants on the far side of the world. Precise arrangements were natural enough in places where there were extensive grants and big capital, especially capital sent from Britain. (During the 1760s Lord Sydney himself had acquired an absentee grant of 10,000 acres in East Florida and, of course, his title was certified with all possible formality.)[44] But a subsistence community, in which all material value was to depend on the labour of the local people, was surely different. The reason for such rigour is explained by events after about November 1786. Important too was the way in which liberty was thought to be tied up with questions of property, especially by Englishmen like Lord Sydney.

For the time being, at least, the convicts to be landed at the Antipodes were not to be under a government of their own making. A government was to be imposed on them. But that government was, in principle, to be strictly limited, especially in its dealings with private property. In short, certified boundaries and freehold title were to be, in New South Wales as in England, the ultimate barrier against incursions by the Crown.

III

It is now time to turn to Robert Ross, the man who might have been wholly in charge on dry land and who represents the other way for European Australia, the alternative to Phillip's way. The alternative was not only there at the beginning, vested in Ross, but it continued in the minds and behaviour of many others after he departed. The priorities of the Lieutenant-Governor appeared during his time in New South Wales and the story must therefore move quickly forward. The First Fleet departed from Portsmouth on 13 May 1787 and, after calling at the Canary Islands, Rio de Janeiro and the Cape of Good Hope, all the vessels anchored in Botany Bay between 18 and 20 January 1788. Finding the place unsastisfactory and discovering a much finer harbour nearby at Port Jackson, Phillip ordered their removal hence, to an inlet on the harbour's southern shore which he named Sydney Cove. Disembarkation began on 26 January – the flag being raised for the first time on the evening of that day – and was complete by 7 February.

Norfolk Island was also occupied during 1788. The soil there was found to be much better than the soil on the mainland, and within two years it was carrying 41 per cent of the population. Lord Sydney's successor at the Home Office, William Wyndham Grenville, was then inclined to think that Phillip might be wise to move his headquarters to Norfolk, 'were it not', he said, 'for the great labor and expence incurred already at Port Jackson'.[45] The two sites were almost equally important, and there was even a chance that Norfolk would outstrip the mainland in due course.

The first superintendent on Norfolk Island was the naval officer (and later Governor of New South Wales), Philip Gidley King, but in March 1790 King was succeeded by Ross. This was a heaven-sent opportunity for Ross to establish his own credentials. He was politically inept but he was a capable administrator within the daily round of garrison life and he also had a fussy interest in theories of good order.[46] On top of his military experience, including several years in North America and the West Indies, he seems to have read enough to have picked up some of the current debate about land-use and citizenship. Unlike Phillip, who thought about farming no more than necessary, Ross had a fashionable interest in scientific agriculture, which at that time was moving ahead in leaps and bounds. He wanted to try his ideas out. In particular, he thought that the convicts should be allowed to work and live independently, which meant growing their own grain and keeping their own livestock. In Phillip's view, everything won by convict effort belonged to the Crown. Ross, on the other hand, told anyone who would listen that while the convicts were sustained by the humanity ('I might have said folly') of the government, 'they will not take the trouble of getting anything for themselves'. At Port Jackson, for instance, he once encouraged two convict men to saw timber on their own account during their spare minutes at breakfast and dinner-time, and, he said, 'they ought not to part with any without they were well paid for it'.[47]

Ross was busy and talkative. He liked to take other men, of all ranks, into his confidence, a habit which was not always good for discipline. His personality became poisonous only when the favour was not returned. Talking was his medium. He was handy with his personnel lists and rosters, his paysheets and stoppages, but, unlike Phillip, he was no good at the lucid and magisterial reports, the careful conversations on paper, with which the empire was now – in principle – governed. This was a type of conversation which people like Ross could only observe as an alien form of life, as they might look at the seagulls which hung in the air above Norfolk. He knew very well that while he suffered in New South Wales, Phillip was writing about him to the Secretary of State. His only resource was to wait, at Port Jackson and then at Norfolk Island, until Lord Sydney should leave office.[48]

The *Sirius*, on which Ross sailed to Norfolk, was wrecked as it was landing stores. Much was salvaged, but a good deal, including the ship itself, was lost. This was a major disaster, and in order to cope with food shortages Ross declared martial law. His commission gave him no power to do so, and to cover the emergency he consulted several officers and then called a full council of such gentlemen, which met at Government House next day. This council, on its own authority, also declared martial law. Not yet satisfied, Ross assembled the whole population of the island, including the convicts and private soldiers, and asked for their active consent to the new regime:

> I proposed [he said], as there was not time to administer an oath to everybody, that passing under the King's colours at the flagstaff, and between the colours of the detachment . . . should be deemed as equal to a voluntary oath of paying a strict obedience to the martial law now in force.

He led this strange procession himself, the rest of the population following (as another officer remarked) with 'solemnity, and . . . chearfulness'. Oath-taking *en masse* had been tried in England in earlier years during times of political crisis.[49] But except for this example, never in Australian history – before universal suffrage in the late nineteenth century – did an entire community take part in a fundamental act of government.[50] It was also the first and last time convicts, men and women, were asked to agree to the way in which they were managed.

Ross showed the same spirit in settling people on the land. During his first months on the island he worked out a plan for making Norfolk self-sufficient in grain. He had done some careful sums, taking account of rates of production and consumption and assuming a population of no more than seven hundred. He proposed to divide the convicts into small parties (including men, women and children), with the idea that they should rely on their own labour. Each party was allowed land of their own. He at first proposed two acres for every six individuals, but also, he said, 'I would . . . encourage them to clear and cultivate some acres adjoining to what they had.' He had no power to grant land in freehold title but in due course, should they want to become permanent settlers, he hoped that they might have grants made out to them: 'This mode, I think, will create a desire among them for living better than their neighbours, and that may create industry, and industry, I think, will cultivate a desire of settling for life.'[51]

Operations began during winter 1790. By February 1791 Ross's plan had succeeded well enough for him to announce a timetable for every convict wanting to be part of it. They were to be allowed Friday and Saturday each week to work for themselves. To spur them on, in three months the flour ration they got from government was to be reduced by a quarter, in six months by another quarter, and when the next harvest was in (early 1792) they were to lose it altogether. He also allowed one sow (with pig) to every three convicts, and within one year thereafter they were expected to live on her progeny. He also offered prizes (an extra free day a week) to those who offered for sale the most pork, the most fowls and the most maize.[52]

During 1791 a total of 198 allotments were given out, and 338 people were committed to working on them. Most were less than an acre and very few were more than two acres, but they might have been expected to grow in time. Many were family enterprises (a man, a woman and a child) and some were run by single individuals, both men and women. But a few were worked by small parties of convicts who apparently chose to be together. Ross had abandoned the idea that the people should combine in parties of six, but there were still openings for shared responsibility. The same corporate spirit can be seen in the order that all convicts with land were to send in to the public store, free of charge, a bushel of grain each year, for the benefit of those 'not able to maintain themselves'.[53] Thus he sought to lay the foundation for an agrarian commonwealth.

Public funds of grain, for the maintenance of the poor, had been common in the original North American colonies, and they were a primitive equivalent of the old system of English poor rates. But taken as a whole Ross's scheme also reflects some of the idealism of his own age. It was to be carefully orchestrated. For instance, the birth of every piglet was to be reported to the Deputy Commissary. Also, the death of every sow was to be followed by an inquiry. If it were found that the cause of death was accident or disease, 'Government shall . . . make good the same', but in case of neglect the three custodians – 'all and every [one]' – were to be considered responsible and were to be punished as criminals.[54] Ross seems to have aimed at a strict discipline, but it was an administrative rather than a physical discipline. His punishment record suggests that he was not a strong advocate of flogging.[55]

His rigour was combined, at least in principle, with a policy of drawing the convicts together, making them responsible for each other and giving them some prospect of family and individual prosperity.

Ross apparently knew nothing of the way ideas had been turned over in the Home Office during the period before settlement, and especially in the mind of Lord Sydney. And yet his own program at Norfolk Island (whether wisely or not) was based on just the same premises. Also, like Sydney, he had no interest in penal discipline. At Norfolk the most incorrigible men – like those on Crusoe's island – were given land of their own. John Coffin had been worked in irons at Port Jackson as a 'public delinquent', and on Norfolk he was also worked in irons and flogged. At the same time he had an allotment and shared a pig with an unmarried couple. The same was true of Henry Wright, a soldier, who had been transported from the mainland after conviction for rape.

At Port Jackson, Phillip was to work under quite different principles. He was much more keenly aware of the convicts as people under sentence. Very little paperwork had been sent with the convicts, and as a result it was impossible to know with certainty when individual terms expired. And yet the knowledge was important for two reasons, especially under Phillip's scheme of things. In the first place, convicts wanted to go home. The Home Office must have foreseen this, but officials had probably hoped that the scarcity of traffic would make thoughts of England merely academic. However, as soon as they arrived convicts began counting the days, and some gave Phillip to understand that they would shortly be needing a return passage. 'Until I receive instructions on this head,' he told Downing Street, 'of course none will be permitted to leave the settlement.' At the same time he asked for a record of all sentences. He had already told the people that their memory and their word were not good enough. They must continue with public labour until their liberty should be proved in black and white.[56] They were bound by paper, and paper alone could release them.

This reply, as Phillip's secretary, David Collins, remarked, must have been 'truly distressing' to the convicts, and some were not prepared to be distressed in silence. Several men told the Governor that when the record was set straight they would want to be paid for their labour. Major Ross (before his time at Norfolk Island) was involved in one dispute. He is said to have told John Cullyhorn, who had finished his term by July 1789, that he could now do what he liked (a notion the major did not use on Norfolk). Subsequently, some heated words followed between Phillip and Cullyhorn in the Governor's tent, and as a result Cullyhorn was sentenced to 600 lashes and six months' labour in irons: a savage (and illegal) punishment for a free Englishman.[57]

The documentation on sentences was important to Phillip for another reason. Unlike Sydney and Ross, he did not believe that convicts should be given any substantial independence until they they had served the terms to which they had been condemned in England. That is to say, he believed that the period of transportation should also be a period of forced labour. He allowed the convicts small gardens, in which they might busy themselves for several hours a week, a scheme aimed at supplementing their diet but by no means making them self-sufficient. The peculiar legal status of convicts in New South Wales gave a convoluted logic to Phillip's point of view. There were no private employers in the Antipodes to whom they (or rather their labour power) could be assigned under the terms of the 1718 Transportation Act. Technically, the Governor became their master as soon as they stepped ashore.

In North America servitude, or bondage to an employer, had been limited to seven years, even when the terms of transportation were longer. But this had been the result of nothing more than local custom and there was no reason why bondage in New South Wales should not extend from the moment of arrival to the far-off bitter end, whether that meant seven years, fourteen years or life. In other words, until His Majesty's Secretary of State produced evidence that convicts were free they were at the disposal of His Majesty's Governor, who put them to whatever labour he liked. They were, as Phillip said, 'servants of the Crown till the time for which they are sentenced is expired'.[58] This principle was to be fundamental to the penal system for the entire period of its existence in New South Wales. It was devised by Phillip at first settlement, but it was not justified by any Act of the British parliament until 1824.

Phillip's approach was never questioned, probably because he stayed in office in New South Wales longer than Lord Sydney did at Whitehall. Sydney ceased to be Home Secretary in June 1789, and his last pronouncements on the subject of New South Wales are to be found in the instructions which Phillip had brought out with him. His Lordship's successors at the Home Office – especially the Duke of Portland, in charge for most of the 1790s – were not interested in the rights of convicted Englishmen on the other side of the world. Besides, the hazards of first settlement had been much worse than anyone had foreseen, and to a casual observer they must have seemed to justify any number of unorthodox principles.

The fact remains that Phillip's instructions had been quite clear. He was to 'emancipate' convicts. He was to 'discharge [them] from their servitude'. Whatever these words might have meant later on in New South Wales, at this point they did not mean that men and women ceased to be convicts, or that their sentence of transportation was cut short. They only meant that convicts were no longer bound to labour under the Governor's control. Servitude meant service, and freedom from servitude meant economic independence. After emancipation, and in spite of convict status, the Governor, 'with all convenient speed', was to grant land to the men, and the precise acreage was set out in remarkable detail.[59] All this Phillip ignored. In England, in strict law, land could not be held by convicted felons. As far as the Governor was concerned, this was to be the case in New South Wales as well. To be landowners they must be free men, and to be free, so he believed, they must, as a rule, finish their terms.

The record of sentences imposed in England on First Fleet convicts was to reach New South Wales in July 1791, and the Governor straightaway ordered a meeting of all the people whose terms had expired. He did not speak to them himself but sent an officer (apparently his secretary, who was also Judge-Advocate) to tell them what their options were. They might go on working for the government (under contract for at least a year at a time), they might take up land, or they might go home. A few volunteered to stay if they could have land, but everyone else wanted to go as soon as they could.[60] There was a misunderstanding about one man, William Bradbury. He had served seven years, and he now volunteered to take land. He was given 30 acres at the Ponds, near Parramatta. But a second look at the record showed that his term was not seven years, but life. 'Hereupon', wrote Watkin Tench, an officer of Marines, 'he grew desperate, and declared he would rather perish at once, than remain as a convict.' After a single spring-time on the soil he disappeared, into the bush or the ocean, and was never seen again.[61] He was a casualty of Phillip's principles.

The Governor's decisions, whether legal or not, were to be profoundly creative in the long term. He was the Shark indeed. Among Europeans in Australia, thanks to Phillip, we can see something remarkable from the beginning. But in laying out these methods he injured the people subject to them. Also, his idea that convicts should be bound to the Crown for their entire term slowed down the process of settling them on the soil. He argued at one point that 'they would starve if left to themselves'. He knew, he said, that the Home Office had hoped for a number of good farmers who might have 'superintended the labour of the rest', but, he argued, there were in fact few or none. In 1788 he put the number at no more than two.[62] Yet he gave land to nearly every man who asked for it as soon as he was certifiably free. And from that point a good number of competent farmers took possession of the soil. Within a period of three years (1792–94), among those who had laboured as convicts on mainland Australia, a total of 78 former convicts were settled with some success on farms of their own. This adds up to 26 per cent, a substantial fraction of the men whom Phillip had hitherto kept in bondage.[63]

At Norfolk, Ross offered independence much more readily than Phillip. It is hard to know how much difference this made in the long term though the spirit of commonwealth which was to appear later among the Norfolk Island people may have been partly due to Ross. Among the men under his government the proportion who stayed as farmers (a few of them going back to the mainland) was only slightly higher than Phillip's (28 per cent). And yet Ross might have argued that his system had not had time to work. In November 1791 Philip Gidley King returned with a commission as Lieutenant-Governor of Norfolk Island, and Ross departed, first for Port Jackson and then for home. By then, presumably, his convict settlers were taking only half a ration of flour and making up the difference themselves. Certainly King, on his arrival, found the crops at Norfolk presenting 'a most promising aspect'. But some of Ross's convicts were fearful about being on their own. They organised a petition, complaining that they had been forced into independence and that they would never meet the major's deadline, now only five months away. King was a young man and an admiring protégé of Phillip. The petition seems to have been signed by less than half the people on allotments, but he made it a reason for calling in the pigs and abandoning the whole project.[64] In this way the entire territory, mainland and island, in so far as it was settled by Europeans, came to be governed according to Phillip's way of thinking.

Over and above this triumph, by the time Governor Phillip departed, in December 1792, his reports to Downing Street had cleared the way for the embarkation of a Second and even a Third Fleet. Grenville, the Home Secretary, had decided that there would in future be two embarkations every year, which, as he told Phillip, would be 'the means of keeping up a regular intercourse between this country and the settlements under your government'.[65] There were not always two embarkations, but this line of communication, this network of 'regular intercourse', was to be the means by which not only men and women in bondage but also paperwork – despatch after despatch, lists, charts, statistical returns – made their way between the centre of empire and this remote section of its periphery.

And so we find, at least on the surface, a very different colony from the one which had been envisaged at the Home Office in August 1786. To all appearances, the ideas of Lord Sydney, and of Robert Ross as well, succumbed to those of Arthur Phillip. The Governor's authority bit into every aspect of life. It almost seemed as if his will bound man to woman, neighbour to neighbour; as if the sharp point of his own self-discipline had marked out a circle of routine and ceremony for everyone else. On paper – so far as we can trust to paper – from the 135th degree of longitude eastward to the sea, from the opal shadows of the bush to the scatter of fires which the convicts lit for warmth and company, there was no other means of order to be seen.

Chapter 5

Argument and Servitude

I

One of the most famous cases tried in the English courts during the eighteenth century was that of Somerset *v.* Stewart (1772). At a time when the rights and wrongs of slavery were hotly debated in polite circles, the Lord Chief Justice was called upon to decide on the rights of Black men and women held as slaves in England. James Somerset was a Black who had been brought from Virginia as a personal servant to Charles Stewart, a planter. When Stewart wanted to go from England to the West Indies, taking Somerset with him (for resale), Somerset was found to be unwilling. He was put on board a ship in the Thames, the *Anne and Mary*, and he would have silently disappeared had not some White philanthropists intervened and brought the case before King's Bench. Thus it came to be announced, within the scarlet panoply of one of the highest courts in the land, that 'the slave . . . refused to serve'.

When the case was settled, an idea quickly, and unjustifiably, gained ground that the Lord Chief Justice, Lord Mansfield, had decided in one fell swoop that slavery was unlawful in England. He had argued, it was said, from the fact that there was no reference to slavery in English precedent or statute, and that the unwilling bondage of human beings was a thing 'so odious, that nothing can be suffered to support it, but positive law'.[1] And yet there were currently large numbers of Black slaves in English households, and, as plain as day, they went on being kept, bought and sold as slaves for some years yet. At Lord Sydney's country house in 1788 there was a little boy who had been sent as a present by the Governor of Dominica.[2] Black or White, slavery was more protean and pervasive within the empire than many seemed to fancy.

Besides, James Somerset had not complained about being a slave. In strict law he had argued with only one aspect of his slavery. He did not want to leave England with his master. As Lord Mansfield himself said, in a later attempt to clarify the case, 'nothing more was then determined than that there was no right in the master forcibly to take the slave and carry him abroad'.[3] In other words Somerset had benefited from that part of the Act of Habeas Corpus which was no longer of any use to convicts, the part which prohibited any subject of the King from being taken out of the country in bondage. This was fifteen years before the First Fleet sailed for New South Wales.

The lawyers in Somerset's case argued backwards and forwards at great length about Englishmen in bondage or, in other words, about Englishmen who had no say in their condition, whose will was in law entirely subject to some superior individual, their identity submerged in his. They could find no obvious precedent for the Black slavery they saw about them, and which had its legal origins in the colonies (and they agreed that 'the law of the plantations' was irrelevant to English law). They found various examples of English slavery nevertheless. They talked about medieval villeinage, Mansfield himself murmuring from the bench that he had once read – 'but does not recollect the author' – that in the time of Charles II two villeins only had been left in England. Villeinage had since died out entirely. They talked about apprentices, especially those who were bound as orphans: 'neither the trade is left to the choice of those who were to serve, nor . . . consent . . . necessary'.[4] They talked about men who were forced in emergency to fight for their country, as soldiers pressed into foot regiments. English law allowed them all the rights of soldiers '(if any rights there are of that state)', but it also imposed on them an iron discipline.[5] They talked, too, about felons who might be forced to labour by Act of parliament or, in in other words, 'Slavery imposed for the performance of public works for civil crimes'. In all these cases bondage, and even forced transportation, might be imposed without consent. But none of them seemed to apply to labouring men and women who happened to be Black.[6]

Slavery, and all kinds of bondage, were a common topic of conversation during the eighteenth century, and the attacks on slavery from the 1760s were symptomatic of an intellectual concern which spanned several generations. There were endless convoluted jokes about it on stage, and no doubt in drawing rooms and taprooms. Freedom and its opposite were puzzling and modish matters. 'I'm a freeborn Englishman', says Silvia, disguised as a gentleman, in Farquhar's *The Recruiting Officer*, 'and will be a slave my own way.' 'Oh Mr Worthy,' says Melinda in the same play, with her thoughts on marriage, 'what you owe to me is not to be paid under a seven year servitude.'[7] (This was the first play performed on Australian soil, and many of the audience on that occasion were bound for seven years.) When Rousseau declared, in his *Social Contract*, 'Man is born free, and yet is universally enslaved', he might have been summing up the witticisms of several generations.

Interest was sharpened by the fact that freedom might be bought and sold in the eighteenth century as a common market commodity. Even men and women in debt might bind themselves to their creditors, as servants for a term of years. More commonly, especially in England, debtors went to prison at the behest of their creditors, until they could pay what they owed. In fact there were many more debtors in English prisons, subject to fellow Englishmen, than there were criminals.

Felons and debtors were not very different. In theory (but only in theory) felons, like debtors, forfeited their property, and property however small was a vital aspect of freedom. The King, or perhaps his agent, whether gaoler or magistrate, became, as it were, their creditor, with the right to dispose of both their liberty and their estate. Their labour power was left as their sole asset, and they might ransom themselves only by servitude. Robinson Crusoe had control of this kind over his 'pyrates'. They began as his prisoners: 'I had some Inclination to give them their Lives, if they thought they could shift on Shore.' Having chosen not to go back to England to be hanged, they became inhabitants of his island, making him, as he put it, their father, benefactor and governor. He had guaranteed their continued existence and through the order he had fashioned he gave them their livelihood. 'I had the absolute Disposal of the Lives and Fortunes of all my Subjects', he said, with a little hyperbole, and yet, 'notwithstanding my absolute Power, I had not one person disaffected to my Government'.[8] In 1722, shortly after Defoe wrote these words, the Privy Council of Great Britain laid it down in similar terms that when the King went as conqueror into a new country he might impose whatever laws he liked there, without asking the inhabitants' consent, 'for there the conqueror by saving the lives of the conquered [in other words, by letting them live], gains a right and property in such people'.[9]

Dealing in freedom thus had a significance beyond the contingencies of buying and selling. Some of the broader implications of the exercise had been spelt out a century before these statements by Shakespeare, in *The Tempest*. On another island, within another imaginary dominion, Ariel was freed by Prospero from a tree in which he had been shut up by the sorcery of the 'blu-ey'd hag', Sycorax, and he was automatically bound in service to his liberator. It was not perpetual service, because Prospero, like Crusoe, was just and honourable, a good master. A time was set and twice reduced. Ariel himself could boast, 'I have done thee worthy service; / Told thee no lies, made no mistakings, serv'd / Without or grudge or grumblings'. At the same time he longed for his freedom, even before 'the time be out', and he sang – one of Shakespeare's sweetest songs – when he was about to get it.[10]

European settlement in Australia was founded and maintained through its earliest years under this principle of redemption, by which human beings were simultaneously freed and bound in obligation to their liberator. It was a profound process, encrusted with an enormous depth of imagery. For centuries it had been essential even to the spiritual order of Christendom, for Christ himself was held to have earned the titles of 'Lord' and 'Redeemer' through the purchase of humanity with his own blood. This argument dated back to St Paul, and it was a peculiarly European (or Graeco-Roman) addition to the Jewish idea of a Messiah annointed by God.[11] Whether as metaphor or reality, it was an understanding foreign to Australia before 1788, and the egalitarian revolutions of the late eighteenth century showed that even in Europe its significance was becoming less concrete than hitherto. The radical poet Blake attacked it as 'a horrible doctrine' incompatible with the dignity of the soul.[12] However, thanks to Lord Sydney and his rigorous attachment to custom and prescriptive liberty, it was transplanted in a relatively flourishing state to the Antipodes.

What did freedom – that vastly complex and supremely European notion – mean for poor men and women? It meant the ability to choose, if only between the frying pan and the fire. In Newfoundland, for instance, there was no regular colonial government, although English, Scots and Irish fishermen were settled in their hundreds along the Atlantic coast. James Kelly was there in the 1730s, when he became involved in the murder of another man. One of the gang (as Kelly later confessed) threw the body into the sea; 'next Day it was found, and according to the Custom of the Place, the People were called together to touch the Corps [sic], imagining by that Means they might discover the Murtherer'. By that or other means, Kelly was caught and was thrown into 'a nasty Gaol'. While he was waiting to be sent in chains to England (there was no legal method of trial in Newfoundland in capital cases), a gentleman offered him freedom 'upon Condition of engaging to be his Bond-Servant for Life'. This would certainly have been tantamount to slavery, which may explain why Kelly rejected the offer. He died instead at Tyburn.[13]

English law was designed, in theory, to enlarge liberties. As Lord Mansfield pointed out, the villeinage, or traditional class of slaves, had long died out in England. Besides, over several centuries various Acts of parliament had assimilated the rights of villeins with those of freemen. When Magna Carta was first written out and signed in the twelfth century its central clauses had affirmed the rights of freemen only. But as early as Edward III these rights had been deliberately extended to every Englishman, 'of what estate or condition that he be'. (Women do not figure in Magna Carta.) About the same time it was enacted that all trials were to be in English, so that '*every man* . . . may . . . the better govern himself' – so that he might speak, understand and reply – when he was brought before the courts.[14] Acts passed under the later Stuart kings, such as Habeas Corpus, had the same general purpose. They were meant to place all the subjects of the King (now making no distinction of gender) on the same footing whenever they came, as accused or injured individuals, before the King's judges. Human beings were, of course, no more equal than before, but (in principle) human *voices* were equal.

And yet, while this was happening freedom was being newly defined, and barriers of a different sort were being built around a new body of unfree men and women. The procedure was a subtle one, and men like James Kelly can hardly be expected to have understood it. The Renaissance interest in the power of reasoning, shaped by a form of literacy dependent on printing, meant that a new villeinage, so to speak, was created just as the other passed away. Many educated men could not believe that the decision-making of the poor and ignorant, those who still lived within an entirely oral culture, was anything more than a legal fiction. The conversation of humble individuals throughout the shires of England seemed quite different in quality and much less valuable than the conversation of men and women who were familiar with books, and had been deliberately taught to think. It followed, apparently, that the former ought to be subject to the latter. They now appeared to be 'slaves in nature', as a Gloucestershire gentleman put it, though not in law. Even during the generation of Habeas Corpus, the Presbyterian divine Richard Baxter declared that 'multitudes in England, and more in Wales, Cornwall, Ireland, the Highlands, are scarce able to talk reason about common things'.[15] Another gentleman said the same about the poor in general: 'The numerous rabble that seem to have the signature of man in their faces . . . are but brutes in their understanding . . . 'tis by the favour of a metaphor we call them men.'[16] They were brutes mainly because, like brutes, they could not read.

Laws were enacted by parliament which reflected and reinforced such ideas, laws which were at odds with the spirit of Magna Carta, in its final form, and with Habeas Corpus. In other words, by the beginning of the eighteenth century the statute book contained some deep contradictions of principle.

Some of the most eminent political theorists of the seventeenth and eighteenth centuries wrote of society as something founded on a contract, real or imagined, among its various members, or between its members and their government, and contract involved independent reasoning. Those who seemed incapable of reasoning must surely be beyond the contract, which must put them within the indefeasible power of others. This seemed to apply wholesale to women and children, who were necessarily subject to the will of men, but the same could be said of some less favoured men. Any man who was given to violent aggression, who injured his neighbour for no obvious reason, was liable to be considered as an outcast from civil society. John Locke, the great theorist of contract, argued that such an individual deserved to be destroyed as if he were a dangerous beast. As for pirates, they lived even beyond the geographical limits of good order, which made them 'Hostis Humani Generis' (enemies of the human race). They were 'Brutes and Beasts of Prey', with whom no promise could be binding.[17]

Convicted felons were individuals who had fallen under the absolute power of their fellow Englishmen, assembled in court as judge and jury. How were they to be treated? There were several possible approaches. Considered in the abstract, there was no place for them in civil life. They must be set apart. If their lives were spared their physical strength might be turned to good, and in a few cases there might be hope of reform. But in general they were a people without rights, to be treated with Christian charity, narrowly defined, but no more. During the middle decades of the eighteenth century this became the usual attitude in Maryland and Virginia, the main destination for convicts transported from Britain and Ireland.[18] However in England, among some of the avant-garde, the notion of convicts as a people under a peculiar type of subjection was easily incorporated within new theories about social order and progress. Among medieval villeins, questions of identity and individuality had been caught within a grid of lineage and lordship. Convicts, on the other hand, were to find their lives defined by mere abstraction. In a growing number of pamphlets and books they were discussed as raw material for highly articulated social experiments. Psychology and penology – the science of punishment – were both disciplines invented in the late eighteenth century.

Nevertheless, some writers and administrators continued to think of the poor and ignorant, including convicts, not as a race apart but as social beings first and foremost. Moral judgment takes various forms. Intellectuals like John Locke and the other contract theorists might like to think of rationality in absolute terms, as the final arbiter of action. Other influential men and women (the third Earl of Shaftesbury being the best known) drew attention to the moral sense, existing, so they said, independent of reason, whose expression was the common voice and body, and on which day-to-day relationships, including unequal ones, were founded. They left room for ancient, unarticulated habits, more aligned with action than with thought.[19] Society was thus a fabric, not of minds only, nor even of hearts, but of souls, for while the first two – minds and hearts – were the source of thought and feeling, it was the soul which determined how the individual was to act, to weave a place in the world (and by the same process, in the world to come). Indeed, the soul was an unarguable matter of fact in the eighteenth century: obvious as bread and lively as wine.[20] The commonwealth was thus to be maintained by rich and poor alike, not by mere intellect, but by the impulse of forbearance, sacrifice, deference, condescension, affection, precept and example. Paley, the philosopher-clergyman, put considerable stress on habit as the basis of society. Habitual action was part of common Christianity.

Such men and women relied on a fabric of behaviour shaped by familiarity, not only with other people but also with material objects, homes and land, sometimes indistinguishable from a deep, unarticulated sense of possession. Marriage, for instance, was understood to be, among other things, an act of shared interest reinforced by Christian inclination. Whatever the inequality of husband and wife, they were mutually committed in marriage for providential motives. Labour relations were meant to work in the same way. As a late-seventeenth-century clergyman put it, masters had a right to expect 'Fidelity and painful industry from their Christian Servants': as Prospero did from Ariel. But they should, all the same, be 'content with their honest endeavours, not Tyrannizing over Christians, as *Turks* do over Galley-slaves, compelling them unmercifully beyond their strength'. Servants must play their part in this Christian interchange, and 'ought to put themselves forth to their utmost power for their Masters Benefit'.[21] There was always debatable ground, a breaking point at which voices might be raised beyond the common conversation of the workplace. (How many exceptions destroy a rule when that rule is a matter of faith?) For instance, on a Sunday in 1719, a day of rest so it was said, a party of English sailors refused to load their ship: 'they were Christians', they argued, 'and not Slaves [and] they would not then work'.[22]

This understanding of Christian commonwealth, in which even the poor and ignorant might be caught up as individuals with spiritual power, survived through the eighteenth century. On it was built an argument about the rights of men and women, spelt out in Sir William Blackstone's *Commentaries on the Laws of England*, first published in four volumes 1765–69. 'Life', wrote Blackstone, 'is the immediate gift of God', and it followed that every individual had a right to life, to the limbs which 'the wise creator' had designed for the defence of life, and to the means of maintaining life; 'For there is no man so indigent or wretched, but that he may demand a supply sufficient for all the necessaries of life from the more opulent.' However, Blackstone was careful not to make the last an absolute right, as it had been in earlier centuries, for fear of leaving the courts incapable of defending the property of the rich from the demands of the starving.[23]

Such ancient notions of commonwealth, and of each soul as it existed within the commonwealth, had their application to convicts. From Europe to ancient Australia, after all, law has always had its spiritual dynamic, and judgment at the highest level has always been tied, if possible, to something transcendant. The criminal law in England depended in essence on Christian principle, on perceptions about the soul, manifest, as the soul must always be, in common behaviour. There was considerable room for disagreement about the overall tendencies of the law, but within its arcane and frequently brutal machinery, beneath the scum of tears and blood, it is easy to find examples of such principle. For instance, judges felt a responsibility to study and classify accused men and women, especially as possible recipients of mercy. Talking backwards and forwards from the bench to the dock, listening to the workings of conscience within the human voice: these were vital parts of the process of justice. In the 1720s and 1730s lawyers began to act as defence counsel in the Old Bailey. They too were allowed to cross-examine.[24]

The eighteenth century saw the rise of a contest of principle within the criminal courts: a constant pull between the need to convict and punish, for the sake of public order, and the need to prove innocence, for humanity's sake; or maybe for the sake of Christian charity. Blackstone stated a very old principle, when he said that 'it is better that ten guilty persons escape, than that one innocent suffer'. But so far, in the English law courts, this had been little more than a high and vague aspiration. During the last decades of the eighteenth century it became fixed as a technical point: from now on, guilt was to be demonstrated beyond reasonable doubt ('the presumption of innocence'). The 1780s, the decade of White settlement in New South Wales, seems to have been the turning point. Beyond any other period of European history, this was a time when common liberties were the theme of many learned conversations, within and beyond the courts.[25]

In principle, felons were free agents making their way through, and stating their own choices at, the various Y-junctions offered by the law. There was always considerable lawyers' fiction in such liberty and, in some ways, the more frequently clients trusted to the eloquence of lawyers the more their poor vestiges of liberty shrank to an article tossed about by gentlemen in powdered wigs. They were subjected to the will of counsel. But the choices were certainly there. For instance, men and women who were condemned to die might, in most cases, choose between death and transportation. Some (like James Kelly in Newfoundland) decided to be hanged almost as a means of celebrating their right to choose: in order to show that they were something better than mere 'objects of mercy'. When Sarah Cowden was offered transportation for life, in April 1789, she gave this answer: 'No, I will die by the laws of my country; I am innocent . . . the people that had the money for which I was tried, are now at their liberty, therefore I will die by the laws of my country before ever I will go abroad for my life.' At about this time the first unpromising reports were coming back from New South Wales, which may explain why an unusual number of men and women made the same choice. 'I would rather die', said one of them, 'than go out of my own country to be devoured by Savages.'[26]

The sense of choice in such cases was greatly reinforced by having one's feet firmly placed on what these two victims of the law called '*my* country', '*my own* country', a well-known space outlined by sea and sky. It depended on an understanding of power, of spiritual and material possession, intermixed with the land, an understanding which, in its broad outlines, pre-literate Europeans shared (say) with Australian Aborigines.[27] Convicts clung to such power even when they left England. The Transportation Act of 1718 made it a hanging offence to come back early. Henry Woodford came home in 1721, and many followed his example even into the Australian period: 'the returning to his Wife and young Children, in order to keep them from Starving in his Absence, was so far from being a Crime,' Woodford said, 'that it was his Duty so to act'. Officially, convicts made an agreement to go away: they might live, but not in England. But while they might understand the need to go, they did not necessarily see the need to stay away. The chaplain of Newgate Gaol might try to explain to them the intricacies of the system: 'the Mercy of the Legislator,' he said on one occasion, 'by giving them back the Life they have forfeited, on certain Conditions, which they were perfectly able to perform, had put that Life in their own Power'. It followed, as the reverend gentleman put it, that 'the violating the very Conditions, on which their Lives were prolonged, . . . not only made these forfeit to all Claim to Life, but . . . exposed them to the

Hazard of being obliged to pay the Forfeiture'.[28] It sounds like rules for a game of cards. In so far as the convicts understood how to play, such rules must have frequently seemed at odds with reality.

From all points of view it was much more than a game of cards. In principle, mercy on the one hand – mercy of an almost divine quality, giving men and women back their lives – was meant to be answered with a willing subjection, with gratitude and a conscientious fulfilment of the conditions of transportation. In Maryland and Virginia it was said that convicts had been sent from England in order to 'work out their Pardon' by seven years of bondage.[29] In New South Wales the ubiquity of government meant that an immediate sense of obligation to the giver of life could be reinforced from day to day. The first Christian sermon in Australia, preached by the Reverend Richard Johnson on 3 February 1788 before an audience of convicts, dwelt on that theme: 'What shall I render unto the Lord, for all his benefits towards me?' (Psalms 116: 12). The King was the Lord's Anointed and the vehicle of divine mercy, and in the Antipodes they proved their subjection to him by grateful labour.

Governor Phillip understood these things. On the King's birthday in 1788 (4 June) he made a strenuous effort to draw the minds of the people back to their sovereign, who had redeemed their very existence and who was the whole basis of the order they lived in. On that day pardons were issued in the King's name to every convict who was awaiting trial or punishment for offences in the colony, and the Governor distributed grog or porter for every convict, soldier and sailor to drink His Majesty's health. Two days' labour had been spent gathering wood for a great bonfire. It was stacked several yards high around a tree and lit in the afternoon, while the gentlemen were all at dinner in the Governor's tent. George Worgan, surgeon of the *Sirius*, called it 'really a noble Sight': 'Here, the Convicts assembled, singing & Huzzaing. On the Governor's Approach, they all drew up on the Opposite Side, & gave three Huzza's, [and] after this salutation A Party of them joined in singing *God Save the King*.'[30]

Worgan did not mean all the convicts. Around the bonfire 'every heart beat with loyalty & joy', but elsewhere a number took the opportunity to raid the officers' tents. It was recalcitrant behaviour like this which did most to shape Phillip's attitude to his community. As a rule he had no confidence in the convicts. They were, he said, 'naturally indolent' and 'never can be trusted'.[31] There were individual exceptions, however, and even refined examples of gratitude. The convict John Grant wrote the following lines after being sent on from Port Jackson to Norfolk Island (making him, perhaps, the inventor of the word 'Australian'):

> I tread an Isle, Great George its King,
> Rising amidst Australian Seas:
> His Clemency gave Life: I sing
> Twice exil'd, ill at ease.[32]

But taken as a whole the convicts were a people beyond both reason and gratitude: so few Ariels, so many Calibans.

Certainly they were hard to reason with. Nor was it possible to deal with them like sailors on board ship. On shipboard everything was strained to a single purpose which even the stupidest men could understand. Seemingly, the convicts had no sense of responsibility at all. According to David Collins, the Judge-Advocate and Phillip's secretary, 'there were many who knew not how to husband their provisions through the seven days they were intended to serve them'. Also, they wandered like children:

> Almost every month since our arrival . . . produced one or more accidents, occasioned principally by a non-compliance with the orders which had been given solely with a view to their security; and which, with thinking beings, would have been of sufficient force as examples to deter others from running into the same danger.

This was in the bewildering first period of settlement. But for long after that, said Collins, the convicts had 'no interest in the success of their labour'. They had no concern for the public good even when it touched themselves. They depended on the government stores, with no thought as to how 'to secure themselves whereon to exist when those stores should be exhausted'.[33]

Phillip seems to have hoped that convict intellect would extend to reading and thinking about the orders he gave, and he made use of public notices. These were read out by overseers, but some were also attached to trees. However, as Collins remarked, the convicts 'had not been accustomed to live in situations where their conduct was to be regulated by written orders'. There was frequent disobedience, and he observed that when any rule was broken the usual excuse was 'that they had never before heard of it'. On one occasion a convict called Ryan protested that 'he did not know of the Notice, that he was never told by his overseer'. Also, he said, he could not read. There was an even more fundamental problem. Convicts like Ryan had no idea that a rule, once announced – on 1 February 1788, for instance: 'In future all trees standing on the ground intended to be cleared are to be grubbed up' – was meant to last from day to day. Many seemed to think that it was issued merely 'for the purpose of the moment'.[34] In short, they had not yet absorbed the central point of the eighteenth-century empire, that writing was a missile designed to penetrate not only places but times unknown.

Before he left England, Phillip had looked forward to a measured system of rewards and punishments, managed by himself and probably modelled on the one used on the convict hulks in the Thames (see Chapter 6).[35] But, except in some isolated cases, he did little with this idea. When it came to the point, he had no profound interest in a people who existed, wilfully as it seemed, beyond the sweetness and light, the higher reasoning, which he so much valued himself. Face to face with the convicts, he found few whose intellectual diet amounted to anything more than the ephemeral echoes of living conversation. In his accounts of the settlement he spent much less time speculating about them than, for instance, Collins did. His detachment from the convicts – even those who cheered him from the other side of the bonfire – also meant that he was probably not in a good position to exchange with them, from day to day, mercy for gratitude. Nevertheless the principle of such exchange was there, fixed within the foundation of government.

II

To begin with, there was no proposal for courts of law in New South Wales. In planning for Lemane it had been thought that the elected chief of the convicts would be told to name one or more from among them 'to try and punish any of them for Crimes'. After all, even pirates elected their 'quartermaster' to act as judge among them. But how far such a procedure was envisaged for New South Wales is not certain. Matra wanted 'the Use of Martial Law and prompt Justice', and this seems to have been the original idea discussed (or taken for granted) in cabinet.[36] The Lord Chancellor, Lord Thurlow, seems to have agreed that at least in capital cases the Governor should be able to order summary convictions. The convicts (we must assume) were to form their own subordinate system of justice, with the Governor intervening in more serious cases. Whatever the methods of trial, punishments were to depend on him. He would also have the power to reprieve condemned men and women.[37]

As far as we can tell, this was the idea during August–October 1786. But early in November Lord Sydney seems to have decided that too much was being left to chance. Radical differences were opening up between the blueprints for Lemane and for New South Wales. The selection of Phillip meant that in the Antipodes there would be an energetic Governor, whose eye would be on everything and whose will would be all-pervasive. A great deal would depend on the decisions of that officer, and, as Sydney said on another occasion, 'no man can think themselves safe in the hands of an individual, who is bound by no rule but his own discretion. In such a situation, an angel would be suspected; nor would satisfaction be given by a god.'[38] In the months before the departure of the First Fleet, the basis of land ownership was tightened up in order to give the convicts absolute rights (see Chapter 4). The same was done with the judicial system.

In short, Sydney decided that the convicts could not be subject to regulations formed for military purposes.[39] In order to ensure that they were treated as English civilians they were to have the benefit of a court system formally established and with a judicial officer commissioned by the Crown. As with landed title, these benefits were not aimed primarily at ex-convicts. In 1786–87 the Home Office took no account of such people. Rather, they were meant for men and women under sentence, who were to have a parcel

David Collins, captain of Marines, first Judge-Advocate of New South Wales and afterwards first Lieutenant-Governor at Hobart Town.

Source: Mitchell Library, State Library of New South Wales

of rights quite different from felons in England. Convicts had traditionally had such rights in North America, or at least in Virginia. Some of these rights had been whittled away by local law before the American Revolution, but in principle there was no reason why the new generation of convicts should not begin in New South Wales with all their rights intact.[40] This was Lord Sydney's intention, and for some years convicts were technically to be allowed the status of free men and women when they appeared before the courts, so that, as a rule, they appear among the records not as convicts, but with 'labourer', 'settler' and so forth written after their names.[41] On other points some compromises were necessary. Cost was one difficulty. Sydney was very ready to spend public money on the settlement, but he could not always carry other ministers with him.[42] This may explain why, when it came to appointing a judge, it was decided that the post should be given to the Marines officer who already had a commission as deputy judge-advocate for the garrison. There was precedent at Gibraltar, where the Judge-Advocate also did double duty for the merchant community settled at the foot of the Rock, using the title of judge-advocate in both courts.[43] The first Judge-Advocate of New South Wales was David Collins. He may have been recommended to the Home Secretary by the fact that his grandfather, Arthur Collins, a celebrated antiquarian, had edited the Sidney Papers at Penshurst. (Lord Sydney himself was a Fellow of the Society of Antiquarians.) David Collins was also to be Australia's original historian, the first volume of his *Account of the English Colony in New South Wales* being dedicated to Sydney. He personified the historical sensibilities which were brought to bear in the shaping of settlement.

The Home Office also had to cope with the fact that there was no sure prospect of finding anyone in the settlement who might act as jurymen in criminal trials. In England jurymen were always local worthies, men of small-to-middling rank and property.[44] Lord Sydney must have been loath to give up the idea of a jury for New South Wales, sanctified as it was by ancient English ideas of liberty. Juries represented the opinion of the people. For that reason, so Sydney argued, they were more important even than the bewigged gentlemen on the bench (an extreme statement even for that time, reminiscent of the radical followers of John Wilkes):

> I have always understood [so Sydney informed the House of Commons], that they [the jurymen] were the sole judges in criminal cases, and that the justices were only expounders of the law, men paid by the public to assist and direct them in intricate and difficult cases.[45]

However, Lord Camden, a former Lord Chancellor, Sydney's neighbour in Kent and with him a stout upholder of common rights, agreed that the people in the new settlement would not be 'of the proper stuff to make jurys'.[46] For the time being, it was necessary to find a substitute. Once again, Gibraltar offered a plausible precedent, a criminal court in which the judge-advocate sat with a number of officers from one or other of the services. Seated in state, the officers looked something like a jury though they were summoned as members of the bench. This was the system adopted for Botany Bay, although it was a confusing compromise. The officers themselves were uncomfortable as judges, at least to begin with. In his account of the first years, Tench explained that the court was like an ordinary English one in some respects but not all. It was meant to administer English common and statute law, but Tench was glad that in making their judgments he and his brother officers might also take account of 'the circumstances and situation of the settlement'. Without this proviso, he said, 'the wisest among us would be now and then puzzled how to act'.[47]

This court dealt with serious offences, from larceny to murder. There was another court, the Judge-Advocate's Bench, which investigated trifling thefts and misdemeanours and which was made up of one or more justices of the peace, including the Judge-Advocate. In Phillip's time Collins usually sat with the Lieutenant-Governor, the Surveyor-General (Augustus Alt), the chaplain (Richard Johnson) and John Hunter, captain of the *Sirius* (and future Governor). Neither Alt, Johnson nor Hunter were members of the garrison, and their presence on the bench helped the notion that this was an ordinary English court of petty sessions – one of the central institutions of English civilian life – and as such a counter-weight to the power of the military, from which the officers were drawn for the higher court.

Flogging was the normal punishment for both courts, and in English common life the main point of judicial flogging was humiliation before one's neighbours, marked mainly by the drawing of blood. In such circumstances the exact measurement of violence was pointless. In the army and navy, on the other hand, men had to be ruled with a systematic rod of iron. Sailors, in particular, were 'like granite, hard and lasting', so that blood and humiliation meant nothing to them.[48] In New South Wales the officers who staffed the criminal court chose to flog entirely by numbers. In Phillip's time the number awarded usually ranged between 300 (for petty larceny, or the theft of an item worth less than a shilling) and 2000, a punishment next to death.[49]

The magistrates in the lower court counted the lashes as well, favouring 25, 50 or 100. But because they were dealing with less serious crimes and with individuals who were not yet beyond the pale they also relied on humiliation, especially in dealing with women. Women were often whipped by instalments, on the weekdays when everyone came in to get their rations, so that a crowd of friends and neighbours might be guaranteed. In May 1788, for instance, Elizabeth Clark was ordered to be 'tied to a Cart's tail, and flogged publicly once up and once down, the Women's camp, on the Western side of the Cove'. On top of a similar punishment, in June 1789, Elizabeth Fowles was condemned to have her head shaved and to wear a canvas cap with 'thief' written on it.[50]

The magistrates and officers felt free to invent other punishments as the occasion seemed to require, just as officers did in regimental tribunals throughout the empire.[51] They condemned convicts to transportation, which meant either a passage to Norfolk Island, a brief period on an island in Sydney Harbour or else, in one case, 'to remain in this Country for Life'. One man, Joseph Elliot, was condemned not only to 300 lashes and a stoppage of his flour rations, but also 'to be chained . . . to Coffin and Bayliss, two publick Delinquents employed at Work on the Roads'. Ann Martin was tried for drunkenness and was ordered 'To make Pegs for a month' (these being used to fix shingles to the roofs of public buildings).[52]

Phillip was interested in the process of punishment. He was no less inventive than the officers and magistrates, but he was more visionary. Before leaving England he had looked forward to a judicial system which would be shaped to fit not only local circumstances but up-to-date ideas. During his naval career he had relied in a conventional way on corporal punishment, but, like some of the best minds of his generation, he hated hanging. In his new settlement, he predicted, '[sentence of] death, I should think, will never be necessary – in fact, I doubt if the fear of death ever prevented a man of no principle from committing a bad action'.[53] On the spot he was forced to compromise and in the second year of settlement he began to take short cuts with the justice system, occasionally sending men to be flogged without formal inquiry. In December 1789, in a particularly angry moment, he ordered a summary one hundred lashes for the man who let Coleby the Aboriginal escape from the settlement.[54]

Even before leaving England, Phillip had wondered what fear might do in binding the wills of the most recalcitrant individuals. Eighteenth-century Europeans were fascinated with cannibalism, an interest encouraged by some lurid detail in Defoe's story of Robinson Crusoe. Two of Crusoe's renegades had been brought to heel by the sight and prospect of it:

> the Thoughts of being eaten up like Beef or Mutton, tho' it was suppos'd it was not to be till they were dead, had something in it so horrible, that it nauseated their very Stomachs, made them sick when they thought of it, and fill'd their Minds with such unusual Terror, that they were not themselves for some Weeks after.

In New South Wales murder and sodomy, Phillip thought, ought to carry the death penalty, and in his early plans he anticipated that anyone convicted of those crimes might be sent 'as a prisoner to the natives of New Zealand, and let them eat him'.[55] Here was vision adrift from reality. But here too was a man struggling like others in his time to marry efficiency – a system of punishment which would put an end to crime – with humanity (see Chapter 6). Europeans in New South Wales were not to be slaves, but they must be forced in many cases directly against their will, and justice itself depended at last on unspeaking fear.

III

Work began on a brick cottage for the Governor within four months of landing. Meanwhile Phillip lived in a prefabricated shelter, more tent than building, set in his future garden. During his private hours, within the tight skin of this edifice, His Excellency's eye was as careful as ever. A chilly night and a warm day in July were remarked on, for instance, in his letters home; but not in terms of discomfort or pleasure, those being issues he rarely embraced on paper. Intimate sensations were distilled to match the calculating language of the Enlightenment. 'I frequently find a difference', he wrote, 'of thirty-three degrees in my chamber between 8 o'clock in the morning and 2 o'clock in the afternoon'. What of the winter light which slanted in as he dressed in the morning? Day by day it threw its comfortable patterns, sweetening the thoughts of a man whose life was in order from the moment he woke up, but it too was translatable: 'the sun', he wrote, 'does not reach the thermometer, which is at the west end of my canvass house'.[56] Private and abstract, gentle and remote, this is as much as we get of Phillip by himself.

Outside the tent, among those who saw only his smooth shadow through the sun-lit walls (as we must do), there was plenty of conversation about his habits, the authority concentrated in his person and the weight he seemed determined to carry on his own shoulders. 'I never herd of any one Single Person having So great a Power in Vested in Him as the Govenour has by his commission', observed Lieutenant Clark of the Marines. The remarks of his brother officer, Captain Campbell, were more personal: 'To establish an infant colony, with any hope of success or satisfaction to those embarked in the attempt, does it not require a man of a Free, Liberal & Generous way of thinking – it surely does. – This man will be every thing himself.' He would be everything, and he gave everything its significance within the Antipodean scheme of things. Campbell might maintain that the opposite was true, that the Governor's moral authority was nil: 'from the greatest rascal among the convicts to his next in command, some Toad eater & talebearer excepted, there is not a man but what despises him'.[57] Certainly some of the officers, such as Campbell and Major Ross, had no time for 'this strange character' – his big nose, his rosebud mouth, his complex, cosmopolitan, un-English physiognomy – believing that the settlement would be better run as a garrison-commonwealth. Others, including some of the more intelligent ones, were able to see into Phillip's up-to-date and highly polished principles. None, however, could escape the force of his personality.

Campbell and Ross were not entirely old-fashioned themselves. Campbell talked about *all* the men in the settlement, from 'the greatest rascal' right up to the Lieutenant-Governor, as one united body of opinion. Campbell and Ross were soul-mates and it is more than coincidence that Campbell's outburst should find a reflection in Ross's methods as commandant at Norfolk Island (described in Chapter 4), especially his effort to get every individual – convicts, soldiers and officers – to pledge him their support. Here was a simple but important notion, shared by two officers, about the way in which government might be fitted to the opinions of all (of the men, at least) who lived under it. Englishmen could never be mere subjects. Their wills and identities could never be shaped entirely by their betters. The English idea of consent was now being enriched in Europe and North America, and it may be that Campbell and Ross (who were Scots) had imbibed newer variations of it. In that sense they were unconscious prophets of democracy.

In fact there is no good evidence to show exactly what the convicts thought about Phillip. It is only possible to say that, apart from a little 'sauciness' here and there, the Governor never seems to have received any abuse to his face from any man or woman in the settlement. The courts were very busy punishing insolence and false rumours among the convicts, but no one of the subject people was ever accused of casting any slur on the Governor. Among the poor and unlettered, he seems to have been awesome even at a distance.

Language was the pivot of good discipline in Phillip's time, but language flowed with disarming ease beyond the circle of subjection which the officers would have imposed on it. Even violent punishment could not entirely confine the vagaries of living conversation. Both the Criminal Court and the Judge-Advocate's Bench were very interested in who said what among the people, and talk was transcribed in great detail in the records of each. Minor theft was the most common offence tried in the courts. But language seems to have been thought the most significant. This was still at bottom an oral culture, and even public life was still drawn in many ways from the spoken word. The transcripts of each trial froze the passing language of the people:

- Joshua Peck, on being told by Surgeon White that he was too drunk to stand up – 'That was Policy'.[58]
- Elizabeth Clark, to the soldier with whom she had slept on shipboard – 'you Bougre', and 'you bloody Bougre'.[59]
- Four adolescent convict girls, at the tops of their voices to Captain Browne of the *Fishburn* as he passed the bakehouse – 'Who bottles Pease Soup? Who puts their Men in the Coal Hole?'[60]
- Ann Powell, in conversation with the constable who informed her that the fire in her hut should have been put out at bedtime –

  she told him, if he would go to the Governor and get her a Pair of Shoes she would [put it out] . . . she told him he was a very busy person to make her get up, . . . he told her what authority he had, . . . she told him, that in the Ship she took him for a Gentleman, but she now found quite the contrary.[61]

- Henry Abrahams, overseer, in conversation with James White, a convict, who questioned him about the siting of a roadway –

  Abra[ha]ms replied, Ask about. White said if Capt. Tench or Mr Long were there, he would not let him come thro'. Abra[ha]ms replied, Damn and bougre Capt. Tench and Mr Long, he would knock their Heads off.[62]

- William Frazer, on being told by Sergeant Connor that he was trespassing too near the soldiers' huts – 'You may kiss my Arse.'[63]

In the very first case heard by the Criminal Court a long story was told which was all about conversation. It began with an argument between two convict men. The drum major of the garrison had been passing and had stepped between the two, as he said, 'To prevent a Quarrel'. One of the convicts walked away, but the other, Samuel Barsby, resented taking orders from the drum major: 'he denied his having any authority over him'. Barsby had an adze in his hand and he hit the drum major, who managed to get him into the custody of the soldiers on guard, until he could be brought to trial. Barsby kept on shouting. '[H]e would not be confined', he said, 'by any Bougre on the Island, that he was brought there by a long Drummer Ben Cook, and was held under by a Parcel of Marines.' The soldiers gagged him, and when this did no good Private Mitchell ordered him to be quiet, 'on Pain of his running him thro' the Body'. Barsby dared him to do it. Mitchell hit him with his bayonet, which was bent 'by his pushing against it near the socket'. 'Had you received Orders to strike him?' asked the court. 'Yes, from the Man I relieved.'[64]

Barsby got 150 lashes, but nothing seems to have been done about Mitchell. Also, no questions seem to have been asked as to whether the drum major was hurt by Barsby's adze, or whether Barsby had been hurt by the bayonet. The evidence was all about the original argument, what Barsby said to the drum major and the efforts to keep him quiet. The courts in New South Wales ignored issues of physical violence, if they could. This was part of their military attitude, violence being central to military life. It was usually condemned only as part of some other offence, such as riot or insolence. Riot, in particular, was a favourite charge at Sydney Cove. For instance, Ann Farmer was charged with 'being in liquor and making a riot' when in fact she was trying to ward off blows from some unnamed assailant and had finished up covered in blood. The court believed her, but nothing more was done.[65]

Disciplining language was a vital matter. 'In oral cultures', as the great scholar of language, Walter Ong, says, 'speech is a conspicuously aggressive weapon.' Officers were expected to fight duels and to use 'manual correction' with their men, but even then the violence was frequently caused by bad or dishonourable language.[66] All military courts took undisciplined talk very seriously, as a potential threat to morale, subordination and/or personal honour. Honour was mainly important where officers were concerned, but soldiers had their dignity too. For the men on guard at Sydney Cove, the voice of Samuel Barsby was a weapon which wounded more deeply than his adze.

This was also the attitude which Phillip and the officers took in dealing with John Cullyhorn, the convict who quarrelled with the Governor as to whether his term was up (see Chapter 4). Here a living voice was raised against the circle of polished and literate men. Cullyhorn was charged with saying things – to the Governor himself – 'to the Prejudice of His Honour Robert Ross, Esqr.' He (Cullyhorn) had said that Ross had said to him that he would always be fed at the public store whether he worked or not. Phillip was sure that the convict was lying, because no officer who called himself a gentleman would make a confidential statement of that kind to a man so much his inferior. Certainly the Governor was troubled by the fact that

Criminal Court was not designed to try questions of honour, but the trial went ahead and Cullyhorn was brutally punished.[67]

In so far as the Criminal Court could be made into a court of honour it was similar to general courts martial in the army or navy. By the same token the Judge-Advocate's Bench resembled not only a court of petty sessions but also a regimental court martial, a court which tried minor crimes in the army and looked into quarrels among the men.[68] In other words, it considered both criminal and civil matters. This partly explains why the bench spent so much time on petty insults, especially where men were the targets. (The insulting of women, as Chapter 7 shows, was another matter.) The convicts soon came to understand that the courts were interested in recording and judging the sudden expressions, the ugly knots in their conversations, the sharp but common words which had hitherto passed among them unheeded.

Some gentlemen spent their time in New South Wales collecting and describing zoological and botanical specimens. Dried leaves and yellow skins, labelled in Latin, supplemented the homeward traffic of paper. Others wrote down the languages of the Blacks. Others again drew lines around the living words of their fellow countrymen, colouring them with the shades of the late Enlightenment. They must have wondered sometimes about doing the same with the speakers, affirming their names in ink for all time, herding them from page to page towards some final judgment, according – for instance – to the tabulated precision of the new penologists. That was, however, a project for another generation.

Speaking out in court, speaking like a free Englishman, went on as well. During his trial Cullyhorn was allowed to argue once more with Governor Phillip: 'Did not Y[ou]r Ex[cellenc]y when you rose from the Table in Warmth, ask me, what the L[ieutenan]t Gov[erno]r said to me?' In answer, Phillip denied rising 'in Warmth' at all, though he was certainly offended, he said, at Cullyhorn's 'manner of speaking'. The right to speak and the need to watch one's 'manner of speaking': these were the two sides of liberty for the convicts, the two seeds from which public order was to grow in the Antipodes.

In March 1791 the Judge-Advocate's Bench added one more form of punishment to its repertoire. Iron shackles had been imposed on delinquents from the beginning of settlement. Now the bench took a further step, ordering iron collars, weighing 7 pounds (3.2 kilograms) each, to be worn by particular offenders for as much as two years at a time.[69] Among Englishmen and Englishwomen, articulate members of Christendom, heirs to the common law, individuals who, by daily conversation, knew about the dumb bondage imposed on Blacks in America, it would have been hard to think of anything more degrading. This was a punishment modelled on slavery. By that time – after three years of settlement – Phillip's system had become so well entrenched as to make the convicts look a little like slaves. So it struck Private Easty, one of the garrison: 'the thoughts of Liberty from Such a place as this is Enoufh to induce any Convicts to try all Skeemes to obtain it'. For, he said, 'thay are the Same as Slaves all the time thay are in this Country'. The labour itself was hard, for the men at least. As Captain Tench admitted, 'necessity compelled us to allot to them the most slavish and laborious employments'. But it was the apparent permanence of servitude which most made it look like slavery. Counting the days and years was no help, and Cullyhorn's case showed that speaking out might make things worse. The people laboured for their entire term. And even after that, said Easty, 'allthough thare times are Expired for which thay are Sentanced by Law thare is no differance between them and a Convict that is jest Cast for trans-portation'.[70]

In fact slavery, the total subjection of men and women, was never entrenched. There was evidence of it and there was talk about it, but in New South Wales, as we see later, slavery was a subject easily exhausted. Meanwhile, the reader is released from the servitude of this chapter.

Chapter 6

Discipline and Cheerfulness

I

The second half of the eighteenth century was an age of humanitarianism, but in that age, as in any age, feelings of humanity – the bright fires of kindness – shone in various colours. They might burn with a strong and steady light, or they might flicker with the merest impulse. Some examples were worth remembering for ever. Some were routine. Some had only the liveliness of passing fashion.

Thomas Townshend, first Baron (and afterwards first Viscount) Sydney, was not a humanitarian, in the commonly understood sense of the word. All the same he was thought to be a good man. He lived an orderly life, avoiding extremes. He was often angry about matters of political principle, as he once admitted, but, he said, 'He thanked Heaven, warm as he was by nature, that his warmth seldom lasted long.' Although he was well-read, he made no boast of being sophisticated. He much preferred his own 'plebeian rusticity', as he called it, his relatively modest house at Chislehurst, his library and his ducks (which he visited each evening when he was at home), to the clubs and gambling dens which were the haunts of other nobleman. 'He was acquainted', he said, 'with no gamblers; he thanked God, that he was never associated with that description of men, let their rank or situation in life be ever so high.'[1] Everything about him was prosaic and unpretentious.

He disliked the 'Asiatic luxury and Asiatic corruption' which he saw coming into England with the new wealth from the East. He thought that much of the British empire had been built on vanity, greed and oppression, and was dangerous to common English virtues.[2] However, he was not especially doctrinaire on this point. For instance, he enjoyed the company of officers of middling rank in the army and navy who were the builders of empire. He liked these unassuming practical patriots, sober men who bore the heat of the day, who lived shoulder to shoulder with their subordinates and who made the hard decisions, as it were, on the outer edge.

This explains why he thought highly of Arthur Phillip. Phillip differed from his minister in so far as he was a man of complicated intellect and sweeping vision. But his obvious sense of duty and his ability to weigh up the practical needs of the people under his control were qualities which Sydney was bound to admire. In principle Sydney thought that convicts had no right to expect kindness from government, beyond the little prescribed in law. The arguments against a settlement at Lemane, he said, had been based on 'mistaken humanity' and 'affected tenderness'. While Africa was certainly an unpleasant place, convicts themselves understood (so Sydney believed) that 'no Climate is worse than that of a Goal [sic]'.[3] But while he was not a humanitarian in the usual sense, he was kind in small matters, and in a number of ways he supplemented Phillip's attempts to lessen the suffering of the people going out to New South Wales.

Besides, humanity in day-to-day things was fashionable too. Throwing crumbs to wild birds was a newly invented source of pleasure, a pleasing affectation among the upper and middle classes.[4] It followed that there should be an unrestrained interest in the suffering of humble individuals, including convicts, and the launching of a great expedition such as the First Fleet provided various occasions for throwing crumbs to wild birds. While the ships were being loaded, there was much talk in London of an act of compassion in which Lord Sydney had joined with the turnkey of Norwich Gaol, John Simpson. Simpson had taken three women to Plymouth to board their transport. One of them, Susannah Holmes, had a baby, Henry, nine months old, which the captain refused to take on board. Leaving the tearful mother behind him, the turnkey carried the child on his lap post-haste to London – a journey the breadth of England – and tackled Lord Sydney on the stairs of the Home Office. '[H]is Lordship very naturally shewed an unwillingness at first to attend to an application made to him in so strange and abrupt a manner; but Mr Simpson described, as he felt, the exquisite misery he had lately been a witness to.' He even suggested that the mother might since have killed herself. 'Lord Sydney was greatly affected, . . . and instantly promised that the child should be restored, commending, at the same time, Mr Simpson's spirit and humanity.' The story appeared in various papers. So many readers were affected in the same way that mother and child found themselves with £20 in donations to carry with them to New South Wales.[5]

Such acts of compassion were easy but precious, to be treasured mainly for what they said about oneself. There was a more long-term, discrete, hard-edged and painstaking humanity, typical of men like Phillip, which piece by piece laid the foundation for a new type of government. During the second half of the eighteenth century, a new generation of officials and opinion-makers were moved by an expansive desire to embrace and permeate the lives of common people as men and women in their position (in Britain, at least) had never done before. Humanitarianism of this kind was one of the great movements reshaping what historians have called the old regime. It did so by creating a new understanding of power, a new sense of responsibility and new methods of subjection.

By the 1780s this approach was already obvious in expeditions across the Atlantic. Health and hygiene were the central concerns. The fleet which had taken the military settlers to Nova Scotia in 1749 had been mounted with the utmost attention to keeping the people healthy. The newly invented 'Sutton's Air Pipes', already in use in the navy, were fitted to all the transports, at a cost of £35 each, to ensure ventilation below deck, and there were lengthy discussions about medical staff and supplies. Contractors for convict transportation to America had also begun to pay more attention to the health of their human cargoes and many fewer were dying at sea.[6] The same is true of slave ships. But here, of course, there were motives apart from sympathy for the poor and miserable. Humanitarianism had its origins as well in a new approach to questions of commercial profit, in what the age called Economy and Policy. There was a new understanding of the way in which profit might emanate from an all-embracing efficiency, and one of the central springs of efficiency was understood to be human health. Europeans at home and abroad showed an almost obssessive day-to-day interest in health. 'Health', said William Paley, ' . . . is the one thing needful . . . no pains, expense, self-denial, or restraint, to which we subject ourselves, for the sake of health, is too much.'[7] If restraint was to be imposed on ourselves, others – the people at large – might also be led or driven towards the same happy discipline. And there were other considerations besides profit. The cutting edge of armies and navies was to be secured in the same way. The power of the empire itself seemed to depend not only on the numbers of its people and on their ability to go forth and multiply wherever necessary. Equally important were the size of its armed forces, their ease of movement, their physical condition, their cleanliness and cheerfulness and, in the end, their wholesome readiness to kill and be killed.

The application of these new principles to large numbers of people – armies, navies, the inhabitants of gaols and transports, slaves, women in childbed, the legion poor who gathered in the new cities – were an intellectual challenge. Sutton's Air Pipes were one contribution. Other ideas came in books and pamphlets:

- Robert Pringle, *Observations on the Nature and Cure of Hospital and Jayl Fevers* (1750);
- James Lind, *An Essay on the Most Effectual Means of Preserving the Health of Seamen in the Royal Navy* (1762);
- Dr Percival, *Essay on the Internal Regulations of Hospitals* (1771);
- W. Black, *Observations on the Small-Pox* (1781);
- Sir Jeremiah Fitzpatrick, *An Essay on Gaol Abuses and on the Means of Redressing Them* (1784);

- Gilbert Blane, *Observations on Diseases Incident to Seamen* (1785);
- John Peter Wade, *A Paper on the Prevention and Treatment of the Disorders of Seamen and Soldiers in Bengal* (1793);

and many, many more. There were numerous medical journals, appearing year by year and dealing with a ramifying series of issues, and for a time there were almost annual publications on one subject alone, the question of scurvy in the navy. Some general periodicals, such as the popular *Gentleman's Magazine*, took it for granted that even lay readers would be interested in detailed technical debate about medicine and methods of keeping well.[8]

Educated men who aimed to be good managers within the departments of state had to keep up with the literature. They had to be effective citizens within their own province of the republic of letters, not only by reading but also by making lucid written reports to their superiors. At sea the fabric of authority was often very thinly stretched, and officers commanded in places which were strange, not only to other officers but to Europeans in general. Efficient pioneering by sea depended on the fluent use of pen and ink. According to John Paul Jones, one of the founders of the United States Navy, a naval officer must be 'capable of communicating his ideas on paper in language that becomes his rank'. In the Royal Navy, whose ships had sailed far abroad for generations, this was a notion taken for granted. Efficiency among underlings, mere clerks, was differently understood. Though they must be literate, their skills called for no sensibility or breadth of vision. '"The [post office] clerks grow expert from habit. [so said Jane Austen's Mr John Knightley] – They must begin with some quickness of sight and hand, and exercise improves them. If you want any further explanation,' continued he, smiling, 'they are paid for it.'"[9] Finer motives and the power of judgment, on the other hand, were expected of officers and gentlemen.

A good deal of attention was paid to the health of the First Fleet, although the effect was uneven. More than a thousand pounds was spent on medical stores, and the medical men who sailed with it treated the expedition as a great and exciting challenge. They knew that success depended not only on the physical condition of the people, but also on their 'cheerfulness', or in other words their willingness to be subject, in every detail of their lives, to humane authority. (In the Royal Navy some captains added musicians to the ship's company, to keep up the spirits of the crew and to get them dancing daily on deck.) The Principal Surgeon appointed for the First Fleet, and for the settlement in New South Wales, was John White. He was young, energetic and up-to-date, and a cheerful man himself. He was also highly literate, and he afterwards published his experiences. His story started with his going on board the convict transports at Plymouth, two months before they sailed. He made it his immediate responsibility, as he recalled, to do something about the 'lowness of spirits' he found among the convicts. He spoke to them in encouraging terms, promised clothing for those in need, arranged for them to be released on deck, 'one half at a time, during the course of . . . [each] day, in order that they might breathe a purer air', and he wrote to his superiors to ask for an allowance of fresh meat rather than salt, together with 'a little wine for those who were ill'. Later he managed to get parts of the interior of each vessel painted with quicklime, wherever the convicts were confined, in order to limit the 'unwholesome dampness' which appeared on the timbers, 'and was occasioned by the breath of the people'.[10]

During the voyage, White remarked on anything that had any connection with public health. Just as a commander's gaze might linger on the skies and seas, White's moved daily over the eyes and skin of his subjects, the dullness, the shining fever, the altered breath. He reported the dying of several convicts, and the causes: dropsy, 'lowness of spirits and debility', 'melancholy and long confinement', and so on. He reported his regular use of creosote, 'three times a week, and oftener if found necessary'. He reported on his treatment of the 'poor fellows' who succumbed to scurvy. He reported on the water rationing:

> people subject to long voyages should never be put to a short allowance of water; for I am satisfied that a liberal use of it (when freed from the foul air, and made sweet by a machine now in use on board his Majesty's navy) will tend to prevent a scorbutic habit, as much [as] if not more than, any thing we are acquainted with.

He also reported a curious but short-lived swelling disease, among both convicts and sailors, and he discussed its possible causes. Was it the verdigris which collected on the cooking utensils? '[T]he coppers were cleaned, and made as bright as they could be, every day, under my own inspection.' Was it venereal? Unable to solve the problem, he published what detail he could for the instruction and future reference of the educated world. (It is now thought to have been mumps).[11]

In New South Wales, White found less to interest him from the point of view of public health, and he filled his pages mainly with botanical and zoological discoveries. However, his reports of death among the convicts continued to combine emotional and physical causes. For instance, Samuel Davis escaped from Aborigines but died from 'fear, united with the cold and wet', after a night in the bush. Among the scientific discoveries, White found that gum from the eucalyptus trees was 'very serviceable' in dealing with dysentery. Native currants could cure scurvy, a great scourge of the first few months, except that there were not nearly enough of them. Native sarsaparilla had a number of uses. Convicts and soldiers made a drink from it like tea, which was sweet even without sugar. 'Indeed,' wrote White, 'were it to be met with in greater abundance it would be found very beneficial to these poor creatures whose constant diet is salt provisions.' He thought it was also good for chest complaints.[12]

John White and Arthur Phillip were men of a similar stamp, except that there was a softness in the surgeon which it is hard to find in the Governor. On the First Fleet and in New South Wales they joined forces in an attempt to marry humanity with good order. Phillip was also interested in public health. On board the *Sirius* on the way out, he was observed by Midshipman Southwell to be 'extraordinary clever in every contrivance and method to render the ship healthy and airy'. Phillip's brand of humanitarianism grew also out of his ideas on naval discipline. Like White and like most humanitarians, he thought it was good policy to promote cheerfulness. For instance, he divided the night watch on the *Sirius* into three short intervals rather than the usual two long ones. As one of the sailors explained, 'he thought it would be much comfortabler for the seamen'.[13]

A matching part of this regimen (as the previous chapter shows) was carefully measured punishment. Phillip had twice before been commander of a King's ship, and in both cases he had used the cat-of-nine-tails to reduce a crew to order. He had better material to work with on the First Fleet, and the high standard of discipline on this expedition has to be numbered among its numerous extraordinary achievements. Seamen were occasionally placed in irons, but for very short periods, the few floggings never extended beyond twelve lashes, and no-one ran the gauntlet. The masters of all vessels were apparently expected to refer to Phillip whenever punishment was called for, and on his own ship, *Sirius*, he took unusual steps to outlaw 'starting', which was the casual beating of the men by their officers. Early in the voyage, according to the sailor quoted above, 'The Govener ordered every officer on board the ship to appear in the cabin, even to the boatswains mate, and told them all if he new of any officer to strike a man on board, he would brake him [that is, strip him of his rank] amediately.'[14] In New South Wales he tried to apply a systematic humanity by keeping a close eye on the floggings dispensed by the courts. To begin with, he made a practice of signing the record of sentence and he often remitted punishments wholly, or reduced them by half. But this was a type of humanity he found hard to sustain, cheerfulness being hard to manufacture in all circumstances. As a formal punishment floggings became very common, and the surgeons' regular duties included attendance whenever men and women were condemned to be whipped. They probably followed the naval practice of keeping count of the strokes on a slate, the sharp lash and the fumbling chalk making their marks in unison.[15]

Better evidence of Phillip's brand of humanitarianism is to be found in the way he dispensed food among the convicts and garrison. The cost of the settlement had been worked out at the Navy Board on the assumption that convict men would receive the same rations as the soldiers, and the women two-thirds. A principle originally designed to make the sums easy at

Whitehall became, for Phillip, a fundamental means of equity. To begin with, all the men under his command, of whatever condition, received weekly a full ration consisting of 7 pounds (3.2 kilograms) of biscuit, bread or flour, 7 pounds of beef (or 4 of pork); 3 pints (1.7 litres) of peas; 6 ounces (170 grams) of butter; and some rice or additional flour. In October 1789, as provisions began to dwindle, the full ration was cut to three-quarters for sailors on the *Sirius* and *Supply* and two-thirds for all other men. Women still got their two-thirds, thanks to the Governor, 'whose humanity', as David Collins remarked on this occasion, 'was at all times conspicuous'.[16]

Phillip insisted that all the officers, including himself, should enjoy, or suffer, the same ration. '[C]ould I possibly have imagined', said Major Ross, 'that I was to be served with, for instance, no more butter than any of the convicts . . . I most certainly would not have left England without supplying myself with that article.'[17] The same principle applied to reductions. When the weekly dispensation was cut to less than half, in April 1790, it was a matter for public emphasis that the same was served 'to everyone without distinction'. Like any officer in command, Phillip entertained subordinate gentlemen at his own table, but the need to demonstrate perfect equity now made that impossible, except under the rubric, 'Bring your own roll.' The 3 hundredweight (about 150 kilograms) of flour which he had kept for the purpose was now mixed with the common store, the Governor 'wishing [as Collins put it] that if a convict complained, he might see that want was not unfelt even at Government house'.[18]

Some historians call this egalitarianism. It was not egalitarianism in any substantial sense. It was meant to prove to the convicts and the soldiers of the garrison that they were ruled according to superior principles of honour and humanity. Collins described the Governor's sacrifice as one 'that did him immortal honor', and so it did. In the same way, as a ship's captain, Phillip had once reduced the water ration for himself and his officers so as to make sure of a full ration for the men.[19] Gentlemen like Ross knew that no-one expected such sacrifices, but it was Phillip's desire always to go beyond common expectation. A perfect, all-encompassing cheerfulness among 'the people' was the great object, the lovely offspring of compassion.

There were lessons to be learnt, and they would be learnt willy-nilly. It must be clear to the people that the officers, and the Governor in particular, deserved to be obeyed. The shining circle which drew the elite apart from the subjects of government was one of peculiar sacredness. The same policy had led Phillip, in July 1789, to place the convict John Cullyhorn on a criminal charge for offending the honour of another officer and so of the regime as a whole (see the previous two chapters), and to have him punished by a bench of officers with 600 lashes and six months in irons. Humanitarianism, at its most thorough, was a policy of subjection wholly in line with an iron code of discipline. In no sense was it meant to promote equality between the gentlemen of New South Wales, the exclusive bearers of humanity, and the mass.

II

Humanitarianism was the force, both good and bad, which shaped authority among the first Europeans in Australia, and it did so partly because this was a settlement of convicts. Criminals were the kind of human raw material which seemed to cry out for the order which humanitarianism offered. The position of criminals within European society had some obvious parallels with the much more deeply understood position of humankind within divine creation. Both were polluted in a distinctive way, and both called for a peculiar effort of cleansing and salvation. In both cases redemption added up, all at once, to new bondage – the bondage of obedience and faith – and to new liberty. New subjection opened the way to new life. The peculiar and contradictory metaphors of Christendom prevailed throughout. In both cases souls were to be bought and brought from evil, as St Paul had originally argued (with slaves in mind), so as to be translated to a better purpose.

The Christian churches had a refined machinery by which they took advantage of the means of divine redemption. During the second half of the eighteenth century criminal wickedness presented itself as a problem which was, of course, less profound than mere sin, but which was urgent and dramatic enough to challenge humanitarian ambition. There was no longer much faith in miracles. Among most educated minds nothing seemed to happen by chance, nor even (some would say) by the magic of divine grace. It was now easier to think that God had laid down perpetual laws which were an expression of his wisdom and by which the world was governed. In this more rational scheme the Creator seemed to stand apart from his creation, as remote, it was said, as the watchmaker from the watch. It was assumed that human government must work in the same way. Good machinery – good laws and good admininistration – was the answer on earth as in heaven. Ancient ideas about sacrifice and redemption survived, but it was now through the painstaking and heroic effort of good men and women that human faults, including crime, might be corrected.

It was difficult to put such ideas into practice where the field was cluttered up with vested interests and old routine. Serious impediments were to be found throughout Britain in the late eighteenth century, but much less so in Ireland, and as a result Ireland was something of a social laboratory in several areas of reform. In 1763 the Irish parliament, acting always with the acquiescence of the British government, took steps to introduce a new type of order into Irish prisons. Two fundamental points were to be observed. In the first place, prisons were to be rearranged from an architectural point of view, to provide the kind of barriers and open spaces thought necessary for health and moral reform. Secondly, there was to be a system of inspection. Inspection was one of the panaceas of the age, but it was not understood to involve the executive itself in constant activity. Motivation of the right kind was believed to come from individuals rather than bureaucracies, and inspectors were to be largely responsible to themselves. Through constant observation and a driving, irrefutable sensibility they were to impose their own sense of humanity within certain boundaries. Little universes were to be created, injected from above with the principle of ordered compassion, and then set spinning along a narrow track to perfection.

The central figure in the early reform of Irish prisons was Sir Jeremiah Fitzpatrick, a medical doctor obsessed with all matters relating to the movement and confinement of large numbers of people. Fitzpatrick was a precise example of an eighteenth-century public figure impelled by a sense of humanitarian duty. Like Phillip, he was a man of obscure origins, but he created authority and prestige for himself by sketching out a new province of authority within which he was to be the indispensible force. The 1760s and 1770s had seen numerous improvements in Irish prisons, but there followed in 1781–83 a far-reaching parliamentary inquiry into the whole system and a movement towards putting it on a new administrative basis. The original initiative came from a few leading members of the Irish House of Commons but it was Fitzpatrick, with his practical experience of the prisons, his 'active genius and exquisite feelings for the distressed', who played the main part in drawing up the Irish Prisons Act (1786). He was soon afterwards appointed Inspector-General of Prisons, under the terms of the Act.[20]

As Inspector-General, Fitzpatrick had no superior except the Irish parliament itself, and parliament was not an executive body. He was his own bureaucracy. His own energy started the machinery and kept it going, and his own sensibility was the final point of judgment. Something like this system appeared in many programmes of late-eighteenth-century reform. A less thoroughgoing example might be found in the hulks moored in the River Thames from 1776, as a place of confinement for convict men. The method of establishing and administering the hulks was worked out jointly by William Eden, one of the under-secretaries of state (see Chapter 3), and Duncan Campbell, for many years the principal contractor for the transportation of convicts to North America. The intellectual inspiration was Eden's (in 1771 he had written a book called *Principles of Penal Law*), but Campbell offered his own ships, he helped draw up the Hulks Act, and he was himself appointed as superintendent under the Act.[21]

In Ireland, Fitzpatrick's main interest was public health. Eden and Campbell, on the other hand, were more concerned with punishment and reform. The hulks were designed to allow hard labour in England to take the place of transportation abroad. But, given the spirit of the times, the health of the convicts could not be ignored. Historians once believed that the hulks were a scene of chaos, but the truth is different. Campbell was responsible to the Secretary of State, and he was not allowed to vary the labour of the convicts: they were to be employed in dredging the Thames. However, in other respects he was largely on his own, and he applied himself to the adminstrative problems with a will. He had to find accommodation. He was responsible for all food, clothing and medical supplies. He decided on his own employees, he dispensed rewards and punishments among the convicts and he established a system of recommending pardons for the best behaved. He was also interested in the health and conditions of his charges and, like Fitzpatrick, he gave considerable thought to details of diet and accommodation. A surgeon was an early appointment. For Campbell, as for Fitzpatrick, regular observation and documentation – once again, pen and ink – were the key to efficiency, and were the only reliable means of guiding individuals towards moral reform. Good record-keeping also allowed for experiments in welfare, like those tried by John White and other up-to-date naval surgeons on shipboard.[22]

The proposal for Botany Bay allowed Arthur Phillip, like Fitzpatrick and Campbell (and also like Oglethorpe in Georgia), to create his own field of action and then made himself captain over it. To use another metaphor (more appropriate to the Newtonian spirit of the eighteenth century), he was not only to mark out his own orbit but to centre it on a principle of his own choice. A less ambitious naval officer appointed to command in New South Wales might have remained at sea, as the Governor of Newfoundland normally did, leaving Major Ross on shore as the main authority from day to day, with a system of government like that sketched out for Lemane and Das Voltas. Instead, both in England before departure and in Australia, Phillip played the part of the heroic humanitarian, one of the great proto- types of the age.

Both the hulks and the settlement in New South Wales allowed for the application of up-to-date penal principles. The new penologists wanted reform in a number of areas. Most of all, they wanted a perfect predictabil- ity. All men and women were to understand that criminal behaviour would be speedily followed by apprehension and punishment. This meant, first, an efficient police. They also believed that crime could be precisely graded in terms of seriousness, and they wanted punishments to match. This explains their dislike for the blunt instrument of capital punishment and their inter- est in prisons, which allowed for carefully measured terms of confinement. They were also interested in moral reform, involving a system of rewards and punishments during the period of confinement (although this was inconsistent with the idea that suffering should match the original crime). They usually argued too that convict effort should be a useful resource to the state, which meant well-organised hard labour. Finally, they hoped to see the entire penal system governed by a spirit of humanity, a rigid articulation of cheerfulness and compassion.

Phillip was interested in the new penology, but it is not clear how well he understood it. He certainly wanted predictability, and he did his best to ensure that judges passing sentence in England might henceforth be confi- dent that transported convicts would suffer penal discipline for the entire period to which they had been condemned. Phillip also wanted his prison- ers to be closely supervised, and on the way out he drew up what he called a 'little plan . . . for the government of these people'. Soon after landing he asked the officers to help with a system of rewards and punishments, but they refused, as he recalled, 'to do more than the duty of soldiers'.[23] He also believed, like Eden and Campbell, that the labour of the convicts ought to be useful to the state. Whatever Lord Sydney might have thought, the founding Governor took this as the guiding principle of the whole operation.

During the 1770s, and possibly in 1781–82 as well, Phillip had commanded in the maritime service of the King of Portugal, and he is said to have transported Portuguese convicts across the Atlantic to Brazil.[24] Whether this last story was true or not, he certainly understood the way in which involuntary labour was used by the Portuguese government in its overseas territories. The Portuguese had a much more elaborate system of management than anything in the British empire, where the operations of the state were hedged about with traditional fears of tyranny. During one visit to Brazil, Phillip made detailed inquiries about the royal diamond mines to the north of Rio de Janeiro. The slaves who worked these mines had been acquired in their thousands by the King, as Phillip noted, on lease from their owners. They were supervised by numerous overseers, which made it possible for them to be managed as individuals. Thus, any man who discovered diamonds was rewarded by the Crown. For 'the smallest spark', so Phillip noted, 'he has a few pinches of snuff', and there were other rewards in proportion. If he did particularly well he was purchased from his owner and given his freedom, although he was expected to go on working for the King, with wages equal to the sum formerly paid for his hire.[25]

The Crown (British rather than Portuguese) figured largely in Phillip's view of the world. He held his commission from the monarch but the impact of royalty on his life went beyond that. Had he been born an English gentleman, his feelings for his King might have been routine and unselfconscious. But he was the son of an immigrant language teacher, and his status in the world hung entirely on the individual whom he called 'my Royal Master'. In New South Wales he paid extraordinary attention to the King's birthday, demonstrating on that occasion an interest in ritual and formality which was uncharacteristic of him otherwise. He once said of his relationship with George III that he was 'faithfully attached to His Royal person, by every tie of duty, gratitude, and affection'.[26] In some mouths such language might have been commonplace, but Phillip was not a man given to flattery.

Phillip's reconstruction of the Crown within his government, his success in transferring the essence of eighteenth-century monarchy to this vast and remote space, was a remarkable labour of imagination. It was partly an exercise in social control. Whether deliberately or not, Phillip was following Rousseau, who had argued in his *Social Contract* that such devices were necessary in settling a new state. Authority must depend on something more than mere force, and the founder must pay lip-service, at least, to 'an authority of an higher order, which may compel without violence, and persuade without [rational] conviction'.[27] Even the lofty principles of humanitarianism were not enough on their own to secure the subjection of the people, to draw them all within the personality of the state. But the Crown for Phillip was something more than an instrument of social control. In most matters he was unemotional, but without his own feeling of obligation to royalty it is unlikely that he could have succeeded in securing an emotional dynamic for both ceremony and discipline in the new land.

Here, and in his experience of Portuguese government abroad, we find the germ of Phillip's idea that the convicts should be 'servants of the Crown'. In both Brazil and New South Wales the ideal, and a distinctive one for the eighteenth century, was that the Crown itself might be a source of commercial enterprise and the master of a considerable labour force. It might also engage in benevolent despotism (or rather, despotic benevolence), in the exercise of an authoritarian conscience. Here, as in His Portuguese Majesty's diamond mines, the working lives of both bond and free – all the material aspects of community – were to be shaped by the agents and interests of the Crown. Whether slaves or convicts, the people were to be encouraged to believe that their lives depended on the Crown and that they would therefore be managed with paternal care and discrimination. And, whether slaves or convicts, the terms of bondage could be relied on absolutely, having been determined from above.

At the same time, the convicts were not slaves, as Phillip himself insisted. Slavery was inconsistent with a genuine redemption. They were certainly tainted for life, and before leaving England he had even imagined that he would make a permanent division between them and any future settlement of free immigrants.[28] But it was obvious to him that no people ruled with true humanity, such as the humanity which shone in his own regime, could be called slaves.

III

The legal implications of this kind of regime were untried, so that the courts of law in New South Wales had to find their way through uncharted territory. In primitive communities it often happens that the courts are also legislatures. Even the parliament at Westminster carried the ancient title of 'High Court'. In more sophisticated circumstances it was possible to separate the two functions, and, as William Paley explained in one of the most influential works of the period, this was highly desirable. Questions of the general good must be separated from the particular:

> The first maxim of a free state is, that the laws be made by one set of men, and administered by another; in other words, that the legislative and judicial characters be kept separate. When these offices are united in the same person or assembly, particular laws are made for particular cases, springing oftentimes from partial motives, and directed to private ends.[29]

The records of the courts in Phillip's time offer plenty of evidence to show that Paley was right. But over time the the magistrates and officers worked out their own 'common law', settling into certain habits of thought and answering certain expectations. The same might be said of the magistrates who staffed the lower court, the Judge-Advocate's Bench, and of Phillip, who was executive, legislator and judge all at once. This 'common law', or rather the sense of justice on which it depended, emerged partly from the ideal priorities of the officers themselves, including their humanitarianism. But its boundaries were shaped from a less sophisticated understanding, from what might be called the moral economy of settlement at Port Jackson.

The settlement was designed to take possession of the territory or geographical space of New South Wales. At its most basic, this was an issue between Aborigines and Europeans. But the Europeans also had to work out what possession meant, and what rights were to apply, among themselves. How were they to use what they found in, and brought to, the Antipodes? In Europe itself, and among Europeans in North America, the rights of property were under fundamental review, in both law courts and workplaces. For instance, the enclosure of common land was a vexed question. So was gleaning by the poor, the gathering of fallen timber in forests, the pocketing of left-overs from one's own labour, and much else. It was against this bitterly controversial background that gentlemen in New South Wales, sitting as judges, had to make up their minds – had to search and shape their consciences – in dealing with common and private property in the Antipodes.

The settlements on Port Jackson and Norfolk Island were thickly populated with ordinary seamen and soldiers, and among such men there were very old and sinewy notions about property in common. According to Marcus Rediker, the sailors' historian, 'Common tars were notoriously generous with what little they had, and they developed elaborate codes of hospitality and sharing. They banded together in units of two, three, four, or more – sharing as brothers, as messes, as gangs.' At Port Jackson the seamen of the *Supply* had a collective vegetable garden on shore, while those of the *Sirius* were allocated an island in the harbour, Garden Island, as their joint property for the time being. A hut was built for them and a soldier posted for their protection. The men from the transport *Charlotte* put up a tent as a similar base for themselves. We know some of its contents: several pounds of biscuit and sugar, a piece of canvas and a bag, all of which was the joint property of John Riddel and Joseph Rimmer, able seamen.[30]

Seamen were driven by a sense of common purpose. They also knew how to stand up for themselves. The first strike in Australian history had occurred, in April 1787, among the seamen on the transports, who had demanded that they be paid before they left England. Also, in May several ships drifted at sea during an argument about rations. Seamen could be dangerous. Like the Governor, they too could resemble sharks who came

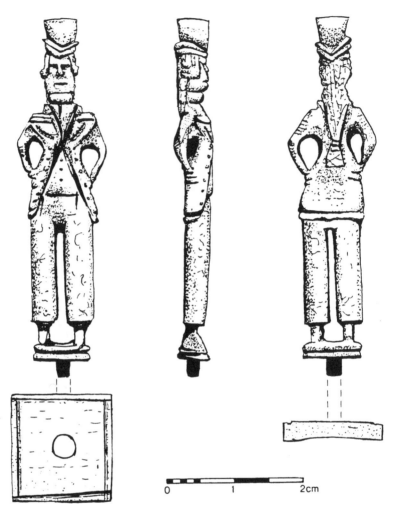

Statuette of a seaman carved in bone, possibly by a seaman, and found at the original place of European settlement at Hobart Town.

Source: Parks and Wildlife Service, Government of Tasmania

ashore. At Port Jackson gangs of them occasionally descended from the ships to the camp. During one vivid episode Cornelius Harragan from the *Supply*, known as 'Captain Ball's Bulldog', caused a tremor among the people as he came to rescue a shipmate from one of the garrison. However, according to David Collins, 'Much less cause of complaint on this score . . . arose than was expected.' Undoubtedly, Phillip was highly skilled in his management of seamen, whether on sea or land. He understood their priorities. Here, indeed, was another explanation for his equal rations policy.

Seamen had fiercely egalitarian notions when it came to the sharing of goods, including scarce food, and they deeply resented officers taking more than anyone else.[31] In sharing food out with scrupulous care, Phillip was answering the kind of demands which an effective captain took for granted at sea.

The convict men included a number of former seamen (one-fifth of all for whom trades are recorded) and they carried some weight among the rest of the people.[32] The leaders of the only attempted convict mutiny on the First Fleet, Philip Farrell and Thomas Griffiths, had been sailors. According to Private Easty of the Marines, one had been a boatswain's mate in the navy and the other master of a French privateer. John Cullyhorn, the most out-spoken of Phillip's convict antagonists on shore, was 'brought up to the sea'. He too was an organiser, and he wrote a petition to the Governor on behalf of himself and five other men about their time being up. They were prob-ably moved by the notion, as stated by another former seaman, William Parish, that once free they were no longer 'under any Person but the Govr'. They appealed to Phillip, a seaman himself, and on Phillip alone they depended.[33] Men who had been sailors also managed the government fish-ing boats, which gave them unusual importance and freedom of action. James Bird, who caught fish for the hospital, sold a good number on his own account, while White, the Principal Surgeon, looked the other way. William Bryant did the same, although eventually he, his wife, children and six other men (including 'a carpenter, and some competent navigators'), took one of the boats and escaped up the coast to Timor. It was a startling demonstration of skill and solidarity.[34] Port Jackson was not 'a nest of pirates', but at the same time clever, unyielding seamen like Cullyhorn, Parish and Bryant must have stood very tall among their fellow convicts.

The network of conversation among the Europeans was shaped a good deal by the seaman's eye and the seaman's tongue; its syntax tasting of salt water. Mutiny, or the thought of mutiny, was a common response to mar-itime life. So was escape, by sea or land: as Phillip put it, 'in this country . . . there are several hundred men, many of whom are seamen, who would at any hour risque their lives, if they saw the least possibility of escaping'. The Governor's own habits of authority were naval habits, and he looked for disorder and complaint such as he might find at sea. Even the most mem-orable jokes among the people might be seamen's jokes. The carpenter of the *Supply* designed a boat for the main highway of the settlement, the waters between Sydney Cove and Rose Hill, waters which included not only pur-ple and green, fathoms deep, but shallows of brown and silver where the Parramatta River ran into the harbour. The vessel was accordingly flat-bottomed and weighty, 'a mere bed of timber' according to Collins, and with saltwater irony the convicts christened it 'the Rose Hill Packet' – after the little packet (or mail) boats which darted among English ports – or else 'the Lump'. Its official name seems to have been the *Prince of Wales*.[35]

Former seamen were among the first regular farmers, and numbers worked the soil together. In the issue of land grants individual names were attached to individual allotments, but labour and tools were frequently shared. The thirteen men who, with several wives and children, made up the first community at Prospect, included three neighbours, Parish, Butler, and Lisk, who had been seamen, and the last two pooled all their resources. These were ex-convicts. William Reid and two brothers named Webb, who had all been able seamen on the *Sirius*, held land together at Parramatta, and eight other men from the same ship made up a neighbourhood along a single watercourse, the Cascade, on Norfolk Island.[36]

Among the soldiers of the garrison there was a more formal kind of shared enterprise. They were divided into four companies. Each company included about forty officers and men, making up a single economic unit, with the captain responsible for sustenance and pay. The records of the Criminal Court give us a brief glimpse of the vegetable garden belonging to Captain Tench's company, in which the soldiers had divided the beds among themselves, and grew cabbages.[37] The division of seeds and cuttings and the sharing of tools must have depended on a considerable spirit of cooperation. (See also Chapter 10.) The same spirit appeared in the language of some of the officers, moved as they were in New South Wales by the sense of common emergency which had also shaped life six generations earlier, in the first settlements across the Atlantic: Virginia, Massachusetts, Newfoundland and so on. In the first palmy days at Port Jackson they spoke of convicts and soldiers together as 'our people', 'our colonists'. It was only to be wished, so Collins remarked, 'that on taking possession of Nature . . . in her simplest, purest garb, we might not sully that purity by the introduction of vice, profaneness, and immorality'. He knew that that was an impossible hope, thanks to 'the habits of youth'. Even so, from the moment of entry they had given the land new conversation and community, 'the voice of labour, the confusion of camps and towns, and "the busy hum of its new possessors"'.[38]

The rights of the Crown frequently pulled against the shared rights of the people. Seamen themselves assumed, from centuries of bitter experience, that the two would always be opposed, that they must be as hard to stitch together as silk and canvas. There were also clear signs that the Crown would insist on proprietory rights in New South Wales like those it enjoyed in England, waging war, for instance, on poachers. Some things at Port Jackson were harvested freely by the people. Elizabeth Chapman, aged eight, daughter of a corporal of Marines, walked by the edge of Cockle Bay (now Darling Harbour) during her second spring in the country, with a handful of un-English wildflowers. Adults, as the spirit moved them, went further afield for the native sarsaparilla, or sweet tea.[39] However, Phillip insisted that by right the Crown possessed all the fruits of convict effort, and besides their daily labour he was interested in any native animals they might catch: 'all the Convicts got was the property of Government'. His Majesty's title to Australian wildlife was very clearly announced within a month of settlement (and underscored with fifty lashes), the object in that case being a little, shivering possum in a bag. It seems to have been well understood by mid-1789, when George Clare, a convict, had the temerity to withstand the claims of Lieutenant Kellow to a wounded bird, arguing that as the Governor himself was absent, Major Ross 'had the right to it'.[40]

There was other debatable ground, especially in the very first days, when all was confused and when some convicts still had hopes of an easy, self-regulated life. Within a fortnight of the Fleet's arrival, Thomas Hill, a convict, was charged with helping himself to twopence worth of bread, part of the general supply. In his view the bread clearly belonged to them all, and he 'had no idea he was committing a robbery'. William Cole took some planks which were lying unused near the tent of the Governor's guard, to hold down the flap of his own tent. According to the corporal of the guard, 'he seemed to think he might take them'. John Boyle's crime was picking up dried grass. Most grass was like native sarsaparilla, there for the taking, but this grass had once been thatch on a hut, now derelict. Cole explained to the court that 'wanting Grass, and seeing that laying about there, scattered and off the Hut, which has long been empty, he took it, thinking no Harm'. George Legge picked up a two- or three-day-old chick, half-dead in a drain – as he might have done in any gutter in London – revived it and gave it to a soldier. All of these men were found guilty of crimes, and indeed Legge received one hundred lashes. The magistrates declared that the chick was 'not his Property', although they made no recorded comment as to whose it was.[41]

Here there are echoes of Virginia in its hard first years, when the *Lawes Divine, Morall and Martiall* had promised death to anyone who stole the smallest item from the common stock. Indeed, Phillip had promised the same in his first address to the convicts, in February 1788.[42] In both places a new state, at the far edge of the known world, was to be cut from the habits and affections, the flesh and blood, of Englishmen and (a separate issue, as the next chapter shows) of Englishwomen. However, the Australian project was in a class of its own. It took place in the age of humanitarianism, when the ambitions of the state were beginning to be shaped by a more pervasive sense of authority and of moral responsibility. There were some who now believed that the management of criminals was a peculiar challenge in itself. But there was also an interest in common suffering which had not existed before, and there was a sense of competence in dealing with it which, however unjustified at times, made a radical difference in the long term.

The dignity of government now depended very much on meticulous administrative effort. It was remarkable that enough food should have been sent, on a single, eight-month journey, to sustain such a large population for a matter of years. It was equally remarkable that at Port Jackson and Norfolk Island every individual, without discrimination, should have been fed at the public store, and through the most difficult times. John Cullyhorn's argument with the Governor turned on the question as to whether he would be fed if he failed to work. Cullyhorn believed, like Thomas Hill, that the provisions sent with them belonged to them all. Ultimately, he was right. It was Phillip's policy to say that the useless would starve, but all the gentlemen and most of the convicts knew that late eighteenth-century humanity had dictates of its own. The Enlightenment had given new priorities to public life which in this case overlapped with the moral priorities of the poor. Cullyhorn might suffer the most brutal of punishments, but Phillip's self-respect, and beyond that the honour of the Crown, required that unless he ran away he would always be fed.

For a while the women, who had very little to do, worried about what the no-work, no-food policy might mean for them. Elizabeth Lock went to the Judge-Advocate to reassure herself. He told her (according to one report) 'that there were 2 y[ea]rs Prov[ision]s for her and that she would not starve. . . . she asked ab[ou]t her working, when the Judge Adv[ocate] told her, [although] there was no work for her at present, she w[oul]d draw her Provisions as usual'.[43] The word quickly got about. The surgeons likewise looked after everyone, however irrelevant they might be to the question of general survival (see the next two chapters), so that sometimes the number of hospital inmates and out-patients made up a very large fraction of the whole population. Here, at the Antipodes, in the strangest emergencies of their lives many Englishmen and Englishwomen learnt to welcome – even to demand – the unfamiliar embrace, the eager conscience and the hard gaze of the state.

The courts were agents of suffering, but the gentlemen in charge loved to proclaim that they were also agents of the Crown at the service of the poor. The Judge-Advocate's Bench heard complaints from the people, and there was also a higher court for this purpose, the Court of Civil Judicature. The latter met infrequently, only one case being tried during the first four years. The applicants on that occasion were Susannah Holmes, who appears at the beginning of this chapter, and the father of her baby, Henry Kable (now her husband). Before leaving England they had benefited from the humanity of Lord Sydney and of London society, but most of the £20 worth of clothes and books which had been subscribed for them, and which had been entrusted to the captain of the transport *Alexander*, had not come ashore. The captain was called to account. He told the court, consisting of the Judge-Advocate, the chaplain and the Principal Surgeon (White), that he had carried the goods from England free of charge and therefore could not be held responsible for them; 'but this objection', said White, 'had no weight with the court, as the ship was in the service of government and paid for the sole purpose of conveying these people, and the little property which they possessed, to this country'. The captain was therefore required to pay up.[44]

The Europeans' investment in Australia came in two parts. In their mouths was the ancient snarling, singing garrulosity of men and women, soldiers and seamen. The common skills of the people and their understanding of shared livelihood, coming from the soil of Christendom, were part of this oral tradition. But secondly, within their extraordinary vessels, rarely seen before in these waters, there was the culture embodied in paper and ink, and with it the administrative aptitude of gentlemen, their pride, their science, their imagination, their self-conscious humanity and high hopes. Australia was obliged to find its own way of accommodating these two things, speech and writing.

Phillip, emerging as it were from the shining vertical blackness of his ocean life, had the task of stitching the two together.

PART 2

Changing

The Transformation of Loglog

As told by Mangurug, of the northern Gunwinggu language, to Catherine Berndt in 1950.[1]

Long ago, that Loglog lizard was a man. He came from the north, and was speaking Yiwadja. He came, he camped, he was eating vegetable foods and meats and kangaroo, and chopping out honey, and he would go back to his camp to sleep. He kept on doing that. He was looking for a place, a country that he had been promising himself he would find. He was still going along, still speaking Yiwadja. As he came, he made a lot of fresh-water places. He would look to see where there was plenty of honey and would pause for a while, eating and camping about, for two days. After that, early in the morning he would get up and keep going.

He went on and saw a big expanse of water. 'Well,' he said, 'Supposing I plant *mandem* water lilies here: then they will grow roots.' He planted them, and he made fish and put them there. He was still following the water, that big water. He went off in another direction, but then he came back and found his old tracks and went straight on. He was killing creatures and cutting out honey, and as he went along he was filling up his honey-baskets, with some grass to keep the honey from spilling. He went on to another place, where he dug a deep hole in the red soil. He saw water come rising up for him, and tasted it: it was a little bit salty, he went and dug again. He said, 'Maybe I'll go to another place and dig there', he went, he dug, and he saw water coming up. He tasted it. 'I've found fresh water!' He drank it all. And he planted a palm tree and that is still standing.

He went climbing higher up to a good place, on top, where he made places and built a stringybark hut for himself. He said, 'Maybe I'll leave the language I'm speaking, Yiwadja, because here I've come to Gunwinggu country, and Maung country.' So he left Yiwadja and was speaking Maung and Gunwinggu. He was still camping where he was making places. He would go hunting, and come back again. He always did that: he was preparing to transform himself. 'I suppose, before, I was a man,' he said. He was hunting one more time, that Loglog. He went and named the place in that country where he planted big paperbark trees. 'Here the place-name is Manbulluyu,' he said, giving it that name. He went on and named various little places. Then he came back along a small creek. He was making places while he was following the stream, and making foliage for various plant foods, and he was making lizards and honey. He kept following that creek, and for three days he was camping at Mardan, where he put the name, eating honey and meats and plant foods, and kangaroos, too, when he speared them. When his days there were finished he set off again. As he went along, he was speaking Maung. He camped for a long time at Indjumal. For a while he was eating fish, when he went to the great water at Mangarubu, Cooper's Creek, and caught fish to bring back to his camp. He would go there when he had finished all the fish he had brought home. He would go hunting too, looking for small creatures. And he would paint himself with white clay, to disguise his human smell, when he went after kangaroos. He would cook them and eat them there. He settled down, when afternoon came, in that country where he had made his camp. He still went along speaking Maung, and Gunwinggu too. He made creeks, and went after long-nosed fresh-water crocodiles, killing and eating them.

Time went on. At last he was 'listening to himself', contemplating what he should do. 'Already they are all gone, all my relatives. They have all put themselves as *djang*. Well, I myself, in my turn, I should follow them, and do what they did first.' He went, and at last transformed himself into a creature. He made himself a tail, and he stopped speaking in human speech as he had before. He made two legs and tried to crawl. He said to himself, in his mind, 'Yes, it's good when I try to go along like a creature: I'm transforming myself, when I crawl along. So then, those people don't eat me. I'm a real creature, and I just go about like that very small *bundjing* lizard does. All we eat is flies,' he said. He went on, and at last made himself completely into a little creature. Everything was all right when he went crawling about, and he had made a proper tail and legs. He just went for ever like those various creatures that go crawling about, such as *bundjing* and *galg-galg*. 'But then, myself, I'm just a different kind of body,' he said to himself. So now he was really transformed. When he wanted to find his relatives, as living people, they had already become creatures. So then he just followed them and tried to do the same. That's what they all did, those first people, so that's what he did too. We see him, crawling about. He does not speak – no words, no language. Long ago he talked like a man, but now he has gone like a creature for ever, crawling on trees and among the grasses, and we see him as he goes about all over the place.

Chapter 7

Men and Women

The first European men and women in Australia settled down among themselves bound by a fabric of words, words which passed among them and words they turned over in their minds in conjuring up their own ideas about the new country and their collective place in it. Among the least regarded of the garrison and convict people, the men and women whom David Collins called 'the common herd', there were some distinctive images of togetherness. In Europe, whether they came from the city or the countryside, the lives of such men and women had been lived in the midst of livestock, and they easily allowed their thoughts of humankind to herd together with those of two other highly social species, namely dogs and fowls. Cats and horses and (in the country) cows and pigs were also part of common experience, but they seem to have done less to nourish the human imagination. The eating habits of dogs and fowls, their mating and their giving birth, not to mention dog fights and cock fights, were part of the continuous theatre of daily life. These offered some enlivening parallels with human existence, and common language was embroidered accordingly.

It is obvious that the imagery sprung mainly from talk among men, because it flattered men and belittled women. 'Bitch', for instance, carried a very heavy burden of meaning from the doggy universe to the human one: an authority of the period called it 'The most offensive appellation that can be given to an English woman.' For another writer, the statesman and philosopher Edmund Burke, it was 'the common mark of the last vileness and contempt in every language', a fact which only showed, he said, how much our feeling for dogs was a mixture of love and derision. (He might have said the same about men's feeling for women.) Poultry, the republic of the fowlyard, offered a slightly more elevated imagery with which to contemplate the way in which human beings behaved together. For instance:

- 'cock', or 'chief cock of the walk' conveyed the pride, liberty and strength of a leading man – say, the best boxer in a village or district;
- 'chicken-hearted' meant cowardly;
- 'hen' meant a woman or mistress;
- 'cock and hen' referred to a party or club allowing women as well as men;
- 'hen-house' meant a house ruled by the wife;
- 'hen-frigate' meant a ship with the captain's wife aboard; and
- 'hen-pecked' described a husband ruled by his wife.[1]

Some of these terms are still used today, when few people much know about the habits of living poultry. Their vivid use in early New South Wales appears in an incident which came before the Court of Criminal Judicature in 1788. Private Thomas Bulmore, of the garrison, had died after a violent struggle with another man, started by himself. He had laid siege by dark to a hut belonging to Mary Phillips, while she was alone in it with a soldier called Baker. At the same time he shouted a number of abusive things to Baker, telling him to come out and fight like a man, jeering at him when he appeared with only a shirt on – 'Damn y[ou]r eyes, put on y[ou]r trowsers, do not be standing there like a woman in petticoats' – and declaring to everyone who would listen 'that no cock would tread his hen that night'.[2]

Even the power of a rooster has its own small mystery, and metaphors like Bulmore's say a lot, not only about the reality of life but about the common eighteenth-century imagination, an imagination fired, as I have said, by notions of slavery and subjection. They show the eagerness of men to divide the rest of the world, including humanity, among themselves, and to fight along their boundary lines. Black slavery was one of the great facts of the age. But beyond that, prevailing economic theory – mercantilism – gave men, women and children, considered *en masse*, a distinct material value (just as the theory which surrounds the term 'human resources' was to do at the end of the twentieth century). Mercantilist writers assessed the capital wealth of a nation or empire partly by the numbers of its people. This view helped to justify the wholesale movement of labouring people from Britain and Ireland and their disposal for varying periods of bondage in North America, their labour power, and so in a sense the people themselves, being shipped as commodities. Many went as teenage children, and it was women and children who were most easily thought of in these straitening terms. Eighteenth-century playwrights, novelists and poets played with slavery as a strangely complex human institution, but there was an added piquancy in the notion of women and children, the intimate, problematic property of Everyman, being considered as a national resource. Among the many hilarious passages of George Farquhar's play, *The Recruiting Officer*, performed at Sydney Cove on the King's birthday, 1789, there was one which made the fathering of children look like a means of adjusting the balance of trade: 'What! No bastards! And so many recruiting officers in town. I thought 'twas a maxim among them to leave as many recruits in the country as they carried out.'[3] Such lines, however ironical, flattered the virility of military men, just as the empire itself did: a field of limitless conquest and limitless possession.

The ownership of human beings, including the ownership of women by men, is never as straightforward as it seems at first sight. Men might aim to manage women as if they were common chattels. At Sydney Cove John Russell, a convict who had been a seaman, got involved in an argument with Mary Love when he tried to persuade her to tell him the whereabouts of Jane Creek, who he said was 'his property'. Then, having found Creek, 'he caught [her] by the hair of the head and was dragging [her] to the ground' when Love stopped him. He then turned again on Love and badly bruised her leg.[4] It was also remarked of many London prostitutes at the time – those whose activities were managed by a 'cock-bawd' or male brothel keeper – that they were as good as slaves: 'nothing, no, not her own Person, is her Property, or at her own Disposal'.[5] Indeed, this was probably the principal meaning of the term 'prostitute': a woman sold not by herself but by somebody else.

The two women in Russell's case were both past middle age and there is no evidence of their having been prostitutes. Russell too is said to have been an 'old man', though he was obviously a robust one. Both women had some reason to nourish a dignified idea of themselves, and it may be that they had no time at all for talk of 'property' and for fowlyard imagery. In the record of the trial Jane Creek appears as 'Nurse Creek', which could only mean that she was a hospital nurse or midwife, a figure of authority at least among the women. Mary Love could also claim a little respectability. She could write. Her signature, large and clear, although shaking slightly with age, appears in the register of marriages nearly two years later (as a witness, not a bride).[6]

The ability to write was unusual in a woman. Between one-quarter and one-third of the women who came as convicts by the First Fleet seem to have had enough schooling to allow them to write their own names. The figure for men was a little more than half. Once or twice in their lives such individuals were able to demonstrate this minimal skill, in most cases when they got married but, as we see in a later chapter, settlement in New South Wales might give them other occasions as well. It is a fine thing to be able to move a pen, like a conductor's wand, through the ceremony involved in signature. The paper gives back one's own image, and a little of the history which resonates in one's own name. The proportion on the First Fleet who could sign was roughly typical of labouring people in England. However, both in England and in New South Wales there were many who could read, however haltingly, without being able to write. Reading was more often useful, and more easily practised. Writing, on the other hand, was a skill not much needed by the poor, especially women. They rarely had command of paper, pen or ink, or time to learn.[7]

Through literacy a minority of educated women had begun to make an impact on public life as early as the seventeenth century, and during the period in which European settlement began in Australia numerous English-women made themselves celebrated in print. Among the twelve best-selling authors in England between 1780 and 1820, ten were women.[8] Nor is this wholly surprising. A woman who stood up to make speeches in public, commanding silence from men, would have been a peculiar sight and, as one gentleman remarked, 'rather too singular to please'. But, as the same author conceded, writing for the public press was another matter. The novelty might be an advantage. For instance, 'the very sound of *sermons written by a lady*, may draw the attention of several, who would not by any other means be engaged to hearken to lectures of religion and virtue'.[9] Here, as in other ways, the magic of print might play startling games with the living voice.

For poor women, the mere ability to read might be important in forming a bridge between the literate and the oral world. Reading was often done aloud. Writing at any length, on the other hand, was a more private skill, manifest in silence. Among the officers in early New South Wales, no-one knew, and few cared, how many of the convicts could write well. Watkin Tench, captain of Marines, was among those who were given the job of checking through letters sent by the convicts to their friends, before they left England and afterwards. (The purpose is unclear.) He found it a tedious chore, but he was impressed with the number who were willing and able to write and with the variety of their messages. Their lives were shaped and coloured by ephemeral voices rather than by writing, but it did not follow, as Tench admitted, that all were 'ignorant and untaught'.[10]

The writing of convicts spanned the oceans much less effectively than the writing of the officers. However, it was just as useful for the writers themselves in making sense of the new world. It served to tear open, for instance, the closed, unthinking, voice-bound world of cock and hens. We can imagine that with pen and ink each letter-writing man or woman (willy-nilly) drew a brief self-portrait, but in doing so they must have uncovered a new self in which the old ingredients were mixed with something daring and exotic. One convict woman (her name unrecorded) who wrote home about ten months after landing, in 1788, described the routine which now shaped her life in what she called 'this solitary waste of creation'. She wrote of the houses – 'most miserable huts' – their windows unglazed and filled up with 'lattices of twigs'. She complained in detail about the 'distresses' suffered at Sydney Cove by herself and the other women. To some extent these were bad only in comparison with the passage out: they were 'deprived of tea and other things they were indulged in in the voyage by the seamen'. However, she said, 'We are comforted with the hopes of a supply of tea from China'.

How often, or rather how seldom, in her earlier life, had she made casual remarks about China? – an exotic place indeed for English minds.

She did not spend her whole letter complaining. There was a serious shortage of clothing, especially for the children, but she mentioned as well some unexpected comforts: 'Our kingaroo rats [sic] are like mutton, but much leaner; and there is a kind of chickweed so much in taste like our spinach that no difference can be discerned. Something like ground ivy is used for tea; but a scarcity of salt and sugar makes our best meals insipid'.[11] Another woman found clothes still very scarce when she arrived, by the *Lady Juliana* in mid-winter 1790, but, she wrote, 'since the Scarborough, Neptune, and Surprize arrived [soon after] we have had a blanket and a rug given us, and we hope to have some cloaths, as the Justinian . . . [is] bring-ing some cloth and linen, and we are to make the cloaths'.[12] In fact, the *Justinian* was wrecked *en route*.

The convicts, with their primitive knowledge of adventure stories, were certainly prepared for the exotic, and ambitious rumours went running through the settlement from the moment of landing. As an officer recalled, 'large fresh water rivers, valuable ores, and quarries of limestone, chalk, and marble, were daily proclaimed'.[13] But in due course continual disappoint-ment, followed by suffering, dampened the excitement. A young man, also a convict, wrote in 1790 to a friend in London. He was struck with the vast gap which now existed between prior imagination and reality. On Robinson Crusoe's island, experience had nourished prosperity. In that ideal spot, time was a cornucopia, from which comforts and pleasures spilt one by one, to settle, one by one, into well-worn familiarity. In New South Wales, after two years, this man saw no such prospect: 'To give a just description of the hard-ships that the meanest of us endure, and the anxieties suffered by the rest, is more than I can pretend to. In all the Crusoe-like adventures I ever read or heard of, I do not recollect anything like it.' All was disappointment, epit-omised by 'the tears that are often shed upon the infants at the breast'. He took no delight in chickweed or 'kingaroo rats'. There was, in theory, a fair ration of salt meat but it had to be boiled to be eaten, which, he said, halved its size. 'All our improvements . . . have lately been quite at a stand . . . from the highest to the lowest, I see nobody that is so contented as they were at first.' For him, as for the women, clothes were a real problem. He asked his friend for needles and some blue thread: 'the cloathes are all wore out that we brought from home, we are mostly in our Woolwich dresses, and the women look like gypsies'.[14]

The vegetable gardens alone, according to this writer, showed some progress. During Phillip's time, gardens were enormously significant. A bark hut might be a very poor thing in itself, but surrounded by a rich and var-iegated pattern of green vegetables it became a place of substance, a testi-mony to the skill and resilience of its occupant. When this last-mentioned letter was written another convict, John Fuller, a carpenter from Kent, had a garden consisting of about 1500 cabbage plants and two or three beds of kidney beans, together with french beans, turnips and potatoes. He was 'in the daily enjoyment of vegetables' while some other convicts were starving.[15] His rows of cabbages were a kind of signature on the Australian soil, and one which he no doubt retraced in his mind each day.

The convict painter Thomas Watling's portrayal of vegetable gardens in High Street (later George Street), 1794, with a line of trees and the Tank Stream at their lower end.

Source: Dixson Galleries, State Library of New South Wales

The signature, so to speak, of Hannah Pugh, another convict, was to be found among the stitches of the bed quilt which she made for herself and her new baby in 1789. It was composed of nine of the worsted caps which were standard issue for the convicts and which she had been given by neighbours in payment for her work as a washerwoman. Her effort shows how the care of one's children might bring out an intimate resourcefulness. Another woman, Jane Chapman, the wife of a corporal of Marines, must have been used to making her home in strange circumstances. She had two little girls, and we know a couple of things about her daily relationship with them. She taught them their Catechism and their Lord's Prayer. Also, each night before she went to bed herself she took a candle and explored their sleeping bodies for lice.[16] She must have done the same wherever her husband took her.

Europeans had been aware of the Antipodes, as a place where human beings might live – albeit upside-down, hanging on to the spinning earth by their feet – long before they arrived to make their home here themselves. A play called *The Antipodes*, first performed in London in 1638, described a country where parrots taught their mistresses to speak and where the women governed the men. Thirty years later Henry Neville's story, *The Isle of Pines*, told of a man wrecked on an antipodean island alone with four women and, in due course, seventeen hundred descendants: a perfect fantasy of cock and hens. Gender might be strangely manifest in such outlandish latitudes. In France in 1676 there appeared a book entitled *Le Terre Australe Connue*, in which the author, Gabriel de Foigny, wrote of a continent inhabited by vegetarian hermaphrodites. But imagination began to narrow slightly with William Dampier's real-life observations of the west coast of New Holland, published in his *A New Voyage Round the World* (1697). Shortly afterwards we catch some common conversation about these lands – now half-illusion and half-reality – in the drunken speech of Sir Wilfull Witwoud, a character in Congreve's play, *The Way of the World*: 'The sun's a good pimple, an honest soaker, he has a cellar at your Antipodes. If I travel, aunt, I touch at your Antipodes – your Antipodes are a good rascally sort of topsie-turvey fellows – if I had a bumper I'd stand upon my head and drink a health to 'em.'[17] In 1726 Jonathan Swift explored several fabulous countries in his great work, *Gulliver's Travels*. Lilliput, a monarchy strangely like England, he discovered a little to the south of New Holland, while the land of the Houyhnhnms was to the south-east. The Houyhnhnms were horses, and it was the nobility of that species (not the pecking-order of the fowlyard) which appears in Swift's story as a model for humankind.

Among the Houyhnhnms the hero, like Robinson Crusoe, had to shift for himself and he led a pleasant though plain existence. 'I often got honey out of the hollow trees,' he told his wondering readers, 'which I mingled with water, or eat with my bread. No man', he said, 'could more verify the truth of these two maxims, *That nature is very easily satisfied; and That necessity is the mother of invention.*'[18] In his story of Crusoe (1719) Defoe taught the same lesson. Through ingenuity a sweet routine might be fashioned from solitary nothing. For instance, houses might be built in the wilderness, meticulous like bee-hives, the walls lined with 'clever convenient' furniture. By a similar jig-saw process families might be drawn together, so as to flourish and multiply, matching ever more closely a type of exquisite domesticity. The women in Crusoe's settlement were natives from the neighbouring mainland, whom the 'pyrate' settlers had saved from cannibals. On his return to the island seven years after their capture, Crusoe found that 'these five Savage Ladies' had been transformed to 'a good Sort of well-govern'd, quiet, laborious Women, modest and decent'. All they lacked was Christianity and legal marriage. The men told him that they thought they were as good as married, their leader declaring 'they lov'd their Wives as well, as if they had been born in their own Native Country'. But Crusoe insisted that the women be christened and wed, which was done by a priest he happened to have with him.[19]

Improvisation had charms of its own. Families, like furniture, might be shaped from material discovered on the spot and be all the better for it. Here indeed was a convenient blue-print for New South Wales. In his proposal for settlement, dated 1783, James Matra had suggested that women be brought as wives from New Caledonia, Tahiti and nearby islands, and this idea was included in Phillip's instructions drawn up at the Home Office. The Governor was told that if either the *Sirius* or *Supply* should be near such islands after arrival they should take potential wives on board. However, he was told to make quite sure that the officers concerned 'do not, upon any account, exercise any compulsive measures, or make use of any fallacious pretences'. The women were to come willingly or not at all.[20]

There was ambivalence in these orders, just as there was in the visions of Daniel Defoe and James Matra. One of the proclaimed purposes of any marriage was to civilise the woman concerned, to draw her from a purposeless existence and to convert her, by Christian authority, into a fully ordered and useful being, to save her with a husband who would be, all at the same time, her companion, her guardian and her guide. Nevertheless, women all too clearly had wills and priorities of their own, regimes which only they themselves understood, and souls which only they could settle for salvation. Most of all – and it is central to much of what appears in the chapters that follow – a polished and 'manly' sensibility involved the understanding that women had rights, rights which might be called passive but which were absolute all the same. In the first place, they might not be married against their will: no native females were to be carried by force to New South Wales. Secondly, once a woman had entrusted herself to a man she was entitled to his support and protection for life. The women on Robinson Crusoe's island lived with men who boasted about their own good intentions. But Crusoe saw to it that the rights of the 'native ladies' were secured by Christian promises.[21]

Both Lord Sydney and Phillip himself were half-hearted about the idea of getting women from the islands. The last-minute shipment of more women convicts, organised in December 1786, made the imbalance of the sexes proposed for the new settlement a little less dramatic (though it remained severe), and on his arrival Phillip did not bother even to make inquiries about willing natives. 'I am certain', he said, 'your Lordship will think that to send for women from the Islands, in our present situation, would answer no other purpose than that of bringing them to pine away in misery.'[22] Phillip, undoubtedly, shared Defoe's admiration for 'well-govern'd, quiet, laborious Women'. His problem was the convict men. Just as he hesitated to make such men into independent farmers, so he refused to cast them in the role of civilising husbands.

II

Phillip gave some thought even before he left England to the way in which a secure and familiar world might be constructed in the Antipodes by matching the men with the women. In fact he was not an expert in this area (his own marriage had failed), and his hopes were clouded by his lack of faith in the convicts. However, he was not a misogynist, quite the contrary, and he placed what confidence he could in the women. His plans for them depended on their 'degree of virtue'. They would be ordered in New South Wales like the colours of the rainbow. The best, whom he did not expect to be either very good or very numerous, were to be shielded from abuse, especially by sailors on the way out. Once arrived they and a certain number of others were to be prepared for marriage, suitable men being allowed to visit them after work, while the remainder, 'the most abandoned', might be encouraged to live as prostitutes. As it turned out there were indeed two camps laid out for the women, on either side of the cove, which may have briefly worked as the Governor had intended. Phillip explained the more reputable part of his scheme in a speech to the convicts soon after landing. 'He gave very good Advice & Encouragement to the Women', so one of his officers recalled, and to the men as well; 'They had his Permission to Marry, and proper times would be allowed for the making up their little Agreements amongst each other.'[23]

Marriages began almost immediately. Five women, the best-behaved on board, had been taken aside by Phillip soon after landing and given tents close to his own.[24] Five also – probably the same ones – were married on the Sunday following the Governor's speech. Some, and probably all five, were well acquainted with their bridegrooms and already committed to a life together. For instance, Susannah Holmes and Henry Kable had known each other in Norwich. It was their baby who had travelled the breadth of England with the turnkey of Norwich Gaol, John Simpson, in his errand of mercy to Lord Sydney (see Chapter 6). At Norwich, Kable, 'a fine healthy young fellow', had shown not only 'a remarkable fondness' for the child but a desperate desire to marry its mother. The three had since been together on the *Dunkirk* hulk in Plymouth harbour and on board the *Friendship* as far as the Cape of Good Hope. They were reunited at Sydney Cove.[25] Two of the other couples had likewise been together at Plymouth and had sailed together. The fourth pair had been acquainted on the hulk, and the fifth in gaol at Liverpool in 1785–86.

All these seem to have been wise marriages. The Kables raised a large family in New South Wales and they were together until Susannah's death in 1825. Two of their companions at the altar, William and Mary Bryant, both West Country people, gave a dramatic demonstration of married love when they escaped together in an open boat, with their two small children and seven other men, in March 1791 (also in Chapter 6). They reached Batavia, where the husband died. Another of these partnerships ended only in 1794 when the husband, Simon Burn, was fatally stabbed after trying to protect another woman from her violent lover.[26]

There were twenty-nine marriages altogether during February 1788, and twenty-three more by the end of the year. After the first five there began a rather different march to the altar. The special attention shown to the first party seems to have encouraged the idea, as David Collins remarked, that 'married people would meet with various little comforts and privileges that were denied to those in a single state'. The first batch had been, for the most part, country people. The remaining marriages during February were typically made between men who had been either seamen or professional thieves, and London women who had, in many cases, lived by sleeping with men and picking their pockets. They had their own understanding of marriage, as an arrangement which mattered only to themselves. The liaisons of seamen often lasted only for the interval between voyages, and for them the terms 'husband' and 'wife' applied to any couple who made a habit of sleeping together. London street thieves used the words similarly, and with no sense of permanence. As a contemporary put it, 'upon the least Disgust they separate'. Some ceremony might be provided when they set up together, especially in London, by clergymen prepared to give their blessing with no questions asked, and a formal type of divorce was also possible. For instance, one London couple, having agreed to part, merely 'declared themselves free of each other, before several Witnesses': a wedding in reverse.[27]

Many of the couples married at Sydney Cove in the second batch saw marriage in this light. Finding soon afterwards that there were few real advantages in it, a good number applied to the Governor to see whether the minister could un-marry them. Several did in fact separate, although there was no predictable logic about the way each relationship worked out. John Leary was a former highwayman, and his bride, Mary Jackson, had lived by picking pockets in London. He gave her permission, so she said, to 'go with Sailors' (though not with convict men), but he also beat her and they lived 'a very unhappy life together'. After eighteen months they were told by the Judge-Advocate's Bench to part 'for a time' and it seems unlikely that their marriage was ever renewed.[28] Another man, Charles Peat, had been, at different times, a sailor and a highwayman, while his bride, Hannah Mullens, was a Londoner who had consorted with sailors and had had three 'husbands' within two years. And yet, they married early and prospered. While Leary beat his wife, Peat became a constable and interfered to stop other wives being beaten. For an interval he returned to England, 'in order', as he said, 'to recover a small legacy', and Hannah took up with another man, but by 1810–12 they seem to have been together again. They then sailed for India, probably with the hope of making money, and the marriage ended with his death at Calcutta.[29]

Some Europeans in New South Wales, especially those who had been country people, saw marriage as a commitment fashioned by God, a fixed part of their existence wherever it might take place in the world. Others thought more in terms of short or middle-term convenience. But cutting across this two-way distinction there were differences of circumstance and personality, which might give a permanent form to the most casual commitments. Human variety was one of the raw facts of colonisation, a prime ingredient in the making of households and enterprises. Defoe had said as much in *Robinson Crusoe*, quoting King Solomon: 'the diligent Hand makes rich', whereas 'I went by the Vineyard of the Slothful, and it was all overgrown with Thorns.'[30] Lord Sydney and James Matra had both anticipated that in a convict settlement the 'diligent' would use a free-enterprise regime to set up families, while the 'Slothful' became their servants. However, the process of differentiation never worked very neatly. It had its best chance at Norfolk Island under Major Ross's regime, in 1790–91. As many as eighty or one hundred couples set up together on the island with Ross's encouragement, about one-fifth of whom had been married in the interval between their arrival at Port Jackson and their departure for Norfolk. But whether married or unmarried, not all these liaisons were permanent. As many as half fell apart before long, and a good number of the men and a few of the women simply disappeared.[31]

The imbalace of the sexes meant that there were always numerous men who never married. At Norfolk there seem to have been about forty who acted on their own in taking up Ross's offer, unwilling or unable to find women to join them. Very few had any interest in staying in New South Wales, but there were exceptions. William Edmunds was a Welshman who had been convicted of stealing a heifer. Thanks to Ross, he was almost self-sufficient by the time his term expired, and by 1794 he had set up on the island as a butcher. He was eventually a small landowner in Van Diemen's Land, but he always seems to have lived alone. James Strong matches more closely the plebeian image of the visionaries. He was a fiddler from Dorchester. At Norfolk Island he was put in irons and sentenced to two hundred lashes for trying to break into the store, but Ross provided him all the same with an allotment and a pig. He did well in the short term, but he was not a man who liked independence, and in early colonial circumstances, where women who wanted husbands might choose from a plenitude of well-settled men, this usually meant living single. Strong left Norfolk in 1792 and spent the rest of his life as a labourer, unmarried, on the mainland.[32]

Phillip had wanted to protect virtuous women from the attentions of seamen on shipboard and in New South Wales the courts made a similar effort,
but with limited precision and success. Within a month of the first landing,
Samuel Barsby was tried on the accusation of Catherine Prior. He had
threatened her with a knife, and abused her 'in terms too gross for her to
repeat'. He was given fifty lashes, but if this was a victory for convict
women it was not maintained. The gentlemen who staffed the courts knew
what to do about masculine dignity but they baulked at making a wholesale
defence of the honour of women. In Phillip's time there was only one other
case which at first sight looks like Barsby's. John Hayes received the same
sentence for his 'infamous behaviour' (unspecified) towards Margaret
Dawson, a convict aged about nineteen. But Hayes suffered because the
woman in this case 'belonged' to a gentleman, William Balmain, one of the
assistant surgeons (who was to look after her for the rest of his life).[33]

A few women found redress after being physically mistreated. John
Boyle, one of the reprobate bridegrooms of 1788, received one hundred
lashes (without the formality of a trial) for 'grievously beating and ill treat-
ing his wife'.[34] In another case, Elizabeth Mason was passing the garrison
lines when she thought to try a little banter with Joseph Abbott, a drummer,
who was standing on guard. She asked him, 'How does your dog's eye do?'
and he replied by kicking her. She went directly to Major Ross and got him
arrested and court-martialled. (The 'dog's eye' was Jane Fitzgerald, who had
friends among the garrison.) Here, however, a tangled series of events led to
the woman being flogged instead of the man.[35] Lydia Munro likewise complained of William Boggis, who tried to rape her as she was going down to
the water to bathe with another woman. There was plentiful evidence of
violence, but Boggis was charged simply with 'wanting to have connexion
with [the woman] . . . against her will'. He was found guilty and sentenced
to one hundred lashes, but he was afterwards 'forgiven'. This means forgiv-
en by the court, not by Lydia Munro.[36]

There is some mystery surrounding the Boggis case. The court took no
notice of the violent struggle which Boggis had initiated, nor of the woman's
injuries. To all appearances, the men on the bench had discovered a relationship, an intimacy however rough, on which they did not want to
intrude. Boggis argued about his own sensibilities – 'it is not likely he should
want to have connexion with the woman when there were two or three
other people present' – and the court showed a similar concern for privacy.
This was a happy policy for rapists. Certainly, there were times when it
could work also to the advantage of women, but in each case their crimes
were much less serious. Elizabeth Clark was tried for insolence to a soldier.
She was proved to have shouted at him 'you bloody bougre' and was
ordered to be flogged at the cart's tail, but further evidence showed that the
two had been on the same ship and that 'there was an intimacy between
them'. The court had stumbled on a lovers' quarrel, and the woman, like

Boggis, was forgiven.[37] Mary Davis escaped punishment for the same reason after breaking a bottle over the head of the gunner's mate of the *Sirius*.[38]

It seems that the officers who staffed the criminal courts were doubtful about handling the slippery and delicate issue of sexual relations. Even in John Russell's case, mentioned earlier, they were solicitous about Mary Love but not about Jane Creek, who was also hurt but with whom Russell had some kind of relationship. This was not because the gentlemen were bemused by the sexual behaviour of the poor, as of a different culture. A hundred years later, no doubt (by the end of the nineteenth century), the lives of many educated people were shaped by a distinctive type of delicacy, making them quite different from the poor. But in this period habits of intimacy were not so clearly differentiated from rank to rank, and neither the poor nor the rich was much surprised by the behaviour of the other. In 1802, at Norfolk Island, a servant told what he had lately seen of his master and a woman. Not only had the two slept together, but the gentleman had 'breakfasted . . . in her room when the [bed]clothes were down so low that I could see part of her breasts, but she pushed them up again on seeing me enter the room'. Also, 'I have heard her also make water in his presence and I saw him do the same in hers', and 'I have seen her sit in my master's lap and he kiss her twice, and', he said, in summing up, 'they behaved in general towards one another like man and wife.'[39] Under this rubric, man-and-wife were the same the world over.

The officers in New South Wales kept up a continual intervention in the lives of the people. Pens in hand, they watched them very carefully. And yet (unlike the servant just quoted) at moments of intimacy, whether sweet or ugly, they averted their gaze. They were possibly guided by a newly fashionable inclination to romanticise sexuality, including the dark and gothic forms of sex which appeared in violence between men and women. Formless passion of this kind was thought of as the necessary basis of community and of humankind.[40]

It would follow that the attitude of the gentlemen was in line with a new type of sensibility, a great movement of ideas in North America and Europe. Settlement at Sydney Cove followed directly on the revolution in America and it coincided with the first years of revolution in France. Both were rebellions against the old order, but the old order had already been undergoing change, in its habits and ideas. In many ways the revolutions picked up these inclinations and carried them forward. In particular, the reconstitution of the state on both continents helped to build a barrier between public and private life, and to affirm different types of citizenship for men and women. In their climax and achievement both revolutions helped to concentrate the educated mind, not only on the moral responsibilities of authority but also on the definition of privacy and the position of private beings under government. Just as the state itself was shaped by public violence, privacy took its life from domestic passion. The French Revolution in particular, as an expression of the brotherhood of men, created a new form of subjection for women. A pamphleteer in Paris declared in 1791, 'Women . . . this revolution must change your manner of thinking, make you see everything differently.' Women had helped to create both revolutions, but their rights were to be coloured henceforth by their purely private existence.[41]

This was also the message embodied in transportation to New South Wales. The sudden movement of so many men and women, fleet after fleet, to the other side of the world was a means of magnifying the authoritarian tendencies of the age: in so far as the people were organised from above, their dealings with each other were transformed and in some cases reduced. They became watchers and receivers. Here too (as in Paris from 1789) a new society was created by force and, where necessary, by bloodshed. From the beginning, the heavy and regular work at Sydney Cove was allocated to the men, and the women were left to look after themselves. Officially at least, the women 'did not labour'.[42] The segregation of men and women was consistent with new patterns of rural labour in England, especially in the south-eastern counties. These counties included Hampshire, where Governor Phillip had lived for a while as a farmer and parish overseer. English labouring women had for centuries worked in the fields on equal terms with men, but from the last decades of the eighteenth century they were given different jobs, or else they stayed at home. Phillip believed in segregation. 'I do not reckon on the little labour which may be got from the women,' he said, two and a half years after landing, and when he added that some worked in the fields ('and their numbers will be increased') he was certainly speaking in marginal terms. Their main duties must be those appropriate to their sex: 'making their own and the men's cloathing, and . . . attention to their children'. Given his urgent need to secure a living for the people, to maximise their labour power and to grow as much food as possible, it was almost perverse of him to insist on the sanctity of womanhood as he did in New South Wales.[43]

In this way the early history of European settlement in Australia embodied two great principles: that of brotherhood, whether the brotherhood of army or navy, the brotherhood by which cocks managed hens, or the brotherhood which was forged in the climax of revolution; and that of benevolent dictatorship, or dictatorial benevolence, a product of the high Enlightenment. The two were frequently intermingled and just as frequently in conflict. Both were concerned with the place of women under (and also within) government, because even among 'brothers' women figured largely: so much so that the man who had no use for them – who could be truly called a 'bugger' or 'bougre' – was thought to be barely a man.[44]

The implications of Phillip's attitude to female labour were not easy to follow through. As far as the courts were concerned, there were two obvious results in the short term. The respect for privacy meant a reluctance to interfere in intimate quarrels between men and women, so that women were frequently left to the mercy of the men they chose to live with. On the other hand – and by a contradictory momentum – women were given reason to hope for more in other aspects of their lives, as individuals with a right to good health, as mothers of families, as managers of houses and even as owners of property. Government had assumed a responsibility for them by the very act of transportation. For instance, men and women who lived together without being married often kept their property separate, each having a box or chest of their own. The distinction was honoured at an early stage by the courts, and in due course such rights were to be amplified so that some women, especially in Sydney, entered into a relationship with the state which gave them an authority beyond anything they could have anticipated in Europe (see Chapter 13).[45] In this respect, the gentlemen who administered the state became, as it were, *in loco maritorum*, a type of collective deputy husband, for all those women who had no good and/or useful husbands of their own.

There were shadowy models for such idealism elsewhere. For instance, one of the schemes of the Irish reformer, Sir Jeremiah Fitzpatrick (see Chapter 6), had involved the Irish government taking direct responsibility for the wives and families of soldiers and sailors sent abroad, even to the extent of allowing annual pensions for widows and orphans. Unlike England, Ireland had no Poor Law to provide for the destitute of either sex, and according to Fitzpatrick a centrally administered system was needed instead. An Irish soldier, when he enlisted for service, deserved to know that, in the event of his death, 'the partner of his Bosom and his Orphan Children' would pass into the care of a paternal government. Fitzpatrick had some success with this idea, though very partial. He was also interested in the women who accompanied their convict husbands from Ireland, and – with motives similar to those of Phillip on the First Fleet – he arranged separate quarters for them on board so as to protect them from abuse by seamen and soldiers. The embarkation of women advanced in pregnancy especially concerned him:

> for there is [he said] no one matter which so soon contaminates the air in a crowded place, and a hot climate as the unavoidable consequences of women's lying in; where they cannot have the necessary means of cleanliness or fresh air and where they must be subject to every inconvenience arising from the crowd and clatter of all about them.

Here too the state was able to replace, to improve on and to eclipse the disabled spouse.[46] When poor men failed so clearly in their duty and their power, even a philosopher-king might aspire to be cock-of-the-walk.

III

Women were drawn by such motives within the dominion of late eighteenth-century humanitarianism. An early beneficiary on this side of the world was Susannah Holmes, the convict whose child was restored to her in England, who was married as soon as she got to New South Wales, and whose property was rescued from a ship's captain by the Court of Civil Judicature. So was Sarah Bellamy, a convict complainant before the Judge-Advocate's Bench in August 1789.

A woman outside a house made of slabs and bark, on the southern edge of Sydney, mid-1790s.

Source: Dixson Library, University of New England

Sarah Bellamy had a house of her own. On 12 August 1789, a little after midnight, a head appeared through the window above where she was sleeping. It was James Meredith, a captain of Marines, and he was drunk. She cried 'Murder!' After pulling at her hair, he got her to open the door and he came in accompanied by James Keltie, master of the *Sirius*. As Meredith afterwards declared, he spoke to the woman 'in the mildest, free and easy Manner he possibly could, asking her why she made so violent a noise, that it was only Mr Keltie who was there, as he was engaged to lay with her'. Sarah Bellamy denied any engagement. On being threatened with imprisonment if she kept up her noise, 'she told him, he was a gentleman and she was a prisoner, therefore she must go wherever he bade her, but [she said] she did not know what she had done, that he had come and disturbed her peace'. The nightwatchman arrived and got the intruders to go away, but she was still determined, she said, 'not to put up with such unmerited treatment from Capt. Meredith or any one else'. With the light of day she reported him to the Judge-Advocate, who staged an investigation.[47]

Meredith knew that there would, as he put it, 'be the Devil and all to pay'. But everyone, including Sarah Bellamy, must have realised that he was not likely to be charged with any offence. She achieved enough through the investigation alone, humiliating him in front of his brother officers and (presumably) getting him a reprimand from his commanding officer. She had also, incidentally, helped to affirm the peculiar relationship which might exist between convict women and the law at Sydney Cove.

This was to be the essence of subjection in the Antipodes. Women's experience set the pace for the entire European project in Australia, as envisaged by Arthur Phillip. The colonial bureaucracy was of a type normally geared to great masculine enterprises, such as the management of defensive expeditions and the waging of wars. However, at Sydney Cove and the out-settlements of New South Wales there was no wholesale movement, no marching backwards and forwards, and there was little of that mass violence which normally gave garrison life its sharp edge and larger purpose. There were challenges all the same, and the lack of military emergency brought such challenges to the head of the queue. Bureaucratic imagination, such as it was, turned to the question of women and families.

Women in response looked to the courts for a power which could override that of the men they saw about them and which could protect them in a range of matters. Even when there was a man available, the bench readily assumed responsiblities which might have otherwise belonged to him. In October 1789 Susannah Allen died in childbirth. The baby's acknowledged father was a soldier in the barracks but the bench issued an order for its future welfare, entrusting it to another woman ('as long as she did Justice to it'), and seeing also to the administration of the mother's will. Some issues were very trivial. For instance, Ann Farmer complained that Sarah McCormick had taken her handkerchief and abused her. The Judge-Advocate's Bench reprimanded McCormick and made her give it back.[48]

But every judgment, large and small, helped to reinforce the courts' power to judge.

These were not efforts of pure generosity. The women were expected to think of themselves as part of an orderly community, a community devised and constructed in the minds of the gentlemen. Here too there were precedents in the recent history of the empire. It was customary in the British and Irish armies to let a certain number of wives go with regiments abroad, and these were looked after as part of the collective enterprise of war. '[I]t is to their labours', so a female observer of camp life remarked, 'that the poor fellows owe all the conveniences of their situation. The contest [among them] seems to be, which shall excel the others in sprucing up their hero for exercise.' They were (in practice, at least) under military control, and the washing and mending they did, the cooking and nursing, might well extend to the company or regiment at large. In North America some wives kept shop and sold rum to the soldiers. In the American revolutionary army they were called to punishment parades carrying buckets of thickly salted water, 'to wash the bloody backs of the sufferers'.[49]

In New South Wales the particular treatment of women related very often to questions of health, including their health as mothers. The surgeons appointed to the settlement made a powerful impression on the female convicts. To begin with, at least, some of the women resented the interest they showed in their physical condition. On the First Fleet, Elizabeth Barber abused the surgeon, Thomas Arndell, 'in a most terrible man[ner] and Said that he Wonted to — her and called him all the names that She could think of'. And yet Arndell and his colleagues were fighting an obvious battle against some of the worst aspects of shipboard life. A week after being abused by Elizabeth Barber, the same man had to deal with another woman who had been sentenced to a period in irons, and he succeeded in having her freed because she was sick.[50] Through such episodes authority presented itself as a kind of theatre, a constant interplay of black rigour, or callousness, and shining humanity which must have made a vivid impression on the people who were its close and captive audience. One woman who arrived by the Second Fleet sent a letter home in which she wrote of dreadful suffering among the convicts on three of the ships, owing to official brutality: 'it would make your heart bleed', she said. She had been lucky to sail on the *Lady Juliana*. On that vessel, she explained, they had been well fed. Also, five or six babies had been born at sea, and 'they had great care taken of them, and baby linen and every necessary for them was ready made to be put on'.[51]

Drama is a great pedagogue. The English poor were already aware of the rights to welfare which followed from their membership of parish communities. Through the startling initiation of shipboard experience the convicts came to believe that transportation likewise endowed them with rights, rights which were frequently denied and which they struggled to maintain, but irrefutable rights nevertheless. These overlapped with the ancient rights of Englishmen – both were fed by argument and demand, by the vigour of living voices – but they had a logic of their own. In so far as they were the rights of an entire population, they were peculiar to European Australia. They were passive rights, rights easily assimilated with the commonly understood rights of women. Most of all, in an age of humanitarianism, the people were taught to imagine that they might demand humanity from their rulers.

Convicts carried this attitude into their time of freedom. Certainly, those who settled as farmers at Rose Hill and elsewhere about Port Jackson were obliged to make certain commitments themselves. In order to ensure that they would turn the soil to good account, they had to promise that they would live on it and cultivate it for ten years. At the same time they had to promise to help each other. Here the immediate beneficiaries were the men, in whose names the freeholds were vested. Men who were given land nearly always had wives with them, but officially these were only assistants. The men had to agree that if any one of them fell sick he might expect from his neighbours two days' labour a month to help him out, for as much as two months at a time.[52]

There is no evidence to show how well this agreement worked in practice. However, it is likely to have been less important than the commitment which the government itself made towards the success of each farming enterprise. For eighteen months after taking up their land the farmers and their families were to be fed with the ration allowed to convicts, and they were to be given the same allowance of clothes and medicine when they needed it. They were to have grain for their first crop and two sows. Also every man and woman was entitled to a hatchet, a tomahawk, two hoes, a spade and a shovel. Cross-cut saws were to be shared among neighbourhoods. All this was received by the settlers as their right, and they complained loudly if they thought they were being short-changed.[53] In fact, such arrangements opened the door to limitless vituperation and trouble. William Parish belonged to a small group of former convicts who had once been seamen, and who settled together at Prospect during winter 1791. He and his wife were also among the batch of couples who had been married by the chaplain soon after landing. They had been settled for less than six months when Parish was brought before the Judge-Advocate's Bench charged with insolence, and with threatening the life of Thomas Arndell, who was now assistant surgeon at Parramatta.

The quarrel between Arndell and Parish had been provoked by the illness of Parish's wife, Phoebe. As with the dispute between Arndell and Elizabeth Barber on board the First Fleet, the surgeon had difficulty getting the Parishes to submit quietly – let alone gratefully – to the healing power of the state. Phoebe Parish had given birth to her second child towards the end of 1791, and she had been unwell ever since. A few days before Christmas,

William came to Parramatta to get provisions from the public store, and Arndell told him that his wife must come in too, for treatment. If she could not come, he said, he would go out and, if necessary, give orders for her to be brought to hospital at Parramatta. Parish refused to let him see her. He had no confidence, he said, in anyone but a convict named Daniel Kelly (who had some medical skill which even the gentlemen recognised). Nor would his wife come in to 'such a lousy place' as the hospital (and 'lousy' was meant literally). They also argued about the quantity of wine she had been given, and as to whether it should be mixed with medicinal herbs. Arndell said that the mixture 'was the only thing w[oul]d do her good'. Parish answered that she would take her wine neat, or not at all.[54]

A conversation and a woman walking alone in the main street of Parramatta, mid-1790s.

Source: Dixson Library, University of New England

Parish had several things of larger significance to say to the surgeon. First, he said, he was a free man, 'nor did he consider himself under any person but the Gov[erno]r'. Secondly, his wife was 'his own property', and it followed that he alone would say what was good for her. He was free, but she was subject entirely to his judgment. Finally, he had a standing claim on the government, and not only for rations. He understood that he was entitled to medical attendance whenever he wanted it for a number of years, 'upon a written ingagement'. And yet, so he said, his wife had been neglected at her confinement and on another, earlier occasion.

Throughout this episode the voice of Phoebe Parish is silent in the written record. She had not come in to see the doctor, and she did not come in to her husband's trial, nor, presumably, to watch him receive a hundred lashes afterwards. He was the first free man to be flogged at Sydney or

Parramatta, but there was no other punishment which seemed appropriate to the bench, given the 'spirit of disobedience, and want of subordination' which appeared in his behaviour.[55] However, Mrs Parish was at the centre of the whole episode. Her husband's trial and punishment were not only designed to deal with his insubordination. They were also meant to prove that his wife was not, in fact, his property. Gentlemen such as Arndell, as representatives of the state, had their own claim to her. It was a claim which enlarged her significance by making her an object of public humanity, a subject of the state in her own right, but it also depended on the notion that neither she nor her husband had voices of their own. In sickness, she was to be fed under their orders, and she might be removed from her husband's roof to theirs – or in other words, to the hospital – whether he liked it or not.

The Parishes lived at the outskirts of settlement, which helped them to keep out of the way of authority. Affairs were more complicated at Sydney Cove. Convict men and women who lived side by side with the civil and military officers at headquarters, overhearing their conversations and frequently confronting them face to face, learnt more thoroughgoing lessons about the new scheme of things. As at Parramatta, the hospital must have been a scene of daily drama, with frequent intimate confrontations like that between Arndell and the Parishes. The hospital at Sydney Cove was also physically conspicuous, and most of the population had some close acquaintance with it in one way or another. In July 1790, for instance – just after the arrival of the Second Fleet – when there were 729 convict men in and around Sydney, 413 (57 per cent) were under medical treatment. To this must be added an unknown number of sick women and soldiers. Six more convict men (and once again an unknown number of women) were employed at that time in looking after the patients, and three worked in the hospital garden and around the building. On top of that, there was usually a team employed in shooting for the hospital and one man in fishing, to ensure a regimen of fresh food.[56]

The hospital was a state enterprise of essential significance for the first Europeans in Australia. New South Wales might be called a penal settlement, but for many years its hospitals – rather than any prisons – were by far the most important buildings used for the confinement of the people. In that way the surgeons continued the regime established on shipboard during the passage from Europe. We know only a little about the way in which the first hospital buildings were arranged, order maintained within, and the patients categorised. The original building at Sydney Cove, laid out within the first few days of settlement, was a single rectangle, 84 feet by 23 (about 26 by 7 metres), with a dispensary and separate wards for soldiers and convicts, but apparently no subdivision beyond that. By the end of Hunter's time there were two substantial brick buildings and one of timber, besides a storehouse and a dispensary.[57] Even with increased space, women inmates must have been under the constant gaze of men – of surgeons, male attendants and other patients – and many, like Phoebe Parish at Parramatta, must have hesitated before entering such a regime.

The care of the sick and dying involved not only the surgeons but the clergy. Richard Johnson, the first chaplain to the settlement, took this part of his duties very seriously. A convict observer, writing home, remarked that 'few of the sick would recover if it were not for the kindness of the Rev. Mr Johnson, whose assistance out of his own stores makes him the physician both of soul and body'.[58] Certainly he seems to have been a very generous man. For the convicts he, more than anyone else, represented the pleasant face and open hand of authority, so much so that they let their imaginations feed on him to excess. They convinced themselves that before the departure of the First Fleet 'a considerable sum of money' had been subscribed for them by English philanthropists, and spent on goods which had been given to Johnson for distribution in New South Wales. It followed that they themselves had a right to everything he handed out. Johnson did all he could to have the story contradicted, and eventually a statement was included by the Governor in General Orders. By this means the chaplain claimed the moral advantage he thought he deserved: 'it was to his bounty they were indebted . . . and . . . consequently the partakers of it were to be of his own selection'. It was probably the same notion – that all he had was theirs – which led the minister's domestic servants to carry off his possessions at a rate beyond anything he could understand. 'I believe', he said, 'few [servants] have been treated better, and perhaps it may be for this very reason that I have met with these returns.'[59]

Once again, such expectations had a particular point among the women. Both Johnson and his assistant, Samuel Marsden, who arrived in 1794, were married men with very young children. Their understanding of themselves as new fathers seems to have done a certain amount to shape their sense of public responsibility. In his first letter back to England, Marsden asked for a consignment of oatmeal. 'The poor', he said, 'when they are unwell and especially the women when they get their beds [that is, in childbirth] are very much in want of this article, as they have nothing but a little indian corn meal to make gruel on.'[60] The paternalism of the ministers supplemented that of Governor Phillip and it continued beyond Phillip's time, even unsettling the succeeding regime. Their following among the convict women, in particular, led to new tensions at headquarters.

The Second Fleet had brought to Port Jackson, during winter 1790, the first detachment of the New South Wales Corps, a regiment raised in England to replace the Marines on garrison duty. The Corps had its own chaplain, the Reverend James Bain, a graduate of the University of Glasgow, who had arrived during 1791. Bain's priorities were clearly different from those of Johnson and Marsden. A naval officer who had travelled with him described him 'a peevish old battchelor' (he was in his early forties) and as a man whom women of all classes declined to take seriously.[61] Bain's significance was greatly increased when the commanding officer of the Corps took over from Phillip as Acting Governor, in December 1792. All the officers now attended at the barracks for Sunday service, conducted by Mr Bain, and orders were given out that convicts should do so as well.

Johnson's congregation had hitherto included several of the convict constables and their wives. Major Grose seems to have been especially keen that they and any other 'decent women' should shift their allegiance to Bain, and the women became the object of a tug-of-war. According to Johnson, 'One of [the constables'] wives fearing . . . least [sic] she s[houl]d be punished for coming to hear me, and not liking to hear Mr Bain, stayed at home once or twice.' But, he said, she afterwards decided to stand by her old minister and other women followed her example. They were punished for their obstinacy by being forced to to shell corn and pick oakum, and seven who were still defiant – their names are unrecorded – had their heads shaved. There was even talk, so Johnson said, of fitting them with iron collars and sending them to public labour at Toongabbie.[62]

Bain was a scholar, and as chaplain to the regiment he had some responsibility for the education of the soldiers' children. He did not stay long in the colony but he contributed a little to the setting up of schools.[63] Education provided another opportunity for families, and mothers in particular, to be drawn within a type of authority which few could have known in England. The first school of which there is any record had been started at Sydney Cove by a convict couple named Richardson at the beginning of 1790. The husband went on to enlist in the Corps and he was also Bain's clerk. On his own initiative he seems to have attached himself to Johnson as well, serving him as clerk through the 1790s. Probably most of the school-teaching was done by the wife, Isabella Richardson, who had been a dressmaker and laundress in London. Johnson supplied her with spelling books, and he and Bain managed to win financial support for her school, and others at Parramatta and Norfolk Island, from the Society for the Propagation of the Gospel, in London.[64]

Johnson insisted that those who came to school during the week should also come to church on Sundays, or risk expulsion. Among some convict and ex-convict families this was no problem: as one of the officers of the Corps conceded years later, 'the women and their children used to seem to take a pride, in general, to make a decent appearance of a sunday'. The school attendance numbers were therefore good: by 1798 there were 150 children enrolled. This was roughly half the total eligible at Sydney (that is, between three and ten years old), a figure better than it might seem because many of the remainder must have attended for some time beforehand or later.[65] Only a few years were necessary for most children to learn to read their testament and to manage the large round handwriting which amounted to basic literacy. Here too, then, the ministers got the response they wanted. The schools worked a small revolution especially in female literacy, in so far as the pattern common among adults – with many women reading but not writing – was not duplicated in the new generation. Invited by the state to share in its bounty, Sydney mothers seemed to have pushed their little girls forward beyond what they would have thought of doing in England. Among the women marrying in Sydney in this period, those locally born were nearly twice as likely to sign their own names as those born elsewhere.[66]

There came into being a distinctive three-way relationship between women, men and the state, essential to European civilisation in Australia. Throughout the period of convict transportation (and beyond) there were always many women, just as there were many men, who resisted the embrace of the state, who declined to receive His Excellency or any of his officers as cock of their particular walk. This was to be true, of course, even when women began to share a little in the exercise of power, as they did at an early stage (see Chapter 13), when the public imagination and the purposes of the state began to be in some respects androgynous. Poor women who refused to cooperate were to be a constant irritant for the gentlemen in authority, not only because they seemed wicked in themselves, but also because they defied the logic of the new humanitarianism, and especially its promise for family life. Their behaviour was – to the discriminating gaze of authority – ugly and old-fashioned: like recalcitrant wives, they seemed to question the good faith of the men who had taken their fortunes in hand. Other women, perhaps the majority, made what they could of the new regime, and especially the life-giving safety it offered: no small matter, after all, among a population so raw and mobile and in a place so wholly strange.[67]

Chapter 8

Black and White

I

Jonathan Swift's story of Lilliput, where the people were less than six inches high, is the first part of his book, *Gulliver's Travels*, and the most famous. But the last part, his account of Gulliver in the land of the Houyhnhnms, has an appeal of its own, a mingling of whimsy, irony and wisdom. Here the hero is finally confronted with a race of creatures whom he has to admire, and whom he never wholly understands.

The country is seen through the eyes of a European, Gulliver himself, and the story is told with his voice. He talks mainly about the Houyhnhnms, beings of sublime intelligence and virtue who rule the country. They are horses. But he cannot avoid the other inhabitants, the Yahoos, who live as vermin and as slaves to the Houyhnhnms and who are men and women. In some ways it is a classic travel story, a combination of familiar and unfamiliar detail, the quaint and the incredible, carried back from a previously unvisited land on the far side of the earth. The trivia of daily life is startling and outlandish, but in this antipodean spot Gulliver also finds a mirror, or two mirrors, for his own humanity: on one side the high example of the Houyhnhnms and, on the other, the vicious squalor of the Yahoos. The story sums up in brilliant metaphor the experience of any number of Europeans over the centuries, who have travelled and settled among strange people and who have thereby, in one way or another, found their own reflections.

For European travellers in the eighteenth century, the best means of understanding the image in these mirrors was through language. They commonly tried to record not only the sense but the method with which people talked. Travellers who had been educated as gentlemen usually knew something about the theories of language which prevailed at that time. Gulliver had nothing but praise for the language of the Houyhnhnms. It sounded, he said, like German or High Dutch, except that it was 'more graceful and significant'. It was a simple language, with relatively few words, because the nobility of the Houyhnhnms was of a straightforward kind. '[T]heir wants and passions are fewer than among us.' Indeed, their simplicity went further than that:

> The Houyhnhnms have no letters, and consequently their knowledge is all traditional. But there happening few events of any moment among a people so well united, naturally disposed to every virtue, wholly governed by reason, and cut off from all commerce with other nations, the historical part is easily preserved without burthening their memories.[1]

The Yahoos, on the other hand, had no language beyond a kind of chatter, and Gulliver took no interest in it. He knew them only by what they did, their strong smells and snarling faces.

Several of the gentlemen who came from Europe in the First Fleet, and in subsequent vessels, were profoundly interested in the people they found in Australia. Here too language was the key. According to Watkin Tench, at first the texture of Aboriginal language seemed 'barbarous' – another officer called it 'excessively Loud & harsh' – but familiarity soon proved that it was rich in vowels. To the experienced ear it was 'sometimes mellifluous, and sometimes sonorous', and Tench offered a list of words to prove it. On one issue, however, the gentlemen at Sydney Cove were unable to agree. Was Aboriginal language simple (like that of the Houyhnhnms), or was it 'copious', with a great variety of words to meet a great variety of uses?[2]

This was an important distinction according to the controversies of the day. The conventional view, dating from John Locke in the late seventeenth century, was that all languages were simple to begin with and directly linked with the experience of the senses. Primeval words denoting particular things had unfolded over time to encompass a range of abstractions and universals. This was understood to be a world-wide phenomenon, and philology was a science beneath whose gaze all humanity was equal. Every humble, short-lived notion, the trivia of daily life, might embody something eternal, and even the conversations of primitive people might carry hints of the sublime. Anyone taking this view would expect to find similarities between Aboriginal language and, say, the languages of Europe in classic times. Tench compared Aboriginal grammar with Latin. Lieutenant William Dawes thought it included a way of expressing plurality similar to Greek. David Collins found three words which resembled their equivalent for sense in European languages, including 'e-lee-mong' which echoed the Greek for 'shield'. 'How these words', he said, 'came into their language must be a mystery till we have a more intimate knowledge of it than I can pretend to.'[3]

However, it was also possible to think of simplicity in other terms. A language which was not yet 'copious' might be evidence of incompetence in its users. This approach depended partly on a theory of language which had emerged in the late eighteenth century, and which was associated with the name of the Scottish lawyer and philologist, Lord Monboddo. In it we see an early inkling of the nineteenth-century theory of evolution, with its assumption of improvement over time. But it was also the result of common prejudice. One of the surgeons on the First Fleet remarked on first seeing the Aborigines that they were 'a most stupid insensible set of beings', with what seemed 'a very short Vocabulary'. This attitude made them more like Yahoos than Houyhnhnms. Tench himself admitted that they had a very limited understanding of number: 'they cannot count with precision more than four. . . . This occasions their computations of time and space to be very confused and incorrect: of the former they have no measure but the visible diurnal motion of the sun, or the monthly revolution of the moon.' And yet, he said, they must improve in due course, for they and the Europeans were all 'Children of the same omniscient paternal care'. The Europeans were distinguished only by 'the fortuitous advantage of birth', and all were equal in the sight of an eternal God.[4]

The first exchanges between Aborigines and Europeans in 1788 were characterised not by spoken language, but by gifts and theft. In this way there was conversation of sorts even during the first landing at Botany Bay. Phillip prepared to come ashore on 18 January, as Tench put it, in order 'to take possession of his new territory, and bring about an intercourse between its old and new masters'. During an exchange across the surf, the Aborigines were given to understand that their visitors needed fresh water and they therefore beckoned them forward. The Europeans, of course, took both land and water, and the Aborigines, in reply, 'condescended to accept of a looking glass, some beads, and other toys'. Also, 'several Gentlemen put Ribbands & Glass Trincketts ab[ou]t their heads'. The Aborigines tried to get their hats from them as well.[5]

During the following weeks the process of exchange entered something of a routine. Two Aboriginal men came to the camp at Sydney Cove during February. They were shown around and presented with hatchets. Others helped the Europeans in pulling in their fishing nets and were given some of the fish, as gift or payment. Elsewhere, however, beyond the eye of authority, men from the settlement picked up spears and other valuables which they found on the rocks and beaches and Aborigines took away tools from the settlement on Garden Island.[6] In this way the interests of Europeans and Aborigines began to merge and ramify, a development which made it important, at least in the eyes of the Europeans, that they should learn each other's language.

The Europeans were anxious to communicate with both men and women among the Aborigines, but they felt a peculiar urgency in dealing with the men, and here the feeling was mutual. But there was some early confusion on the issue of gender because the visitors were clean-shaven. Even their voices, overlaid with peculiar intonations, did not prove that they were men, and the Aborigines considered the possibility that they were misshapen females. On 21 January, while the fleet was still at Botany Bay, a party of Black men signalled that they wanted to know 'of what Sex we were', and some of the humbler European men, no doubt under orders, 'satisfied them in that particular': a display of stark white skin under their own blue sky. 'When they found we were men like themselves they express'd their joy & astonishment by loud Exclamations & grotesque gestures, & immediately shook hands with us.' This first shaking of hands, this welcoming ashore of 'men like themselves', established a détente on which much else depended.[7]

Mirrors were among the first trinkets offered by the Europeans to the Aborigines. However, like the Europeans, the Aborigines needed no glass in order to find distorted images of their own humanity wherever they looked within the new culture. For instance, they admired the movements and colour of the military and in time some of them picked up the more intricate ceremonies of the dinner table. 'They are wonderfully expert at the art of Mimickry,' remarked one of the officers, 'they will say – 'Good Bye' after us, very distinctly.'[8] Conversely, Aboriginal ritual fascinated the Europeans. Several gentlemen were very keen to see an Aboriginal dance and when they did so, in March 1791, they were much impressed. It seemed 'truly wild and savage', and yet there was evidence of 'order and regularity' such as appeared in dances everywhere. Most remarkable was a movement in which the Aboriginal men stood with their feet wide apart and set their knees trembling, 'by an extraordinary exertion of the muscles of the thighs and legs'. Several officers tried it themselves, but only proved the ineptitude of their own ivory shanks.[9]

Useful progress in the learning of new tongues, European or Aboriginal, was very slow during the first year of settlement, and incidents of violence led the Governor to conclude that only force could open the way to a satisfactory relationship. In December 1788, therefore, a man named Arabanoo was carried off by boat from Manly Cove, with the hope that he would not only teach the newcomers some of his language but in time convey their friendly intentions to his own people. He turned out to be 'a very good natured talkative fellow' and, once again, a great mimic. However, his understanding of English never went much beyond the names of the men who tried to talk to him, before he died in May 1789, a casualty of the great smallpox epidemic which devastated the Aboriginal population.[10] Two children, Boorong and Nanbaree, were brought in during the same crisis. By the end of the year they 'understood almost everything we said, and could make themselves well understood'. But children were not good enough. The Governor still wanted one or two men, and as a result Bennelong and Coleby were captured in November.[11]

This was an important step forward. Coleby escaped within a few weeks and Bennelong in May 1790, but acquaintances formed in the interim played some part thereafter in drawing their people within a European circle of communication and exchange. Bennelong was especially useful. He learnt English more quickly than Arabanoo had done. Even in captivity he 'sang, danced, and capered', and he answered questions willingly. Afterwards both he and Coleby came back for occasional visits. They brought women and children with them and others followed: 'whenever they were pressed for hunger, they had immediate recourse to our quarters, where they generally got their bellies filled'. Knowledge of the English language was overlaid by knowledge of English food: 'the little children . . . learnt the words, hungry, bread; and would, to shew that they were hungry, draw in their belly, so as to make it appear quite empty'. A few equivalent gifts were made in exchange. For instance, in September 1790 Bennelong and Coleby sent the Governor a parcel of flesh cut from the side of a stranded whale.[12]

In this way, a peculiar pattern of conversation and ritual was worked out between Black and White which depended only partly on spoken language. The Governor and some others made a point of collecting a vocabulary of Aboriginal words, but they had trouble applying them. Much the same was true of the Aborigines. Bennelong seems to have been unusual: other Blacks learnt very little English, using mainly a kind of pidgin, 'a mutilated and incorrect language formed entirely on our [own] imperfect and improper application of their words'.[13] Phillip himself initiated a typical series of exchanges after receiving the present of whale's flesh, a kind of pidgin mixture of manners. He took a boat to the place where the whale had been washed up, and as his men rowed close to the beach he stood up and called out in the local tongue, asking where Bennelong was. Bennelong replied, 'I am here', at which Phillip announced, in the same language, 'I am the governor your father.' He then got out of the boat and walked up the beach with his arms out. The Aborigines retreated towards the bush and Bennelong disappeared, but the Governor persuaded a number to accept presents of knives, jackets, wine, beef and bread, and to shake hands.

Eventually Bennelong and Coleby both emerged and spoke with Phillip and an officer named Waterhouse. John Hunter, the naval captain and later Governor, describes the interchange as follows:

> Ba-na-long [that is, Bennelong] had at this time two jackets on, which he had received from the governor and Captain Collins; Co-al-by [Coleby] had also a jacket given him; after Ba-na-long had been asked several questions, he took Mr Waterhouse round the neck and kissed him . . . Co-al-by shook hands again with Mr Waterhouse, and begged him to put on [him] the jacket which he had been given, and which he held in his hand, not knowing how to put it on himself, which Mr Waterhouse did for him. Ba-na-long, on the governor's first meeting him, had a remarkable fine spear, which the governor asked him for, but he either could not or would not understand him, but laid it down on the ground.

In spite of every appearance of harmony, this ceremony ended in violence. After being introduced to several other Aboriginal men, Phillip eventually took his leave, promising to send more presents, including hatchets for both

Bennelong, as he first appeared to the Europeans.

Source: Watling Collection, Natural History Museum, London

In 1792 Bennelong went to Europe with Governor Phillip, where he met Lord Sydney, and on his return he dictated this letter to be sent to Sydney's steward, Mr Phillips. The voice of the Aborigine here carries the burden of eighteenth-century European politeness.

Source: National Library of Australia

Bennelong and Coleby. Bennelong made him stop to shake hands with one more stranger, but the man, Willemering – 'not understanding this civility' – picked up Bennelong's spear and sent it though the Governor's shoulder.[14]

The wound was not fatal, but this was the most dramatic assault made hitherto on the Europeans in Australia. It had in it a certain justice. For their part, indeed, the newcomers had offered no violence – none sanctioned, at least, by Phillip himself – but they had bit by bit pressed their advantage. The Governor's advance on Willemering, smiling and holding out his hand, may stand as a small symptom of their invasion. They had moved in that way from the beginning, pressing against the Aborigines – killing them softly – propelled by confidence not only in their own superior strength but also in their good intentions. There was a fathomless power in Phillip's politeness. We do not know whether the mythology of the Port Jackson area included any notion of the Shark who came ashore (see Chapter 3).[15] But the Shark's fearful symmetry was a quality which might well have been mirrored, once again, in the first Governor.

The women were subject to such pressure as well as the men. Swift, in his story of the Houyhnhnms, was not much interested in distinctions of gender. In that fantasy all depends on the difference between Houyhnhnms and Yahoos, and the females of either species have no importance of their own. However, Swift had written in the early years of the eighteenth century. Two or three generations later the focus of European ideas had shifted. Women were now independently subject to the gaze of travellers, writers and public men. In Australia Phillip and his officers wanted to deal directly with Aboriginal women, overriding any barriers which the men might throw up. Hunter tells of an exchange during the first weeks at Sydney Cove, when he and others came across some Aboriginal men and behind them some women partly concealed. He and his friends refused to be put off by the men's belief that their own authority was 'absolute'. He told the men that he had presents for the women. The men offered to take them themselves, 'but to this proposal I positively refused to agree, and made them understand, that unless they [the women] were allowed to come forward, they should not have any'. The men gave in and the women advanced in a state of high excitement: 'during the whole time that we were decorating them with beads, rags of white linen, and some other trifles, they laughed immoderately, although trembling at the same time, through an idea of danger'.[16]

In an exchange like this there was apparently no thought among the men, Black or White, that the women might give anything material in reply. They were receivers only, to be decorated just as the land itself was to be decorated, in due course, with artefacts from Europe. And yet some Europeans went to great lengths for the women. John White, the Principal Surgeon, was especially eager to please. During a passing conversation with a woman at Broken Bay he tore up both his pocket and neck handkerchiefs, tying the strips around her head, neck and arms. Then, 'Having nothing left, except the buttons of my coat, on her admiring them, I cut them away, and with a piece of string tied them around her waist.' This was during winter, when a buttoned coat might have been useful. Certainly, White's was an act of common gallantry, a sacrifice such as any officer might make for an engaging woman of lesser rank. In Farquhar's play, *The Recruiting Officer*, Rose, a 'country wench', says of Captain Plume that 'He took the very ribbands out of his shirtsleeves and put 'em into my shoes.' In dealing with such women talk was perfectly unnecessary, and John White found in the woman at Broken Bay a response as simple as any he might have looked for at home. 'Thus ornamented, and thus delighted with her new acquirements, she turned from me', he said, 'with a look of inexpressible archness.'[17]

II

During the first years of invasion, the Europeans had much that they were anxious to give to the Aborigines. But giving is like commerce: it binds and defines both the parties who engage in it. How was it to be done when each was wholly ignorant of the habits and intentions of the other? In settling relations as a whole, were the newcomers to dispense their gifts with some show of equality and reciprocity, as in the dealings between Phillip's party and the Aboriginal men? Or were they to give from a position of obvious power, with no thought of return, as they did with the women? A similar dilemma had recently confronted the agents of British power in India. The East India Company had traded since the 1660s with the native merchants of Calcutta, Madras and Bombay, but during the eighteenth century its authority in those parts had increased so as to become virtually sovereign. In other words, the European relationship with the Indians was still reciprocal, but it was now one of superiority as well. Subsequently, in 1783, the British government itself took possession of several provinces and the people became British subjects. At the same time reformers set about imposing a new order, redefining the rights of property and the relationship of native proprietors with government. This new legitimacy was similarly meant as a gift.[18] The Europeans not only dealt, man to man, with the wealth of Indians. They also guaranteed it.

In Australia, transactions between Black and White likewise depended on the legal relationship the Aborigines might be understood to have with the British government. The terms of Phillip's commission gave him authority extending from the east coast of New South Wales westward to the 135th degree of longitude. However, in principle this was nothing more than a territory, a geographical space. It was not a province, like Bengal or Bihar. In law its boundaries did not comprehend a body of people requiring government. It was understood to be *terra nullius*. In other words, its people were considered to have no systematic pattern of relationships – such as Europeans might recognise – either with the soil or among each other.

And yet, at the same time, British officials took it for granted that there was in fact some form of order and authority among the inhabitants of the new territory. In the instructions issued to Phillip before his departure the Aborigines were given a paragraph to themselves. They were referred to as an ordered community, and also as aliens – though innocent ones – which meant that in dealing with them the Governor was to behave as an agent at the frontier of empire. He was required 'to open an intercourse' with them and 'to conciliate their affections', and he was to make sure 'our subjects' (the inhabitants of the new settlement) did nothing which might gratuitously annoy them.[19] There were numerous models for instructions of this kind. In issuing orders for the Mosquito Shore, admittedly, the King assumed an equal sovereignty over both natives and settlers – 'Our Indian and Our other Subjects' – as he was not yet prepared to do in New South Wales. But it was understood that the Indians would look after themselves in their own way.[20] On the continent of North America the work of the Superintendents of Natives had mainly involved negotiation with fiercely independent Indians, and in Africa the proposed agent at Lemane was to have juggled affairs with an unknown number of Black princes.

Order appears partly in the eye of the beholder, and once on the spot different Europeans saw different types of order among the Aborigines. Some, certainly – those whose imagination had been formed by *Robinson Crusoe* and little else – looked for, and found, 'savages' and 'cannibals'. Such semi-literate vision was probably widespread among the convicts and it might well have affirmed that Australia was an empty land, ripe for invasion. Others saw a type of order but with nothing much to recommend it. To Watkin Tench, the Aborigines looked something like the French at the height of revolution. 'Without distinctions of rank,' he wrote, 'except those with youth and vigour confer, theirs is strictly a system of *Equality*.' As a result, power belonged to the strong, and he thought that it was probably exercised through an ugly system of injury and revenge.[21] However, Tench's view was that of a young man, excited by the great events of his day and eager to make sense of shocking new distinctions between liberty and law. John Hunter, who was old enough to be Tench's father, looked on the Aborigines with the more benign eye of a Scot who had been educated, like others of his generation, to believe in the world-wide virtues of reason. Recent revolutions could not affect his faith in the careful self-ordering of societies. All human institutions, he thought, must have some clear purpose, and if authority was hard to find among the Aborigines that was not surprising. In their case leadership was needed only in battle, and then, he said, 'they put themselves under the direction of a chief'. Such chiefs were chosen, presumably, not for their personal prestige but 'from an opinion of their dexterity in war'.[22]

Phillip's view was radically different to all of these. He soon realised that among the Aborigines age conferred authority, although he concluded that this meant the rule of One – the oldest, perhaps. He does not seem to have recognised any councils of the elderly. As his secretary, Collins, remarked, in any encounter with the Aborigines 'we were always accosted by the person [that is, the man] who appeared to be the eldest of the party, while the women, youths, and children were kept at a distance'.[23] An admirer of monarchy himself, Phillip concluded that the population was divided among a number of dominions faintly resembling feudal lordships. Territory seemed to him to be the essential point (and his ideas about it were at odds with the spirit of *terra nullius*). He suggested that Aboriginal chiefs, like European noblemen, took their titles from their territories, and that the people were subjects, in the full sense of the word, being 'distinguished by the name of their chief'. Thus, on the north-west shores of Port Jackson, 'The district is called Cammerra; the head of the tribe is named Cammerragal, by which name the men of that tribe are distinguished.' And, he added, 'A woman of this tribe is called a Cammerragalleon.' Certain powerful chiefs were also able to establish a type of suzerainty over surrounding tribes, signified, so Phillip believed, by a tribute of front teeth. However, he said, 'Some [intended subjects] refuse paying this tribute.'[24]

Certainly close observation suggested that the Aborigines were not frightened of authority as Europeans were taught to be. '[T]hese Savages', wrote John Harris, surgeon of the New South Wales Corps, 'tho the[y] own a Chief seems [sic] to be under no kind of awe with regard to passion before him.'[25] It followed (sadly for the invaders) that they must be very hard to govern.

Nevertheless, Phillip's hierarchical understanding prevailed from a policy point of view. It even encouraged ideas about degrees of status quite apart from those of age. In spite of Harris's observation, Hunter was persuaded that Coleby had the bearing of a man of rank, particularly as Bennelong seemed in awe of him: 'he was always very silent in his company'. Bennelong himself seemed to enjoy some prestige among his own people, even resembling a small landed proprietor. His estate, inherited from his father, said Collins, was 'Me-mel', or Goat Island, in Port Jackson: 'To this little spot he appeared much attached; and we have often seen him and his wife Ba-rang-a-roo feasting and enjoying themselves on it.' There were others too, so he understood, who held 'this kind of hereditary property', by common consent.[26] The Port Jackson communities may indeed have been patrilineal, like some others elsewhere in Australia. Among the first Europeans, such shreds of evidence produced a complicated understanding of the place of rank and property, owing something to Aboriginal reality and something, much more perhaps, to their own perceptions.

Once again, the Aborigines responded in parallel fashion. The spirit of reciprocity which existed between Black and White at the very beginning involved a confrontation of images and imagination, of mirrors shining on mirrors.[27] However, Phillip and his officers were luckier than the Aborigines.

In dealing with their opposite numbers, they were not compelled to make any great effort of mind. They could well believe that they understood the essence of what they were looking at. (They were, of course, wrong.) They already knew something of the variety of humankind and they had elaborate theories to comprehend it. Into such theories they could fit the Aborigines, or what they perceived of them, with more or less ease. The Aborigines had only one narrow paradigm, their own collective sense of self. It was particularly difficult for them to sift and explain the personification of authority they witnessed in Governor Phillip. When Captain Cook first landed on Hawaii in January 1779 a series of coincidences had made it easy for the island people to identify him with the god Lono, who likewise came from the sea, and they fashioned their relationship with him accordingly: they adored him and then they killed him.[28] Phillip could not be accommodated in such a straightforward way by the Aborigines. His physical presence, his European dignity of rank and the material things with which he surrounded himself, especially his house and garden, were phenomena which must have made a dramatic impact on the local understanding of humanity.

Bennelong, and in due course other Aborigines, called Phillip 'Be-anna' (otherwise spelt, in the European record, 'Be-ah-nah', 'Beanah' or 'Been-én-a'), meaning 'Father'. According to Collins, it was a title commonly given to old men with some kind of supreme authority.[29] It must have been the best word they had for the power they saw in Phillip, and in that way they unknowingly mimicked the people of Georgia, who had used the same title for General Oglethorpe (see Chapter 3). For both Aborigines and Georgians, no doubt, the name 'father' suggested an individual who guaranteed life and good order. However, for the Aborigines it must have had especially strong connotations of kinship. Also, its use must have raised important questions about Phillip's relationship with the land.

In Australia, according to beliefs which had evolved over endless generations, all human and animal life was embedded within a precise pattern of locality. It seems to have followed that the spot with which Phillip identified himself, and the peculiar shelter he raised on that spot, had a life-giving, even a spiritual, significance as well. Government House – and the web of huts, tents, roads and gardens which radiated from it – constituted a new item of topography, whose creation was to be attributed somehow to the Dreaming and the Ancestors. The Aborigines seem to have recognised the authority of this new site by their own movements within the settlement. In due course they took possession of the fenced space around the house, which thus became, as Hunter put it, their 'head quarters' within the settlement. One day in November 1790, for instance, sixteen (including Bennelong) arrived early in the morning, and, 'some fish being distributed amongst them, they made a fire in the governor's yard, and sat down to breakfast in great good humour'.[30]

Government House, Sydney, in 1791. Here the naval officer, William Bradley, has made the house look taller than it really was and has also shown the garden fence which helped to determine this new focal point of Aboriginal life.

Source: Mitchell Library, State Library of New South Wales

The first short phase of European settlement was absorbed into Aboriginal thinking in a peculiarly creative fashion, thanks to Phillip and to Bennelong. Bennelong was a man of imagination – 'His powers of mind', wrote Tench, 'were certainly far above mediocrity' – and he was a master of ritual, passing backwards and forwards between his own people and the remarkable personage who had come among them.[31] Bennelong held the Europeans at bay by redefining them. He had his own understanding of European artefacts, especially blankets – a variation on the highly prized possum-skin rugs – which he used in his own family birth and burial rituals. Among the Aborigines, objects of material culture, especially if they showed ingenuity, were understood to embody a method and form derived from the creative power of Ancestors and cultural heroes.[32] Their exchange from people to people was a means of spiritual innovation, a dispensing of life. In that sense, the Aborigines were like the Europeans, in so far as trade among them (of ideas, language and goods) might be a sacred process: a buying, binding and redeeming of souls. Both were lovers of commerce. The knowledge of particular dances was transmitted likewise, and it was Bennelong who organised the dance mentioned earlier, at which the gentlemen of the settlement were deliberately placed in a ring as witnesses and, presumably, as students. No-one was merely an onlooker in Aboriginal dances. It also seems to have been Bennelong who first called Phillip 'Father', taking in return the name 'Governor' (although there is no evidence of him using it).[33]

Bennelong was particularly keen to be connected, in a spiritual sense, with Government House, and he built up the importance of the house within the Aboriginal scheme of things. Among the Aborigines, birthplace had enormous spiritual significance in so far as it guaranteed particular ties with the land, and so with a spiritual Ancestor. The Ancestors, who were both the creators and the inhabitants of the Dreaming, had a continuing existence in topographical features, and the human body and identity were formed by the circumstances of birth. Bennelong seems to have had no children living when the Europeans arrived, but in the early spring of 1791 his wife, Barangaroo, was well advanced in pregnancy. Bennelong predicted the birth of a son (he was wrong), and he seems to have been anxious that its arrival should extend the type of spiritual lineage or fabric which already bound him to the Governor. Thus, he asked beforehand that the baby might be born at Government House: 'the governor persuaded him', as Hunter put it, 'that [his wife] . . . would be better accommodated at the hospital'.[34] As we see below, the hospital was itself a place of significance for the Aborigines, so that it might well have been a satisfactory second-best.

In December 1791, following the death of the young man Ballederry, the yard surrounding Government House became an Aboriginal burial site. Ballederry and Bennelong had both lived with Phillip occasionally, and Bennelong asked that his friend be buried in the yard. Arabanoo had already been buried there, but that had been the Governor's idea: it proved his own fondness for the individual rather than any feeling for the place. Bennelong's motives must have been different. Now, he and Coleby took charge of the funeral rites, and Phillip's place was among the audience.[35] About the same time Bennelong also lost both his wife and his baby daughter, Dilboong. The baby too was buried in the yard, and her father and two or three others sat by the grave all night. However, Barangaroo's body was burnt, in the presence of the Governor, John White and David Collins, and the site is unrecorded.[36]

Through such ceremonies the Governor, and the place near Sydney Cove with which he had identified himself, became part of the ritual life of the area, at least in the remarkable mind of Bennelong and among those who were prepared to follow his lead. In a patrilineal society old men and fathers might well be conflated with the Ancestors, and it is likely that Phillip's arrival, his movements through the country, his mere presence, became, in a sense, imbued with a type of creative, ancestral dignity.[37] Indeed, the whole fabric of mutual learning and exchange was overlaid with spiritual significance. But such an understanding could flourish only in the original, pristine period of European settlement, and as long as Aborigines could find openings for their own authority.

III

At the same time the Europeans were not only shaking hands. They were also enfolding the Aborigines within an embrace from which, in principle, there could be no escape. Like the Aborigines, the people of Europe in the late eighteenth century still believed in a type of transcendent order, a pattern of being which tied together the whole of creation. They might disagree among themselves on its shape and purpose, but few doubted that one system prevailed. Within two or three generations, certainly – by the mid-nineteenth century – such an understanding was to be broken up and dispersed, so that the particular instant and the immanent fact were to be given a self-sufficient reality of their own. Each object of creation was then to be believed in and examined for itself, and not for its relationship to the greater whole. European poets of that period looking back to the time of their parents and grandparents were to mourn, very often, the end of a single certitude. Like the great ocean, wrote Matthew Arnold, 'The Sea of Faith / Was once, too, at the full, and round earth's shore / Lay like the folds of a bright girdle furled.'[38] However, during the period with which this volume is concerned, that seeming disaster was still a matter for the future. The Europeans who first came to Australia were travellers on Arnold's Sea of Faith, although it was already a sea on which the lights of secular and religious understanding played with equal significance. Thus their imagination was sometimes capable of reaching out with a sense of fellowship to the Aborigines, just as the imagination of the Aborigines reached out to them.

Unlike the inhabitants of, say, Bengal after 1783, the Aborigines were not clearly understood to be subjects of the King. And yet they lived within the King's dominions and they were obviously capable of benefiting from the humanity and the high sense of honour which, in this age of Enlightenment, were supposed to adorn British power abroad. In the months before the departure of the First Fleet, a correspondent to a London newspaper had asserted that the government intended nothing but good towards the people currently living in Australia: 'they wish to form them into a more civil community,' he said, 'so as that they and our countrymen may reciprocally contribute to the felicity of one another'.[39] This formula stated the superficial ideal of empire. It described precisely the current project in India. It also summed up the attitude of the first gentlemen at Sydney Cove. Like 'our countrymen' – in other words, the convicts – the Aborigines were to surrender to lessons in civility. Together, all were to be taught happiness.

The disciplining of the Aborigines, as if they were British subjects, began in Phillip's time. To some extent, the purpose was defensive and designed for the safety of the settlement. Whatever the state of race relations at headquarters, the Aborigines went on throwing occasional spears at Europeans who dared to make their way by old paths through the bush. During 1790 efforts were made to get them to stop, on the understanding that otherwise 'numbers of them would be killed'. At last John Macentire, a convict employed to shoot game, was fatally wounded by Aborigines, and Phillip decided that the threat of retribution must be carried out. It was to be a measured ritual, orchestrated so as to evoke from its victims not only fear but thought. Troops were sent out with very precise instructions. They were to capture or kill six Aboriginal men. Any Aboriginal weapons they found were to be broken and the pieces left where their owners might see them, so as to prove that this was punishment for wrong-doing and not a wanton exercise of power. Also, the overwhelming virtue of empire was to be exhibited by the scrupulous attention which the troops were to show to Aboriginal women and children. These, said the Governor, 'were not to be injured on any account whatever'.[40]

The exercise achieved nothing, because the Aborigines managed to keep out of the way, and no-one was either killed or captured. The Governor was no more successful in the way he tried to impose on the Aborigines who chose to come and go within the settlement. Bennelong valued his relationship with Phillip, but he was rarely deferential. He was so violent during an altercation in January 1791 that the Governor threatened to have him put to death, 'for his behaviour was the height of savage insolence, and would have been immediately punished in any other person'.[41] However His Excellency's anger achieved very little.

An empire of the high Enlightenment was necessarily an empire of knowledge, and the Europeans wanted to know as much as they could about the Aborigines. They were curious not only about their methods of government and their ties with the soil, but also about the relationship of male and female. Any such detail would help in drawing Aboriginal society within the intelligent gaze of British power, and nothing, as Watkin Tench remarked, was more puzzling than 'the behaviour of these people . . . which relates to their women'. The officers noticed that many women lacked two joints of their left little fingers, and they debated at length as to what that might mean. It was a custom so much like the wearing of wedding rings in Europe that they seized on the notion (wrong as it turned out) that it must be a distinction allowed to wives.[42] The to and fro of married life was watched with equal eagerness. The gentlemen soon decided that the women were subordinate to the men (as if equality were the rule in Europe). Wives suffered from continual beating, they had to carry the heavier burdens, and they had to labour incessantly for food. David Collins drew a plaintive picture of the women of Port Jackson,

> forced to sit in their canoe, exposed to the fervour of the mid-day sun, hour after hour, chanting their little song, and inviting the fish beneath them to take their bate; for without a sufficient quantity to make a meal for their tyrants, who were lying asleep at their ease, they would meet but a rude reception on their landing.

One officer spoke of the women as 'slaves', and indeed – whether correctly or not – many recorded comments conjured up the classic forms of slavery, such as the late-eighteenth-century humanitarian knew by heart.[43]

Phillip's views on slavery have been mentioned in Chapter 3. He also shared in the idea which prevailed among enlightened Europeans that no power could be honourable which allowed a systematic brutality towards women. Violence among the Aborigines sometimes seemed romantic, but not in this case. The Governor was greatly disturbed by the way in which Bennelong treated his wife, Barangaroo, and he told him several times that it was wrong to beat a woman. But Bennelong only laughed. He beat her, he said, because 'she was bad'. Phillip took stronger steps to prevent him killing another woman, against whom he had some claim to revenge, telling him that 'if he did kill her, or even beat her any more, he should lose his life'. Bennelong was undeterred by any such threats, but the woman was kept safe until his mood had changed.[44]

Episodes like this suggested that the Aborigines might lack the capacity for a European type of citizenship, as defined by the gentlemen of Sydney Cove. An impulsive pride, such as Bennelong possessed, was very fine and feudal, but it had little else to recommend it. Highly conscious of their own humanity, the gentlemen were struck by what they considered a lack of a polished sensibility among the Aborigines. Bennelong had attacked the woman just mentioned while she was surrounded by her friends, but no-one had moved to help her. The Blacks also seemed very perfunctory in the way they mourned their dead. Nor did they understand the making of promises. Like the convicts, whose marriages were temporary and who thought that orders were given only for the moment, they did not seem to make long-term commitments. In other words, they seemed unable to exert that memory of the will which was understood to be fundamental to the fabric, especially the commercial fabric, of European society.[45] Memory of this kind was exercised and strengthened by literacy, by the familiar permanence of the written word. With writing there can be monuments for every other minute. Societies bound together mainly by talk, on the other hand, could offer to the individual mind's eye no lasting self-image, no balance-sheet of conscience. Among both Aborigines and convicts, even the notions of honour and reputation were dissimilar from those of literate Christendom.

Nevertheless, as early as Phillip's time the Aborigines had begun to incorporate themselves within the settlement. There was no intermarriage, although one woman, who had lived briefly in Government House, 'granted favours', as Hunter put it, to a number of the convict men, and others made a habit of visiting the barracks at night. Aborigines had also begun systematically exchanging fish for bread, rice and vegetables, and by the time Hunter himself became Governor in 1795 boys and men were finding employment fetching wood and water and otherwise helping on some of the farms. Women and children lived as domestic servants, and at the end of the decade there were as many as ten Aborigines fed at the government store.[46]

Most important of all, Aborigines began to look to the hospital and to the surgeons to ease their pains and to cure their wounds and diseases. In that way, as with the regular acceptance of food, they made themselves sub-

jects of European power, venturing within the imprisoning circle of humanity and cheerfulness. There were times when the Europeans, acting under the
aegis of the Father-Governor, seemed to offer not only sustenance but life
itself. The naval officer William Bradley recorded an episode early in 1788
when John White, the Principal Surgeon, shot a bird and threw it to some
Aborigines in canoes. They would not come ashore, and straightaway the
bird, which was only wounded, stirred and flew away. According to Bradley,
this succession of events made the Blacks think that White had given the
bird back its life. They were so astonished, he said, 'that they remained quite
silent sometime & then all joined in a loud exclamation of wonder'.[47]
Among the Aborigines themselves, the power of healing was a great power
indeed. Not long after the episode with the bird, some were invited to watch
the Europeans amputate a leg. At first they took it for granted that the
patient would die, 'but when they saw the torrent of blood stopped, the vessels taken up, and the stump dressed, their horror and alarm yielded to
astonishment and admiration, which they expressed by the loudest tokens'.[48]

In Phillip's time the hospital at Sydney Cove became a place of resort for
the Aborigines second only, it appears, to Government House. They used
their own cures as well, but a few quickly saw the greater efficiency of
European medicine. Arabanoo on his deathbed, in May 1789, 'suffered himself to be bled & took all Physicks that was offered to him with a Great deal
of Confidence'. Bennelong was once discovered trying to cure his wife's
stomach pain by singing, barking and blowing on the sore spot. 'How long
this ceremony would have continued was uncertain,' Hunter remarked, 'for
Governor Phillip sent for the doctor, and she was persuaded to take a little
tincture of rhubarb, which gave her relief, and put an end to the business.'[49]

The gentlemen offered not only their medicines and their skill but also
their sensibility, and, true to form, they paid special attention to Aboriginal
women. During winter 1789 the Governor organised a party to explore the
area of Broken Bay. There its members found hidden in the grass a girl of
seventeen or eighteen years old, cold and wet and still weak from smallpox.
Hunter tells the story and in doing so he gives an exquisite picture of inarticulate suffering matched by that firm-handed fondling of the will which
summed up the invasion of Australia:

> she was very much frightened on our approaching her, and shed many tears, with
> piteous lamentations: we understood none of her expressions, but felt much con-
> cern at the distress she seemed to suffer; we endeavoured all in our power to
> make her easy, and with the assistance of a few expressions which had been col-
> lected from poor Ara-ba-noo while he was alive, we soothed her distress a little,
> and the sailors were immediately ordered to bring up some fire, which we placed
> before her: we pulled some grass, dried it by the fire, and spread [it] round her
> to keep her warm; then we shot some birds, such as hawks, crows, and gulls,
> skinned them, and laid them on the fire to broil, together with some fish, which
> she eat; we then gave her water, of which she seemed to be much in want, for
> when the word *Baa-do* was mentioned, which was their expression for water, she

put her tongue out to shew how dry her mouth was; and indeed from its appearance and colour, she had a considerable degree of fever on her.

Nor was this all. As night fell, in order to make the invalid as comfortable
as possible, the gentlemen 'got some fire-wood laid within her reach, with
which she might, in the course of the night, recruit her fire'. They also cut
more grass – or, more likely, had the sailors cut it – dried it and covered her
with it, and then, like a good husband tip-toeing from the bedroom, they
'left her to her repose'. Hunter did not look for any hidden scabs of resentment, any lingering recalcitrance, treasured though they might have been by
the woman herself. Several visits next day made her, he believed, perfectly
aware that 'we had nothing in view but her comfort'. She no longer hesitated to ask for fish and water, 'and when she did, it was always supplied her'.[50]

Four years later, in France during the first period of the revolution, the
poet Wordsworth was travelling with his friend Beaupuis when they too saw
a girl, 'hunger-bitten' and wretched, walking in a country lane. Wordsworth
was then a radical youth looking forward to the remaking of government
throughout the world, or at least throughout Europe and its empires. He
kept a record of the encounter as Hunter had done, but in verse. As he
recalled, Beaupuis,

> In agitation said, "'T is against *that*
> That we are fighting', I with him believed
> That a benignant spirit was abroad
> Which might not be withstood.

By contrast with that of Hunter, Wordsworth's sensibility was not backed
up by action. But the poet's dreams were larger than the naval officer's. He
was sure that very soon a new order shaped by the spirit of humanity would
blot out such wretchedness, 'whence better days / To all mankind'.[51] For
Wordsworth, the solution to misery lay in marrying an irresistible power to
feelings as fine as his own. The same was exactly true of gentlemen like
Hunter in the Antipodes.

This visionary spirit was typical of what might be called the revolutionary age of European settlement in Australia, the 1780s and 1790s. Phillip's
time was the high-water mark of early race relations, and to some extent his
policies had a long-term effect on official dealings with the Aborigines. For
three years after his departure the officers of the New South Wales Corps
managed the settlement, but Aborigines continued to live at Sydney Cove.
Indeed, for a time, they seemed so easy-going that a few of the officers,
equivocal humanitarians, began to wonder whether they might be harnessed
to a form of slavery on the current American model.[52]

Government House was now, apparently, deserted, but Blacks camped in
the main street of the settlement without being disturbed. A party of
Spaniards who arrived by the *Descubierta* and the *Atrevida* in 1793 were

impressed with the open-handed way in which the natives were treated by some of the British officers. While guests at dinner, for instance, the travellers were occasionally startled to find themselves in the company of Aborigines, both men and women, who had been brought in, 'although entirely naked and disgustingly dirty', to be 'regaled with one or other dainty from the same Table'. It is likely that the officer responsible in this case was John Macarthur, then a lieutenant in the Corps, who continued to ask Aborigines to his table for many years. During a vivid episode in 1817–18, for instance, two men emerged from the bush to see Macarthur at dinner time. They were seated and given wine, and one of them made a short speech – a remarkably eloquent one, as Macarthur's son recalled – in which he complimented the master of the house.[53]

Unlike Phillip, Macarthur was moved partly by a love of the sensational. Besides, he was married and the presence of women and children in families like his no doubt inhibited the movements of unclothed Black men. Elizabeth Macarthur may well have been more restrained than her husband in such matters, and yet their farm at Parramatta became a common resort for the Aborigines. One man, whom the Macarthurs called Bill, died from spear wounds in their care, his last words including a farewell for Mrs Macarthur.[54] As Chapter 14 shows, John Macarthur was a considerable visionary in the European uses of power in Australia. His attempts to mediate boundaries of race were part of his own brand of idealism.

There were other signs of cooperation between Europeans and Aborigines. With the growth of local fishing and sealing, Aborigines went to sea. They are said to have been properly paid, and they adopted the habits of their workmates, swearing, smoking and drinking like European seamen. Also, one Aboriginal man was allocated four acres on the outskirts of settlement which he planted with maize.[55] Nevertheless, hatred gradually became the prevailing sentiment between Black and White. Uneducated Europeans, including the convicts, were not much interested in grand projects in humanity, and on the whole their own dealings with the Aborigines were differently directed. Besides, the expansion of settlement brought home to Aborigines themselves the ghastly momentum of invasion. As more and more convicts were freed and settled on remote farms, it was no longer possible for race relations to be as well managed as the Governor might have liked. Aborigines began the wholesale theft of corn, the burning of crops and the destruction of other European property, and farmers learnt to organise themselves in savage retaliation.

It is impossible to know how long the image of Phillip which had formed in the mind of Bennelong and his followers survived the Governor's departure. Among much later generations, both of Aborigines and of Europeans, Phillip was to be confused with the discoverer, Captain Cook (just as, among the English in England, several real figures probably exist within the remembered personality of King Arthur). The first Governor came to represent for Aborigines not an Ancestor but the inversion of life. There was a recognition too that the written word was death: an alien knowledge, a rising and relentless sea. 'And Captain Cook went longa Sydney Harbour', explained Hobbles Danayari, of the Northern Territory, nearly two centuries after Phillip's arrival, 'and people been live over there. And why didn't you ask them? You, Captain Cook, when you came through.' Invasion meant death: 'Captain Cook been shooting there for, I think, nearly three weeks time. Shooting all, all the people. Women get shot, kids been get knocked out.' And it meant the triumph of writing over ancient voices, with all that that implied for sacredness and order: 'Him been bringa lotta book . . . from Big England right here now. They got that book for Captain Cook from England. And that's his law. . . . Not only one book, book all over. And he still got it today.'[56]

In 1797 the first of a number of attempts was made to use the law as a means of governing relations between Europeans and Aborigines. The initiative came, presumably, from Governor Hunter, and it was founded on the understanding (which not everyone shared) that Aborigines were under the full protection of the law. In October, William Millar was charged with murdering an Aboriginal man known as Tom Rowley (the name proves a connection with Captain Thomas Rowley of the Corps), and Thomas Bevan was charged with aiding and abetting. The crime took place on the north shore of the harbour, and the only witnesses seem to have been other Aborigines. The court decided that such evidence was inadmissible and the two were acquitted. It was a fundamental rule in English courts that witnesses could be heard only if they understood the risk of divine retribution should they vary from the truth. Men and women who were Christians were assumed to know it, but even the children of Christians were suspect. A little girl, Mary Cole, was heard before the Criminal Court about this time: she understood, she said, that if she lied, 'God Almighty will hate her, but if she tells the truth he will love her.' A boy, Patrick Silk, on the other hand, at ten years of age, admitted to the court that he knew nothing of oaths and his evidence was refused.[57]

In February 1799 Thomas Hewitt was charged with having shot and killed Willi Cuthie. In this case the Judge-Advocate, William Dore, seems to have invited the wife of the murdered man to appear as prosecutor, but only for formality's sake because the same obstacle immediately appeared. She was 'incapacitated from giving such testimony as could be admissable in law to affect the life of the prisoner'. However Dore was clearly anxious not to let Hewitt escape, and he was charged instead with being 'an incorrigible rogue and vagabond' and sentenced to three hundred lashes, to be inflicted 'at a time when the greatest number of natives can be assembled together to witness the punishment'. The sentence also included twelve months in a gaol gang.[58] In September a more momentous case came on. Following the murder of two farmers by Aborigines, some of their victims' neighbours took revenge by tying up, stabbing and shooting some Aboriginal boys who lived with them. Two of the boys were killed, and five Europeans were tried for murder (see Chapter 9). This time there were European witnesses and the culprits were found guilty, but now another problem arose. The members of the court could not agree that the Aborigines were strictly entitled to the full protection of the law, a point which affected the punishment of the murderers. In no official document were they described as subjects of the King, and all the cases so far had been based on mere assumption. The minority of the officers on the bench, who were naval men, voted to flog the offenders and let them go. But the remainder, members of the New South Wales Corps, insisted on referring the case to Whitehall.[59]

By this time the Corps was involved in the regular policing of the frontier. It may be that their officers genuinely wanted to know whether the Aborigines were aliens or fellow subjects, but no doubt they also realised that referral home meant no punishment at all. The answer, as it turned out, was noncommittal. Nevertheless, the Governor (Philip Gidley King) made the most of it. He immediately issued a proclamation to the effect that the Aborigines would henceforth be protected by law against 'any . . . injustice or wanton Cruelty'. They were not (apparently) British subjects but, he announced, from now on they would be treated precisely as if they were. In other rules issued about the same time for the informations of ships' crews entering the harbour, he declared, in less ambiguous terms, that 'If any of the Natives are killed, or Violence offered to their Women, the Offenders will be tried for their Lives.'[60]

King had his proclamation read and explained to numbers of Aborigines. While it promised them protection against 'Injustice or wanton Cruelty' it also stated that settlers would be justified in doing whatever was necessary to prevent their own property being 'invaded' and themselves killed. The Governor was confident that both sides now understood their rights. The Aborigines, he told the Secretary of State, had 'paid great attention' to the proclamation. Some had since complained to the magistrates about offending Europeans instead of using violence themselves, and had been 'well satisfied' with the result.[61] In fact, the situation was not so straightforward. For some years Aborigines within the areas of settlement had been fighting under the leadership of Pemulwuy, one of the Bediagal people from Botany Bay. Some Blacks, certainly, refused to follow him, but Pemulwuy's influence, reaching as it did over at least two language groups, the Dharawal and the Dharug, suggests that the Aborigines had found new methods of authority to cope with the new emergency that faced them. Pemulwuy was a man of dramatic courage, and the gentlemen of the settlement showed him a grudging admiration. He too became a subject for their humanity. In a brief pitched battle near Parramatta in March 1797 he was wounded in the head and body with buckshot, and after his people had been beaten off he was carried to the hospital. He was kept in irons while he recovered, but he got away with the shackle on his leg.[62]

Pemulwuy's recovery and escape gave him added charisma among his people. The credit for his survival belonged to European medicine, but the

magic seems to have been transferred in local imagination to the man himself. From this time his followers believed that he was proof against bullets,
and he became even more active, so that, by common report at least, he
headed every party in the attack on crops and farmhouses. Finally, in spring
1802, not long after King's proclamation, he was shot and killed. At the
request of the peace party among the Aborigines, his head was cut off and
sent as a trophy to the Governor.[63]

Several years of extreme violence left the policy of humanity badly com-
promised and the implications of invasion wholly exposed. King was
pleased with the effect of his proclamation, but following more trouble in
1805, with violence coming from both sides, he consulted the Judge-
Advocate (now Richard Atkins) on the possibility of charging Aborigines
for criminal offences. In his answer, Atkins drew attention to the technical
difficulties which must follow from offering equal protection under the law
to Black and White. Fundamental to his answer was the idea that the
Aborigines were, as he put it, 'Persons not bound by any moral or religious
Tye'. This and their ignorance meant that whatever they said in court must
be worthless: 'The Natives are within the Pale of H.M. Protection; but how
can a Native, when brought to Trial, plead Guilty or not Guilty to an
Indictment, the meaning and tendency of which they must be totally ignorant of?' Besides, a common acquiescence in the truth depended on the
swearing of oaths, and they were not Christians. Nor could the rules be bent
for the sake of natural justice. Due process, especially in criminal trials, was
too sacred for that: 'Penal Laws cannot be stretched to answer a particular
exigency.'[64]

Atkins's logic was more sweeping than that which might have been used
by Dore, his predecessor. He was less interested in the Aborigines than were
some of the other officers and gentlemen in New South Wales, and his idea
that they were 'not bound by any moral or religious Tye' was not, or not
yet, the ruling orthodoxy. He might have been more at home in contemporary North America, where a rule had been long observed in some places
which banned men and women who were not Europeans from being heard
in court because (as it was said in Virginia) they were usually 'of such base
and corrupt principles, that their testimony cannot be depended upon' (see
Chapter 1). In spite of Atkins, this was not the principle so far used at Port
Jackson. Certainly Blacks and Whites who spoke with each other from day
to day exchanged a faulty currency: one of the first Aboriginal words to
enter Australian English was 'whanga', meaning 'liar'.[65] But in the courts
Aboriginal disqualification was on narrower and more technical grounds.
Nor did it apply to Blacks (West Indians and others) who had come with the
invaders (and who probably made up about one in a hundred of their number).[66] The attitudes of the high Enlightenment dictated that skin colour
should not be noticed for its own sake within the early colonial courts.

Moral ties among the Aborigines, and between Aborigines and
Europeans, had been evident to the interested European eye from the begin-

ning. Even now, in Governor King's time, there survived cross-currents of commitment. For instance, during Pemulwuy's rise to fame among the Europeans, his young son Tjedboro (or Tedbury) had been taken in by John Macarthur, presumably with the father's consent. Tjedboro's 'reclaiming' was an interesting experiment from Macarthur's point of view, but even as a boy he was fiercely independent. He was not above taking care of the Macarthur children and he became 'devotedly attached' (as one of the children later put it) to their father, whom he called 'Master', but in adolescence he went back to the bush. Thereafter he was drawn to visit the Macarthurs often, but he chose to live among his own.[67] At liberty, he won something of Pemulwuy's reputation among the Europeans. He leapt into notoriety in 1801–05 and again in 1809 – both times when Macarthur was out of the colony – although, unlike Pemulwuy, his sins seem to have been limited to a type of highway robbery backed up with 'diabolical' threats. He was jailed once, but let out when other Aborigines promised his reform. In 1810 he appeared before the Criminal Court as a victim of violence, when a young gentleman was tried in Sydney for shooting and wounding him. (As usual, the culprit was acquitted.) This injury was said to be the cause of Tjedboro's death not long after.[68]

The experiences of Tjedboro's short life neatly sum up the deep ambiguities which characterised the first dealings of Black and White. Exchange was at the heart of it all. A grateful silence was expected from the Aboriginal women. Nevertheless, conversation was born as soon as possible, in the surf at Botany Bay, and it was always there, shaping and moderating the mutual fear, the mutual fascination, the giving and the theft. The balance of power, however, had shifted, in the period between Phillip's equal exchange of names with Bennelong and the moment of Tjedboro's apparently happy understanding that Macarthur's name was 'Master'.

Chapter 9

God and Humanity

I

On 3 July 1784, at about nine in the morning, a wagon pulled up at the sign of the Three Cups in Bread Street, City of London. The landlord of the Three Cups managed the conveyance of goods around London, and among other things the wagon carried a leather portmanteau, or 'cloak bag', addressed to the Honourable Miss Boscawen, a middle-aged lady who was maid-of-honour to the Queen at St James's Palace. It contained three silk gowns, a silk skirt, two great coats and a number of waistcoats. During the afternoon, the landlord had it transferred to a cart for final delivery. The driver, John Wayte, made several calls on his way towards the West End, and in the process he attracted the attention of one Christopher Magee, alias Charles Williams, a young man apparently living by his wits. Magee managed to snatch the portmanteau while the cart passed through Fleet Market and dashed away with it, nearly knocking over a child as he went. It was a daring and foolish theft, perfectly visible in the summer twilight. Besides, Magee ran no further than a nearby alehouse, the Artichoke, where he stuffed the portmanteau under a seat. Wayte's back had been turned, but, as he later recalled, a nearby shopkeeper '*subscribed* the man' to him, and they both went to look for him at the Artichoke. On being cornered, Magee demanded, 'can any body swear I stole it out of the cart[?]'.

The judge at the Old Bailey four days later had no problem finding sufficient evidence on that point. Nor did His Honour spend much time on Magee's explanation – 'A gentleman asked me to carry this portmanteau for him into Smithfield, to the Ram, and he would give me sixpence' – before sentencing him to seven years' transportation.[1]

Although a foolhardy man, Magee, or Williams, as he was usually known on this continent, was one of the more unusual characters in very early New South Wales. Only twenty-two years old in 1784, he had already been transported, or so it seems, among the last shipments of convicts before the

American Revolution. Certainly he had spent his adolescence in the North American colonies and had there, or perhaps on shipboard, imbibed strange notions of morality and religion. He was wayward without being vicious. He knew how to behave well, when he liked, but the things he said among his fellow convicts gave him the reputation of a man whose soul was at war with its Maker. In August 1788 he was married at Sydney Cove to Eleanor McCabe, a woman who had given trouble on the First Fleet. In April 1791 the two began to clear some ground at Parramatta, which Williams received as a grant when his term expired in July. There he was neighbour to James Ruse and to three former seamen from the *Sirius*. (He seems to have liked seamen.) He and his wife worked hard, and within six months he had very promising crops of wheat, maize and tobacco. He had done well, he said, 'by industry, and by hiring all the convicts I could get to work in their leisure hours, besides some little assistance which the governor has occasionally thrown in'. He hoped to grow tobacco in a big way, inspired no doubt by the plantations he had seen in North America.[2]

However, during 1792 both man and wife seem to have changed their habits for the worse. In the springtime (by his own account) Williams was visited at night by an acquaintance, Richard Sutton, one of the boat crew, who got him out of bed and told him to come with him into the bush. When they reached a secluded spot Sutton said to him, 'Now you Buggar, will you stand firm[?]'. Williams asked what for, and Sutton replied, pirate-like, 'suppose it was for Gold and Silver[?]' Williams hesitated, but he agreed to meet Sutton again next day. At their second meeting Sutton told him that he would swear him. '[He] drew a knife, and telling him he would not hurt him, swearing by some saint, he cut himself and him in the face, drawing blood, and swearing him never to divulge what [it] was he told him.' Presumably Sutton mingled the blood to make sure of Williams's fidelity. He then brought from the undergrowth a watch, which he said was gold, and a pair of knee-buckles encrusted with what he said were diamonds, which he wanted Williams to sell to one of the gentlemen of the garrison.

Sutton told a different story. Among other things, Williams, he said, sought him out, among the boatcrew. He 'made him drink,' he said, 'and asked him to get him water, . . . he went with him to a Place where there was water, and . . . Williams in a drunken Bravado cut himself, and swore no man could have him; that he would be Boatswain's Mate in Hell, and a good deal of such Blackguardism'. (Boatswain's mates were men chosen for agility and fierceness, who dealt out casual beatings with knotted ropes on behalf of the boatswain.) Whatever the exact truth of Sutton's account, on examining the loot Willams seems to have realised that his friend was deluded about its value (the 'diamonds' were paste), and seeing no advantage for himself he gave it up to a member of the night-watch.[3] Sutton was tried for theft, but he produced an alibi and, on top of that, a gentleman offered disturbing evidence about Williams, to the effect that he had lately been heard to say 'that he did not consider an Oath as binding'. This might have freed him from his obligation to Sutton, but it also cast doubt on his value as a sworn witness. Indeed, he had put himself even further beyond the pale by stating, according to this witness, that 'he was not of any Religion at all, but that of the Cock and Hens'.[4]

According to the Judge-Advocate, Williams left the court 'much degraded in the opinion of every man who heard him'.[5] Was he degraded because he had betrayed a friend, or was he degraded because he denied the transcendant faith expected of all decent Englishmen? What was the religion of the cock and hens? It seems likely that Williams subscribed to a rough type of deism, or atheism, long popular among those of the poor (especially seamen) who were sceptical of the great orthodoxies of the age. It was a set of beliefs which left no room for divine revelation or for miracles of any kind, which denied the immortality and even the existence of the soul, and which made Christian teaching about sin, judgment and redemption nothing but a fraud practised by the rich upon the poor.[6] Here there was no firm foundation for promises.

By this teaching, the real requirements of humanity were few, no more than those of the cock and the hens. One need only scratch a living from the soil, eat and drink, enjoy the company of one's fellow creatures, fight when necessary, and perpetuate the species. Sergeant-Major Thomas Whittle, of the New South Wales Corps (illiterate, like Williams), made the same point when he corrected the swearing of his fellow soldiers. They should not say 'Damn my soul!', for they had no souls: they must 'damn their gizzards' instead.[7] These, perhaps, were the principles which governed the Williams household at Parramatta. It was a creed more boldly articulated by men than by women, and Williams probably liked to think that under the aegis of this anti-theology he ruled the roost at home. After the first months of hard work he and his wife had turned to drinking and arguing, but some bond continued between them nevertheless. On 21 January 1793 they, their year-old baby girl and a second woman were returning by water from Sydney to Parramatta, arguing as usual – Williams was presumably at the oars – when their boat capsized. Williams got the baby ashore, half-dead, but Eleanor, who was heavily pregnant, and the other woman sank like two stones. None of the females survived, and Williams buried his wife and child near the door of his house. He went on drinking with Eleanor nevertheless, pouring her share on her grave, 'declaring how well she had loved it during her life'.[8] Nothing was certain, nothing was immortal, but appetite.

Williams decided to sell his farm. He and Ruse made this move together, and together they agreed (presumably with the acquiescence of Ruse's wife, Elizabeth) to move to the remote edge of civilisation, to the valley of the Hawkesbury, where they took up land side by side. The two men were obviously friends. They had spent nine or ten months on the same First Fleet vessel, *Scarborough*. Williams had followed Ruse to Parramatta when that was the perimeter of settlement, and they now persuaded each other to take an even more dramatic step. The Hawkesbury had been discovered by an expedition led by Governor Phillip in June 1789, and other visits had been made since. The margins of the river were rich alluvial flats, but it was a long way from either Sydney or Parramatta. There seems to have been no official plan for peopling it with Europeans before Williams, Ruse and a small number of others formed their own.

The dream of an alternative settlement in New South Wales, a settlement managed by the people, had been born before the First Fleet left England. It had its blueprint in Robinson Crusoe's island, in the real and fabled 'nests of pirates' at Madagascar, Sierra Leone and the Mosquito Shore, in the plans for Lemane and Das Voltas Bay, and in the imagination of many of the men and women who came by the First Fleet ships. Governor Phillip would not consider any settlement at all at the Hawkesbury without 'proper people' to manage it. However, methods of government were somewhat different after his departure, when the colony was run by the senior officers of the New South Wales Corps. Thus a settlement suddenly appeared in that remote spot, a mushroom growth, in January 1794. As Collins put it, Williams, Ruse and some others had been allowed to settle there: 'They chose for themselves allotments of ground conveniently situated for fresh water, and not much burdened with timber, beginning with much spirit, and forming to themselves very sanguine hopes of success.' They seem to have been free, as in the blueprint, to work out their own mutual boundaries, although the whole settlement was to be properly surveyed later in the year.[9]

The Hawkesbury people spent their first years revelling in their liberty and in the ease of their new life. Reports came back of 'a rich black mould of several feet depth' from which potatoes might be harvested within three months of sowing. Indeed, wrote the Acting Governor, 'whatever they have planted has grown in the greatest luxuriance'. During their second year, while everyone else was putting in their crop, according to David Collins, the settlers at the river did nothing, 'consuming their time and substance in drinking and rioting; and trusting to the extreme fertility of the soil, which they declared would produce an ample crop at any time without much labour'. Governor Hunter, on his arrival in September 1795, was appalled that such a community could exist virtually independent of headquarters. At his first attempt to assert his authority there, the reply came back, in no uncertain terms, 'that they did not care for the Governor or the Orders of the colony – they were free men, and wou'd do as they pleas'd'.[10]

Worst of all, a perverse Providence seemed for a time to reward their intransigence. By 1796 only the settlers on the Hawkesbury seemed to be getting anywhere with their farms, and yet they spent their time, as ever, 'immersed in intoxication'. Their numbers rapidly multiplied, and that corner of the world very shortly became a repository towards which most of the available alcohol flowed, and also a refuge for criminals. According to

Collins, 'the Hawkesbury settlers afforded [shelter] to every vagabond that asked it'.[11] It was indeed a nest of pirates.

David Collins made these remarks in his celebrated history of the colony, published in London in 1798. As Judge-Advocate he was well qualified to say who dwelt within, and who beyond, the bounds of orthodoxy in New South Wales. He was also the Governor's secretary, so that in his voice echoed the original spirit of the state, its transcendant means of judgment and its measured beneficence. And yet, strange to say, the private ideas of Collins himself resembled those of Williams, and the same scepticism appeared indeed among some other educated men in New South Wales. William Gore, for instance, who arrived in 1806 as Provost Marshal, seems to have avoided the Christian ceremonies of baptism and burial. He sanctioned neither in his own family and for many years (much later in the nineteenth century) his own coffined remains and those of his wife and daughter were to stand – exposed to the air and brushed, no doubt, by the brown antipodean grasses – on trestles in a back paddock at Artarmon, his property on Sydney's North Shore.[12]

Such men, of whatever rank in life, were sceptics, though for varying reasons. The imagination of David Collins allowed a little room to all processes of thought. His account of the Aborigines in Van Diemen's Land in 1804 – 'We have every reason to believe them to be Cannibals, and they may entertain the same Opinion of us' – was symptomatic of a mind undisciplined by notions of cultural superiority.[13] Like Charles Williams, Collins understood that Christian faith was a medium of social control; but unlike Williams, he saw a state Church as utterly necessary. Unlike William Gore, he did not ostentatiously avoid it. The story Collins told of the early years reveals almost no inkling of religious faith. A dark thread runs through his narrative, an interest in death, and in humanity as the plaything of an irresponsible Providence. In 1794, for instance, he described the colony as 'doomed to be the sport of contingency'. It struggled, he said, against a pernicious combination, 'the dangers of the sea' and 'the jarring interests of men'. He delighted in stories such as that of Richard Burton, a botanist who had been sent out to Port Jackson by Sir Joseph Banks, and who had experienced presentiments of death before going to shoot ducks. His gun accidentally went off without hurting him, which made him think the danger past. But he was wrong and soon shot himself very effectively. Collins also took a morbid interest in the drowning of Williams's wife, Eleanor. His story records the fact that in her drunkenness she had cursed herself and her unborn child just as she stepped into the boat, drawing fate about her, as it were, like a leaden blanket.[14] In Collins's universe, haphazard curses were more interesting than prayers.

Appetite might be the rock on which people like Williams founded their faith. Collins was more sophisticated, and as an officer and gentleman it is not surprising that among the chaos of circumstance he put his trust in the rigid exercise of authority. Ultimate power belonged to Providence. It might be worth guessing about the discretion of the Almighty by looking out for omens, but these were clearly unreliable. Much then depended on human authority, on a settled hierarchy and on strong men within it, like Phillip. In his book, Collins cited only two texts from the Bible: 'There is but a step between me and death', and 'By me kings reign.' The 'madness' of the Hawkesbury settlers upset him profoundly because they seemed to align themselves with chaos. They danced at the edge of death by putting themselves, as he remarked, 'above all restrictions'.[15]

In fact the people at the river found a type of order among themselves. Not only Williams and Ruse, but four other pioneers had come out together on the *Scarborough*. Three more men among the first settlers had come on the *Friendship* and two on the *Alexander*. The women and the rest of the men had scattered origins. There was one well-publicised quarrel among them, during the winter of 1795. Mary Pawson and Mary Mandeville, or Butler, lived with their men on adjoining farms. Mary Pawson harboured some deep resentment against her neighbour – they had come together from Ireland by the *Queen* – and when the other's hut burnt down in the middle of the night, she was blamed. The Court of Criminal Judicature found no useful evidence, although a conversation between the two a few weeks earlier had ended with Pawson clapping her hands and remarking, 'You bloody, bloody Whore, before this Day Month I will give you a Warm Arse.' She was acquitted, but her neighbours banished her nevertheless: 'the husband . . . sold a very good farm . . . and withdrew to another situation, remote and less advantageous'.[16]

Such events must have reinforced the community that remained, although by this time it was a very considerable one. James Ruse seems to have made himself a master of ceremonies for some among them, and in due course he too was summonsed to appear in Sydney, charged with having gathered together, at various times, 'at his dwelling House and Barns and outhouses great numbers of disorderly persons', thereby encouraging them 'to gamble and Illegally Squander away their property'.[17] The trial seems to have been abandoned at the last minute, possibly for the very good reason that although squandering was wicked, and might even seem diabolical, it was not illegal.

The authorities in Sydney made another attempted assault on the Hawkesbury people in 1799. The murder of two Aboriginal boys mentioned in the previous chapter took place on the Hawkesbury. Some of the original settlers at the river were implicated in the deed, but the leading man was Edward Powell, a farmer and constable who had been a seaman. He had come late in the piece. This episode shows once again the solidarity of the Hawkesbury people, because the killing was a deliberate act of revenge for the deaths of two of their neighbours, the widow of one – 'a worthy good fellow' – having announced beforehand that Aborigines must die. It was a matter of inevitable judgment issued against a people whose complexions demonstrated clearly enough that they were beyond the edge of Christendom. In this age it seemed right that all questions of justice, on earth as in heaven, should depend on ceremony. A settled magic transformed revenge into righteousness. Just as the Almighty seated in splendour separated thunder from lightning, the wicked from the just, so one of the murderers had planned a mock trial for the Aborigines he caught: 'What sentence shall we pass upon these black Fellows – I will pass sentence myself – they shall be hanged.'[18] They were, however, stabbed and shot in an unceremonial frenzy.

The trial of the murderers themselves was a formal one, but in spite of conviction they went back unpunished to the Hawkesbury. Questions of right and wrong which seemed simple enough on the frontiers of settlement were much more difficult from the perspective of the empire at large.

II

Throughout the British empire in the eighteenth-century, as we have seen in earlier chapters – and throughout Europe – there were two worlds, two types of sensibility, one nourished by writing and the other by living conversation. Each had its own habits of thought and means of judgment. For educated men and women, much seemed to depend on extending their own reach beyond the dividing frontier. Left alone, the world of living speech was not only dangerous but an indictment on the other. This was part of the reason for David Collins's resentment of the very existence of the community on the Hawkesbury, and there were other gentlemen in New South Wales more devout than he was who thought in the same way.

An Englishmen, unnamed but of obvious respectability, tackled the broader issue in 1774, some years before European settlement began in Australia:

> I set before my imagination [he wrote] a ballad-singer, standing in the chief place of concourse, with a crowded audience round him, inflaming their appetites and passions, winning his way into their hearts, by means of music often too sweet, and raising at his will the various devils of unbridled lust, shameless lasciviousness, discontent, sedition, and malice: His hearers swallow with open mouth every sentence he utters, suck in the delicious poison, and go away to spread it among their neighbours, to speak evil of Dignities, to rail against their Sovereign, or to plunge in lewdness and debauchery.

This living conversation could not be stilled, at least not to begin with. However, so this author argued, it could be reformed to a better purpose. He put his faith in the power of the printed word. Educated men and women, he said, should collect and publish ballads which were not only far more moral but just as sweet. So they might hope to reshape the language of the poor.[19] This and similar projects were understood to be of fundamental significance, because language was not only a symptom of thought, but its very foundation. Language was held to determine ideas, at least as much as the other way around.

Such projects set the pace. An oral culture was to receive the imprint of a written one. It now seemed necessary to go down among the poor, to learn their language, to listen to their common conversation and, under the guidance of a higher civilisation, to work to do them good; just as one might do the same for Blacks. And what limits might there be within the fabric of a well-organised empire? The settlement of Georgia was a very early project of this kind, and there was a gathering of pace through the last decades of the century. Writing was the answer. This was precisely the attitude adopted by the Reverend Richard Johnson, the first clergyman in New South Wales, who arrived in 1788 and who was to go home, exhausted with the effort, twelve years later.

The Reverend Richard Johnson, a portrait drawn in 1787 shortly before his departure to be the first minister of religion in New South Wales.

Source: Mitchell Library, State Library of New South Wales

Johnson was accompanied on the First Fleet by more than a thousand eternal souls. He brought with him as well 4262 books and pamphlets, supplied by the Society for Promoting Christian Knowledge, one of the leading evangelical societies of the Church of England. Most of these publications were multiple copies, and there were only fifty-one different titles. All the same, it was a very substantial public library and, at least in terms of quantity, it was remarkable evidence of European civilisation suddenly transferred to the Antipodes. Fifteen titles came in very small numbers, no more than six or a dozen each, and were obviously meant for the guidance of the minister and any future assistants, and perhaps for circulation among the officers of the garrison. They included one copy of the Reverend James Talbot's book, *The Christian Schoolmaster*, and twelve of Bishop Wilson's *Essay Towards an Instruction for the Indians*, presumably meant as a first step towards enlightening the entire continent. For distribution among the people, there were 500 Bibles and testaments, 500 Church of England psalters and 600 copies (500 of them broadsheet and 100 bound) of the Reverend Dr James Stonhouse's *Admonitions against Drunkenness, Swearing, and Sabbath-breaking*. There were also 200 copies of *An Exercise against Lying* and, for the garrison, 200 of *The Christian Soldier*. There were 100 each of *Most Important Truths and Duties of Christianity*, and of *Friendly Advice to a Patient* (both by Stonhouse), of the Reverend Stephen White's *Dissuasive from Stealing*, of William Burkitt's *An Help and Guide to Christian Families* and of another work called *An Exhortation to Chastity*. There were also some purely educational texts, including 100 spelling books (probably Henry Dixon's *The English Instructor*).[20]

Behind this gift to Australia was the belief that moral reform and eternal salvation would come through everyone reading. The aims of evangelism were total. The common language of the people was to be tackled and reshaped by exposing them to sermons and to daily advice, but most of all by the written word.[21] The great enemy, perhaps the greatest enemy of all, was swearing, as in Mary Pawson's 'You bloody, bloody Whore', because it proved the self-sufficiency of a squalid and corrupt culture, one engrimed in centuries of sin. The wickedness of swearing was the subject of Johnson's first sermon at sea in 1787, and he stressed it continually thereafter:

> Our Lord assures us, that for every idle word that men shall speak they shall give an account in the day of judgment! How dreadful then will be the case of those persons, who during their whole life have employed their tongues in cursing, swearing, lying, and all manner of vile and unclean conversation. Oh! think of this in time, and tremble and repent, and learn to use your tongues to better purpose in future!

They sinned by their living speech, and they would be both reformed and judged by the power of the written word:

I must and will tell you, that there is not a profane oath which you have uttered, not a lie which you have told, nor a sabbath which you have broken, nor a single act of adultery, fornication, theft, or any wickedness of which you have been guilty; in a word there is not an evil you have committed, nor a duty you have omitted to perform, but what is noted down in the book of God's remembrance, and will be produced against you in the day of judgment, unless you repent, and believe the gospel.

The response he asked of them was silence. They must pray quietly, they must listen well – for before God, '*I* must answer for my preaching, and *you* for your hearing' – and they must read. Prayer might be difficult at home, in the convicts' huts, amid 'those who ridicule and scoff at every appearance of religion'. In that case, he advised, 'Retire from them, and pray to him who seeth in secret.'[22] They must break the link of common conversation in order to speak directly to God.

But most of all, they must read. In 1792 Johnson wrote a two-part sermon which was printed and bound in London for distribution in New South Wales. We do not know how widely it was read in the colony, but it was shaped by several years of the minister's experience, of preaching and counselling among a peculiar congregation, and of watching the response. It was therefore born of Australian circumstances. Its appearance was the first occasion on which Europeans in Australia were invited – urged, in fact, as a matter of eternal life and death – to find their image on paper, against the background of their new home. Its publication was provoked, so Johnson told his readers, by their rapidly growing numbers, following the arrival of the Second and Third Fleets, and by the spread of settlement, which made it impossible, he said, 'either to preach, or to converse with you so freely, as my inclination and affection would prompt me to do'. But beyond this necessity the written word had its own value, its own authority. Talking about religion depended on the minister's movements, on his initiative rather than theirs. The process was ephemeral, whereas with books they could help themselves, and beyond that they could rely on something certain and unchanging, a part of their furniture and a part of their thoughts. They must, he said, 'read this plain, affectionate Address seriously. Read it a second, a third, and a fourth time, till your hearts are affected by it.'[23] That was the way forward.

Johnson was a vigorous preacher and a compassionate man, and he made an impact on the convicts and soldiers. His following among some of the women appears in Chapter 7. He was often disappointed: 'They prefer their Lust before their Souls, yea, most of them will sell their souls for a Glass of Grogg, so blind, so foolish, so hardened are they.' But this was because he aimed at nothing less than conversion, a complete change in habits. The great hope of the evangelicals was echoed in advice given to the Reverend Samuel Marsden, who came to join him in 1794: 'if . . . you take forth the precious from the vile you shall be as God's mouth'. Just as frequently

Johnson noticed small improvements, demonstrating hints of religious feeling among numbers of his people. For several days after his shipboard sermon on swearing, 'I . . . scarcely heard an oath from any of them.' After one of his efforts on dry land, 'one at least went away sorrowful and heavy-hearted, and some others rejoicing in the Son of God', while his first address to the women who came by the *Lady Juliana* drew tears from many. In October 1794 a sermon specially written for a man about to be hanged failed to make any obvious impression, and yet the victim was 'visibly touched' by the singing of a psalm: 'Purge me with hyssop, and I shall be clean: wash me, and I shall be whiter than snow. / Make me to hear joy and gladness; that the bones which thou hast broken may rejoice'.[24] In Phillip's time, although attendance at Sunday services was practically voluntary, between a quarter and half the convicts turned up, which could mean congregations of six or eight hundred at Sydney. On top of this, the minister travelled by demand to preach at places as remote as the Ponds and Prospect Hill, and he gave well attended 'private lectures' in his own house. On such occasions many were prepared to confide in him, complaining, for instance, that they could not pray at home in peace. Meanwhile, by 1794 he seems to have exhausted his supply of Bibles.[25]

On the other hand, there were certainly obstacles. From 1791, with the arrival of the Third Fleet, a considerable minority of the convicts were Catholics from Ireland, unfamiliar with the religious idiom of Protestant clergy. Even more difficult was the garrison, both officers and men. Soldiers in the late eighteenth century were not notably religious and, although several Marines officers – Ross, Dawes, Clark – had been friendly to Johnson, none was particularly devout. Among the New South Wales Corps there was a feeling which amounted to an active dislike for religion, or Johnson's type at least, even an organised desire to destroy it. For the soldiers of the Corps, the judgment of humanity depended on opinions born of their own garrison-commonwealth, a world of brotherhood. Personal antipathy soon flared up between the minister and the commanding officer, Major Grose, who gave a clear impression that he 'held Religion in Contempt'. However, Grose may have been more weak than irreligious (his own son was to be a clergyman) and Thomas Whittle, the sergeant-major mentioned above – who told his comrades not to swear by their souls – probably did more to shape the attitude of the men. The departure of Governor Phillip gave Whittle, who was then drum-major, the chance to make war on Johnson's evangelical efforts. Once, when the minister was about to take morning service with a congregation of soldiers and convicts, he heard Whittle tell the drummers to interrupt at a certain point by beating the call to parade. Johnson hurried through, reading only part of the service and dropping the hymns so as to leave time for his all-important sermon. But he was ambushed all the same. With the beating of the drums halfway through the sermon, 'the soldiers instantly got up, took their arms, fell into their ranks, and marched away'. Left with a scattering of convicts, 'I could not go on with my discourse, and therefore returned home, greatly distressed in my mind, at such barefaced profanity and infidelity.'[26]

The Hawkesbury people avoided religious discipline, and postponed judgment, by living a long way away. Johnson made regular visits to Parramatta, but there is no evidence of him visiting the Hawkesbury. He later recalled that the people of New South Wales were very conscientious in bringing in their children to be baptised: 'They were perhaps more regular than some parishes in England.' But this was not true of the Hawkesbury parents. James and Elizabeth Ruse, for instance, had children baptised in 1791, 1793 and 1794, but of the three or four born thereafter only one seems to have been brought to Johnson for admission to the Church. Other Hawkesbury families were equally remiss.[27]

Another obstacle was the lack of any building dedicated to worship. Phillip began one, but the structure was converted to another purpose, so that for five years Johnson's congregations had no settled place to meet, and sometimes no place at all. They were sometimes reduced to gathering within the hollow dug in the ground for the sawyers, which had had a roof built over it to keep off the sun. The indignity and uncertainty of accommodation was, as Private Easty (of the Marines) remarked, 'a thing much to be Lamented by a Searous mind'. Some of the gentlemen found it amusing, and when Johnson complained in their hearing they offered to turn 'the Lump' (the flat-bottomed boat which sailed between Sydney and Parramatta) upside down on top of posts; 'or, you shall have a *Centry Box* to stand in, or, well, *never mind Doctor* [a common term for ministers], *you will still buffett Satan in the saw pit*'.[28]

Despairing of government assistance, during June 1793 Johnson began to build of his own accord, using whatever resources and labour he could find. The result was ready for use in August. It was a remarkable building, considering the current state of settlement. The poor materials at hand and the minister's lack of architectural skill seem to have limited the roof-span to 20 feet (6 metres), but Johnson managed all the same to enclose a space of about 210 square metres, accommodating five or six hundred people. He did this by designing three long, thin naves, arranged in the form of a 'T' and meeting in an open space dominated by his reading desk. Even with this great achievement, there were still problems. He frequently had to put up with dogs and children playing between the pews, 'or persons talking, laughing, sleeping or otherwise behaving improperly'.[29] It may be that some of the congregation preferred the happy distractions of the open air.

It was now possible for most of the convicts at Sydney to come to church, and when Governor Hunter arrived in 1796 Johnson got him to make attendance compulsory (as it had been only in theory hitherto). Ideally, the minister liked to draw his congregation to him by the power of argument, but in New South Wales such ideals had often to be turned upside down. So

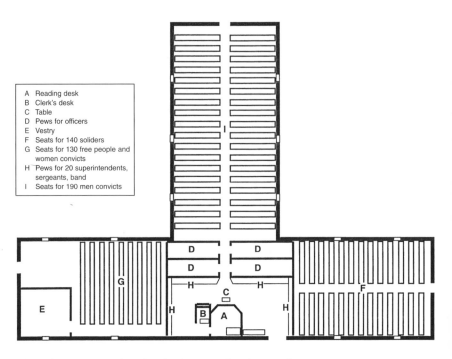

A   Reading desk
B   Clerk's desk
C   Table
D   Pews for officers
E   Vestry
F   Seats for 140 soliders
G   Seats for 130 free people and
     women convicts
H   Pews for 20 superintendents,
     sergeants, band
I   Seats for 190 men convicts

Plan of the Reverend Richard Johnson's church at Sydney

many of the people were, as he put it, 'totally destitute of all pious senti-ments' that they had to be forced to hear him. By the grace of God, horses thus brought to water might be persuaded to drink.[30]

This was the most ambitious scheme of compulsion Australia had so far seen, apart from transportation itself. Unlike forced labour, forced worship extended equally to men and women among the convicts. It reached to the edge of their freedom to make up their own minds, and in that way it promised a fabric of community, subjection and judgment more tightly drawn than any which might be designed by secular authority. Such rigour was perfectly consistent with the great evangelical effort which rode on the back of European settlement of Australia. Even in Hunter's time, however, success depended on the cooperation of the convict overseers. Besides, larg-er events intervened. On 2 October 1798, apparently moved by resentment at this remarkable invasion of their lives, a convict or convicts unnamed burnt Johnson's great building to the ground.[31]

Johnson also found that the books which he handed out to the people were not always used with piety and devotion. He noted sadly, 'One sold his Bible for a glass of liquor; others tear them up for waste paper.' Others again, as they themselves told him, had no time to read, to which he answered, 'You might find time, if you could find a will'; or else they could not read, and to that he said, 'you might prevail on some of your comrades to read to you'.[32] He was very anxious, however, that they should learn to read, and his great ambition was that they should teach each other on Sundays – 'I have often expressed my longing desire that such a plan was set on foot among you' – and he promised to help as far as he could. However, he had more success with schools for the children.[33]

III

Captain Cook discovered Australia. By the same token, Bennelong and his compatriot Yemmerrawannie, who both sailed with Phillip from Port Jackson in December 1792, discovered Europe. Geography is a profound science, and visits to new continents have a strange impact on one's ideas about existence. The Aborigines' view of the world had always been conditioned by their total isolation (modified in the far north by contact with islanders), and by their dependence on the vegetation about them, on familiar rivers, creeks and inlets, and on the soil they walked over. They were bound to believe that humanity consisted only of themselves and others like them, and that the coastal seas were the edge of reality. The land in which they found themselves was fundamental, in both a spiritual and physical sense, and therefore absolute. Their ideas about place – concrete and all-embracing – were at the bottom of all their ideas. Such thinking left no room for heaven or hell. Nor did it allow for a divine being embodying some sacred ideal, leading a separate existence and casting its shadow on a disparate and transitory creation.

A cosmology such as this is vulnerable to any hint that another world does in fact exist. That hint makes a chain of new ideas possible. New knowledge produces doubt and doubt produces adaptation. During the last three decades of the eighteenth century, the cosmology of the people who lived within reach of Port Jackson – first the Cadigal, but almost immediately others beyond – suffered a number of drastic shocks. The visit of Cook's *Endeavour* in 1770 must have affected them as it affected others along the east coast. As one new ceremonial song of the time put it: 'These strangers, where are they going? / Where are they trying to steer?' Awareness of people coming from, and departing to, a place beyond the water must have given the Aborigines a new sense of themselves. They were now an audience for events of an unprecedented character. The arrival of the two expeditions of January 1788 (the British under Phillip and the French under La Pérouse) must have confirmed this new self-image in a dramatic way. More was to come. The British settlement – cutting down trees, digging holes, building enclosures – posed large questions about Aborigines' relationship with increasingly large areas of terrain. Also, the great smallpox epidemic of 1789 killed enormous numbers. The wholesale destruction of families left a gap in the equation of land and people which must have cast serious doubt on the regenerating powers of the earth, hitherto taken for granted.[34]

At the same time, the Aborigines began to be acquainted with other ideas about the boundaries and foundation of existence. As Eleanor Dark puts it, 'the real world grew misty, dimmed by miracle, shaken by magic made visible'.[35] It seems likely that the heavens and the seas took on a new complexity for them. New questions met with new answers. By 1791, despite difficulties with language, 'every gentleman's house was . . . a resting or sleeping place for some of them every night'. Some of the Europeans began to interrogate their visitors by pointing to the sun, moon or clouds, as an officer recalled, 'to strike them with some idea of reverance [sic] – or, more properly, to see if they have any'.[36] Richard Johnson, in particular, pushed Aboriginal curiosity in certain directions. For a while he hoped to set up 'a school to instruct the natives', and he did what he could (which was very little) to stop them being infected by the conversation and habits of the convicts. He and his wife adopted an adolescent girl, Boorong, and within a year Johnson had begun to teach her to read, to say the Lord's Prayer, and to struggle with the idea of a Supreme Being. She and other Aboriginal children who lived from time to time in officers' houses were apparently happy to sit through Christian services. According to David Collins, 'I have often seen them take a book, and with much success imitate the clergyman in his manner.'[37]

What ideas did they pick up as well, and what explanations and arguments did they take back to their friends, about the tangible world and about the world beyond? Here is a question which embraces, sometimes on similar terms, not only the Aborigines but also the convicts, soldiers and seamen who were the bulk of Johnson's audience. Johnson certainly thought of the two parts of his 'parish', Black and White, as equally in need of redemption and, in many cases, equally ignorant. David Collins told a story which seems to prove such equality, although the White men in question were an extreme case. They were the boat crew and they had probably been seamen, the most superstitious of Englishmen: 'They had procured some shell-fish, and during the night were preparing to roast them, when they were observed by one of the natives, who shook his head and exclaimed, that the wind for which they were waiting would not rise if they roasted the fish.' The crew took no notice. The wind did in fact turn against them, and as a result they abused the man who had warned them, 'attributing to him the foul wind which detained them'. As another officer, Watkin Tench, put it, 'untaught, unaccommodated man, is the same in Pall Mall, as in the wilderness of New South Wales'.[38]

Richard Johnson was a clergyman of the Established Church, the Church of England, and his enthusiasm for questions of common morality and for preaching the Word meant that he belonged to the Church's Evangelical wing. The Methodists, who had originated with John Wesley in the 1740s, had not yet wholly broken away from the Church of England, and Johnson can be called a Methodist. His wife, Mary, as he once said himself, was half Methodist and half Baptist.[39] Among such people, distinctions of theology, ritual, social status and even race were not very important. Like all earnest Protestants, Johnson frowned on what he called the 'superstition and idolatory' of the Catholic Church, and yet he was remarkably kind to the Spanish priests who visited New South Wales with the Malaspina expedition in 1793. He liked to quote 1 Corinthians 2:2 ('For I determined not to know anything among you, save Jesus Christ, and him crucified'), and he believed that he benefited from the prayers of 'true Christians of every denomination'. With all he dealt on equal terms.[40]

Questions of social status were more sensitive. Johnson was a man of relatively humble origins, and he took seriously the fact that his military commission, as chaplain to the settlement, made obedience a duty. At the same time, he was able to muster up enough courage to reprimand the officers of the garrison, even in his published sermons, for 'unclean' living. 'The declaration of God, Thou shalt not commit adultery, is equally binding', he declared, 'upon persons of all ranks, to whom it is known, at all times, and in all places.' Statements like these offended what he called '*the delicate* feelings of some', including, perhaps, Major Grose.[41]

Johnson believed in the universal significance of the gospel, a vital point in shaping his work in Australia. For men and women like him, distinctions of geography made no difference, and all places were equally close to the Almighty. It was all the same, he said, whether 'Church or Meeting; a store house or Barn, a Cathedral or a Chapel'. He declined to attach any sacred significance to the great T-shaped edifice he built for worship at Sydney Cove. At its opening, he told his congregation that it was nothing but a shelter – 'there was holiness in every place' – and he made no attempt to dignify it with a saint's name, altar or pulpit.[42] Under this rubric the same everpresent holiness applied from continent to continent, whether on one side of the globe or the other, at Westminster or Toongabbie, just as, indeed, the power of the secular empire extended with increasing efficiency throughout the known world. These were well-established ideas among evangelicals, but they had to be more than ideas in Australia. The minister could make an impact on his audience only by persuading them of the truth of his own belief, that God was not embedded in the churches and cathedrals of England. Good Christians carried among them the Ark of the Covenant: there was something numinous within themselves, the means of a new discipline, and the Church was recreated, and a home made for their own souls, wherever they prayed together.[43]

The belief in 'One God, World without End' is a central tenet of the Christian Church. And yet, it is much easier for Europeans, as it is for anyone else, to believe in a God who lives in familiar places, who has his home in buildings sanctified and set apart, who blesses some nations rather than others, who favours certain kings and certain causes, and who is, at least, of a certain race, gender and complexion. Except in the matter of gender, the official creed of Christians warned against the enticements of such a being: a particular god shaped by the demands of language and place might be arbitrary and unpredictable, qualities inappropriate to any father, let alone an Almighty one. Nevertheless, as long as Europeans lived in a world without much geographical movement, at least beyond national boundaries, a world of living and dying conversation, the One God of the priesthood could not wholly prevail against this kind of local Providence. Place was an unyielding reality – as it was for the Aborigines – and God was mainly the god of place. However, the ocean traffic which evolved during the seventeenth and eighteenth centuries, and the conversations of pen and paper that went with it, created a wider world. Contact with alien peoples created God out of nothing for the Aborigines. For the Europeans in Australia, such contact expanded a residual sense of the Almighty, as the one, ubiquitous, abstract, all-encompassing, imperial 'I am.' Here too was a fatherly Providence, stern but merciful, whose inscrutable bounty offered a pattern for mortal rulers, such as their King or their Governor.[44]

The existence of Australia, beneath their own feet, proved to Europeans just how vast the world was, and also how profound the power of God (and the imagination of humanity) might be. As one of them exclaimed in verse in 1805, during an Australian thunderstorm:

> Now hark! The Voice of the Most High
> In awful accents rends the Sky:
> Earth trembles! Nature all in tears
> The Eye of Her Creator fears:
> Yet *some*, who feel his chast'ning rod
> Listen with transport to their God:
> Sure of *His* presence round the poles,
> When Thunder, as in England, rolls.[45]

An interest in big things, in mightiness of size or distance, and a feeling for the sublime were part of the fashionable sensibility of the day. The impact of such power was no doubt especially strong among educated travellers to the Antipodes, but perhaps it had a broad impact among all those inclined to think of themselves as subjects and created beings.[46]

A God who is equally everywhere complicates an understanding of heaven and hell. So did the idea of a world which was not only very big, but spherical. Here was a puzzle which dated back at least to the seventeenth century: 'if they whose feet are towards us, / At the lower part of the world have heaven too / Beyond their heads, where's hell?'[47] Damnation remained, nevertheless, an idea in common currency. When an officer of the garrison at Sydney Cove described the convict women as 'damned whores' and 'damned bitches', the adjective was more than an empty ejaculation. These were women who had, apparently, betrayed their own souls and set their faces against salvation, quite as much as men like Charles Williams had done. Very different were the prospects which Christianity held out for that 'dear Heavenly woman', the same officer's wife, and their two-year-old son, 'my dear heavenly Boy'.[48]

Obvious difficulties notwithstanding, Richard Johnson had a keen sense of the geography of the hereafter. Hell, he informed his congregation at Sydney Cove, was 'the most gloomy and dreadful [place] that can be conceived'. It promised 'the torment of devils, and of all impenitent sinners, for ever and ever': 'May backsliders from God be reclaimed! May every one be stirred up to consider, What will become of him in another world! For who amongst us can dwell with everlasting burnings? Yet such *must* be our lot, unless we repent.' This was an image which affected even David Collins, who was shocked, for instance, at the sight of a convict defiant at the gallows, going, as Collins put it, 'unprepared before his Maker'.[49]

Heaven was equally real. Johnson's vision in this case was of a place which offered 'every thing that an immortal soul can want or desire to make it happy'. There, in 'those happy and holy mansions', we 'live with God, with angels, and glorified saints'. However confusing terrestial geography might be, the destination of the just was certain. Convicts who had left pious relatives at home and who turned to God in the Antipodes might be sure, the chaplain said, of seeing their loved ones hereafter. And, in view of the spiritual divorce, the uprooting of souls from their native land which was central to the whole process of transportation, such advice might well have been a means of fundamental comfort. Johnson himself knew that he would be with his English friends again, if not on earth, then in 'a better world when we shall part no more for ever'.[50]

Johnson, like many of his generation, also believed that the end of the world itself was not far off. He conveyed this urgent message to the convicts, and to those Aborigines who were listening in:

> the Lord Jesus [he said] will shortly appear in the clouds of heaven, the last trumpet shall sound, the graves shall open, the sea give up her dead, and all who have lived upon the earth, from the creation to the final consummation of time, will then be judged, and rewarded or punished according to their works.

This was something which he thought they might well see within their own lifetime, and he gave a vivid description of the way in which those men and women – including some among his listeners – who had sinned together at Port Jackson might be 'companions in misery' on the Final Day. On the other hand, attentive and penitent convicts, 'however obscured and reproached on earth', would find themselves 'standing before the throne, clothed in white robes, with palm branches (the emblems of victory) in their hands, and singing to their harps their Redeemer's praise'.[51] All this, he said, could happen *soon*.

The Aborigines were undoubtedly affected by this news, although they absorbed it in their own way. Events since Cook's visit must have made them eager to know about worlds beyond Australia, of whatever dimension. Bennelong's visit to England (Yemmerrawannie had died there) might well have encouraged him, and others as well, to think that his native soil and the life he lived on it were now contingent on some greater whole, some new absolute. These lines from the nineteenth-century American poet Emily Dickinson may hint at his experience:

> Exultation is the going
> Of an inland soul to sea,
> Past the houses – past the headlands –
> Into deep Eternity –
>
> Bred as we, among the mountains,
> Can the sailor understand
> The divine intoxication
> Of the first league out from land?[52]

Bennelong came back to Australia determined that he would reshape his people towards a utopian ideal: 'he should no longer suffer them' he said, 'to fight and cut each other's throats, as they had done; . . . he should introduce peace among them, and make them love each other'.[53] David Collins talked to him in an effort to compare European and Aboriginal ideas about the hereafter. Bennelong now knew England, and Collins asked him whether he thought his own people might also have their origin in an island somewhere. 'His answer was, that he knew of none: they came from the clouds . . . and when they died they returned to the clouds.' This reply was at odds with traditional Aboriginal thinking about the birth of souls and spirits and the timeless anchoring of individuals to certain places, and it must surely have been shaped by Bennelong's experience of the Europeans and his time abroad. Most of the local people now agreed with it, but some had decided that after death 'they went either on or beyond the great water'.[54] Bennelong knew better than that, having sailed on the water himself.

Bennelong also had some ideas about the particular joys of paradise. He explained to Collins that the souls of the dead 'ascended in the shape of little children, first hovering in the tops and in the branches of trees'. There, or at some point beyond, they feasted upon little fishes. Collins, a sceptic in all things, thought this a perfectly ridiculous idea, but no more so, he remarked, than the belief cherished among 'some of us' (including Richard Johnson) about the resurrection of the body at the Last Day. 'The savage here treads close upon the footsteps of the Christian.'[55]

The Christians themselves had a range of ideas about their own immortality and about the hereafter. They shared a pattern of belief which had evolved very gradually, the product of centuries. Some, and they were not necessarily the most tractable and docile, were deeply impressed with the possibility of judgment such as Johnson described. John Macentire was a man of great size and strength, a former north-country highwayman, who became a good bushman in New South Wales and was employed shooting game. He made his own way in the world and was not much trusted, either by Europeans or Aborigines. He was fatally speared, by Pemulwuy, in

December 1790. Isolated in life by his own behaviour, his initial fear was of dying in the bush, cut off from the little companionship that Sydney Cove could give him. Paradise aside, he struggled against the wretchedness of 'dying in a ditch', a proverbial source of terror for poor men and women. However, having been carried back to the settlement, his thoughts turned instead to the prospect of being abandoned for eternity. On being told there was no hope of recovery, he 'began to utter the most dreadful exclamations, and to accuse himself of crimes of the deepest dye; accompanied with such expressions of his despair of God's mercy, as are too terrible to repeat'.[56]

Other dying men and women were more optimistic, but their hopes of the hereafter were not necessarily based on an officially sanctioned Christian faith. Many must have followed the example of a convict in Newgate Gaol who is said to have looked forward to the gallows merely with the idea, as he put it, that 'I am going from a Life of Trouble and Noise and Confusion, to a World of Quiet.' This was an old hope among the English poor: it had helped to shape the thinking of some of the radical sects during the seventeenth-century civil wars. Bound up with such a prospect was the hope of being cherished in the immediate aftermath of death by one's friends and relations, of eternal sleep in a familiar place. It was a hazardous hope when death happened on the wrong side of the world. Here, however, the ubiquitous God might intervene. Another man, Samuel Peyton, hanged at Port Jackson in 1788, spoke of leaving 'this vale of wretchedness, to enter into an unknown and endless eternity'. Peyton, 'a very pale faced young man' and an inveterate thief, saw the promises of Richard Johnson as a highway to 'the world to come . . . [in which] I shall yet experience that peace, which this world cannot give'.[57]

Others again thought of a different kind of triumph, and for them the authorised version of heaven was much too passive. Instead of endless suffering or endless singing, they looked forward to forging a special relationship with the Almighty, or whomever else they might find in charge. Mary Green, a woman in Newgate Gaol, wrote as follows to her victim, a lady of influence (and her godmother), in a last attempt to escape hanging: 'when my soul has got rid of my body, and happens into the hands of a kind keeper, I will tire him with my prayers, till he lets me loose to haunt you at your sunday evenings diversions. I will, d[am]n my e[ye]s if I don't, unless you get me my pardon.' Hell too might be a useful place. In New South Wales, Mary McDonough cursed at the funeral of her husband's betrayer, William Howarth: 'she hoped the bloody devil would fly away with his bloody soul before he got to the bloody church. . . . her bloody husband had not half the attendance of that bloody informer'.[58] For his part, Charles Williams apparently contemplated (when he was drunk) being 'boatswain's mate in hell', as if the glorious disorder of a seaman's life could be carried on for ever in some stormy underworld.

It is not clear what European men and women, newly settled in Australia, thought about the location of heaven and hell, but much must have depended on their understanding of the geography of the earth itself. Probably the most ignorant had no clear sense of the earth as a sphere, and no knowledge of the distance which divided one place from another on its surface. Escaped convicts who went north from Port Jackson looking for China had some true sense of direction. But in spite of the time they had taken to sail from England, they seem to have resisted any notion of the vastness of the world. China, or some other place inhabited by 'copper coloured people', they thought was 150 miles away, about as far as Bristol was from London, or Dublin from Cork: about a fortnight on foot.[59] For such people, heaven might have been just as it had been in Europe, a visible, tangible, level domain just above the clouds, fixed in eternal balance with hell beneath their feet.

For others, the very experience of sailing half-way around the earth must have offered a new challenge to the imagination. On the one hand, the universal power of God may have become a sustaining link between the two hemispheres and between the two phases of their existence, offering a type of spiritual continuity just as Johnson said it should. God now rose, very persuasively, beyond restrictions of place.[60] On the other hand, heaven and hell, in so far as they were places like any other, might have assumed a feebler significance. They did not fit well into the newly understood universe, and for some they must have seemed less substantial than before. Many of the English poor believed, as Johnson did, that the Second Coming was imminent, that the velvet canopy of the sky would soon be torn open for the final drama, a cataclysm that would merge heaven and earth.[61] Could that drama be played out on a spherical stage?

In a curious way, Richard Johnson's preaching reversed the common significance of place and time. He argued that, under God, all places were, like all souls, of equal value. As the Evangelical hymn put it, 'In Christ there is no east or west, / In Him no south or north.' One could worship anywhere, and one could find redemption at Sydney Cove as easily as one could find it in the oldest church in Christendom. However, some times were much more precious than others. The Sabbath was to be set aside for sacred purposes, and, even more important, the Day of Judgment was the Day towards which all lives were to be directed. Preaching directly from the Word tended to focus listening souls on imminence, on a future soon to be unveiled.[62] These priorities were at odds not only with the Aboriginal understanding of place and time, but also with the traditional understanding of most uneducated Europeans.

And yet, it may be that Johnson's priorities were in keeping with the new order of things in Australia. Souls need settled habitations, and both the Aborigines at Port Jackson and the convicts had been forced away from places they knew as their own. In that sense, arguments about territory were already over as far as they were concerned. But arguments about the possesion of time were another matter. Who would enjoy the future? The convicts learnt very effectively to measure the time within their own lives which had been taken over by government, an empty, wasted time, and to separate it from the blessed time which would be their own, even before they died. Johnson tried to persuade them that, even as free people, their Sundays still belonged to God, and he also asked them to think that, however they might suffer in life, they could hope for victory in death. The conquered would conquer. The Last Day would mark a revolution in humanity which would make earthly revolutions look tame.[63]

For many Australian generations to come, indeed, there was to be a tangled fabric of claims on time, and on the shape it might be given. What (and whose) was the jewel, the last nugget of all, which change must uncover? Eternal happiness? Moral reform on earth and the redemption of the nation? Material progress? Expanding liberty? One's own republic? Even William Gore, lying on trestles in his paddock at Artarmon, was presumably waiting for something. If God was not a god of place, he must be a god of time, an elusive Providence, a vacancy in the present but a sweet certainty for the future.

PART 3

Putting Themselves

Biriwilg (As Told by Women)

As told by Gararu, Gunwinggu language, to Catherine Berndt in 1950.[1]

Biriwilg set off, coming and camping on the way, looking for honey and meats and vegetable foods. She came to Wiridjeng, where she met Ngalmoban, who was carrying *man-gindjeg*, bitter yams, and asked her, 'Where shall we go?' Ngalmoban said, 'We'll go this way, north, in search of a place.' So they came on together. They camped at Gun-roidbi-boro, a red-ochre place name, and talked together. Ngalmoban told her, 'I'm going higher up, and you go this way. We'll go separately. I'm taking *man-gindjeg* yams.' Biriwilg agreed: 'I'm going to the Garigen area, I'm not going that way.' Ngalmoban went off with her yams. She was throwing them about at different places so they would grow there, and naming the places as she did so.

Biriwilg went on by herself. At Gara-morug on the plain, eating *man-gulaid* nuts, she said, 'I'll go north and look for a place to put myself!' She came on, crossing the fresh water at Mula, and settling down for a while at Ngaraid-wodi-daidgeng where White Cockatoo had cut the rock with a boomerang. Still she came on. 'I'm looking for a house where I can put myself and stay always.' On the way she was eating long yams. 'I'll stay here for a while, at Inyalbiri, eating these yams.' Then she went on again. At Gun-ngad-bo she gave the place its name, because 'here I dug a soak, and I drank water'. She came on, climbing up, camping on the way, and crossing the water at Yawagara. She said, 'I'll go this way, where there is a big stretch of water, and I'll cross over.' She crossed a big creek at Wolgal, went on, looked at the place, and said, 'Here I'll put myself, where the place is good and the cave-house is good, where I'll stay always.' She went on, and was digging for soak water. As she dug the ground, she saw that it was only a little hole. She got up, and dug in another place. This time she was digging a big hole. Then she went, and was swimming about in it. When she had finished swimming, she climbed up out of the water and went to the cave. She said, 'Here I put myself. I am Biriwilg. I came a long way. Ngalmoban and I came together, then we said farewell to each other. She went on. I came this way, and here I'll stay for ever: I put myself. I stand outside, like a drawing [painting] I stand. But I am a woman. I started off far away. Here the name of the place is Gun-gangin, where I put myself. I stand like a person, and I keep on standing here for ever.'

Chapter 10

Boundaries, Homes and Money

I

Small as they were, it took a while for the conquered parts of Australia to be mapped out with anything like a dense fabric of permanent European place-names. Explorers who came with the First Fleet, and afterwards, fastened names to the most obvious geographical features, but such names were not necessarily fixed in common memory. For instance, in April 1788 Governor Phillip honoured a pair of prominent ranges which he could make out to the west of Port Jackson with the names of two British marquises, Lansdowne and Carmarthen. Lord Lansdowne was a former Prime Minister, while Lord Carmarthen was a distinguished diplomat and future Duke of Leeds. In Australia these names have not survived. 'Lansdowne' died immediately, and 'Carmarthen' lingered for a few years only. The two ranges which were intended as monuments to their lordships formed part of the first horizon of settlement, a hem to the enclosing circle of sky. To the busy eye of ordinary men and women they were indistinguishable within the dazzling band which they called, in common conversation, the Blue Mountains.

This name, 'the Blue Mountains', had travelled from evanescent word of mouth – from the tip of the tongue – to the written record, as early as 1793–96, which is good evidence of the seductive power of the vulgar. Some of those poor men and women who believed in an Australian utopia, a place where they would be welcomed and live easily, looked to that western skyline as its gateway.[1]

The people whose imagination fashioned the name of the Blue Mountains, those eighteenth-century forebears and forerunners, are now as dimly opaque to us, perhaps, as the land was at first to them. We can conjure up something of the way in which they looked at the mountains, but we can know very little about the finer vision with which their minds encountered the smaller stretches of scrub, brown grassland or river bank, the jabbing sunshine, the tangled silver of magpie song, which made up the

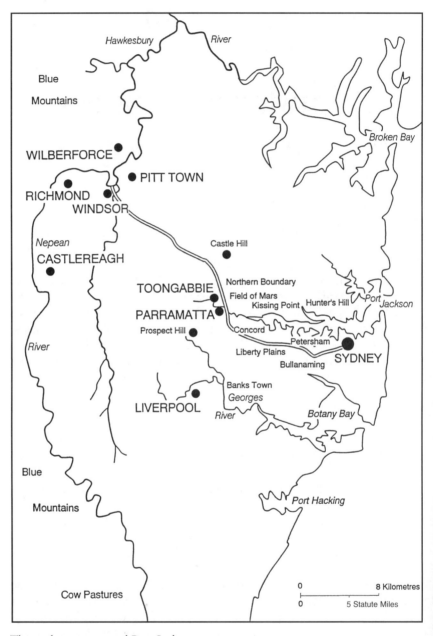

The settlements around Port Jackson

more immediate territory of their lives. Having been brought here by force, in most cases (and from a country which they did not need to be told was their own), they did not eagerly become Australians. As a community they were like the bones in the vision of Ezekiel, parched and scattered, waiting for the breath of God. For a long time the language they used for the bush was vague and indiscriminate, and their sense of local geography was primitive. The place-names they commonly used had little particularity. The passage of time among the Europeans had not yet made Australia a palace of memory. Encircled by the Blue Mountains on one side and, on the other, the yellow sandstone smashed by salt water, we find the Camp, the Crescent, the River, the Flats, the Ponds, and numerous small farms distinguished only by the names of their owners: denominations so sketchy as to suggest a failure of engagement within European minds.

The names chosen by Governor Phillip sometimes seem equally thin, especially those which he used to commemorate individuals living in another hemisphere – Sydney Cove, Rose Hill, the Hawkesbury River – but these at least were distinctive, and they gathered Australian associations in time. Attempts were also made by him and others to describe physical appearance or to commemorate events, with names such as Prospect Hill, Shell Cove, Manly Cove and Cockle Bay. Picking his way through the formless scrub, George Caley, the botanist who explored the approaches to the Blue Mountains in 1804, let his considerable fancy light on Luminous Valley, Dismal Dingle, Skeleton Rocks and Pincushion Hill.[2]

The naming of towns called for thought of a higher order. Phillip was romantic enough to believe, with many of his generation, that the spirit of community might be distilled in a name, and he struggled to find expressive ones for the places where men and women would gather together in large numbers. Soon after landing he drew up a plan for the first town at the site of his headquarters and decided to give it the name 'Albion', a poetic term for England, resonant with ancient, golden order. In the short term this scheme came to nothing. The place (now Sydney) offered a superb anchorage, but there was little in the soil which could encourage farmers, and farming seemed a necessary foundation for a good community. The settlement was allowed to take its name, by default, from the adjacent Sydney Cove, and in 1790 the Governor turned his hopes inland, to Rose Hill, 20 kilometres away at the head of the harbour. There his planned capital and 'first township' (as he described it) was named 'Parramatta', a European rendering of the Aboriginal place-name. With its subsidiary settlement, christened 'Toongabbie' in 1792, this foundation offered a clumsy echo of names as ancient, perhaps, as 'Albion', but closer to hand.[3]

By that time Phillip had begun to build primitive and fragile bridges between European and Aboriginal conversation. The choice of such names as 'Parramatta' and 'Toongabbie' is evidence of his respect for local language, and of his hope that future Europeans might somehow replicate an indigenous sense of place. It was an important ambition, but it involved

European minds negotiating the elephantine fact of conquest, a task which the founding generations found hard even to contemplate.

Settlement at Parramatta opened to European view a gently undulating extent of land to the westward, the Cumberland Plain, more than 20 miles across. The soil, for the most part, was fairly heavy clay and loam, liable to saturation in wet weather and at other times hard, but light patches were found around Parramatta, at Prospect and, most important of all, along the banks of the two rivers which bordered the plain to north, south and west, namely the Hawkesbury and its great tributary, the Nepean. Other small areas of relatively good soil were discovered to the east of Parramatta, on the north side of the harbour at Kissing Point, the Field of Mars, the Ponds and the Northern Boundary. These last-named places, together with Parramatta, Toongabbie and Prospect, were all settled with farmers in Phillip's time.

This chapter and the five which follow explore the succeeding twenty years, the period managed by Phillip's successors: by the senior officers of the New South Wales Corps (1792–95), by Governors Hunter (1795–1800), King (1800–06) and Bligh (1806–08), by another succession of officers from the garrison (1808–09) and, at last, by Governor Macquarie, though we go no further than Macquarie's first two or three years. The most dramatic movement outwards from Sydney and Parramatta occurred during the first of these regimes (1792–95), when Major Grose and Captain Paterson were Acting Governors. According to extant lists, the area officially granted in this short interval totalled 21,225 acres (8590 hectares), six times the area given by Phillip, settlers being dispersed to the Hawkesbury, Hunter's Hill, and along the Sydney–Parramatta road, at Liberty Plains, Concord, Petersham and Bullanaming. John Hunter, Governor from 1796 to 1800, was less expansive, and while farmers kept on multiplying the only new set- tlement in his time was at Banks Town, on George's River, the main tribu- tary to Botany Bay.[4] King was likewise a consolidator, though on new prin- ciples, and Bligh gave out hardly any land at all.

In 1800 Hunter sanctioned a count of the landholdings in New South Wales. He found a total of about 420, with roughly half on the Hawkesbury. Crops and livestock were included in the estimate, and it was found that nearly all the farmers grew wheat and/or maize, but that very few had yet managed a large crop. Three-quarters had no more than 10 acres (4 hectares) in wheat, and the plots of maize were even smaller. The usual livestock were pigs, and hardly a farm was without them. Milking cows were rare but there were numerous goats, and indeed these helped to define the various farming communities. In each locality there were either one, two or three individuals with herds of goats big enough to supply milk to their neighbours (mainly to their neighbours' children) on a hopeful commercial basis, and, in summer at least, it was impossible to take milk much beyond this immediate market.[5] More durable items were carried for sale by small dealers, men and women whose skin was beaten to new shades by continu-

ous movement under a hard sun. In 1800 the total European population of
New South Wales numbered nearly five thousand. With resources such as
these – wheat, maize, pigs' flesh, goats' milk and assorted vegetables – the
people had now become largely self-sufficient. Largely, but not wholly;
because seasonal difficulties and declining yields, where the soil had been
overcropped and unmanured, meant that supplies still had to be brought
sometimes from Britain, India or the Cape of Good Hope. Also, the ration
allowed to those individuals fed by the government (still 60 per cent of the
population) continued to be regularly topped up with imported produce.[6]

The broad extent of the Cumberland Plain was settled last by the
Europeans, and for a time it lay as a boundary between Port Jackson and
the Hawkesbury. A rough track linked Parramatta and Green Hills, the
embryonic village on the river, but the scarcity of horses and oxen made carriage slow and difficult. Labouring men and women might have walked the
distance, but otherwise the way was by water, as if the Hawkesbury valley
were an island, down the river to Broken Bay and by sea around to Sydney
Cove, three days' journey. The 41-ton schooner *Francis* carried goods and
passengers by that route from the beginning, and it was joined in time by
other vessels, mostly much smaller. The *Francis* had been built from pre-cut
materials brought out from England, but its colleagues were the work of
local shipyards.[7] Common rowing-boats were put together for communication along the river itself, and spent their lives crossing hither and thither to
any number of little beach-heads, havens in which the mud picked up wandering light from the water. Many poor men and women thus had the pleasure of a private vehicle.

A sense of place depends on the understanding that a sum may be more
than its parts, that a geographical point, whatever its mere black-and-white-
ness on a map, can house something absolute, even some immortal spirit.
Such a sense crept very gradually into the collective imagination of
Europeans in Australia. They were, of course, still inhabitants of an ocean
empire: 'Bone soldered by coral to bone, / mosaics / mantled by the bene-
diction of the shark's shadow'.[8] But they were beginning to be subject also
to the land itself. On the Hawkesbury the very power of the river, its wealth
and beauty, the sparkling serenity with which it lay at the service of its
people and the ease with which it occasionally destroyed them, would have
made it godlike to Europeans of an earlier age; and who knows what hints
of piety its sudden, adamantine judgment evoked in one or two minds even
now? In the years 1799–1801 annual floods, more than 20 metres deep, tore
down from the south. The last was the worst:

> the river [as one colonist recalled] . . . rushed impetuously to renew its former
> devastations. Flocks and herds were swept away by its irresistible influence; the
> houses, which had been re-built [since the last disaster], were once more levelled
> to the earth; and a settler was deprived of his existence, after witnessing the cat-
> astrophe which had robbed him of the whole of his possessions.[9]

The man who drowned was John Stogdell, once a gentleman's valet, who had come as a convict on the First Fleet ship, *Alexander*. At his death he was a considerable farmer, with 140 pigs, 160 goats, 450 sheep, and several hundred acres under crop, and was licensee as well of a local public house called 'the Bush'. In short, he was someone whom the river had previously made rich.[10]

The house and farm of John Palmer, the Commissary, at Walloomoolloo (now Woolloomooloo), at the water's edge near Sydney. Palmer was unusual in choosing an Aboriginal name for his antipodean home.

Source: Mitchell Library, State Library of New South Wales

Europeans who were given land grants by government chose, or were allocated, places which they were to hold almost unconditionally. A certain quantity of soil was measured out for them and within their boundaries they were allowed virtually all the rights of an English freeholder. There, in most cases, they lived and made a living, but what they thought of their homes is hard to tell. Some chose names for their land just as Phillip had done for Parramatta and Toongabbie, with the idea that the word itself, turned over in the mind from day to day, would create a parcel of happy associations with the soil. This was most common among men and women with some education, familiar with the romantic notions of the age, who liked to commemorate former homes in England, as if the name re-used might duplicate the old domestic virtues and fondly remembered scenery. George Johnston, an officer in the New South Wales Corps and a native of the Scottish

Lowlands, thus took possession of his grant, Annandale, 290 acres near Sydney, and James and Elizabeth Badgery, free immigrants from Devon, established themselves at Exeter Farm, on the Nepean. John Macarthur was even more romantic, but less misty-eyed. He named his Parramatta land Elizabeth Farm after his wife, she having made herself part of its unfolding character. On the opposite bank of the Parramatta River, a spot named Mount Hester likewise commemorated the wife of its owner, 'General' Joseph Holt, the Irish rebel. ('I', said Holt, 'was eager to tell my wife the conversation of the day, and she, poor soul, was contented with anything that pleased me.') In each case, marriage worked as an anchor, powerful and deeply felt, throughout a tempestuous and egotistical career.[11]

Living relationships manifest in talking – the caress of words in the air – were part of the means by which places were built in the European imagination. The original plan for settlement had assumed that farmers taking up land would find wives from among the female convicts, or perhaps from among the indigenous people. There were difficulties in fulfilling this vision. Of the farms listed in 1800, less than 60 per cent had women living on them, and on the Hawkesbury it was less than half. Wives had not been brought from the Pacific, as had once been suggested, and Aboriginal women stayed with their own people. Among the Europeans, female inclinations contradicted those of the men. Whereas the frontier at the river exercised an extraordinary drawing power on men, women tended to stay close to headquarters. This is not to say that Sydney was overcrowded with them. Even there, in 1800 there was only one woman for every six men: nevertheless, Sydney was much more wholly a place for women.[12] Not only women's scarcity but their inclinations held back the making of families on the frontier.

A few women actively looked for independence in what was already coming to be called 'the bush'. Margaret Catchpole lived alone on 15 acres, running sheep, goats and pigs and growing maize: 'I hire men to put in my corn and I work a great deal myself.' Her sense of community was shaped by her being a woman, aware of other women and of children and at ease with the fragile underside of common life. As with the goats' milk, the fabric of need within which she worked was also a fabric of collective self-help. 'I have a good many friends that I go to see when I think proper,' she said, 'such as I have nursed when they lay in.' In other words, she was a midwife. The women among her neighbours, as she boasted, 'cannot do without me'.[13] The 1800 list mentioned about twenty women as owners in their own right of land and/or livestock, such as pigs, goats or sheep.[14] Some of these lived in town nevertheless. Mary Mullett had a valuable allotment at Sydney Cove where she kept a shop, and the large crops of wheat and maize, ten sheep and one horse which also appeared against her name must have been somewhere else. Women with children were ocasionally given grants of land so that they might support themselves. Jane Poole lived for several years with a soldier called McManus, and when he died, in 1797, she was given

160 acres at the Hawkesbury, 'as a provision for herself and family'. She was not McManus's widow but only the mother of his children, and probably for that reason her right to dispose of the land – the children's inheritance – was limited by the deed of grant. On the other hand, it was sometimes prudent for women to avoid marriage, because under English common law a wife had no property separate from that of her husband. Indeed, the whole relationship of woman and man might be much more egalitarian without marriage. As Joseph Holt remarked,

> a mistress has more command over a man than a wife, for a wife is to be com-
> manded by her husband, and if you don't be very obliging to a mistress she will
> be disobliging to you perhaps in the middle of the night, and very like you would
> not have her the next night.[15]

Eleanor Fraser was given 40 acres at Concord soon after her husband died, in 1791, leaving her with two small sons. She then took up with William Morgan, a soldier with land of his own, but she never married him. They lived together for years, but they seem to have kept their farming interests separate. Her rights as an independent proprietor were publicly affirmed in November 1798, when she took Morgan to court for detaining some of her pigs.[16]

Some couples were very thoroughly anchored to the soil. Ann Thorne arrived by the *Surprise*, in October 1794. She soon took up with an earlier arrival, James Shephard, under the very tangible blessing of the Acting Governor, Major Grose, who immediately gave her (though still a convict) a grant of 20 acres at Kissing Point. This piece of bounty was quickly followed by conditional pardons for them both. Shephard seems to have been in government employment, possibly as a clerk, so that much of the management of the land may have devolved on his wife. Within ten years they had four children – the beginning of a local dynasty – and 150 acres on the Kissing Point site.[17] Children could be a useful addition to the fund of family labour. However, in the time of Hunter and King the newness of most marriages meant that few children were old enough to help. Also, many ex-convict women were no longer young when they finally settled, and had few child-bearing years left to them. Among all the farming couples listed for the Hawkesbury in 1800, nearly a quarter seem to have been permanently childless.[18] Even more, perhaps, than the small number of women, the scarcity of children on the farms ate into any sense of long-term interest in the land. It reinforced the farmers' belief that the state alone – a power, like Caesar, 'constant as the northern star' – gave direction to their lives. In that regard, *they* were children.

The first farmers on the mainland did not use bonded labour, because there was no regular system of assigning convicts, except to officers and civil officials. On Norfolk Island, Lieutenant-Governor King invented an

assignment system in 1791, handing over to farmers both the labour of convicts and the responsibility for feeding them, a detailed record being kept of
the whereabouts of each.[19] On the mainland, however, the regime was much
looser, at least until 1800, when King succeeded there as Governor.
Labourers were left to work out their duty to their employers as they went
along. John Rayner, who arrived in 1791 with five years left of a seven-year
sentence, first worked for the government and then looked further afield.
Early in 1795 he went to Walter Rouse, a farmer at Liberty Plains, and told
him 'that he had permission from the Gov[erno]r to take himself off the
stores, and agreed to work with him for a pig [that is, for payment in kind]'.
He did a week's work when he asked to vary the agreement, and then left.[20]
All this was quite in order.

Skilled men, especially, might find their own way in the world. William
Orman, or Norman, arrived on the Second Fleet with four-and-a-half years
left. He seems to have been a bricklayer, and he immediately found work
with James Bloodsworth, the colony's principal builder. He stayed with
Bloodsworth three or four years before making other arrangements. In 1796
he was living on a farm at the Ponds, doing mainly unskilled work, when
the following conversation occured, as recalled by the farmer's wife,
Elizabeth Anderson:

> as soon as she got up . . . she went and let the stock [pigs] out of the yard, and
> saw the men belonging to her go to work. She asked Norman . . . if he was going
> to work, he said he was not, that he had paid Jos[eph] Dunstan a dollar and like-
> wise a dollar [to] James Hodgston to work on her husband's ground, that he
> then should go and earn something for himself and then pay her husband what
> he was indebted to him. She asked Norman if he was not going to work at
> Marshalls, he said that first he was going to work at Tynans and that afterwards
> he would work at Marshalls.

It was skilled work he was going to do on the neighbouring farms – 'he
asked her for his trowel and a piece of wood with a hole in the middle with
a stick to carry mortar on, . . . she gave them to him' – which is why he
could afford to find other men to do his work for the Andersons. Note, too,
the way in which Mrs Anderson spoke of 'the men belonging to her',
although it was 'her husband's ground' and, indeed, he paid the men.
Marriage and farm life created a very subtle fabric of ownership, duty and
obligation.[21]

The experience of a few years of settlement laid down a fragmentary
wisdom about antipodean resources, seasons and soil. The authorities
soon came to insist on ironbark and bluegum, of certain tested dimensions,
for the building of bridges.[22] Some imported species flourished and some
did not. The most successful flower gardens featured myrtle, wallflowers,
stocks, sweet william, columbine, candy tuff and lupins. Geraniums, according to one convict woman, were everywhere, 'and they run 7 or 8 feet high',

the effect (she wrote from Sydney in summertime) being 'very beautiful'. Yams, ginger, bananas and sugar-cane were bound to fail, but kidney-beans, parsley, watermelons, pomegranates and broom all did well. Winter cauliflowers were 'very fine'.[23]

The Hawkesbury River, showing a hut, two small boats on the water and the low, rich alluvial flats in the distance.

Source: Dixson Galleries, State Library of New South Wales

On the Hawkesbury, among skilful farmers, the sowing of wheat began in mid-April. Elsewhere it was left for another couple of weeks. Lambing might be planned for May but, according to one authority, not all ewes then giving birth could keep up their strength without help, 'the nights being long, and the grass bad in the woods at this season'. In November the wheat harvest began. But note: 'No wheat ought to be stacked upon the ground, as the moisture which arises from the earth ascends thro' the stack, & tends much in this warm climate to increase the weevils.' These were rules distilled by the most enterprising farmers, compiled and published in 1806 under government imprimatur. Not everyone agreed with them. Some farmers liked to plant their wheat in March, and as most had only a limited area of cleared land this meant sowing among the stubble of recently harvested maize, cluttered as it was with weeds and rubbish. The logic here, according to our author, was deceptive: 'a farmer seldom calculates upon the probable quantity of grain his farm may produce, but upon the number of acres he has in cultivation'.[24]

Regard for one's neighbour was part of customary understanding about life on the land. Mutual rights and expectations were aspects of habit, and had developed in vast complexity in Europe over many hundreds of years. The European use of Australian land during the first period of invasion involved a range of agreements, with ancient notions complicated further by new ideas worked out on the spot. The 1800 list already mentioned was compiled shortly after the arrival of Philip Gidley King as Hunter's designated successor, and it was made at his request.[25] Several other lists were made after King had taken command, in which he similarly aimed to comprehend his people in neat statistical form. The effort succeeded to a degree, but it could not conceal the disparities, the awkward categorisations, and the stretching of fact to fit a paper pattern.

The idea of individual landed title was the basis for all the lists. Governor King was a man with commercial instincts and a feeling for the technicalities of both urban and rural property. To his mind, good possession of the soil depended on two things: efficient surveying, including the documentation of boundaries; and the vesting of title in individuals, because only individuals had a neat and tangible existence in law. In the same way, the best farmer was also a self-sufficient unit, a man applying his intelligence to the exploitation of his acreage: the archetypal 'he' in the farming advice quoted above.

As a reformer, King cut across common habits. Individual title was by no means paramount in the thinking of the people of New South Wales. It tended to weaken the position of women by limiting authority to husbands and fathers, the usual title-holders. Also, it was less appropriate to the poor, for whom farms were a means of mere sustenance, than it was for the rich, whose imagination was shaped by the law and the market. Methods of taking up the land had been determined to begin with by Governor Phillip, whose views were similar to King's. But since December 1792 they had been recast by the priorities of the New South Wales Corps. The senior officers of the Corps had ruled without restriction for nearly three years, and the process of settlement which they had established continued unabated during the succeeding five years of Governor Hunter. The officers took up large grants for themselves, which they naturally thought of in exclusive and individual terms. But they also used the land as a resource for the regiment, and in that case they followed the inclinations of the soldiers, frequently the final word in army life. This meant duplicating the notions of combined enterprise which had been tried by Major Ross with the convicts on Norfolk Island. As soon as the Corps arrived, company commanders secured not only gardens in which the men might grow vegetables for their own use, as the Marines had done before them, but also areas which they might sow with grain.[26] This opened up the possibility of combined profit.

Late in 1793 Major Grose began to allocate land to soldiers in freehold title, a scheme carried out in full by Captain Paterson, as Acting Governor, in 1795. According to one of the men, speaking some years later, 'Every Soldier that applied for it had it.' To begin with, the grants were made out to individuals; but they were allocated in groups, beginning with a number at Concord, and the quantities were very small (normally 25 acres each). We cannot know the basic purpose of the exercise because it is impossible to penetrate beyond the only surviving record, the registration of title, which is inconsistent and incomplete.[27] The paymaster of the regiment, John Macarthur, and the company commanders were currently investing regimental funds for their own purposes (see below), and they were fastening on various alternatives for paying the wages of their men. Land grants may have been one substitute. There were more than four hundred men serving in the garrison, and most, if not all, received land.[28]

They took up their allotments in various ways. The movements required of them as soldiers must have made management difficult, and it is impossible to know how many were given title only so that they might sell it. However, soldiers were used to cooperation. The practice of looking after each other's interests probably allowed for a number of haphazard agreements in the seasonal use of the soil. From March 1795, and during Hunter's time, the collective nature of such land grants was affirmed by the registering of joint title in some cases. Groups of two, three or four names, even up to seventeen, were inserted in the register, often, no doubt, securing possession already settled in practice. A total of 170 men, more or less, were given shared title before 1800, when King put a stop to it.[29] The entire exercise grew out of a system of land-use full of short-term expedients. Where there were women there might be an interest in the security of family life. But for the most part cooperation on the land among the first Europeans worked only from season to season, with little thought for the period beyond. King aimed to change all that.

II

Trade took place in New South Wales from the moment the people of the First Fleet disembarked. Even the lack of money in the beginning did not stop useful exchange, and surviving fragments of evidence point to the kind of prices paid. For instance, within the first two years of settlement Mary Phillips bought a tin quart pot from Peter Opley, at the cost of a silk handkerchief. John Turner gave one loaf of bread to Mary Kennedy, wife of a sergeant of Marines, for a pint of rum, and two to a man called McLean for a quart (an exact pattern of exchange, since a quart equals two pints). These were Turner's earnings – one loaf a week – as baker to the purser of the *Sirius*. Ann Davis, alias Judith Jones, required a white shirt, 'to make her a Bedgown', from a soldier, unnamed, as the price of sleeping all night with her. William Boggis paid over some of his rations to Samuel Woodham for the privilege of living in his hut. William Hambly, carpenter's mate of the

Sirius, bought a young pig from David Killpack for a silk handkerchief and a bottle of rum.[30]

Over a period of months in 1789, Mark Hurst, a soldier, sold a white shirt, part of the garrison's standard issue, to William Whiting for two pounds of flour, a low price, as the shirt was 'a very bad one'. Thomas Kidner acted as intermediary, and possibly in payment Hurst gave him some flour. With a pair of shoes and another white shirt, Hurst bought two bottles of rum from Thomas Bryant (who got them from Joseph Abbott, drummer). He tendered rum himself to Joseph Morley in purchasing some fish, but they agreed instead on a pair of white stockings, a second pair of which he gave to John Hall in exchange for stockings of worsted.[31] Hurst took an unusually commercial attitude to the various parts of his uniform, and he was court-martialled and flogged for it. But he represented only one point of exchange in a flourishing market in small goods, a pattern of implicit agreement about the value of things, which continued to expand and ramify thereafter. The garrison was a rich source of manufactured items, and the convicts were prepared to pay for them with objects they made themselves, objects they caught, objects they stole, and objects they purchased from somebody else. Some men and women quickly gathered capital as a result, building up authority for themselves within the headquarters of exchange, which was, of course, the camp at Sydney Cove.

Sydney in the middle 1790s: a watercolour view by the convict artist Thomas Watling, looking up the east bank of Sydney Cove. Government House is in the distance on the right and the hospital in the right foreground. The commercial parts of the town grew within the embrace of these two sets of public buildings.

Source: Mitchell Library, State Library of New South Wales

'Sydney', the other name commonly used for this place (it appears among the convicts as early as July 1788), was formally adopted by government during the winter of 1790, a tacit admission that something like a town had already begun there, in spite of the current plans for Rose Hill.[32] The name was directly linked with the recent Secretary of State, Viscount Sydney, but (as I say in Chapter 3) in the minds of most men and women in the late eighteenth century it had much richer associations, going back to Algernon Sidney, the minister's famous ancestor, a martyr to common rights who had been vindicated by the Glorious Revolution of 1688. Sidney's arguments about commonwealth, about order married to popular liberty, about rights formed from the initiatives and conversation of daily life, reflected the orthodoxy of the age. 'Thus we find a few Men assembling together upon the Banks of the Tiber,' he had written, 'resolv'd to build a City, and set up a Government among themselves.'[33] The origins of Sydney, in New South Wales, did not exactly fit this classical prescription, but in some humble respects they were very close. The town was built on the exchange of language and goods.

Barter was to be the main method of commerce for many years, just as it had been generations earlier in the first English settlements in North America. In early Virginia the main item of exchange was also the main item of produce, namely tobacco. In New South Wales there was a variety of goods, known locally as 'property' (especially wheat, flour and rum), whose value was relatively well settled and which were a regular standby in the market. None of these was important enough to become an absolute standard of value, as Virginian tobacco had been, and partly for that reason (even when money was absent) everything was measured in money terms.[34] Besides, cash began to penetrate the local market as the traffic from Europe multiplied. It was eagerly welcomed among the convicts. In March 1791, John Le Roi, a seaman from the Dutch vessel, *Waaksamheyd*, spent a little time on shore with 'a girl' and paid her a dollar, 'when coming out of the House, he was struck by [Thomas] Smith and robbed of 4 Dollars by [John] Thomas'. A fight ensued: 'there was a great Crowd of People who advised the convicts to run away, which they did', and no doubt the dollars went with them.[35] This is the first record of cash stolen in New South Wales.

Late in the following year, several thousand Spanish dollars arrived from London for official expenditure. Governor Phillip did not permit gambling, but with the arrival of this and other quantities of coin, and with Phillip's departure not long after (December 1792), the settlement was overtaken by a hectic enthusiasm for games of chance:

> To such excess was this pursuit carried among the convicts [wrote David Collins], that some had been known, after losing provisions, money, and all their spare clothing, to have staked and lost the very clothes on their wretched backs, standing in the midst of their associates as naked, and as indifferent about it, as the unconscious natives of the country.

Cribbage and all-fours were the favourite games, and cash was the ultimate object. With it, 'they could purchase spirits, or whatever else their passions made them covet'.[36]

The new eagerness for drink, and therefore for money, only reinforced the dependence of the people on the government. The promissory notes drawn on His Majesty's Treasury became the great desiderata of commercial life, and many farmers spent their labour growing things for which they knew they would get paid at the government store. Making no effort with vegetable gardens, their resources were disastrously narrow. 'Growing wheat and maize', as Philip Gidley King remarked, ' . . . has been their only object, and when that has been obtained it has often occurred that one night's drinking . . . has eased them of all their labour had acquired the preceding year.'[37]

The same fevered interest affected other types of commerce after Phillip's departure. The importing of goods for sale had already begun. In October 1792 the officers of the Corps formed a syndicate to charter the storeship *Britannia*, commanded by William Raven, with eleven shares of £200 each (another example of pragmatic combination within the regiment). Raven was to take the ship to the Cape of Good Hope and bring back livestock and provisions for sale at the settlement. By this time vessels were also beginning to come to Port Jackson on speculation, and the officers were able to dominate the purchase of goods. They had not only their own salaries to draw on, but all the financial credit of the regiment, including the soldiers' pay and various other allowances. For the period 1792–98 they were thus able to invest a total of £36,844. (Private drawing of interest from government funds was common practice and not thought dishonest.) A visiting ship's surgeon liked the Sydney people he mixed with. They were, he said, 'affable, polite, and hospitable to a stranger', but he was obliged to add that '*many* of them only *appear* so, having always some latent motive in view'.[38] The usual motive was a wish to turn acquaintance into profit.

Retailing shops had been opened up, in which the press of business must have fluctuated very much with the arrival of overseas cargoes. The possibility of profit began to affect everyone more or less, and the settlement became a different place as a result. The Reverend Richard Johnson, writing in 1794, complained that 'Little other conversation is heard but buying, selling, bartering, &c.'[39] David Collins, the Judge-Advocate, also felt it. He too was inclined to complain, describing the way in which farmers now looked 'to their immediate interest' in managing their crops, even in times of scarcity. And yet in principle Collins, as a clear-thinking, educated man – and as a young man, open to new ideas – should have admired this kind of ambition. Rational free enterprise was one of the emerging panaceas of the age, though Collins was not alone in believing that it was better cultivated by gentlemen than indiscriminately among the mass of the people.[40]

A likely exemplar of such polished energy was the gentleman convict Shadrach Shaw. In earlier life, Shaw had laboured in a position of trust at the Transfer Office of the Bank of England. After a long and apparently blameless career, he had made a bumbling attempt to defraud a customer of £167 5s. and was sentenced to seven years' transportation. Arriving in New South Wales in October 1792, he was almost immediately given a conditional pardon by Grose and a little land at Concord. He was also allowed to set himself up on a site at the head of Sydney Cove, secured by government lease in May 1794. His was the first building in Sydney to be dedicated to external trade. Thus positioned, and with the favour of the senior officers of the Corps, Shaw must have dominated the import business. It was presumably on his premises that the officers disposed of their goods by the *Britannia* (which was to make four voyages altogether during the period 1792–95) and by other vessels.[41]

In September 1798, when his sentence was nearly up, Shaw sold the whole concern to Simeon Lord. He presumably sailed home as soon as he could, and he is not heard of in this country again. Lord, his successor, was a very different character. Shaw had a wife and four children in London, affluent connections, and some hope of renewed respectability to go back to.[42] Lord's future, on the other hand, was in Australia. He was a man of meagre education who had begun to make his way at Sydney Cove as a servant, using his native wit and patiently waiting his chance. He was also a generation younger than Shaw, with his life ahead of him.

Conditional pardons were usually given to men and women with life or fourteen-year sentences. The recipients became, in local language, 'free on the ground' or 'free of the country'. In other words they were free as long as they stayed in New South Wales. Such people were released from labour, or 'emancipated'. This last word was one whose meaning was to become much looser among Australians in later years, so as to include everyone who had been through the convict system. But to begin with, it referred only to those with pardons.[43]

The market dictated agreements about the value of land and goods, and the status of certain kinds of property. Much the same process, a living consensus, defined the status of people. Just as freehold tenure was the ultimate form of landed title, so the condition of a free man was the absolute means of participation in society, whether in Britain or New South Wales. Other forms of civil existence were partial and relative. All the same, the criteria for freedom varied, contingent on time and place, on custom and community. The criteria in early New South Wales reflected English habits of mind, but also the circumstances of the Antipodes. In England, convicted felons lost all effective property rights. Freehold tenure might continue in their name, but its proceeds and all other possessions were forfeit to the Crown. However, transported convicts were all assumed to go abroad under pardon, and they took whatever property they liked with them. In Virginia and Maryland, the destination of nearly all transported men and women before the American Revolution, they had been subject to local law and (unless they came back before their time) the British authorities took no more notice of them. They were normally absorbed within the bonded workforce, Black and White, on which those colonies depended, but those with money could buy their freedom on stepping ashore. They then became, as it were, 'free on the ground', just as emancipated convicts did in New South Wales. In Virginia, for a time, they might give evidence in the courts and the propertied men among them might vote in local elections, both rights withheld in England.[44]

In New South Wales the situation was never so clear-cut. Lord Sydney had envisaged a settlement in which transported men and women would be 'free on the ground' from the beginning, enjoying the land in freehold tenure, suing and giving evidence in the courts. (See Chapters 3 and 4.) However, this was impossible while the people depended on the government for survival, because such dependence was inconsistent with the common understanding of freedom. But also from a legal point of view, Phillip had taken an approach radically different from that of his minister, believing that the convicts were 'servants of the Crown' until they were pardoned or their time expired. This policy was never applied in any absolute way, but it was to be central to the convict system in New South Wales, and the main point of difference with American practice.[45]

Convicts coming to Australia were still free to bring money with them, and during the early period of transportation money might make all the difference to their experience of transportation. Shadrach Shaw probably brought enough to set up in trade on his own account (thus establishing his right to a conditional pardon), even without the officers of the Corps. In 1800 the passage of the convict Joshua Palmer by the *Royal Admiral* was rendered much more comfortable by the fact that his wife, who came with him, paid for a cabin for them both and fresh provisions from the captain's table. On the same ship forty-three convicts died as a result of close confinement.[46] John Grant (*Coromandel*, 1804) brought considerable personal luggage.

> The Black Sattin Waistcoat and Breeches [he told his mother on departure] are very beautiful and the shirts, I fear very expensive. The white hat is also handsome. . . .
>
> You may, if you please, send me a small pair of Knee Buckles. Your chocolates are very acceptable and the small knife very useful. Thank Mrs Mallett for the beautiful spun Watch pocket and the Silver Cream Jug.

During a stop-over at San Salvador he bought 60 gallons of rum, for resale in New South Wales. It was confiscated on his arrival, but because it was alcohol, not because he was a convict.[47]

The activity of men and women like these, of farmers with produce for sale, and of salaried officials and army officers, created the means of independence among the population. It was possible for men and women of small pretensions to remain dependent on, and employed by, the government (even after their time was up) if they chose to do so.[48] However, from the last year of Phillip's time some former convicts began to support themselves, taking advantage of convict labour. Very rapidly traders with what might be called indigenous resources came forward, and a few, such as Simeon Lord, managed to emerge in a remarkably short time as the principal managers of capital in Sydney. The commercial supremacy of the officers within the colony was indeed brief, limited perhaps to the first half of the 1790s and certainly past by 1800.[49]

During the same period, the private employment of convict labour began. To begin with, all convicts were thought of as servants of the Crown, whoever they worked for, and were fed and clothed by the Crown. Only in 1798 did the Governor move, under orders from London, to see that private employers (except for magistrates, officers and some others) supported their own servants, whether convicts or not.[50] Technically, members of the workforce was thus divided into two, depending on whether or not they ate the King's bread. However, there was already a third category (self-defined, because no comprehensive lists were kept before 1800). Women convicts had always been free agents from an economic point of view, 'seldom thinking themselves included in the restrictions that were laid upon others', and there were also large numbers of men who chose to find a living where they could. Some were skilled men like William Orman, mentioned above, but others were 'worthless fellows who have deserted from the work of Government, or from those to whom their labour had been given'. During the wheat harvest in 1799 the Hawkesbury was said to be full of such men, 'styling themselves free people', and demanding very high wages for bringing in the grain.[51]

The existence of this third category shows that, given a little luck and cunning, everyone had some choice as to what they did. In these first years of European settlement (after Phillip's time and up to Macquarie's) even convict men and women who came with no money entered a market fully as much as they did a penal system. Men were often able to insist that in working for the government their labour should be measured by the job to be done, the 'task', and not by the hour. They also had time to themselves. As late as 1804, according to Governor King,

> Among the convicts victualled by the Crown there are but few, and those are of the worst description, who have not comfortable little dwellings at the places they are stationed at; many have the convenience of small ovens, or iron pots, they bake under [sic]; and not a few have their wives and families of children, who they maintain by their labour when their Government work is finished, with the help of small pieces of ground round their dwellings.

They might also, if they had the resources, hire others to do their government work.[52] The sheer quantity of work to be done throughout the settlements gave them room to negotiate, but a strict form of bondage would have been hard to impose in any case, given the prejudice which still survived against making slaves out of white-skinned Christians. In the days of transportation to North America, convicts destined for servitude had also been free agents to a limited extent, even having a limited choice as to who would employ them when they arrived.[53] Early New South Wales is best understood against the background of American precedent such as this. The harder regime of the 1820s and 1830s was still to come.

Like the American convicts, women had to make their first decisions as soon as their ship tied up in the new land. The scarcity of European women in New South Wales meant that men came on board straightaway looking for partners. Men of superior status could not be resisted. But otherwise a woman was not always obliged to go, especially if she had been able to think ahead and could say that 'that there is another person who will apply for her, and with whom she would more readily engage herself'. Also, once landed there was no rule to prevent her making fresh arrangements.[54] A convict man might also abandon a master to whom he was assigned. Even if he stayed, as with the men working for government, he was allowed to look for other work during a large part of every afternoon.[55]

Variety is everything. Besides this liberty, there were also examples of total subjection – especially among men 'of the worst description', as King had admitted – where opportunity was dead, at least for the time being. The Christian metaphor which makes suffering the road to freedom leaves room as well for absolute misery. In early New South Wales the burgeoning market, which offered so much freedom, also allowed for the treatment of both men and women as voiceless objects of order. Lord Sydney's vision had stressed the first. The administrative scheme devised by Governor Phillip (however much he might have regretted it), even his high humanitarianism, had led inexorably to the second. Holt recorded the following exchange between himself and two officers as they watched convicts at work, tightly disciplined and virtually naked, soon after his arrival in 1800:

> The gentlemen walked about and, at length, Captain Johnston says: 'Mr Holt, you are a proper farmer sir.'
> 'I understand tilling the ground with horses and oxen, but with men I do not.'
> Says Doctor Thomson: 'Don't you think them men would know what you would say to them better than horses or bullocks?'
> 'Yes sir, but give me leave to tell you I think it is a brutish comparison."
> 'Well sir, you will think nothing of it by and by.'

The same author recorded the other side of the picture for women too, and here we hark back to the cock-and-hen imagery of Chapter 7. A woman might argue for her own choice on arrival and might still be forced to go with a man she did not like. And, 'in a few days, perhaps that fellow in his drunken schemes would sell his interest to some other fellow'. Customary prices for women under these circumstances, says Holt, were 'a gallon of rum, some five pounds and so forth'.[56]

Liberty and subjection were two sides of a single phenomenon. Australians are commonly bound, through the experience of centuries, by European imagery. So it seems fair to say that, although this was a hard and strange country, especially for the weak, under European settlement a certain grace clearly issued from it. In Australia (before and after its remaking by European sensibility) red sap suddenly appears on dead-white trees. The land yielded fitfully, but then so did the royal fountains of mercy in Europe.

The Court of Civil Judicature was designed for the benefit of convicts as much as anyone else (see Chapter 5), and for the time being nothing official seems to have been done to disqualify them from coming before it as free agents. In 1801, for instance, a party of six men, all or nearly all convicts, sued for wages they said were due to them, probably for harvest labour.[57] Indeed, a type of legal immunity worked in the opposite direction, for the benefit of convicts. In 1798 Governor Hunter ordered that no free individuals might bring before the court debtors who happened to be servants of the Crown. Convict men in public employment made their own arrangements as to where they lived and whom they lived with, and in their dealings with local shopkeepers and landlords they often asked for credit. This could cause difficulties, because debtors under prosecution were liable to imprisonment until they paid up. 'Government', announced Hunter, 'will by no means dispense with the labour of its servants for the partial accommodation of any private dealings whatever', and this rule was taken to cover all convicts who had not served their time.[58]

Governor Hunter also tried to persuade anyone moving about the colony to carry a form of identity, or 'passport', to be obtained from a magistrate. Officers were exempt, and afterwards 'settlers', meaning employers of various kinds, as well.[59] In so far as the rule was enforced, it might have helped to define a class in bondage. Governor King acted more precisely in inventing 'tickets of leave' ('annual certificates' or 'certificates of leave') which every convict not fed and employed by the government or officially assigned to settlers was supposed to carry. All men still serving their time were henceforth to come under one or other of these three headings – tickets of leave, public labour or private assignment – and men and masters who disregarded the distinctions were to be punished.[60] This was a vital step in the forging of pen-and-paper links between government and people. Chains of command, entire patterns of responsibility both benevolent and oppressive, were manufactured from tickets of leave and certificates of right. By such paperwork the governors, and King in particular, aimed to make colonial lives more predictable, more orderly and more tightly bound to the soil.

III

During the 1790s the British government openly acknowledged for the first time that New South Wales and its nearby seas were places in which money might be made. Hopes of this sort had been in the minds of visionaries in

England for years beforehand. James Matra's original proposal for settlement at Botany Bay, presented to the government in 1783, had been linked with a scheme to harvest flax and timber on Norfolk Island, and Matra's associate, Sir George Young, had pursued that possibility, together with his brother-in-law, John Call, as late as 1791.[61] There was serious difficulty in all such plans for private enterprise in so far as the East India Company enjoyed a monopoly, guaranteed by a series of royal charters since the time of Elizabeth I, over all British commercial operations throughout the Indian and Pacific Oceans. The Company was sometimes prepared to license private traders in its area, but it would not allow a permanent operation whose success might tempt more to follow.

The British government did not want to encourage activity which would upset the company. The original details for settlement at Botany Bay, worked out at the Home Office in 1786–87, had included nothing which might open the way to any enterprise beyond subsistence farming by the convicts. The character of Lord Sydney, the minister originally responsible for the settlement, was an added guarantee for the Company, because Sydney was not interested in matters of profit and loss. No speculator himself, he thought he was doing English merchants a favour by dismissing dreams about New South Wales. The projects of those with 'lucrative views of their own' were, he said, merely 'ridiculous', and with regard to flax and timber he was probably right.[62]

Governor Phillip was instructed to take possession of Norfolk Island, but nothing was done with it from a commercial point of view. Dreams of flax and timber were quickly replaced by more realistic plans for the discovery of whales and seals in the south-west Pacific. Whales were Britain's principal source of oil, and the whaling industry was enormously valuable. Seals supplied not only oil but skins, for which there was a very good market in Europe and China. Hitherto the northern Atlantic had been adequate for British fisheries of all kinds, but increasing demand, government bounties, and competition from the French and the newly independent Americans had encouraged British whalers to move southward. The number of vessels at work and their geographical range quickly increased beyond all expectation.[63] For a short time they were accommodated within the southern Atlantic, but in May 1786 the directors of the East India Company were obliged to let them go east of the Cape of Good Hope, as far as Madagascar. Two years later, whalers wanting to hunt beyond Cape Horn were given access to the western two-thirds of the Pacific Ocean.[64]

These areas were not vital to the Company because they did not affect the all-important trade between the southern Chinese port of Canton (Guangzhou) and Company bases at Calcutta, Bombay and Madras. The seas in which that trade was carried on, however – defined by lines of longitude all the way down to the Antarctic and taking in most of the Indian Ocean and the waters around New Holland and New Zealand – were another matter. That area was considered fundamental to the Company's existence, and given the power of its shareholders at Westminster it could be taken for granted that other British enterprise would be kept out for the foreseeable future.

In January 1789, Samuel Enderby, the most active of the London whaling merchants, told the Board of Trade that he and his colleagues wanted unlimited access to all the oceans of the world. With it, he said, 'The British Adventurers would soon explore the most distant parts.' In particular, 'the settlements of New Holland would be often visited as there are many whales in those seas'.[65] Enderby was guessing about 'many whales', but his guesses were shortly followed by certain knowledge. Two months after the date of his letter, one of two whaling vessels which had been used for the First Fleet, as convict transports, returned to England with good news of whales in the Indian Ocean. Soon equally encouraging information came back from the western parts of the Pacific. Hurried into hopes of finding ever richer areas, London whaling firms now began to think of convict transportation as a means of breaking into the last remaining region of the Company's monopoly. The Third Fleet, which sailed in March 1791, included five whalers, all of which went on from Port Jackson to various parts of the Pacific to look for whales, several of them hunting along the coast of New South Wales itself.[66]

Phillip had apparently not thought of New South Wales as a whaling ground. When he had left England, in May 1787, it must have seemed unlikely that whalers would want to push into the area of his government for many years, and even less likely that they would be allowed to do so. On the other hand, even at that time there were members of the British cabinet who may well have foreseen such a possibility. Nothing but the urgent need to dispose of convicts could have forced ministers to plan a settlement in such a remote place as New South Wales. But once the decision had been taken, it would have been prudent to make the most of it, and to look for other ways in which the territory might someday be useful to British enterprise. The land itself, taken as a whole, might never amount to much, but the coastal seas were more promising.

Apart from the eastern edge, which had been charted by Captain Cook, and parts of the west, which had been discovered much earlier by the Dutch and by William Dampier, the exact outline of the continent was unknown. It was even possible that there was no single land mass and that Cook's New South Wales was quite separate from the western remainder. Such ignorance notwithstanding, the British government defined its new territory as extending westward to the 135th degree of longitude, a line which passed through what was later to be the Northern Territory and South Australia. A lengthy coastline in the south and north, never seen by Europeans as far as anyone knew, was thus claimed by the British for future contingencies. Phillip's appointment may well have been due partly to his cartographic skills, and he was certainly ordered to see to the exploration of the seas and coasts 'within the limits of [his] . . . government'.[67]

Phillip knew a little about whaling from his service with the Portuguese, whose whalers fished off the coast of Brazil. Following the arrival of the Third Fleet, Captain Thomas Melville, master of the *Britannia* (not Raven's *Britannia*), asked him for permission to hunt along the coast of New South Wales, having seen 'a great Plenty' of whales off Van Diemen's Land. The Governor was very much aware of his duty to safeguard the monopoly of the East India Company, but his doubts were diminished on reading letters Melville had brought from England. According to Melville, 'He [then] took me into a private Room . . . and told me he had read my letters and that he would render me every service that lay in his power . . . which he did accordingly and did everything to dispatch us on our Fishery.'[68] The documents which made the difference possibly included something from Enderbys, who owned the *Britannia*, and something unofficial from Whitehall. A short voyage by the *Britannia* and other Third Fleet vessels was enough to assure the Governor that 'a fishery will be established on the coast', and the settlement itself, so Melville said, was 'all alive' with the prospect.[69] The Governor wrote home for copies of relevant legislation and some explicit instructions on the matter. Nothing was forthcoming, probably because negotiations were under way which ministers hoped would lead to the fisheries being wholly opened up.[70]

This came to pass only in June 1798. The Act of parliament then passed (38 Geo. III, c. 57) made a profound difference to the European impact on Australia by opening the seas about New South Wales to British whalers. For whalers such as the Enderbys it only affirmed a process which had already begun, but within the broad perspective of the British empire it was another matter. From now on it was possible for the British government to think about the Australian continent (and New Zealand too) in deliberately economic terms. Enterprise, both British and local, might be deliberately tied to the process of settlement. All future British communities along the coastline – in other words, all those dating from the nineteenth century – were thus to be established as integral parts of the empire. All were to be pieces within an economic and constitutional whole, driven from the centre. None, in other words, were to demonstrate the loose open-endedness, the backward-glancing ambiguity which had characterised Lord Sydney's plans for Botany Bay.

By the 1790s Sydney himself was becoming a man of the past. (He died in 1800, aged sixty-seven.) The revolution in France – the formation of the National Assembly in 1789, the execution of the King in 1793, the Directorate and the reign of terror – epitomised an age in which public debate unfolded with extraordinary speed. Throughout Europe, customary freedoms such as Sydney cherished were now overshadowed by a terrifying, or exhilarating, mixture of bloodshed and intellectual sophistication, and by apparently irresistible arguments about abstract rights. By a parallel process, chartered privileges like those of the East India Company were giving way to new notions about free enterprise, to a belief that the resources of the earth ought to be exploited by all men equally. The Company's ban on trading in its area of monopoly, as distinct from whaling, remained in place beyond 1798 (it disappeared only in 1819), but even that was soon treated as the remnant of a past age.

Australian commerce moved forward very rapidly. At Sydney what had begun in 1788 as 'the Camp' now became a port, in the formal sense. In 1799 Governor Hunter was instructed to keep an account of maritime traffic, similar to those which had been always kept in the older colonies, and a Registrar of Exports and Imports (otherwise called Naval Officer) was appointed.[71] But the most significant effect of the new regime was the foundation of British settlement in Van Diemen's Land, the island now called Tasmania, which lay a week's travelling time in good weather south of Port Jackson. The whale and seal fishery in those waters was the main reason for colonisation.[72]

Britain was at war with France from 1793, but late in 1801 peace negotiations began, leading to the Treaty of Amiens (and war again very quickly afterwards). The older economic rivalry continued, and when the French vessel *Naturaliste* reached Sydney in April 1802 on a voyage of exploration, followed by the *Géographe* in June, Governor King saw them as the advance guard of French enterprise in neighbouring seas. He had already dreamt of outstations, under his government, which might help to prove the economic potential of Australia: an indigo plantation on the far north coast, for instance (beyond the present site of Bowen). He now wrote immediately to London urging that British rights be affirmed by a new settlement to the south. Bass Strait, dividing Van Diemen's Land from the mainland, had just been discovered, and King suggested that settlers be sent to some island or harbour commanding the strait.[73] Without waiting for an answer, in March 1803 he despatched a party of his own under the naval lieutenant John Bowen, not to Bass Strait but to the mouth of the Derwent, on the south-west coast of Van Diemen's Land.

At Whitehall, his suggestion was treated as a matter of urgency. A new department, called War and the Colonies, had just been created, with Lord Hobart (afterwards 4th Earl of Buckinghamshire) as Secretary of State. Hobart had served as Governor of Madras, which may explain his interest in the East. During the European winter, 1802–03, he organised an expedition, on a much more ambitious scale than King could manage, to settle Bass Strait. The timing was fortuitous because for the previous eighteen months there had been increasing public interest in New South Wales as a place of free settlement. Recent wheat harvests in southern England had been very poor, and hardship had increased with the partial demobilisation of the troops, always a stimulus to crime and unemployment. Rumours were rife that government was prepared to let free emigrants go to the Antipodes, and a stream of inquiries came in:

in consequence of a rumour and it having been mentioned of late several times to me, that Y[ou]r Grace did with the permission of Government give leave, permits, grants of land &c to natives of this country . . .

Having a great desire to go to Botany Bay, and having been informed by a gentleman in your Lordship's office that the proper channel . . . should be through an application to Your Lordship . . .

I here that there is some of His Majesties Subjects gone to Botney Bay as Free Settellers . . . [74]

It was soon widely understood that skilled men, or 'mechanics', and farmers were wanted. In fact, to all appearances deliberate free settlement was afoot, although no-one seems to have been sure, as one applicant put it, what 'purpose Government hath in view in sending persons there to colonize the place'.[75]

There were various purposes. Lord Hobart was a civiliser, and he was the first minister since Sydney whose imagination was stirred by the idea of European settlement in the Antipodes. He showed a constant interest in the possibility of new food crops (especially rice) in New South Wales; he appointed a mineralogist to serve both settlements; and he sent numerous gifts with the people going to the southward – silver communion plate (described as a present from His Majesty), twelve compasses, two surveying chains and a theodolyte, and various reference books of law, science, agricuture and religion – with the obvious hope that ambition and piety would both in future be more finely measured in that part of the world. He also hoped that that by diverting transportation in that direction for a period he would give King room at Port Jackson to negotiate what he understood to be a crucial stage in the evolution of settlement there.[76] In other respects, he was more pragmatic. The main purpose of the new settlement was the security and extension of the British fisheries. The command in the south was given to David Collins, the former Judge-Advocate of New South Wales, and besides 306 convicts (some with families) twenty free settlers were sent with him. The twenty (eleven men, five women and four children) included a ship's carpenter and two seamen, one of the latter being William Collins (no relation to David), formerly a master in the navy, who immediately reported back on the local prospects for whaling. He may have been asked to do so before he left.[77]

The two ships carrying David Collins's party, *Calcutta* and *Ocean*, left England in April 1803. A larger group of free people, thirteen men, fifteen women and twenty-one children, had already departed for Port Jackson aboard the *Perseus* and *Coromandel*. They arrived during winter 1802 and most of the men were given grants of 100 acres each at Portland, on the Hawkesbury. This was also the acreage allowed to free people at the southern settlement. Collins first disembarked at Port Phillip (near the present site of Melbourne) but, considering it unsuitable, he followed Bowen to the mouth of the Derwent, where his people landed in February 1804. The final settlement, at Sullivan's Cove, was called Hobart Town (now Hobart).[78]

To make doubly sure, yet another party was sent from Sydney to the north coast of the island, at Port Dalrymple, in November 1804, under Lieutenant-Colonel William Paterson, commanding officer of the New South Wales Corps. In this case, Lord Hobart ordered that settlers be brought from Norfolk Island, with a promise of four times the acreage each possessed on the island.[79] King was quite ready to measure up large farms anywhere under his government. It was currently a matter of debate among Englishmen as to whether large farms were better than small ones from both a social and economic point of view. Small farming, in which the people were egalitarian, cooperative, self-sufficient and inward-looking, had been the model hitherto for New South Wales, thanks to Lord Sydney's original inspiration. But it was a model which was losing favour among younger European writers on agricultural science. A proper concentration on individual profit, and on markets beyond the immediate horizon, was said to need not only energy and intelligence but also substantial capital. The counter-argument that numerous acres caused high prices was cast aside.[80] The policies of both Lord Hobart and Governor King show that they too believed that only large farms would allow farmers to think in enterprising terms.

Grants of 25 to 60 acres (10 to 24 hectares) had been normal for the first decade after 1788. The officers of the Corps, while they were in charge (1792–95), had distributed grants of 100 acres each to themselves, the civil officials and a few others, but there had been no fundamental change of policy until near the end of Hunter's time. The Governor then made a deliberate effort to create a class of landowners who might be substantial mixed farmers, big employers and men of authority. He gave grants of 200, 300 and 400 acres each, and of nearly 1000 in one case of joint title. King, his successor, carried this policy forward. The normal thing now was either 60 to 200 acres, an area suitable for yeomen (not peasants), or 500 to 1500, for hopeful landed gentlemen. On farms such as these, there was room for pasture and for the rapid expansion of flocks and herds. King also distributed government livestock with the idea of making farmers relatively rich.[81]

This was a community with a few individuals now ready to take risks in a larger market, whether rural or maritime, and to gaze into the future. Its maritime leaders looked first to the adjacent seas and to Asia. The building of sea-going vessels was forbidden from London, because it might threaten the Company's monopoly, but they were built all the same and by early in King's time, if not before, some had been sent to Bass Strait to hunt for seals. The most active colonial shipbuilders were the former convicts, James Underwood and Henry Kable (husband of Susannah Holmes), partners for a time with Simeon Lord.[82] Lord had attempted the export of New Zealand timber to Calcutta (without success, thanks to the Company) and there was movement in the opposite direction. In 1798 Robert Campbell, junior partner in the firm of Campbell and Co., Calcutta, arrived in person with a cargo for sale. Pleased with the result, two years later he took up residence in Sydney as his firm's local agent, operating under licence from the Company for the carriage of goods within the area of its monopoly.[83]

Trade with Europe was more difficult because of the distance, but more desirable, if only because it was a means of reminding the real world – the sheet-anchor of colonial imagination – of the existence of the Antipodes. '[I]t is natural for Us,' wrote a naval surgeon on the First Fleet, 'in such a distant part of the World, to snatch greedily at every Opportunity to convey our Hopes & Wishes to our Friends.'[84] It was equally natural to want to dispatch the fruits of one's labour in the same direction. Here the crucial figure to begin with was John Macarthur. As paymaster of the Corps, Macarthur had begun to make himself familiar with the lines of trade which might be drawn between Sydney and neighbouring places, especially India and the Cape. In 1801 he returned to England, nominally under arrest (see Chapter 13), and he used his time to open up new opportunities. At Elizabeth Farm he and his wife had begun to experiment with the growing of fine wool, and he now succeeded in making British woolbuyers aware of New South Wales as a possible future source of supply. From Whitehall he secured an order for a grant of 5000 acres, by far the largest so far allowed in Australia. Publicity was Macarthur's strong point. Campbell and Lord had made some small trials with seal skins and oil in London, but it was Macarthur who did most to build up the English image of Australia as a place of opportunity.

Macarthur's formal ties with London had so far been shaped by his needs as an officer of the Corps and, besides the regimental agent, he and several others had a personal agent, Thomas Thompson, of Castle Street, Leicester Square. During this period in England, Macarthur saw a good deal of Thompson's family, including his son-in-law, Thomas William Plummer. A City merchant and politician, Plummer was twice, briefly, a Whig member of parliament, and he was known as 'Little Bacchus' in Whig circles. He was an eager young man at the heart of events. Macarthur's affairs seem now to have passed to him, and it must have been through Macarthur that Plummer's firm also became, from this time, London agent for Lord, Kable and Underwood. They began to act as such immediately, and by June 1805 they had disposed of thirty-four cases of seal skins sent from the colonial partnership, and more, to the value of about £40,000, by 1810.[85] Plummer is a small figure – physically and historiographically – in the story of European settlement, but he is pivotal nevertheless. Through him, individuals who had found freedom in Australia, and who had remade themselves as rich men 'on the ground', began for the first time to transmit the fruit of their labours back to Europe. There were numerous Englishmen in England who thought of New South Wales as a place of their own creation. Plummer was the first whose imagination ran in the other direction: whose job it was, in other words, to witness and respond to life in the Antipodes.

Chapter 11

Vicissitudes of Commonwealth

I

Eighteenth-century European life was governed by living speech, less than that of previous centuries but more than that of the ages to come. Oratory was an art loved by the poor, especially if the language was rich with pomp and artifice. Within an oral culture, speech laden with stereotypes and with formulaic themes will always be a matter for admiration.[1] During the first years of European settlement, good speeches were one of the most effective means by which the hearts and minds of the poor might be touched, momentarily at least, by men in authority. But speeches made by people of their own kind were even more welcome. Nor were the poor alone in listening to the poor. A vestigial authority remained in all English voices, of a kind which the literate culture of the high Enlightenment had not yet quite destroyed.

Words from the mouths of men (as I say in Chapter 1) had an authority which women could not hope for. The last statements made by condemned male criminals, in speeches from the gallows, concentrated the thoughts of everyone who heard them. They were a careful exhibition of humanity, and they were judged and discussed accordingly. Among gentlemen observers, the agony of the hanging itself was a black background against which one might display a glittering sensibility. When John Bennett was hanged at Sydney Cove in May 1788, Captain Watkin Tench was not impressed with his performance. He 'met his fate', he said, 'with a hardiness and insensibility, which the grossest ignorance, and most deplorable want of feeling alone could supply'. Tench's brother officer, David Collins, disagreed, and indeed the note he made of Bennett's speech shows that it followed the standard formula for such occasions: 'He confessed that he had often merited death before he committed the crime for which he was then about to suffer, and that a love of idleness and bad connexions had been his ruin.' There were minor variations on this theme from hanging to hanging. William Smith, executed in November 1795, advised his audience 'to guard against breaking the Sabbath', as he had apparently failed to do. A mixture of boasting, contrition and advice, underlined by a peculiar, numinous authority, the power of the almost-dead, was the usual thing.[2]

The hanging of the poor, besides being a brutal act of authority, was a performance in which a variety of individuals – directors, audience and actors – met on the same ground, working for a shared effect. A type of deference and cheerfulness, like that which John White had hunted for among the convicts on the First Fleet, was expected of the victim. Standing centre-stage, he eagerly used language otherwise more common among gentlemen. The audience absorbed not only the words but the spectacle, whose ghastly details had been orchestrated for them, or rather the series of spectacles, from trial to burial. Sometimes the criminal had been condemned not only to hanging but to dissection afterwards, and everyone had a right to see that too: not the cutting up, but the result. John Fenlow, a Hawkesbury farmer who shot his convict servant, was hanged and dissected in August 1796. The surgeons had to announce when the body was ready. No sooner had they done so with Fenlow, says Collins, 'than the hospital was filled with people, men, women, and children, to the number of several hundreds'. But in this case Collins, godlike in his own sensibility, fixed his own gaze on the audience and on the dramatic quality of their response. None 'appeared moved with pity for [Fenlow's] . . . fate, or in the least degree admonished by the sad spectacle before their eyes'.[3]

The poor created theatre themselves, mimicking the forms used by the educated. In England gangs of thieves might double as acting troupes, for their own entertainment at least. One former gang member gave an account in Newgate Gaol of their 'Mock-Masquerades, and particularly one in Meeting-House Alley, Wapping, when Men and Women met'. Criminal court procedure offered similar entertainment and through mock trials criminals joined in their own judgment, with a strange parcel of replication and antithesis. They were also good practice for the real crises of life. 'The novice', by one report, was 'tutored in a mock tribunal, with a defence of his guilt'.[4] Charles Lucas, a captain among thieves in London, directed performances in which even his victims took part. Once a man was escorted in from the street, half drunk, by two of Lucas's women. Lucas sat as judge in 'a chair of state' and he had his 'counsel' and 'jury' properly placed. The man 'was brought up to the bar, where his indictment was read in the face of the court'. The charge was the carriage of valuables (his own) through London:

Judge.   Prisoner, hold up your hand at the bar, guilty, or not guilty?
Culprit.   Guilty, my Lord.
J.   How will you be try'd?
C.   By your Lordship's will and pleasure.
J.   Will you have counsel assigned you?
C.   If your Lordship pleases.

> *J.*   Then give him a fee.
> *C.*   What fee will your Lordship order me to give?
> *J.*   Let me see how able you are first; lay your store down at the bar. – Oho! it is very well, Sir, you are convicted without evidence: why, Sir, what an impudent fellow you are, to run about in the night with prohibited goods?

Lucas himself, when his own time came, was careful with his hanging. Few so wicked, said the Newgate chaplain, had died so well, 'I may say so heroically good, so much like a reasonable creature, and a Christian.'[5]

As with novels (a largely new medium in the eighteenth century), theatre drew together the familiar and the fantastic in a combination which was momentarily dazzling to its audience. Within an intimate space, carefully defined, well-known identities, male and female, were undone and strangely elevated. Theatre's appeal was universal. At least one play was performed by convicts on board the First Fleet on the night of 2 January 1788, as they entered the Southern Ocean. What it was we do not know, except that it included, or was followed by, 'many songs'.[6]

This performance may not, indeed, have been a properly scripted drama. The word 'play' covered a range of performances, but the literature carried on the Fleet must have included at least one script because at the second celebration of the King's birthday, 4 June 1789, George Farquhar's *The Recruiting Officer* was performed at Sydney Cove, to an audience of convicts, marines and officers. The *Pitt*, which arrived in February 1792, included on board at least three keen actors, the convicts Henry Green, John Sparrow and William Chapman, and it was presumably owing to their efforts that a proper playhouse was built less than three years later, complete with pit, gallery and boxes, at a cost of over £100. Such buildings had appeared in the North American colonies only within the last thirty years, so that the Europeans in New South Wales were keeping pace with the times.[7]

The new building opened on 16 January 1796 with a performance of the popular tragedy, *The Revenge*, under Sparrow's management and with Green and Chapman among the players. It was once again a spectacle open to all comers: 'we cannot command success,' so the company's motto declared, 'but will endeavour to deserve it.' David Collins conceded that 'their performance was far above contempt'.[8] The costumes included some from the theatre at York, and since Chapman had been tried in that city, they probably came in his baggage.[9] More were put together on the spot, and words might be improvised as well. One evening, in March 1800, after another performance of *The Recruiting Officer*, there was a 'musical entertainment' called 'The Virgin Unmasked', probably adapted for the occasion. The virgin, Lucy, was played by Frances Parry (Sylvia in the preceding item), a woman of many masks who had been transported as Frances Ferguson, alias Frances Grosvenor, alias Frances, the wife of George Herbert Fox. She was now newly married to Philip Parry, who took bookings for boxes. A month later she appeared as Lady Hotspur in *Henry IV*, Part I, and afterwards in 'a new dance' called 'The Drunken Swiss'.[10] Among the male actors Henry Green, an educated man and once a London tradesman, was an exceptional performer. In July 1796 his colleagues paid him the compliment of a benefit performance, and a year later he received an absolute pardon and returned to Europe. The theatre suffered a similar loss in 1800, after the performances mentioned above, when both the Parrys had their sentences cut short and went home.[11]

Like the meetings of the courts of justice, the plays were carefully orchestrated occasions which drew everyone's attention. They were very popular, and convicts would hand over their rations when they had no money for a seat, 'and thus, by the frequent privations of their regular food . . . were unable to pursue their labour with proper energy and activity'.[12] The theatre was a ceremonial site where convicts, as members of the company, managed the agenda, choosing the plays (as far as we can tell), devising the props and costumes, and setting the candle footlights which divided their fancied world from its audience. It was mostly convict voices and movements which shaped the imagination of the large numbers who came to watch, but not entirely because the New South Wales Corps also joined in. British soldiers liked to put on a show, not only fighting in what was called the theatre of war but also displaying themselves wherever they could gather admirers for their movements and costume. On service abroad they frequently put on plays, and during the American Revolution buildings in Philadelphia and New York were taken over by the British troops especially as theatres.[13] In New South Wales, the second female in the cast of both *Henry IV* and *The Recruiting Officer*, the two plays we know to have been performed in 1800, was Mrs Barnes, probably the wife of Corporal Barnes, and there were several actors taking men's parts who were almost certainly soldiers. Sergeant-Major Jamison and Sergeant Field sold tickets, and the 'Master Haddocks' who played Lucy in *The Recruiting Officer* was probably a soldier's son. Both these plays had military themes, and good use must have been made of uniforms from the garrison.

There was also a theatre on Norfolk Island, from May 1793, and plays were performed there weekly, to begin with, and afterwards every month or so. But at Norfolk there was too much bitterness between convicts and soldiers for them to cooperate as they did at Sydney. A soldier had been among the group who started the theatre, but divisions formed very quickly. A party of soldiers led by Sergeant Whittle turned up one evening 'with a determination of making a disturbance', and there was a fight over seats. Whittle sat down forcibly on the lap of the ex-convict constable and theatre manager, Thomas Restell Crowder, and Crowder pushed him off.[14] The superior harmony in Sydney must have been partly owing to the people in charge. Robert Sidaway, the government baker, was active in the management throughout, with Sparrow. Philip Parry and Daniel Parnell (Coupee in 'The Virgin Unmasked' and Mrs Parry's partner in 'The Drunken Swiss') were both employed in the commissary's office, as clerk and bookbinder respectively. Another actor, George Hughes, was government printer. The playbills came from his press.[15]

The theatre was an arena for the use of memory, commonly believed to be one of the constituent aspects of the soul. By this I mean not only the memory of one's lines (the lines written out in multiple copies, presumably, by Parry and his friends in the commissary's office), but also the memory of histrionic form, inflection, gesture and affectation which the actors had picked up in earlier years. The memory of such discipline served to knit together not only the theatrical performances but other pieces of art as well. Sermons, hangings, plays and skilful narrative were contrived and enacted in New South Wales during the first decade of European settlement. So was music, for Lieutenant George Worgan, R. N., brought out his piano, and there must have been smaller instruments at hand too. For every such performance we can say that a spot was found by the power of imagination, an area cleared and circumscribed, a new sphere of action, an antipodean Globe, erected in the mind's eye, an audience conjured up and characters placed and set in motion. For each the script and stage were adapted to the time and place, so that Australia, or Sydney at least, became a home for the active souls of Europeans.

We can take a wider view. All such performances can be considered sideshows within a larger, more truly global enactment. Theatre involved not only memory but a bending of voice and action to the power of the written word. Acting in scripted, published plays was only one of the characteristic art forms of the new age of literacy, dating from the seventeenth century. It was only one means of expressing the transformation in society which writing had brought about. Playwrights were playwrights because they gave orders in writing. Through writing, the thoughts of Shakespeare (*Henry IV*), of George Farquhar (*The Recruiting Officer*, 1706), of Susanna Centlivre (*The Busybody*, 1709; played in Sydney 1796), of Edward Young (*The Revenge*, 1721) and of other authors shaped the actions and words of individuals who were remote in space and, in these four cases, remote in time as well. The obedience of antipodean actors shows the power of playwrights, a power similar to that which guided the eighteenth-century empire itself. The will of playwrights and of the King's ministers worked by the same process, through a faith in pen and ink.

It was impossible to force the submission of all limbs and voices. Many convicts in early New South Wales had little experience and no regard for literacy, or at least no wish to act the parts allocated for them. They were not, remarked Collins, 'accustomed to live in situations where their conduct was to be regulated by written orders'.[16] Nor, of course, were the Aborigines. But the rest of us (we living men and women and those of our ancestors who cast in their lot with the future) live necessarily under new rules. The business of writing and acting in plays was an imperial system which depended on literacy. Like the British empire itself, it proved the extraordinary and increasing willingness of men and women to be bound, in the merest detail, by script.

The authorities in Britain had themselves defined Australia, or its newly mapped landscape, as a stage on which men and women might eventually enact the forms of daily life in a cogent and laudable way. In 1779 Joseph Banks had presented to a committee of the House of Commons a summary vision of a settlement in New South Wales made up of convicts (see Chapter 3). In his imagination it was to be a community capable of managing itself, one which would be shaped by its own energies. 'If the People formed among themselves a Civil Government, they would necessarily increase, and find occasion for many European Commodities', while at the same time, he said, 'they might, undoubtedly, maintain themselves without any Assistance'.[17] This phrase, 'formed among themselves a Civil Government', and the idea of self-sufficiency which underpinned it, would have been well understood by the committee, because the processes of civil government had been scripted and polished in England for generations, so thoroughly that most men and women knew them by heart. Banks was predicting that New South Wales would become, not an open-air prison, but rather an open-air playhouse exhibiting to the world the various forms of English public and semi-public life.

But how far the performances contained in it should be shaped by mere memory of the way things *ought* to be done, a memory unfolding in common conversation, and how far they were to be bound by the written word sent frequently from Whitehall, was a difficult question to answer.

II

There was a third possibility, one which proceeded directly from the ideals of the Enlightenment. This third option had a peculiar significance for the Europeans in Australia, and I have sketched it out in earlier chapters. The despotic, paternal benevolence of great men like Phillip, humanitarian heroes, might well (it seemed) be the answer for this country, cutting through the difficulties arising from the character of its new population, from resistant memory and from the impediments imposed by vast distance, so as to meet the demands of an up-to-date sensibility. Humanitarian methods had been shaped by a polished and highly literate culture. They were born in books, but they were carried abroad as an active, living principle by powerful and cultivated minds, such as Phillip's. It was the founding Governor who devised the permanent blueprint for authority in the Antipodes, cutting short common inclination and living voices. He could not prevent it being complicated by other priorities, especially after his departure. Nevertheless, his successors, each in his own way, continued the Enlightenment project, by dispensing laws – with varying success – from a position of high humanitarianism. It was Philip Gidley King, however, as the rest of this chapter shows, who as Governor (1800–06) built most immediately and profoundly on what Phillip had done.

Looking back, we like to think of 26 January 1788 as the beginning of a story, the raising of a curtain. Phillip himself thought so as early as 1790, when the anniversary of the 'Day of Landing' was marked for the first time by the flying of the flag. But there can be no connected drama without an active, thinking audience – without an audience which knows it is an audience – and for the time being none existed. A common sense of theatre stretched no further than the playhouses at Sydney and Norfolk Island. It took about fifteen years for there to be any popular understanding of one large narrative, a chain of vicissitudes linking the antipodean past and future. Even then not many people thought that as settlers at Botany Bay they were involved in any splendid and riveting drama, a building of nations or empires. The Aborigines thought differently, as we see by the dazzling and absolute image constructed by Bennelong, for whom the first Governor moved across the land as a type of Ancestor (Chapter 8). The Aboriginal imagination was much readier than that of the local Europeans, although time was partly to remedy the difference.

But narrative does not need to be dazzling in order to work. Imagination can be drawn to little things, to one-dimensional characters and to trivial battles. In due course, even for the Europeans, Australia began to look something like a stage for the enactment of stories. They were themselves remade as a single audience, drawn to one drama. The gaze of power was answered by the gaze of the powerless, and leading players were invested with an otherness, a magic durability – time out of time – typical of theatres.

Phillip himself was not easily forgotten. In England he continued to behave as Governor until his official resignation at the end of 1793, giving instructions, for instance, to the Reverend Samuel Marsden when that gentleman was about to depart. In Whitehall he was referred to as 'old Govr. Philip [sic], the father of N.S. Wales' and in the colony he long seemed a model for governors.[18] And yet the command structure within European Australia complicated itself very quickly, so that the close-knit authority initiated by 'the father' was soon obsolete. In the first formal sub-division of power, as early as 1789, King had been appointed Lieutenant-Governor of Norfolk Island. He was responsible to Phillip and afterwards to the Acting Governors at Port Jackson (Grose and Paterson), but he also dealt directly with London. The first Lieutenant-Governor at Hobart Town (1804), David Collins, was glad to feel that his settlement had been founded directly from England and he struggled against the indignity of reporting to Sydney. He had some reason to consider himself the head of a separate and self-sufficient community because in practical terms both he and the Lieutenant-Governor at Port Dalrymple, on the north coast of the island, were largely on their own. They were certainly responsible for their own expenditure, and the governors in Sydney were happy to disentangle their own budgets from those of the out-settlements.[19]

The colonial courts of justice were a type of piecemeal theatre and the surviving evidence of their proceedings allows us the catch a little of the dramas of daily life. An interchange in the Court of Civil Judicature in 1804, in the case of Rowley *v.* Newton, shows how talk became a kind of vortex, drawing in various parties until it reached its climax in a carefully orchestrated performance before one of the central tribunals of the state. The growing use of the Civil Court, in which contendants met and spoke as equals, is significant in itself because it shows that Joseph Banks's prescription for a self-made civil community was indeed being played out in New South Wales, and especially in Sydney. The discipline inherent in rank was still important, and also the silence imposed by fear, but so was the unfolding of meaning, the half-predictable point and counterpoint of ideas, the common appeal to principle and custom. In March 1804, a meeting of various leading inhabitants of Sydney had been held at Simeon Lord's house to consider the recent bankruptcy of the paymaster of the Corps, William Cox. There was some heated discussion among those whose property was at stake, and afterwards Captain Thomas Rowley, Cox's brother officer and one of his trustees, brought an action against Mary Newton for traducing his character. Mrs Newton owned (or had owned) the government bakery. She also dealt in pork and she had supplied a considerable quantity to the Corps on the paymaster's credit. John Palmer, the Commissary, was called as a witness at the trial and his interrogation by Rowley went as follows:

Q. Was you in the house of Mr S[imeon] Lord on the 19th of March last?
A. I was there at the time the trustees met on Mr Cox's affairs.
Q. Did you see Mary Newton the Def[endan]t there?
A. I did.
Q. Be so good as to mention to the Court the language made use of by Mary Newton to me on that day.
A. I heard Mary Newton tell Capt[ain] Rowley that he had taken a false oath, and that a man that went up in the boat to Parramatta can prove it.
Q. If I had not brought this action should I not have suffered in your opinion?
A. Yes, you certainly would, for on the same day I made the remark to you, that I would not labor under such abuse, without bringing it forward.

Rowley brought it forward. He chose a type of public display designed, of course, to vindicate his public image, but a trial in the Civil Court showed as well that the voice of Mary Newton was powerful enough to hurt him. At the same time, indeed, in suing Cox, Mrs Newton was ordered to plead her own case in court rather than employing a male attorney to speak for her. She too was an actor within the commonwealth, though a mere woman and a former convict incapable of signing her own name.[20] Her justification, in spite of her obvious disabilities, was her property. Her trading achievements had given her a voice both at Lord's house and in court, and her authority throughout the town had the same foundation.

Property established interests, and interests led to active rights. A variety
of rights, entrenched in property and scattered throughout the populace,
meant a variety of voices. This process of commonwealth had been well
understood in England, and among the English abroad, for generations. In
European Australia the owners of a little property, enough to make them
independent householders, were the main bearers of commonwealth. Their
potential authority was especially clear on Norfolk Island, a genuine cru-
cible of constitutional method in the Antipodes. Here the future seemed to
lie with the farmers, often called 'settlers', most of them ex-convicts. It was
always assumed that commonwealth was the proper offspring of small agri-
culturalists (though Chapter 13 shows how wrong it was to overlook
Sydney). 'As they grow rich they [will] naturally grow honest', James Matra
had predicted in 1783, and all the early rulers of New South Wales thought
thus of the farmers.[21] Nor was honesty only a private virtue. It included that
businesslike candour, that manly ability to speak out (a virtue, it seemed,
women might hope to emulate), which was the essence of commonwealth.

The disastrous wreck of the *Sirius* at Sydney Bay, Norfolk Island, in March 1790.
In this picture by one of the ship's officers, William Bradley, men are organised to
bring ashore all that they can before the vessel sinks.

Source: Mitchell Library, State Library of New South Wales

The curious history of law-making on Norfolk Island went back to
the meeting on 20 March 1790 of all the inhabitants of Norfolk Island,
called by Major Ross to approve his declaration of martial law, following
the destruction off-shore of the *Sirius* (see Chapter 4). The regime thus

established gave legislative authority to a council of officers, which met monthly, in March, May and July, until martial law was discontinued. Three of its members also sat as a criminal court.[22] Another meeting of the same kind took place on Norfolk in March 1798, when the people faced extreme shortages and had no means of communication with the mainland. The officers, having convened, signed an agreement 'to build a boat of sufficient dimensions to convey the information of our distressed situation to His Excellency Governor Hunter at Port Jackson'.[23] These were situations like shipwreck, a fact nicely exemplified by the wreck of the *Isabella* in 1813 at one of the Falkland Islands, on the way home from New South Wales. Passengers and crew having all struggled ashore, a ruling 'committee' was formed, as a member recalled, 'to appoint new laws of our own, as we had neither King or government, law or constitution'. Seven members were elected by vote from among the men – shouts of 'Aye!' – and rules were drawn up for common signature: 'all private stores should go into the main stores', and 'nothing should be done without the voice of the people'. On Norfolk Island the population was too large for such absolute democracy. Neither council (1790 and 1798) was elected, and while in 1790 Ross thought of getting signatures for the declaration of martial law, in the end everyone showed their consent by marching past the flag.[24]

When Phillip heard of the wreck of the *Sirius* he also called a meeting, the first council of Europeans on the mainland. But he allowed for no consultation among the people. The officers of the garrison and the gentlemen of the civil staff were assembled by invitation to decide on several proposals. Among other things the food ration was cut and 'All private boats were to be surrendered to the public use' to facilitate fishing.[25] Both communities, at Norfolk and Port Jackson, faced starvation unless, like the survivors of a shipwreck, they were able to marshal the few provisions they had and make the most of whatever the country provided. Conventional methods of agreement, more or less understood by everyone, led to general acquiescence. All concerned knew that decisions would take their force from general consent. In calling his council Phillip relied on the moral authority which, he thought, men bearing the King's commission must enjoy among British subjects everywhere. Major Ross relied on the same gentlemanly prestige, but he backed it up with a vote at the beginning. The castaways from the *Isabella*, on the other hand, put no faith in traditional hierarchy, and they all met to consider every proposal made by their committee. The vital point in all cases was property, and especially the way individual claims (mainly claims to food and the means of getting it) might be brought into line with the public good. These little assemblies therefore mimicked in principle the most august legislatures in Europe. Even the House of Commons was confronted throughout the eighteenth century by questions about the legitimacy of some of its decisions and about related rights of property. Among the arguments on Norfolk Island there were hints of the ancient notion of taxation only by representation (an issue central to the American

Revolution), the rights of private property being managed by forms of general consent.

In each case there were also echoes of fashionable debate about commonwealth, about the way men living together – pirates, thieves, the settlers at Honduras, Rousseau's founders of nations – might meet and cooperate for the common good. Writers liked to consider how the spirit of commonwealth, which they believed to be inherent among Christians, especially Christian householders, might be drawn out and shaped to more elaborate ends. Projects of this kind appear in the blueprint for the settlement of former slaves at Sierra Leone and of convicts at Lemane and Das Voltas Bay (Chapter 3). Plans were made in England for incipient commonwealths – primitive and prosaic but new and inspiring all the same – places in which poor but independent men, heads of small households (containing wives, children and labouring people), would meet, debate and legislate for the common good. Female heads of households, such as Mary Newton, had no place in the theoretical fabric, but they made their way sufficiently in practice.

It was thought that such commonwealths should be watched by some selfless and highly principled eye and guided where necessary by an educated hand. Experience might contradict this wisdom. In September 1793 the small farmers on Norfolk Island met of their own free will to form a 'Settlers and Landholders Society'. Their main aim was the regulation of prices for produce, labour and commodities, but they also wanted to establish a fund on which members might draw, as with a benefit society.[26] The members asked King, their Lieutenant-Governor, to back their decisions with his own authority, and he agreed to do so, believing that consensus was the only way of keeping prices down. He was optimistic about the moral character of his people as evident in such movements, but he was determined all the same to change the constitution of the society. There were ninety original members and he ordered that the number be reduced to thirty, including four nominees (three representing men without land). The remaining twenty-six were to be elected annually by the farmers from among themselves and were to meet quarterly in a building erected for the purpose (to serve also as a market house). This body, to be called the 'Settlers Meeting', was to transmit its decisions to the two island magistrates (to be known collectively as the 'Higher Meeting'), who were to pass them on to the Lieutenant-Governor for his consent.[27] It was a parliament in miniature, but one in which King kept for himself the power of a Tudor sovereign.

The first Settlers Meeting took place on 22 October 1793. Its resolutions, all relating to the cost of goods and labour, were, as King remarked, 'corrected by the Magistrates and sanctioned by me; after which a proclamation rendered those prices binding on every description of people on the Island'. There was one more meeting, and then the institution died. The Lieutenant-Governor attributed its failure to 'the unsteadiness of those People' – 'I found them too wavering, irresolute and self-interesting to persevere in what they had resolv'd on' – but it seems equally likely that the settlers were not charmed by the improvements he had made to their society.[28] Their September meeting demonstrated an efficient spirit of commonwealth as far as it went, similar, say, to the gatherings of 'inhabitants at large' which had worked for many years at the Honduras. King's method, on the other hand, divided the people into electors and elected. Meetings were not to be a common theatre in which members of the audience were all engaged and in which eloquence gave its sanction to the rules they made. Instead they became business sessions with no audience (presumably) beyond the thirty themselves. On top of that, agreements were liable to be 'corrected' by the magistrates, before being laid before His Honour.

King disliked large, uncontrolled gatherings. The Norfolk theatre had begun with his permission five months before the first of the Settlers Meetings, but he had immediately banned it after the fight, mentioned above, between soldiers and convicts. (It seems to have been resurrected in 1805–06, when John Piper was commandant.)[29] Perhaps this unhappy experience made King decide that convict theatres were always unwise, because on taking office on the mainland as Hunter's successor, in September 1800, he ordered the cessation of the plays there as well. The officers had already lost interest, possibly because the number of women of their own class had increased so that their evening gatherings had become more private and circumspect. The Sydney playhouse itself, for four years a brilliant stimulant to popular imagination, was levelled to the ground.[30]

Like King, Hunter had tried to work up effective methods of cooperation among mainland farmers. He found that they were concerned to begin with only about wage levels, the cost of labour being so high, as he remarked, 'that it runs away with the greatest part of the profits of their farms'. He hoped that a joint effort would help them to counter the demands of labouring men. On 14 January 1797 he therefore issued an order requiring the farmers of each district to organise meetings every quarter. The agreements on wages made from meeting to meeting were to be signed by them all, registered with the Governor, and enforced by the Civil Court. The meetings were also to decide on penalties for infringement, to ensure the collection of fines and to manage their expenditure 'for the general benefit of their own district' (a provision which would have led to considering a range of public issues). In short, the signatures of participants were to create a general civil contract, actionable at law, and maintained by an ongoing spirit of commonwealth.[31]

Meetings were accordingly held, and within three months Hunter was able to announce that wage levels had been set, 'agreeable to the wishes and opinions of the settlers'. But the mainland farmers did not see why they should do the Governor's job for him. Doubtful about getting the scheme to stick, Hunter was forced to announce that he himself would punish any man going back on his bond, an arrangement which he said (no doubt correctly) 'the settlers cannot but approve'.[32] Even this authoritarian sanction was not enough to make the farmers hold together against the demands being made by labouring men, and the quarterly meetings, having failed in their object, ceased to meet.[33]

Like King, Hunter was acting in response to local demand, but whereas King had aimed to prune the spirit of commonwealth among his farmers Hunter had been trying to plant it. Norfolk had its own hierarchy of status and expertise, sufficient even to maintain a theatre. (Thomas Restell Crowder, the theatre manager, was also a leading figure in the Settlers Meetings.) The community there was well defined. Its island boundaries gave it a sense of shared responsibility, that feeling, familiar on shipboard, of one-and-all and all-as-one against adversity. There was no acrimony between town and country as on the mainland, and there were more women and children on the farms, reinforcing day-by-day habits of cooperation and a pride in accumulating for the future. In 1801, among the entire population of the island, 28 per cent were children: a substantial human glue. (It was only 11 per cent around Parramatta and 6 per cent on the Hawkesbury.) Also, at a very early stage the islanders had felt the impact of Robert Ross, and especially his belief that while government fed its people with an open hand 'they will not take the trouble of getting anything for themselves' (Chapter 4).[34] King likewise, though he trod carefully in Phillip's footsteps, expected more self-reliance than Phillip had done.

On the mainland farmers lived more frequently as individuals, for the man alone and for the short-term. They hung on their Governor's high humanity. Hunter might ask them to pull together as neighbourhoods, to fix on places of meeting and on patterns of local leadership, on forms of rhetoric which might crystallise as legislation. Highly literate himself, he might expect that each man would be bound by his own signature, his name set out with a little effort before his neighbours. But it was asking too much.

Certainly there were more meetings of a kind among the mainland farmers. Early in 1800 numbers gathered at the Hawkesbury and at Parramatta to discuss their mounting grievances. They now raised their voices not only about wages but also about the price of commodities coming up from Sydney. Unwilling to debate and decide, they were ready to complain. Unwilling to act, they were ready to watch, to be pleased or displeased with the performance of government. At the Hawkesbury fourteen men met as representatives, 'appointed from the different districts', but they did not aspire to legislate or even to meet on a regular basis. Their only concern was to work out the average prices already paid for labour and goods throughout the valley as proof of what they suffered.[35] This was nevertheless a significant effort and was obviously the result of some hand now unknown orchestrating events. Elsewhere the farmers similarly chose deputies who met at Parramatta, two from each of seven districts (Toongabbie, Prospect, Parramatta, Kissing Point, the Field of Mars, the Ponds and the Northern Boundary), to compose a petition on the same theme addressed to the Secretary of State. Hunter now showed scant sympathy. The farmers had only themselves to blame for their problems, he said, because they had failed to make use of the little legislatures he had designed for them.[36]

Both Hunter and King saw themselves as shaping free communities. Their views echoed the original belief, held by the Home Office in Lord Sydney's time, that a military form of government would prevail in New South Wales only 'while the Settlement is in an Infant State'.[37] A count on the mainland in December 1799 showed that already convict men serving their terms made up only about two-fifths of all European men, and many of those (and most of the convict women) were living virtually as free individuals.[38] Also, the use of bonded labour had never before stopped free Englishmen, anywhere in the world, from enjoying rights themselves. But though the aims of the two governors were similar, their methods were different because they disagreed about the purpose of freedom. The antipodean experience of both went back to the beginning – both had been on the First Fleet – but Hunter was a generation older than King. He was already fifty-nine when he arrived for the second time, as Governor. He had an optimistic view of human nature, and of the way in which society must always move towards higher things. His beliefs were typical of an educated Scotsman, a civic humanist born of the Scottish Enlightenment. To such a mind, the phases of human progress, as described by contemporary historians, were all legitimate and necessary, each opening the way to its successor. In each, one could glimpse the unfolding spirit of cooperation, fellow-feeling and patriotic virtue which was the means of genuine citizenship.[39]

The failure of the mainland farmers to keep up their quarterly meetings showed a sad lack of civic virtue. Much the same happened with Hunter's attempt to get the people in each district to elect constables or watchmen every year from among themselves, as in England. Within three years, election seems to have changed to nomination by the magistrates.[40] There were three magistrates (William Balmain and Richard Johnson at Sydney and Samuel Marsden at Parramatta), and from the beginning of Hunter's government they had been given a larger part to play in civil administration, supervising road works for instance. The helplessness of the farmers added to their responsibilities. They were particularly active in controlling weights and measures (to prevent cheating in the shops) and in keeping an eye on the bakers, on whom the farmers depended for bread made directly from their household flour.[41] The magistrates were gentlemen, and during 1799 Hunter seems to have decided that individuals of that kind were more hopeful bearers of constitutional progress. Certainly he now began asking the gentlemen of the colony and other men of superior status to consult together in a formal way. In January he called a meeting of all the senior military and naval officers, the Principal Surgeon (Balmain), the Surveyor-General (Augustus Alt) and the two chaplains, 'to consider various matters of a public nature'. In June the same people (plus, as it turned out, certain unnamed 'principal inhabitants, and landholders') met by his order to decide on the best means of building a gaol in Sydney, and to appoint a committee for the purpose. The speech with which the Governor opened this meeting, the largest so far held among the Europeans in Australia for the purpose of free discussion, still survives.[42] In July a concern for the number of robberies in Sydney and Parramatta led him to ask 'the principal inhabitants' of each town to elect representatives, 'whom they may authorize to consider of the most effectual means of detecting the robbers and bringing them to trial'. Their deliberations were to be followed by a meeting of the magistrates to sift and decide on their suggestions, but it is not clear whether either meeting took place.[43]

Finally, in November 1799 there was a series of meetings to consider the recurring problem of the bakers. By now whatever public interest there had been in such gatherings had lapsed. Once again, civic virtue proved sadly lacking. Some stayed away in spite of the Governor's positive orders, and 'the Chairman of the Assembly', in conveying messages from His Excellency, sometimes found it hard to get those who came to listen.[44] The chairman in each case was almost certainly the Governor's chief minister, William Balmain. Hunter called no more meetings, and in the following year the government on the mainland passed to King.

III

The governors kept at a little distance from the daily lives of the other officers. Their dignity required it. They made their will known among the elite and gathered information by the use of go-betweens, men in whom they had particular confidence. Phillip had relied mainly on the Judge-Advocate, David Collins, and the Principal Surgeon, John White, and these two were also his personal attendants: Collins his secretary and White his physician. Major Grose, when he became Acting Governor in December 1792, turned to John Macarthur, then a lieutenant in the Corps, as his right-hand man. Macarthur was only twenty-six but his ability and self-confidence were just what Grose needed. He was already paymaster of the regiment, and he was now given the additional title of Inspector of Public Works. His responsibilities embraced all 'the civil duties' at Parramatta and Toongabbie, the management of the public stores of grain and the government farms, and he probably influenced all measures of policy.[45] Hunter agreed with the appointment on his arrival late in 1795, but within a few months he and Macarthur quarrelled and Macarthur resigned. Balmain was henceforth the Governor's leading assistant, and Hunter also relied on George Johnston, a captain in the Corps, 'an old and kind acquaintance' for whom he created, or revived, the post of aide-de-camp. Johnston managed the labour of all the convicts employed by the Crown.[46]

Governor King confirmed Balmain's authority in 1800 by making him the colony's first Naval Officer, which meant that he controlled the traffic in Port Jackson.[47] But a year later Balmain sailed home. The new Naval

Officer was John Harris, surgeon of the Corps, whom King described as 'a most indefatigable and useful assistant to the Governor'. His administrative virtues – 'general knowledge of every person in the colony' and a readiness with pen and paper – were precisely what King needed in his efforts to tighten up the relationship of government and people. Equally important was the work of the Governor's secretary, once done by the Judge-Advocate but now given a full-time dignity and purpose of its own. King defined the duties of his secretary as follows:

> Has the custody of all official papers and records belonging to the colony; transcribes the public despatches; charged with making out all grants, leases and other public Colonial instruments; also the care of numerous indents or lists sent with convicts of their terms of conviction, and every other official transaction relating to the colony and Government.

This was pivotal work within the bureaucracy which King envisaged, but owing to the lack of both men and money he had trouble fitting the ideal to reality.[48]

At the same time the failure of commonwealth among the farming people made it necessary to look for other means of moral order. In 1802 Balmain, now in England, drew up a proposal for the appointment of a number of senior officials to be known as Commandants or Residents, one for each district. The officers of the Corps were an important body of gentlemen, but they could not play the part expected of gentlemen in British communities. They could not offer genuine leadership to the farmers because they were not trusted, and also because most of them had no wish to. As Balmain remarked, they were 'only anxious to see the day of relief arrive that they may withdraw from a scene which they have never enjoyed'. The men he wanted appointed in their place must be capable of winning popular confidence, offering advice and encouragement, and stiffening the common resolve to do well. Such men might also, he said, make up a council to advise the Governor and to pass laws for the colony.[49]

Lord Hobart was now Secretary of State. He had similar ideas about the need for a superior class of men in the colony, but he aimed to create one by encouraging free settlement, larger grants of land, and the local cultivation of capital. This was also King's approach. King relied on individual ambition much more than Hunter had done, on private interest rather than on civic virtue, on energy rather than custom. He had no great faith in public gatherings and free discussion, and nothing approaching the shape of a legislative council met in his time. He ordered daily meetings, at nine each morning, between himself, the Judge-Advocate, the Commissary, the Principal Surgeon and the Provost Marshal, but in shaping laws and policy he looked mainly, as he himself remarked, to his own judgment, 'my own opinion of men and things'.[50] He nevertheless succeeded in fixing those common rights he most valued himself, rights embedded in homes and property, among the Europeans in Australia. His method involved taking full advantage of his authority and also of the written word, using writing to draw the people within a precisely regulated, risk-reduced community. He closed down the theatre at Sydney, but he started the first newspaper and he published the first two books (both government manuals). He was a governor who performed best on paper.

In Europe itself, governments were in the process of being remade by the astute use of written instructions. Skilled bureaucracy had evolved very considerably during the eighteenth century, and in England it was brought to a high pitch while William Pitt the Younger was prime minister (1783–1801). The Home Office had been created just before Pitt came to power, partly replacing a haphazard system of government departments, and within it there appeared a gradual concentration of domestic policy, a more highly articulated concern for common loyalty, law and order. This was only possible because of continuously faster and fuller communication among the people themselves, a process remarked upon by Jane Austen through one of her characters in *Northanger Abbey*: England was a country where 'social and literary intercourse' was now so thorough that 'every man is surrounded by a neighbourhood of voluntary spies, . . . roads and newspapers lay every thing open'. William Godwin's brilliant story of *Caleb Williams* (1794) likewise explored the idea of a single Englishman caught under what seems to be an ubiquitous eye. The miscellaneous gaze of society matched and overlapped the gaze of power. In republican France the government took advantage of similar developments for its own purposes, and with the suddenness of revolution. The need to effect a radical change in the minds of the people consistent with changes in Paris led to a wholesale reliance on paper by the men who took charge in the revolutionary years, the result being, as one historian puts it, 'a magnificent experiment in organised social communication.'[51] King's New South Wales can be seen in the same terms.

King was a protégé of Governor Phillip, and like Phillip he believed in strong, centralised power on which all might learn to depend. The authority which Phillip had formed was used by King to draw his people – now (ideally) putting themselves forward as active, skilled individuals – within the embrace of government. His entrepreneurial approach to land-use and land ownership (see Chapter 10) was a case in point. The survival of settlement from year to year depended on foodstuffs grown on the spot. The government had its own farms, but they were not adequate as a source of supply, and they became steadily less significant in the overall scheme of things. Life was therefore shaped and maintained for the long term from two directions: not only the despotic benevolence of government but also the independent energy of the ex-convict farmers. King worked hard with this strong tissue of mutuality and even as early as 1791, soon after becoming Lieutenant-Governor of Norfolk Island, he acted among his people there by establishing a type of social contract, or rather a fabric of daily agreements, in writing.

Large numbers of people could be managed well, or so King believed, only if they were frequently listed. Their circumstances were to be described in detail by the government clerks, and their names carried forward, from list to list, under the Governor's eye. (The system of coupling the names of convicts with the names of their ships, for easy identification, dated from this time.)[52] From the beginning at Norfolk, many of the lists included the signatures of the people themselves, for in his own mind King was dealing not only with subjects but with individuals who were themselves participating in the minimisation of risk. These signatures mostly acknowledged payment for grain and pork sold to the public store, and the Lieutenant-Governor himself signed the promissory notes given in return, which entitled the recipient to draw on the British Treasury.[53] The exchange of signatures was significant beyond the merely instrumental. Names attached to persons – among Europeans, one's own Christian name and surname – are like jewels, the badges of the soul. They are objects of custom and ceremony. The exchange of signatures was something like the exchange of names among Aborigines, or the shaking of hands. It worked as a mutual salute in which each side gratified the dignity of the other.

John Hunter, captain in the Royal Navy, who became Governor of New South Wales in 1795, aged 58.

Source: National Library of Australia

Such a system was hard to keep up in dealing with large numbers, and only King succeeded. Hunter tried to follow his example as Governor on the mainland, but his request for signatures from farmers dealing with the store was soon a dead letter.[54] Among other things, this meant that individuals could muster stray pigs and sell them to the Commissary as their own: 'any Name they chuse to give in is considered sufficent'.[55] Hunter knew the importance of signatures, but whereas King valued them as a means of binding people to government, Hunter was more concerned with encouraging such ties among the people themselves. He had tried to use his own moral authority to promote a sense of community among the farmers, but he had none of King's reverence for names collected on paper: columns and columns of names. King, when he took over as Governor at Sydney, was nonplussed to find 'no general list whatever of the inhabitants'. But even more than names, King wanted signatures. His own was everywhere: 'nor is there a nail issued', he said, 'but by my written order'.[56] Within weeks of taking command at Port Jackson, he tightened up the pen-and-paper connection which existed between farmers and the state, by multiplying the number of signatures required when goods were taken into the store. He also immediately insisted that employers taking convict labour should sign indentures, by which they undertook to share with the government in the welfare and discipline of labouring men. Thus the system of convict assignment was established on the mainland.[57] Hunter had tried to promote written agreements among the people but King went a step further by setting up government registers in which contracts of all kinds could be entered. In the first nine months of his time, the number of government clerks doubled, from seven to fourteen, and by 1802 the annual cost of stationery, set at £20 in the parliamentary estimates, was three times that amount.[58] The community was bound together, in a new way, by paper.

No-one during the time of Hunter and King could have predicted the enormous influx of convicts which was to follow the end of the war with France, in 1815, and which was suddenly to reinforce the bureaucratic ties between Britain and Australia. Nor was it possible then to foresee the impact of unfolding ideas about public responsibility. In due course (after the period of this volume), such developments were to make New South Wales and Van Diemen's Land into authoritarian states of a type unprecedented in two hundred years of empire. However, King drew together the energies of government by a process which foreshadowed these changes. An embryonic civil service came into existence, an increasing number of individuals living within the very body of government. In Hunter's time, some clerks had spent their spare time organising plays. Such men now amused each other. One of them, the young convict James Hardy Vaux, told in later years of the camaraderie at work among so many civil servants and of the 'expensive and dissipated' hours spent afterwards at various public houses. He was the principal spark, 'entertaining . . . my fellow-scribes at my own cost' and ruining himself in the process.[59]

King's project was a very large one, and likely to fail in some respects. A settler might glow with the dignity of writing his own name on paper, but the individuality of the deed might seem to him less significant. Some were happy to sign for their friends. Nor did they necessarily see that writing (especially their own writing) was an activity with lasting implications. For other reasons too, a settler might carry his commitment to government fairly lightly. As a visiting naval officer remarked, 'Government conveys an idea of remoteness and generality that leads him [the settler] to consider a debt to it, in a very different light from one due to an individual. Government he knows cannot distress him for payment without defeating its own ends.'[60] Nevertheless, this very confidence in government strengthened the bonds on which everything else depended. A literacy in which all played some part helped to embody the splendour of the state, and it added to the sense of general security. The state was thus reinforced as the nexus and medium, the conversation point, of common rights. At the same time, this was not an egalitarian arrangement. The signature of the Governor himself had a weight far beyond subject signatures, so much so, indeed, that promissory notes thus adorned now pushed down even the value of coin.[61]

This chapter ends with another of King's innovations. When he left Norfolk for the last time in October 1796 he was presented with a farewell address signed by seventy-four 'settlers and landholders'.[62] It was the first free-will, or acquiescent, demonstration of commitment to government by the people, and it suggests that public opinion on the island was already intermeshed, through writing, with the state. The same thing happened a number of times during King's government on the mainland, and afterwards during that of William Bligh. A libellous verse written in 1803, and handed around among the garrison has a fictional ruler ('the great King') amusing himself with looking over signed addresses full of gratitude from the farmers ('poor tools'), and boasting that they were 'An invention alone of my own undertaking'. The real Governor, in his comments on this scandalous piece of writing, gave himself a more heroic part. He informed the Secretary of State that 'acknowledgements' of his efforts did in fact come in 'daily, monthly, and yearly'. They were the free offerings of 'those oppressed and industrious people who [sic] I have rescued from debt, poverty, and destruction'.[63]

The libeller of 1803 gave the fictional King the role of a tyrant, a common part in popular theatre. He (the author was almost certainty an officer of the Corps) added other aspects of the stereotype in an accompanying piece of scripted dialogue: gluttony, for instance, both calculating and arbitrary. Salt pork from Tahiti was not good enough for the tyrant's table:

> The brig be damned, the crew and all the meat,
> Fresh beef and sheep is what I like to eat;
> A royal mandate brings them from Toongabbe,
> Excepting only what are sick and scabby.[64]

King had pulled down the playhouse at Sydney, but theatrical forms lived on, and indeed these verses signalled a clearer common focus within local thinking and a heightened sense of place, so that the colony itself was now expounded as a type of theatre: backdrop of limitless, ambiguous green with stems of silver, black and pinky-brown. The performance of the ruler appealed in a new way to the imagination of his people.

The author gave King a classic but unlikeable image. The Governor himself chose the part of his people's saviour, the hero to whom they offered endless gratitude. But the making of any image at all, the very fact that such an audience and such a theatre of the mind could exist, was an important step forward. Much was due to King's vivid concentration of energy, his patent busyness, and to the fact that the settlement itself now became a point of new interest to the wider world (Chapter 10), especially from a commercial point of view.

The application of judgment and taste is expected of any audience, but where is the moral effort involved in merely watching? King had drawn the attention of the people in a new way. But whatever the quality of his own performance, his audience were largely men and women who in 1798 had gazed, engrossed but unmoved, on the remains of their neighbour, John Fenlow, transparent to the bone.

Chapter 12

Varieties of Brotherhood

I

Numerous far-sighted Europeans in the late eighteenth century nourished the idea of a single humanity, or, as they sometimes put it, a brotherhood of man. The Antipodes was part of the silver sphere of such radical imagination. But any community, including a global one, depends on mutual understanding among its members, which means conquering divisions of language. A code of signs and gestures was deliberately laid out among the avant-garde, rich and poor, within Europe and elsewhere, a project without precedent in its global ambitions (except for the evangelism of the Christian Church). The republic of letters, born of the seventeenth-century traffic in print, was overlaid by a republic of symbols passing current world-wide. For instance, the *bonnet rouge* was adopted as the ritual headgear of anyone, anywhere, who longed to replicate France's great revolution, and, indeed, the revolution itself was an event – a new myth – which seemed to belong to all humanity (once again, like the Crucifixion). The Tree of Liberty might be of any species, might grow in any soil. In June 1792 a crowd invaded the royal gardens at the Tuileries, in Paris, aiming to plant such a tree. Two years later a party on their way to the Antipodes not only got hold of a red cap to take with them but also raised their glasses to the toast, 'May a Branch of the Tree of Liberty be transplanted to the Dreary and Desolate Shores of New Holland.'[1]

Nineteen years later again, at the Falkland Islands in the southern Atlantic, the shipwreck of the *Isabella* on a voyage from Sydney to London led to similar echoes. Aboard was Joseph Holt, who had been one of the leaders of the Irish uprising of 1798 – a man well versed in the language of revolution – together with his wife, Hester, son and servants. Nearly two months passed on that remote spot before another ship was sighted. Holt's stilted literacy shows what happened then:

They bore in for shore and sent their boat to the shore. By this time there was fourteen of our people standing on the beach. The first man came ashore was Captain Edward [rightly Edmund] Fanning, from Nantucket in America. He look at me very earnest and came over and shook hands with me and asked: 'How was the settlement of the world?' I answered: 'Very well.'

This was code, and the meaning is hidden even now, but Holt was willing to explain a little to the unitiated:

My Good Reader in order to let you know the cause of him coming to me: I wore my beard under my chin as a mark of what I was, and he had his in the same manner. He and I spoke two or three words together which made us to know more than I am going to tell my reader.[2]

Such cryptic gestures might be understood all over the world, by certain travellers among obscure islands as much as at the heart of Europe. Some were more common than others. The beard worn under the chin might have been relatively rare, but it was typical in one sense at least. The brotherhood of man was closed to women.

This exclusiveness of gender might have brutal implications, depending on the men concerned. Women did not belong to the new, free world, but the pride of brotherhood might well make a man glory in his care for women and children. The image of the cock and hens might be recast to suggest a new model of manhood in which the cock was sweetly monogamous. The French-American author, Hector St John de Crèvecouer, in his famous book, *Letters from an American Farmer* (1782), used his own farmyard as an image of citizenship in the age of revolutions, telling his readers of the 'gentle useful hen leading her chickens with a care and vigilance which speaks shame to many women', and herself attended by the male of the species, 'arrayed with the most majestic plumes, tender to its mate, bold, courageous, endowed with an astonishing instinct, with thoughts, with memory, and every distinguishing characteristic of the reason of man'.[3] At the Falklands Captain Fanning, with the tenderness of a good man and a brother, made the safety of Holt, his wife and son a top priority, and he would take no money from Holt for doing so. 'Make yourself easy, and family,' he told him, 'for we are in duty bound to protect you and to let you know that if every one else was to pay, you, and family, must go free as a citizen of the world.'[4]

Fanning was himself a citizen of the world in a very active sense, and the same was probably true of most of the men who were with him. He was master of a whaler from Nantucket. This island off the coast of Massachusetts was the home of a community of whalers, intricately linked by blood and marriage, whose abilities were famous throughout the Atlantic and Pacific. They were highly moral men, a good number being Quakers, but like the pirates who had lived on the same waters two generations before, they spent their lives either at sea or on their own island, and their sense of national patriotism was very weak. Even apart from the peculiar circumstances of Nantucket, sailing ships notoriously drew their crews from a variety of nations, and the loyalty of the men to each other, for the time being at least, might override any other consideration.[5] The fraternal and egalitarian habits of seamen extended easily into remote waters. 'The sea which surrounds them', wrote St John de Crèvecouer, who much admired the men of Nantucket, 'is equally open to all, and presents to all an equal title to the chance of good fortune.'[6] There were several methods by which Atlantic seamen were paid, the most ancient being by shares, all taking a cut of the profits of each voyage. By the eighteenth century payment by shares was still used by pirates and privateers, and also on some whaling and fishing vessels. At Nantucket shares were called 'lays'. Numbers of Nantucketers were taken up by British whaling firms after the American Revolution and they took with them their preference for shares, so that it was soon common in Australian seas. The former convicts who worked the whaling and sealing vessels during the first decades of European life in the Antipodes were shareholders: a telling example of salt-water brotherhood.[7]

Citizenship of the world had a rainbow quality. Anchored, in principle, to nothing beyond self, family and a protean and limitless fraternity, it made its impact differently from man to man. It appeared in the humanity of the early governors of New South Wales – allowing not only for the protection but also for the occasional authority of women – and in Joseph Holt's suspicion of the same governors: 'O what a pity it is to take a tiger on land, or a shark out of the water, and place them in the room of a man.' The pride and plainness in Holt's idea of brotherhood was further demonstrated by his saying, not long after he was rescued by Fanning, 'I don't care a farthing for one nation no more than another but what honour and manhood requires.'[8] Among men who subscribed to such an understanding, brotherhood might take life instantly – even at moments of chance meeting, as Holt and Fanning found at the edge of the icebergs.

Holt and Fanning almost certainly recognised each other as initiates in the great international code of Freemasonry, currently at the height of its power. No institution more thoroughly enshrined the virtues of liberty, equality and fraternity, as understood in the late eighteenth century. The lodges, as one historian has remarked, were 'the strongest social institution of the eighteenth-century moral world'.[9] The Masonic code embodied powerful ideas about the new manhood, erecting peculiar hierarchies of knowledge – secret opening into secret, successive illuminations veiled in words – within which many thousands of men were drawn as if dazzled. The language of its rituals made it an institution fixed in living male voices, its activities shut off from the sound of women and children, and (what might amount to the same thing) from the ephemera of any particular place. It was an ideal community, maintained by the 'tongue of good judgment' and by the shining abstractions of honour and manhood. Though governed by speech, Freemasonry offered a type of virtue as certain as any defined in print.[10] As with communities of worship among evangelical Christians, lodges might be formed anywhere and were often a great help to men who found themselves a long way from home. Brothers thus initiated found their imaginations cradled in arcane myth and themselves bound, as tightly as they liked, by the sympathy of their fellows.

Thoroughly established in England and Scotland during the early eighteenth century, Freemasonry spread quickly through Europe and the British empire. There were lodges in Bengal and Gibraltar by 1730, and soon afterwards in Africa, South America and the West Indies. In North America the craft multiplied especially after the 1750s.[11] Freemasonry stood for a new ideal of frankness and mutuality among men ('candour' was one of the favourite words of the age), so that joint-enterprise and investment abroad might issue from brothers' meeting places. There was a lodge in the London suburb of Blackheath called the Knuckle Club, whose members played a part in planning the European settlement of Australia. Most were City merchants, and a good number were Scots. Duncan Campbell, superintendent of convict hulks on the Thames and, in 1786–87, the government's advisor on transportation to Botany Bay, was a captain of the club. So was George Macaulay, Lord Mayor of London, a whaling merchant interested in the First Fleet vessel, *Lady Penrhyn*.[12]

Within each lodge the brothers were men among men: 'a new world', as a writer of the time remarked, 'hidden among the old'.[13] However, since the 1750s the craft had been divided. Once dominated by high-minded noblemen and other men of property, a new breed had since emerged. Brotherhood in the handling of power was answered (as with Joseph Holt) by brotherhood in the resentment and resistance of power. Men with more aggressive ideas about equality, artisans, publicans and small shopkeepers, had frequently taken the lead. New lodges were formed, called 'Ancient' and boasting a theoretically older and purer code. The Ancients reduced entrance fees and drew in vast numbers, each candidate being merely 'of mature age, upright in body and limbs, free from bondage, [and possessed of] . . . the sense of a man'. They also helped brothers and their families who fell on hard times.[14] The craft thus made its way into the army and the navy, where it helped to create a more careful and self-conscious *esprit de corps*. Among officers and men, a new sense of discipline and self-discipline was abroad and if a good soldier must, as up-to-date training manuals put it, be 'master of his person', he might also certainly possess, in Masonic style, 'the sense of a man'. Most British infantry regiments had their own lodges, typically affiliated to the Grand Lodge of Ireland, a citadel of Ancient Masonry.[15]

Here there were ambiguities. The Ancient code became part of the British presence throughout the world, but it did not always add to British power. It was triumphant throughout the North American colonies by the time of the American Revolution and lodge friendships reinforced revolutionary clubs.[16] In New South Wales several officers of the Corps were Masons, and members twice attempted, in 1796 and in 1803, to form a lodge.[17] A fraternal spirit showed in soldiers' collective land grants (Chapter 10), especially where officers and men participated on equal terms.[18] Masonic ideas might also explain the Corps's little war on Christianity, or at least on the evangelism of the colonial chaplains. Freemasons were not necessarily anti-religious, but the dictates of honour and manhood might crowd out revealed religion, manifest as it frequently was in the voice of authority. Such contradictions of ethos became increasingly hard to sustain, and in 1813 the War Office banned Freemasonry to private soldiers. Within the New South Wales Corps, where the spirit of Masonry flourished in spite of there being no lodge, the officers managed the clash of principle by a twofold strategy. They stood by their men on all occasions, guarding their welfare and insisting on privileges (especially in contrast with convicts), but at the same time they would not forgive any insolence against themselves. A soldier of the Corps might be hanged for mutinous words.[19] Savage cross-currents of loyalty and disorder within the garrison were among the central facts of early colonial life.

In New South Wales, as elsewhere, soldiers taught civilians about the virtues of Freemasonry. The society formed on Norfolk Island in 1793, which King had tried to convert into a 'Settlers Meeting' (Chapter 11), clearly had Freemasonry for its model. It was a benefit and burial society, as Ancient lodges normally were, and something of the international flavour of Freemasonry can be seen in the provision that the widows of members were to be provided with part of their passage money should they decide to leave the island, whether for Europe, Asia or America.[20] The society's original moving spirit was a former soldier, the Provost Marshal of Norfolk, Fane Edge. (The Provost Marshal did the executive work for the courts, issuing summonses, receiving bonds and levying for debt.) Edge was the eldest son of a clerical family and had grown up in Ireland where his father was prebend of Drumholme, county Donegal. His Christian name shows his kinship with the Earls of Westmorland, and so does the principal family heirloom: twelve silver tablespoons engraved with the Fane arms.[21] He had fought as a British officer in America during the revolution, but in 1781 he sold his captain's commission to pay his debts. Cast off, as it seems, by his family, he lived as a recluse on £30 a year, inactive as never before and feeling, as he said, 'a heavy and tedious Dislike to myself'. In 1786 he asked to go with the expedition to New South Wales, and on being left out he seems to have decided to give up what he called his gentlemanly 'birthright'. He married a woman of whom nothing is known save her name – Sarah Rushton – and in 1790 he joined the newly formed New South Wales Corps as a private soldier.[22]

He was promoted as far as possible at Port Jackson and then went as Provost Marshal to Norfolk, where he also made up for the absence of a chaplain, taking prayers and visiting the sick. This may explain his popularity and his success in drawing the settlers within his own imagined commonwealth.[23] He had once thought of settling in Canada, and at Norfolk he made a virtue of being even more remotely at the edge of his class, and at the edge of the world, a Crusoe or Gulliver within that sea-bound, pine-shadowed fragment of European life. In 1789 there had appeared in Europe the second volume of the celebrated and scandalous *Confessions* of Jean-Jacques Rousseau, with its story of Rousseau's escape from the sophistication of Paris to a small house named the Hermitage, on the outskirts of the forest of Montmorency, where the hero lived in isolated simplicity with his humble lover, Thérèse. It was a story about redefined manhood, the apotheosis of the man of feeling, a variation on the American dream of St John de Crèvecouer. Fane Edge fled with Sarah in the same way, and when they came to a halt on the far side of the world he named his home after Rousseau's, the Hermitage. It was a stone building, a step away from the main settlement and overlooking the surf at Turtle Bay.[24] At such secluded places one could envisage the fabled union of heart and head, the beautiful and the sublime (as eighteenth-century writers understood those terms), the womanly object and the gentle, superior manly gaze.

But the allusion was not only romantic, because the reputation of Rousseau was now bound to the wheels, bloody and accelerating, of the French Revolution. Signals like the name of his little estate were probably the reason for Edge's ambivalent relationship with the local agents of empire, who admitted that he was 'extremely useful and active' as Provost Marshal, but who also spoke of his behaviour as 'improper', 'disgraceful', 'notorious'. In 1802 he was dismissed.[25] Although he had often thought about going home, he died on Norfolk in the following year.[26]

The Masonic colouring of the Settlers' Society was apparently not lost on King, who not only altered its constitution but also banned Edge's title of 'President', which he (King) associated with Freemasonry.[27] King departed on leave in October 1796 and within eighteen months the settlers (presumably under Edge's leadership) had once more begun to meet, this time as the 'Fraternal Society of Norfolk Island', a name which Governor Hunter, when he heard of it, vigorously condemned as 'seditious'. By 1800 they boasted an unmistakeable Masonic lodge, the Lodge of St John, no. 1, and sufficient funds to buy land for a meeting place; enough, indeed, in 1806, to answer an appeal from one of the initiated, a small landholder on the far-off Hawkesbury ruined by recent floods.[28] King's successors on the island were all officers of the Corps, and were more sympathetic to Masonic principles. One of them, Captain John Piper, was saluted as 'brother' by the local fraternity.[29]

Even King was not always hostile to Freemasonry. In September 1804, for instance, when he was Governor on the mainland, he allowed his new *Sydney Gazette* to carry a paragraph announcing the death of a Norfolk Island settler, Charles Wood, a young man of 'extreme good character' and a Freemason: 'his funeral was one of the most respectful that had been witnessed for a length of time, being followed by a numerous procession of the fraternity'.[30] King was a changeable man, prepared to act the stern ruler, but grasping also at more popular parts. He may have come to understand that the principles of brotherhood were also changeable. Freemasonry offered to the mind's eye a new order, embellished with secrecy and masculine pomp. With a slight imaginative effort, men who were otherwise merely governors of daily life, their hearths and farmyards, might think themselves citizens of the world. But in real terms – if a sense of place prevailed (as it very easily did on Norfolk) – then Freemasonry might do little more, in fact, than up-date old notions of commonwealth. This was a process easily worked by the magic of Rousseau which justified, at once, both revolution and contentment.

II

The European settlement in New South Wales was mostly English, but from the beginning it was also a mixture of nationalities and ethnic backgrounds, drawn especially from the shores of the Atlantic Ocean. On the First Fleet, for instance, there were at least eight seamen who seem to have been natives of Portugal, France, the Netherlands and Scandinavia. Former inhabitants of Britain's empire on the far side of the Atlantic were even more common.[31]

The brotherhood of man had grown mainly from increased traffic and communication throughout the eighteenth-century Atlantic world. The power of writing had given its own impetus to the cancelling of distance and the erosion of old peculiarities of language. Such changes overran the boundaries between regions and dialects. But besides the hints of globalism they led as well to a contradictory result, a better understanding of nationhood among the mass of the people. The nation state, raised on a pedestal of paper, commanded popular attention as never before, so that among Europeans nationality – the imagined community of the nation – now had much to offer for the common sense of self.

In New South Wales, from 1788, national origins were the main point of distinction (especially the difference between English and Irish). Men and women coming from the same counties or regions in England rarely sought each other out, as they might have done had settlement happened in an earlier generation. Confronted by radically new circumstances, as if by a common enemy, they were merely English. From the beginning convicts lived together in groups of various sizes, sharing a roof (often put up by their joint labour), a fire and cooking implements, and they made their own choice as to whom they shared with. Londoners sometimes kept clear of country people, but otherwise such choices seem to have been dictated not by place of origin but mainly by shipboard friendships. Very early domestic life probably duplicated the daily meals at sea, in which men and women took their food in small parties, or messes.[32]

Convicts born in Ireland had a keener sense of regional difference, but for them too Irishness was now all-important. During the 1790s nationality had become suddenly central to the political agenda in Ireland, crystalised by a more sharply focused antipathy to England.[33] Numbers of Irish were to be found on the First and Second Fleets (sailing from southern England), but the first transport to leave an Irish port for the Antipodes, with men and women sentenced in Ireland, was the *Queen*, arriving in September 1791. Two followed in 1793, one in 1796 and one in 1797, so that by New Year 1800, 894 convicts (687 men and 207 women) had arrived from Ireland compared with 5808 (4723 men and 1085 women) from England. The Irish, thus calculated, were 13 per cent of the whole.[34] Some became land-holders. A list of individuals with land and livestock drawn up by Governor King in 1802 included fifty-one men who had come on one or other of these first five ships from Ireland, a figure which shows that the Irish were just as ready to occupy land as the English.[35] A few had settled together. Two Dublin men who had come out together on the *Sugar Cane* (1793) had bought 12 acres as a joint enterprise at the Field of Mars. On the Hawkesbury, Dennis McCarty, with 30 acres free grant and 40 more purchased from two soldiers, shared it with James Dun, who had been with him on the *Marquis Cornwallis* (1796). But there was nothing in New South Wales which could be called an Irish neighbourhood.[36]

The Irish who came by the *Queen* were very confident about their rights. On board they had elected one of their number to attend at the regular weighing of provisions (he was sent away by the master of the ship after the third day).[37] In New South Wales they were obvious in a crowd in front of Government House, Parramatta, in December 1791, protesting about a change in the issue of rations, from daily to weekly. The first such gathering among the convicts, it was shaped largely by Irish anger. The Irish, notwithstanding the farmers among them, soon proved a people (in the words of Governor Hunter) 'so turbulent, so dissatisfyed with their situation here, so extremely insolent, refractory, and troublesome, that, without the most rigid and severe treatment, it is impossible for us to receive any labour whatever from them'.[38] During Hunter's time their fury posed no fundamental threat. It was not exactly aimless, but for the time being Irish imagination usually operated on a level of its own. Irish ambition focused mainly on escape.

The Irish never came to terms with their geographical situation and with the remoteness of New South Wales from Europe. Though some could read and write, they moved within a largely oral culture, Gaelic and English, and they pieced together a knowledge of their position on the globe (assuming they thought of a globe) from oral sources, none of which was capable of dealing with vast distance. To begin with, they picked up the stories, which dated back to the First Fleet, of a settlement somewhere nearby, where they might live happily without labour. There was also still talk of China being within reach. The Irish were dispersed throughout the settlements, but they managed to direct all their efforts towards reaching one or other of these paradises, passing messages among each other and laying elaborate plans for provisioning and flight. No argument – necessarily framed by an alien and literate understanding – seemed to deter them. When they failed, according to Collins, 'they only regretted their ill fortune, never attributing the failure to their own ignorance and temerity'.[39]

The Irish were imprisoned in Australia, not only by the processes of transportation, but also by their inability to cope with the imaginary scheme of things manifest in pen and paper, maps and terrestial globes. They were not hopeless geographers as long as they could depend on speech and memory. In Ireland itself, men of their kind had long made their immediate landscape work for them. By word of mouth they could conjure up, as a near-contemporary put it, a 'mysterious engine of secret combination, shifting from place to place . . . [and] wielded by some invisible hand'.[40] In New South Wales they worked together to escape by the same means, but beyond a certain distance they were surrounded by a glass wall which their abilities could not broach. In November 1791 twenty men and one pregnant woman walked north from Parramatta. Most were found within a week, scattered and starving. In September 1794 Lieutenant Macarthur's six-oared boat was stolen, filled with provisions and rowed from Parramatta round to to Botany Bay, where it was abandoned, the rowers – all Irish – having set out, as they thought, for Broken Bay: they had turned south at the Heads instead of north. In January 1798 sixteen or more assembled at the outskirts of settlement, equipped with food and with two pieces of paper, one piece with written directions and the other with a compass drawn on it. In this case the constables intervened before a start could be made at all.[41]

The attempt to use the drawing of a compass, as Hunter said, was fair proof of '[t]he ignorance of these deluded people'.[42] But there might have been more to this drawing than immediately meets the eye (our eye or the Governor's). The most politically active of the Irish convict men had been Defenders, members of a secret brotherhood dedicated to a shifting range of purposes, including the expulsion of British power from Ireland. They were not necessarily in favour of Irish independence: among their oaths was one which spoke of 'the United States of France and Ireland'. They were bound to each other by a wilderness of catechisms and code-words, memorised formulas invested with a kind of talismanic authority, as usual among people who think of writing as a semi-sacred skill. Drawings on paper passed among them as icons for the initiated. (In remote parts of Wales at the same time, pieces of paper cryptically inscribed were family heirlooms among the poor.) Three years before the paper compass appeared in New South Wales, the authorities in Dublin received from one of their spies 'a paper full of drawings', and among the designs was one of a compass enclosed within a heart, signifying brotherhood, with a French fleur-de-lys at the north point.[43]

Perhaps the antipodean compass was like this one. Among Freemasons (as in the medieval Church) the north point had a powerful significance. The north, where no sun shone, was a place of profanity and ignorance. In initiation ceremonies new brothers approached from the north, as it were towards the light. Such symbolism must have been complicated for the Defenders because in Ireland the radical headquarters were to the north, in

Ulster. Also, Catholic and revolutionary symbols were mixed together in their thinking, and the north point of the compass could also be read as the head of the Cross. Other items sent to the Irish government about the same time included the following chatechisms:

> How far did you brave? From the north.
> Where are you going? I am going to the north.
> What to do there? To see my new made brothers.
>
> Where are they [our brothers] gone? To the river.
> What river? The River Jordan.
> When will they return? When they are cleared and purged from their sins, they will return back and wear white love.[44]

It is hard to pick one's way through the web of imagery to be found in such ideas, much less to map the confines of the Defenders' imagination, whether in Ireland or New South Wales; to know how far they sought white love among the blue leaves and barbed undergrowth of the Australian bush. Hunter spoke of a 'fancied paradise' and the Defenders were indeed men whose hopes reached easily in the direction of paradise. They believed that good times were coming, although they differed from month to month, and from man to man, as to how, when and where. Theirs was not a heaven which would swallow up the earth, like the Reverend Richard Johnson's, but a heaven on earth, and one which they might have to search and fight for. In Ireland the theme of deliverance from bondage, a sudden and final victory, under the leadership, say, of the Stuart Pretender, had long been spoken of by Gaelic poets.[45] In New South Wales it was China or another settlement which they sought to the north. However, Broken Bay proved more impassable than the River Jordan, and here the Irish lacked a Moses, a Joshua or a 'pretended Prince of Wales'.

Brotherhood revived old millenarian ideas among the Irish. Ancient ideas of baptism and redemption were mingled with hopes of sudden liberty and with the exhilaration which came from belonging to a band of heroes. Freemasonry was more popular in late-eighteenth-century Ireland than in any other country on earth; 'scarcely a village', it has been said, 'was without its Masonic meeting', and 951 local lodges were listed with the Grand Lodge in Dublin.[46] Masonic meetings were held in the houses of some of the Protestant Ascendancy, both merchants and aristocrats, so that Freemasonry helped to build bridges, momentary for the most part, across divisions of creed and status. However, this was done only by reinforcing, in a peculiarly rigid way, distinctions between men and women. The Defenders, or Sons of Liberty, found their prototype in Freemasonry. Irish Masons sometimes took up political causes and Masonic lodges were a recruiting ground and a front for more radical purposes. Masons and Defenders used similar oaths and images. The point within the circle, the essence of any compass, was a symbol of virility among the Masons, of a generative power like the sun's. For both, fraternity was the highest bond and the best virtues (as for Joseph Holt) were honour and manhood.[47]

In 1800 the plans of the Irish in New South Wales took a sudden leap forward. In January the convict ship *Minerva* arrived from Ireland with the first men condemned for taking part in the rising of 1798, the rebellion of the United Irish. This loose confederation of secret societies (the Defenders, in particular) had organised to take advantage of Britain's war with the French Republic. The leadership had timed their uprising to coincide, as they hoped, with a French invasion of Ireland. An army of Irish and French had beaten the British forces in August 1798, but not long afterwards the republican alliance was crushed, and in due course another series of transports from Ireland began to arrive, carrying not only prisoners of the familiar kind but also men condemned for rebellion. Eight vessels came between the beginning of 1800 and the end of 1802 with about five hundred men convicted of political crimes.[48]

The brutality of 1798, on both sides, was beyond anything known in Ireland for generations. The total death toll was around 30,000, and 336 men were condemned to death (a quarter of these had their sentenced commuted). The men who were sent to New South Wales were more inured to violence than their predecessors and they seemed more dangerous. They were equally visionary, but their thoughts were less engaged with finding a utopia on this side of the globe and more with the freedom of Ireland. They dealt in news, or rumours, about international relations, and they gave a new turn to Irish conversation in Australia. Those who came early in 1800 included several men who had been leaders among the United Irish, including Joseph Holt, and there were immediate signs of new activity. In Ireland the rebels had worked hard, and often successfully, to win over soldiers from British regiments, and there was especially good reason to hope for success in the Antipodes.[49] As soon as he arrived, Holt was invited to dine with his 'brother' (self-described) and fellow Irishman, William Cummings, lately an officer in the Corps. The sharpened edge of radical feeling was evident too in March, at a night-time drinking session including an Irish ex-convict, Edward Dogherty (a friend of Holt's), and Thomas Whittle and Thomas Jones of the Corps. Among other things, Dogherty told Jones that if he (Jones) 'could get 20 soldiers in the barracks that would be true, he [Dogherty] . . . could plant the Tree of Liberty in this country'. Whittle and Jones seem to have thought it wise to turn Dogherty over to the constables before they could be implicated in such talk, and he was sentenced to 200 lashes.[50]

The officers and men of the Corps trod an uncertain path between dissidence and loyalty. Some of the officers were interested in the political ideas currently galvanising Europe. 'Read Paine's Rights of Man,' Ensign McKellar told Ensign Piper in 1793, when that book, though new, was selling in its hundreds of thousands (cheap editions had been scattered through Ireland). But he added a word of warning: 'he is a violent republican, and

tho' he says many true things, is apt to lead us too far into republican principles'.[51] In 1797 it was reported to Hunter that an officer (probably John
Macarthur) had been heard haranguing a party of Irish convicts, trying to
get them to disregard a public order and telling then that 'that he had not
yet begun with the Governor'. The culprit's denial, on the word of a gentleman, ended the matter. Humble men like Thomas Whittle had to be more
careful. Besides, most of the soldiers, whatever their political principles,
were committed above all to the regiment, where brotherhood worked for
them in concrete terms from day to day. When it suited them they savaged
republicans, behaving, as soldiers were meant to do, as the teeth and claws
of empire.[52]

More consistent friends of the brotherhood of man were to be found else-
where. The republican merchant, John Boston, and the five 'Scottish
Martyrs' – Thomas Muir, William Skirving, Thomas Fyshe Palmer, Maurice
Margarot and Joseph Gerrald – had all come to New South Wales in 1794,
Boston as a free man and the Martyrs under sentence of transportation, con-
demned in the Scottish courts as political offenders. Muir and Skirving were
Scots radicals, Palmer was an English-born member of the Dundee Friends
of Liberty, and Margarot and Gerrald had been arrested as English delegates
to the British Convention of the Friends of the People, in Edinburgh.
Skirving and Gerrald had died soon after reaching New South Wales and
Muir had escaped, but this left Boston (who was Edward Dogherty's master), Margarot and Palmer. The presence of such educated men was important for the Irish, who were always on the lookout for leaders of superior
social status, a Moses or a Joshua. Liberty and fraternity meant much more
to them than equality, and Boston was especially attractive as a man with
access to shipping.

There was a good deal of plotting among the newcomers from Ireland
during the winter of 1800. There were hopes of recruiting Boston, Margarot
and Joseph Holt, but the preliminary leadership consisted of five men by the
Minerva, including the transported schoolmaster, Farrell Cuffe, who seems
to have acted as secretary. There were rumours of a written list of supporters, every man recruited – 'made' was the term used – being expected to find
another ten, none being told (in theory) who was involved beyond the one
who made him. Also, according to one of Governor King's spies, 'Every man
is sworn to secrecy by receiving a ticket', a system which had been used by
the Defenders in Ireland, where pieces of paper were carried as proof of
identity when a man moved beyond his immediate circle.[53] The initiation
was easily managed. On Norfolk Island in 1800 one of the charmed circle
took a convict by the *Minerva*, Henry Grady, into an empty house, and there
'swore him in a united man'. (Grady was afterwards a soldier in the
Corps.)[54] More readily concealed than the rituals of Freemasonry, which
tested and made men before meetings of their fellows, such ceremonies also
lacked the polished mystery by which one became, among Masons, a citizen
of the world.

In September, Governor Hunter ordered an inquiry into the reports of Irish activity and eighteen leaders, including Cuffe, were sentenced to transportation to Norfolk Island, and some to flogging as well. New men immediately came to the fore, agreeing this time to move on the moment, before they could be betrayed again. Parramatta was to be attacked on 28 September, a Sunday, while everyone was at church. The gentlemen were to be killed but the soldiers were to be seized and held, presumably with the hope that they might change sides. But once again word got to the authorities in time.[55]

On Norfolk Island the transported leadership waited for a ship which – so they told each other – John Boston would send for them, and they planned an uprising for Christmas Day. One of the government surgeons, Gaunt ('who', they said, 'was better than a dozen men like us'), they hoped would lead them. At the same time, they saw the bright side of their present situation. During one furtive conversation over breakfast, according to Farrell Cuffe (it was summer on that shining island and they cannot have been far from the sea), someone said, 'who would go and bathe, Grady said he would go, McClaine said the same'. Cuffe was asked 'would he go[?]', but – ever the scholar, the note-taker and looker-on – he replied, 'he would go to the waterside but was too ill to go in'. During the plotting Cuffe showed a similar delicacy, murmuring without avail against the need for slaughter.[56]

The rebel leadership on the island also looked for help from the local detachment of the Corps, and they won the support of six or seven soldiers, two of whom, said Cuffe, were 'masons and friends of his, and two good men'.[57] The quality of brotherhood among the Irish is evident in the way the conspirators talked about each other: 'a fine fellow', 'a good civil fellow', 'a very good man', 'an open hearted man', 'a very good sort of lad'. Their cause was founded on affection, the comfortable sound and touch of other men. It was an iron citadel of souls, forged by manly voices and symbolised by the drawings of hearts which were common talismans in Ireland; 'the nature of it', the Irish on Norfolk said, 'was to love one another'. But here was none of the gentle patriarchy of St John de Crèvecouer. Women, including Irishwomen, were usually beyond the pale, a distinction which occasionally proved unwise. Plans for an attempted mutiny on the transport *Hercules*, which carried both men and women from Ireland in 1801–02, included an agreement among the men to kill everyone, including their female fellow prisoners. The women returned the compliment by raising the alarm.[58] On the other hand, 'sisters' were sometimes found among the Defenders in Ireland. Also, during an earlier planned mutiny on an Irish transport, the *Marquis Cornwallis* (1798), the women had played their part by mixing ground glass with the flour issued to the seamen.[59] On Norfolk Island in 1800, after heated debate, the harder line prevailed among the men. The officers were, of course, to feel the sharp end of the pikes being secretly manufactured for the rebellion, but also 'all the women should be put to death'. The traitors to freedom this time, the men who upset the timing and let the word out, were men who loved their brothers too little and the women too much.[60]

Apart from Boston's ship, there were various hoped-for ways of escape from New South Wales. In 1800 the Irish on the mainland, once successful, 'intended to live upon the Farms of the Settlers until they heard from France whither [they] . . . meant to dispatch a ship', namely H.M.S. *Buffalo*, then in harbour, many of whose crew were thought to be Freemasons and republicans.[61] American vessels sometimes took away individuals. Muir escaped by one in 1796. Especially promising were the French vessels of exploration, *Naturaliste* and *Géographe*, which arrived in 1802. The French officers had, in fact, no room for numerous Irishmen (forty hopeful escapees were returned to the colonial government), but some of them deliberately encouraged dissidence. A treaty had lately been signed between Britain and the French Republic, but the peace was not expected to last, and the visiting Frenchmen were particularly interested in the Corps, its strength and willingness to defend the colony, apparently believing that with Port Jackson in republican hands the British possessions in India might be more easily invaded. They must have been heartened to hear rumours about this time of a great stockpile of weapons, guns, blunderbusses, pistols and pikes, prepared by the Irish. Another current story had it that William Cummings was to be 'commander' in the imminent uprising, which (whatever the truth) shows the equivocal reputation of the Corps in which he had lately been a lieutenant.[62]

The French officers drew a map of Sydney and they also managed to get a complete list of members of the Corps. In September, shortly before they left, some of them invited a group, including at least two English officers, to take part in a Masonic ritual on board. They themselves were members of the Masonic order of the Rose Croix (the rosy cross). The ceremony was cut short by Governor King's intervention, but not before Captain Anthony Fenn Kemp had been admitted to the order. '[I]f it were allowed to continue its sitting,' so Jacques St Cricq, a lieutenant on the *Naturaliste*, is alleged to have said afterwards, 'the candidates would be after their third step in Masonry initiated into the principles of the illuminati', making them committed republicans.[63] The arrival of H.M.S. *Glatton*, however, in March 1803, brought more hope for brotherhood. As with the *Buffalo*, there were Masons among the crew and Thomas Whittle took this opportunity to try to establish a lodge in Sydney, including the bosun of the *Glatton* and under the presidency of the gentleman convict, Sir Henry Browne Hayes, who had been initiated in Cork five years before.[64] Once again, King was alerted in time and sent in the police. During the ensuing fracas everything was done to hurry through the essential formalities, the bosun shouting 'Masons, Masons' and taking up 'a position of defence', while someone else barred the door to stop hopeful members from being removed.[65] They apparently failed. Had he not acted, the Governor said, Hayes 'would very soon have made every soldier and other person Freemasons'.[66]

The climax of such efforts came in March 1804, when the United Irish in New South Wales were at last able to circumvent the Governor's network of police and spies. On the evening of 4 March the convicts, Irish and English, employed on the government farm at Castle Hill, near Parramatta, were led out in rebellion by one of their overseers, Philip Cunningham, once a captain of the United Irish in county Kerry. Their cry, as in Ireland, was 'Death or Liberty!' They raided all the neighbouring settlements looking for weapons, and their numbers were said to have grown to between 400 and 600 men. Governor King was awoken a little before midnight and hurried to confer with Major George Johnston, currently the Corps's senior officer, at his house near Sydney. Demonstrating his usual obsession with the written word, King presented Johnston with hastily scribbled orders. The Governor's writing was bad at the best of times. '[S]eeing I could not make it out,' Johnston recalled, 'he said he supposed I cou'd not read it, I told him no, he might as well have given me Greek, he then read it himself.'[67]

Major George Johnston defeats the rebels at Castle Hill, 5 March 1804. On the left Quartermaster Laycock fights with an Irishman, with 'Thou Rebel Dog' from the first and 'oh Jasus' from the second. On the right Trooper Anlezark shouts 'Croppy lay Down' ('croppy' meaning Irish rebel) to a man who cries 'We are all ruin'd'; a rebel addresses Johnston, 'Death or Liberty Major', and Johnston answers, 'You Scoundrel. I'll liberate you'; while in the background the Catholic priest, Father Dixon calls out, 'Lay down yr Arms my deluded Countrymen'.

Source: National Library of Australia

The major made a forced march with a detachment of officers and men, reaching Parramatta about sunrise. At Toongabbie he was told that the main party of rebels was drawn up nearby. He chased them along the road westward, catching up with them at Castle Hill, where he persuaded two of the leading men to come forward to speak with him. The two seem to have hoped that they might be able to negotiate 'a ship to take us home', but they were seized and the troops charged the main body. Cunningham fled to the

Hawkesbury, where he was captured and hanged at the store house. A court, convened under martial law three days later, condemned ten more leaders to death, though two were later reprieved. About twenty rebels were said to have already died in what was called, in memory of a much bloodier clash in Ireland in '98, the Battle of Vinegar Hill.[68]

After the aborted uprising of December 1800 on Norfolk Island, two men had been summarily hanged, and in March 1803 two Irish escapees, who had robbed with violence, were also executed.[69] For twelve and a half years Irish rebels unsettled the peace of New South Wales, but in the end no lives were lost except these forty-five or so from among their own ranks.

III

The language of brotherhood included several ancient images of slavery and emancipation. The *bonnet rouge* was associated with the *pileus*, the cap given to Roman slaves when they were set free by their masters. In Ireland the Gaelic poets had spoken of their country as a woman enslaved to foreigners, while the imagery which the Defenders took from Exodus compared the Irish to the people of Israel in Egyptian bondage.[70] In other words (or rather in the same words), talk of the enslavement of individuals was mixed up with the idea that entire nations might be captive as well. To most minds New South Wales, however, did not yet qualify as a nation, whether ripe for freedom or not. The main concern of most colonial republicans was escape; to climb, like Persephone from Hades, back into the world.

But even at this stage there were a few men of radical imagination prepared to wonder how a revolution might improve life in the Antipodes. Maurice Margarot kept a notebook in which he jotted down thoughts about the future. A few years' experience in the colony had proved to him that the people were hardly prepared to use their freedom well, and that they needed instruction. The Reverend Richard Johnson had aimed to spread the Word of God through books and pamphlets, and Margarot's agenda was similar. 'When a revolution at home takes place', he told himself, 'it will afford a fine opportunity of introducing a number of books here, and also of directing the public attention to the perusal of those of a proper and salutory authority.' He also thought of starting a cheap weekly newspaper to convey the republican message, to be called the *People's Friend*. The educational system would also need reform, and Margarot followed Thomas Paine and other contemporary radicals in thinking that Latin and Greek should be kept out of the schools in favour of subjects useful to a plain-speaking, forward-looking, egalitarian population.[71]

All the same, he was not entirely sure that a revolution would take place, and he let his thoughts move in other directions as well. To ensure the prosperity of New South Wales, even within the British empire, he thought that agriculture and fishing ought to be further encouraged and the towns reduced. Farmers, he told himself (and he was ready to tell Governor King), should not be allowed to choose their own land, and they should be ordered to live on their allotments. They should also be made to lodge part of each harvest with the government, to be preserved for times of shortage as a guarantee against fluctuations in price. Also, the government should set a limit to all prices and interest rates (or better, no money should be lent at all). [72]

The main difference between Margarot's two projects lay in the fact that the first was to be the result of the people rising against their government (in Britain), while the second was to be imposed by the existing government (in New South Wales). The mingling of the two in Margarot's mind shows that radicals might easily be authoritarians, allowing no room for compromise or commonwealth. Indeed, the very word 'republican' carried connotations of energy, virtue and intelligence so strict as hardly to allow for chance agreements among the uninstructed. True republican revolutions must take place simultaneously from above and below. They must be managerial revolutions, bending all minds towards an ideal future. Dissent like this, the white-hot dissent of a man like Margarot, conceived of an orthodoxy beyond orthodoxy. But he was before his time. More common within the poorly focused parameters of early European New South Wales were dissenters who looked to the past, who insisted most of all on the old right of free speech. They argued from their understanding of the British constitution.

Within Freemasonry, members passed through a process of enlightenment, in which they gathered knowledge about the craft, moving forward stage by stage until they were wholly bound to, and simultaneously set free by, a single sacred Truth. The British empire and the British constitution, properly understood, offered a similar sense of belonging, a finely articulated bondage-cum-emancipation. Some subjects of the empire lived all their lives oblivious to 'the glorious constitution' of which they, as Britons, were supposed to be part. Some, especially women, were not interested in such arcane matters, which had very little, it seemed, to offer them. The peculiarly inchoate protest of Elizabeth Buckner (who lived with ex-Sergeant Tuckwell) makes the point. She appeared before the Criminal Court in March 1799 as 'a pernicious and seditious woman' because, when the Provost Marshal came to order the filling up of backyard wells in Sydney, so as to return the flow to the public wells, she demanded whether the Governor's well was being blocked too. She was told that orders were orders, to which she replied, 'She did not know how long that would be and . . . she hoped some person would put poison into his well.' [73]

There was little mileage in such hopes. Working in the opposite direction, however, the rules which formed the inner structure of the constitution might be broached, even at the Antipodes; this great well of Truth might be opened up and its mystery penetrated by those few who aimed at a higher form of liberty. They were themselves a type of brotherhood.

In New South Wales to begin with, the main issue had not been liberty but survival, plus a little comfort. The European settlement of Australia was a humanitarian project, in which the British government and its agents agreed that all who submitted to authority in this part of the world would be fed and maintained. A certain implicit agreement, underwriting settlement, apparently bound all concerned, at least on this side of the world. For instance, in 1798 the Secretary of State, the Duke of Portland, wrote to Hunter to say that he could not see why the convicts fed by the government should receive sugar – the full ration was several ounces a week (one ounce equals 28.35 grams) – and he forbade its issue in future. Hunter himself believed that the bounty of the Crown was dispensed too freely. But sugar was part of the original ration, sanctioned in Lord Sydney's time, and therefore, he dared to tell the minister, it could not be discontinued: 'if we had none we shou'd find it necessary to serve either an additional quantity of salt meat or of grain'.[74] In short, a diet agreed upon at Whitehall in 1786–87 as a matter of grace and humanity was now received as a matter of right: sugar was embedded somehow (like artifacts set under a foundation stone) in the very fact of settlement. King was even more anxious to cut costs than Hunter, but even he baulked at making the convicts give up their sugar, when it was available, and the matter was dropped.[75]

There is no way of knowing just how the convicts might have voiced their displeasure at such a loss, but the governors' ears were certainly open to murmurs of discontent. King, as he himself explained to Whitehall, visited every convict ship on its arrival:

> I go on board and enquire into the behaviour of the prisoners and passengers during the voyage, interrogating them respecting their treatment, if they received the ration and other comforts allowed by Government, and finally whether they have any cause of complaint against any person in the ship.[76]

This was the ideal. The reality may have been a little less on occasion, but King's statement is a partial summary of convicts' rights, inherent in their setting foot in this country. It included their right to complain.

The Governor's prestige, as the living heart and mind at the centre of things, was much strengthened by his being the recipient of complaints. Everything indeed seemed contingent on this one personage, including even the courts, as if the royal charter of justice was somehow cast into shadow by His Excellency. It may be that the early doubts of Major Ross and Captain Campbell about the Governor's power and the womanly cynicism of Elizabeth Buckner – 'she did not know how long that would be' – were more widespread than appears in the written record, but certainly in public conversation, until the time of Governor Bligh (1806–08), vice-regal authority was beyond debate. In this part of the world, as Richard Atkins, a magistrate and later Judge-Advocate, remarked, 'power . . . hangs by a thread'. That thread was the Governor.[77]

The governors all understood that their power was unusual within the context of British tradition, and in their different ways they tried to take account of the fact that old expectations about common rights were not likely to be met in New South Wales. Hunter and King (as Chapter 11 shows) experimented with more or less elaborate forms of consultation. Failing these, the law courts remained the only mediator between government and people. In any eighteenth-century British community, indeed, the main principles of public order were manifest in the courts. In New South Wales the administration of justice began to be publicly debated soon after Governor Phillip left the country. Major Grose, who took command in December 1792, halted much of the judicial machinery which had been set in motion by the Home Office under Lord Sydney, and by Phillip himself in 1788, implementing instead a regime of so-called military government. Not only were soldiers preferred to convicts under the law. The Judge-Advocate's Bench ceased to sit and all misdemeanors were punished and disputes settled by order of the Acting Governor. According to Atkins, if anyone alleged, for instance, that someone else owed him twenty shillings, 'the Com[andin]g Officer without hearing what the person complain'd of has to say sends a constable and orders him to pay up'. The Court of Civil Judicature was also effectively suspended.[78]

There were arguments in England about the merits of military justice. It had been condemned by Sir William Blackstone, the greatest legal authority of the age, as 'entirely arbitrary', a system to be 'indulged rather than allowed', and although other writers protested to the contrary, Blackstone's verdict prevailed in most minds. Atkins agreed with Blackstone. Whatever Grose might think, Atkins told his diary, by right the colony was 'a civil government, and the military are subordinate to it'. The courts ought therefore to be independent, as in England, dispensing as far as possible the ancient common law. Punishment awarded otherwise he condemned as 'a strong symptom of military government'.[79]

Under Grose, justice was unpredictable but it was not necessarily severe because the Acting Governor was not interested in cruelty. He ordered the cat-of-nine-tails used on the convicts to be trimmed back, and for a time it was rumoured among them that he would never hang anyone. He also set up the first inquiry into the administration of justice, following the complaint of a seaman-settler, Thomas Webb. Webb had come on the *Sirius*, and then, having returned to England, sailed again on the *Bellona*. On arriving in New South Wales for the second time, in January 1793, he had married Catherine Buckley, a convict on the same ship, and Grose had given him 80 acres at Liberty Plains. About a year later his wife was ordered to testify at the trial of the man who had sold her a pair of stolen shoes, and who was subsequently sentenced to 300 lashes. He collapsed under the whip, dying soon afterwards of either dysentery or consumption, and Catherine Webb, who was expecting her first child, seems to have been so much upset that she miscarried. The combined tragedy rankled with her husband. He was illiterate himself, but during the winter he hired a convict labourer named Ebenezer Sampson, who could write, and by this means made his feelings known to Major Grose.

Webb's complaint may stand as an example of the way in which resentment, born of an unlettered knowledge of the world, assumed the shaky authority of pen and ink. On 18 September the two sat down together, Sampson, as he himself recalled, writing 'as exactly as he could in his master's words'; 'while he was writing the letter he occasionally stopped to read it to him [his master] as he went and . . . [Webb] approved of it'. He also 'read the whole over [aloud] when he had finished it', and having done so 'he folded it up and gave it to his master who returned it to him to deliver to the Lieut. Governor'. The points thus gathered on Sampson's piece of paper seem to have tumbled from Webb's mouth in no particular order, but they can be placed in order here. He said that he had not received all the help he was entitled to in taking up his farm: 'I have not had stock, nor no assistance, for a house, nor seed, or slops like any settler.' But he wanted mainly to protest about the suffering which had been caused by the trial of an offence which, he said, 'the Laws of England would not call a crime'. For, he said, 'a man is been flogged to death'. And from his own point of view, 'I think it is very hard', he said, 'for a woman to be so long separated from her husband'; and worse, 'the usage that she received made her be delivered of a dead child, after three days agony'. 'Sir,' he ended, mingling deference with determination, 'I hope you will look into this, for if I do not receive the satisfaction I could wish, I am fully determined to put it in force in England, and to have it tried by the laws of my King and Country. Sir, your humble servant, Thomas Webb.'[80]

The only part of this letter which seems to have made an impact on Grose was the suggestion that he had had a man flogged to death. The ensuing investigation dealt with that point alone, and in due course Webb was fined £50 for making scandalous and unjustified statements about the Acting Governor. It called for better scholarship than Webb's to question the way justice worked in New South Wales. Even the courts themselves were not always repositories of high learning. In Hunter's time, the post of Judge-Advocate passed from David Collins, himself an amateur, to Richard Atkins. Atkins presided over the courts from 1796 until 1797, when Richard Dore, a qualified lawyer – the first to come of his own free will to New South Wales – arrived from England; and then again on Dore's death in 1800 until another lawyer, Ellis Bent, took up the post in 1810. Atkins was intelligent – 'exceedingly clever', according to Governor King – and he had the education of a gentleman. (He must have been the first in New South Wales to own a copy of Edmund Burke's *Reflections on the Revolution in France*, published in 1790.)[81] But he had no legal training. He was also timid and gentle, loved by women but inept in the manly codes of brotherhood, incompetent with money (among the property he had already lost was the lordship of the manor of Clapham) and addicted to drink.

Atkins regarded the law of England as a sublime system which he was bound to admire and defend, however little he understood it. He was high-minded, and a visitor to his house in 1804 found him 'the perfect delicate gentleman when himself'.[82] But he lacked worldly discrimination. Relying on his law books, he often using precision rather than equity, and, a good-natured innocent himself, he was oblivious to lying and corruption.[83] However, as Judge-Advocate he was determined to resist what he knew of military government. In his time the court avoided trying questions of honour (they now went to court martial), and its methods of punishment were almost wholly sanctioned by civil precedent.

And yet there were still peculiarities, not only in the structure of the colonial courts but in the way in which trials were conducted. According to James Tuckey, a visiting naval officer, procedure was 'not only contrary to the usual forms of law and evidence, but even contrary to every principle of common sense'.[84] This was due partly to ineptitude and corruption but partly also to the way in which the needs of the people had been interpreted by governors and judges. The courts had invented their own common law. The place of colonial women under the law was especially remarkable. In England, as Blackstone said, 'husband and wife are one person in law', so that during marriage 'the very being or legal existence of the woman is suspended'.[85] This rule was impossible to apply in many cases in New South Wales because husbands were often convicts and as such had no legal existence themselves: in England, felons could neither sue nor be sued in the courts. Lord Sydney had intended that convicts should not be disabled in the Antipodes, but by the mid-1790s local opinion began to suggest the contrary. The free wives of convict men therefore became self-sufficient in law. The first to appear in the courts on this basis was Sarah Fielder, she being allowed to sue an officer of the Corps for debt in July 1795.[86] From the beginning the local authorities had made up for the moral incompetence of poor men by setting up as a substitute husband: the judge-advocates dealt similarly with the legal incompetence of male convicts. The governors themselves gave land to married women (even, occasionally, when the husbands were not convicts), and both Dore and Atkins, for all their admiration of English precedent, let such women use the courts, on their own account, to defend their property.[87]

This was mere local custom. Within the law of England there were larger principles, deeper mysteries, mansions of understanding which were beyond humble and illiterate men like Thomas Webb, and which were irrelevant to Richard Atkins. The process of enlightenment, by which a man was initiated into a higher comprehension of the law – drawn step by step towards an elaborating, liberating knowledge – appears in the case of the gentleman convict, John Grant. Grant arrived on the *Coromandel* in May 1804. His first wish, declared on his stepping ashore, was to make money. Writing home to his mother and sister, he spoke of trading to India, and he looked forward to sending some of his takings home: 'If I ever become affluent, you shall also.' It took him about a fortnight to see that matters were not so simple. He was not allowed to sell the cargo of spirits he had brought with him, and as a result he had no capital. Most convict men without resources would have been forced to enter immediately into bondage, as servants and dependants of the state, 'to be disposed of', as Grant put it, 'like a Slave'. He chose instead to wait, to 'live, literally speaking, upon a crust', until he could find work of his own choice, of a kind 'not grating to the feelings of a gentleman'.

He then found that he could take full advantage of money he earned only if he had a conditional pardon, which would enable him to sue and be sued. A conditional pardon became the great object. Without it, 'I come within the Eye of the Law, incapable of making engagements of any kind and my hands tied up from all exertions.'[88] This prize was won in February 1805, but Grant then wrote home to announce a more fundamental truth. He now understood, at last, he said, that the whole system of colonial authority was flawed, and here he expounded the principles which had motivated Lord Sydney in his founding of the settlement. He was emancipated, thanks to a condescending Governor, but, he said, 'The idea of emancipation itself is an atrocious bug-bear.' He now believed that King had been legally incapable of limiting his rights, or those of any convict, at any stage after arrival. As various old-fashioned members of parliament had understood very clearly in the 1780s, in strict law the sentence of transportation involved nothing more than banishment. No Transportation Act made any reference to hard labour or other penalties. Grant had nothing to say about the rights of women convicts. It was a sense of brotherhood under the constitution that made him declare that transported men were rightly 'under the influence of the Grand Magna Charta of England in the two great points we are taught at home to hold most dear to us, viz. "their persons and property are sacred"'. In New South Wales, however, nothing was sacred: 'Men are sent forcibly to the hoe under pain of dreadful flagellation and made slaves of, and others (as is my case) suffer a plunder of their little property, without means of redress.'[89]

Two years before, in England, the radical lawyer Jeremy Bentham had come with surprise to a similar conclusion. Bentham wrote up his argument, with much more learning than Grant could command, in a pamphlet called *A Plea for the Constitution: Shewing the Enormities Committed, to the oppression of British subjects, innocent as well as guilty; in breach of Magna Charta, the Petition of Right, the Habeas Corpus Act, and the Bill of Rights. As likewise of the Several Transportation Acts, in and by the Design, Foundation, and Government of the Penal Colony of New South Wales.* The argument dealt especially with the power of the Governor, that thread on which all else hung, and which Bentham concluded was unsupported, in most respects, by any Act of Parliament. He was keen to alert the government to the fragile legitimacy of its achievement in New South Wales. But he was also afraid of letting such ideas loose in the Antipodes and his work, though printed, was not published.[90]

Bentham's discovery reached Sydney nevertheless. He had decided to entrust a copy of his pamphlet to David Collins on his being appointed to govern the new settlement to the south. Before his departure Collins seems to have mentioned it to John Macarthur, currently in London, who passed on the idea to an incredulous Governor King when he returned to New South Wales in 1805. In the colony itself, the pressure of events and the accumulation of property in King's time had begun to draw the minds of educated men – especially those who argued with government – in the same direction. During a dispute with King in 1804, the ex-convict attorney, George Crossley, maintained that 'there is no Authority in this Colony to make local Laws', and he meant laws touching property in particular. The Governor, he said, possessed no more power than could be given him by the King-in-Council, and that was strictly limited. Among others it was said that the Governor, 'except in extraordinary cases, is only an executive officer'.[91]

King's efforts to raise money on the spot, mainly through customs duties, hurried debate to the heart of the problem. Taxation without the consent of the people, or of some representative body of men, was a classic infringement of common rights. It had been one of the celebrated causes of the American Revolution. Surely, said Major Johnston, writing to a friend in England, ministers cannot have agreed to its happening here: 'that a single Individual (and without even a Council) can have a right to impose taxes upon any of His Majesty's subjects unless authorized by . . . Parliament'.[92] In August 1806, 244 individuals holding land on the Hawkesbury, including George Crossley and William Cummings, sometime lieutenant in the Corps, presented an address of welcome to Governor Bligh, in which they told him of their hope that they would soon have 'a Legal Authority to make Local Laws'. They assured him, all the same, that every 'recommendation' he might promulgate for them they would readily comply with.[93]

The empire was built on debatable truths and it would have been easy to find, in England, men who thought of the law as a medium of order rather than liberty, who would have disputed the oppositionist understanding of advocates like Crossley.[94] But this the lesser fraternity of New South Wales could not know. Nor is it likely that many of the 244 signatories to the Hawkesbury address understood the fine line between acquiescence and obedience. Among a small number in the colony, however, including Johnston and others who had been Cummings's brother-officers, men who stood at the edge of high learning, this was a sublime and precious distinction. It was a fine line dividing ignorant bondage from rational liberty. It was better than the insight they might have won from Lieutenant St Cricq and others of the order of Rose Croix during their rituals on board the *Naturaliste*. Pleasant it may have been for a man to call himself a citizen of the world. As with the humbler circle on Norfolk Island, it was much more obviously useful to live within the brotherhood of one's native tongue and native place.

Chapter 13

Sydney's Rebellion

I

The management of New South Wales by the regular use of print began with Governor Hunter. A printing press had come on the First Fleet, and shortly after his arrival as Governor in September 1795 Hunter found a skilled printer, the convict George Hughes, who used the press to publish government regulations. A press was also part of the cargo which the first Lieutenant-Governor at the Derwent, David Collins, brought with him in 1804 and he used it from the beginning.

Through printing, the will of governors and lieutenant-governors was broadcast with a new immediacy: copies of orders appeared, each in a single, definitive form, wherever there were people to read them. Properly managed, printing added to the authority of the living voice in these small settlements. On the mainland 'Government and General Orders' were announced at garrison morning parade at Sydney Cove, and then repeated at various centres of population. On 29 September 1795, for instance, the soldiers and anyone else within earshot heard first the two passwords for that day and then, interspersed by the miscellaneous clatter of the port and the whining of seagulls, the following announcement read from the printed page:

> His Excellency the Governor recommends it to all persons who have lands in cultivation to plant as much of them as may not be under any other grain with Indian corn, and this being the proper season for putting it into the ground, he hopes no one will lose the opportunity, particularly as it is an essential article in the nourishment of live stock, the increase of which is of such importance to the settlement that he cannot but advise the utmost care and oeconomy in the use of what may now and hereafter be in the possession of settlers and other persons.[1]

Although the voice belonged to someone else, the words were Hunter's. He was here speaking to the free people about their own concerns and characteristically used tones of persuasion rather than command. It is hard nevertheless to know what the various listeners might have made of the result, echoed as it was in due course by numerous other voices, gnarled and fumbling, from one outpost to another, until it was finally laid to rest as a merely printed notice.

The Governor's own voice continued to be an instrument of extraordinary power. At Norfolk Island the smallness of the place and population made it especially obvious. Following the riot at the island's theatre, in 1794, Lieutenant-Governor King made a carefully polished speech to his people in which he refuted the gossipping accusation that he favoured convicts over soldiers: 'I now here, most solemnly and openly, disavow having ever harboured in the most distant point of view such a base thought as that which has been laid to my charge.'[2] He called the speech a 'proclamation' but it was also a parade of feeling. Laws which issued from the heart and mind of an individual such as the Lieutenant-Governor – an officer living among his people, most of whom heard his voice daily – were naturally a mixture of gentlemanly cliché, tenderness and iron.

King was a complicated man and the larger responsibilities of government on the mainland, where he succeeded Hunter in 1800, exposed the tensions in his character. Although he could make polished speeches, he was less mild and urbane than Hunter. Even his attempts at gravity, according to an educated listener, could sound 'serio-comic'.[3] He also had a quick temper and, for a man dignified as 'Excellency', his language was sometimes unduly coarse. In the interval between his own arrival and Hunter's departure King organised a muster of every soul in the settlement as a means of drawing up the first of his comprehensive lists. Hunter, who did not wholly understand the point of the exercise, gave the gentleman radical Maurice Margarot and his wife permission to stay away so as to avoid mingling with the labouring people. But no: King insisted that Mrs Margarot turn up among the women and her husband with the men. Margarot recorded the result as scripted dialogue (as if a play could be written *after* the performance). On Mrs Margarot's day the exchange went as follows:

G[overnor] King – Who are you (in a surly tone)?
Answer – Mrs Margarot.
G[overnor] King – Oh! very well; go along, go along; get out.

And next day, when Margarot's name was announced:

G[overnor] King – Mr Margarot, I would advise you to be very quiet, very quiet, and deserve the continuance of the indulgence Governor Hunter has shown you; be very cautious not to give us any suspicions.
M.M. – I hope, sir, my behaviour has given you no cause of suspicion.
G[overnor] King – No, sir, no; to be sure, we have not found you out yet; but take care, sir, mind you do not give any reason for complaint; sir, go along.
M.M. – Sir, I know my duty, and you may depend upon my fulfilling it.

Margarot's reputation being what it was, this last comment sounded like a double entendre, a little hint of fraternity, and the conversation took a sudden turn for the worse.

> G[overnor] King – Now, for that insolence, sir, get along out of my house. Commissary, strike him off the store, and send his man to the campgang. (Then uprising from his chair in a maniacal rage) Go, get along out of the house; what do you mean by insulting me thus?

Such abuse from a public official, so Margarot informed the Colonial Office in Downing Street, was 'not sanctioned by the laws of my country, nor . . . consonant with the humanity due to a fellow-creature'.[4]

Liberty and order both depended on the conventions of civil society, and a Governor who could so easily forget himself (it seemed) was not likely to heed the law at all. Joseph Holt was similarly struck with King's rough and vulgar language. But what Margarot called brutality, Holt called weakness. King was quick-tempered, and he acted on the first idea he heard or thought of, 'but', said Holt, 'when he would reflect on his rashness, he would make an atonement'.[5] King understood his own faults and as Governor he tried to avoid random situations in which his tongue might take control. In January 1801 he announced that in future he was not to be 'interrupted when passing through the streets'. He was to be consulted only by appointment, so that his secretary was to be the bridge between Governor and people.[6] Such formality, like the exchange of signatures, offered a medium by which both parties might know just where they stood.

Printing, rhetoric and punctuality were part of the process of enriching the face of government. They promoted harmony by circumventing the aggressive power of speech, always peculiarly dangerous in oral cultures. Anything which made officialdom more splendid encouraged obedience and trust, and indeed governors might already be looked up to also as the shadow of Majesty. In Britain at this time and throughout the empire, the Crown was becoming an object of renewed veneration.[7] Thanks to an amplified public imagination and a readier sense of global power, British subjects now made their King into a vivid, sacred presence even in the far Antipodes. Government was strengthened but at the same time the replication of royalty abroad also meant the replication of Britishness and British rights. It made public officials more clearly accountable to one supreme conscience (a theory especially dear to Lord Sydney) and the King became part of libertarian language as he had never been before. In New South Wales the immediacy of power, the daily appearance of the governors, their murmuring, shouting and swearing without discrimination of audience, told against their being the King's replica. The King himself was therefore especially important, his dominion in Australia being prized, for instance, even by the Irish rebel, Joseph Holt, and the English radical, John Grant. 'I know', Holt told Governor King, 'you are His Majesty's representative. Yet and all I hope you will not disgrace your power or go beyond the power of the happy and well adapted laws made for the protection of His Majesty's subjects.' John Grant wrote verse on the same theme: 'Ye Captains to a Monarch, lov'd, rever'd, / Draw on his Head and yours disgraces down'. For, he said, 'tho' Britons rule the Waves, / Great George's subjects – Britons – here are slaves'.[8]

Governor King embellished his power in more independent ways. Shortly after taking command he gave himself a mounted personal bodyguard, consisting of six private soldiers (afterwards four) and a corporal. Following his quarrel with the officers of the New South Wales Corps in 1802, these were replaced with civilians, but appropriately dressed.[9] He also extended his dignity by assuming the full title of 'Excellency' and 'Governor-in-Chief' as soon as he took command, although it was not until 1802 that he heard of his promotion from Acting Governor. He went further by setting out some of his public orders under the splendid title 'proclamations'. (In one, dated April 1802, he announced his own adaptation of various Acts of Parliament.)[10] He imposed customs duties, something which Hunter had been afraid to do without permission from England.[11] And in spite of his obsession with the written word, he often relied on instructions from home which had never been written down and which he may well have invented. He admitted to the under-secretary in the Colonial Office that many of the orders he gave were 'no ways provided for by any instructions'. For that, he said, he took full responsibility.[12]

By such calculated means King built up his armour, overlaying the fragility of the man underneath. He knew he lacked the powerful presence and self-control of the figure who was frequently before his mind's eye, his patron and friend, Governor Phillip. He strengthened his hand by bluff, by careful formality and also by a genuine munificence of feeling. He easily lost his temper, but no governor knew better the usefulness of public praise. Even when he was forced to disband his original bodyguard, he used General Orders to announce his debt to the soldiers concerned, 'for their attachment and alacrity'.[13]

'Governor King', according to the free settler, George Suttor, 'was a singular character, sometimes a gentleman sailor; at other times fond of low jokes.' Among his low jokes was his habit, when a ship arrived in Sydney Cove with convict women, of having them distributed among male householders by ordering the government bellman 'to go and ring the bell and ask if anybody wanted cows or sows or mares that they should be served out to them'.[14] In other respects, King's treatment of women was much more elevated. It was Mrs Philip Gidley King who began the reshaping of female authority in New South Wales, so that during her husband's government, on Norfolk Island (1791–96) and afterwards on the mainland, womanly accents can be heard for the first time within the brief and narrow corridors of European power in Australia. Here too, King's authority was embroidered beyond that of his predecessors. Governor Phillip had been separated from his wife and Hunter was unmarried (though Eliza Kent, wife of his favourite nephew, was sometimes hostess at Government House). Anna Josepha King therefore had a significance of her own.

A picture of Governor and Mrs King and their three surviving children (one daughter having died), painted in England during the period 1797–99.

Source: Privately owned; copy from the Mitchell Library, State Library of New South Wales

Mrs King arrived on Norfolk as the new wife of the lieutenant-governor in 1791 (one officer of the island garrison told his diary that she was 'a Genteel woman not very pretty'). She returned with King and their three children to England in 1796 – a fourth was born on the way – and when he was named as Hunter's successor she sailed again, this time leaving the eldest two at home.[15] On Norfolk she had been a novice encumbered with babies, but her presence at Sydney made a marked difference to executive power. The empire in Australia had always been designed partly for the protection of women. Some thereby became independent householders and participants in public conversation. Now a small space was opened for the authority of women such as Mrs King, whose voices were reinforced by rank and gentility.

The understanding in Sydney that important decisions might now be subject occasionally to female influence caused suspicion and even a sense of scandal. The officers of the Corps, brothers as ever, spoke of 'Queen Josepha'. William Maum, an educated Irishman who had been implicated in the 1798 rising, told a story about this 'Queen' reminiscent of those which had tainted Marie-Antoinette in the years before 1789. Mrs King managed her own accounts and was said to be 'a rigid economist', highly inventive in the cutting of costs. In June 1803 she settled in her own way a bill from Ferdinand Meurant, the convict jeweller, which itemised the making of necklaces and earrings for herself and for her seven-year-old daughter, Elizabeth, some filigree work and the weekly mending of her husband's spectacles. The account came to £66 5s., of which £50 was written off (as Meurant's receipt testified) 'By a free pardon'.[16] Pardons were given for miscellaneous reasons, but never before – or so Maum implied, when he complained to the Secretary of State – as private items of exchange.

Mrs King's significance went a long way beyond mixing up private and public concerns. Her authority helped to focus and enlarge that of other women in New South Wales who could call themselves ladies. It offered an immeasurable alternative to brotherhood and an arena for women's imagination at a time when women in Britain were making new (if mainly hesitant) claims as creators and interpreters of public culture, especially through writing and reading. A political establishment which was easily literate and secure in its authority – always more or less the case in Britain – was a good medium for female voices. Brotherhood never prevailed among the British as it did in France. Jane Austen revelled in what she called 'this age of literature'. Mary Wollstonecraft's book, A Vindication of the Rights of Women (1792) – though scandalously radical – the pamphlets of Hannah More, the publications of numerous female novelists besides Austen, the drama of Joanna Baillie (which made her the most admired playwright of her age), the performances of Sarah Siddons, and the private thoughts of all those women who read and heard about them; taken together these partly affirmed and partly challenged the status quo in Britain. They added a new dimension to public life.[17]

The Kings' addition of a drawing room to Government House, Sydney, a room which in any house was meant mainly for women's conversation, was the most concrete sign of change in this part of the world. Public ceremonies involving women – in 1803, for instance, the consecration of St John's church, Parramatta (ladies turned up in force), a dinner on board the Buffalo managed by Mrs Kent, wife of the commander, the King's birthday ball in June – were as different as they could be from the wholly masculine rites observed by Freemasons, United Irish and Scottish Martyrs. At the height of the French Revolution, women with public power had become the ultimate enemy, the negation of égalité. Marie-Antoinette had been exhibited and killed as the epitome of wickedness, since only modest women, purely private and hiding in men's shadows, could coexist with the new democracy. In France, even female authors became a target of hatred.[18] In New South Wales, as in Britain, there were deliberate, though frequently challenged, movements in the opposite direction.

In New South Wales, to begin with, the scarcity of their own kind had limited the conversation of ladylike women, and their ideas were wholly overshadowed by those of their men. Elizabeth Macarthur, wife of John Macarthur of the New South Wales Corps, had been virtually alone in that respect when she arrived in 1790. The only other woman approaching her in rank was Mary Johnson, the chaplain's wife: unhappily, said

Mrs Macarthur, 'a person in whose society I could reap neither profit nor pleasure'.[19] She was to find the company of Eliza Marsden, who came soon afterwards with her husband, the assistant chaplain, more rewarding and Mrs Marsden in turn thought her 'a very pleasant agreeable lady'. They both lived at Parramatta. By 1794 there were also at Sydney 'several ladies', as Mrs Marsden remarked, 'so that we have some respectable society'. But only in King's time did the number of such women allow for anything like a rewarding exploration of friendship. In 1802 Mrs Marsden reported that 'our society of married ladies' had reached unprecedented dimensions: 'we have now twenty'. Two years later she was one of an entirely female party, including Mrs King, Mrs Kent and Mrs Macarthur, who met for dinner together in Sydney in the absence of their less friendly husbands.[20]

Mrs Marsden's twenty probably included the recently arrived Elizabeth Atkins, wife of the Judge-Advocate and, in terms of gentility, the most distinguished of them all. John Grant met Mrs Atkins about this time, and he found her 'a sensible woman, [with a] very fine figure' (and thanks to her husband's failings 'she wears the breeches completely'). Having been 'a Miss Antrobus' she belonged to one of the oldest families in Cheshire, a county where good blood was prized beyond rubies. These facts were cold comfort to Mrs Marsden, because Mrs Atkins's pride of lineage prevented her from having anything to do with the other married ladies, their origins being 'so obscure'. What she thought of the new country we do not know, although in due course it claimed her bones.[21]

Conversation among women such as these – even their consciousness of rank, from officers' and officials' wives down – strengthened their sense of place. Their authority was contingent on the territory they lived in. A similar combined sense of place and of hierarchy appears in Jane Austen's novels (currently in the process of composition). Such women were less apt than their husbands to think of New South Wales as a promotional step on the way to somewhere else. They might take a merely passive view of the future, placing their trust in the narrower world which they themselves could manage: neighbours, households and budgets, the lives and occasionally the deaths of their children, matters whose ends were frequently concealed in what Eliza Marsden called 'the dark womb of Providence'.[22] On the other hand (unlike other colonial women), they understood the ideals shaping local society and they were capable of looking about with a trained eye, obedient to the dictates of an up-to-date sensibility. 'The country is very romantic,' said Mrs Marsden, 'beautifully formed by nature, and will be most delightful when it becomes a little more opened.' In contrast with this sweet substantiality, 'Old England', she said on another occasion, 'is no more than like a pleasing dream; when I think of it it appears to have no existence but in my own imagination.' Elizabeth Macarthur said of herself that she was 'never . . . more sincerely happy than at this time'. Long before her husband, she thought of her children as future inhabitants of their native country.[23]

Anna Josepha King's most substantial achievement was the foundation of the Female Orphan School in Sydney, a project begun within a month of her arrival in 1800. This she undertook with the help of the wife of the commanding officer of the Corps, Elizabeth Paterson, a woman described as 'benevolent . . . beautiful and spirited' but also 'very sharp'.[24] A large brick house, newly built by Captain Kent, was bought on behalf of the Crown and a management committee appointed, including Mrs King, Mrs Paterson, William Balmain, John Harris and Samuel Marsden.[25] Mrs Paterson believed the school would benefit not only the children but the colony as a whole, 'for certainly,' as she informed her friend Maria Sophia Bentham, sister-in-law of the philosopher, 'if we ever hope to see worth and honesty in this settlement, we must look to them for it'.[26] For Marsden, it was a logical step beyond the early efforts which he and Richard Johnson had made in Sydney, which had done so much for the literacy, especially of little girls (see Chapter 7). Officially the school was designed to rescue 'deserted female orphans', and the Secretary of State, in giving his approval, told King to make sure that no others were admitted. The committee decided to ignore this order, receiving without charge any girl who seemed likely to benefit from the regime they had to offer.[27]

By the end of 1801 the establishment consisted of a matron, three women teachers, a housemaid, a porter and forty-nine girls aged from seven to fourteen, who were taught needlework, spinning, reading and writing. Mrs Atkins seems to have condescended to take tea with the matron, and Mrs King and Mrs Paterson were daily visitors.[28] Moral discipline and womanly skills were the great desiderata. The girls were trained to be competent, humble wives and mothers, and in the interim before marriage they might also be good servants, a point of interest to all members of Mrs Marsden's 'society of married ladies'. Sarah Bockerah, or Bockrea, for instance, had been born about 1792 and was an orphan very early. She was one of the school's first pupils and she behaved well enough to find employment afterwards with Elizabeth Atkins, whom she served for three years. She then married a convict, John Laurie, and (possibly on Richard Atkins's recommendation) was given fifty acres in her own name, as the foundation of a permanent prosperity.[29] Her story, to all appearances, matched Mrs King's idea of a configuration of womanly souls scattered through a God-given hierarchy – an Australian hierarchy – a pattern of households, fortunes and families, interrelated and interdependent. It was a vision which relied on men as good husbands and fathers, and for which brotherhood was irrelevant.

Elizabeth Paterson embarked on the *Buffalo* in March 1805 to join her husband, who had gone as commandant to Port Dalrymple, Van Diemen's Land. The pinnace by which she joined the ship, and which was laden mostly with ladies, was saluted by cannon as it crossed the water, in the first piece of public ritual offered by European Australians wholly to a woman.[30] For her part, Anna Josepha King ceased to be the Governor's wife in August 1806, when William Bligh arrived as her husband's successor. The Kings did not leave until February 1807, but by that time a very different regime was in place. Governor Bligh had a wife and five daughters, but he was accompanied only by his second daughter, Mary, and her husband, John Putland, a lieutenant in the navy. Mrs Putland took Mrs King's place on the Orphan School committee but her time was mainly taken up with her husband, who was dying of consumption.[31] Nor was she interested in philanthropy. She was said to be 'very accomplished' and her fashionable abilities were immediately obvious. She brought with her a piano and a lute, and it was presumably she rather than her father who redesigned the garden at Government House so as to give it an up-to-date pattern of paths and vistas. She was also conceited ('you have but to observe the mode of her sitting down'). She loved the latest dresses and she owned one – common in London – in which the skirts were so diaphanous as to need pantaloons underneath. The outfit she chose for church on Sunday, 27 September 1807, may explain the 'highly indecent and improper' behaviour of the soldiers on that occasion (as Richard Atkins observed), 'making faces and looking over each other's shoulders, fixing their eyes on her'.[32]

By this time, thirteen months after their arrival, Mary Putland and her father had lost much of the public respect which had belonged to their predecessors. Bligh, like King, was quick-tempered, but unlike King he made no effort to manage himself. Though better educated, he did not anchor his inclinations with pen and ink. His language was arbitrary. Painstakingly kind when he had his own way, and highly moral, there was brutality in his anger. Just as Mary Putland's appearance disconcerted her audience, so the terms Bligh used in talking to his subordinates were surprising and painful. He was 'so uncertain in his manners, so violent in his conduct', according to one acquaintance (otherwise friendly), 'but at the same time so eloquent in his diction, that he overpowers or affronts every person that has any dealings with him'. 'There might be no particular gesture', according to Richard Atkins, struggling to describe a reprimand several years old. And yet 'the expression of his countenance' was deeply upsetting, 'and is at present impressed upon my mind'. Most memorable were the penetrating, unstinting insults, all the more unseemly – and cutting all the more deeply – because of his superiority of rank.[33]

II

Sarah Wills (born Sarah Harding) and her husband Edward Wills lived in High Street, Sydney, near the head of Sydney Cove. They had several small children, three being born during Governor King's time. Both parents, with the eldest, had come by the *Hillsborough* (1799), Edward as a convict with a life sentence for highway robbery and Sarah as a free woman. They must have brought money too, because they were able to buy a small farm in her name and by 1806 they owned 150 sheep, a bull and ten cows. But they lived in town, where they were importers and retailers. Edward Wills received his conditional pardon in 1803, but although he thus recovered the prerogative of a husband under the common law his wife continued to invest on her own account. In May 1805 she appeared as a plaintiff before the Civil Court, in an attempt to secure money she had put into the building of a house near her own.[34]

The Wills were beginning to prosper when Governor Bligh took command. Bligh's impact among people like them was immediate, and Sarah Wills gave a telling account of it in a letter she wrote to her mother in England. From the moment of his arrival, she said, the Governor took 'every shameful advantage of those that lay in his power'. She was especially angry with the way he treated town investors and householders.

> From some [she said] he took good houses and gave them bad ones – from others he took their houses and turned them into the street and made them no recompense whatever. Some he stopped building. Others he made make improvements against their inclinations and on the whole endeavoured to crush every person as much as possible.[35]

For Bligh, Sydney, its appearance, its moral character – commercial greed and cohabitation outside marriage both seemed to him very wrong – its profiteering at the expense of the farmers, its power to resist unwelcome change, summed up all that was wrong with New South Wales. Neither he nor Mary Putland seems to have sympathised with Mrs King's gentle vision. He moved very quickly to reform and rearrange the town, its homes, shops and warehouses, giving a clear impression at the same time, as Mrs Wills remarked, that he aimed to undermine the prospects of families like hers.

Sydney had taken shape as a port settlement mainly in Hunter's time (1796–1800). Phillip, certainly, had played with the idea of a town to be called 'Albion', with a Government House, guard house and courts of justice crowning the hill at the head of the cove. A parade ground 200 feet (61 metres) wide was to lead down to the water, lined by lesser public buildings and giving the Governor a view of all who stepped ashore at the main gateway to European Australia. But by 1790 Parramatta had taken the place of Albion in Phillip's imagination, and indeed the visionary blueprint had cut across lines already emerging in the process of settlement.[36] At the very beginning, the officers of the garrison had pitched their tents in a row beside the only supply of fresh water, the Tank Stream. The path worn from tent-door to tent-door became the settlement's main thoroughfare, extending in due course southwards towards the brickfields and to Parramatta, and northward to the marketplace and hospital beside the cove and taking the name 'High Street'. This and other rows were lined with one or two-roomed houses built by the convicts for themselves, of timber from the local cabbage-tree palms, plastered with clay and thatched with grass or rushes. The government also erected small barracks made of brick, designed to accommodate ten. Bridge Street ran eastward from High Street across the head of the cove to Government House, lined on its south side by the homes of the Commissary, the Judge-Advocate, the surveyor and the chaplain. '[T]heir houses are neat, charming, and delightful,' wrote a visiting ship's surgeon (here in summertime), with gardens back and front 'in which are the most fragrant and delicious flowers and fruit'.[37]

The usual means of tenure among householders was the Governor's word, whether spoken or written. His word in writing was preferable, and signed 'letters of occupation' might pass through a series of owners, the receipts being the only paper evidence of ownership.[38] Leases, subject to survey, were better still. Phillip had ordered on his departure that no land was to be granted freehold within the peninsula on which Sydney stood, but fourteen-year leases were given sporadically (to a total of forty-six) up to the end of Hunter's time. Most went to civil officials and to officers and sergeants of the Corps, but former convicts had some as well.[39] Leases pushed up the value of land in Sydney, making rents, at 2s 6d per annum, virtually nominal. In 1798 Simeon Lord paid £160 for Shadrach Shaw's lease at the head of Sydney Cove, a price which was presumably near the top of the market for town allotments and much more than was currently paid for most rural land, including freehold.[40] The quality of building improved as well. As early as 1793, the houses of the officers had shown where prosperity might lead. These were of whitewashed brick and designed in rectangular form, with two to four rooms divided by a central passage, each with its own fireplace and with detached kitchens and servants' rooms.[41] Within ten years, a few ex-convicts enjoyed comfort even superior to this. When in 1803 Simeon Lord built on the land he had bought from Shaw, it was a house of three storeys (four at the back), superior to Government House itself, of stone, cedar-lined, and worth £15,000.[42]

By that time the trading community in Sydney had begun to settle into fixed habits of business. Simeon Lord and his two partners, the shipbuilders Henry Kable and James Underwood (all former convicts), and the free-immigrant merchant, Robert Campbell, led the way in directing local interest to whaling and sealing in southern waters, and these were now making a handsome return.[43] Profits and security depended on intelligent method. There was no representative decision-making within the town, but leading traders took an active interest in institutions maintained by the government, especially the police, the courts and the *Sydney Gazette*. Sydney's police were managed by its magistrate, John Harris, also surgeon to the Corps. Governor King's quarrel with the officers in 1802 forced Harris to give up his civil duties, but the leading townspeople immediately protested at the loss of an official whom they saw as their own. 'Under his magisterial eye', they said, 'we have enjoyed perfect security in person and property. We could lay down in safety, knowing that Mr Harris was always awake.' In June 1804 he was reappointed.[44]

The Court of Civil Judicature was even more vital to the underpinning of Sydney property. Hunter had restored its authority after the lapse of

1792–95 and in his time it was eagerly used by the townspeople in hunting down their debtors and – thanks to the high prices they charged, their willingness to give credit, and their use of an ephemeral currency (mainly spirits, grain and flour) – their debtors were very numerous. Farmers were the usual victims, some of them simply failing to cope with the freedom of the market. The court usually awarded future crops to the creditor but, failing that, the debtor might be forced to pay by personal servitude, entering briefly into a type of bondage as rigorous as that of any convict. In due course, farms themselves might be forfeit. Meanwhile, the dealers happily made the court integral to their buying and selling, and it was swamped with work. During February 1797, for instance, it heard ninety-four cases, taking up nearly a fortnight and altogether worth more than £3000.[45]

Both Hunter and King condemned the voracious habits of the retailers, and in King's time a government store was set up in an attempt to control the prices charged in the shops. But both governors believed that it was beyond their power to interfere with claims in the courts, which must offer justice freely to all comers.[46] Whatever the faults built into the judicial system, as long as it was treated as sacred by the governors it worked as the bedrock of legitimacy in the common dealings of the people. The Civil Court was central to Sydney's economic life, and the retailers, for their part, won a little of that dignity, that sense of self-worth, which comes from knowing that the law is a weapon ready to one's own hand. The number of debtors declined in King's time, partly owing to the government store, but the quantity of capital, especially in Sydney, vastly increased. An elite, the unusually rich, emerged among the colonial middle class, with Simeon Lord pre-eminent. Individuals who had once been convicts, 'by their good conduct [as an observer remarked] are now considered as respectable characters, and are in possession of horses, carriages, and servants, with a sufficiency to secure their independence during the remainder of their lives'. Several were bold enough, in 1803, to offer the Governor advice on the regulation of the local currency, conveying, as they said, 'the wish of the people at large'.[47]

The Civil Court drew to itself increasingly complex cases, and those townspeople who followed its proceedings found themselves engaging in public debates more momentous than any New South Wales had hitherto known. The *Sydney Gazette*, founded in 1803, gave detailed accounts of the court's proceedings, besides offering news of auctions, shipping and other commercial events. Like the court, the *Gazette* gave a new legitimacy to trade, and Simeon Lord figured just as much in its pages as did Philip Gidley King and John Harris. It similarly gave a voice to women, literate or not, whose names and stories appeared not only in the reports of cases at law but also in announcements of goods for sale. Print makes a pretence, at least, of lacking gender, so that the court and the newspaper were a combined force of great significance.

The *Gazette* fed the public imagination. Mere talk, footpath gossip, was stimulated by print. In March 1805, for instance, there appeared the following story ('Gretna' means Gretna Green, on the Scottish border, where runaway couples could be married outside English law):

> A grey goose last week eloped from its owner, after a long and faithful servitude [fifteen years] in different families. It came originally from the Hawkesbury, and is, or possibly *was* considered of sixteen *brothers* and *sisters* the only survivor. In its younger days it made an excursion to Norfolk Island, and there remained to the completion of its *eleventh* year; had been a favorite to several masters, and would doubtless have retained its fidelity *durante vitae*, but for the mal insinuation of a licentious gosling, who is supposed to have accompanied the *old lady* in a trip to *Gretna*.

We can only guess how detail of the goose's natal origins passed from owner to owner, from far western to far eastern hinterland – and through most of the period of settlement – before alighting at Sydney. There, however, in the *Gazette*, word-of-mouth was finally translated, partly into Latin and wholly into print.[48] Through such snippets, through the description of events in court and in other ways, the *Gazette* took up the project begun with Richard Johnson's published sermons (1794), in which he had predicted and explained the archangelic trumpet blast over Sydney Cove. In its pages the *Gazette* unfolded the idea of this spot as one where events of moment, or mock-moment, might be ordered and printed out. Local stories were thereby fixed within the mind of every reader.

Of all the nascent communities in European New South Wales, Sydney had the most robust public opinion. It also enjoyed a sense of place, enhanced by landmarks. Its skyline was punctuated by a tall Norfolk Island pine planted by Phillip in front of Government House, several windmills ('which gave the whole an appearance peculiarly English') and a clocktower 150 feet (about 46 metres) high. Much of the area originally intended as a parade ground, and known as 'the Old Parade', was still open. It included the town market place (with a fresh-water well), and was bordered at the top by the clocktower and the foundation-work of St Phillip's church. Beyond was a large quadrangle used by the military. These central points and spaces, and the water on three sides, defined the place. Hunter had subdivided both Sydney and Parramatta for police purposes and numbered all the houses, but in Sydney the numbers made no immediate impact, presumably because (like Phillip's Albion) they had nothing to do with the way in which the people already understood the layout of their town.[49] Most Sydney streets were short, with perhaps a dozen houses each (so that addresses were obvious), and they began and ended within one or other of the three main suburbs: the upper High Street area (mainly reserved for the garrison), the Rocks at the bottom of High Street, and a number of rows behind Government House. Households within the town were said to total between 460 and 500, but in King's time numbers grew very quickly and some of the rows in this last district began to lengthen eastward.[50]

During winter 1803 King made a general offer of leasehold tenure to householders. The normal term was, as ever, fourteen years, but the annual rent now went up to 10s. Before his resignation in August 1806 he issued seventy-four new leases, so that that entire streets were surveyed and occupied in a clearly legal sense and a numerous class of artisans and shopkeepers entered into a settled commercial relationship with the government.[51] The added security of property encouraged an interest in the improvement of the town, including the tidying up of boundaries and street surfaces, and King also established a system for 'regulating and forming the Streets', three housekeepers from each being asked to marshal the energies of their neighbours. The Governor found the people very willing, as he said, 'to Second my Wishes'. A new stone bridge at the junction of Bridge and High Streets proved that public and private initiative marched step and step.[52]

In 1803 even unleased land, in a good position, could sell for more than £100, and in 1806–07 a large allotment, capable of subdivision, went for the remarkable price of £900, a larger sum than most labouring men and women could earn in a lifetime.[53] Prosperity was widely shared, and shopkeepers made themselves rich selling to the population at large. Women were conspicuous consumers. Silk handkerchiefs, flowered muslin and chintz gowns were common and 'ladies shoes' were imported as if for a mass market. 'Articles of female apparel and ornament are greedily purchased', wrote David Dickenson Mann, an ex-convict and King's principal clerk, 'for the European women . . . spare no expense in ornamenting their persons'. Good local products began to appear in the shops beside imported goods. The pottery of Samuel Skinner earned a high reputation: 'His dishes, plates, basons, covers, cups and saucers, teapots, and chimney ornaments, were in a very superior style of workmanship; and other useful articles equally handsome.'[54]

The officers of the New South Wales Corps had been deeply involved in colonial commerce during the first half of the 1790s, and some were still interested in a marginal way, though they had mostly turned their attention to building up their livestock and landed property.[55] But it was the non-commissioned officers – sergeants and corporals – who now represented the commercial face of the Corps and who gave it its stake in Sydney life. The sergeants used their pay to set themselves up as traders. They were 'connected by the ties of common interest' among themselves; the result was a sense of moral and financial independence distinctly unmilitary and, according to Mann, 'fatal to that strict subordination which ought to be maintained and enforced'. At times as many as one-third of Sydney publicans were non-commisisoned officers, although it is likely that their wives managed such enterprises.[56]

In King's time a military district was set apart within Sydney, but the Governor went on giving town leases to soldiers. One of the publican-sergeants, Thomas Whittle, who succeeded John Fleming as sergeant-major in 1805 (and who was also a licensed butcher), had two allotments; one of them, presumably, was the site of his public house and the other his home in Spring Row. The public house was the venue, in March 1803, of Whittle's attempt to form a Masonic lodge. Such a lodge would have been a ritual meeting ground for the men among Sydney's elite, including soldiers like himself, adding even further to the town's political voice. Whittle, indeed, was a respectable burgess, though he could neither read nor write. The brick house in which he lived with his family possessed, he said (when he came to sell it), 'four capital rooms in front, with a kitchen and servant's room adjoining, [and] a capital garden well manured, in which are a number of excellent fruit trees', all adjoining 'a continual stream of pure water'.[57] The last was the Tank Stream, by this time, in fact, disgustingly dirty.

These were the words of an illiterate man polished and printed. Such little artifices show how the sample of literate Europe which had come to Australia in 1788 had taken root in the antipodean soil. Its growth was nourished especially by Governor King, so that by the time he departed, in August 1806, living speech echoed in writing and writing echoed in living speech, print was enlivened and voices given certainty – especially in Sydney – more thoroughly than anyone could have anticipated within a mere eighteen years.

Governor Bligh, within a few months of his arrival as King's successor, had proved to the people of Sydney (according to Elizabeth Macarthur) that

William Bligh, a pencil drawing by his son-in-law, H. A. Barker, done in 1805 shortly before his departure for New South Wales.

Source: Mitchell Library, State Library of New South Wales

he was 'violent, rash, tyrannical'. His views were not urban in fact, but agrarian. Before being sworn in, he had received from King three grants of land, including a thousand acres on the Hawkesbury, making him the first Governor to take up farming during his time in office.[58] He also moved immediately to help farmers ruined by recent flooding, supplementing their food supply by the slaughter of government cattle.[59] He showed no interest in trade. More significantly, his preference for the spoken over the written word made a vivid impact on the townspole – especially those whose interests King had defined with printed edicts, title deeds and multiple signatures – and on those households which Mrs King had aimed to nourish with new standards of patient, hopeful female industry. Bligh gave no town leases. Instead, he offered security of tenure simply on 'his verbal permission', which he said 'was better than a lease, for that he could take away'. Under such a regime, as one of his officials remarked, 'all property of whatever nature must be uncertain'.[60]

Bligh wanted, as far as possible, to resurrect Phillip's plans for Sydney, and he aimed to clear two spaces: one at the Old Parade, including St Phillip's church, and the other around Government House.[61] The account which Sarah Wills gave her mother was a fair summary of his readiness to intervene in private building programs in order to achieve this end. Simeon Lord bought a lease next to his own at the head of the Cove, in front of Government House, but the Governor forbade him to build on it, the order coming as a verbal message through Charles Grimes, the surveyor. Lord, already aggrieved by Bligh's lack of interest in his commercial vision, resented such off-hand treatment and he asked for a written order. Grimes, as he himself recalled, went back to the Governor: 'he told me, in a very violent manner, at my peril to give any message in writing.'[62]

Such methods were wholly at odds with the project of European settlement in Australia, and especially with the way in which it was designed to draw life – a settled hope of order and prosperity – from the security of pen and ink. Not only were improvements stopped. Houses were pulled down – as Sarah Wills said, without compensation – the occupants being allowed only to remove the remains and build elsewhere. John Davis, a soldier, was said to have lost two homes, one after the other. David Dickenson Mann, who lived on a lease a few steps from Government House, was offered another site, but he declined, telling Bligh that the exchange would ruin him, and, he added, 'I conceived, by the laws of England, I was entitled to a just and quiet possession.' Sergeant-Major Whittle received a visit from the Governor at his house in Spring Row at seven o'clock in the morning:

> I saw him coming towards the gate [Whittle recalled], and I went and paid him the compliment that was due to him. He asked me, who owned the house, or whether I owned it. I told him [in some detail] . . . that I had exchanged it for a house that I had lived in before . . . . He bawled out in a very violent manner, (and all the neighbours heard it,) that I might chop and change as I pleased, but he would have the house down by ten o'clock, and that I was welcome to take

the bricks off the ground. 'Sir,' says I, 'I have got a lease of this house:' then he paused a bit, and afterwards says he, 'How long has that lease to run?' Says I, 'It has about six or seven years to run and it is signed by Gov. Hunter.' 'Well,' says he, 'I will have the house down again by ten o'clock, and you shall neither take bricks nor any thing else away, but it shall be all mine, house, and ground, and all.'

Whittle immediately signed his lease over to Major Johnston, his senior officer, 'for his protection', and nothing more was said.[63]

Performances like this made a deep impression. Richard Atkins, as judge of the Civil Court, was well qualified to know the concerns of the towns-people. 'They complained very much', he said; 'whenever I went along the streets, the people were talking about those houses being pulled down.' It was always, he said, 'My turn will be the next.' Like Sarah Wills, he saw this grievance as the main cause of the townspeople's hatred for their new Governor. Such men and women could make no effective resistance on their own (so Atkins testified), but 'if they could have done anything they would'. Another witness, the botanist George Caley, was not so sure of their inabil-ity. The leadership in Sydney, the rich ex-convicts, so he believed, were 'among the first who . . . opposed and overturned the Governor'.[64]

III

The story of Governor Bligh's deposition on 26 January 1808 is complicat-ed. Like many much greater revolutions, it was mainly the result of cross-currents within the capital. Sydney was a tiny metropolis, a centre of power and, like many others – from Paris to Beijing – a theatre where men and women could watch the unfolding of sovereign events (or sovereign for the moment). There too a concentrated public opinion, the gossip of towns-people living face to face, could be easily brought to bear on politics. But grander issues were also brought to bear, including imperial ones. Some dated back to a comparable crisis in Bligh's career, the mutiny on H.M.S. *Bounty* (1789). He and eighteen of his crew were then set adrift in a small boat in the mid-Pacific, making their way, without loss of life, from Tofua, near Tonga, to Timor, a journey of enormous hardship, before getting back to England. Fourteen mutineers were later caught, of whom four drowned on the way home and three were hanged. Several had powerful friends and thanks to their efforts the story of his heroism in the open boat, a story which the newspapers had given national currency, was eclipsed in the pub-lic imagination by details of tyranny. Among many navy men he became an object of lasting hatred.[65]

He had several powerful allies nevertheless, including Sir Joseph Banks, President of the Royal Society and a close friend of the King. It was Banks who got Bligh his governorship, in 1805. Bligh took two naval vessels to

New South Wales, but the master of one, Joseph Short, refused to obey his orders on the way out, firing once across his bows. When they got to Sydney, Short was accused of drunkenness and cruelty by one of his own officers and he was ordered back to England for court martial.[66] Mrs Bligh, who was on the spot, kept a careful watch over her husband's interests. 'When Captn. Short began his defence', she told her husband, 'they [the officers on the bench] listened with every complacency, and sat for a long time to hear him defame and belie the Govr. of N.S. Wales, who was no party in the trial, and had nobody to defend him.' The Admiralty, moved partly by prejudice and partly by tales of 'extreme hardship' suffered by Short, even suggested to the Colonial Office that Bligh be recalled.[67]

In New South Wales, Short's triumph had been taken for granted. Bligh made enemies in this part of the world very early. Soon after his arrival he met John Macarthur, now the largest landowner in the colony. Macarthur's original 200 acres had now grown to more than 8000 and he had flocks and herds to match, including a number of Spanish merinos brought from the Cape of Good Hope in 1797. In 1801 he had been involved in a quarrel with a visiting naval lieutenant and had deliberately entangled both Paterson, his commanding officer, and Governor King. King had sent him to England under arrest, asking that he be court-martialled, but Macarthur used the expedition to build up his own power.[68] His ship was forced to call en route at Ambon, where he made the acquaintance of Robert Farquhar, a young man who managed the East India Company's commercial affairs in the Moluccas.[69] Farquhar had just been reprimanded from Calcutta, and Macarthur advised him to stand on his dignity (a rule Macarthur always made for himself) and to take his story to the top. This advice, immediately taken, won Farquhar the patronage of Lord Wellesley, Governor-General of India. In England Macarthur found himself befriended by the young man's family, including his father, who was physician to the Prince of Wales, and his cousin, George Watson, private secretary to Lord Camden, the new Secretary of State for War and the Colonies.[70]

On this chance foundation, Macarthur built a fabric of patronage which was to do him endless good. He was not court-martialled (no witnesses were available), and he now resigned his commission in the army. He had taken with him to England samples of wool from his Spanish sheep. He was one of a number of settlers trying to breed fine wool, but he was the first to publicise the result at the centre of the empire. Wool manufacturers in England currently relied on Spain and Germany and they were attracted by the possibility, however remote, of finding a source of supply which would be safe in wartime. Macarthur's energy and his new connections made a powerful impact and before he left England in November 1804 he had been promised a grant of 5000 acres, with another 5000 when his flocks were properly established. He also bought back to Australia six merinos purchased from the King's flock at Kew.

Macarthur was on the eve of his fortieth birthday when Bligh arrived in New South Wales, and the new Governor was fifty-three. Macarthur had fought his way upwards and had just begun to shine as he thought he ought to do. He had begun to make plans for the prosperity of the colony and of himself, and his mind was never still. He loved theatre and he eagerly watched his own behaviour on the stage he had chosen. Shakespeare's *Coriolanus* was his favourite play and his own performance mimicked the hero: 'Such a nature, / Tickled with good success, disdains the shadow / Which he treads on at noon.'[71] Bligh, on the other hand, was entering on the evening of a chequered career. He had no shrewdness in his observation of himself or of others. Macarthur had land, livestock, financial credit and powerful connections, but he needed a good supply of labour. He therefore depended on Bligh, who was responsible for the system of convict assignment. Macarthur soon sought out the new Governor, hoping to make sure that he was friendly to his scheme for breeding fine-wooled sheep. They met in the garden of Government House, Parramatta, and, according to Macarthur, the conversation went as follows. On Macarthur's broaching the subject of his visit, Bligh

> burst out instantly into a most violent passion, exclaiming, 'What have I [to] do with your sheep, sir; what have I to do with your cattle? Are you to have such flocks of sheep and such herds of cattle as no man ever heard of before? – No, sir!' I endeavoured [said Macarthur] to appease him, by stating that I had understood the Government at home had particularly recommended me to his notice. He replied, 'I have heard of your concerns, sir; you have 5,000 acres of land in the finest situation in the country; but, by God, you shan't keep it.'

After some further heated words – including Bligh's celebrated outburst, 'Damn the Privy Council! and damn the Secretary of State too! . . . What have they to do with me?' – they went inside and took breakfast with the Kings, who had not yet departed. Bligh was so much worked up and spoke in such insulting terms to his predecessor 'that Gov[ernor] King burst into tears'.[72]

Macarthur began to contemplate Bligh's removal. Short was sent home not long after this conversation and the Governor's new enemies predicted that his court martial would force the hand of the Secretary of State. But Macarthur's imagination reached towards a crisis within New South Wales itself, with himself as its pivot. He foresaw a re-enactment of the *Bounty* mutiny, declaring that unless Bligh made himself more pliant he would 'get another voyage in his launch again'.[73] But the new crisis was to be more elaborate and more tightly orchestrated. Macarthur knew of Bentham's argument that most of the Governor's orders were unsupported in law (see Chapter 12). He was also aware of Bligh's preference for the spoken over the written word and he began to question publicly 'whether this [ought to] be the tenor on which Englishmen hold their property in N.S. Wales'.[74] It was indeed Bligh's language – the sound of his voice from day to day in Sydney – which made him criminal even for men and women with no exact legal knowledge. Public opinion, formed in the mouths of Sydney people, made him a target for anyone with courage to advocate the rights of Englishmen in New South Wales.

During the winter and spring of 1807 several local trials strained the relationship between Bligh and the law, eating at the legitimacy of his government among those who already disliked him. In October 1806 Macarthur had begun a number of prosecutions for debt. One of the defendants was Andrew Thompson, a leading Hawkesbury settler, and the case turned on the value of a promissory note which specified payment in grain but which had been made out when grain was cheap. Thompson offered the original value and Macarthur demanded the quantity of produce written on the face of the note. The court ruled for Thompson and in July 1807 Macarthur turned to the Governor as the authorised court of appeal. Bligh heard only Thompson's argument before dismissing the case.[75] His contempt for due process had at least a hint of favouritism, not only because Thompson was a farmer but because he managed the Governor's Hawkesbury enterprise.

During August and September there was a concerted attack, through the courts, on William Gore, the Provost Marshal and Bligh's ally. Gore (the irreligious sceptic mentioned in Chapter 9) was an illegitimate scion of the Gores of Lissadell, county Sligo – 'The light of evening, Lissadell, / Great windows, open to the south' – and a graduate of Trinity College, Dublin. He had a reputation for cavalier dishonesty (Mary Putland herself said so) and he boasted of being able to do anything with the Governor. He was not a magistrate, but he had taken Harris's place in the management of the Sydney police. His constables, according to Harris, ran a stand-over system among the townspeople: 'he has everybody in some way or other under contribution to him thro' Sydney'.[76] On 19 August the Civil Court began to hear a suit brought against him by Simeon Lord for the allegedly illegal sale of a house, and on the 21st the magistrates took notice of two unrelated criminal charges, in one of which James Underwood seems to have deliberately laid a trap for him. The Governor was at the Hawkesbury, and on the 23rd Atkins heard from him that neither the Civil Court nor the magistrates were to sit again until he got back to Sydney.[77] Bligh had already told Atkins that his own authority was 'equal, or of the same effect, as the laws of England' and such interference with judicial proceedings implied that even the courts were subject to his will. Appalled as he was, Atkins made no protest, only copying this new message into his diary with the caption, 'Thus is the Civil power suspended.' And he added, 'The Spirit of party never manifested itself so strongly as in this business.'[78] The townspeople, including Lord and Underwood, might have hoped to undermine Gore through the courts. In fact he won every case brought against him and, given that Bligh's wishes had clearly prevailed, his enemies might well have believed that the

Governor had beaten them by changing the rules of the game. It was a game fundamental to European order in New South Wales.[79]

In November the schooner *Parramatta*, of which Macarthur was part-owner, arrived with a cargo of salted pork from Fiji. It had left Port Jackson in June with a convict hiding on board and on its return Robert Campbell, whom Bligh had made Naval Officer, required payment of the bond (£900) which every out-going vessel entered upon to prevent the escape of convicts. Meanwhile, such was Bligh's suspicion of Macarthur that constables were sent on board to stop cargo being removed, the ship's papers were seized and the vessel itself was brought in to shore where it could be watched, and where it was in danger of running aground. Macarthur decided to give up the ship altogether – 'I considered myself as completely dispossessed' – and the crew, unpaid and unfed, appealed to the Governor and Judge-Advocate. On 14 December Macarthur received a message requiring him to appear in Sydney on the following morning, 'to show cause of . . . your conduct'. He refused to go and there followed a warrant for his arrest. This time he sent the constable back with a scribbled reply: 'I will never submit to the horrid tyranny that is attempted until I am forced, . . . I consider [the warrant] . . . with Scorn and Contempt as I do the persons who have directed it to be executed.'[80] Having now offended far more seriously, he went down to Sydney of his own accord, where, on 16 December, he was arrested and committed for trial. The case was set down for 25 January and Bligh used the interim to persuade the magistrates, who were not inclined to go so far, that the charge should be sedition.[81]

The main actors from this point were, besides the Governor, Macarthur himself and Thomas Whittle, sergeant-major of the regiment, radical Freemason, butcher, publican and householder. Macarthur, the Coriolanus and Cromwell of his little community, ordered the formalities and justified the event in the written record. Whittle, illiterate himself, provided the spark of Jacobinical energy moving at the heart of things.[82]

Whittle was now in his late forties, grey-haired, with a small, dark face. He had been a soldier virtually all his life, having begun as a drummer boy, and he had served in Ireland and in the American revolutionary war. In March 1791, at thirty years old, a married man with a young family, he had succumbed to rheumatism, and he had chosen a warm climate, taking appointment as a sergeant in the Corps in preference to a military pension.[83] Promoted sergeant-major in December 1805, he had since shown himself an eager politician. He had already learnt, with some of his fellows, how to mix military duty with commercial success. He was in his own mind a soldier-citizen, a model exemplified in his youth by the Irish Volunteers and by the revolutionary troops in America, and as sergeant-major he was in a position to forge the men of the regiment into a single body of opinion, as a band of local patriots. In July 1806, in a typically inflated gesture, he committed them all to a joint subscription of £1000, offered for the discovery of the author of an anonymous letter reflecting on their loyalty to government.

In February 1807 he addressed Governor Bligh, on behalf of 'the non-commissioned officers and rank and file at head-quarters', thanking him for an increase in their food ration, 'which', he said, 'we are aware would have long since taken place were it in your Excellency's power to have given it'.[84] These were words to make any governor wince: terms of politeness among gentlemen but pure egalitarian presumption when addressed by mere soldiers to their captain-general. Besides, Whittle also broadcast irreligious ideas among the soldiers. He was shortly to encourage less pleasant notions also about the civil power.[85]

The code of brotherhood, which prescribed an absolute loyalty to the regiment, was not for everyone. Recruits were continually arriving from England, and some new sergeants resented antipodean methods, now thoroughly ingrained in the character of the Corps. During the wars with republican France, the army at home had been much reformed. Among officers, commissioned and non-commissioned, there was a more professional attitude to discipline and to regimental finances, and newcomers to the Corps could not help noticing 'many irregularities and several customs not agreeable to the present [reformed] system'.[86] Such dissent made little difference to Whittle for the time being. He had a dominion of his own within the commercial life of Sydney, and as sergeant-major he presided over the lives of the men; his officers, absorbed in their own affairs, left him to manage in his own way.

Whittle's campaign against the Governor must have begun when or before Bligh visited his house, in December 1807, and told him to pull it down. The news of their confrontation, he said, was all over town in less than half an hour: 'I had a little business at the Hospital Wharf, and every body had it in their mouths . . . saying what a pity it was that such an elegant house should be pulled down.' John Macarthur could not hope to enjoy sympathy of the same kind among the Sydney people. His own origins were commercial, but he liked to act the landed gentleman disdainful of mere money-making. His thoughts lingered with both scorn and fascination on Sydney. His imagination echoed Coriolanus – 'Who deserves greatness / Deserves your hate'. He wavered between a contempt for lesser beings, such as the men and women who populated the town, and a wish to have his way at the heart of the market.[87] Also, at this crisis, in his advocacy of the rights of Englishmen, Macarthur needed the express backing of public opinion. In order to be plausible, demands for common liberty must spring in a demonstrable way from commonwealth.

In August 1806 Macarthur had taken it upon himself to represent 'the Free Inhabitants' in an address of welcome to Bligh. The Sydney people, in a document with 135 signatures and entrusted to Simeon Lord ('as their Representative'), had protested that he had no right to speak on their behalf; 'had we deputed anyone, John McArthur would not have been chosen by us'. They charged him especially with making them pay too much for their mutton by keeping his wethers from the butcher.[88] However, by winter 1807

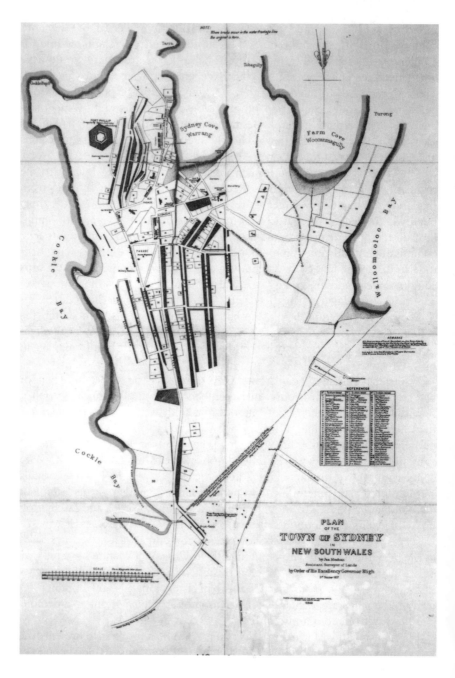

Map of Sydney drawn by the government surveyor, James Meehan, in October 1807, showing current leases. This map was presumably commissioned by the Governor as a means of preparing for the redesign of the town.

Source: Mitchell Library, State Library of New South Wales

the gap between Macarthur and the town was beginning to close. The argument about Thompson's promissory note helped to prove that, under the current regime, Macarthur had much in common with other managers of capital, and the case of the *Parramatta* did the same. In about November some of them, including Lord, were involved in a move to send him to England as their agent, to carry to the seat of empire their complaints about the Governor.[89]

In mid-January 1808 Macarthur crowned the alliance between himself and the townspeople with a public performance at the centre of Sydney. Bligh had lately begun what was, to all appearances, a sweeping attack on leaseholds, calling in title-deeds for inspection and ordering a new town survey.[90] The area which he wanted to clear near the church included one and a quarter acres leased by Macarthur. On 13 January Macarthur prepared to fence his land, intending, he said, to build on it. Under Bligh's instructions, the Superintendent of Convicts, Nicholas Divine, arrived at the site on horseback and told him that whatever he put up would be pulled down. As Macarthur recalled, 'I immediately fixed one of the posts myself.' They were, after all, his own posts and the holes had been dug within his own boundary. Divine 'then alighted from his horse, pulled down the post, declared he did it by the order of the Governor, and added, in a very emphatic tone, "When the axe is laid to the root, the tree must fall."'[91] Both parties knew that a point had been reached beyond which there could be no return.

Besides making friends with the town, Macarthur, as the botanist George Caley remarked, 'secured himself by the soldiers'.[92] Whittle was his medium. At some point, probably towards the end of 1807, the men had been caught up in a grand effort of propaganda. Gore had inadvertently prepared the ground by fomenting rivalry between them and his town constables.[93] But Private Thomas Finnegan, a new recruit from England, also noticed, as he put it, 'the strange conduct in the Officers and non commiss[ione]d Officers respecting the Governor . . . Much Calumny was propagated among the Soldiers . . . that the Governor was a Tyrant, and dismissed on account of Short's Business.' It became safer, he said, 'to praise Bonoparte, than to speak respectfully of Governor Bligh'. And yet, some did. Macarthur, as a former officer, sent to the barracks for volunteers to put in his fence-posts in January and several men refused. Private Collinan said that Macarthur was acting in defiance of the Governor, at which Whittle called him 'a damnd Scoundrel': 'why should he object more than any other man, would not half a pint of rum be as acceptable to him as any other person[?]' But Collinan would not go.[94]

Macarthur's trial on 25 January brought the final explosion. The courtroom was lined with soldiers ordered to resist any sudden move by 'the Damnd Constables', giving the whole an air of danger and suspense.[95] Proceedings opened with the six officers being sworn in, but before Atkins could take the oath as Judge-Advocate, Macarthur stood up in the dock and demanded to be heard. He read out an impassioned speech (he loved the entrenched, enamelled magic of the written word) in which he protested against Atkins being one of his judges because he was his debtor and eager to see him imprisoned. He ended with a peroration addressed to the six officers on the bench:

> [Y]ou have the eyes of an anxious public upon you, trembling for the safety of the property, their liberty, and their lives.
>
> To you has fallen the lot of deciding a point which involves perhaps the happiness or misery of millions yet unborn; and I conjure you in the name of the Almighty God, in whose presence you stand, to consider the inestimable value of the precious deposit with which you are intrusted.
>
> ... It is to *the Officers of the New South Wales Corps* that the administration of justice is committed; – and who that is just has any thing to dread![96]

Great confusion followed this speech. Atkins, deeply offended, shouted, 'I will commit you to jail, sir!', and Anthony Fenn Kemp, the senior officer on the bench, shouted back, 'You commit, sir! No sir, I will commit *you!*' Atkins: 'You commit *me*, sir!' Kemp: 'I would, sir.' Atkins then left the room declaring there could be no court without him. As the audience made to follow, Kemp called out, 'Stay, stay! Tell the people not to go out. We *are* a court.'[97]

This last assertion – 'We *are* a court' – led directly to revolution. Were they indeed a court? Where did legitimacy lie? The six officers demanded that the Governor name another Judge-Advocate for Macarthur's trial, but Bligh refused to notice their collective existence without the Judge-Advocate appointed from Downing Street. He decided indeed to charge them with treason, and since there was no court to try them it followed that he must have planned something like martial law. All, including the lives of reputed traitors, would then depend on the Governor's word. The news reached some of the six a little later and the following conversation (remembered by a soldier three years later) ensued among them. Clearly, not all were equally in command of events:

> *Lieutenant Thomas Laycock:* '[B]y God we are all going to be hanged'.
> *Another, unnamed:* 'Why so[?]'
> *Laycock:* 'Old Bligh has summoned us to appear before him.'
> *Adjutant Minchin:* 'Mr Laycock if you are afraid I am not and will find a way to cool him.'
> *Laycock:* 'How is that[?]'
> *Minchin:* '[B]y arresting him before he arrest us.'

Laycock argued that that was mutiny – they ought to go – but Minchin 'swore he would be damn'd if [he] would not go for Major Jo[h]nston and have him [Bligh] arrested first, which was applauded by the rest, particularly [Lieutenant] Lawson, who replied, that is the best thing to be done'.[98]

Minchin had already been plotting with Macarthur and with Johnston, currently the senior officer at Sydney. Both of the latter believed that the Governor was acting beyond what could be justified by his orders or by the British constitution. It followed that any move they might make against him would be safe in law. Surgeon Harris and Captain Abbott (on duty at Parramatta) had almost certainly been drawn in as well, but the other officers were involved only at the last minute.[99] Harris and Minchin fetched Johnston from his house at Annandale, outside Sydney, on the afternoon of the 26th. Johnston drove up to the barracks, arriving at about five o'clock. Throughout the day the soldiers had been increasingly agitated. Macarthur, through Whittle, had plied them with alcohol, but many already hated the Governor and they were angered by the idea of their officers being arrested for treason. They were on the point of mutiny (or so it was later alleged), some of them, such as Whittle, embracing mutiny as revolution.[100] By now Kemp and Lieutenant Bayly had each written letters of protest addressed to Bligh which were in the process of being checked for grammar and syntax by Robert Townson, a settler and Doctor of Laws. Macarthur having now appeared, these feeble productions were brushed aside and Simeon Lord and other leading townspeople were sent for.[101]

Macarthur now took charge, himself drawing up a paper (which no-one needed to check) designed for general signature and addressed to Johnston, in which he called for the Governor's arrest. He himself signed first, the gentleman settler John Blaxland second, the surgeon James Mileham third and Simeon Lord fourth. A total of 147 other signatures followed, nearly all of them after the event.[102] Macarthur also directed the movement on Government House, telling the band what tune to play ('The British Grenadiers'), and, as they moved up Bridge Street, raising his hand and shouting, 'My Boys, the Memorable day shall be the most Glorious day the New South Wales Corps ever experienced.' Whittle added his counterpoint: 'Men, I hope you will do your duty, and don't spare them' (the soldiers replying, 'Never fear us'), and to Sydney's offspring, 'Children, go out of the way, for some of you I expect will be killed.'[103]

As they entered the gates of Mrs Putland's new garden, the order was given, 'Make good your way, but use no violence if you are not opposed', but Mrs Putland herself was in fact their only opposition. Following a search lasting two hours, the Governor was found in a small back room. Three men located him, apparently lying behind a bed (they said later that he was under it). They called out, 'Here he is, here he is', and 'Man, take care of yourself, he is going to take a pistol out of his bosom!' Another four joined them, and after a brief exchange Minchin arrived and escorted the prisoner downstairs.[104] In the drawing room Johnston, reading from a script prepared by Macarthur and acting, as the document declared, 'in His Majesty's sacred name' (that index of liberty), informed the Governor that his authority was at an end. One reason alone appeared on the paper: 'the respectable inhabitants' had charged their Governor with 'crimes' which made him unfit to hold office.[105] Gore was arrested the same evening, while sitting with his wife after supper. Mrs Gore was naturally upset, and the soldier who came for her husband told her 'not to make herself uneasy, as for his own part, his wife was accustomed to see him confined daily without expressing a murmur'. It was a statement, Gore said, replete with 'the true spirit of Jacobinical equality'.[106]

A picture of Governor Bligh's arrest by two soldiers of the New South Wales under the command of Adjutant Minchin. There is no conclusive evidence that the Governor had hidden under a bed, but this picture, painted soon afterwards for propaganda purposes, aimed to establish his cowardice as part of the common memory of the rebellion.

Source: Mitchell Library, State Library of New South Wales

Johnston took the title of lieutenant-governor but power rested with Macarthur, who styled himself 'Secretary to the Colony' and assumed all the customary pomp of a governor. The revolution, as the leaders themselves called it, was marked on the following day by fireworks, by a salute of cannon, by a service of thanksgiving and by the erection of a new gallows. On that day, too, Pemulwuy's son Tjedboro turned up in Sydney prepared for blood. He had heard that Macarthur was in gaol and he had come, he said, to spear the Governor.[107] The final act in this considerable drama began on the afternoon of 8 February, when the town bellman announced a meeting to be held in St Phillip's church. This was to underline the legitimacy of the revolution and to prove its roots among the people. Macarthur's business partner, Garnham Blaxcell, was in the chair and, large quantities of wine and spirits having been distributed beforehand, the attendance was large and noisy. Blaxcell could hardly make himself heard, but he managed to open the proceedings by announcing that Johnston had acted to affirm 'the laws of the British nation, and the rights and liberties of Englishmen'. No distinctions were observed either of status or gender, and indeed the first voice from the crowd was that of a woman, unnamed, who led the vote appointing a delegate to take their grievances to England. Macarthur was chosen (a decision obviously preordained), and he was thereupon brought into the room. He made a well-rehearsed speech in which he reminded his audience of the 'diabolical' schemes from which he had escaped and of the 'villains who [had] wanted to drink his blood': 'he betrayed much emotion, frequently clasping his hands together with much energy'. Money was then voted to pay his expenses to England. The partnership of Lord, Kable and Underwood offered the enormous sum of £500, and lesser townspeople made promises in proportion. Among thirteen other original signatures (ten men and three women) were those of Sarah Wills's husband, Edward (£30) and Mary Skinner, the potter's widow (£10).[108]

All now came undone. The rebels quarrelled among themselves, and Macarthur soon proved too autocratic for the townspeople. None of their money was forthcoming and as early as April the idea of his being their delegate was abandoned. The officers decided in spite of him to send for their commanding officer, Paterson, now at Port Dalrymple, as the rightful lieutenant-governor but meanwhile, in July, Joseph Foveaux, Paterson's second-in-command, returned from leave in England. He took command for the time being, and Macarthur went back to Elizabeth Farm.[109]

The interregnum lasted until the end of 1809. Gore was tried once more by the Criminal Court and sent as a convict to the coal mines at Newcastle. Bligh, after thirteen months under house arrest, embarked with his daughter on the *Porpoise*, living as commodore on the waters of Port Jackson or the Derwent. He did not give up hope of winning in the end. In July 1808, while the ship lay at the entrance to Sydney Cove, he ordered the acting commander of the *Porpoise*, William Kent the younger, as Kent later recalled, to train his guns towards the shore, and 'to Blow down the Town of Sydney, for the purpose of reinstating him in his Government'. He later made the same '*most extraordinary* proposal' to the commander, John Porteous. The responsibility being so grave, both refused to act without a written order, which Bligh declined to give.[110]

Bligh had always thought of Sydney as a 'sink of iniquity', a place to be made over by strong measures.[111] But it was also a place whose people had hitherto trusted their rulers. Bligh's predecessors had struggled to make themselves predictable and therefore dependable. These last exchanges, in which the Governor relied, as always, on taking the place by surprise, were symptomatic of his battle with the town.

Chapter 14

The Ocean and the Little Fish

I

The first Europeans in Australia still believed in a kind of transcendent order, an immanence which justified creation (as I say in Chapter 8). Not until the middle decades of the nineteenth century did that belief begin to lose its comprehensive power to shape European thought and conversation. Only then did Matthew Arnold think to lament the 'melancholy, long, withdrawing roar' of what he called the 'Sea of Faith': 'Retreating to the breath/ Of the night-wind, down the vast edges drear / And naked shingles of the world'. But even Arnold underestimated the earlier power of the Sea of Faith. He also underestimated the ocean itself, and the way it echoed, as a source of terror, in the minds of his forebears. No-one of an earlier generation would have used the image of that infinity of waters as Arnold did: as a means of comfort, the lifeblood of civilisation. For Arnold there was too little sea and too little faith. For him a richer humanity receded with the tide. In earlier times both sea and faith were frequently overwhelming.

The generation which lived through the first decades of European settlement in Australia was one for whom the sea was still appallingly large. Human beings might certainly grow rich on it, but they could too easily be lost in it. The parameters of the sea, its depth and breadth, its perpetual movement, were still far beyond common comprehension. Byron's image of a 'glorious mirror, where the Almighty's form / Glasses itself in tempests', catches something of the current sense of fear and wonder.[1] Nor at this time – the years about 1800 – could one turn one's back on the sea as easily as one might have done during previous moments of world history. Increasing ocean traffic meant that the voice of the world's waters forced itself upon the European imagination even more powerfully than hitherto.

The age was equally drawn to the idea of the manly individual, the genius of the one man all alone. Fraternity, as among the Freemasons, was designed to flatter and comfort such a person. A genuine manhood required communion with self, accountability to one's own soul. Women, on the other hand, seemed to be wholly made for dependence and society. They were shaped by the places they lived in, while men were considered wanderers, so many Napoleons, so many Newtons, universal rule-makers and universal types. The poet Wordsworth, filling his own imagination with Isaac Newton's 'silent face' – the genius himself was long dead – placed a fashionable mask on that antique flesh: 'The marble index of a mind for ever / Voyaging through strange seas of Thought alone'.[2] The bright energy and mystery of the individual man seemed a noble thing indeed. Napoleon waged war on Europe. Similarly, so John Keats remarked, 'the commonest Man shows a grace in his quarrel'.[3]

'Help! Help!': the picture drawn by William Blake to illustrate his poem, *The Gates of Paradise*.

Source: National Library of Australia

But even singularity is relative. Napoleon, like Newton, was mortal. With all the fineness of the individual, there remained a sublimity beyond men, calling up a painful contrast, for instance, between the image of the single man – insect-like, fragile and angular – and that of vast objects like the ocean. Set against the serenity of Wordsworth's ideal Newton was the terror of Coleridge's Ancient Mariner:

Alone, alone, all, all alone,
Alone on a wide wide sea!
And never a saint took pity on
My soul in agony.

Drawn by the same cheerless mystery, in 1793 William Blake published his illuminated work, *The Gates of Paradise*, with its picture, entitled 'Help! Help!', of a single arm extended from an otherwise featureless sea. That picture was partly inspired, it seems, by a picture in oils called 'Watson and the Shark' (1778) by John Singleton Copley, which was copied and widely distributed as an engraving. A naked man there struggled alone in the black and emerald-blue water, his friends apparently powerless to save him from the teeth of a sea-monster.[4]

Watson and the Shark: the popular engraving from J. S. Copley's oil painting.

Source: British Museum

Napoleon was important in another way. His regime as emperor in Europe (1804–14) carried to fruition the idea that states might remake themselves as oceans of authority, as profound and inevitable as Copley's shark, entire bodies of power whose denizens were the mass of the people. The heroism of the emperor was combined with a new administrative finesse, the people being bound by chains of paper, their habits assessed and minds recast by a civil service wholly accountable to Paris. The ideas which had evolved in Europe during the Enlightenment thus reached their apotheosis in the extended gaze of the state. The British empire was similarly drawn within the purview of Whitehall and that of increasingly busy intellectual and philanthropic bodies cooperating with government. Australia had been opened up to the intelligence of Europeans since the arrival of Captain Cook, and Cook's travelling companion, Joseph Banks, as President of the Royal Society, continued to collect information about this continent for the rest of his life. For the well-informed mind, wrote Thomas Fyshe Palmer, the Scottish Martyr, on his arrival in New South Wales, this was a place of 'infinite entertainment'. 'It is certainly a new world, a new creation', he exclaimed, 'Every plant, every shell, tree, fish and animal, bird, insect different from the old.'[5] Among the governors alone, Hunter drew and collected much of what he saw, Paterson was a Fellow of the Royal Society who sent seeds and plants to Banks and to Samuel Bentham, while Bligh's daughter, Mary Putland, packed up shells for her mother, a well-known conchologist.

The urge to control and collect was linked with military and territorial power. The Seven Years War, 1756–63, had been the first world war, in which Britain and France had fought in almost every quarter of the globe. With victory, Britain had increased its authority in India, North America, Africa and the West Indies. Large numbers of British troops were afterwards stationed permanently abroad, and squadrons of the Royal Navy were scattered thickly through the world's waters. The first British settlements in Van Diemen's Land were a direct result of competition between Britain and France in that most remote spot. A capacity to think efficiently in such world-wide terms depended not only on a better sense of geography. It also required a continuous polishing of administrative skills, improved habits of command and improved habits of obedience. Such skills took a leap forward during the war with revolutionary and Napoleonic France. In other words, the ideological effect of Napoleon – the new imprint of the state – was felt not only within his own empire but among his adversaries.

The wish to rule large numbers and large spaces was easily justified. Success ensured immortality for self, dynasty and nation, but to such timeless reasons the eighteenth century had added two more. A scattered empire was good for trade. European settlement in New South Wales had opened the way for whaling and sealing, and by Governor King's time, especially with the new southern bases, the colony began to be fully drawn within the network of imperial commerce. Australia was now subject to systematic thinking about profit in Europe. But also, the more numerous one's subjects, the better enlightenment could be dispersed among the human race. Europeans sent to the Antipodes were subject to the dictatorial benevolence of the British government from the moment they left their native soil. Governor Phillip had been its eager medium, and through Phillip and his successors humanitarian order was established in New South Wales. In principle, all Europeans who came to New South Wales under the aegis of government were offered a regime of welfare and discipline and, especially in King's time, paths were laid down for the making of homes and the accumulation of property.

Such security depended on New South Wales being part of a larger whole. Enlightenment thinking prevented any single place from being sacred or absolute of itself. Every spot on earth was contingent on the whole, and even ancient centres of authority needed their margins in order to make sense. The dignity of human life lay in usefulness rather than custom, in the mutuality of power from place to place rather than the pomp of names, in geography more than history, unless it was the sort of history which said that men and women had always been the same. Jeremy Bentham showed how far these priorities could be taken. During the 1790s he worked out two schemes to end Britain's difficulties with crime and poverty. He argued for the building of new prisons, 'panopticons' or 'inspection houses', whose architecture would allow all the inmates to live continuously under the eye of a single inspector. Their cells were to be in a great storied circle, each open on its inner side and the inspector housed at the central point. This engine of discipline was to be powered not only by the vigilance of the inspector but also by the ignorance of the prisoners, who could never know whether he was looking at them or not. They were subject to the institution and to what Bentham called 'an invisible omnipresence', a power recording their behaviour and managing rewards and punishments. His other plan was for the building of a network of new settlements throughout Britain to house the destitute. The guiding principles were like those of the inspection houses, but from a geographical point of view the configuration was looser and more vast. Instead of a citadel, he sketched a net flung over the face of the country.[6]

Bentham was against convict transportation because he thought that transported men and women escaped from such vigilance. But his panopticon principle was quite capable of being given a world-wide dimension, making Britain the final point of reference for the control of individuals whose cells were continents and islands. The first person to make this suggestion seems to have been Governor Bligh's opponent, John Macarthur, a man forever thinking, forever wielding a finely drawn genius, 'a grace in his quarrel'.

Macarthur, in his ideas for New South Wales, drew on two common and inconsistent visions of the settlement, one looking backwards and the other forwards, and only the second could have owed anything to Bentham. The old vision was in line with traditions of commonwealth, with notions of English energy making its way, unimpeded, anywhere it liked. When Phillip's expedition to New South Wales was announced in 1786, English imagination of this antique kind was fired by the idea of an antipodean settlement as strange as Crusoe's island, squalid in its origins but of an independent spirit, with an upside-down morality like that of the London gangs from which it was to be recruited:

John Macarthur, a miniature painted during one of his periods in England,
1802–04 or 1809–17.

Source: Mr John Macarthur-Stanham, copy from Historic Houses Trust of New South Wales

> They go of an island to take special charge,
> Much warmer than Britain, and ten times as large;
> No custom house duty, no freightage to pay,
> And tax-free they'll live when at Botany Bay. . . .
>
> As scores of each sex to this place must proceed,
> In twenty years time – only think of the breed;
> Major Semple, should fortune much kindness display,
> May live to be king over Botany Bay.

James Semple was a gentleman pickpocket who was never in fact transported. He also figured in newpaper skits published about the same time
which pretended to report news from Botany Bay in the remote 1850s. He
there appeared as Governor with an elite made up of similar men, living in

places whose names replicated the London underworld: 'Old Bailey Plains', 'Gallows Town', 'New Drop Bay'. The news told of a revolution like America's, of 'unhappy disturbances occasioned by the tyrannical acts passed in England, to the injury of our natural rights, our constitution, and our liberties', and it announced another Declaration of Independence, that of '*the States of New-Holland*'.[7]

These burlesques sometimes featured another gentleman pickpocket, George Barrington, who was indeed transported and whom Hunter made a superintendent of convicts. Barrington's notoriety led to his name being attached as author to books about the colony so as to promote sales, and in 1801 the *Annual Register* printed a verse written as a pretended prologue for 'the Theatre, at Sydney, Botany Bay, to be spoken by the celebrated Mr Barrington':

> From distant climes o'er wide-spread seas we come,
> Though not with much eclat or beat of drum,
> True patriots all; for be it understood,
> We left our country for our country's good.

And much more, all arguing the small difference between crime, theatre and the building of nations.[8] To the literary eye, Botany Bay, the 'island', was this theatre expanded – 'Newgate . . . become a quarter of the globe' – and designed to bear the performances of characters like Barrington. '[T]he time may come,' said the *Edinburgh Review*, in one the finest visions of this kind, 'when some Botany Bay Tacitus shall record the crimes of an Emperor lineally descended from a London pick pocket, or paint the valour with which he has led his New Hollanders into the heart of China.'[9]

John Macarthur, though less whimsical, made much of the idea of New South Wales as a separate community with separate interests, like the old American colonies, entitled to its own energies, its own heroes and its own history. During the weeks following the rebellion, he seems to have put together a number of ideas for colonial reform which he sent to Plummer, his London agent, for presentation wherever they might make a mark.[10] He proposed the appointment of an agent for the colony in London, just as other colonies had, to stand up for the interests of its people. He also wanted a local council of seven, including two chosen by the magistrates from among themselves, with legislative and judicial powers like similar bodies throughout the empire (including the House of Lords). But, he said, such a council should not limit the Governor and there should be no elected lower house: this colony needed a firmer hand than others because it was 'so distant . . . and composed of such discordant materials'.

These were telling reservations. However powerful his sense of place (it was less powerful than his wife's), in the end Macarthur was more interested in the usefulness of New South Wales to the empire at large. In his mind the new order took precedence over the old, Bentham over Algernon Sidney.

He thought more of efficiency than of pickpocket emperors. He had a ready understanding of geography, evident in his hopes of exporting fine wool to Britain and in a remarkable scheme he worked out, in theory only, in 1806–07 for a quadrangular trade system independent of Europe and linking Sydney, Fiji, Calcutta and Canton.[11] In 1808 he showed the same vast sense of space in suggesting a new system of transportation. It revolved around several points: Port Jackson, Newcastle, Port Dalrymple, Hobart Town and possibly Norfolk Island. Punishment should differ in severity from one to the other, and the convicts should move by 'rotation' through lessening stages of misery until they reached the last, Port Jackson, where they might be set free. Each year a ship was to make the voyage from point to point, dropping and picking up, exchanging the reformed for the partly reformed, in what was to be another quadrangular system. The minimum periods at each place should be arranged so as to add up to seven years, even for convicts with life sentences, so that an individual's suffering was to depend not on the sentence handed down in Britain or Ireland but on his behaviour as he moved along the antipodean path laid out for him. Bureaucratic efficiency was to be the anchor of the entire system. Besides the careful records of behaviour which such a scheme called for, there were also to be certificates for each convict at the end of each stage and none was to be delayed without full inquiry. At the heart of the system, like the inspector in Bentham's panopticon, was the Governor, the medium of whose gaze was to be, not the naked eye as with Bentham, but pen and paper.[12]

The subjects of this scheme were to be men. Female convicts, so Macarthur suggested, were to be married off or kept in asylums at Port Jackson. The recent revolutions in Europe had celebrated the now undeniable fact that men were public beings, a quality which laid on them a peculiar burden, which exposed them absolutely to the new means of power. Unlike women, men were obliged to belong either to the light of public liberty or the catacombs of public bondage, and Macarthur thought the eyes of male convicts might be fed with the dazzling contrast of brightness and blackness as they were enticed towards the first. Hope and its opposite were everything to romantic minds like his.

James Hingston Tuckey was an officer on the *Calcutta*, which carried convicts and settlers to Port Phillip in 1803, and, when that site proved unsuitable, on to the Derwent. He afterwards gave an account of his own sensibility – like Macarthur's, but more literary – 'sitting', as he said, 'on the carriage of a gun, in front of the camp' at Port Phillip, where he simultaneously watched the movement round about and the drama among his own emotions. The male convicts provoked in him a finely wrought melancholy:

When I viewed so many of my fellow-men, sunk, some of them from a rank in life, equal to or superior to my own, and by crimes degraded to a level with the basest of mankind; when I saw them *naked*, wading to their shoulders in water to unlade the boats, while a burning sun struck its meridian rays upon their uncovered heads, or yoked to and sweating under a timber carriage, the wheels of which were sunk up to the axle in sand, I only considered their hapless lot, and the remembrance of their vices was for a moment absorbed in the greatness of their punishment.

The women were a more comfortable prospect. Women's lives were shaped by the places in which they found themselves. Private and particular beings, they were freed more easily from universal notions of right and wrong:

> When, on the other hand, I viewed the lively appearance of the camp, the employments of the women, and the ridiculous dilemmas into which they were every moment thrown by the novelty of their situations, I smiled, and inwardly admiring the pliability of mind, which enables us to accommodate ourselves to the vicissitudes of fortune, confessed that the pride of independence, and the keen sensibility of prosperity, like marks imprinted on the sand, are soon effaced by the current of adverse circumstances.

Among women all was relative, so that nothing about them could be truly tragic. Indeed, Tuckey admitted to himself and to his readers that even female chastity, which seemed so important among some people, 'grows weaker by degrees, and at last falls a sacrifice to present convenience'.[13] Women belonged, each enduring her own circumstances, on dry land; but men, even on this far side of the world, remained the 'hapless' subjects of sun and water.

The implementation of ideas like these – palpable subjection – depended on the structure and power of the empire, including its military power. It also depended on the response of the human material. The events of Bligh's government and its aftermath drew some of the issues together. Neat visions like those of Macarthur and Tuckey lived mainly on paper, but as imperial power began to make an impression (very gradually, even as yet very slightly) on the common mind, gentle and simple, bond and free, there was talk about what it meant to be its subject. Whoever you were, when you turned yourself to the centre – in Blake's terms, when you shouted from the deep – did you meet an eye or a conscience, a sharpened sensibility or another soul?

II

Bligh had his supporters in New South Wales, including the merchant Robert Campbell (whom he had made Naval Officer), the Commissary, John Palmer (Campbell's brother-in-law), William Gore, and a number of lesser officials. A few outspoken free immigrants, men who had come with enough money to set themselves up as respectable small farmers, were also among his supporters. They were leaders within some of the outlying communities: not rich, but moral men, literate (up to a point), untainted by crime or, in most cases, by association with Sydney's port-life. They recognised in Bligh an attitude of moral superiority like their own. He enabled them to believe that Whitehall itself mirrored their virtues, as indeed it now did. At the Hawkesbury about a dozen, mostly arrivals by the *Nile* in 1802 and the *Coromandel* in 1803, signed a series of addresses, first to Paterson, asking him to come up from Port Dalrymple to restore the Governor, and afterwards to Bligh and to the Secretary of State in London. They cooperated with another group at Baulkham Hills led by Andrew MacDougall (*Barwell* 1798) and George Suttor (*Porpoise* 1800).[14] Suttor was a botanist who, like Bligh himself, had come out under the patronage of Joseph Banks and who was incarcerated for six months by the rebels.

Bligh thought that free immigrants must always be a cut above ex-convicts, and the Baulkham Hills people had been flattered, as they told the minister, with his 'affable manner of receiving them and Visiting them at their habitations'. But they and their friends also praised his more general efforts to relieve distress after the 1806 floods and to break the power which the traders and large livestock-owners had over prices. In particular, they said, he had set up branches of the government store in outlying parts, undercutting the travelling dealers and saving trouble for the farmers.[15] How much impact such changes had really made before January 1808 we cannot know. More fundamental was the understanding, among these few farmers at least, that Bligh was at odds, as they were, with Sydney and its ex-convict managers.

These declarations reached England late in the day. One of the rebels, the surveyor Charles Grimes, had arrived with Johnston's despatches and the first news of Bligh's deposition as early as 12 September 1808. Short notices had appeared in the London papers three days later and on 17 September the *Morning Post* gave a description of three days' rejoicing in Sydney.[16] The Whig journalist William Augustus Miles wrote to a friend to pass on the gossip that Bligh, 'who ought never to have been sent there, except for life', had been dragged by the rebels from under a feather bed. 'All tyrants', he said, 'are cowards in adversity . . . capable of being seized by a child, as soon as their authority is attacked.' Bligh's friends spoke differently. 'I fear', wrote the Honourable Charles Greville to Banks on the same day, 'the plans against Bligh have been extensively laid and artfully conducted. Certainly prejudice has been more barefaced in any case I ever saw.'[17]

John Macarthur's nineteen-year-old son, Edward, a passenger with Grimes, immediately contacted Plummer and Johnston's patron, the Duke of Northumberland. Macarthur and Johnston themselves arrived in October 1809. The Secretary of State, Lord Castlereagh, seems to have been in two minds about the rebellion. He was prepared to reprimand Bligh, in one instance, for behaviour 'not reconcileable with the Principles of British Justice', and he refused to reinstate him. But he also wrote to assure him that the news of the 'Mutinous Outrage' had caused 'the strongest Sensation' at

Whitehall.[18] The law officers advised that Johnston was liable to court martial on a charge of mutiny, whatever justifying facts might emerge during his
trial. Macarthur might be indicted for conspiracy, but only in New South
Wales.[19]

Such trials would involve assuming Bligh's innocence and casting the burden of proof on his enemies. There was another view, which followed from
the idea that Englishmen, wherever they were in the world, ought to be as
free as possible. Accountability rested with government and not with those
who advocated the rights of the people. This was the classic Whig understanding. The Duke of Northumberland, though a distinguished soldier
himself, argued that the rebellion ought not to be judged from a military
perspective. A court martial, he said, was uncalled for, at least in the first
instance. Investigations should start with the Privy Council – as they had
lately done in the case of Governor Picton of Trinidad, accused of torture by
one of his people – and they ought to depend less on Bligh's allegations and
more on the assumption, as the Duke told Johnston, 'that the Troops, which
accompanied you, were for *his* Protection against an enraged people'.[20]

In short, according to Northumberland, 'it was in your *Civil*, and not in
your *Military* Capacity, that you superseded the Gov[erno]r'.[21] But what was
Johnston's civil capacity? As senior officer of the garrison at Sydney he had
the temporary status, though not the name, of Lieutenant-Governor, with
the right of succession should the Governor be suddenly absent, disabled or
dead. What of his right to remove the Governor from power? Here the Duke
implied a more shadowy type of civil capacity, an ability to step between the
supreme magistrate and the people, as it were 'in His Majesty's sacred
name', to use military force for civil ends, to marry order with liberty under
the sanction of gentlemanly judgment. The British constitution was understood to be held in trust by gentlemen, as the natural leaders of the people,
and discretion such as Northumberland referred to was expected of a gentleman, whether a soldier or not. But beyond that issue was another. The
civil power of a gentleman depended on his being part of a civil community
and subject to a civil government. Did any such exist in New South Wales?

In short, was New South Wales to be taken seriously, as a fragment of
customary British order, or was it to be thought of as a place whose very
existence was an act of power? John Macarthur, throughout the long drama
of his own life, struggled to prove that he and the stage on which he performed must be taken very seriously indeed. Soon after his arrival in
England, he began to think of himself once again as an advocate of local
interests. He was flattered by the attention of influential men, mainly Whigs
among the parliamentary opposition. They included Hugh Elliot, brother of
the Earl of Minto and close friend of the Comte de Mirabeau, one of
the bright early lights of the French Revolution. Elliot said that everyone
(meaning his own circle) thought the rebellion 'indispensible for the preser-
vation of everything worth saving in the Colony'.[22] Support among such
people opened up the possibility of new legislation for New South Wales.
But nothing could be done without some official verdict on the rebellion,

which was impossible until Bligh returned. When that at last happened, in October 1810, the moment for government action seemed almost past.[23] Macarthur himself prepared to sue his enemy for £20,000 damages, presumably for the loss of the *Parramatta*, and to think of entering parliament himself.

> Be patient [he wrote home to his wife] and all will be well, – for I have found a powerful body of Friends in this Country, who are not only able but willing to give me their support in my endeavours to obtain satisfaction for the past and *security* for the *future*, *depend* upon it, the Colony will soon undergo *a radical reform.*[24]

Johnston himself, sure of being able to prove Bligh's 'tyranny and oppression', applied to the Colonial Office for an inquiry.[25] That and Bligh's eagerness to prosecute secured him a court martial, and meanwhile Macarthur's own pursuit of Bligh was put off.

Johnston's court martial, held at Chelsea Barracks between 7 May and 5 June 1811, was the first occasion on which methods of government in New South Wales had been examined in any detail in England. The result justified Northumberland's fear that a military trial would throw Johnston onto the defensive. It also fulfilled Macarthur's prediction, made at a gloomy moment: 'The *precedent* [of the rebellion] is not liked, for men in power prefer *unlimited* authority over those they govern.'[26] The president of the court was Lieutenant-General William Keppel, equerry to the newly appointed Prince Regent (the King had just become permanently mad), but the most distinguished figure was Sir David Baird, a veteran of India, Egypt, southern Africa and the Peninsula, a popular hero since 1801 when he had led a great trek from the Red Sea to the Nile. He was brave, terrifying and efficient, a perfect type of the new professional. Among the other thirteen officers, including members of the royal household and of parliament, political and family ties pulled in numerous ways. Major-General the Honourable Edward Paget was first cousin to Nicholas Paget Bayly, one of the Corps deeply involved in the rebellion. However, at a moment when the war with France had reached a desperate point, and when there were fears of revolution even in England, the verdict in such cases tended to lie with men like General Baird.[27] The same authoritarian view appeared in the Judge-Advocate-General, a civilian and a lawyer who was present throughout such trials and who managed every detail. This was Charles Manners Sutton, a man young enough to have been the son of Keppel or Baird but who was in fact the son of the Archbishop of Canterbury. He was a young Tory, one of the leaders of a generation dedicated to good order and rigorous private virtue.[28]

The legal basis of government in New South Wales was central to the trial. It was an old issue for the rebels, Johnston having once privately complained about colonial taxes being imposed without the sanction of parliament and Macarthur having publicly demanded whether Englishmen ought to hold their property at the Governor's discretion.[29] The appeal which the people of Sydney had made during the assembly at St Phillip's church in February 1808, about 'the various grievances they have for a length of time laboured under', had some obvious recent precedents in Britain and Ireland. Since the days of John Wilkes in the 1760s ('Wilkes and Liberty!'), Englishmen had become more and more ready to make organised demands for constitutional change. Leaders were frequently individuals of middling rank, small property owners like the men and women of Sydney.[30] In some minds, on the other hand, such movements were now identified with revolution. Officers on the bench of a general court martial at the climax of a great war could not easily imagine that any legitimate order could exist within popular meetings, even when the spokesmen only asked that their property be safe against arbitrary power. For their part, Johnston's lawyers seem to have decided that it would be wise to narrow the argument to the finest point possible, limiting their case to the question of the breakdown of order and avoiding any large problems of law.

Bligh's authority was therefore never debated, and misunderstandings on this point drew the military net even tighter, not only around Johnston but around New South Wales. The first witness for the defence (though he had no wish to be on either side) was Richard Atkins, who referred in passing to the trial of D'Arcy Wentworth, a government surgeon court-martialled on Bligh's orders. This led the bench to inquire what sort of trial Wentworth might have been liable to and Atkins handed in his own commission, which was modelled on that of a regimental judge-advocate. Nearly all officials, he said, were commissioned in that way, 'being all placed under the Governor, according to the rules and discipline of war', at which the bench remarked, 'In short, it is made a military government.'[31] This conclusion took no account of the civilian jurisdiction in New South Wales, but it reassured the members of the bench in the belief that they were dealing with a situation which they, as soldiers, understood. They dealt with Macarthur's evidence on that basis. Sutton asked him, 'By what law is the colony governed; is it by military law or by civil law?' Macarthur answered, 'By civil law'. Sutton let this pass but he went on to ask why he had not obeyed the Governor's order that he go to Sydney to answer for the *Parramatta*: 'it is every man's duty to obey the laws of his country; the Governor sent for you, and you should have gone', which amounted to saying that the Governor's order was law. One of the bench (probably Baird, who had governed at the Cape of Good Hope when it was conquered from the Dutch) interjected, 'I was once at the head of a colony myself, and if the orders which I sent were disobeyed, how could I govern the colony?' Sutton now put his hand on the royal patent of 1787 by which the two principal courts of law in New South Wales had been established, and which stated that in criminal cases the laws of England were to apply only 'as nearly as may be' and that even civil judgments could be overturned by the Governor. He seems to have hoped that Macarthur would retreat to the fundamental question of the legality of the Governor's orders. As a lawyer he must have been aware of Bentham's ideas on that point, and he must have hoped that Johnston's counsel or one of his witnesses might be driven onto such ground. For six days the point had been ignored by the defence and even now Macarthur was able to double back, holding off his interrogator with trifling answers: 'I beg pardon'; 'I intended no disobedience.' Sutton had to give up, remarking as he put down the patent, apropos of nothing, that that document was the constitution of New South Wales, 'as far as it was necessary to give it a constitution'.[32] It followed that New South Wales was nothing like a civil community.

The officers on the bench struggled to discover why the insurrection had happened at all. At the opening of the trial, Bligh had told a simple story of enemies created by his own success. But he named only one achievement, his banning of the barter of spirits and, as his own witnesses testified, very few had complained about that.[33] On the fourth day a voice came from the bench, 'What was Mr M'Arthur tried for?' Another member: 'We have never understood, though he seems to have been the main-spring of every thing.' The former member: 'It would be a satisfaction to know what was the cause of so great a revolution.'[34] The defence had not intended to make Macarthur look like the main-spring, but he was central to their case. Macarthur was a gentleman, 'an opulent and respectable settler', as they called him, 'of unblemished character both in public and private'. As such his rights and dignity were, by most criteria, peculiarly sacred, and defence witnesses told of the people being worked up to a dangerous pitch of fear and anger by his injuries.[35] Macarthur knew the part well, but he played it with such conceited enthusiasm as to become, for the bench, not only the main-spring but the villain of the piece. He affected to be a gentleman in a place where gentlemen were irrelevant. In the end Johnston's lawyers even changed their story so as to make him no longer essential, as he had been made to seem at the beginning, but incidental on the evening of Bligh's arrest.[36] This made the event even harder to understand.

Sergeant-Major Whittle, who might have been a crucial witness, was useless to both sides. The prosecution asked him a string of questions in a tone which anticipated a string of lies, before pressing him on his story about Bligh's threat to pull down his house. Whittle began to tremble:

> What was the date of that conversation? – Upon my word, I cannot tell.
> Do you know the year?– Yes, sir, it was the same year, 1808.
> You are sure it was in 1808?– I think it was, I am not positive.
> Was it a few days before the arrest of the Governor? – It was four or five months. [It was one month.]
> How could it be four or five months before the arrest of the Governor, and yet in 1808? – I think it was in 1808.
> Who was present besides yourself and the Governor?

At this point the witness collapsed and was carried from the court.[37]

Johnston was found guilty and cashiered. That is, he was stripped of his rank and cast out of the army. He was saved from hanging only by agreement among the bench that there might have been some crisis which had forced him to act. But, as Sutton reported to the Prince Regent, they thought he should have reasoned with Bligh first. Johnston had already explained during the trial that Bligh was not a man for reasoning with and that no agreement with him could be binding.[38] This had been a point central to the whole crisis, but it was lost on the bench since none had lived among the forest of conversation which existed in European New South Wales. They could only assume a type of order familiar to themselves, the order of an empire shaped both for war and for the full tide of Enlightenment.

The result of the court martial was a major setback for Macarthur's hopes, but not all was lost. New South Wales was a topic of parliamentary conversation, not only because of the rebellion but also because of a revival of interest in penal discipline. A House of Commons select committee with George Holford as chairman was currently inquiring into the English penal system and had produced two reports during the trial, both dealing with new prisons. Early in 1812 Holford turned his attention to the hulks, and a second committee, with George Eden in the chair, was appointed to look at transportation.[39] Eden was a young man who was to be very distinguished in later years as Governor-General of India but whose main qualification for the chair lay in his being a member of the Whig opposition and son of William Eden (see Chapter 3), author of *Principles of Penal Law* (1771). He was also Lord Hobart's brother-in-law, and nephew both to Hugh Elliot and to Sir Robert Eden, who had been Governor of Maryland at the outbreak of the American Revolution. Governor Eden had been honoured by both the King and the Maryland rebels, a proud matter of family memory likely to have shaped George Eden's understanding of the difference between a good governor and a bad one.[40]

Eden's report vindicated the rebellion in Sydney, but only by implication. Hugh Elliot had said that among his circle the event was thought indispensable. Eden would not go so far in a public document but, unlike the officers at Johnston's court martial, he made local public opinion central to his conclusions. He strongly condemned Bligh for taking up land while he was Governor. He also suggested that the courts of justice be reformed, 'to give the inhabitants that confidence and legal security which can alone render them contented with the Government under which they are placed'. He took it for granted that the subject of his inquiry was (as Maryland had been under his uncle) a civil community with a civil government, and he was especially critical of the Criminal Court, which, he said, ought to look less like a court martial. And, like Macarthur, he suggested that the Governor be given a council made up of leading men, if only to provide the inhabitants with a legitimate and orderly avenue of protest against him. For, wrote Eden, it could hardly be expected, 'where so much authority and responsibility are thrown into the hands of one man, that his will however just, and his administration however wise, will not at times create opposition and discontent among men unused, in their own country, to see so great a monopoly of power'.[41] He argued here in terms not of absolute right but of expectation and usefulness.

This was the Whigs' measured verdict on the revolution in New South Wales. If it contradicted the assumptions of the court martial, it could not cancel the spirit of the age. For all his Whig heritage, in the last resort Eden had considered the lives of free people in New South Wales as if they were incidental to the business of transportation. Even for him, the rights of Englishmen were no longer the final point of reference in public debate, as they had been for Lord Sydney. They were part of larger picture and as such to be described, measured and, where necessary, adjusted to new standards of virtue and to the needs of empire.

III

Eden had tried to find out how many convicts there were in New South Wales, what was happening to them there and how they responded. The first point was the most difficult. Statistical records of a kind had been kept since first settlement, but mainly in order to quantify health, sustenance and survival. The numbers in hospital and the numbers dead had been carefully counted by the surgeons and placed among the systematic facts of settlement. From 1791 the Commissary had begun to make regular surveys (six-monthly to start with), in which he divided up the population according to the type of ration they received: whole, two-thirds, half or a quarter. Within his tabulation there was a category for convicts, but it also included male convicts' free wives and children. Also, when some convicts ceased to be fed by the government they were moved indiscriminately into a column headed 'People not Victualled from the Stores'.[42] The Commissary was not interested in legal status except where it helped in showing who was to be fed.

Governor King's lists offered the first effective means of counting men and women still serving their terms. It thus appeared that in 1805, among a total mainland population of 6980 Europeans, 30 per cent were convicts (1561 men and 516 women). Similar tables compiled by David Collins at Hobart Town that year showed 66 per cent (274 men and 35 women) in a total of 467.[43] But Bligh made no effort of this kind, and when he was called as a witness before the Eden committee he could only offer guesses. He believed, he said, that among ten thousand souls in all the settlements (a muster of March 1810 made it 10,452) about a fourth or fifth were convicts. But for Bligh, 'convict' did not include men and women with tickets of leave who were allowed to look after themselves.[44] Like the Commissary, he defined convicts, not by the sentence they carried from Europe, but by the degree of freedom they had in New South Wales.

The new penology was built on precision, and George Eden was glad to be able to note that Whitehall had already moved to remedy ignorance on convict numbers, the Secretary of State having asked Macquarie, the new Governor, for twice-yearly returns.[45] But Eden was not a penal theorist as his father had been. In his report he did not press for strict congruity between European crime and Australian suffering. All the same, he understood the importance of good administration in the management of large numbers of men and women. He was most concerned with the transportation process, including the work of the surgeons appointed for each ship. He described a regime which depended on a combination of humanity, medical skill and ready literacy. Each surgeon, he reported, had to keep a daily record of ill-nesses, of the scraping of the decks, the cleaning of the berths and related matters. He had to visit all the sick twice a day and the healthy once. He was in full command of medicines and food given to the sick. And 'He is further instructed to transmit to the Secretary of State, any observations which may occur to him productive of improvement in the mode of treat-ment, and he is paid a gratuity of 10s 6d for every convict landed in New South Wales.' All this was very correct. Eden only regretted that the souls of the convicts were not as carefully tended as their bodies, there being no pro-vision for religious worship on the voyage.[46]

Refined administrative methods – progressively more and more refined – had been central to the traditions of eighteenth-century empire. But so was the idea of independent life abroad. Eden wanted New South Wales to be an efficient repository for convicts, but this, he thought, would follow from its being a place in which both men and women had a chance of reform and, beyond that, of independence and respectability. He went out of his way to condemn Bligh's statement, given in evidence to the committee, that neither former convicts nor their children should ever expect to be received as visi-tors at Government House. In Eden's view, individual ambition, nourished without restraint by local circumstances, ought to drive the engine of reward and punishment.[47]

Women convicts figured largely in Eden's report. They were essential to his understanding – inherited from the long experience of eighteenth-century empire – that good administration lays the basis for new life. Like others who had thought about transportation to New South Wales, he believed that in the business of settling families on the soil women convicts were a mixed blessing. But they *were* a blessing. Many women would fight to the end against the authority of literate men and not all knew, or wanted to know, how to negotiate with promises on paper. But all, said Eden, must be considered as mothers, because as mothers they were vital to the whole enterprise: 'from this stock only can a reasonable hope be held out of rapid increase to the population; upon which increase, here as in all infant colonies, its growing prosperity in great measure depends'.[48] He overlaid this judgment with an interest in female wickedness characteristic of his genera-tion. There was an ancient distinction between good and bad women. It appeared in the words of Mary Farrell in Sydney in 1804 on being proposi-tioned by John Green (he leaping through her door with a knife): 'My sweet fellow, I am a married woman, the mother of children, and I am not a per-son of that description you want.' It was a distinction which might matter very little to a determined rapist (it made no difference to Green), but it was useful to statesmen. Governor Phillip, in his first remarks about women in

New South Wales, had hoped to divide the marriageable ones ('who still retain some degree of virtue') from those ('the most abandoned') who were to be considered prostitutes.[49] George Eden, forty years younger than Phillip, took a further step, struggling with the task of drawing the wicked as well as the guilty within the moral view of government. He was scandalised by the discovery that on ships taking out female convicts the seamen and women made their own arrangements, two by two, for the duration. And he was pleased to learn that Macquarie had stopped the practice of allowing newly arrived women to be taken as common-law wives.[50] For young gentlemen such as he, rulers of post-revolutionary Europe, public security depended on private morality and anything less than certified marriage implied the unravelling of the state.

Methods of government in New South Wales, he thought, should make the inhabitants secure in their lives and property. Relationships among them ought to be sanctioned on paper: blessed by the church, recorded by the state and capable of affirmation by the courts. Bad men and women might be bad subjects, but they were subjects all the same – subjects of a new morality – and they were not to be given opportunities for wickedness. Such a view had already been expressed in New South Wales, but mainly by the chaplains. In 1806 Samuel Marsden, building on the bureaucratic work already done by Governor King, compiled a list of all the European women on the mainland, distinguishing each as either wife or 'concubine' and numbering the children as legitimate or illegitimate. It thus appeared (and the list is full of mistakes) that among a total of 1430 women, 1035 were 'unmarried and concubines'. Marsden's 'concubines' were women who lived as wives without marriage and indeed, as King remarked on looking over the figures, there were 'Very few of the unmarried but who cohabit openly with one man'.[51]

Through successive efforts, the Europeans in Australia were thus drawn together in the imagination of authority, first – from 1788 – within an economic calculus (concerned with the keeping together of body and soul), and only afterwards within a moral and a penal calculus. The net of literacy and list-making was tightened one stage at a time and not, as some historians say, all together at the first moment of settlement. Another world, crossed by new roads and footpaths, shaded by eucalypt, high and dry, wholly antipodean and warmed by a buzz of voices, found its own life nevertheless, according to Lord Sydney's blueprint. Conversation and the calculus worked simultaneously in the Antipodes.

From the official point of view, the myriad inclinations of good and bad subjects were to be managed against an increasingly complex administrative backdrop. The Holford committee had already found to their satisfaction that London convicts hated going to New South Wales because they thought they would lose everything they enjoyed in England, especially money and friends.[52] What about when they arrived? Eden pressed his witnesses as to whether the length of sentence made any difference to behaviour and whether many wanted to come home at the end. The second was a question no-one in authority had considered in 1786–87, when settlement was first planned. Governor Phillip had thought that all his people were in effect transported for life, and only in 1796 did the Secretary of State make it clear that governors had no right to hold those who had served their terms.[53] As many as possible should be settled, but the decision to settle must be theirs. Eden's dislike of oppression led him to follow up this idea. He argued that in practice it was too hard for women to make their way home, except by 'prostituting themselves on board the ships whose masters may chuse to receive them'. Unless the government were to condone and promote vice, he said, it must provide some other way for them.[54]

Such arguments would have seemed eccentric twenty years before. They were now driven by enough fashionable moral energy to ensure action at the Colonial Office.[55] They were also evidence of new movement in the long debate – one of the main concerns of this book – about the transfer of people, bond and free, within the empire. In New South Wales in King's time the debate had been revived, when it was decided to relocate at least part of the population of Norfolk Island, an administrative exercise unparallelled in Australia since the arrival of the First Fleet. Hitherto the fertility of the Norfolk soil had made the island worthwhile in spite of its isolation and its lack of safe anchorage, but ten years of settlement had left the soil over-worked. With crops failing and costs rising, in June 1803 Lord Hobart ordered King to see to the transfer of some of the people to Van Diemen's Land. Families choosing to go were to get four acres for every one they gave up, and for a year after their arrival they were to be fed from the public store and allowed two convicts each.[56]

Hobart's order was announced to the people of the island by Joseph Foveaux, then their Lieutenant-Governor, and forty-one settlers immediately gave in their names. But they were worried about relying on the government for food and they were disturbed to hear of King's belief that only freeholders and young and energetic men, without big families, should go. King was well known on Norfolk and his apparent doubts shifted the balance of risk. Many of the people, thinking back ten or fifteen years, remembered what it meant to start from scratch. 'They . . . feel but little inclination', said Foveaux, 'to remove from habitations and other little enjoyments which they actually possess, to an unknown Country, where they will have to provide themselves, and begin the World again.'[57] Set in the balance against 'actual possession', against familiarity and certainty, government could only offer its promise of full compensation. Much depended on the people's ideas as to how engagements might work between the subject and the state.

Foveaux understood the principles at stake in the evacuation. He knew about the variety of attitudes among the people and he warned his superiors, for instance, of a small number, 'tolerably comfortable . . . having large Families and being advanced in Years', who would refuse to pull up their roots whatever they were offered, at least as long as there was an official presence on the island. He knew about the need to be, or to seem to be, generous in order to ease the task of persuasion. But he also understood that, even in the uprooting process, government in the end was master. It was not the judgment of the poor that mattered but the judgment of the high-minded men in charge. As if to underline this aspect of the system (and just as Marsden categorised women as wives or 'concubines') Foveaux suggested that prospective emigrants from Norfolk be distinguished according to their moral status. All who owned land and buildings were to be fully compensated, but those whose reputation was good should be offered a bonus. They should be fed and clothed by government and have the labour of two convicts for two years, compared with one year for the remainder.[58]

Foveaux was well connected and highly thought of at Whitehall, and his plan was adopted without variation. In December 1806 William Windham, Secretary of State for War and the Colonies, ordered Bligh to begun evacuation on that basis. Not just part, but the entire establishment was now to be closed. The Governor was to see that the people were wholly removed and carried to wherever they chose to live, their options being the mainland and the two new settlements in the south.[59] Bligh sent copies of Windham's instructions to the two Lieutenant-Governors in Van Diemen's Land, Collins at Hobart Town and Paterson at Port Dalrymple. He did not, however, wait to find out whether either could fulfil the promises made on behalf of the Crown. A copy was sent at the same time to John Piper, commandant at Norfolk, with orders that he get the people ready. They must know what they were entitled to and they must understand the need for 'chearful compliance', everything being 'solely directed to their good'. They were not to argue or to ask for different conditions, and they must be convinced, said the Governor, that 'on my part they may rely on the most particular care and watchfulness over everything which appertains to their future Interests and Comforts'.[60]

None but the wicked, so Bligh believed, would resist this parcel of promises. He underestimated, as he did in Sydney, the affection and sense of dependence which men and women felt for their homes and for their own part of the antipodean soil. His letter to Piper was entrusted to the commander of the *Porpoise*, one of the vessels to be used in the evacuation, who in taking charge of it mentioned to the Governor that there might be difficulties: on an earlier visit to Norfolk he had heard some of the settlers say 'they would not quit the island, and that they would run [to] the woods first'. The Governor therefore gave him verbal orders together with the written ones (as ever, an important distinction for Bligh): '[If] any of them refused to go, he [Piper] was to use military force; and if any of them took to the woods, he was to outlaw them and to shoot them.'[61] There were five embarkations, from November 1807 to September 1808, the last three managed by the rebel government but all with Bligh's emphasis on haste. There is no certain evidence of shooting but family memories told of two men by the last vessel, James Belbin and Robert Nash, who did indeed take to the bush (Nash owned a large house with 'farandra at back and front' and had just spent nearly £300 on a new watermill) and who were 'according to the practices of the good old times . . . hunted down by the crew of the boat employed to take them aboard'. Both had families, but as to whether all ten individuals, young and old, resisted, the story is silent.[62]

Between 550 and 580 individuals were moved during 1807–08.[63] Some still remained, together with a skeleton establishment, even until February 1814, but their numbers were small. The migrants added enormously to the European population in Van Diemen's Land. In spring 1806, a year before the Norfolk Island people began to arrive, there were 478 men, women and children at the Derwent and and 276 at Port Dalrymple, convicts, soldiers and officials making up the majority in both places. At the Derwent the settlers included only twenty-six men, thirteen women and twenty children, most of whom had come free with Collins and were living on hundred-acre farms at New Town, up the river from headquarters. At Port Dalrymple there were only three men described as settlers, whose few livestock grazed on Crown land.[64] The influx from Norfolk Island made Van Diemen's Land at last look like a place for free men and women.

Both settlements were currently run on authoritarian lines. David Collins had never been a conciliatory ruler. During the short period at Port Phillip, from October 1803 to January 1804, he had had trouble with semi-organised protest among both convicts and soldiers.[65] As Lieutenant-Governor, he aimed to replicate the authoritarian order which Phillip had formed at Port Jackson, and which he had seen first hand as Judge-Advocate and the Governor's secretary. He was also a stickler for personal cleanliness. Once arrived at the Derwent, he had had combs and brushes issued and demanded the name of anyone who failed to keep his head clean; and he ordered that a list of inmates be posted outside each hut, headed by the name of the man elected to answer for the cleanliness of all within.[66] But he was more ready to consult than Phillip. At Port Phillip he approved an 'Association of the Civil Officers', formed by the gentlemen to guard against trouble among the convicts.[67] At Hobart Town, when the convict men presumed to ask 'an unjust and enormous price' for their labour on the open market, he ordered all the commissioned gentlemen to meet with three of the settlers to resolve what they would pay. He called weekly meetings of the magistrates, apparently for administrative purposes, and he also made some attempt to consult among his officers when he was forced to decide how to deal with the deposed Governor Bligh, who arrived by the *Porpoise* from Port Jackson during 1809.[68]

Neither Bligh nor the Norfolk Island settlers were very welcome in Van Diemen's Land. On Norfolk itself everything possible had been done by Piper, as commandant, to record what the people had left behind and what they were entitled to get on arrival. Precise lists of heads of families had been drawn up, the clerk struggling to express by neat tabulation a complicated flesh-and-blood reality. On the mainland at that time about two-thirds of couples living together were not married and the proportion was about the same on Norfolk.[69] There too, as at Port Jackson, women might deal face to face with public authority, as individuals with a direct claim on government, and that also complicated matters. Elizabeth Bradshaw, listed with her five children, had come to Australia as a convict's wife (or widow, since her husband seems to have died in transit) and she had since bought land on Norfolk. She now left behind 84 acres (making her one of the largest landholders on the island), a house measuring 17 by 11 feet with a timber floor (some floors on Norfolk were earth), thatched and boarded, and a barn of thatch and logs. In the same embarkation, but listed separately, was Robert Jillet, apparently her children's father, a labouring man and according to Piper, a 'Convict for Life, [and] a bad character'. His claim was nil. Cath Kearney, or Kearnon, with her two sons, likewise husbandless and 'a very seditious troublesome character', nevertheless had 'a claim to a Town lease of 1677 [square] feet'. Susan Burn, called the 'wife' of James Dodding (they were not married), could look forward to sharing whatever he got in Van Diemen's Land, but she also had 'a separate claim' of her own: '10 acres, 5 of which is cleared'.[70]

Such details sank very early beneath a mass of more urgent difficulties. Nearly all the people ended up by choice at the Derwent, and the first arrivals, in November 1807, immediately asked for clothes and bedding, demands which Collins could not satisfy, though he assumed (wrongly) that such articles were on their way from somewhere else. Several who came by the last shipment complained that articles they thought had been sent with them had been lost or stolen. On inquiry the magistrates at Hobart Town concluded that some people had lost 'a great deal of Property' but exactly how much was guesswork, because the vouchers had been left at Norfolk.[71] There was also no way of giving the people what they had been promised by the Secretary of State. Houses could not be built because the labour was not available, and the number of convicts and livestock on hand fell far short of that required. Collins, whose experience in negotiations of this kind went back to Sydney Cove (it was probably he who had been sent by Phillip in July 1791 to make offers to convict men who said their time was up: see Chapter 4), did his best to deal with the settlers' disappointment. Some among them, he said, 'had sense enough to perceive that, without more assistance arrived in the Settlement, it would be impossible for this Government ever to fulfil the promises held out to them'. Others, 'ignorant and low Characters', blamed the Lieutenant-Governor himself for not giving them all that they had been told to expect.[72]

When Bligh arrived, many of the people had been allocated land, but they possessed little else. They had even, to all appearances, lost their right to complain. The system of government they had found in Van Diemen's Land was much more dictatorial than they had been used to, especially while Piper had governed Norfolk. Many were old settlers who had been comfortable and independent for years. They had numerous children, some already grown up, a multiplying audience for their own manly and parental dignity. (Women householders were strangely silent during this crisis.) Among them were the men who had organised the Settlers Meeting in 1793, the Fraternal Society in 1797 and – that epitome of self-sufficient ritual – their own Masonic lodge. They did not know that Bligh's decision to move them without any previous inquiry was the main reason for their trouble, and they looked to him, 'the true and only Representative of our August Sovereign', as the rock on which the public faith must rest. The ex-Governor, himself now dispossessed, was received with similar deference by Collins. However, within a month orders to the contrary came from Paterson in Sydney; after consulting with his officials and with Edward Lord, commandant of the garrison (a detachment of Marines), the Lieutenant-Governor decided to take his chance with the rebels.[73]

The officials were already split into two parties, and the minority remained loyal to Bligh. The Norfolk people rallied in the same way, and James Belbin, who had resisted being taken from the island, joined with James Dodding to draw up a loyal petition. Belbin had already made an enemy of Lieutenant Lord after speaking out against the summary flogging of a woman who had fought with Lord's own woman. 'Can this be a land of Christians,' Belbin said (or was remembered to have said), 'or one of savages only, where such an exhibition is permitted[?]' When Lord heard that Belbin and Dodding were appealing to Bligh against Collins he went to the house which Belbin, a widower, and his children shared with another family and after a certain amount of reciprocal violence the document was destroyed. It was said to have read like a 'Bill of Rights', a shout against 'despotism' and a call to the conscience of the true Governor.[74]

On 21 May two proclamations were issued at Hobart Town, one from Paterson and the other from Collins, both forbidding any communication with Bligh, an order especially urgent because some of the people had taken it upon themselves to ply his ship with food. On the same day eighteen men from Norfolk presented an address to the Governor in which they declared their 'determined abhorrence of those measures which have been taken by a set of Disloyal and Unprincipled Men, who in the most daring manner have subverted your Government'. They mingled their references to public loyalty with compliments to Bligh's 'Amiable daughter' and to 'Parental Kindness and filial duty', both important virtues for these humble householders. The first signature was that of Belbin's friend, Thomas Restell Crowder, who had directed the theatre at Norfolk Island and who had been second only to Fane Edge in the Settlers Meeting. Belbin and Dodding signed second and third. Last was Michael Lee, once a leading member of the Norfolk Island Masonic lodge.[75]

John McCloud, though his name was not on this document, was another dissident. He had come to Van Diemen's Land with Mary Potter and her five children, leaving behind a boarded and thatched house, a nanny goat and five pigs, and had taken up land in her name. In June 1809 he was caught carrying grain on board the *Porpoise* and was bound over at a penalty of £100. In August he still deeply resented the failure of government promises: 'he had been robbed by Govr. Collins . . . there was neither Law nor Justice to be had in this Country'. Bligh was his only hope: 'he would go', he said, 'to Governor Bligh and let him know how he been treated . . . Governor Bligh . . . had come in time to save the People from ruin who came from Norfolk'. Nor was he afraid of forfeiting his £100 bond: 'he had nothing to lose, the Farm was the Woman's'.[76]

But it was the ex-convict widower James Belbin who fought the longest fight for His Majesty's Governor, a cause which he identified not only with his own claims but with the broader question of public justice throughout the empire. Belbin was one of those individuals whose sense of right was all the stronger from their being at the perimeter of the world. Surrounded by profiteering and by men and women shifting for themselves, he aimed to be a good subject and a painstaking father. Legitimacy of power and principle had its root, for him, partly in Britain and partly in the familiar order of his own household (or what was left of it). He kept a diary, a record of family events and of his injuries, which still survives. It opens with part of a speech made by a celebrated lawyer in the court of King's Bench on the subject of injustice in remote parts of the empire: 'the meanest British subject if Oppressed would one day have an opportunity of meeting his Oppressor face to face in a country [namely Britain] where equal Justice was administered to the Rich and Poor'.[77] Such an idea, picked up as a jewel of faith, a light on the ocean of power, by humble men like Belbin, shows how far the moral power of the state had penetrated – without regard to rank or distance – during the last decades of the eighteenth century. It is hard, however, to find humble women saying such things. They were much more local beings, as James Tuckey had perceived, and much less willing to pin their hopes on speeches in King's Bench.

In September 1809, while the *Porpoise* was still at the Derwent, Belbin went on board to see Bligh. He was arrested and held in gaol until 4 December when he was sentenced to 500 lashes, 'for denying Col. P[aterson]'s proclamation and because I would not acknowledge any Person but H[is] E[xcellency] W[illiam] B[ligh] Esqr as the Govr in Chief, without a legal cause for changing my opinion'. He was unwell ('from being confined 27 Days from my motherless Children') and received only fifty. He was then imprisoned for ten weeks more, James, his youngest, aged six, being with him part of the time: he had 'Rec[eive]d a hurt that obliged me to apply for Medical assistance'. No land grant was yet forthcoming and in February 1810, eight months before the right time, Belbin and his children were taken off the list of those fed by the government.

David Collins died on 24 March 1810 and Edward Lord became Acting Lieutenant-Governor. Among Collins's last acts was to sanction the publication of a local newspaper, the *Derwent Star*, a fortnightly medium of

orders and news edited by the surveyor, George Prideaux Harris. It continued for a short time after Collins's death, but its pages offered no evidence
that Lieutenant Lord loved freedom of speech.[78] In July, Belbin pinned up a
notice at Hobart Town, 'with the Settlers thanks for the impartial conduct
of Corpl Pennington' (there is no record as to what the conduct was), which
earned him another 300 lashes. In November 1811, after many months of
trying, he was given permission to quit the settlement. Leaving his four girls
behind, he embarked with James, worked his passage to England (the cost
of a fare was £50), found Bligh in his house at Lambeth, on the south bank
of the Thames, and got him to write a letter to the under-secretary at the
Colonial Office. He wanted a free passage back again for himself and
the boy, and he wanted the land and everything else promised him by the
Crown. He had no money left, and Bligh asked in his letter to the under-
secretary that part of his entitlement be given to him now, 'to shelter himself and child from the Weather'. (It was December in London.)[79]

Bligh's letter and the under-secretary's response justified Belbin's persis-
tent piety, though the end result was to be bungled a little on the other side
of the world. He found another wife in England and – having proved the
good faith of government at the price of three years' struggle – he was back
in Van Diemen's Land in 1814.

Chapter 15

The Coming of the Macquaries

I

Elizabeth Henrietta Macquarie, poor but well-born, romantic and capable, with a frequently cooperative husband and a new world to remodel, was more advantageously placed than any European woman had hitherto been in this part of the world. She was a Scot, daughter of John Campbell of Airds, county Argyll, and cousin of the fourth Earl of Breadalbane. She was born on 13 June 1778 and, both her parents dying early, she was mistress of many aspects of her life from an unusual age. She was to say years later that the events of her younger days ('and the attention I have bestowed on the management of landed property') had qualified her to command even men of her own class.[1]

She was a woman of vivid sensibility, describing once a moment of serious loss: 'I felt as tho' cold water had made itself all over me, between the body and the skin.'[2] Like many other women of her generation, probably including Mary Putland, she understood new methods of assembling landscape, arrangements which drew the cultivated eye towards the sublime, towards hills and mountains, wood and water. (Water was one ingredient among others, a backdrop only, working not between the body and the skin but at a happy distance. Imagination's home was stillness and dry land.) Observers were to be placed so as to catch the best view, or they were to be moved by preconcerted means – stopping at selected resting places – through a series of views. Nature might be complimented by some building, preferably rich with moral associations – with some solid truth – positioned to focus the eye. The young Elizabeth experimented with part of the grounds at Airds House, laying down a winding gravel pathway which opened up a kaleidoscope of scenes through the garden and across the adjacent loch.[3]

She met Lachlan Macquarie, whom she was to marry, at Lochbuy House, Argyll, home of her sister, Mrs Maclaine of Lochbuy, in June 1804. She was twenty-six and he, a childless widower, was forty-three: 'clean-shaved, strong, lusty-looking [so he was to be remembered in Australia] . . . about 5ft 10 in in height and very broad-shouldered'. She may well have noticed, as his portraitists have done, his 'dark, penetrating eyes'. He had spent seven years as an officer in North America and the West Indies and fifteen years in the East. He was passionate and generous but also a man of pen and paper. He had been paymaster in various regiments, major of brigade to the troops at Malabar, military secretary to the Governor of Bombay and deputy adjutant-general in Egypt (where he had been with General Baird on his celebrated march from the Red Sea to the Nile). At Lochbuy they went fishing with his brother, Charles, as Macquarie noted the same evening, 'at which last diversion Miss Campbell is particular expert and successful in'. Next morning he was astonished by her setting off on a journey across the loch in a small open boat, 'without any other Company or Society than the Boat's Crew!!! This Girl is quite a Heroine!'[4]

He proposed to her in London on 26 March 1805 and she accepted straight away, although it was understood that they could not be married until he came back from another period in India. This he did in 1807, with the rank of lieutenant-colonel and command of the 73rd Regiment, and they were married on 3 November at Holsworthy, in Devon, where Elizabeth was then governess at the rectory. Macquarie was a man for dates and anniversaries. He kept a careful diary and these particular days were for him steps in the gradual exposition of his life.

Macquarie thought highly of his wife's robust energy, her almost manly self-sufficiency, and what he called her 'most excellent judgment and sound understanding'. All were to be evident in New South Wales. During their first progress through the antipodean countryside by carriage and horse-back, they sat down to dinner in tents with everything, as he was delighted to find, just as it should be, 'Mrs M. tho' so young a campaigner having provided every requisite to make our tour easy, pleasant, and happy'. He likewise discovered, during rough seas on a trip to Van Diemen's Land, that 'she makes a most excellent brave sailor'. He had a high regard for the power of women (older women were among his favourite correspondents) and he did not set himself up as his wife's moral guide. His being her husband, he said, made him 'no more responsible for her sentiments than for those of any other Lady'. And yet she had, for him, some of the virtues of an eager sub-altern – the young campaigner, the novice sailor – who might aim to become his own mirror image. She needed someone whose judgment she could satisfy. Without such a person, she once told herself (when he was dead), 'all energy is at an end, and life becomes like stagnate [sic] water'.[5]

Macquarie had not been an obvious choice as Governor of New South Wales because, in spite of his administrative experience, he lacked seniority and effective patrons. In December 1808, three months after news of Bligh's deposition had reached England, the appointment of Brigadier-General James Nightingall had been announced from the Colonial Office. There were to be no more naval governors and Macquarie's regiment was to replace the New South Wales Corps, which was to be recalled. He was therefore to be Lieutenant-Governor. However, in April 1809 Nightingall decided not to go and almost by default Macquarie was appointed. He, Mrs Macquarie and the regiment, together with a new Judge-Advocate, Ellis Bent, his wife and baby son, departed on board the *Hindostan* and *Dromedary* in May.[6]

During the next seven months, while they were at sea between Europe and Australia – the longest path she had ever traversed – Elizabeth Macquarie kept a journal of things and people and their impact on her feelings. There were two high points in her story. At Madeira, while she and her husband were looking over the island, they happened upon a church in which a girl was being received, in tears, into an order of nuns. From bystanders Mrs Macquarie heard enough about the convent ('the strictest ever known') to conjure up a tragic future. Here was her own life in reverse. She had lately made herself a wife and was now travelling towards increasingly fine prospects. She briefly imagined the woman giving up 'her dreadful intention', forsaking the convent for 'my protection' so that they might make their way in some sense together. 'I cannot say that I ever felt so much distress at the fate of a stranger, as I did on this occasion . . . I could not bear the subject mention'd without considerable emotion for some time after.' The episode closed with doubt nevertheless, an uncertainty about her own power: that gap between heart and eye, between *your* bleeding, untaught soul and *my* polished imagination. 'I hope', she remarked before turning to something new, 'her situation does not *feel* to her, as it *appeared* to me.'[7]

At sea in the south Atlantic a young ship's carpenter whom she had glimpsed the day before ('a very pleasant handsome looking man') was drowned. The captain took charge of his possessions, which included letters from a woman and some of the carpenter's answers; a collection such as novels at the time were frequently composed of. Mrs Macquarie was given a sight of them. The woman's letters, she observed, 'in my opinion contain'd more fine affection, express'd in a more natural & affecting manner than any I ever read'. His too were 'very interesting'. But it was once again the pain beyond imagination which occurred to her at the end: 'What her sufferings will be when she hears of this event it is dreadful to think on.' Such verdicts were typical of the high humanity which this second Governor's wife, this worthy successor to Anna Josepha King, brought to New South Wales. As Jane Austen wrote of her character Marianne Dashwood, 'Her sensibility was potent enough!'[8]

The Macquaries arrived with the idea that they would find serious disorder at the Antipodes. The Governor's first task, as he saw it, would be to establish his own dignity as firmly as possible, to set aside the consequences of rebellion and to beat back any last opposition to the dictates of empire. He was a natural authoritarian, and he and his wife both had an ample idea of their future importance. They came to anchor in Sydney Harbour on 28 December 1809. On the 30th Macquarie sent a message to the

Lieutenant-Governor, William Paterson, informing him that he and his party would come ashore on New Year's Eve and ordering that the soldiers of the Corps receive him by lining the street from the wharf to Government House. He landed accordingly, to a salute of fifteen guns from each of the two ships, cheers from the seamen and answering shots from the fort. In the evening Aborigines who had come in from as far as the Hawkesbury performed what a young officer of the 73rd called 'a regular battle in honour of the new Governor'.[9]

On New Year's Day, 1810, the day of his swearing in, Macquarie began the business of proving (as both King and Bligh had tried to do in their time) that his authority was to have a much higher colouring than that of any of his predecessors. His first proclamation, composed by the new Judge-Advocate, declared that he had come directly from the King to bring 'Quiet and Harmony' after 'the late Tumultuous Proceedings'.[10] Macquarie's mind was sufficiently romantic and up-to-date for him to warm to the idea of Majesty immanent throughout the empire, of George III ruling in the hearts of men and women even in the Antipodes. He aimed to varnish his regime with ideas of monarchy. But he was also eager to shine himself as the vehicle of power. On the following Sunday the chaplain at Sydney, William Cowper (who had arrived during 1809), preached a sermon at St Phillip's to mark the Governor's accession, using the text, 'Arise, anoint him; for this is he': God's naming of David as King of Israel.[11] If the message matched Macquarie's bearing, it was a high compliment indeed: equalled only by the apotheosis of Phillip long ago in the mind of Bennelong.

Macquarie's hope of making a place for himself in the history of the country depended on its having a history, a local sense of past, present and future, a connected antipodean drama-with-audience. Such an understanding had begun to lodge itself in colonial minds during King's time, and Bligh's deposition had produced several ill-formed historical statements. John Macarthur's idea of himself was powerfully historical: he had deliberately played before the audience of posterity in telling the officers in the Criminal Court on the eve of the rebellion that they had in their hands 'the happiness or misery of millions yet unborn'.[12] On 27 January 1808 the town had been illuminated, bonfires lit and salutes fired in the name of liberty, while Sergeant-Major Whittle had put up a picture showing Bligh dragged from under a bed, attended by three manly figures in the uniform of the New South Wales Corps. Other imagery was more miscellaneous and confused. William Evans, once Macarthur's servant, had a picture done of Charles II hiding in the oak after the battle of Worcester (1651), and even his contemporaries must have wondered what that meant. The gaoler Daniel McKay, a Scot, confronted passers-by with a portrait of Johnston dressed as a Highland officer, his sword through the snake of tyranny and something like a *bonnet rouge* above his head, while John Reddington, an Irishman, stuck up the harp of Ireland without its customary royal crown. Afterwards the 27th was set down in the colonial calendar as a 'Public Day' (the 26th being already the 'Day of Landing'), presumably with the idea that its lessons, whatever they were, might be rehearsed from year to year by Macarthur's millions.[13]

In 1810 a more coherent understanding of the past was called for (leaving out the rebellion). The country was now ruled by individuals who had not been there at the beginning, for whom the First Fleet and the pioneering years belonged not to memory but to piecemeal stories. This had been true of Bligh, but the Macquaries were more willing than Bligh to talk to old settlers and to come to terms with the deeds of those who had gone before. Macquarie had a powerful sense of lineage and as early as the King's birthday, 1810, he began including Governor Phillip's name among the toasts at official dinners, as 'the Founder of the Colony'.[14] Such details appeared in the *Sydney Gazette*, and Macquarie obviously hoped that their publication would help to instil a more deliberate sense of local tradition and of the dynasty of governors to which he belonged. For him, and therefore for everybody, the past was now to be recalled by artifice. Also, now that he was a public man, the weekly *Gazette* became in a sense his personal journal. (His diary had been demoted to a series of memoranda.) In it he told his people, as he otherwise might have boasted to himself, of his successive achievements as their ruler, his sentiments – 'His Excellency the Governor has seen with great regret . . . ', 'His Excellency cannot forebear to make known his indignation . . . ' – and the anniversaries which were important to him as markers on the road between past and future. Eager too for 'the Founder's' blessing, in October 1811 he sent a large parcel of recent *Gazettes* to Phillip, now living in Bath: a very expensive surprise for the old Admiral, since recipients paid postage.[15]

Macquarie cast himself as a new founder. Following his first two tours beyond Sydney (to the nearby settled districts in November–December 1810 and to Van Diemen's Land a year later) he published accounts of what he had seen, explaining that they would be 'Documents of importance to refer to at some future period' when everything would be 'much improved'. The rebels' anniversary, 27 January, was already forgotten and Macquarie looked instead to 1 January, the day on which he had taken power. In 1813 it was declared a public holiday (as it had been, at one time, merely as New Year's Day), the Governor himself was hailed in the *Gazette* as 'our Patron and Ruler', and there was a 'Commemoration Dinner', including a toast to 'Governor Macquarie! May the Anniversary of his assuming the Command of this Territory be commemorated and reverenced by our latest Posterity!'[16]

A larger sense of time was married to a larger sense of space. Macquarie immediately put his mind to the better arrangement of the territory over which he presided. He began building a turnpike road from Sydney to the Hawkesbury. At his recommendation, the two settlements in Van Diemen's Land were placed under a single lieutenant-governor, and in 1811 he and his wife travelled from the Derwent to Port Dalrymple, south to north, on horseback, affirming a barely existent road, as if to prove that the future lay with dry-land methods and with dry-land traffic. At his own request he was made ultimately responsible for everything on the island, including finances, a burden his predecessors had been glad to avoid. The oceanic parts of New South Wales were not wholly forgotten, however. Macquarie confirmed that Norfolk Island served no useful purpose, but he proposed a new settlement on the north island of New Zealand, wholly tributary to Sydney and to be managed for profit by several local traders interested in growing flax. (This was short-lived.) Also, like previous governors, he took it for granted that his authority extended eastwards into the remote Pacific and he was the first to appoint justices of the peace in those parts, not only at the Bay of Islands (in New Zealand) but also at Tahiti.[17] At no time before Federation in 1901 did anyone in the Antipodes seek effective government over a territory so large.

He also asked for the creation of numerous new offices at Sydney, as a means of strengthening his hand. His private secretary, John Thomas Campbell (who had arrived with him), currently something like a senior clerk with a salary of £182 10s per annum, ought to be converted to Colonial Secretary, with twice the income. There should be a government architect. There was already a government printer, George Howe (successor to George Hughes), who earned what he could from the weekly production of the *Gazette*. He ought to have a regular salary. The Naval Officer, a local individual employed part-time, should be appointed from England, and perhaps with a salary instead of taking, as at present, 5 per cent of what he could collect in customs duties. Macquarie aimed to raise a Veteran Company from among the soldiers of the New South Wales Corps (now the 102nd Regiment) who chose to stay, and the increased military business called for a barrack master and a colonial paymaster.[18] There were doubts at Whitehall about the cost of so many new jobs, but Campbell's salary was increased a little and £60 a year was approved for the printer.[19] Macquarie dealt with three Secretaries of State (Lord Castlereagh to October 1809, then Lord Liverpool and from 1812 Lord Bathurst) and all of them agreed with him on the need to focus his power and to build anew in a country which had been too long neglected.

Macquarie aimed to make himself into a ruler of the kind best called the Good King. A universal type, the Good King is a man of order and a peacemaker. He preserves the harmony of the universe. He is predictable like the seasons. He is a medium of grace, an easy distributor of words, goods and justice among his people, and they are listeners wholly drawn within his sense of right. He is both manly and patriarchal, and in the continuous ritual reproduction of society he is both author and creator, an originating 'I am.' The latter notion is of perennial importance: it provoked in the twentieth-century author, Anaïs Nin, the remark, 'I suppose they mean "I am God, I am not a woman." '[20] Mrs Macquarie, for her part, wrestled in a surprising way with the role of the Good King's wife.

The new epoch was meant to be one of forgiveness and reconciliation among warring parties. Macquarie managed to persuade both small farmers and townspeople that he had their interests at heart, and a little experience with ex-Governor Bligh (who arrived back from the Derwent in mid-January) persuaded him that the rebels of 1808 were not wholly in the wrong. He was surprised to find such tolerable order, and he attributed it mainly to Lieutenant-Colonel Joseph Foveaux, second-in-command of the Corps, Acting Governor during the second half of 1808 and the real ruler even during Paterson's government, from January to December 1809. Macquarie made Foveaux his principal guide to begin with. D'Arcy Wentworth, who had been one of Bligh's bitterest enemies, was likewise loaded with authority during 1810: confirmed as Principal Surgeon in February, appointed treasurer of the Police Fund (one of the two repositories of government money) in March, named one of the commissioners of the new turnpike road in April, and given the management of Sydney itself, as superintendent of police, in December.[21] At a humbler level Charles Whalan, an ex-convict and a sergeant in the Corps who transferred to the 73rd, was given command of the Governor's bodyguard (a post he had held under King) and the position of 'confidential orderly sergeant', making him a central wheel within the Macquaries' household.[22]

Some found it hard to reconcile the distribution of such plums with Macquarie's first proclamation, in which he had announced the King's 'utmost Regret and Displeasure' at the conduct of the rebels. Joseph Arnold, a visiting surgeon, observed that Bligh was very unpopular – 'people who dare hoot him' – and yet, he thought, if the rebellion had been wrong, Macquarie was 'too peaceable' in dealing with those responsible. Fears of retribution had run through the Corps on Macquarie's arrival and, according to Joseph Holt, 'The soldiers and sargents began to split and inform.' But no such fears were realised. John Hillas, one of the free immigrant settlers bold enough to sign addresses of loyalty to Bligh in 1808–09, wrote to his patron in England marvelling that the entire Corps had not been put under arrest: 'why they where [sic] not I cannot tell'. But he added, with that attitude of deference which had attached him to Bligh in the first place, 'Neither do I want or mean to pry in to the Policy of Legal Govement, Neither is my abilities sufficient if I where desirous so to do.'[23] Such acquiescence was the key to Macquarie's success. It was reinforced by his order that no magistrate, gaoler or constable who had acted in the period since Bligh's deposition was to be sued for damages merely because he had lacked authority. And he promised that 'His utmost Displeasure' would be directed against those who tried to stir up arguments in the courts about the events of 1808.[24]

Besides his role as the representative of 'Legal Govement' Macquarie's power lay in his voice and in his physical presence. Elizabeth Macarthur, now alone at Elizabeth Farm, found him most agreeable, 'one of the most pleasing men, but then he is the Governor, and it is not possible to forget that he is so'; 'when he knitted his brow', said a woman married to a soldier of the 73rd, 'he meant something, and woe betide anyone offending him'.[25] He was a man of certainties, a fluent writer but neither a reader nor a debater. His wife was quicker and less deliberate than he was, which may explain her liking for the feminist taunt, 'The grey mare is the better horse.' Macquarie was given, as a Good King ought to be, to high-sounding, formulaic phrases, clichés of the day which gave predictability (after some initial surprises) to both his public and private life. His diary is full of the expression 'better to be conceived than described', a term so hackneyed as to be laughable in some circles.[26] He was a Freemason from his bachelor days, but he was one of those Freemasons who liked polished manhood and good friends more than arcane knowledge. There were hints of Masonic feeling in the salute with which he began his first speech in New South Wales, on New Year's Day, 1810 – 'Fellow Citizens, and Fellow Soldiers!' – a set of words as startling in its power to embrace as the formula of a later age: 'Men and Women of Australia!'[27]

His subjects, as they listened, might have wondered what exactly the timbre, the smell, the touch of fellowship would be like in Macquarie's time, just as the historian wonders on looking back. The ambition was clear. On the island of Madeira Mrs Macquarie had hoped that the situation of the weeping novice 'does not *feel* to her, as it *appeared* to me'. An equivalent hope was an early part of the Macquaries' regime in New South Wales. But here they wanted the reverse. Their feelings had to be powerful enough to force a change in the way things looked. They stood on a high vantage point, with a fine view to past and future (cast within a frame of their own making), and with the noble hope of reshaping the landscape of souls which also lay about them.

II

The Macquaries' first celebration at Government House, Sydney, was the wedding of Bligh's daughter, Mary Putland, and Maurice O'Connell (who had replaced Macquarie in command of the 73rd) on 8 May 1810. For Bligh it was a matter of bitter disappointment that his daughter was to stay in this part of the world. But for the Macquaries, Bligh was surprised to notice, the marriage was a cause of 'exultation', and the Governor affirmed his pleasure by giving the O'Connells 2500 acres in the husband's name and 1055 in that of the wife (she already had a grant from Governor King), together with £762 worth of livestock, the latter to be paid for several years hence.[28] The new rulers had an insatiable wish to scatter replicas of their own contentment: a scheme which proved both their generosity and the tightly drawn simplicity of their ideas. Mrs Macquarie might argue with her husband at dinner, as a guest once observed (her 'rudeness' producing from him

Lachlan Macquarie, Governor of New South Wales 1810–21, and Elizabeth Henrietta Macquarie, his wife, miniatures painted during their early years together, before their departure from England in 1809.

Source: Mitchell Library, State Library of New South Wales

'a most happy smile'). She might, as rumour remarked, 'rather be the Governor than the Governess'. They were still, according to the same guest, blissfully devoted to each other, 'a perfect pattern of domestic tranquillity'.[29] Central to their scheme for New South Wales was the infinite replication of that 'most happy smile'.

Until the birth of their first and only child in 1814, when Mrs Macquarie began sometimes to stay at home, husband and wife travelled about the country together. They both took pleasure in the landscape, and the shared experience was one of a peculiarly inward and private kind, social sensibility at its most intense. During their tours they used spare moments to ride or walk alone together; 'to enjoy the cool of the evening and the tranquil scenes of the forest'; to explore Yellow-Mundie Lagoon; to look at two Aboriginal huts and then to venture into the bush at Jervis Bay ('to view the different sorts of trees and the soil'); to inspect Hobart Town; and to climb to the top of a hill at Port Stephens: 'a very fine extensive prospect'. On such occasions the Governor submitted to his wife's judgment, describing for instance a farm at Bringelly, 'the beautiful situation . . . the picturesque scenes . . . the great order and regularity', a combination with which, he said, 'Mrs M was much pleased.'[30] The names they gave to objects in the country proved the way they – she, more than he – looked at it. Their vision was so intimate that even Henrietta Annabella Meredith, the friend of Mrs Macquarie's spinster years, was remembered with an island, a sizeable feature which closed a view for them at Port Stephens. Their travelling was self-consciously punctuated with points of rest and reflection, like a well-designed garden path. In December 1811, when they made their way overland from Hobart Town to Port Dalrymple, the most remote territory they ever saw together, they scattered private names along the way as mem-oranda: Glenforsa (after Macquarie's brother's land on Mull), Elizabeth Valley, Governor Macquarie's Resting Place, Prospect Hill ('on account of the fine view'), Macquarie Springs, Meehan Valley and Antill's Ponds (after two travelling companions), Mount Henrietta, Argyle Plains, Macquarie River, Mount Campbell and Maclaine Plains (two more companions), Antill Plains, Elizabeth River, Macquarie Plains, Henrietta Plains and Gordon Plains (after the commandant at Launceston, who now came to meet them). No public figures were remembered except, once, the Duke of York, the army's Commander-in-Chief, and they gave no thought to Aboriginal names.[31] They made larger compromises with the public world during their travels on the mainland, but there too the tendency was the same.

This was the kind of nuptial sweetness they wanted to see copied in other households. Antipodean marriage mattered at Whitehall too, for more for-mal reasons. Lord Castlereagh had told Macquarie on his appointment that his 'Great Objects of attention' were to be the improvement of morals, which meant getting people married, building schools, and restricting drunkenness. He must also as Governor 'increase the Agriculture and Stock, so as to ensure the Certainty of a full supply to the Inhabitants under all Circumstances', but this aim was closely linked to the first. Virtue, order and security were all part of a single parcel, both for the colony as a whole and for every man and woman who agreed to settle together with the sanc-tion of Church and state. On 24 February 1810 Macquarie issued a lengthy proclamation in which he announced 'his high Disapprobation' of 'the shameless and open Manner' in which men and women were living together unwed, 'to the utter Subversion of all Decency and Decorum', and 'his firm Resolution to repress, by every Means in his Power, all such disgraceful Connections'. On the same day he also stated the great regret with which he had noticed 'a number of Children about the Town of Sydney, who appear to be wholly neglected in their Education and Morals'. He would, he said, establish a charity school, in which such children might learn obedience to their parents and superiors, so as to become 'honest, faithful, and useful members of Society, and good Christians'.[32]

It was easy to set a charity school going – it was done by April – and to gather a number of children into it. Persuading people to marry was another matter, harder in some ways than the older project of getting families to move from one part of the world to another. It involved a capacity to work on the wills of grown men and women (couples who each had, at most, one place to name after themselves), to change their intimate inclinations and to give them new ideas about the order of their lives. In his proclamation, apart from his talk of indecency, Macquarie placed before his listeners, whoever they were, two arguments about the practical wisdom of marriage. Marriage meant material security. In the first place, he said, '*Illegal Cohabitation* (for whatever Length of Time) with any Man, confers no valid Title upon the Woman to the Goods and Effects of such Person, in case he should die intestate.' Secondly, men and women who lived in that way could expect from the Governor 'neither Favour nor Patronage'.

The proclamation made no straightforward impact. During the Macquaries' first six months a total of 174 marriages were recorded by the chaplains, about equal to the number for the last three years altogether, 1807–09. But two-thirds of the bridegrooms were soldiers of the New South Wales Corps, who had to marry the women they were living with before returning with them to England, or even before transferring to the 73rd or the Veteran Company. And among the remaining one-third only a few were men and women who might have been chastened by Macquarie's proclamation. For instance, of all the women whom the Reverend Samuel Marsden had listed as 'concubines' in 1806 (apart from soldiers' women) in these six months only three chose to marry their men. Propertied couples who may have been frightened at the threat about intestate estates were also scarce, or even non-existent.[33]

Marriage in New South Wales had never had much to do with the security of property. Men and women had agreed to marry for a number of reasons, but rarely because they thought that it could help a widow's claims to the family estate. The decision to marry arose mainly from an age-old desire to do the right thing at the beginning, a desire which in New South Wales affected only a few. A change had begun in Bligh's time. It was Bligh rather than Macquarie who first tried to impress on the people the importance of marriage; or rather, if we cast further back, it was Bligh who first revived the official concern shown by Phillip and by Richard Johnson as early as 1788. Bligh had tried to stop men taking convict women directly from the ships, and he had done very well, with a marriage rate more than twice King's and not far short of Macquarie's in 1810 (if we exclude the soldiers).[34] But common attitudes were not easily transformed. The new Judge-Advocate, Ellis Bent, himself a young husband and father ('we are never more happy than at home together'), was appalled by the wickedness of 'the common people'. 'The Women constantly live with the Men in a state of prostitution,' he said, 'and openly avow it. To use their words, "'It is the Fashion of the Country."'[35]

Bligh was still in Sydney in February 1810 when Macquarie issued his proclamation on marriage, and he later spoke of it with scorn. But Macquarie used more concrete methods of persuasion as well. Like Bligh, he refused to let men take convict women from the stores without marrying them. Those women who had left lawful husbands in Europe had to be married again, which involved describing themselves as widows, a practice very soon 'notorious'.[36] He also tried to back up his warning about women's claims to property. In January 1810 Andrew Thompson, magistrate on the

Hawkesbury, had reported the sudden death of a farmer, George Wood, who left a certain amount of property, 'the fruit of many years earning between him [and] Martha Parlthorpe [or Palethorpe]'. But the two had not married, and Wood left no will. Many men had so died in previous years without inquiry, but Thompson now wrote asking what was to be done. The answer which came back from the Governor's secretary referred merely to 'the woman who had been in the service of the deceased' and it was unnecessary to add that she had no rights whatever. This was severe, but the sting was drawn by Martha Palethorpe's being named in the *Gazette* a month later as Wood's administratrix. Presumably the land and goods which she had always thought of as jointly hers became wholly hers in law. A woman in her position might be safe as long as her man left no blood kin who could act against her, and few ex-convict men had any such relations on this side of the world. Marriage was to be more important among the native-born, the new generation now beginning to emerge, because a woman setting up with a native-born man had to make herself safe against his family on the spot. Thus, to secularise St Paul, 'shall a man leave his father and mother, and shall be joined unto his wife'.[37]

Such lessons, whether from Paul or Macquarie, were only gradually learnt. On 5 November, Richard Partridge and Mary Greenwood, who had a large farm near Parramatta and who had been together for more than eighteen years, were married at St John's, and a fortnight later two similar couples on the Hawkesbury, John Gregory and Anne Ferrol (or Farrell) and Thomas Gosper and Mary Hipwell, came in to receive the blessing of their new, and first resident, chaplain, Robert Cartwright. In January 1811 Henry Lamb and Elizabeth Chambers, with numerous children and a Hawkesbury grant dating back to 1798, did the same. The Macquaries' recent tour of the Hawkesbury–Nepean, during which they had called on numbers of small farmers, may have had some effect, the Governor listing their names in his journal as if he meant to remember them. Some he had scolded for their lack of attention to 'their own personal cleanliness and comfort', and he may well have commented likewise on their doubtful condition in the eye of God.[38]

In August–September 1811 the inhabitants of that region were taught a more profound lesson. It was now to be understood that the proper relationship of men and women added to the dignity of reach. Ralph Malkin, a labouring man, and the woman he lived with had agreed to separate and to seal their parting with an ancient ritual involving the mock sale of the woman to another man. She was led into the streets at Windsor with a rope around her neck and after something like a process of bidding her new 'owner' took her at the price of £16 and several yards of cloth. The magistrates found out and launched an inquiry. Both men freely admitted what they had done and the woman was happy with the change, but such an 'odious' transaction – similar to many such 'divorces' in King's time, though more open, formal and expensive – could no longer be allowed. It amounted to a dereliction of womanhood, for the individual sold (she was not named in the record) was clearly devoid of womanly pride, 'those feelings which are . . . the most valuable in her sex'. Malkin likewise was a mere 'person', a 'no-man', for so using a woman under his protection. He was sentenced to 50 lashes and three months in the Sydney gaol gang. She was sent to Newcastle 'for an indefinite time'.[39]

Cohabiting couples might marry in mere ones and twos, but public conversation – the descant of respectability over and above the common songs of life – changed its tune much more quickly, a fact evident in the widely broadcast 'indignation' of the Windsor people at Malkin's transgression. But the common songs, the individual agonies and delights, continued. Through marriage, women normally gave up the right to hold property in their own name. No doubt for some, even without marriage, this right had always been a fiction. Elizabeth Mumford, or Cassidy, a publican, congratulated herself that she and Michael Cassidy had been married during the interregnum between Bligh and Macquarie. All pardons and grants of land issued in that period had been declared null and void and she was under the impression (wrongly) that marriages had been invalidated too: 'thereby he has no power or authority over me'. But he sold what she owned all the same, besides beating her so that she was, as she put it, 'most crippled and and black and blue all over my body'.[40] Some women looked after themselves when they married by securing their property by deed of settlement. The publican Rosetta Marsh (who had offered £20 after the 1808 rebellion to send Macarthur as a delegate to England) married the shopkeeper Samuel Terry (he and Malkin had come on the same ship) in March 1810, drawing up a deed by which she kept control of her own assets. The marriage involved Terry's separation from another woman, Mary Shipley, and a division of their property, an arrangement similarly secured by settlement.[41]

Macquarie's main contribution to the dealings of such people was not his marriage proclamation nor even the more concrete ways in which he urged people to wed. It was his assertion of what John Hillas called 'Legal Govement', a legitimacy well founded on the past – on both common memory and the written word – and thereby secure for the future. Men and women were led to underpin their lives with signatures, confident that they were doing something reliable. It was a legitimacy doubly assured by the presence of a new Judge-Advocate, Ellis Bent being a qualified and hardworking lawyer willing to talk to all comers. By March 1810 as many as twenty people a day were knocking at his door with questions, anxious to make themselve safe in law.[42]

One of Macquarie's favourite words was 'comfortable', but comfort depended on material security. The O'Connells were the first of many couples to profit from the Governor's liberality in the distribution of land. The records are imprecise, but the quantity of soil now given in free grants seems to have been more than twice and possibly four times per annum the average hitherto.[43] Picking out men and women, distinguishing them by name (lists were once again among the necessary paraphernalia of government) and endowing them with goods was indisputable evidence of power. Macquarie's popular image, as a soldier's son remembered long after, was that of 'a generous-hearted man . . . very liberal to those who befriended him or did him a slight service. He had more power than any Governor before or after him.' The second idea followed in many minds from the first. It was an image made up of small stories like that of Thomas O'Neil, once Governor King's tailor and the first settler at Mosman, on Port Jackson's north side. 'His Excellency Governor McQuarie', O'Neil remembered afterwards, 'finding ide like to reside out of Sydney Bid me go and pick out a small farm where I chused . . . [and] when the Governor handed me the order [for the grant] he said Tommy O'Neil here is your order, let me see you get rich.'[44]

Macquarie also acted immediately to finalise the claims of the Norfolk Island settlers in Van Diemen's Land, asking the commandant at Hobart Town to get them all to hand in vouchers describing the property for which they needed compensation. These were to be forwarded to Sydney and the people were to be told that their claims would be fully paid in cash and/or livestock. As for the building of homes, they were to understand that the Crown's original promise could not be met, but in 1811 Macquarie asked the Secretary of State to see that the next ship with male convicts be sent direct to the Derwent, with the idea of supplying Norfolk Islanders with labouring men.[45] He made a point of visiting the claimants during his first inspection of Van Diemen's Land late that year, by which time most were settled in the district of New Norfolk, up the river from the capital. There he laid out a town for them. He briefly made his base at the house of Dennis McCarty, the district constable, and on the evening of 27 November a large number came there to see him. He was for them Bligh's undoubted successor and as such he had finalised their future. Beginning with 'many cheers and huzzas . . . they continued drinking, singing, and making bone-fires the greater part of the night'. Next day the Governor returned the compliment with the language of a ruler whose promise mattered, 'speaking to them all', as he noted on his journal, 'on their several claims, and exhorting them to persevere in their present habits of industry, honesty, sobriety, and morality'. He took away with him a written address in which they informed him that 'our Children shall be instructed, as soon as their articulation commence, to lisp the Name of Governor Macquarie'.[46]

Macquarie made his way with his voice. He was a man for whom language was an uncomplicated tool, a stately highway to the heart. Speech was not for him an object of curiosity as it had been for Phillip and some of the other officers who had come at the beginning. He was not immediately interested in the Aborigines because their words, and therefore their feelings, made no sense to him. His wife took more trouble in that direction. In July 1810 a brief note signed 'Philanthropus' appeared in the *Gazette*, asking for advice on the best means to 'civilize and evangelize' the Aborigines, a request curiously made: as if from a position of authority and yet under cover. A man wanting such advice would normally call a meeting, but a woman might work thus anonymously through print. Any answers to the letter were to be published, or else 'privately . . . left at the Gazette Office'. We cannot know the author, but this second option was so roundabout and delicate as to suggest it may have been Mrs Macquarie.[47]

Two answers appeared, both anonymous. The first, published at length over four issues of the paper, explained that relations between Black and White were not what they had been in earlier years:

> Formerly our intercourse with the natives was much greater than at present; they frequented the settlements in numbers, and performed their exercises, most of which were hostile to each other, frequently among us; they were then familiar, almost every one was known as well by an European name, which he assumed, as by his native appellation: – but that intimacy has subsided; for as the elders have fallen off, the younger, not receiving the encouragement their parents met with upon our frst acquaintance, seldom come among us.

We seemed, the writer said, no longer interested in them, and our own violent habits had ended the 'good opinion' they had once had of us.[48]

Among the Aboriginal elders who had lately died was a man well known among the Europeans for his gentleness, and who had long ago named himself Collins, after the first Judge-Advocate, his brother (still alive) having apparently paid the same compliment to Governor Phillip.[49] No Aboriginal man had since offered to call himself King, Bligh or Macquarie. Only a systematic effort, declared the writer in the Gazette, could restore the old mutuality. He argued that if a few Aboriginal parents could be persuaded to lend their offspring to 'sedate' European families then much good might be done. Our children must learn their language too, he said, and far from being cut off from their own people the young Aborigines 'must be taught to honour their parents, [and] to esteem their relatives'. They would thus participate in 'the general work of civilization' by 'counsel and example'. The other answer to 'Philanthropus', published in September, trusted less to the children, Aboriginal or European. Easy association such as that proposed, the second author argued, would instil in the Blacks the vices of the Whites. Also, if the children were allowed to teach each other their respective languages the end result must be 'a jargon'. New South Wales would cease to be part of the empire of pure English. (In 1786 the Home Office had hoped that indigenous women might marry convict men. The risk to language was then unimportant in a place so utterly remote.) Instead, said this writer, the Black children should be placed in a public institution, where they would be safe from the 'individual caprice' of European householders and where they might be subject to the uninterrupted light of Christianity and civilisation.[50]

Neither the Governor nor his wife was interested in Aboriginal culture for its own sake. Macquarie seems hardly to have noticed the Blacks before his first tour, in November 1810, and for Mrs Macquarie theirs were souls even more opaque than that of the novice at Madeira. She confronted the problem nevertheless. Whether or not it was she who provoked the debate in the *Gazette*, she immediately took up its agreed point, the need 'to civilize and evangelize'. Her opportunity was the Queen's birthday ball in January 1811, an occasion entirely under her control. The ballroom featured a large picture done by the botanical artist John Lewin showing (as the *Gazette* reported) 'our Native Race in their happy moments of festivity', including 'a striking full-sized figure, drawn in one of the most animated attitudes of the *corrobori* [who] pointed with his *waddy* at the Church of St Philip'. This was meant to be 'symbolical of the Christian Religion inviting them to happiness'. The ex-convict poet, Michael Robinson, read an ode written for the occasion in which he averted to 'yon sable Race', including the warrior – directing the thoughts of the dancers to that landscaped image, whose own thoughts were directed to the church on the hill – and in which he lamented that the Blacks were 'Lost to each social Interchange of Thought, / Their Youth neglected, and their Age untaught'.[51]

The Governor was proof against even such a public demand for action. Next summer, during a visit to Port Stephens, as they were putting out to sea, he and his wife saw a man running down the beach waving a fish. Mrs Macquarie, once again the first to move, held out a piece of tobacco in exchange. The man, after taking it, 'strutted and walked about', as the Governor noted, 'in a very conceited fantastical manner, dancing and capering and making a number of signs which we did not understand'.[52] Macquarie could not copy his wife's spontaneity (itself a faint echo of Phillip's numerous encounters). No detailed thoughts about the Aborigines appeared in his despatches home until October 1814, when he had been more than four years in New South Wales. He then announced his intention to found a school at Parramatta, 'the Native Institution', in which Black children might receive the rudiments of a European education. He forwarded as well the arguments of William Shelley, a former missionary, who was obviously aware of the Governor's priorities because he spoke mainly of the need for marriage among the Aborigines. None, he said, would ever be properly attached to European civilisation unless they could look forward, like men and women everywhere, to something like domestic happiness. The Native Institution was to take both sexes, and it was to teach not only reading and writing but the skills which would lead to indigenous people settling together as husbands and wives.[53]

In order to promote the school and the wider business of assimilation, the Macquaries organised a meeting at Parramatta with the Aborigines of the Cumberland Plain, and from 1816 there were to be annual feasts, at which they distributed clothes and food. Already used to the process of giving among the Europeans, the Governor at last made the imaginative step which might draw Aborigines within the same ritual circle. Besides the more tangible goods, he also offered routine. Phillip and his officers had made many gifts to the people they found here, but Macquarie made giving into a system. He chose a day (28 December, the anniversary of his own arrival in Australia) and he chose a place (Parramatta), both of which were to be affirmed from year to year.[54] Though late in the day compared with what he had done among the Europeans, Macquarie relied as ever on what he understood of the certainty of habit and the power of expectation in order to send his authority even further abroad, and even further inland, from White to Black.

III

The Macquaries came to Australia thinking they would stay for no more than four or five years. Waiting for them in Scotland was the estate which the Governor had bought on the Isle of Mull, a new village to be tended there, a house to be built, a grove of birches to be planted (Mrs Macquarie once contemplated orange trees, a forced union of luxurious scent and icy northern air), a local hierarchy to be formed and a line of lairds, Macquarie of Jarvisfield, to be established.[55] The vision of a community tightly drawn about themselves and within daily reach of their voices was the apple of their mind's eye. They had now, however, come to 'an island', as the verse of 1786 put it, 'Much warmer than Britain, and ten times as large', a space which dwarfed their Isle of Mull. But their daily energies could be concentrated to a point for many practical purposes, a point where voices did make a difference. That point was Sydney. To begin with, Sydney was a surrogate Jarvisfield and nothing else so much engaged their minds and hearts.

Governor King had succeeded in making Sydney a mirror for the colony's business, not only a market but a bureaucratic centre. It was to Sydney that the farmers now looked for the final adjustment of their debts, for their certificates of title, for the final word on boundary lines and for continuing statements about wages and prices. The main property owners in town had done well under King, and they had asserted themselves in combination against Bligh. They now wanted a ruler who could underwrite their interest in good order, their definition of public faith, and their sense of progress. Macquarie and his wife did all that. The Governor was deeply interested in town-planning. One of the main purposes of his first tour of the rural districts in the early summer of 1810 was the siting and mapping of new towns, and on his way back he spent an afternoon looking about Parramatta, where, as he recorded, he 'planned several new streets, alterations, and improvements for the ornamant of the town and the accommodation of its inhabitants'.[56] Hobart Town received the same attention during their visit to Van Diemen's Land a year later, and arrangements were made for a new establishment, George Town at Port Dalrymple.[57] Mrs Macquarie accompanied him on these tours, but she found something else to do while he ordered streets and squares. At George Town she and a young officer went off to sketch the scenery.[58]

But Sydney, with its ancient, eight-foot geraniums, its wallflowers, pome-granate trees and winter cauliflowers, its crumbling hovels and sparkling shop-fronts, offered the best and largest challenges. Among those now in command at the heart of the empire, town life was important because towns were centres and symbols of public order, places where the remodelling of citizenship must necessarily begin. Macquarie saw in Sydney a town which had been left too much alone and which had corrupted its garrison. He wanted the process reversed so that something like a military regime might prevail, a systematic parade of public duty and private virtue. Within twelve months of landing, he had decided on a plan which imposed a new cogency on existing streets and which allowed for two great open spaces (where Bligh had wanted them) around St Phillip's church in the west and in front of Government House in the east. A new set of names publicised the bal-ance. The west was to be dominated by memorials to the King and Queen – George Street and Charlotte Square – and to a series of princes (streets called York, Clarence, Kent and so on), and the east was to feature Macquarie Place and streets named for every governor since the beginning. The names were painted on notice boards, and it was announced that 'the Streets are henceforth to be known and called *only by the new Names* now given them': the first explicit order on this continent for the daily use of lan-guage. The market place, currently part of the area which stretched up from Sydney Cove to the new Charlotte Square, was to be moved to the southern edge of town, conveniently open to country roads and to a new wharf at Cockle Bay (later Darling Harbour). Also, public ground to the south-east hitherto used for various purposes was now clearly marked out, named Hyde Park and put down for military exercises and for 'the Recreation and Amusement of the Inhabitants'.[59]

Henceforth pigs, goats and dogs were not to be allowed to wander on to Sydney's public places. The soil of Hyde Park was not to be cut up by work-men coming over from the adjacent brickfields. Men were not to splash about naked at the government wharf and at the dockyard on hot days. Such order, and the more efficient suppression of crime, was to be guaran-teed by a refurbished town police force. Sydney under Macquarie was a place of experiment for up-to-date ideas about policing: active, interven-tionist ideas based on the need not only to teach the poor that they might not use public areas as they liked, but also on the ready identification of places and people and on continuous inspection and surveillance. The num-bering of houses was revived and householders were ordered to send in lists of all in residence, with every new lodger to be reported within 24 hours of arrival. Besides forty-four ordinary constables there were to be five district constables, each with his own part of the town, a chief constable and, at the head of the entire system, a superintendent and deputy superintendent, and these individuals were to be subject to a daily regimen of walking, watching, listing and reporting, as elegant in its symmetry (set out in the *Gazette*) as some extended polonaise. The resulting 'Regularity and

Efficiency', according to Macquarie, were 'not surpassed by that of any City in Europe'.[60]

Like Bligh, Macquarie had to remove houses in order to make the public spaces he wanted. At Macquarie Place, in front of Government House, a number of 'old Buildings and Inclosures' were swept away at an early stage, but whoever lived in them made no recorded resistance. Bligh's designs for this area had hurt Simeon Lord, whose property was threatened, but Macquarie moved more carefully. Whatever pain he caused was silently borne because it was restricted to lesser householders. Lord's boundary line and those of his neighbours, Andrew Thompson and Thomas Reibey, were to make up the northern edge of Macquarie Place, so that in fact those properties were now improved rather than jeopardised. Macquarie also offered freehold tenure in town, an idea which had been Foveaux's and which likewise added to the capital of its leading people.[61]

Lord, Thompson and Reiby were all important men within the new dispensation. Lord, Sydney's richest merchant, and Thompson, who normally lived at the Hawkesbury, were both appointed magistrates for their districts, the first ex-convicts to be raised to the bench. They also sat together as trustees for the Sydney–Hawkesbury turnpike road, Macquarie's earliest building project. Thompson had increased his credit with the new regime by making his very fine Sydney house available to Ellis Bent, the Judge-Advocate. However he died in October: Lord and the Governor himself were the main beneficiaries of his will. Thomas Reibey was a merchant absent from the colony during most of 1810, his concerns being managed by his wife, Mary, a publican in her own right, and his partner Edward Wills (both of whom had once been convicts). Edward and Sarah Wills (see Chapter 13) also managed a retail warehouse and eating place in George Street. Before being transported, Wills had learnt some of the skills of a printer and he and his wife were close friends of George Howe, editor of the *Gazette*. In December the printing business – Macquarie's voice in black and white – was moved to the Wills's premises.[62]

Governor Macquarie was not a man of ideas himself, but he admired the ideas of other people. Foveaux pointed the way for the Sydney police, and the scheme was worked out in detail by Ellis Bent. Campbell, the Governor's secretary, suggested a colonial bank modelled on one in which he had been employed at the Cape (which came to pass only with the founding of the Bank of New South Wales in 1817).[63] The leading townspeople, including those just named, taught Macquarie especially important lessons. Joined with the merchant families were the new chaplain at St Phillip's, William Cowper, and the government surgeons, William Redfern and D'Arcy Wentworth. Cowper was the Macquaries' favourite clergyman and, given his interest in the Aborigines, he was probably one of those who pushed forward the idea of the Native Institution. Redfern (who married the Wills's eldest daughter) and Wentworth both attended as physicians at Government House, sharing that intimate influence which John White had once enjoyed with Governor Phillip. Both were victims of the law, though Wentworth had left England before he could be transported. The new Sydney Hospital, designed in 1811 as the town's most prominent and splendid edifice – a fitting continuation of the hospital-building begun in 1788 – owed much to the Governor's two doctors.

Others magnified the personal image of His Excellency. Ellis Bent (though he later had doubts about the colonial constitution) drew up proclamations among whose phrases the executive power was enthroned with unprecedented splendour, and Howe of the *Gazette* did the same in his own way. The commemorative poetry which began to appear on public occasions, and to which Howe gave up whole columns of his paper, was written by Michael Robinson, once Lord's clerk and now a senior figure in Campbell's office. It hailed Macquarie in lavish terms:

> And Thou! whose firm and philanthropic Mind
> Glows with warm Sympathy to all Mankind, –
> To whom a grateful People fondly bend,
> At once their CHIEF, their PATRON, and their FRIEND.[64]

The mind thus praised was a territory happily cultivated by a number of tenants, including, of course, Macquarie's wife. Besides shaping the Governor's idea of the picturesque, Mrs Macquarie had her say in several buildings, including a new Female Orphan School at Liverpool (to replace the Sydney one) modelled on her father's house at Airds, and the spires for St John's, Parramatta, likewise copied, by her wish, from those of a seaside church in Kent.[65]

Charmed by the salty margin between land and sea, a fisher, a paddler, a walker on wet rocks, Mrs Macquarie also ordered the planting of several Norfolk pines, presents from Simeon Lord and D'Arcy Wentworth, at intervals along the edge of Sydney Harbour, where the surf ran against the Government House domain.[66] She also designed the path through the domain now named after her, a route punctuated by yet another resting place, the rock seat called Mrs Macquarie's Chair. She made the sea part, but part only, of her own land-based vision, holding it off in her own mind: just as Bennelong had tried to manage the European invasion by imagining it as part of the world he already knew.

The finest early celebration of the new regime was the Sydney races. The idea for a properly managed race course seems to have begun with officers of the 73rd, but Lord's partner, Francis Williams, was among the three stewards. Preparations went so well that an interim dinner was held in August (the Prince Regent's birthday) and a bachelors' ball at Lord's house in September. In October, the course being ready, there was a week of horse-racing, a little foot-racing and cock-fighting, another ball and dinners each night at Edward Wills's establishment. Macquarie's new magistrates and some women described only as 'the Ladies of the Colony' (presumably including Mary Reibey and Sarah Wills, both of whom commanded their own wealth) donated prizes, the latter being presented by the Governor's wife with a speech which Howe published verbatim. It was the closest Elizabeth Macquarie came to using words with the pomp of a Governor: 'In the name of the Ladies of New South Wales, I have the pleasure to present you with this Cup. Give me leave to congratulate you on being the successful Candidate for it; and to hope that it is a prelude to future success, and lasting prosperity.' The races drew the farming people in numbers never before seen in Sydney, and Howe congratulated his readers on the fact that 'Entertainments were given all over the Town, to welcome our country friends to our first *jubilee.*'[67] It was a significant boast about *our* celebrations and *our* grateful visitors, affirming, if it could be doubted, that 'the Town' was now truly 'ours' as well. The doubts of Bligh's time were past.

The men and women who managed the races helped to carry the new weight of public authority, a burden both frightening and comfortable in its omnipresence. For lesser townspeople, it was mainly frightening. In 1811 Ann Chapman, a publican, received a visit from another woman who offered to sell her some spirits. 'I told her', said Mrs Chapman, 'I would not have it, and if she had any to be very careful for the governor had given very particular orders last week and that I would not have it in my house for £20, poor as I was.'[68] The constables were ordered to pay special attention to men and women who were still convicts – a distinction never made so keenly before – who were to be off the streets and in their own houses by nine o'clock each night. Not long after the rules were promulgated, James Richards and Benjamin Grainger, both convicts, were seen very late on the wrong side of their fence in Phillip Street. They slipped inside but the constable followed them, an invasion which Richards resented: 'he was within his own gate-way', he said, 'when [the constable] . . . insisted upon his giving an account of himself'. The constable's jaw was broken in the fight which followed, but it was his own fault, so Richards said, because 'he had no right to intrude upon his . . . premises at all'. The court affirmed the power of the constable by ordering a sentence of 100 lashes.[69]

Dogs were less effectively penned up, and in spite of Macquarie's orders they were said to 'traverse as usual, and attack whom they please'. But then dogs were not beings whose morals mattered. It was also hard to organise their owners because, according to George Howe, 'those who have half-a-dozen dogs breathing perpetual vengeance . . . are yet as liable to feel and complain of a bite as other people'.[70] This was less strange than he implied. The business of complaining was built into local public order, and the right to complain, justifiably or not, was a fundamental right, vital not only to those bitten by dogs. The new surveillance gave added chances for complaint. Women in particular had always been ready to go to the authorities when they had trouble at home, and they seem to have welcomed a more numerous and watchful police. Men like James Richards might resent invasion, but the new force meant an even wider avenue by which women could appeal and by which the authorities could oversee the dealings of men with women, in their varying degrees of brutality, whether married or not.[71]

By such means the Macquaries met halfway the pattern of order which they found within the emerging commonwealth of Sydney. Sydney, now the most sinewy and dynamic creation of the Europeans in Australia, did the same for them. The inclinations of Mrs Macquarie, or some of them, were built into the arrangement. Her love for her husband was the foundation of her soul, and the fond tension between them was the axis of government. Once, probably late in life, she read Samuel Johnson's remark that a wise woman ignores her husband's infidelity. This was possible, she retorted, only where she felt nothing for him; 'but, if she is bound to him with true love and affection, she cannot bear it but with the most dreadful & alarming paroxisms of despair & desperation to which the human mind is liable'. It was this understanding of private faith which now began to shape the minds of Sydney's leading women, and to colour the understanding of public faith among all couples who wanted to subscribe to the new respectability.

It also affected ideas about common rights. Mrs Macquarie agreed with the maxim (Dr Johnson again): 'Political liberty is good only so far as it produces private liberty', or in other words, a secure family life.[72] This was the ruling orthodoxy from the first year of the Macquarie regime. The Governor had no interest in any expansion of public liberty which would curtail his own power, condemning out of hand George Eden's suggestion, in his report of 1812, that the colony needed a legislative council: 'I . . . indulge a fond Hope that this Measure will never be resorted to in this Colony.'[73] Here, too, the Sydney people were well suited. With friends at every level of authority they had all the influence they needed. Only a new Governor, in the 1820s, was to change their thoughts on public rights, leading them to argue at last for changes such as Macquarie had hated to foresee.

He was the first Governor, except perhaps for Bligh, who refused to think of the local constitution opening out by progressive steps, the first to say 'never' in that context. He did argue for a judicial system more in keeping with English custom, including trial by jury. But freedom of expression among jurymen – shopkeepers and small farmers – fell far short of that which could be expected within a council of gentlemen. Nor did he make any effort, as Governor Hunter had done, to encourage the people from district to district to meet, discuss and legislate for themselves.

Mrs Macquarie also consulted in a way peculiar to her own sense of authority. She liked dealing with men rather than women, and plain, rough-hewn men, men embodying bluntness and transparency, most of all. There was a striking directness in her dealings with such men. The orderly sergeant, Charles Whalan, was one of her favourites: he was to be for her 'My dear Sergeant', and during her years as a widow in England she was to hang his picture in her bedroom.[74] She did not choose to gather a circle of friends and allies like Mrs King's, from among women educated as she was; and her interest in the Female Orphan School, that women's project, was equivocal. In writing to married couples, and presumably in talking to them, unlike other ladies she habitually addressed herself to the husband. Government House ceased to be a place for women's conversation, and even men must have behaved differently there depending on whether they were married or unmarried. A young officer of the 73rd might recall 'those pleasant family dinners which the Genl and Mrs Macquarie used to make every one so happy in', but Ellis Bent, who visited with his wife, found that Mrs Macquarie lacked 'the art of making people feel happy and comfortable about her'.[75] Ladies ceased to come, even when invited. On the King's birthday, 1810, among eighty-one at dinner there were only three female guests, Mrs O'Connell, Mrs Bent and Mrs John Murray, whose husband was about to go as commandant to Hobart Town. Next year there were four among seventy-two.[76]

Ex-convict men benefited most under this dispensation. Elizabeth Macquarie inherited the vision which had inspired European settlement in the first place: a vision of humble men turned rich and honest, freed from degradation and standing within a new territory as classic bearers of commonwealth; a vision rendered all the more static and all the more brightly enamelled – 'as a painted ship / Upon a painted ocean' – by her own sensibility. James Matra, in 1783, had said that even convicts freshly transported should be allowed to forget their mistakes. Lord Sydney had established law courts on that basis, and for years the principle had prevailed at least a little in daily life. Condition depended on social origins, so that even a gentleman convict remained a gentleman. Ostensibly, the Macquaries aimed at nothing more than acceptance of this kind. In fact they also managed the way in which individuals crossed the boundary between bond and free by making their own patronage part of the privileges of freedom. Their refashioning of the moral landscape included giving the name of gentleman even to ex-convicts who had never thought to claim it – Simeon Lord and Andrew Thompson were largely self-educated – whose only qualifications were wealth, self-conscious freedom and attachment to the Governor. Many such (in spite of Macquarie's strictures) lived with women not their wives and therefore came alone to Government House. Mrs Macquarie held large parties nevertheless, although as one lady remarked they were not very select: another good reason for staying away.

In due course the Macquaries, almost in a spirit of defiance, extended the principle so as to define the character of the whole European community. The future of this country was to be identified, so the Governor said, with 'those who have been convicts or are descended from convicts', with those plain and unpretentious people who had been locally redeemed, who were now in perpetuity (as the term went) 'free on the ground'. Convict origins

quickly became the pivot on which all social distinctions turned. The officers of the 73rd, for instance, largely ignored it when they arrived in 1810,
but the regiment which took over from them in 1814 showed their independence by declaring ex-convicts beyond the pale.[77]

The distinction was all the more powerful because from this time penal
discipline itself was harder, heavier and more exact. Macquarie was the first
governor required to keep an accurate account of men and women still in
bondage. Even the chaplains were ordered to note at each burial whether
the deceased was a convict, distinguishing each by their ship and year of
arrival.[78] The rule about convicts being off the streets and in their own houses after nine o'clock at night – evidence of the same principle – was to lead
in 1817 to the building of the Hyde Park barracks, as a place of accommodation for Sydney's convict men, a four-square symbol of penological precision. For the women there was already the Female Factory at Parramatta,
built by King to hold a small number employed in the spinning of wool and
flax. Most women in King's day had made whatever arrangement they could
with male householders. Now they were in theory removed from the eye of
government only by marriage or deliberate assignment, and the Factory
became more truly a place of confinement. But although Macquarie saw the
need to restrain male and female convicts, he was not himself a penologist.
The Female Factory figured very little in his thinking, and the women themselves, unless they married, he considered a dead weight on his larger
hopes.[79]

Thanks to these new ideas, a finer contrast was drawn between the bond
and the free, and there was a lively interest in the use of power in polishing
the blackness and the brightness of those two conditions. Mercy is in the gift
of kings, and Macquarie made effective use of it. In July 1810 he announced
in General Orders in that he had commuted the sentence of death lately
passed on James Hutchinson, a celebrated burglar and escapee. George
Howe expatiated for his readers on what the order called 'this Act of Grace
and Clemency'. He dwelt at length on Hutchinson's dreadful situation,
'Unfit to live, yet more unfit to die', when 'His Excellency was pleased to
order him into his presence.' There 'Contrition became his mediator at the
seat of Mercy', and his life was saved.[80] Who among the inner circle gave
him these details to work up? What sense of sacred power led him to use
terms such as 'grace', usually reserved for God and the sovereign?[81]

Such deeds proved that in the end giving and receiving were the essence
of government, a larger and deeper process, certainly, than buying and selling. (As they are still.) Similarly, promises proceeding from the heart of
authority overshadowed – even engendered – the business of commonwealth and agreement among equals.

Macquarie was the first governor who made his own voice a true reflection, echoing day by day, of the paper-based order of empire, an order vested in the memory of ages. This was the Shark's secret: it made its home

ashore through an ancient, self-justifying certainty, a Truth which echoed in the ear. If one cut along its shining sides they fell open like a book, full of gilded imagery and familiar stories, but edged also with terror.

More than any other governor since Phillip, Macquarie was commonly thought to direct the way in which the courts dispensed justice, achieving with ease a fearful image such as Bligh had only dreamed of. Early in 1813 he allowed the hanging of five men involved in one crime. The ringleader was the butcher Matthew Kearns, once a respectable figure in Sydney, involved with the Sydney playhouse in Hunter's time, a business partner of Thomas Whittle's, and now a considerable land and stock-holder whose bay mare, 'Creeping Jenny', had won 50 guineas at the Sydney races. Kearns, with his son and brother, had stolen government cattle and, facing discovery, they had paid two other men to kill an informer. The latter two were hanged at Parramatta, on a gallows erected close to the site of the murder, but the three Kearnses died in Sydney, walking by their own request through the streets from prison to the place of execution. The bodies of all five were afterwards carried to the surgeons for dissection. So many dramatic deaths made a vivid impression, as they were meant to do, and the event was linked long afterwards with the name of Macquarie, as significant among his subject people as his roads and buildings have been among historians. His image as a man of unwavering justice was reinforced by a popular (and improbable) story that Mrs Macquarie begged without success for Kearns's life.[82]

It is one of the great facts of empire that provincial grace may be measured and curtailed from places beyond. The extent of Macquarie's grace was questioned in 1812, when George Eden recommended that governors in New South Wales should have no power to pardon transported convicts in their own right, only making recommendations to Whitehall. Macquarie objected. The dignity he had taken to himself – the high, justifying power of his own voice – depended on the fuller prerogative, and he argued especially about the problem of time and distance. 'There is a Feeling,' he told Lord Bathurst, 'not far removed from that of Despair, very generally felt by those men who are most worthy of Consideration amongst Convicts, which can only be known by Persons who have much Intercourse with them.' He was such a person. The new rule would force men to wait many months before they discovered what substance there might be in the Governor's promise. He spoke only of men, perhaps believing that women had all the moral sanction they could need – as his own wife was forced to recognise – within the common fabric, the asking and answering, the ordering and acquiescence, of their daily lives. Men's sense of justification under the state, as represented by His Excellency, was a much vaster and more frightening issue. Most of all, he said, 'At the Hour of Death a Convict feels more from the Idea of dying a Convict than for Death itself.' It was therefore important that he should be able to issue pardons at a moment's notice. '[M]ore than once', so Macquarie informed the Secretary of State, he had been asked for pardons by dying men who lacked for nothing in their daily lives but this single evidence of grace.[83]

Exaggeration, or rather the conversion of ephemeral facts into stories of moment, was part of Macquarie's style, a skill shared with the Good King. Surviving evidence suggests that at this stage he had pardoned only one man who thought he was dying. In May 1810 Edward Wills, the Sydney trader, Sarah Wills's husband and Thomas Reibey's partner, made out his will, though he was only thirty-one years old. On 4 September he was given an absolute pardon, and in his case – a possible symptom of urgency – the Governor departed from his usual method of waiting until a batch of men and women could be dealt with all at once. If Wills was ailing, he now rallied; he fell ill again, however, in February 1811 and died at last on 14 May, happily possessed of a secular blessing all the more absolute from its being set out on paper and entered in the books of the Governor's secretary.[84]

He had been 'free on the ground' (having a conditional pardon) for seven years. With his wife he had made a considerable fortune and settled a new family on the soil. Within the island of his imagination he now died redeemed.

Afterword

Blaise Pascal (1623–62) was one of those long-dead writers admired by highly literate Europeans at the opening of the nineteenth century. In his *Pensées* Pascal wrote of how much it hurt him to think of the apparently purposeless existence of humanity: 'I am overcome by fear like a man who has been carried off during sleep and deposited on some terrifying desert island, who wakes up without knowing where he is and without any means of escape.' On that island time was dissolved. Memory was undermined and the will was enslaved by the horror of distance. The poet Cowper wrote in 1803 about much the same kind of fear, reflecting on the imagination of a man fallen overboard at sea: 'He long survives, who lives an hour / In ocean self-upheld.'[1] Both told of the agony, momentary but infinite, of a soul suddenly displaced.

The first Europeans in Australia experienced this sense of loss, and of being lost, in various ways. Terror prevailed for William Bradbury (Chapter 4), who was told after being given a farm that there had been an administrative mistake and that he had seven years more in bondage. Announcing that 'he would rather perish at once, than remain as a convict', he disappeared. Numbers, especially among the early Irish, talked of a paradise within a fortnight's walk, as real to them as the purgatory in which they found themselves, and the physical remains of some who searched for it were to litter parts of the bush. Within Eliza Marsden's surviving letters, on the other hand, the desert island had a familiar solidity. She was a palpable Crusoe. 'He long survives, who lives an hour', but for her the hour was so crowded and amplified that ancient safety itself became an illusion. 'Old England is no more', she said, 'than like a pleasing dream; when I think of it it appears to have no existence but in my own imagination.'[2] Elizabeth Macquarie was comforted by a desire to wander within the moment, by a love of stillness. On the Hawkesbury there were ex-convict farmers who built boats to serve their purposes up and down the river and who demonstrated a similar adaptation. Unskilled with pen and ink, they constructed their vehicles not from plans but from scale models, and they taught themselves to work with antipodean timber, especially blue gum and mahogany, spending a day sometimes, Crusoe-like, hunting through the bush for a single item properly shaped, a floor piece, beam, knee or breast hook.[3]

The European settlement in Australia, having begun in an age of revolution, was characterised by a kaleidoscope of ambitions whose object, in many cases, was to start anew. In Europe itself, the French revolutionary leadership aimed to rearrange a number of nations all at once. In the new United States, thirteen colonies were combined and republicans tried to instil among the federated people a new sense of public duty. In the Antipodes, the Macquaries came to an empire which was much smaller than either of these. And yet the Governor similarly made himself supreme, not only on the mainland but at the Derwent and Port Dalrymple, as no man had ever done before. In 1817 he officially proposed the name 'Australia' for the entire continent.[4] In that sense he invented Australians, and his hopes for a better-ordered people were built into the invention. In an age of revolution, popular obedience was no longer to be taken for granted, whether in Europe, North America or Australia. On the other hand, in an age of improved roads and postal services, among a people more and more familiar with writing, obedience was all the more easily secured. Everywhere within the European world the subjects of government were now asked to admire a system of power at once sublime, efficient and good.

Macquarie partly succeeded in conveying this message because his people included many, especially in Sydney, who were making new homes for themselves and a competence for the future. They had passed beyond the stage of piecing together accommodation, furniture, a food supply and human company. '[W]e are rising', they told him in 1812, in one of their complimentary messages, 'from the rude and unconnected state consequent and inseparable from the first Efforts of Colonization.'[5] A sense of order and 'connection', such as he and his wife offered in their first years, came next. And what beyond that? Macquarie himself, though powerfully energetic, was not a man for perpetual movement, and his early achievements exhausted his imagination. His wife's mind was more expansive, but she was not the Governor.

In spite of such newness the Macquaries also looked backwards, making links with Phillip, 'the Founder', and coming to terms with the ex-convict people who had learnt to be free in New South Wales. Even Napoleon, in Europe, modelled himself a little on Charlemagne, and the new federation in America also looked for roots which were distinctly local, rough-hewn, ancient and customary. Men and women of romantic sensibility admired old kingdoms and primitive origins, and it was natural for the Macquaries to build on the well-worn moral economy worked out on the spot during the twenty-two years before their arrival. The period of their honeymoon with New South Wales was therefore the climax of the first period of European settlement, the end of the beginning. Or so it must appear to those of us, coming long afterwards, who interest ourselves in the patterns they left. This volume has told the story of a single generation. At the end of it the Europeans, though more sophisticated and self-conscious, had not yet changed in any dramatic way. They were still scattered in a few insular settlements. The entire population numbered little more than 10,000, and it still consisted largely of men and women who had passed through the cruel distinguishing ceremonies of criminal trial and transportation. The Macquaries themselves, when they arrived, aimed only to improve the existing human landscape.

However, not only a new generation but two great changes – both beyond the scope of this volume – were soon to overtake them. In 1813 Gregory Blaxland and William Lawson organised an expedition to cross the Blue Mountains, together with D'Arcy Wentworth's son, William. Their success meant a sudden expansion of territory open to European settlement and a new sense of the size of the continent. Sydney's original hinterland, the mainly agricultural settlements within a day's ride, was enclosed within a further circle, a vast margin thick with pale green and purple beauty, a keen, dry brilliance – a place of 'mountain ash and kurrajong', of 'stringy barks and saplings' – which only a series of generations could hope to comprehend. The farms themselves became by comparison small and familiar. Ideas of limitless bush and of large, remote possessions began to enter the Australian-European imagination.

The other change, or combination of changes, came directly from Europe. The end of Britain's war with France in 1815 released large quantities of capital for use throughout the empire. It also let loose many educated men, former officers in the army and navy, who had more hope of living well in this and other colonies than in Britain. Enormous numbers of soldiers and seamen were demobilised as well, and owing to high prices and scarce employment they added to the incidence of British crime. The numbers of convicts sent to New South Wales therefore multiplied. So far, for most of the period of settlement, the annual average had been less than 500. In 1815 it was 1074 and from 1818 (with the exception of 1823) it was never less than 2000.[6] Sheer numbers altered the purposes of administration. At the same time the dictates of the new penology became much more pervasive, and increasing contact between Europe and Australia allowed the transportation system to be much more tightly managed. From 1815 the antipodean settlements became a penal colony on a more vast and elaborate scale than their founders had ever anticipated. Hitherto, since 1788, convict men and women had been merely banished, and what happened to them on arrival had been a matter of chance. Now their suffering was meant to be deliberate, methodical and rooted in theory.

Lord Sydney, the instigator of European settlement, had seen no usefulness in New South Wales except as a place of banishment. From about 1815 its uses began to seem limitless and it was to be much more tightly drawn within the empire. Macquarie might protest about being cramped and curtailed in his dispensing of mercy, but in this and other ways antipodean governors were never again the self-sufficient vehicles of grace they had once aimed to be. He might hand out some of the riches of Europe to Aborigines, but even there his efforts were badly counterbalanced by the growing European eagerness for Australian land, which helped to entrench the mutual fears of Black and White. In immediate response a new leader came forward on the Aboriginal side, a man from the south named Carnabyagal or Carnanbigal, who inspired a fresh resistance. Macquarie answered with outright warfare. He also ordered that individual Blacks who wanted peace were to receive monthly certificates bearing his own signature, little pieces of paper to be carried about their person which he hoped might save their lives in arguments with Europeans.[7]

Among the enormous flood of paper which had already reached Australia, these certificates were among the most whimsical and hopeless. Macquarie's commission gave him the power to create and to countermand both life and death, to condemn and to forgive, but these fragments of writing fell far short of such great aims. Those issued must have ended up at length among the more ancient debris of the bush, the Governor's majestic signature a piece of landscape for ants. They were a typical echo of one man's justifying tongue and, at the same time, so many little monuments to the vast ambitions of pen and ink.

Notes

Abbreviations

ADM	Admiralty records, Public Record Office, London
BL	British Library, London
CO	Colonial Office records, Public Record Office, London
HO	Home Office records, Public Record Office, London
HRA	*Historical Records of Australia* (31 volumes, Sydney 1914–25)
HRNSW	*Historical Records of New South Wales* (8 volumes, Sydney 1892–1901)
KB	King's Bench records, Public Record Office, London
ML	Mitchell Library, Sydney
NL	National Library of Australia, Canberra
NSWSA	New South Wales State Archives, Sydney
PROB	Probate records, Public Record Office, London
SP	State Papers, Public Record Office, London
T	Treasury records, Public Record Office, London
WO	War Office records, Public Record Office, London

Foreword

1   William Paley, *The Principles of Moral and Political Philosophy* (Boston 1810), p. 98.

2   Evidence of Edward Abbott, 30 May 1811, in John Ritchie, *A Charge of Mutiny: The Court Martial of Lieutenant Colonel George Johnston for Deposing Governor William Bligh in the Rebellion of 26 January 1808* (Canberra 1988), p. 351.

3   William Wordsworth, *Lyrical Ballads and Other Poems, 1797–1800* (ed. James Butler and Karen Green) (Ithaca, N.Y., 1992), p. 351.

4   Jonathan M. Hess, 'Wordsworth's Aesthetic State: The Poetics of Liberty', *Studies in Romanticism*, vol. 33 (1994), pp. 3–29.

5   Thomas Jefferson, 'Draft of Instructions to the Virgina Delegates in the Continental Congress', July 1774, in Julian Boyd and others (eds), *The Papers of Thomas Jefferson* (25 vols) vol. 1 (Princeton 1950), pp. 121–5.

6   John Hirst, *A Republican Manifesto* (Melbourne 1993), p. 1.

7   M. Barnard Eldershaw, *Phillip of Australia: An Account of the Settlement at Sydney Cove, 1788–92* (London 1938), p. 9.

8   W. K. Hancock, *Australia* (London 1930), p. 73.

9   Ibid.

10   Ged Martin (ed.), *The Founding of Australia: The Argument about Australia's Origins* (Sydney 1978); Alan Frost, *Convicts and Empire: A Naval Question, 1776–1811* (Melbourne 1980).

11   Mollie Gillen, 'The Botany Bay Decision, 1786: Convicts not Empire', *English Historical Review*, vol. 97 (1982), pp. 740–66; David Mackay, *A Place of Exile: The European Settlement of New South Wales* (Melbourne 1985).

12   John West, *The History of Tasmania* (Launceston 1852; republ. Sydney 1971), p. 30; Lloyd Robson, *A History of Tasmania*, vol. 1 (*Van Diemen's Land from the Earliest Times to 1855*) (Melbourne 1983), pp. 32–3.

13   Margaret Steven, *Trade, Tactics and Territory: Britain in the Pacific, 1783–1823* (Melbourne 1983), pp. 90–5.

14   Alan Atkinson, 'Sunshine from Frost', *Push from the Bush*, no. 26 (April 1988), pp. 9–23.

15   David Neal, 'Free Society, Penal Colony, Slave Society, Prison?', and John Hirst, 'Or None of the Above: A Reply', *Historical Studies*, vol. 22 (1987), pp. 497–524; Alan Atkinson, 'The Free-Born Englishman Transported: Convict Rights as a Measure of Eighteenth-Century Empire', *Past and Present*, no. 144 (August 1994), pp. 88–115.

16   Marian Aveling (now Quartly), 'Imagining New South Wales as a Gendered Society', *Australian Historical Studies*, vol. 25 (1992), pp. 1–12; Patricia Grimshaw, Marilyn Lake, Anne McGrath and Marian Quartly, *Creating a Nation* (Melbourne 1994), pp. 27–54.

17   Marcus Rediker, '"Under the Banner of King Death": The Social World of Anglo-American Pirates, 1716 to 1726', *William and Mary Quarterly*, series 3, vol. 38 (1981), pp. 203–27; Marcus Rediker, 'The Anglo-American Seaman as Collective Worker, 1700–1750', in Stephen Innes (ed.), *Work and Labor in Early America* (Chapel Hill 1988), pp. 252–86; Marcus Rediker, *Between the Devil and the Deep Blue Sea: Merchant Seamen Pirates and the Anglo-American Maritime World, 1700–1750* (Cambridge 1993); Mollie Gillen, *The Founders of Australia: A Biographical Dictionary of the First Fleet* (Sydney 1989), p. 446.

18   Miriam Dixson, *The Real Matilda: Woman and Identity in Australia, 1788 to the Present* (Melbourne 1994; first publ. 1976), pp. 155–74.

19   Marshall Sahlins, *Historical Metaphors and Mythical Realites: Structure in the Early History of the Sandwich Islands Kingdom* (Ann Arbor 1981), pp. 17–28; Greg Dening, *Mr Bligh's Bad Language: Passion, Power and Theatre on the Bounty* (Cambridge 1993), pp. 168–71; Ann McGrath, 'The White Man's Looking Glass: Aboriginal–Colonial Gender Relations at Port Jackson', *Australian Historical Studies*, vol. 24 (1990), pp. 189–206; Tony Swain, *A Place for Strangers: Towards a History of Australian Aboriginal Being* (Cambridge 1993); Grimshaw et al., op. cit., pp. 7–26.

20   P. L. Gregory, 'Popular Religion in New South Wales and Van Diemen's Land from 1788 to the 1850s', PhD thesis, University of New England 1995.

21   Paula J. Byrne, *Criminal Law and Colonial Subject: New South Wales, 1810–1830* (Cambridge 1993).

22   See also Alan Atkinson, 'Jeremy Bentham and the Rum Rebellion', *Journal of the Royal Australian Historical Society*, vol. 64 (1978), pp. 1–13; Alan Atkinson, 'The British Whigs and the Rum Rebellion', *Journal of the Royal Australian Historical Society*, vol. 66 (1980), pp. 73–90; Alan Atkinson, 'Taking Possession: Sydney's First Householders', in Graeme Aplin (ed.), *A Difficult Infant: Sydney before Macquarie* (Sydney 1988), pp. 72–90.

23   George Mackaness, *The Life of William Bligh, R.N., F.R.S.* (Sydney 1931), vol. 2, pp. 224–5.

24   Ibid., pp. 288–9; Ross Fitzgerald and Mark Hearn, *Bligh, Macarthur and the Rum Rebellion* (Sydney 1988), pp. 120–1; Dening, op. cit.

25   Alan Atkinson, 'The Primitive Origins of Parliament', *Push from the Bush*, no. 24 (April 1987), pp. 48–76.
26   Brian Fitzpatrick, *British Imperialism and Australia, 1783–1833* (London 1939), pp. 13–15.

Part 1

1   Ronald M. Berndt and Catherine H. Berndt, *The Speaking Land: Myth and Story in Aboriginal Australia*, (Ringwood, Vic., 1989), pp. 44–5.

Chapter 1 Talk

1   David Collins, *An Account of the English Colony at New South Wales* (ed. Brian H. Fletcher) (Sydney 1975), vol. 1 (first publ. 1798), p. 2; L. F. Fitzhardinge (ed.), *Sydney's First Four Years* (that is, Watkin Tench, *A Narrative of the Expedition to Botany Bay and A Complete Account of the Settlement at Port Jackson* (Sydney 1979), pp. 30–1.
2   Quoted in Christopher Hill, *The World Turned Upside Down: Radical Ideas during the English Revolution* (Harmondsworth 1975) (London 1972), p. 219.
3   Thomas Dekker, *The Dead Tearme*, quoted in Arthur F. Kenny (ed.), *Rogues, Vagabonds and Sturdy Beggars* (Barre, Mass., 1973), p. 33.
4   J. M. Beattie, *Crime and the Courts in England, 1600–1800* (Oxford 1986), pp. 352–62. See also, in relation to these paragraphs, Caroline Robbins, *The Eighteenth-Century Commonwealthman: Studies in the Transmission, Development and Circumstance of English Liberal Thought from the Restoration of Charles II until the War with the Thirteen Colonies* (Cambridge, Mass., 1959).
5   31 Car. II, c. 2.
6   Jeremy Bentham, 'A Plea for the Constitution, etc.', in John Bowring (ed.), *The Works of Jeremy Bentham* (New York 1962; first publ. 1838–43), vol. 4. (first printed as a pamphlet and privately distributed 1803).
7   Michel Foucault, *The History of Sexuality*, vol. 1 (London 1979), pp. 58–60.
8   John Saltmarsh, quoted Hill, op. cit., p. 47; and Lawrence Clarkson, quoted ibid., p. 273.
9   John Everard, quoted ibid., p. 149.
10   John Milton, 'Areopagitica', in *John Milton: Complete Poems and Major Prose* (ed. Merritt Y. Hughes) (New York 1957), p. 742; Johnson quoted in Paul Langford, *Public Life and the Propertied Englishman, 1689–1798* (Oxford 1991), p. 465.
11   William Thornton, 30 May 1753, *Parliamentary Debates*, vol. 14, cols 1321–2.
12   Karen Ordahl Kupperman, 'Apathy and Death in Early Jamestown', *Journal of American History*, vol. 66 (1979–80) (Patrick Copland quoted pp. 26–7).
13   Collins, op. cit., p. 57.
14   Quoted in Edmond S. Morgan, 'The First American Boom: Virginia 1618 to 1630', *William and Mary Quarterly*, series 3, vol. 28 (1971), p. 169.
15   Quoted in Richard L. Morton, *Colonial Virginia* (Chapel Hill 1960), vol. 1, p. 5.
16   John Smith and others, 'A Map of Virginia' (1612), in Philip L. Barbour (ed.), *The Jamestown Voyages under the First Charter, 1606–1609* (Cambridge 1969), vol. 2, p. 384.
17   Collins, op. cit., p. 72.
18   Governor Phillip's Instructions, 25 April 1787, *HRA*, series 1, vol. 1, p. 12.
19   J. H. Lefroy, *Memorials of the Discovery and Early Settlement of the Bermudas or Somers Islands, 1515–1685* (London 1877), vol. 1, pp. 63–4, 74, 109–13; Virginia Bernhard, 'Bermuda and Virginia in the Seventeenth Century: A Comparative View', *Journal of Social History*, vol. 19 (1985–6), pp. 59–62.

20   J. A. Doyle, *The English in America: The Puritan Colonies* (London 1887), pp. 72–8; William T. Davis (ed.), *Bradford's History of the Plymouth Plantation, 1606–1646* (New York 1908), p. 96; Julius Goebel, 'King's Law and Local Custom in Seventeenth Century New England', in David H. Flaherty (ed.), *Essays in the History of Early American Law* (Chapel Hill 1969), p. 116.

21   J. F . Maclear, 'New England and the Fifth Monarchy: The Quest for the Millenium in Early American Puritanism', *William and Mary Quarterly*, series 3, vol. 32 (1975), pp. 241–2.

22   Introduction, and John Guy to Sir Percival Willoughby, 6 October 1610, in Gillian T. Cell (ed.), *Newfoundland Discovered: English Attempts at Colonisation, 1610–1630* (London 1982), pp. 5–8, 61.

23   Goebel, op. cit., pp. 96–7.

24   Minutes of Assembly, 25 January 1637, *Archives of Maryland*, vol. 1 (Baltimore 1883), p. 4.

25   Sebastian F. Streeter, *Papers Relating to the Early History of Maryland* (Maryland Historical Society Fund Publication no. 8) (Baltimore 1876), p. 259.

26   Davis, op. cit., pp. 236–43; *Dictionary of National Biography*, vol. 13, pp. 1055–6.

27   James Harrington, *Oceana* (ed. S. B. Liljegren) (Heidelberg 1924), p. 19.

28   Thomas Seals' deposition, 10 July 1816, and Michael Howe and ten others to William Sorrell, November 1816, *HRA*, series 3, vol. 2, pp. 163, 643–4.

29   John Peachey's deposition, 9 September 1816, ibid., pp. 590–1.

30   Quoted in A. F. Madden, '"Not for Export"': The Westminster Model of Government and British Colonial Practice', *Journal of Imperial and Commonwealth History*, vol. 8 (1979), p. 14.

31   Lord Baltimore to William Stone, 20 August 1649, *Archives of Maryland*, vol. 1, pp. 263–4.

32   Petition of the inhabitants of the Mosquito Shore to Lord Sydney, 4 April 1787, CO 123/5, ff. 11–14; Former inhabitants of Mosquito Shore to London merchants, 26 August 1787, CO 123/5, ff. 128–31; 'Narrative of Mr Daniel Hill upon oath', 4 July 1788, CO 123/11, p. 328. I owe the last reference to Mollie Gillen.

33   Quoted in Lyle Koehler, 'The Case of the American Jezebels: Anne Hutchinson and Female Agitation during the Years of Antinomian Turmoil, 1636–1640', *William and Mary Quarterly*, series 3, vol. 31 (1974), pp. 58, 64.

34   *Archives of Maryland*, vol. 1 (Baltimore 1883), p. 215 (21 January 1648, new style). See also *Dictionary of American Biography*, vol. 3, pp. 18–19.

35   Anon., 'On the Languages', *Monthly Miscellany*, February 1774, pp. 55–6.

36   *Coriolanus*, Act V, scene v; Jane Austen, *Pride and Prejudice* (Harmondsworth 1972; first publ. 1813), p. 85; Lynn Hunt, 'The Many Bodies of Marie Antoinette: Political Pornography and the Problem of the Feminine in the French Revolution', in Lynn Hunt (ed.), *Eroticism and the Body Politic* (Baltimore 1991), pp. 108–30.

37   Trial of John Elkin, 24 March 1643 (new style), *Archives of Maryland*, vol. 4 (Baltimore 1887), p. 180.

38   Warren S. Billings, 'The Cases of Fernando and Elizabeth Key: A Note on the Status of Blacks in Seventeenth-Century Virginia', *William and Mary Quarterly*, series 3, vol. 30 (1973), pp. 460–70; James Walvin, 'Black Slavery in England', *Journal of Caribbean History*, vol. 7 (November 1973), pp. 79–80.

39   Graham Greene, *The Quiet American* (London 1973), p. 102; Quotation from Keith Thomas, *Man and the Natural World: Changing Attitudes in England, 1500–1800* (London 1983), p. 42.

40   See, for example, 22 Geo. II, c. 13: William Waller Hening (ed.), *The Statutes at Large; Being a Collection of all the Laws of Virginia* (Richmond, Va, Philadelphia and New York, 1809–23), vol. 5, pp. 546–7.

41   R. H. W. Reece, *Aborigines and Colonists: Aborigines and Colonial Society in New South Wales in the 1830s and 1840s* (Sydney 1974), pp. 179–82.

42 Henry Lawson, '"Water them Geraniums"', in John Barnes (ed.), *The Penguin Henry Lawson Short Stories* (Ringwood, Vic., 1986), p. 163. And see '"Some Day"', ibid., p. 65 ('to live like a Christian').

43 Maryland legislation of 1728, quoted Basil Sollers, 'Transported Convict Laborers in Maryland during the Colonial Period', *Maryland Historical Magazine*, vol. 2 (1907), pp. 32–3.

44 Alan Atkinson, 'The Free-Born Englishman Transported: Convict Rights as a Measure of Eighteenth-Century Empire', *Past and Present*, no. 144 (August 1994), pp. 97–8, 105.

45 Walter Allen, *The English Novel: From* The Pilgrim's Progress *to* Sons and Lovers (London 1958), pp. 108–18; Walter J. Ong, *Interfaces of the Word: Studies in the Evolution of Consciousness and Culture* (Ithaca, N.Y., 1977), pp. 253–5, 292; Walter J. Ong, *Orality and Literacy: The Technologizing of the Word* (London 1982), pp. 17–28.

Chapter 2 Writing

1 Jeffrey Kittay, 'Utterance Unmoored: The Changing Interpretation of the Act of Writing in the European Middle Ages', *Language in Society*, vol. 17 (1988).

2 Lawrence Stone, 'Literacy and Education in England, 1640–1900', *Past and Present*, no. 42 (February 1969), pp. 108–9; John Miller, 'Public Opinion in Charles II's England', *History*, vol. 80 (1995), p. 363; *Short Title Catalogues*; and see Maureen Bell and John Barnard, 'Provisional Count of *STC* Titles 1475–1640', *Publishing History*, no. 21 (1992), pp. 49–64.

3 D. C. Coleman, *The British Paper Industry, 1495–1860: A Study in Industrial Growth* (Oxford 1958), pp. 12–15, 19, 54–9.

4 Ibid., pp. 353–5.

5 John Brewer, *The Sinews of Power: War, Money and the English State, 1688–1783* (London 1989), pp. 94–5, 114–26, 153–4.

6 George Farquhar, *The Recruiting Officer*, Act IV, scene ii.

7 Ian K. Steele, *The English Atlantic, 1675–1740: An Exploration of Communication and Community* (New York 1986), pp. 114, 119–31.

8 Ibid., pp. 92–3, 168–72.

9 Barbara J. Shapiro, *Probability and Certainty in Seventeenth Century England: A Study of the Relationships between Natural Science, Religion, History, Law and Literature* (Princeton 1983), pp. 239–46; Keith Thomas, *Man and the Natural World: Changing Attitudes in England, 1500–1800* (London 1983), pp. 80–9; Julian Hoppit, 'Reforming Britain's Weights and Measures, 1660–1824', *English Historical Review*, vol. 108 (1993), pp. 83, 92–4.

10 Steele, op. cit., p. 305.

11 William Congreve, *The Way of the World*, Act II, scene v.

12 Norman S. Fiering, 'The Transatlantic Republic of Letters: A Note on the Circulation of Learned Periodicals to Early Eighteenth-Century America', *William and Mary Quarterly*, series 3, vol. 33 (1976).

13 Benedict Anderson, *Imagined Communities: Reflections on the Origins and Spread of Nationalism* (London 1983), pp. 62–3; Steele, op. cit., p. 159.

14 See the Act of parliament 6 Ann. c. 30 (1707), 'for ascertaining the rates of foreign coins in her Majesty's plantations in America', and incorporating a proclamation of 1704.

15 Sarah Tyacke, *London Map-Sellers, 1660–1720* (Tring, Herts., 1978), pp. xi–xv; Leo Bagrow, *History of Cartography* (Chicago 1985), pp. 181–9; Defoe quoted in Glyndwr Williams, 'Buccaneers, Castaways, and Satirists: The South Seas in the English Consciousness Before 1750', *Eighteenth-Century Life*, no. 18 (November 1994), p. 123.

16   William Neate Chapman to his mother, 18 October 1791, ML A 1934, pp. 18–19.
17   *The Way of the World*, Act III, scene xv.
18   Brewer, op. cit., pp. 159–60.
19   Dora Mae Clark, 'The Impressment of Seamen in the American Colonies', *Essays in Colonial History Presented to Charles McLean Andrews by his Students* (New Haven 1931), pp. 202–24.
20   Robert G. Albion, *Forests and Sea Power: The Timber Problem of the Royal Navy, 1652–1862* (Cambridge, Mass., 1926), pp. 248–9, 255–9; Joseph J. Malone, *Pine Trees and Politics: The Naval Stores and Forest Policy in Colonial New England, 1691–1775* (London 1964), p. 10.
21   Brewer, op. cit., pp. 31–7, 66, 160.
22   Daniel Parke to the Council of Trade and Plantations, 3 November 1708, 24 May 1709, 26 June 1709, *Calendar of State Papers (Colonial)*, 1708–9, pp. 136, 311, 386, 396–7; Same to same, 21 March 1710, *Calendar of State Papers (Colonial)*, 1710–11, p. 60.
23   Testimonial of officers of the regiment in the Leeward Islands, 13 November 1708, *Calendar of State Papers (Colonial)*, 1708–9, p. 145; Address to Daniel Parke signed by 110 soldiers, n.d., enclosed with Parke to the Council of Trade and Plantations, 24 April 1710, James Jones to Lord Sunderland, [27 November 1710], and Lieutenant-Governor and Council of Antigua to Queen Anne, 26 January 1711, *Calendar of State Papers, Colonial (America and West Indies)*, 1710–11, pp. 81–2, 286–7, 390–3.
24   William Mathew to [?], 24 February 1711, ibid., pp. 395–6; Abel Boyer, *Quadriennium Annae Postremum; or the Political State of Great Britain During the Four last Years of the late Queen's Reign* (London 1718), pp. 243, 244; *Dictionary of National Biography*, vol. 15, p. 225.
25   Peter Clark, 'Migration in England During the Late Seventeenth and Early Eighteenth Centuries', *Past and Present*, no. 83 (May 1979), p. 89. Quotation from the prologue of John Day's play, 'The Travailes of the Three English Brothers' (1607), in A. H. Bullen (ed.), *The Works of John Day* (London 1963), p. 320.
26   Walter Allen Knittle, *The Early Eighteenth Century Palatine Emigration: A British Government Redemptioner Project to Manufacture Naval Stores* (Philadelphia 1936), pp. 29–30.
27   Ibid., pp. 3–5.
28   Ibid., pp. 84, 99–101.
29   William Lowndes (Treasury) to Josiah Burchett (Admiralty), 12 July 1710, ADM 1/4283; Robert Hunter to William Popple, 16 June 1710, and Hunter to Board of Trade and Plantations, 24 July 1710, *Calendar of State Papers, Colonial (America and West Indies)*, 1710–11, pp. 119, 139–40; Knittle, op. cit., pp. 128–48.
30   A. Roger Ekirch, *Bound for America: The Transportation of British Convicts to the Colonies, 1718–1775* (Oxford 1987), pp. 26–7.
31   Norma Landau, 'The Regulation of Immigration, Economic Structures and Definitions of the Poor in Eighteenth-Century England', *Historical Journal*, vol. 33 (1990), pp. 541–72.
32   Alan Atkinson, 'The Free-Born Englishman Transported: Convict Rights as a Measure of Eighteenth-Century Empire', *Past and Present*, no. 144 (August 1994), pp. 99–100, 102–7.
33   *Maryland Gazette*, 27 June 1776.
34   Ekirch, op. cit., pp. 196, 149–50.
35   Robert Eden to Lord Hillsborough, 4 August 1771, Fisher Transcripts (MS 360), vol. 7, Maryland Historical Society; Knittle, op. cit., pp. 163–75; Rachel N. Klein, 'Ordering the Backcountry: The South Carolina Regulation', *William and Mary Quarterly*, series 3, vol. 38 (1981); Ekirch, op. cit., pp. 206–9.

36   Peter Linebaugh, *The London Hanged: Crime and Civil Society in the Eighteenth Century* (London 1993), pp. 120–1; Jay Fliegelman, *Declaring Independence: Jefferson, Natural Language, and the Culutre of Performance* (Stanford 1993), pp. 81–3.

37   Sir John Vanbrugh, *The Provok'd Wife*, Act III, scene iii.

38   Archer, in George Farquhar, *The Beaux' Stratagem*, Act I, scene i.

39   Martin Green, *Dreams of Adventure, Deeds of Empire* (London 1980), p. 69.

40   *The Ordinary of Newgate his Account*, executions on 11 September 1721, Bodleian Library; Gerald Howson, *Thief-Taker General: Jonothan Wild and the Emergence of Crime and Corruption as a Way of Life in Eighteenth-Century England* (New Brunswick, N.J., 1985), pp. 107, 125.

41   Robert McCrum, William Cran and Robert MacNeil, *The Story of English* (London 1986), p. 93; Linebaugh, op. cit., pp. 130–4.

42   Anon., 'Ode on a Storm' (1758), in Jonathan Raban (ed.), *The Oxford Book of the Sea* (Oxford 1992), p. 118.

43   Charles Johnson [that is, Daniel Defoe], *A General History of the Robberies and Murders of the most notorious Pyrates, and also Their Policies, Discipline and Government* (London 1724), pp. 37–40; Marcus Rediker, '"Under the Banner of King Death"': The Social World of Anglo-American Pirates, 1716 to 1726', *William and Mary Quarterly*, series 3, vol. 38 (1981).

44   Alan Atkinson, 'The First Plans for Governing New South Wales, 1786–87', *Australian Historical Studies*, vol. 24 (1990), pp. 24–5.

45   Johnson [Defoe], op. cit., pp. 194–6.

46   Deposition of John Vickers, n.d., enclosed with Alexander Spotswood (Governor of Virginia) to Council of Trade, 3 July 1716, CO 23/12/1, ff. 105–6; Johnson [Defoe], op. cit., pp. 46–52.

47   Woodes Rogers to Council of Trade, 31 October 1718, CO 23/1, ff. 20–1; Gale to [?], 4 November 1718, CO 23/1, f. 47.

48   William Dampier, *Dampier's Voyages* (ed. John Masefield) (London 1906), vol. 2, pp. 122–3. See also Johnson [Defoe], op. cit., pp. 289, 292.

49   Ibid., pp. 169–74; Rediker, op. cit., pp. 208–12.

50   Dampier, op. cit., pp. 179–80; Alexander Harris, *Settlers and Convicts: Recollections of Sixteen Years' Labour in the Australian Backwoods* (Melbourne 1953; first publ. 1847), p. 86.

51   Robert Hodgson, 'The first Account of the State of that Part of America called The Mosquito Shore, In the Year 1757', CO 123/1, f. 63.

52   Ibid.

53   Ibid.; 'Narrative of Mr Daniel Hill upon Oath', p. 328; E. M. Despard to Lord Sydney, 24 August 1787, CO 123/5, ff. 174–81.

54   Despard to Sydney, 23 February 1787, CO 123/5, f. 51.

Chapter 3 Towards Botany Bay

1   This statement is true for practical purposes and agrees with every other published authority, the Governor having departed in December 1792, but he did not in fact resign until December 1793.

2   Daniel Southwell to his mother, 7 August 1790, *HRNSW*, vol. 2, part 2, p. 722; James Campbell to Lord Ducie, 12 July 1788, in John Cobley, *Sydney Cove, 1788* (London 1962), p. 192; L. F. Fitzhardinge (ed.), *Sydney's First Four Years* (that is, Watkin Tench, *A Narrative of the Expedition to Botany Bay and A Complete Account of the Settlement at Port Jackson*) (Sydney 1979), p. 228. Another joke appears in John C. Dann (ed.), *The Nagle Journal: A Diary of the Life of Jacob Nagle, Sailor, from the Year 1775 to 1841* (New York 1988), p. 101.

3   Robert Ross to Philip Stephens, Secretary of the Admiralty, 10 July 1788, and Ross to Evan Nepean, under-secretary at the Home Office, 16 November 1788, *HRNSW*, vol. 1, part 2, pp. 173, 212.

4   Marshall Sahlins, 'The Stranger-King; or, Dumézil among the Fijians', in his *Islands of History* (Chicago 1985); Howard Morphy, *Ancestral Connections: Arts and an Aboriginal System of Knowledge* (Chicago 1991), pp. 103–5, 196; Wally Caruana, *Aboriginal Art* (London 1993), pp. 44, 177; Greg Dening, *Mr Bligh's Bad Language: Passion, Power and Theatre on the Bounty* (Cambridge 1993), pp. 160–1. The line of poetry is from Algernon Charles Swinburne's 'The Return' (1866).

5   Quoted in Jay Fliegelman, *Declaring Independence: Jefferson, Natural Language, and the Culture of Performance* (Stanford 1993), p. 60.

6   Martin Green, *Dreams of Adventure, Deeds of Empire* (London 1980), pp. 93–4.

7   Daniel Defoe, *Robinson Crusoe* (Oxford 1928), vol. 3, p. 80.

8   John Nicol, *The Life and Adventures of John Nicol, Mariner* (London 1822), p. 4.

9   George B. Worgan, *Journal of a First Fleet Surgeon* (Sydney 1978), pp. 27, 49.

10 [James Oglethorpe], *A New and Accurate Account of the Provinces of South-Carolina and Georgia* (London 1733), pp. 49–50.

11 'Rules for the Year 1735' (and apparently for earlier years as well), in Allen D. Chandler (ed.), *The Colonial Records of the State of Georgia*, vol. 3 (Atlanta 1905), pp. 407–11; Paul S. Taylor, *Georgia Plan: 1732–1752* (Berkeley, Ca., 1972), p. 54 (note).

12 Oglethorpe, May 1731, quoted ibid., pp. 14–15; Benjamin Martyn, 'An Account Shewing the Progress of the Colony of Georgia in America from its first establishment', in Chandler, op. cit., pp. 379–80, 394.

13 Martyn, op. cit., p. 378; Taylor, op. cit., p. 41.

14 [Samuel Eveleigh?], 1733, quoted Taylor, op. cit., p. 73.

15 John Robertson's deposition, 28 November 1741, in Anon., *A Brief Account of the Causes that have retarded the Progress of the Colony of Georgia, in America* (London 1743), pp. 18–19.

16 James Edward Oglethorpe, 'On Starving, A Scetch', ms, n.d., Granville Sharp Papers (Lloyd Baker Archive), Gloucestershire Record Office.

17 Paul Langford, *Public Life and the Propertied Englishman, 1689–1798* (Oxford 1991), pp. 438, 446–8.

18 'Extract of a Plan presented to His Majesty by the Earl of Halifax for the Settlement of His Majesty's Colony of Nova Scotia', enclosed with Duke of Bedford to Board of Trade, 6 March 1749, House of Lords Record Office, Nova Scotia Papers, Bundle A, no. 1, f. 3740; Albert Berry Saye, *A Constitutional History of Georgia, 1732–1968* (Athens, Ga, [1971?]), p. 3.

19 Lord Halifax, 'Proposals for the Establishment of a Civil Government and the Settlement of a Number of Protestant Subjects in the Province of Nova Scotia', enclosed with Duke of Bedford to Board of Trade, 6 March 1749, loc. cit., f. 3748.

20 Ibid., ff. 3748–9.

21 William Wordsworth, 'The Prelude', book 6, ll. 339–41.

22 Board of Trade to Lord Halifax, 2 December 1763, CO 123/1, f. 27; Halifax to Joseph Otway, 9 December 1763, CO 123/1, f. 31; Robert Hodgson's commission, 31 July 1767, CO 123/1, f. 33.

23 Inhabitants of the Mosquito Shore to Lord Sydney, 4 April 1787, CO 123/5, f. 11; Minutes of a meeting of inhabitants, Belize River, 23 July 1787, CO 123/5, f. 156; Committee of Honduras settlers to Paul Le Mesurier and other London merchants, 27 August 1787, CO 123/5, ff. 128–48.

24 J. Lawrie to Alured Clarke, 9 March 1786, CO 123/4, ff. 85–6; Return of Mosquito Shore inhabitants supplied with provisions, [August–October 1787], CO 123/5, ff. 194–7.

25   Committee of Honduras settlers to Paul Le Mesurier and other London merchants, 27 August 1787, CO 123/5, ff. 128–48; E. M. Despard to Lord Sydney, 24 August 1787, and to Evan Nepean, 21 October 1787, ibid., ff. 174, 181, 198–207.

26   Committee of Honduras settlers to Paul Le Mesurier and other London merchants, 27 August 1787, CO 123/5, ff. 128–48.

27   Ibid.

28   Caroline Robbins, *The Eighteenth–Century Commonwealthmen: Studies in the Transmission, Development and Circumstance of English Liberal Thought from the Restoration of Charles II until the War with the Thirteen Colonies* (Cambridge, Mass., 1959), pp. 10, 318; Bernard Bailyn, *The Ideological Origins of the American Revolution* (Cambridge, Mass., 1969), pp. 224–5; Robert A. Selig, 'Emigration, Fraud, Humanitarianism, and the Founding of Londonderry, South Carolina, 1763–1765', *Eighteenth–Century Studies*, vol. 23 (1989), p. 15 (including note 37).

29   Sydney to Despard, [6] February 1788, CO 123/6, f. 99. After Sydney's resignation Despard fell from favour, lost his post and after years of increasing bitterness concocted a scheme to assassinate the King, which led to his execution in 1803: *Dictionary of National Biography*, vol. 5, pp. 858–9.

30   See, for instance, T. Boulden Thompson to Philip Stephens, 4 February 1787, and minute thereon, ADM 1/2594; and Sydney to Lords of the Admiralty, 21 February 1787, HO 28/5, f. 394.

31   Sydney to Lords of the Admiralty, 7 December 1786, HO 28/5; and see Sydney's speech in the House of Lords, 25 June 1788, *Parliamentary Debates*, vol. 25, cols. 646–7; Christopher Fyfe, *A History of Sierra Leone* (London 1962), p. 14.

32   Sydney to Lords of the Admiralty, 7 December 1786, and 21 February 1787, HO 28/5, ff. 356–7, 394; Fyfe, op. cit., p. 20.

33   T. Boulden Thompson to Lords of the Admiralty, 21 March, 26 May, and 23 July 1787, ADM 1/2594; Captain's log, *Nautilus*, 7, 16 July 1787, ADM 51/627/4; Thompson as reported by Sydney, 25 June 1788, *Parliamentary Debates*, vol. 27, cols 646–7.

34   'Civis', writing in the *Morning Chronicle*, 16 September 1782.

35   Debate of 9 May 1776, *Parliamentary Register*, vol. 4, pp. 104–5; *Gazetteer*, 11 May 1776; G. C. Bolton, 'William Eden and the Convicts, 1771–1787', *Australian Journal of Politics and History*, vol. 26 (1980); J. M. Beattie, *Crime and the Courts in England, 1660–1800* (Oxford 1986), pp. 223, 554–9.

36   Bamber Gascoyne, speaking in the House of Commons, 23 March 1778, *Parliamentary Debates*, vol. 19, col. 970.

37   'Report from the Committee who were appointed to consider the several returns, which have been made to the Order of the House of Commons of the 16th day of December 1778' (Sir Charles Bunbury's committee), *House of Commons Journals*, vol. 37, pp. 378–85.

38   Ibid., pp. 379–80, 391.

39   Ibid., pp. 379–80.

40   Alan Atkinson, 'The Free–Born Englishman Transported: Convict Rights as a Measure of Eighteenth-Century Empire', *Past and Present*, no. 144 (August 1994), pp. 94–8.

41   Anon., 'Extract from an Essay on Punishment, of Felony, &c., written in the year 1751', SP 36/117, ff. 121–5; Capt. John Luttrell, speaking in the House of Commons, 11 March 1784, *Parliamentary Debates*, vol. 24, col. 755.

42   Ibid.

43   William Hussey, speaking in the House of Commons, 11 March 1784, *Parliamentary Debates*, vol. 24, col. 757. A fuller account of this statement shows that Hussey was referring to New Zealand (*Morning Chronicle*, 12 March 1784).

44   Algernon Sidney, *Discourses concerning Government* (London 1704), p. 66; Caroline Robbins, 'Algernon Sidney's *Discourses Concerning Government*:

Textbook of Revolution', *William and Mary Quarterly*, series 3, vol. 4 (1947), pp. 267–72; Bailyn, op. cit., pp. 34–5, 45; Hugh Cunningham, 'The Language of Patriotism, 1750–1914', *History Workshop: A Journal of Socialist Historians*, 12 (Autumn 1981), p. 14.

45   Maurice Cranston, *Jean-Jacques: The Early Life and Work of Jean-Jacques Rousseau, 1712–1754* (London 1983), p. 291.

46   William Jones, *The Principles of Government, in a Dialogue between a Scholar and a Peasant* (a pamphlet distributed by the Society for Constitutional Information, of which Lord Sydney was a member, London 1782).

47   Henry Fielding, *An Enquiry into the Causes of the Late Increase of Robbers and Related Writings* (ed. Malvin R. Zirker) (Oxford 1988), p. 76.

48   Evidence of John Teague, Report of the Committee on the State of the Gaols of the City of London, ordered to be printed 9 May 1814, *Crime and Punishment: Prisons* (Irish University Press series), vol. 7, pp. 299–300; Arthur Griffiths, *The Chronicles of Newgate* (London 1884), vol. 2, pp. 90–1; Henry Fielding, *The Life of Mr Jonathan Wild the Great* (Oxford 1926), pp. 171–6 (I owe this reference to Joanna Innes); W. J. Sheahan, 'Finding Solace in Eighteenth–Century Newgate', in J. S. Cockburn (ed.), *Crime in England, 1550–1800* (London 1977), pp. 233–4.

49   [John Roberts?] to Gilbert Ross, December 1784, HO 42/5, ff. 465–9. I owe this reference to Mollie Gillen.

50   Speech in the House of Lords, 4 February 1784, *Parliamentary Debates*, vol. 24, col. 523.

51   House of Commons debate, 9 May 1776, *Parliamentary Register*, vol. 4, p. 105. See also John Brewer, 'The Wilkites and the Law, 1763–74: A Study of Radical Notions of Governance', in John Brewer and John Styles (eds), *An Ungovernable People: The English and their Law in the Seventeenth and Eighteenth Centuries* (London 1983), p. 160.

52   [Roberts?] to Ross, December 1784, HO 42/5, ff. 465–9; Mollie Gillen, 'The Botany Bay Decision, 1786: Convicts not Empire', *English Historical Review*, vol. 97 (1982), p. 749.

53   Robert White to Evan Nepean, 25 January 1785, CO 123/3, ff. 86–7; Nepean to Despard, 15 September 1785, CO 123/11, ff. 166–7. As recently as 1783 Lord North had tried to force convicts on Nova Scotia: Gillen, op. cit., pp. 746–7. But see W. W. Grenville to Lord FitzGibbon, 2 December 1789, Dropmore Papers, *Report of Historical Manuscripts Commission*, vol. 30, part 1, pp. 548–9.

54   Robert White to Nepean, 25 January 1785, CO 123/3, ff. 86–7.

55   Sydney to Lords Commissioners of the Treasury, 9 February 1785, and enclosures, HO 35/1; Mollie Gillen, 'The Botany Bay Decision, 1786: Convicts, not Empire', *English Historical Review*, vol. 97 (1982), pp. 749–80; David Mackay, *A Place of Exile: The European Settlement of New South Wales* (Melbourne 1985), pp. 42–9. A similar plan for a convict settlement in the River Gambia, dated 1779 (the year of the Bunbury committee), is to be found in a volume of papers by John Roberts, and once belonging to William Wilberforce, now among the Egerton Papers, BL Mss 1162A; see especially ff. 262–4.

56   Jean-Jacques Rousseau, *A Treatise on the Social Compact; or the Principles of Politic Law* [that is, *The Social Contract*], (London 1764), pp. 60–8; Defoe, op. cit., vol. 2, p. 59. See also Marian Aveling (now Quartly), 'Imagining New South Wales as a Gendered Society, 1785–1821', *Australian Historical Studies*, vol. 23 (1992), pp. 1–4.

57   Sandra M. Gilbert and Susan Gubar, *The Madwoman in the Attic: The Woman Writer and the Nineteenth–Century Literary Imagination* (New Haven 1979), pp. 3–16; Jay Fliegelman, Prodigals and Pilgrims: *The American Revolution against Patriarchal Authority* (Cambridge 1982).

58   Evidence taken by the Select Committee of the House of Commons inquiring into Transportation, 26 April–25 May 1785, HO 7/1; First Report from the Committee, 9 May 1785, *Journals of the House of Commons*, vol. 40, pp. 955–8.

59   *Journals of the House of Commons*, vol. 40, p. 1162.

60   Alan Frost, 'Historians, Handling Documents, Transgressions and Transportable Offences', *Australian Historical Studies*, vol. 25 (1992), pp. 192–8.

61   Gillen, op. cit., pp. 751–2; Mackay, op. cit., pp. 51–6.

62   'Memo. of matters brought before Cabinet', Sydney Papers, Dixson MS Q522. For the correct date of this paper, see Frost, op. cit., pp. 204–7.

63   Inquiries made of Duncan Campbell, and Campbell's answers, n.d., HO 42/10, ff. 425–6; Mackay, op. cit., p. 55.

64   Edward Thompson, 'Some Account of the Country on the West Coast of Africa . . . ', CO 267/9; Evan Nepean to Thomas Steele, 190 June 1786, T 1/632, f. 40; [Evan Nepean?], untitled memorandum ('It is proposed that Commodore Thompson . . . '), n.d., CO 267/9.

65   Draft and fair copies of the budget for New South Wales, August 1786, HO 42/7, ff. 23–4; Alan Atkinson, 'The First Plans for Governing New South Wales, 1786–87', *Australian Historical Studies*, vol. 24 (1990), pp. 30–1, 35–6.

66   [Evan Nepean] to Sackville Hamilton, 24 October 1786, in Michael Roe, 'Motives for Australian Settlement: A Document', in Ged Martin (ed.), *The Founding of Australia: The Argument about Australia's Origins* (Sydney 1978), pp. 54–5.

67   *Public Advertiser*, 20 September 1786.

68   Sir Charles Blagden, quoted in Mackay, op. cit., p. 1.

69   *Daily Universal Register*, 10 October, 18 December 1786.

70   Arthur Phillip to Evan Nepean, 18 November 1791, *HRA*, series 1, vol. 1, pp. 308–9; David Collins, *An Account of the English Colony in New South Wales* (ed. Brian H. Fletcher) (Sydney 1975), vol. 1 (first publ. 1798), pp. 54, 158, 163, and vol. 2 (first publ. 1802), p. 57; D. D. Mann, *The Present Picture of New South Wales,* (London 1811), p. 10; Anne–Maree Whitaker, *Unfinished Revolution: United Irishmen in New South Wales, 1800–1810* (Sydney 1994), pp. 79–80, 82.

71   *Morning Chronicle*, 26 September 1786. For the reference to 'superintendent' as the officer who was not the naval commander, see Sydney to Lords of the Treasury, 18 August 1786, *HRNSW*, vol. 1, part 2, p. 15; and for the distinction of titles, see an enclosure in the same letter ('Staff Establishment for the Settlement at New South Wales', p. 19). The first contradicts the second; see also draft and fair copies of budget [August 1786], HO 42/7, ff. 23–4; Major Ross's commission, 24 October 1786, is at ibid., p. 26. See also Atkinson, 'The First Plans for Governing New South Wales, 1786–87', op. cit., pp. 32–3.

72   Watkin Tench to an unknown correspondent, 1788, in 'An Officer', *An Authentic Journal of an Expedition under Commodore Phillips to Botany Bay* (London 1789), p. 24.

73   Alan Frost, *Convicts and Empire: A Naval Question* (Melbourne 1980); Robert Hughes, *The Fatal Shore: A History of the Transportation of Convicts to Australia, 1787–1868* (London 1987), p. 2.

Chapter 4   Arthur Phillip and Robert Ross

1   'Report from the Committee who were appointed to consider the several returns, which have been made to the Order of the House of Commons of the 16th day of December 1778' (Sir Charles Bunbury's committee), *House of Commons Journals*, vol. 37, pp. 379–80, 391. See also the opening question to Sir Joseph Banks, 10 May 1785, evidence taken by the Beauchamp committee, HO 7/1. The discussion in the latter case dealt with a settlement of 500 convicts.

2   'Phillip's Views on the Conduct of the Expedition and the Treatment of Convicts', n.d. (1786–7), *HRNSW*, vol. 1, part 2, p. 53.
3   King's speech, 23 January 1787, *Parliamentary Debates*, vol. 26, col. 211.
4   Henrietta Drake-Brockman, *Voyage to Disaster: The Life of Francisco Pelsaert* (Sydney 1982), pp. 73–5, 209–11, 229–30.
5   Governor Phillip's Instructions, 25 April 1787, *HRA*, series 1, vol. 1, pp. 9–10, 13. These were copied from a late rough draft, CO 201/1, ff. 29–40. Instructions for Ross were foreshadowed in Sydney to Lords of the Admiralty, 31 August 1786, *HRNSW*, vol. 1, part 2, p. 22.
6   Phillip to Nepean, 22 December 1786, T 1/639; James Adair to Nepean, 26 December, 1786, HO 47/5; Sydney to Dorning Ramsbotham, 1 January 1787, HO 13/4, f. 354; Nepean to Thomas Shelton, 1 January 1787, *HRNSW*, vol. 1, part 2, pp. 42–3.
7   Nepean to Mary Fowell, 12 December 1787, and Nepean to John Fowell, 23 May 1788, in Nance Irvine (ed.), *The Sirius Letters: The Complete Letters of Newton Fowell* (Sydney 1988), pp. 57, 97.
8   L. F. Fitzhardinge (ed.), *Sydney's First Four Years* (that is, Watkin Tench, *A Narrative of the Expedition to Botany Bay and A Complete Account of the Settlement at Port Jackson*) (Sydney 1979), p. 162; *A Voyage to New South Wales: The Journal of Lieutenant William Bradley RN of HMS Sirius* (Sydney 1969), pp. 97, 99, 101, 103, 106; Paul G. Fidlon and R. J. Ryan, *The Journal of Arthur Bowes Smyth: Surgeon, Lady Penrhyn, 1787–1789* (Sydney 1979), p. 62.
9   Sydney to Lords of the Treasury, 31 October 1788, HO 35/9 (I am grateful to David Mackay for help with this reference); *Gentleman's Magazine*, 8 December 1788, p. 1116; Jed (rightly Ged) Martin, 'Convict Transportation to Newfoundland in 1789', *Acadiensis*, vol. 5 (1975), pp. 85–6; Ged Martin, 'The Alternatives to Botany Bay', in Ged Martin (ed.), *The Founding of Australia: The Argument about Australia's Origins* (Sydney 1978), p. 160.
10   Evan Nepean's evidence before Lord Beauchamp's committee, 27 April 1785, HO 7/1; 'A Description of the Island Lemain . . . ', n.d., enclosed with Sydney to Lords of the Treasury, 9 February 1785, HO 35/1.
11   Walt Whitman, 'To Him that was Crucified', *Leaves of Grass and Selected Prose* (ed. Lawrence Bell) (New York 1981), p. 303.
12   'Phillip's Views on the Conduct of the Expedition and the Treatment of Convicts', op. cit., p. 53.
13   Phillip to Evan Nepean, 2 September 1787, *HRNSW*, vol. 1, part 2, p. 114; Phillip to Lord Lansdowne, 3 July 1788, *HRNSW*, vol. 2, pp. 410–11; Phillip to Nepean, 22 August 1790, *HRA*, series 1, vol. 1, p. 207.
14   Phillip to Sydney, 1 November 1786, Sydney Papers, Dixson MS Q162; John Elliot to Sydney, 28 February 1787, CO 194/37, ff. 1–2; Alan Atkinson, 'The First Plans for Governing New South Wales, 1786–87', *Australian Historical Studies*, (1990), pp. 25–7. In 1794 John Hunter offered another explanation for the 'naval government' of New South Wales, but this looks like rationalisation after the event; nor does it preclude the explanation given here (Hunter to Philip Stephens, 7 April 1794, *HRNSW*, vol. 2, pp. 199–200).
15   'Phillip's Views on the Conduct of the Expedition and the Treatment of Convicts', and Ross to Nepean, 10 July 1788, *HRNSW*, vol. 1, part 2, pp. 51, 176.
16   Speech in House of Commons, 25 February 1777, *Parliamentary Debates*, vol. 19, cols 80–1.
17   Sydney to E. M. Despard, [6] February 1788, CO 123/6, f. 98.
18   James Campbell to Lord Ducie, 12 July 1788, in John Cobley, *Sydney Cove, 1788* (Sydney 1962), p. 193.
19   Ross to Nepean, 10 July 1788, *HRNSW*, vol. 1, part 2, p. 176: John H. Moore, The *First Fleet Marines, 1786–1792* (St Lucia, Qld, 1987), pp. 35–6.

20   Phillip to Sydney, July 1788, *HRNSW*, vol. 1, part 2, p. 179.

21   Sydney to Lords of the Admiralty, 31 August 1786, ibid., p. 21.

22   Various letters, from Sydney and Nepean, dated between 14 October and 25 November 1786, HO 13/4, ff. 214–328; Mollie Gillen, *The Founders of Australia: A Biographical Dictionary of the First Fleet* (Sydney 1989), pp. xxiii–xxiv.

23   R. B. Knight, 'The First Fleet – Its State and Preparation, 1786–1787', in John Hardy and Alan Frost (eds), *Studies from Terra Australis to Australia* (Canberra 1989), pp. 128–9, 133.

24   John Hunter, *An Historical Journal of the Transactions at Port Jackson and Norfolk Island . . .* (London 1793), pp. 2–3.

25   *Daily Universal Register*, 27 November 1786; Philip Stephens to Capt. Marshall, 3 March 1787, *HRNSW*, vol. 1, part 2, p. 56; Mackay, op. cit., pp. 68–9.

26   'The King agt Lord George Gordon (de *Newgate*): Copy of *Record* to the End of Interlocutory Judgment', London, Trinity 27 Geo. 3, 1787, KB 33/14/2; Kathleen Wilson, 'Citizenship, Empire, and Modernity in the English Provinces, c. 1720–1790', *Eighteenth-Century Studies*, vol. 29 (1995), p. 83.

27   Debate in House of Commons, 15 February 1773, *Parliamentary Debates*, vol. 17, col. 729; Phillip's instructions, final draft, (April 1787), CO 201/1, f. 36.

28   Petition of the inhabitants of Mosquito Shore to Sydney, 4 April 1787, CO 123/5, ff. 11–14; 'Narrative of Mr Daniel Hill upon Oath', 4 July 1788, CO 123/11, p. 320.

29   Henry Smeathman, *Plan of a Settlement to be made near Sierra Leona, on the Grain Coast of Africa* (London 1786), p. 6 (my emphasis). I am grateful to Mollie Gillen for a copy of this pamphlet.

30   William Paley, *The Principles of Moral and Political Philosophy* (Boston 1810), pp. 80–1, 95.

31   Granville Sharp to Sydney, 20 January 1785, Granville Sharp Papers (Lloyd Baker Archives), Gloucestershire Record Office; Granville Sharp, *An Account of the Constitutional English Polity of Congregational Courts: And More Particularly of the Great Annual Court of the People, called the View of Frankpledge* (London 1786; first printed 1784), pp. 264, 265–6, 292.

32   Jean-Jacques Rousseau, *A Treatise on the Social Compact; or the Principles of Politic Law* (that is, *The Social Contract*) (London 1764), pp. 83–4; Caroline Robbins, *The Eighteenth-Century Commonwealthmen: Studies in the Transmission, Development and Circumstance of English Liberal Thought from the Restoration of Charles II until the War with the Thirteen Colonies* (Cambridge, Mass., 1959), p. 15.

33   James Mario Matra, memoranda attached to his 'Proposal for Establishing a Settlement in New South Wales', 23 August 1783, *HRNSW*, vol. 1, part 2, p. 7; 'A Description of the Island Lemain . . . . ', n.d., enclosed with Sydney to Lords of the Treasury, 9 February 1785, HO 35/1; Forster quoted (in translation) in Lesli Bodi, 'Georg Forster: The 'Pacific Expert' of Eighteenth-Century Germany', *Historical Studies*, vol. 8 (1959), p. 359.

34   Isaac Barrow, 1696, quoted in Ernest Lee Tuveson, *The Imagination as a Means of Grace: Locke and the Aesthetics of Romanticism* (Berkeley 1960), p. 45.

35   Navy Board to Thomas Steele (Treasury), 13 November 1786, T 1/639; Christopher Fyfe, *A History of Sierra Leone* (London 1962), p. 17; Daniel Defoe, *Robinson Crusoe* (Oxford 1928), vol. 1, p. 149, and vol. 3, p. 58.

36   Governor Phillip's Instructions, 25 April 1787, *HRA*, series 1, vol. 1 , pp. 11, 12.

37   Ibid., p. 14.

38   Matra, memoranda, op. cit., p. 7.

39   Banks's evidence before the Beauchamp committee, 10 May 1785, HO 7/1; Budget, rough and fair copies, n.d. [August 1786], HO 42/7, ff. 23, 24. In the rough copy 'Second Year' has been hopefully altered to 'First Year'.

40   Matra, memoranda, op. cit., p. 7.

41   Banks's evidence before the Beauchamp committee, 10 May 1785, HO 7/1.

42 Phillip's first commission, 12 October 1786, *HRA*, series 1, vol. 1, p. 1; Henry Reynolds, *The Law of the Land* (Ringwood, Vic., 1992), pp. 7–9, 13–14, 51–4.

43 In the final draft of Phillip's instructions, 25 April 1787, the words 'any such Person as you may think competent to discharge the trust' were replaced with 'the Surveyor of Lands' (CO 201/1, f. 38).

44 Charles Loch Mowat, *East Florida as a British Province, 1763–1784* (Berkeley 1943), p. 60; Bernard Bailyn, *Voyagers to the West: A Passage in the Peopling of America on the Eve of the Revolution* (New York 1986), p. 456.

45 W. W. Grenville to Phillip, 19 June 1789, *HRA*, series 1, vol. 1, p. 121; Phillip to Grenville, 1 March 1791, ibid., p. 229.

46 John H. Moore, *The First Fleet Marines, 1786–1792* (St Lucia, Qld, 1987), pp. 215–17.

47 Trial of Edward Varndell and John Allen, 23 May 1788, Judge-Advocate's Court, NSWSA 1/296; 'Remarks and Observations on Norfolk Island by Major Ross' (c. December 1790), *HRNSW*, vol. 1, part 2, p. 419; Edgars Dunsdorfs, *The Australian Wheat-Growing Industry, 1788–1948* (Melbourne 1956), p. 4.

48 Ross to Grenville, 29 August 1790, *HRNSW*, vol. 1, part 2, pp. 402–3.

49 Hunter, op. cit., p. 179; Paul Langford, *Public Life and the Propertied Englishman, 1689–1798* (Oxford 1991), pp. 104–5.

50 Ross to Phillip, 22 March 1790, and enclosures, *HRNSW*, vol. 1, part 2, pp. 319–23; Paul G. Fidlon and R. J. Ryan (eds), *The Journal and Letters of Lt Ralph Clark, 1787–1792* (Sydney 1981), p. 123.

51 Ross to Grenville, 29 August 1790, and 'Remarks and Observations on Norfolk Island by Major Ross', op. cit., *HRNSW*, vol. 1, part 2, pp. 402–3, 416–20.

52 General Orders at Norfolk Island, 8 January and 9 February 1791, *HRA*, series 1, vol. 1, pp. 241–5.

53 Ibid.; Reg Wright, *The Forgotten Generation of Norfolk Island and Van Diemens Land* (Sydney 1986), pp. 63–5; Reginald Wright, 'Land Usage', in Raymond Nobbs (ed.), *Norfolk Island and its First Settlement, 1788–1814* (Sydney 1988), pp. 115–16.

54 General Order, 9 February 1791, *HRA*, series 1, vol. 1, pp. 243–5.

55 Moore, op. cit., pp. 237–8.

56 Phillip to Sydney, 9 July 1788, *HRNSW*, vol. 1, part 2, p. 154; David Collins, *An Account of the English Colony in New South Wales* (ed. Brian H. Fletcher) (Sydney 1975), vol. 1 (first publ. 1798), p. 60.

57 Trial of John Callaghan (Cullyhorn), 29 July 1789, Judge-Advocate's Bench, NSWSA 1/296; same, 31 July 1789, Court of Criminal Judicature, NSWSA 2391; Collins, op. cit., pp. 60–1; Gillen, op. cit., p. 90.

58 Phillip, 'Instructions for Philip Gidley King, Esq., Superintendant and Commandant of the Settlement of Norfolk Island', 12 February 1788, *HRA*, series 1, vol. 1, p. 34; Alan Atkinson, 'The Free-Born Englishman Transported: Convict Rights as a Measure of Eighteenth-Century Empire', *Past and Present*, no. 144 (August 1994), pp. 108–9.

59 Instructions, op. cit., pp. 14–15.

60 Lord Grenville to Phillip, 19 February 1791, *HRA*, series 1, vol. 1, p. 217; Collins, op. cit., p. 141.

61 Fitzhardinge, op. cit., p. 252; Gillen, op. cit., pp. 43–4.

62 Phillip to Sydney, 9 July 1788, Phillip to Evan Nepean, 9 July, 28 September 1788, Phillip to Grenville, 17 July 1790, *HRA*, series 1, vol. 1, pp. 46, 56, 87, 195.

63 These figures, and those in the following paragraph, depend on a comparison of lists in R. J. Ryan (ed.), *Land Grants, 1788–1809: A Record of Registered Grants and Leases in New South Wales, Van Diemen's Land and Norfolk Island* (Sydney 1981), and Wright, *The Forgotten Generation*, p. 68. For the permanence or otherwise of individual settlers I am indebted to the prodigious work to be found in Gillen (op.

cit.). I have counted only grantees from 1792–94 who were still on their land in 1796. Nearly all were there for much longer.

64   King to Phillip, 17 November 1791, ML C187; King to Evan Nepean, 23 November 1791, *HRNSW*, vol. 1, part 2, p. 562. There were 158 names on the petition, which unfortunately does not survive.

65   Lord Grenville to Phillip, 19 February 1791, *HRA*, series 1, vol. 1, p. 215.

Chapter 5   Argument and Servitude

1   Somerset *v.* Stewart, *English Reports, King's Bench*, vol. 98, p. 510.
2   E. A. Webb, G. W. Miller and J. Beckwith, *The History of Chislehurst, Its Church, Manors, and Parish* (London 1899), p. 175.
3   Quoted in James Walvin, 'Black Slavery in England', *Journal of Caribbean History*, vol. 7 (November 1973), p. 83. See also James Walvin, *Black Ivory: A History of British Slavery* (London 1992), pp. 12–22.
4   Somerset *v.* Stewart, loc. cit., p. 507.
5   Ibid.
6   Ibid., p. 500.
7   George Farquhar, *The Recruiting Officer*, Act II, scene ii, and Act V, scene iii.
8   Daniel Defoe, *Robinson Crusoe*, (Oxford 1928), vol. 2, p. 71, and vol. 3, p. 200.
9   Privy Council, 1822, quoted in Alex C. Castles, *An Australian Legal History* (Sydney 1982), p. 10.
10   *The Tempest*, Act I, scene ii, and Act V, scene i.
11   Its Christian origins are to be found in Paul's Epistle to the Romans.
12   E. P. Thompson, *Witness against the Beast: William Blake and the Moral Law* (Cambridge 1994), pp. 163–4.
13   *The Ordinary of Newgate his Account*, executions on 23 June 1736, pp. 6–7, 17–18, Bodleian Library.
14   28 Edw. III, c. 3; and see also 36 Edw. III, c. 15 (emphasis added).
15   John Smyth of Nibley, *A Description of the Hundred of Berkeley in the County of Gloucester and of its Inhabitants* (1639), quoted in David Rollison, *The Local Origins of Modern Society: Gloucestershire, 1500–1800* (London 1992), p. 247 (and see also Rollison, op. cit., pp. 247–64); Baxter quoted in Christopher Hill, *The World Turned Upside Down*: Radical Ideas During the English Revolution (Harmondsworth 1975), p. 59.
16   Quoted Keith Thomas, *Man and the Natural World: Changing Attitudes in England, 1500–1800* (London 1983), pp. 43–4.
17   Ibid., p. 47; Marcus Rediker, *Between the Devil and the Deep Blue Sea: Merchant Seamen, Pirates, and the Anglo-American Maritime World, 1700–1750* (Cambridge 1993), p. 274.
18   Alan Atkinson, 'The Free-Born Englishman Transported: Convict Rights as a Measure of Eighteenth-Century Empire', *Past and Present*, no. 144 (August 1994), pp. 101–8.
19   Ernest Lee Tuveson, *The Imagination as a Means of Grace: Locke and the Aesthetics of Romanticism* (Berkeley 1960), pp. 51–5; Barbara J. Shapiro, *Probability and Certainty in Seventeenth-Century England: A Study of the Relationships between Natural Science, Religion, History, Law, and Literature* (Princeton 1983), pp. 89–92, 106–7; Karen Halttunen, 'Humanitarianism and the Pornography of Pain in Anglo-American Culture', *American Historical Review*, vol. 100 (1995), pp. 304–7.
20   See, for instance, Nancy Armstrong and Leonard Tennenhouse, 'The Interior Difference: A Brief Genealogy of Dreams, 1650–1717', *Eighteenth-Century Studies*, vol. 23 (1990), pp. 469–71.

21 Reverend Paul Williams, 1678, quoted in T. H. Breen, James Lewis and Keith Schlesinger, 'Motive for Murder: A Servant's Life in Virginia, 1678', *William and Mary Quarterly*, series 3, vol. 40 (1983), p. 120.

22 Dunkin *v.* Revit, deposition, 21 February 1720, HCA 24/133, no. 71; Rediker, op. cit., pp. 270–1.

23 Sir William Blackstone, *Commentaries on the Laws of England* (4 vols, London 1783), vol. 1, p. 129–31; Douglas Hay, 'Property, Authority and the Criminal Law', in Douglas Hay, Peter Linebaugh and E. P. Thompson (eds), *Albion's Fatal Tree* (London 1975), pp. 35–6.

24 J. M. Beattie, 'Scales of Justice: Defense Counsel and the English Criminal Trial in the Eighteenth and Nineteenth Centuries', *Law and History Review*, vol. 9 (1991), pp. 223, 224–6, 231–2. I am grateful to John Beattie for a copy of this paper.

25 Ibid., pp. 226–30, 247–50.

26 *Old Bailey Sessions Papers*, April 1789, p. 483; Thomas R. Forbes, 'A Study of Old Bailey Sentences between 1729 and 1800', *Guildhall Studies in London History*, vol. 5 (1981), pp. 32–3.

27 A suggestion which appears also in Rollison, op. cit., p. 73.

28 *The Ordinary of Newgate his Account*, executions on 3 April 1721, Bodleian Library; ibid., 11 October 1752, pp. 138–9, Bodleian Library.

29 *Legislative Journals of the Council of Colonial Virginia*, vol. 2, pp. 1034–5 (11 April 1749).

30 George B. Worgan, *Journal of a First Fleet Surgeon* (Sydney 1978), p. 54.

31 Phillip to Lord Sydney, 15 May, 9 July 1788, *HRA*, series 1, vol. 1, pp. 19, 46.

32 John Grant, 'Ode on His Majesty's Birth-Day, 1806', ML FM4/1141.

33 David Collins, *An Account of the English Colony in New South Wales* (ed. Brian H. Fletcher) (Sydney 1975), vol. 1 (first publ. 1798), pp. 26, 42, 47.

34 Trial of P. Ryan, 26 July 1789, Judge-Advocate's Bench, NSWSA 1/296; Collins, op. cit., p. 44. The rule about grubbing trees appears, in Captain Campbell's spelling, in John Cobley, *Sydney Cove, 1788* (London 1962), p. 50.

35 'Phillip's Views on the Conduct of the Expedition and the Treatment of the Convicts', [1787], *HRNSW*, vol. 2, part 2, p. 52.

36 'A Description of the Island Lemain . . . ', enclosed with Sydney to Lords of the Treasury, 9 February 1785, T 1/164; Matra's evidence before the Beauchamp committee, 9 May 1785, HO 7/1; Rediker, op. cit., p. 263.

37 Nepean, 'Observations', n.d., August–October 1786, HO 48/1B, f. 565.

38 Speech in the House of Commons, 6 December 1770, *Parliamentary Debates*, vol. 16, cols 1262–3.

39 Nepean to Sydney, 9 November 1786, ML An 53; Alan Atkinson, 'Beating the Bounds with Lord Sydney, Evan Nepean and Others', *Australian Historical Studies*, vol. 25 (1992), p. 218.

40 Alan Atkinson, 'The Free-Born Englishman Transported . . . ', op. cit., p. 108–11.

41 The term 'convict' was not used, except in very rare cases, in any of the courts after February 1788.

42 John Hunter to Lord Sydney, 30 July 1797, Dixson MS Q522; Atkinson, 'The First Plans for Governing New South Wales, 1786–87', *Australian Historical Studies*, vol. 24 (1990), pp. 39–40.

43 'Notes relative to the Act to Settle N.S. Wales', [1786], ML Dixson MS Q522; Nepean, 'Observations', August–October 1786, HO 48/1B, f. 565; C. P. R. Clarke, 'Gibraltar as a British Possession till 1783', BLitt thesis, University of Oxford, 1934, pp. 116–20.

44 Atkinson, 'The First Plans for Governing New South Wales, 1786–87', op. cit., pp. 36–8.

45 Speeches in the House of Commons, 27 November, 6 December 1770, *Parliamentary Debates*, vol. 16, cols 1162–3, 1262–3; John Brewer, 'The Wilkites

and the Law, 1763–74: A Study of Radical Notions of Governance', in John Brewer and John Styles (eds), *An Ungovernable People: The English and their Law in the Seventeenth and Eighteenth Centuries* (London 1983), pp. 155–8.

46   Lord Camden to William Pitt, 29 January 1787, PRO 30/8/119, f. 131.

47   Phillip to Sydney, 16 May 1788, HRA, series 1, vol. 1, p. 35; James Campbell to Robert Ross, 27 April 1789, Ross to Phillip, 6 May 1789, and 'Questions to Officers', 28 May 1789, ibid., pp. 114–19; Collins, op. cit., pp. 8–9; Ellis Bent to Edward Cooke, 7 May 1810, *HRA*, series 4, vol. 1, p. 49; L. F. Fitzhardinge (ed.), *Sydney's First Four Years* (that is, Watkin Tench, *A Narrative of the Expedition to Botany Bay and A Complete Account of the Settlement at Port Jackson*) (Sydney 1979), p. 43; Tench to [?], 1788, in 'An Officer', *An Authentic Journal of the Expedition under Commodore Phillips to Botany Bay* (London 1789), p. 25.

48   W. N. Glascock (1831), quoted in Greg Dening, *Mr Bligh's Bad Language: Passion, Power and Theatre on the Bounty* (Cambridge 1993), p. 115; Arthur N. Gilbert, 'Military and Civilian Justice in Eighteenth-Century England: An Assessment', *Journal of British Studies*, vol. 17 (1978), pp. 51–5; J. M. Beattie, *Crime and the Courts in England, 1660–1800* (Oxford 1986), pp. 462–4.

49   Records of the Court of Criminal Judicature, 1788–97, NSWSA 1147A.

50   Trials of Elizabeth Clark, 27 May 1788, and of Elizabeth Fowles, 25 June 1789, Judge-Advocate's Bench, NSWSA 1/296.

51   Gilbert, op. cit., p. 43.

52   Trial of Ann Martin, 21 August 1788, Judge-Advocate's Bench, NSWSA 1/296; Trial of James Castle, 2 December 1788, of Joseph Elliott (or Trimby), 23 May 1790, and of William Harris and Edward Wildblood, 26 October 1790, Court of Criminal Judicature, NSWSA 1147A.

53   'Phillip's Views on the Conduct of the Expedition and the Treatment of the Convicts', [1787], *HRNSW*, vol. 1, part 2, pp. 52–3.

54   Collins, op. cit., p. 68; Gilbert, op. cit., pp. 53–5. Some, at least, of these are listed with the records of the Judge-Advocate's Bench (NSWSA 1/296), beginning with 13 April 1789. For the Coleby case, see ibid., 14 December 1789. An earlier order, by Ross, appears at 16 March 1789.

55   'Phillip's Views . . . ', op. cit., pp. 52–3; Defoe, op. cit., vol. 2, p. 171; Martin Green, *Dreams of Adventure, Deeds of Empire* (London 1980), pp. 80–1.

56   Phillip to Sydney, 9 July 1788, *HRA*, series 1, vol. 1, p. 57.

57   James Campbell to Lord Ducie, 12 July 1788, in John Cobley, *Sydney Cove, 1788* (London 1962), pp. 192–3; Paul G. Fidlon and R. J. Ryan (eds), *The Journal and Letters of Lt Ralph Clark, 1787–1792* (Sydney 1981), p. 96 (7 February 1788).

58   Trial of Thomas Chadwick, Joshua Peck and John Small, 16 July 1788, Court of Criminal Judicature, NSWSA 1147A.

59   Trial of Elizabeth Clark, 27 May 1788, Judge-Advocate's Bench, NSWSA 1/296.

60   Trial of Ann Smith, Ann Mather, Mary Mitchcraft and Phoebe Flarty, 27 September 1788, Judge-Advocate's Bench, NSWSA 1/296.

61   Trial of Ann Powell, 14 June 1788, ibid.

62   Trial of Henry Abrams, 28 October 1788, ibid.

63   Trial of William Frazer, 5 January 1789, ibid.

64   Trial of Samuel Barsby, 11 February 1788, Court of Criminal Judicature, NSWSA 1147A.

65   Trial of Ann Farmer, 2 August 1788, Judge-Advocate's Bench, NSWSA 1/296; G. A. Steppler, 'British Military Law, Discipline, and the Conduct of Regimental Courts Martial in the Later Eighteenth Century', *English Historical Review*, vol. 102 (October 1987), p. 884.

66   Walter J. Ong, *Interfaces of the Word: Studies in the Evolution of Consciousness and Culture* (Ithaca, N.Y., 1977), p. 113; Walter J. Ong, *Orality and Literacy: The Technologizing of the Word* (London 1982), p. 43–5; Steppler, op. cit., p. 864.

67   Trial of John Callaghan (Cullyhorn), 31 July 1789, Court of Criminal Judicature, NSWSA 1147A.
68   Steppler, op. cit., pp. 866, 867.
69   Judge-Advocate's Bench, 30, 31 March 1791, NSWSA 1/296. Men seem to have been shackled without any official record kept: see John Hunter, *An Historical Journal of the Transactions at Port Jackson and Norfolk Island . . .* (London 1793), p. 133.
70   John Easty, *Memorandum of the Transactions of a Voyage from England to Botany Bay, 1787–1793: A First Fleet Journal* (Sydney 1965), p. 127; Fitzhardinge, op. cit., p. 134.

Chapter 6   Discipline and Cheerfulness

1   Thomas Townshend (Lord Sydney), speech in Parliament, 30 April 1777, *Parliamentary Debates*, vol. 19, col. 208; ibid., 30 April 1781, vol. 22, col. 121; ibid., 8 February 1787, vol. 26, col. 614; ibid.,15 December 1788, vol. 27, col. 681; E. A. Webb, G. W. Miller and J. Beckwith, *The History of Chislehurst, its Church, Manors, and Parish* (London 1899), p. 167.
2   Compare Bernard Bailyn, *The Ideological Origins of the American Revolution* (Cambridge, Mass., 1969), pp. 133–6.
3   Sydney to Lord George Cavendish, 20 May 1785, Townshend Papers, Beinecke Library, Yale University; Sydney to Sir John Wrottesley, 6 November 1785, HO 13/3, f. 239.
4   Keith Thomas, *Man and the Natural World: Changing Attitudes in England, 1500–1800* (London 1983), p. 279.
5   'Distress of a Convict Ordered to Botany Bay', *Push from the Bush*, no. 17 (April 1984), pp. 39–42; David Neal, *The Rule of Law in a Penal Colony: Law and Power in Early New South Wales* (Cambride 1991), pp. 1–4.
6   *Journal of the Commissioners for Trade and Plantations, 1742–9* (London 1931), pp. 392–3, 396–7, 399–403, 405–6, 408; Arnold Zuckerman, 'Scurvy and the Ventilation of Ships in the Royal Navy: Samuel Sutton's Contribution', *Eighteenth-Century Studies*, vol. 10 (1976–7), pp. 229–34; A. Roger Ekirch, *Bound for America: The Transportation of British Convicts to the Colonies, 1718–1775* (Oxford 1987), pp. 104–8.
7   William Paley, *Principles of Moral and Political Philosophy* (Boston 1810), p. 47; Roy Porter, 'Lay Medical Knowledge in the Eighteenth Century: The Evidence of the *Gentleman's Magazine*', *Medical History*, vol. 29 (1985).
8   Christopher Lloyd, 'Cook and Scurvy', *Mariner's Mirror*, vol. 65 (1979), p. 25; Porter, 'Lay Medical Knowledge in the Eighteenth Century . . . ', op. cit.
9   Bernard Smith, *European Vision and the South Pacific* (Oxford 1989), pp. 1–2; Jane Austen, *Emma* (London 1966; first publ. 1816), pp. 296–7; John Paul Jones quoted in Greg Dening, *Mr Bligh's Bad Language: Passion, Power and Theatre on the Bounty* (Cambridge 1993), p. 152.
10   John White, *Journal of a Voyage to New South Wales* (ed. Alec H. Chisholm) (Sydney 1962); first publ. 1790, pp. 48–51; Sir James Watt, 'The Colony's Health', in John Hardy and Alan Frost (eds), *Studies from Terra Australis to Australia* (Canberra 1989), p. 147.
11   White, op. cit., pp. 52, 53–4, 58, 62–3, 65; Watt, op. cit., p. 140.
12   John Nicol, *The Life and Adventures of John Nicol, Mariner* (London 1822), p. 131; White, op. cit., pp. 133, 134, 144, 155; Watt, op. cit., pp. 148–9.
13   Daniel Southwell to Mrs J. Southwell, 4 June 1787, *HRNSW*, vol. 2, p. 671; John C. Dann (ed.), *The Nagle Journal: A Diary of the Life of Jacob Nagle, Sailor, from the Year 1775 to 1841* (New York 1988), p. 85.

14   Captain's log, *Ariadne*, 1781–2, ADM 51/60, and *Europe*, 1783–4, ADM 51/324 (I am grateful to Gillian Hughes for help with this material); Dann, op. cit., p. 85; Dening, op. cit., p. 117.

15   For an example of such record keeping at sea, note the evidence of James Thomas Ricketts, 14 June 1797, before an inquiry convened by Governor Hunter, *HRA*, series 1, vol. 2, p. 41.

16   Phillip to Nepean, 5 July, 28 September 1788, and Phillip to Sydney, 12 February 1790, *HRA*, series 1, vol. 1, pp. 44, 86, 145–6; David Collins, *An Account of the English Colony in New South Wales*, (Sydney 1975), vol. 1 (originally publ. 1798), pp. 7, 68–9.

17   Ross to Philip Stephens, 10 July 1788, *HRNSW*, vol. 1, part 2, pp. 173–4.

18   Phillip to Sydney, 11 April 1790, *HRA*, series 1, vol. 1, p. 167; Collins, op. cit., p. 88.

19   Captain's log, *Europe*, 20 February 1783, ADM 51/324; Marian Aveling (now Quartly), 'Imagining New South Wales as a Gendered Society, 1783–1821', *Australian Historical Studies*, vol. 25 (1992), pp. 5–6. See also Jay Fliegelman, *Declaring Independence: Jefferson, Natural Language, and the Culture of Performance* (Stanford 1993), p. 62.

20   Oliver MacDonagh, *The Inspector General: Sir Jeremiah Fitzpatrick and the Politics of Social Reform, 1783–1802* (London 1981), pp. 42–83, and quotation p. 119.

21   G. C. Bolton, 'William Eden and the Convicts, 1771–1787', *Australian Journal of Politics and History*, vol. 26 (1980); Dan Byrnes, '"Emptying the Hulks": Duncan Campbell and the First Three Fleets to Australia', *Push from the Bush*, no. 24 (April 1987), pp. 5–6.

22   Wilfrid Oldham, *Britain's Convicts to the Colonies* (Sydney 1990), pp. 36–46; Alan Frost, *Botany Bay Mirages: Illusions of Australia's Convict Beginnings* (Melbourne 1994), pp. 21–39.

23   Phillip to Sydney, 16 May, 30 October 1788, *HRA*, series 1, vol. 1, pp. 34–5, 96–7. See also Phillip to Evan Nepean, 4 January 1787, *HRNSW*, vol. 1, part 2, p. 45.

24   Alan Frost, *Arthur Phillip, 1738–1814: His Voyaging* (Melbourne 1987), pp. 111–12.

25   'Extract from the Journal of Capt. Arthur Phillip', n.d., Sydney Papers, vol. 17, William Clements Library, University of Michigan; Frost, *Arthur Phillip*, pp. 86–90.

26   Phillip to W. W. Grenville, 14 June 1790, *HRA*, series 1, vol. 1, pp. 175–6.

27   Jean-Jacques Rousseau, *A Treatise on the Social Compact; or the Principles of Politic Law* (that is, *The Social Contract*) (London 1764), p. 67.

28   'Phillip's Views of the Conduct of the Expedition and the Treatment of Convicts' [April 1787?], *HRNSW*, vol. 1, part 2, p. 55.

29   William Paley, *The Principles of Moral and Political Philosophy* (Boston 1810), p. 374.

30   Trial of John Bennett, 29 April 1788, and of Cornelius Harragan and William Russell, 12 September 1789, Judge-Advocate's Bench, NSWSA 1/296; Collins, op. cit., pp. 13, 23–4; Marcus Rediker, *Between the Devil and the Deep Blue Sea: Merchant Seamen, Pirates, and the Anglo-American Maritime World, 1700–1750* (Cambridge 1993), p. 244.

31   Trial of Cornelius Harragan and William Russell, 12 September 1789, Judge-Advocate's Bench, NSWSA 1/296; Collins, op. cit., pp. liv–lv, 153; Paul G. Fidlon and R. J. Ryan (eds), *The Journal and Letters of Lt. Ralph Clark, 1787–1792* (Sydney 1981), p. 12; Rediker, op. cit., pp. 246–8.

32   Mollie Gillen, *The Founders of Australia: A Biographical Dictionary of the First Fleet* (Sydney 1989), p. 446. Peter Linebaugh says that 'About a quarter of those hanged at Tyburn in the first half of the eighteenth century belonged to the "deep-sea

proletariat"', or in other words were seamen: 'The Tyburn Riot against the Surgeons', in Douglas Hay, Peter Linebaugh and E. P. Thompson (eds), *Albion's Fatal Tree: Crime and Society in Eighteenth-Century England* (London 1975), p. 85.

33   Trial of John Cullyhorn (Callaghan), 29 July 1789, and of William Parish, 8 January 1792, Judge-Advocate's Bench, NSWSA 1/296; John Easty, *Memorandum of the Transactions of a Voyage from England to Botany Bay, 1787–1793: A First Fleet Journal* (Sydney 1965), p. 79.

34   Trial of William Bryant, 4 February 1789, and of James Bird, 26 July 1789, ibid.; L. F. Fitzhardinge (ed.), *Sydney's First Four Years* (that is, Watkin Tench, *A Narrative of the Expedition to Botany Bay and A Complete Account of the Settlement at Port Jackson*), (Sydney 1979), pp. 219–20; Collins, op. cit., pp. 76, 86, 128–30.

35   Phillip to Lord Grenville, 5 November 1791, *HRA*, series 1, vol. 1, p. 269; Collins, op. cit., pp. 69, 549.

36   Fitzhardinge, op. cit., pp. 250, 257; Gillen, pp. 221, 302. Lisk had also been a watchmaker.

37   Trial of Richard Knight, 31 March 1790, Court of Criminal Judicature, NSWSA 1147A.

38   Collins, op. cit., p. 4.

39   Trial of Henry Wright, 10 September 1789, Court of Criminal Judicature, NSWSA 1147A; Collins, op. cit., p. 47.

40   Trials of James Stow and of Frederick Meredith, both 22 February 1788, and of George Clare, 20 June 1789, all Judge-Advocate's Bench, NSWSA 1/296; Paul G. Fidlon and R. J. Ryan (eds), *The Journal of Arthur Bowes Smyth: Surgeon, Lady Penrhyn, 1787–1789* (Sydney 1979), p. 74.

41   Trial of Thomas Hill, and of Thomas Cole, both 11 February 1788, Court of Criminal Judicature, NSWSA 1147A; trial of George Legge, 9 January 1789, Judge-Advocate's Bench, NSWSA 1/296; trial of John Boyle and Thomas Pritchard, 20 June 1789, ibid. See also the trial of James Price, Anthony and Elizabeth Rope and Samuel Day, 2 June 1788, Court of Criminal Judicature, NSWSA 1147A, the trial of Thomas Eccles, 20 September 1788, and of James Brown, 17 January 1789, both Judge-Advocate's Bench, NSWSA 1/296.

42   Fidlon and Ryan, *The Journal of Arthur Bowes Smyth*, p. 68.

43   Trial of John Cullyhorn (Callaghan), 31 July 1789, Court of Criminal Judicature, NSWSA 1147A.

44   Complaint of Henry and Susannah Cable (rough minutes), 1, 2, 5 July 1788, Court of Civil Judicature, NSWSA 2/8147; White, op. cit., p. 149.

Part 2

1   Ronald M. Berndt and Catherine H. Berndt, *The Speaking Land: Myth and Story in Aboriginal Australia* (Ringwood, Vic., 1989), pp. 199–200.

Chapter 7 Men and Women

1   Edmund Burke, *A Philosophical Enquiry into the Origin of our Ideas of the Sublime and Beautiful* (ed. James T. Boulton) (London 1987), p. 67; *1811 Dictionary of the Vulgar Tongue: A Dictionary of Buckish Slang, University Wit, and Pickpocket Eloquence* (facsimile, foreword by Max Harris) (London 1981); Eric Partridge, *The Penguin Dictionary of Historical Slang* (abridged by Jacqueline Simpson) (Harmondsworth 1972).

2   Trial of James Baker, Luke Haines, Richard Askew and Richard Dukes, 17 November 1788, Court of Criminal Judicature, NSWSA 1147A.

3   Kathleen Wilson, 'Empire of Virtue: The Imperial Project and Honoverian Virtue *c.* 1720–1785', in Lawrence Stone (ed.), *An Imperial State at War: Britain from 1689 to 1815* (London 1994), pp. 139–41. The quotation from *The Recruiting Officer* is from Act I, scene i, ll. 218–20.

4   Trial of John Russell, 12 January 1789, Judge-Advocate's Bench, NSWSA 1/296.

5   John Cleland, quoted in Paul Langford, *Public Life and the Propertied Englishman, 1689–1798* (Oxford 1991), p. 6.

6   Mollie Gillen, *The Founders of Australia: A Biographical Dictionary of the First Fleet* (Sydney 1989), pp. 85, 224, 319, 559. I am here relying, to a considerable degree, on Miriam Dixson's understanding of control within gender relations: Miriam Dixson, *The Real Matilda* (Ringwood, Vic., 1994), especially pp. 274–8.

7   Roger Schofield, 'Dimensions of Illiteracy, 1750–1850', *Explorations in Economic History*, vol. 10 (1972–3), p. 446; Barry Reay, 'The Context and Meaning of Popular Literacy: Some Evidence from Nineteenth-Century Rural England', *Past and Present*, no. 131 (May 1991), pp. 93–6; Bethia Penglase, '1788: That Illiterate "Freight of Misery"?', *Journal of the Royal Australian Historical Society*, vol. 75 (1989), pp. 101–7.

8   Anne K. Mellor, 'Joanna Baillie and the Counter-Public Sphere', *Studies in Romanticism*, vol. 13 (1994), p. 560.

9   Anon., review of *Sermons* 'written by a Lady [that is, Rachael Roberts]', *Monthly Review*, July 1770, p. 79. I am indebted to Ludmilla Jordanova for this reference.

10 L. F. Fitzhardinge (ed.), *Sydney's First Four Years* (that is, Watkin Tench, *A Narrative of the Expedition to Botany Bay and A Complete Account of the Settlement at Port Jackson*) (Sydney 1979), pp. 11–12, 61–2.

11 'Letter from a Female Convict', 14 November 1788, *HRNSW*, vol. 2, pp. 746–7.

12 'Voyage of the Lady Juliana. Extract from a letter by one of the female convicts transported in the Lady Juliana', 24 July 1790, *HRNSW*, vol. 2, p. 767.

13 Fitzhardinge , op. cit., p. 137.

14 'A Convict's Letter. Extract of a letter from a young man at Port Jackson to Mr Thomas Olds, of James-street, Oxford Road', 9 April 1790, *HRNSW*, vol. 2, pp. 758–9.

15 Adjudication of the complaint of John Fuller, 29 May 1790, Judge-Advocate's Bench, NSWSA 1/296. See also Alan Frost, *Botany Bay Mirages: Illusions of Australia's Convict Beginnings* (Melbourne 1994), pp. 92–4.

16 Trial of Hannah Pugh, 15 August 1789, ibid.; Trial of Henry Wright, 10 September 1789, Court of Criminal Judicature, NSWSA 1147A.

17 *The Way of the World,* Act IV, scene x. Gabriel de Foigny's book has been republished (trans. and ed. David Fausett) as *The Southern Land, Known*, (Syracuse, N.Y., 1993).

18 Jonathan Swift, *Gulliver's Travels* (London 1960), pp. 297–8 (original emphasis).

19 Daniel Defoe, *Robinson Crusoe* (Oxford 1928), vol. 2, pp. 221–2, and vol. 3, pp. 29–30; Louis James, 'From Robinson to Robina, and beyond: *Robinson Crusoe* as a Utopian Concept', in Krishan Kumar and Stephen Bann (eds), *Utopias and the Millenium* (London 1993), p. 37.

20 'James Maria Matra's Proposal', 23 August 1783, *HRNSW*, vol. 1, part 2, p. 3; Governor Phillip's Instructions, 25 April 1787, *HRA*, series 1, vol. 1, p. 14.

21 Defoe, op. cit., vol. 3, p. 29; Joan Wallach Scott, 'French Feminists and the Rights of "Man": Olympe de Gouges's Declarations', *History Workshop*, issue 28 (Autumn 1989), p. 5.

22 Arthur Phillip to Lord Sydney, 15 May 1788, *HRA*, series 1, vol. 1, p. 23.

23 'Phillip's Views on the Conduct of the Expedition and the Treatment of Convicts', 1787, *HRNSW*, vol. 1, part 2, pp. 51, 52; George B. Worgan, *Journal of a First Fleet Surgeon* (Sydney 1978), p. 36.

24   Paul G. Fidlon and R. J. Ryan (eds), *The Journal of Arthur Bowes Smyth: Surgeon, Lady Penrhyn, 1787–1789* (Sydney 1979), p. 66.

25   'Distress of a Convict Ordered to Botany Bay', *Push from the Bush*, no. 17 (April 1984), pp. 39–42.

26   Gillen, op. cit., pp. 47–8, 60, 169 (William Haynes), 276 (William Parr).

27   *The Ordinary of Newgate his Account*, executions on 18 March 1740, p. 8, Bodleian Library; Ibid., 14 September 1741, pp. 4, 16–17, Bodleian Library; John Nicol, *The Life and Adventures of John Nicol, Mariner* (London 1822), p. 73; David Collins, *An Account of the English Colony in New South Wales* (ed. Brian H. Fletcher) (Sydney 1975), vol. 1 (first publ. 1798), p. 14.

28   Trial of John Leary, 8 August 1789, Judge-Advocate's Bench, NSWSA 1/296; Charles Peat to John Sullivan, 26 July 1802, CO 201/24, f. 43; Gillen, op. cit., pp. 189–90, 216.

29   Trial of Joseph Marshall and William Bell, 21 July 1788, Judge-Advocate's Bench, NSWSA 1/296; Collins, op. cit., p. 14; Worgan, op. cit., p. 25; Gillen, op. cit., pp. 256–7, 280.

30   Defoe, op. cit., vol. 2, pp. 192–3. The quotations are taken, loosely, from Proverbs 10:4 and 24: 30–1.

31   I am here relying on the list which appears in 'An Account of the Sows and Supplies delivered to the Convicts of Norfolk Island for their Own Support . . . Commencing the 5th day of February 1791', CO 201/9, ff. 31–40.

32   Gillen, op. cit., pp. 116, 257, 280, 348.

33   Trial of Samuel Barsby, – February 1788, and of John Hayes, 11 August 1789, Judge-Advocate's Bench, NSWSA 1/296; Gillen, op. cit., p. 102.

34   Trial of John Boyle, 2 November 1789, Judge-Advocate's Bench, NSWSA 1/296.

35   Trial of Elizabeth Mason, 29 August 1789, ibid.; Gillen, op. cit., p. 128.

36   Trial of William Boggis, 13 September 1788, Judge-Advocate's Bench, NSWSA 1/296.

37   Trial of Elizabeth Clark, 27 May 1788, ibid.

38   Trial of Mary Davis, 27 September 1788, ibid.

39   Evidence of Samuel Babey, in the case of Zachariah Clark, 25–26 March 1802, CO 201/29, f. 284. This inquiry was a special case and as such does not contradict my argument, because Clark was accused of incest, the woman being his daughter.

40   Exceptions can be seen in cases of gang rape and where the victim was a child. See the trial of Henry Wright, 10 September 1789, Court of Criminal Judicature, NSWSA 1147A; trials of Joseph Marshall and others, 15 March, 22 April 1795 (the same offence, called rape in the first trial and assault in the second), and trial of William Merchant and others, 7 November 1795 (clearly rape but tried as assault, probably through experience gained in the earlier case), both Court of Criminal Judicature, NSWSA 1147B. See also Michel Foucault, *The History of Sexuality*, vol. 12 (London 1979), pp. 24–7; Doris Sommer, 'Love and Country in Latin America: an Allegorical Speculation', in Marjorie Ringrose and Adam J. Lerner (eds), *Reimagining the Nation* (Buckingham 1993); Roy Porter and Lesley Hall, *The Facts of Life: The Creation of Sexual Knowledge in Britain, 1650–1950* (New Haven 1995), p. 117.

41   Mary Beth Norton, *Liberty's Daughters: The Revolutionary Experience of American Women, 1750–1800* (Boston 1980); Elizabeth Colwill, 'Just Another *Citoyenne*? Marie-Antoinette on Trial, 1790–1793', *History Workshop*, issue 28 (Autumn 1989), pp. 63 (the quotation), 74–5; Dena Goodman, 'Public Sphere and Private Life: Towards a Synthesis of Current Historiographical Approaches to the Old Regime', *History and Theory*, vol. 31 (1992), pp. 14–20; Barbara Clark Smith, 'Food Rioters and the American Revolution', *William and Mary Quarterly*, series 3, vol. 51 (1994).

42   Collins, op. cit., p. 69.

43   Michael Roberts, 'Sickles and Scythes: Women's Work and Men's Work at Harvest Time', *History Workshop*, issue 7 (Spring 1979); K. D. M. Snell, *Annals of the Labouring Poor: Social Change and Agrarian England, 1660–1900* (Cambridge 1987), pp. 15–66, 155–8; Alan Frost, *Arthur Phillip, 1738–1814: His Voyaging* (Melbourne 1988), p. 51; Phillip to W. W. Grenville, 17 July 1790, *HRA*, series 1, vol. 1, p. 194.

44   See, for instance, the quarrel between Lieutenant Charles Ingles and Acting-Lieutenant Alexander Forsyth, both of H.M.S. *Buffalo*, in King to Sir Evan Nepean, 29 March 1803, and enclosures, *HRA*, series 1, vol. 4, pp. 53–9.

45   Compare, for instance, the burglary trial of John Bevan, 14 July 1794, and of Abraham Whitehouse and others, 7 November 1795 (both Court of Criminal Judicature, NSWSA 1147A and 1147B respectively), in which the victims were married and all the property, including women's and children's clothes, was described as the husband's, with the trial of John Pierson and Samuel Lunt, 12 February 1794, of John Flemming, 14 July 1794 (both NSWSA 1147A), and of John Rayner, 22 April 1795 (NSWSA 1147B), in which the victims were only cohabiting and in which a clear distinction is made between the property of men and women. See also the trial of William Smith, 19 May 1791, Judge-Advocate's Bench, NSWSA 1/296. For more on boxes, see Paula J. Byrne, *Criminal Law and Colonial Subject: New South Wales, 1810–1830* (Cambridge 1993), p. 83.

46   Sir Jeremiah (here called John) Fitzpatrick to A. Graham, 26 January 1802, *HRA*, series 1, vol. 3, pp. 372; Oliver MacDonagh, *The Inspector General: Sir Jeremiah Fitzpatrick and the Politics of Social Reform, 1783–1802* (London 1981), pp. 257–67, 269.

47   Deposition of Sarah Bellamy, 15 August 1789, Judge-Advocate's Bench, NSWSA 1/296.

48   Trial of Ann Farmer, 21 August 1788, complaint of Deborah Herbert, 5 December 1788, trial of John Leary, 8 August 1789, memorandum of 24 October 1789, and trial of Andrew Roman, 25 January 1791, ibid.

49   Frederick Bernays Wiener, *Civilians Under Military Justice: The British Practice since 1689 Especially in North America* (Chicago 1967), pp. 83, 89; 'Coxheath Camp. A Novel in a series of letters by a Lady', (1779), quoted Charles Herbert, 'Coxheath Camp, 1778–1779', *Journal of the Society for Army Historical Research*, vols 45–6 (1967), p. 146.

50   Fidlon and Ryan, op. cit., pp. 27, 29–30.

51   'Voyage of the Lady Juliana. Extract from a letter by one of the female convicts transported in the Lady Juliana', 24 July 1790, *HRNSW*, vol. 2, p. 767. The good treatment of convicts on this ship is mentioned also in Nicol, op. cit., pp. 110, 126.

52   Fitzhardinge, op. cit., p. 251.

53   Ibid.; John Hunter, *An Historical Journal of the Transactions at Port Jackson and Norfolk Island* (London 1793), p. 537.

54   Trial of William Parish, 9 January 1792, Judge-Advocate's Bench, NSWSA 1/296. I am here assuming that a word in the manuscript record of the trial which looks like 'buch' refers to buchu, a medicinal herb found at the Cape of Good Hope. For Kelly, see also Hunter to Duke of Portland, 25 July 1798, *HRA*, series 1, vol. 2, pp. 172–3.

55   Trial of William Parish, 9 January 1792, Judge-Advocate's Bench, NSWSA 1/296.

56   Trial of James Bird, 26 July 1789, Judge-Advocate's Bench, NSWSA 1/296; Hunter, op. cit., p. 457; Collins, op. cit., pp. 23, 179; John White, *Journal of a Voyage to New South Wales* (ed. Alec H. Chisholm) (Sydney 1962; first publ. 1790), pp. 113–14.

57   Collins, op. cit., p. 15; J. W. Price, 'A Journal kept on board the Minerva Transport from Ireland to New South Wales', 12 February 1800, BL Add. Mss 13,880, f. 80.

58   'A Convict's Letter. Extract of a letter from a young man at Port Jackson to Mr Thomas Olds, of James-street, Oxford Road', 9 April 1790, *HRNSW*, vol. 2, p. 758.

59   Johnson's notes on his grievances, 6 August 1794, pp. 14–15, Lambeth Palace Library, Arch/P/Moore 22; Collins, op. cit., p. 98. See also Reverend John Newton to Sir Charles Middleton, 7 December 1786, Wilberforce Papers, Rosemary House, Catterick, Yorkshire.
60   Samuel Marsden to [William Wilberforce?], 4 May 1794, Lambeth Palace Library, Arch/P/Moore 22.
61   John Gardiner (first lieutenant, R.N.), 'Voyage of the "Gorgon" to Australia, Capt. John Parker', ML Doc. 1176, pp. 22–4; Note on James Baine [sic], *The Matriculation Albums of the University of Glasgow, from 1728 to 1858* (Glasgow 1913), entry no. 2403.
62   Johnson's notes on his grievances, 6 August 1794, pp. 34–6; Johnson to John Hunter, 5 July 1798, in Mackaness, op. cit., p. 25.
63   Bain to [William Morice?], January, 13 February 1790, and Morice to Bain, 30 January 1790, A3584. Bain's grandfather had been Professor of Divinity at the University of Glasgow, and his father was a Presbyterian minister eminent enough to listed in the *Dictionary of National Biography* (vol. 1, pp. 909–10). Bain himself was later honoured with a doctorate in law from Aberdeen: *Scots Magazine*, vol. 92, part 2 (1823), p. 640; *Fasti Ecclesiae Scoticanae*, vol. 3 (Edinburgh 1920), pp. 171–2. (I owe this last reference to Mr Stuart Allan of the Scottish Record Office.)
64   Evidence of William Richardson, Johnson to Secretary of the Society for the Propagation of the Gospel, 6 December 1794, and Johnson's rules for the Sydney school, 1798, in Mackaness, op. cit., part 2, pp. 9–10, 31; John F. Cleverley, *The First Generation: School and Society in Early Australia* (Sydney 1971), pp. 23–6. In 1792 Johnson refers to Isabella Richardson (formerly Rosson) as wholly in charge: Johnson to William Morice, 21 March 1792, ML A3584.
65   Johnson, note dated 6 August 1794, pp. 25–6, Lambeth Palace Papers Arch/P/Moore 22; Johnson to Secretary of the Society for the Propagation of the Gospel, 6 December 1794, précis of Johnson to Secretary of the Society for the Propagation of the Gospel, 31 August 1798, Johnson's rules for the Sydney school, 1798, and Johnson to William Morice, 21 September 1799, in Mackaness, op. cit., part 2, pp. 28, 29–32, 42; Evidence of George Johnston, 13 April 1812, before the House of Commons Select Committee on Transportation, *Parliamentary Papers*, 1812, II, 341, p. 74. See population returns, *HRA*, series 1, vol. 1, pp. 492–3, 598, and vol. 2, pp. 385–6.
66   I am indebted to Trin Truscett's research for these conclusions. They affirm, more or less, the statement in Vernon W. E. Goodin, 'Public Education in New South Wales before 1848', *Journal of the Royal Australian Historical Society*, vol. 36 (1950), pp. 204–5. The period used for both studies is the eleven years 1804–14. Sydney brides numbered (in the Truscett study) 489, and of those, 16 of the 33 native-born signed their own names; only 88 of the 456 born elsewhere could do so. Goodin's conclusions for other parts of the colony (which are much less remarkable) have not been checked.
67   Compare Wendy Brown, 'Finding the Man in the State', *Feminist Studies*, vol. 18 (1992), pp. 7–34.

Chapter 8   Black and White

.1   Jonathan Swift, *Gulliver's Travels* (London 1960), pp. 253–4, 261, 294,
2   L. F. Fitzhardinge (ed.), *Sydney's First Four Years* (that is, Watkin Tench, *A Narrative of the Expedition to Botany Bay and A Complete Account of the Settlement at Port Jackson*), (Sydney 1979), pp. 290–3; David Collins, *An Account of the English Colony in New South Wales* (ed. Brian H. Fletcher) (Sydney 1975), vol. 1 (first publ. 1798), p. 506; Paul G. Fidlon and R. J. Ryan (eds), *The Journal of Arthur*

Bowes Smyth: Surgeon, Lady Penrhyn, *1781–1789* (Sydney 1979), p. 58; Alexandro Malaspina, 'Loose Notes on the English Colony of Port Jackson', in Robert J. King, *The Secret History of the Convict Colony: Alexandro Malaspina's Report on the British Settlement of New South Wales* (Sydney 1990), p. 149.

3   Collins, op. cit., p. 513; Fidlon and Ryan, op. cit., p. 293; Stephen K. Land, *From Signs to Propositions: The Concept of Form in Eighteenth-Century Semantic Theory* (London 1974), pp. 18–19; Bernard Smith, *European Vision and the South Pacific* (Oxford 1989), pp. 41–3.

4   Collins, op. cit., p. 466; Fitzhardinge, op. cit., pp. 293–4; Fidlon and Ryan, op. cit., p. 58.

5   Fitzhardinge, p. 35; Fidlon and Ryan, op. cit., p. 58.

6   Collins, op. cit., pp. 12–13; John White, *Journal of a Voyage to New South Wales* (ed. Alec H. Chisholm) (Sydney 1962; first publ. 1790), p. 113.

7   William Bradley, *A Voyage to New South Wales: The Journal of Lieutenant William Bradley RN of HMS Sirius, 1786–1792* (Sydney 1969), p. 60, 63, 71; Fidlon and Ryan, op. cit., p. 58; Nance Irvine (ed.), *The Sirius Letters: The Complete Letters of Newton Fowell* (Sydney 1988), p. 68; Ann McGrath, 'The White Man's Looking Glass: Aboriginal–Colonial Gender Relations at Port Jackson', *Australian Historical Studies,* vol. 24 (1990), p. 192.

8   George B. Worgan, *Journal of a First Fleet Surgeon* (Sydney 1978), p. 18. See also White, op. cit., p. 153; McGrath, op. cit., p. 189.

9   John Hunter, *An Historical Journal of the Transactions at Port Jackson and Norfolk Island* (London 1793), p. 212; Bradley, op. cit., p. 231.

10   Hunter, op. cit., pp. 132–3; Newton Fowell to John Fowell, 31 July 1790, in Irvine, op. cit., p. 114.

11   Hunter, op. cit., p. 166.

12   Ibid., pp. 205–6, 476; Fitzhardinge, op. cit., p. 160.

13   Collins, op. cit., vol. 1, p. 174; Bradley, op. cit., p. 231.

14   Hunter, op. cit., pp. 206–9; Collins, op. cit., vol. 1, pp. 110–11. Hunter's account seems to have been taken nearly verbatim from a record made by Waterhouse: see Bradley, op. cit., pp. 225–30.

15   The Aborigines' refusal to eat sharks points to their having some kind of spiritual significance: Phillip to Lord Sydney, 28 September 1788, *HRA,* series 1, vol. 1, p. 77. Also, sharks figure largely in stone carvings in the Sydney area: Peter Stanbury and John Clegg, *A Field Guide to Aboriginal Rock Engravings, with special reference to those around Sydney* (Sydney 1990), pp. 118, 119.

16   Hunter, op. cit., p. 56.

17   George Farquhar, *The Recruiting Officer,* Act IV, scene i; White, op. cit., pp. 118, 160.

18   Ranajit Guha, *A Rule of Property for Bengal: An Essay on the Idea of Permanent Settlement* (New Delhi 1981).

19   Governor Phillip's Instructions, 25 April 1787, *HRA,* series 1, vol. 1, p. 14.

20   Lord Halifax to Joseph Otway, Superintendent of the Mosquito Shore, 9 December 1763, and Robert Hodgson's commission as Superintendent of the Mosquito Shore, 31 July 1767, CO 123/1, ff. 31, 33.

21   Bradley, op. cit., p. 142; Fitzhardinge, op. cit., p. 285.

22   Hunter, op. cit., p. 62.

23   Collins, op. cit., p. 452. See Ronald M. Berndt, 'Law and Order in Aboriginal Australia', in Ronald M. Berndt and Catherine H. Berndt (eds), *Aboriginal Man in Australia: Essays in Honour of Emeritus Professor A. P. Elkin* (Sydney 1965), pp. 167–83.

24   Phillip to Sydney, 13 February 1790, *HRA,* series 1, p. 160.

25   John Harris to an unknown correspondent, 20 March 1791, ML A1597.

26   Hunter, op. cit., p. 168; Collins, op. cit., vol. 1, p. 497; Irvine, op. cit., p. 115.

27   Compare Eleanor Dark, *The Timeless Land* (Sydney 1960), p. 48.
28   Marshall Sahlins, *Historical Metaphors and Mythical Realities: Structure in the Early History of the Sandwich Islands Kingdom* (Ann Arbor 1981).
29   Hunter, op. cit., pp. 502, 532; Collins, op. cit., pp. 452–3; Fitzhardinge, op. cit., p. 160.
30   Hunter, op. cit., pp. 480, 508, 512.
31   Fitzhardinge, op. cit., p. 160.
32   Collins, op. cit., pp. 500, 502; Franz Josef Micha, 'Trade and Change in Australian Aboriginal Cultures: Australian Aboriginal Trade as an Expression of Close Culture Contact and as a Mediator of Culture Change', in Arnold R. Pilling and Richard A. Waterman (eds), *Diprotodon to Detribalization: Studies of Change among Australian Aborigines* (East Lansing, Mich., 1970), pp. 289–302; Michael Smithson, 'A Misunderstood Gift: The Annual Issue of Blankets to Aborigines in New South Wales, 1826–48', *Push: A Journal of Early Australian Social History*, no. 30 (1992), pp. 86–9. For a similar, more recent example of adaptation of burial ritual, see Howard Morphy, *Ancestral Connections: Art and an Aboriginal System of Knowledge* (Chicago 1991), pp. 304–5.
33   Hunter, op. cit., p. 545; Bradley, op. cit., p. 231; Fitzhardinge, op. cit. p. 160; Stephen Wild, 'Australian Aboriginal Drama', in A. M. Gibbs (ed.), *Masks of Time: Drama and its Contexts* (Papers from the Australian Academy of the Humanities Symposium 1993) (Canberra 1994), pp. 181–2.
34   Hunter, op. cit., pp. 544–5; Nancy D. Munn, 'The Transformation of Subjects into Objects in Walbiri and Pitjantjara Myth', in Ronald M. Berndt (ed.), *Australian Aboriginal Anthropology: Modern Studies in the Social Anthropology of the Australian Aborigines* (Nedlands, W.A., 1970), p. 146.
35   Hunter, op. cit., pp. 513, 534, 566; Collins, op. cit., pp. 499–501; Fitzhardinge, op. cit., pp. 150, 160.
36   Collins, op. cit., pp. 502–3.
37   Munn, op. cit., p. 149; Morphy, op. cit., pp. 103–5.
38   Matthew Arnold, 'Dover Beach'. See also Richard Sennett, *The Fall of Public Man* (Cambridge 1977), p. 21.
39   *Public Advertiser*, 28 September 1786.
40   Hunter, op. cit., pp. 492, 494–5.
41   Ibid., p. 502.
42   Phillip to Lord Sydney, 15 May 1788, 28 September 1790, *HRA*, series 1, vol. 1, pp. 26, 76; Hunter, op. cit., p. 510; Collins, op. cit., vol. 1, pp. 457–8; White, op. cit., pp. 118, 160; Fitzhardinge, op. cit., pp. 49–50, 230, 277.
43   Hunter, op. cit., p. 475; Collins, op. cit., vol. 1, pp. 485–6, 499; Fitzhardinge, op. cit., p. 290.
44   Hunter, op. cit., p. 475, 480–6.
45   Ibid., pp. 482, 534; Fitzhardinge, op. cit., p. 53; Thomas L. Haskell, 'Capitalism and the Origins of the Humanitarian Sensibility', part 2, *American Historical Review*, vol. 90 (1985), p. 552.
46   Hunter, op. cit., pp. 503, 532–3; Collins, op. cit., vol. 1, pp. 249, 339; 'State of the Settlements . . . ', 31 December 1799, *HRA*, series 1, vol. 2, p. 468; Alexandro Malaspina, 'Loose Notes on the English Colony of Port Jackson', in Robert J. King, op. cit., p. 148.
47   Bradley, op. cit., pp. 98–9.
48   Fitzhardinge, op. cit., pp. 282, 284.
49   Hunter, op. cit., p. 476, 480, 545; Newton Fowell to John Fowell, 31 July 1790, in Irvine, op. cit., p. 114.
50   Hunter, op. cit., pp. 139–41.
51   William Wordsworth, 'The Prelude', book 9, ll. 517–19, 531–2.

52 Diary of Richard Atkins, 12 February 1795, NL MS 4039.
53 Alan Atkinson, 'A New John Macarthur', *Push from the Bush*, no. 17 (April 1984), p. 49; Robert J. King, op. cit., pp. 74–5, and Alexandro Malaspina, 'A Political Examination of the English Colonies in the Pacific', ibid., p. 106.
54 William Macarthur, 'A few Memoranda respecting the aboriginal Natives', (1835?), ML A2935, pp. 171–82. See also Alan Atkinson, *Camden: Farm and Village Life in Early New South Wales* (Melbourne 1988), p. 228.
55 D. D. Mann, *The Present Picture of New South Wales* (London 1811), p. 47.
56 Hobbles Danayari, quoted in Deborah Bird Rose, 'The Saga of Captain Cook: 'Morality in Aboriginal and European Law', *Australian Aboriginal Studies*, vol. 2 (1984), pp. 31–4; Tim Rowse, 'Mabo and Moral Community', *Meanjin*, vol. 52 (1993), pp. 229–32. Paul Keating, speaking as Prime Minister in 1993, referred to Cook 'establishing a settlement in Australia': *Sydney Morning Herald*, 11 June 1993, p. 1.
57 Trial of William Millar and Thomas Bevan, 9 October 1797, Court of Criminal Judicature, NSWSA 1147B, pp. 353–4; Trial of James Daily, 1 October 1805, and of John William Lancashire, 4 January 1806, Court of Criminal Judicature, NSWSA 5/1149, pp. 241d, 253.
58 Trial of Thomas Hewitt, 1 February 1799, NSWSA X905, p. 68.
59 Hunter to Duke of Portland, 2 January 1800, and enclosed transcript of the trial of Edward Powell, Simon Freebody, James Metcalfe, William Timms and William Butler, 14–18 October 1799, *HRA*, series 1, vol. 2, pp. 401–22; Collins, op. cit., vol. 2, pp. 200–1, 279–80.
60 Lord Hobart to King, 30 January 1802, King's proclamation, 30 June 1802, and King's 'Regulations to be observed By the Commanders of English or Foreign Merchant Vessels, arriving in Port Jackson; and by all Merchants, Importers, and Consignees, resident in His Majesty's Territory called New South Wales', 10 October 1802, *HRA*, series 1, vol. 3, pp. 366–7, 592–3, 714.
61 King to Hobart, 9 May 1803, *HRA*, series 1, vol. 4, p. 73.
62 Collins, op. cit., vol. 2, pp. 20, 24, 25–6.
63 Ibid., p. 70; King to Hobart, 30 October 1802, *HRA*, series 1, vol. 3, pp. 582–3.
64 'Judge-Advocate Atkins' Opinion on the Treatment of Natives', 8 July 1805, *HRA*, series 1, vol. 5, pp. 502–4.
65 See, for example, 22 Geo. II, c. 13: William Waller Hening (ed.), *The Statutes at Large; Being a Collection of all the Laws of Virginia* (Richmond, Va, Philadelphia and New York, 1809–23), vol. 5, pp. 546–7. For 'whanga' see Paula J. Byrne, *Criminal Law and Colonial Subject: New South Wales, 1810–1830* (Cambridge 1993), p. 271. 'Murry', meaning 'great', similarly appears in a report of the trial of John Gould, *Sydney Gazette*, 7 March 1811.
66 For the number of Blacks arriving during the convict period, see Mollie Gillen, *The Founders of Australia: A Biographical Dictionary of the First Fleet* (Sydney 1989), p. 424; Ian Duffield, 'Martin Beck and Afro-Blacks in Colonial Australia', *Journal of Australian Studies*, no. 16 (May 1985), pp. 9–10.
67 Macarthur, op. cit., pp. 171–4.
68 *Sydney Gazette*, 19 May, 4 August 1805, 3 September, 1 October 1809, 24 February, 17 March 1810; Macarthur, op. cit., p. 174.

Chapter 9 God and Humanity

1 *Old Bailey Sessions Papers*, 7 July 1784, p. 877–8.
2 L. F. Fitzhardinge (ed.), *Sydney's First Four Years* (that is, Watkin Tench, *A Narrative of the Expedition to Botany Bay and A Complete Account of the Settlement at Port Jackson*) (Sydney 1979), p. 256. One Christopher Magee had been sentenced

to transportation at the Middlesex Quarter Sessions, 6 September 1773: Greater London Record Office, Indictments MJ/SBP 18/387, and Sessions Book MJ/SBB 1275 (I am grateful to Gillian Hughes for this research).

3   Trial of Richard Sutton, *Old Bailey Sessions Papers*, 16 February 1791, pp. 228-9; Trial of Richard Sutton, 15 October 1792, Court of Criminal Judicature, NSWSA 1147A; John Masefield, *Sea Life in Nelson's Time* (London 1905), p. 101; Michael Lewis, *A Social History of the Navy, 1793-1815* (London 1960), p. 105.

4   Trial of Richard Sutton, 15 October 1792, Court of Criminal Judicature, NSWSA 1147A.

5   David Collins, *An Account of the English Colony in New South Wales* (ed. Brian H. Fletcher) (Sydney 1975; first publ. 1798), vol. 1 pp. 201-2.

6   Christopher Hill, *The World Turned Upside Down: Radical Ideas during the English Revolution* (Harmondsworth 1975); Marcus Rediker, *Between the Devil and the Deep Blue Sea: Merchant Seamen, Pirates, and the Anglo-American Maritime World, 1700-1750* (Cambridge 1989), pp. 172-86.

7   Untitled paper [1811?], with information apparently from Reverend Henry Fulton, among documents relating to Lt-Col. George Johnston's court martial, WO 72/35.

8   Collins, op. cit., vol. 1, p. 223.

9   Ibid., pp. 285, 338-9; Brian Fletcher, 'Grose, Paterson and the Settlement of the Hawkesbury, 1794-1795', *Journal of the Royal Australian Historical Society*, vol. 51 (1965). See also the Journal of Richard Atkins, 12 May 1794, NL MS 4039.

10   Hunter to Duke of Portland, 20 June 1797, *HRA*, series 1, vol. 2, p. 23 (the original is in italics).

11   Francis Grose to Henry Dundas, 29 April 1794, *HRA*, series 1, vol. 1, p. 470; Collins, op. cit., vol. 1, pp. 347, 388, 394, 395.

12   Lewis Rose Macleod, *The Northern Suburbs of Today* (Sydney 1903), p. 12. Although Gore and his wife Ann seem to have had four children born in New South Wales, there is no record of any being christened, nor do any family burials appear in the church registers, though Gore announced both births and deaths in the press. His wife died in 1833 and he in 1845. The daughter was probably Ann Stanhope Gore, died 1836.

13   David Collins to King, 15 May 1804, *HRA*, series 3, vol. 1, p. 238.

14   Collins, op. cit., vol. 1, pp. 171, 223; Alan Atkinson, 'Isaac Transported', *Labour History*, no. 50 (May 1986), p. 50.

15   Collins, op. cit., vol. 1, pp. 96, 192, 268, 330, 388.

16   Trial of Mary Pawson, 20 July 1795, Court of Criminal Judicature, NSWSA 1147B; Collins, op. cit., vol. 1, p. 354; Michael Flynn, *The Second Fleet: Britain's Grim Convict Armada of 1790* (Sydney 1993), p. 471.

17   Indictment of James Ruse, [between 6 February 1796 and July 1798], Court of Criminal Judicature, NSWSA 1145, p. 5. See also Jan Barkley and Michelle Nichols, *Hawkesbury, 1794-1994: The First 200 Years of the Second Colonisation* (Windsor, N.S.W, 1994), pp. 85-7.

18   Transcript of the trial of Edward Powell, Simon Freebody, James Metcalfe, William Timms and William Butler, 14-18 October 1799, *HRA*, series 1, vol. 2, p. 405; Barkley and Nichols, op. cit., p. 87.

19   'An Essay on the present State of Music among the Common People, and the Influence of Bad Music on their Morals', *Monthly Miscellany*, February 1774, pp. 54-5.

20   The full list appears in Neil K. Macintosh, *Richard Johnson, Chaplain to the Colony of New South Wales: His Life and Times, 1755-1827* (Sydney 1978), pp. 105-6 (but with some mis-spellings).

21   Richard D. Altick, *The English Common Reader: A Social History of the Mass Reading Public, 1800-1900* (Chicago 1957), pp. 99-108.

22   Richard Johnson to Henry Fricker, 30 May 1787, in George Mackaness (ed.), *Some Letters of Rev. Richard Johnson, B.A. First Chaplain of New South Wales* (Sydney 1954), part 1, pp. 12–13; Richard Johnson, *An Address to the Inhabitants of the Colonies established in New South Wales and Norfolk Island* (London 1794), pp. 17–18, 45–6, 56–7.

23   Ibid., pp. iv, 72.

24   Richard Johnson to Henry Fricker, 30 May 1787, 15 November 1788, 9 April 1790, 4 October 1791, in Mackaness, op. cit., part 1, pp. 13, 24, 29, 41, 42; Henry Foster to Samuel Marsden, 10 June 1794, ML A1992, p. 3; Collins, op. cit., vol. 1, pp. 99, 328. And see Psalm 51.

25   Johnson to Secretary of the Society for the Propagation of the Gospel, 6 December 1794, and Johnson to Fricker, 4 October 1791, 15 August 1797, in Mackaness, op. cit., part 1, p. 41, and part 2, pp. 9–10, 19; Johnson, op. cit., p. 46; Johnson to Arthur Phillip, 29 February 1792, *HRNSW*, vol. 1, part 2, p. 594; Johnson to Francis Grose, 12 November 1793, Lambeth Palace Papers Arch/P/Moore 22; Evidence of William Richardson, 20 March 1812, before the House of Commons Select Committee on Transportation, *Parliamentary Papers*, 1812, II, 341, p. 57.

26   Johnson's statement of grievances, 16 April 1794, pp. 3–10, Lambeth Palace Papers Arch/P/Moore 22; Johnson to John Hunter, 5 July 1798, *HRA*, series 1, vol. 2, pp. 178–9; R. J. B. Knight and Alan Frost (eds), *The Journal of Daniel Paine, 1794–1797* (Sydney 1983), p. 34. See also Johnson, note dated 6 August 1794, p. 19, Lambeth Palace Papers Arch/P/Moore 22.

27   Johnson's evidence, 25 March 1812, p. 67; Janice Ruse Israel, *'My Mother Reread Me Tenderley': The Life of James Ruse* (Sydney 1988), pp. 10, 53, 66. I rely here also on the reconstitution of Hawkesbury families which appears in the three volumes of C. J. Smee and J. Selkirk Provis, *The 1788–1820 Association's Pioneer Register* (Sydney 1981, 1983, 1987).

28   Johnson's statement of injustices, op. cit., pp. 9–10; John Easty, *Memorandum of the Transactions of a Voyage from England to Botany Bay, 1787–1793: A First Fleet Journal* (Sydney 1965), p. 144.

29   Johnson's statement of grievances, op. cit., p. 18. A plan of the building appears in Macintosh, op. cit., facing p. 81.

30   Johnson to Henry Moore Archbishop of Canterbury, 8 May 1793, quoted Macintosh, op. cit., p. 72.

31   Macintosh, op. cit., pp. 86–7.

32   Johnson, op. cit., pp. 39, 72; 'Extracts from the Rev. Mr Johnson's Copious Journal of Events at New South Wales', in Macintosh, op. cit., p. 107.

33   Johnson, op. cit., p. 39; Johnson to Moore, 8 May 1793, Lambeth Palace Papers Arch/P/Moore 22.

34   Quoted Tony Swain, *A Place for Strangers: Towards a History of Australian Aboriginal Being* (Cambridge 1993), p. 114.

35   Eleanor Dark, *The Timeless Land* (Sydney 1960), p. 50.

36   Daniel Southwell to Reverend W. Butler, 14 April 1790, *HRNSW*, vol. 2, pp. 709–10; John Hunter, *An Historical Journal of the Transactions at Port Jackson and Norfolk Island* (London 1793), p. 205.

37   Johnson to Fricker, 9 April 1790, in Mackaness, op. cit., part 1, p. 29; Johnson, op. cit., pp. 67–8; Johnson, notes attached to copies of correspondence, n.d. [1794], p. 52, Lambeth Palace Papers Arch/P/Moore 22; Collins, op. cit., vol. 1, p. 54, 455; Fitzhardinge, op. cit., p. 280.

38   Fitzhardinge, op. cit., p. 294; Collins, op. cit., vol. 1, p. 494.

39   Johnson to Fricker, 30 May 1787, in Mackaness, op. cit., part 1, p. 14; Francis Grose to Henry Dundas, 4 September 1793, *HRA*, series 1, vol. 1, p. 451; Johnson to Grose, 16 November 1793, Lambeth Palace Papers Arch/P/Moore 22; Macintosh, op. cit., pp. 76–7.

40   Johnson to Fricker, 30 May 1787, 4 October 1791, in Mackaness, op. cit., part 1, pp. 14, 39; Johnson, op. cit., p. viii; Macintosh, op. cit., p. 80.
41   Johnson to Fricker, 4 October 1791, in Mackaness, op. cit., part 1, p. 39; Johnson, op. cit., pp. 57–8, 59; Grose to Dundas, 4 September 1793, *HRA*, series 1, vol. 1, p. 451.
42   Johnson to Fricker, 4 October 1791, in Mackaness, op. cit., part 1, p. 41; Collins, op. cit., vol. 1, p. 258.
43   Johnson, op. cit. p. 47.
44   Philip Gregory's work on the significance of ideas about providence among early settlers has been especially useful here.
45   John Grant, 'Ideas awakened before Day-Break by a terrible Storm', December 1805, ML FM4/1141.
46   Gary Hentzi, 'Sublime Moments and Social Authority in *Robinson Crusoe* and *A Journal of the Plague Year*', *Eighteenth-Century Studies*, vol. 26 (1992–3), pp. 419–34.
47   Diana, in Richard Brome's play, *The Antipodes* (first acted 1638), Act I, scene vi. See also Martin Green, *Dreams of Adventure, Deeds of Empire* (London 1980), p. 40.
48   Paul G. Fidlon and R. J. Ryan (eds), *The Journal and Letters of Lt. Ralph Clark, 1787–1792* (Sydney 1981), pp. 20, 32, 54.
49   Johnson, op. cit., pp. 3–4, 6; Collins, op. cit., vol. 1, p. 328.
50   Johnson to Fricker, 9 May 1790, in Mackaness, op. cit., part 1, p. 30; Johnson, op. cit., pp. 3–4, 12, 66. See also Thomas Muir to [?] Moffat, 10 November 1793, *HRNSW*, vol. 2, p. 826.
51   Johnson, op. cit., pp. 16–22. See also Andrew Porter, 'Religion and Empire: British Experience in the Long Nineteenth Century, 1780–1914', *Journal of Imperial and Commonwealth History*, vol. 20 (1992), pp. 378–9.
52   Thomas H. Johnson (ed.), *Final Harvest: Emily Dickinson's Poems* (Boston 1961), verse 14, pp. 8–9.
53   Collins, op. cit., vol. 1, p. 367.
54   Tench, p. 280; Collins, op. cit., vol. 1, p. 454; Knight and Frost, op. cit., p. 41.
55   Collins, op. cit., vol. 1, p. 454.
56   Fitzhardinge, op. cit., pp. 205–6. In the libellous verses written about him in 1803, Governor King is made to say, 'I shall actually die in a ditch – / And be damned!' ('Extempore Allegro', enclosed with King to Hobart, 9 May 1803, *HRA*, series 1, vol. 3, p. 168).
57   *The Ordinary of Newgate his Account*, executions on 4 January 1725 (Charles Towers), Bodleian Library; Fitzhardinge, op. cit., pp. 62–3; Mollie Gillen, *The Founders of Australia: A Biographical Dictionary of the First Fleet* (Sydney 1989), p. 284.
58   *The Ordinary of Newgate his Account*, executions on 4 April 1746, pp. 14–15, Bodleian Library; Trial of Mary McDonough, 10 November 1811, Court of Criminal Judicature, quoted Paula J. Byrne, *Criminal Law and Colonial Subject: New South Wales, 1810–1830* (Cambridge 1993), p. 248. See also Peter Linebaugh, 'The Tyburn Riot against the Surgeons', in Douglas Hay, Peter Linebaugh and E. P. Thompson (eds), *Albion's Fatal Tree: Crime and Society in Eighteenth-Century England* (London 1975), pp. 105–9.
59   Phillip to Evan Nepean, 18 November 1791, *HRA*, 1st series, vol. 1, p. 308; Hunter, op. cit., p. 563; Collins, op. cit., vol. 1, p. 154, 163, and vol. 2 (first publ. 1802), p. 57; Fitzhardinge, op. cit., pp. 243–4, 246.
60   I am very much indebted here to Philip Gregory.
61   J. F. C. Harrison, *The Second Coming: Popular Millenarianism, 1780–1850* (London 1979), p. 41.
62   Walter J. Ong, *Interfaces of the Word: Studies in the Evolution of Consciousness and Culture* (Ithaca, N.Y., 1977), pp. 261–4.
63   Johnson, op. cit., p. 51.

Part 3

1   Ronald M. Berndt and Catherine H. Berndt, *The Speaking Land: Myth and Story in Aboriginal Australia* (Ringwood, Vic., 1989), pp. 58–9.

Chapter 10   Boundaries, Homes and Money

1   David Collins, *An Account of the English Colony in New South Wales* (ed. Brian H. Fletcher) (Sydney 1975), vol. 1 (first publ. 1798), p. 262; Editor's introduction in Alan E. J. Andrews (ed.), *The Devil's Wilderness: George Caley's Journey to Mount Banks, 1804* (Hobart 1984), pp. 7, 9, 12, 14.

2   Editor's introduction in Andrews, op. cit., pp. 55, 70, 89.

3   The town was laid out in July 1790 and named in June 1791: Phillip to Grenville, 17 June 1790, *HRA*, series 1, vol. 1, pp. 181–2; John White, *Journal of a Voyage to New South Wales* (ed. Alec H. Chisholm) (Sydney 1962; first publ. 1790), p. 140; Collins, op. cit., vol. 1, pp. 103, 189; L. F. Fitzhardinge (ed.), *Sydney's First Four Years* (that is, Watkin Tench, *A Narrative of the Expedition to Botany Bay and A Complete Account of the Settlement at Port Jackson*) (Sydney 1979), p. 239.

4   Collins, op. cit., vol. 2 (first publ. 1802), p. 227; Brian H. Fletcher, *Landed Enterprise and Penal Society: A History of Farming and Grazing in New South Wales before 1821* (Sydney 1976), p. 232.

5   'Land and Stock held by Free Settlers, and Emancipated or Expired Convicts', July–August 1800, in Carol J. Baxter (ed.), *Musters and Lists: New South Wales and Norfolk Island, 1800–1802* (Sydney 1988), pp. 2–14; B. H. Fletcher, 'The Development of Small Scale Farming in New South Wales (excluding Norfolk Island) 1787 to 1803', MA thesis, University of Sydney, 1962, p. 177.

6   Fletcher, *Landed Enterprise and Penal Society*, pp. 59–61, 83.

7   Henry Dundas to Phillip, 5 July 1791, *HRA*, series 1, vol. 1, p. 266; Jan Barkley and Michelle Nichols, *Hawkesbury, 1794–1994: The First 200 Years of the Second Colonisation* (Windsor 1994), pp. 13, 99, 101, 102.

8   Derek Walcott, 'The Sea is History' (1979), in Jonathan Raban (ed.), *The Oxford Book of the Sea* (Oxford 1993), p. 500.

9   D. D. Mann, *The Present Picture of New South Wales* (London 1811), p. 8.

10 Mollie Gillen, *The Founders of Australia: A Biographical Dictionary of the First Fleet* (Sydney 1989), pp. 346–7; Baxter, *Musters and Lists, 1800–1802*, p. 13; Barkley and Nichols, op. cit., p. 104.

11 Joseph Holt, *A Rum Story: The Adventures of Joseph Holt Thirteen Years in New South Wales (1800–12)* (ed. Peter O'Shaugnessy) (Sydney 1988), pp. 53, 101.

12 The muster of September 1800 shows 1859 free men (not counting garrison and officials), of whom 744 lived in Sydney and 753 on the Hawkesbury; and 241 free women, 121 in Sydney and 40 on the Hawkesbury: 'State of the Settlements . . . ', 29 September 1800, *HRA*, series 1, vol, 2, p. 680. See also Collins, op. cit., vol. 2, p. 198; Marian Aveling (Quartly), 'Imagining New South Wales as a Gendered Society, 1783–1821', *Australian Historical Studies*, vol. 25 (1992), pp. 1–8.

13 Margaret Catchpole to her aunt and uncle, 2 September 1811, in Patricia Grimshaw, Susan Janson and Marian Quartly (eds), *Freedom Bound I: Documents on Women in Colonial Australia* (Sydney 1995), p. 18.

14 Baxter, *Musters and Lists, 1800–1802*, pp. 2–14.

15 Holt, op. cit., p. 89.

16 Rough minutes, 3 November 1798, Court of Civil Judicature, NSWSA 2/8147; R. J. Ryan, *Land Grants, 1788–1809* (Sydney 1974), pp. 136–7; Gillen, op. cit., pp. 134–5, 290–1.

17   Carol J. Baxter (ed.), *Musters of New South Wales and Norfolk Island, 1805–1806* (Sydney 1989), pp. 140–1. The entire family was victualled from the stores as late as 1800, and Shephard may have been a government clerk: Baxter, *Musters and Lists, 1800–1802*, pp. 3, 5.
18   From a comparison of the lists for 1800 and 1806, in Baxter's two works, already cited.
19   King to Phillip, 29 December 1791, ML C187, p. 89.
20   Trial of John Rayner, 9 April 1795, Court of Criminal Judicature, NSWSA 1147B.
21   Trial of Elizabeth Anderson and William Norman, 10–11 August 1796, ibid., p. 185; Michael Flynn, *The Second Fleet: Britain's Grim Convict Armada of 1790* (Sydney 1993), p. 465.
22   'Account of the Produce of N.S. Wales as Exports', enclosed with King to Lord Hobart, 9 May 1803, and Thomas Moore to King, 13 May 1803, *HRA*, series 1, vol. 4, pp. 105–6, 265; *Sydney Gazette* (supplement), 8 September 1805.
23   Margaret Catchpole to Mrs Cobbold, 21 January 1802, in Helen Heney (ed.), *Dear Fanny: Women's Letters to and from New South Wales, 1788–1857* (Canberra 1985), p. 23; 'List of Plants in the Colony of New South Wales that are not Indigenous', 20 March 1803, *HRA*, series 1, vol. 4, pp. 234–9; Alan Frost, *Botany Bay Mirages: Illusions of Australia's Convict Beginnings* (Melbourne 1994), pp. 216–20.
24   *New South Wales Pocket Almanack and Colonial Remembrancer* (Sydney 1806), pp. 17, 18, 24, 25.
25   King to Hunter, 24 June 1800, *HRA*, series 1, vol. 2, p. 652.
26   See, for instance, Elizabeth Macarthur to Bridget Kingdon, 7 March 1791, in Sibella Macarthur Onslow (ed.), *Some Early Records of the Macarthurs of Camden* (Sydney 1914), p. 33.
27   On his arrival in September 1795, Hunter found 150 landholders without grants: Hunter to Duke of Portland, 10 June 1797, *HRA*, series 1, vol. 2, pp. 17–18. The register itself refers incidentally to four private soldiers (Podmore, Ewer, Barton and Prentice) who were given land but for whom there is no formal record of title: Ryan, op. cit., pp. 131, 135, 140, 141.
28   Journal of Richard Atkins, 14 February 1795, NL MS 4039; Evidence of Richard Roome and of Stephen Smith, in Crossley *v.* Edwards and others, 7 August 1804, NSWSA 2/8148, pp. 660–2; Evidence of Edward Abbott, 31 May 1811, in John Ritchie (ed.), *A Charge of Mutiny: The Court Martial of Lieutenant Colonel George Johnston for Deposing Governor William Bligh in the Rebellion of 26 January 1808* (Canberra 1988), pp. 352–3; S. J. Butlin, *Foundations of the Australian Monetary System, 1788–1851* (Sydney 1953), pp. 34, 53–5; D. R. Hainsworth, *The Sydney Traders: Simeon Lord and his Contemporaries, 1788–1921* (Melbourne 1972), pp. 26–7.
29   All 174 participants in shared grants (allowing for several mistakes with Christian names) can be identified as private soldiers or non-commissioned officers of the Corps, except for three pairs of men and nine scattered individuals: comparison of Ryan, op. cit., with the 'Register' in Pamela Statham (ed.), *A Colonial Regiment: New Sources Relating to the New South Wales Corps, 1789–1810* (Canberra 1992), pp. 245–63. There seem to be a small number of omissions in Statham's list.
30   Trial of Peter Hopley (Opley), 30 April 1788; trial of John Turner, 6 September 1788; trial of Ann Davis, 3 January 1789; trial of Amelia Levy and Elizabeth Fowles, 24 February 1789; Amelia Levy's deposition, 2 March 1789; and trial of Samuel Woodham, William Boggis and Carolina Laycock, 25 July 1789: all Judge-Advocate's Bench, NSWSA 1/296.
31   Trial of Thomas Kidney and others, 26 July 1789, ibid.
32   Alan Atkinson, 'Taking Possession: Sydney's First Householders', in Graeme Aplin (ed.), *A Difficult Infant: Sydney before Macquarie* (Sydney 1988), pp. 73–6. Phillip began occasionally dating his letters from 'Sydney', rather than 'Sydney Cove', on

12 April 1790, and he used the older term for the last time on 17 June that year: *HRA*, series 1, vol. 1, pp. 168, 179. Similarly, the formal notation, 'at Sydney Cove in the County of Cumberland', was used for the last time in the records of the Criminal Court on 28 May 1790, being replaced by 'at Sydney in the County of Cumberland' at the next sitting, on 24 August: NSWSA 1147A.

33 Algernon Sidney, *Discources concerning Government* (London 1704), p. 66.

34 James Hingston Tuckey, 'A Sketch of the Present State of the Colony of New South Wales', [1804], ML A2001, pp. 8–10; Butlin, op. cit., pp. 18–26.

35 Trial of John Thomas and Thomas Smith, 21 March 1791, Judge-Advocate's Bench, NSWSA 1/296. See also trial of James Cottington, 7 January 1792, ibid.; trial of Thomas Jones, 15 September 1791, and of William Pugh, 9 April 1792, Court of Criminal Judicature, NSWSA 1147A.

36 Collins, op. cit., vol. 1, p. 282.

37 'State of His Majesty's Settlement in New South Wales', 31 December 1801, *HRA*, series 1, vol. 3, p. 422.

38 J. W. Price, 'A Journal kept on board the Minerva Transport from Ireland to New South Wales', 12 February 1800, BL Add. Mss 13,880, f. 82; Hainsworth, op. cit., pp. 25–7; Pamela Statham, 'Making Sense of the Cox & Greenwood Ledger', in Statham, op. cit., pp. 210–3.

39 Richard Johnson to Jonathan Stonard, 11 August 1794, in George Mackaness (ed.), *Some Letters of Rev. Richard Johnson, B.A. First Chaplain of New South Wales* (Sydney 1954), part 2, p. 7; Collins, op. cit., vol. 1, pp. 198–9; Hainsworth, op. cit., pp. 22–5.

40 Collins, op. cit., vol. 1, pp. 300, 308.

41 *Old Bailey Proceedings*, 1791–2, pp. 139–42; Rough minutes, 27 August 1796, Court of Civil Judicature, NSWSA 2/8147, pp. 173–5; Hainsworth, op. cit., pp. 23–4, 39; Ryan, op. cit., pp. 17, 219.

42 Hainsworth, op. cit., p. 40.

43 Collins, op. cit., vol. 1, p. 327; Evidence of William Richardson, 20 March 1812, before the House of Commons Select Committee on Transportation, *Parliamentary Papers*, 1812, II, 341, p. 57; Alan Atkinson, 'The Free-Born Englishman Transported: Convict Rights as a Measure of Eighteenth-Century Empire', *Past and Present*, no. 144 (August 1994), p. 110.

44 Ibid., pp. 89, 93–107.

45 Ibid., pp. 107–12.

46 Rough minutes, 29 December 1800, Court of Civil Judicature, NSWSA 2/8147, pp. 312, 316–17, 326–7; King to Duke of Portland, 30 November 1800, *HRA*, series 1, vol. 2, p. 697.

47 W. S. Hill-Reid, *John Grant's Journey: A Convict's Story, 1803–1811* (London 1957), pp. 30, 32, 50.

48 Hunter to Portland, 25 June 1797, *HRA*, series 1, vol. 2, p. 32; Collins, op. cit., vol. 1, p. 141.

49 This is one of the principal findings of Hainsworth, op. cit.

50 Portland to Hunter, 31 August 1797, *HRA*, series 1, vol. 2, p. 107; A. G. L. Shaw, 'Labour', in G. J. Abbott and N. B. Nairn (eds), *Economic Growth of Australia, 1788–1821* (Melbourne 1969), p. 111. Shaw does not allow as much free agency to convict labourers as I do.

51 Government and General Orders (hereafter 'Orders'), 11 July 1796, *HRA*, series 1, vol. 1, p. 695; Collins, op. cit., vol. 2, pp. 194, 198.

52 Orders, 15 May, 19 July, 30 October 1798, 3 October 1800, *HRA*, series 1, vol. 2, pp. 214, 218, 359, 625; King to Hobart, 1 March 1804, *HRA*, series 1, vol. 4, p. 468; J. B. Hirst, *Convict Society and Its Enemies: A History of Early New South Wales* (Sydney 1983), pp. 34–6.

53   *The Ordinary of Newgate His Account*, executions on 7 November 1744, p. 5,
     Bodleian Library; F. H. Schmidt, 'Sold and Driven: Assignment of Convicts in
     Eighteenth-Century Virginia', *Push from the Bush*, no. 23 (October 1986), pp.
     13–16.
54   Stephen Hutchinson to John Fogle, 5 September 1798, Dawson Transcripts, vol. 11,
     ff. 74–6, British Museum (Natural History); Tuckey, op. cit., p. 39; Evidence of
     William Bligh, 21 February 1812, before the House of Commons Select Committee
     on Transportation, op. cit., p. 35; Holt, op. cit., p. 89.
55   Hunter to Portland, 10 June 1797, *HRA*, series 1, vol. 2, p. 17; Shaw, op. cit.,
     p. 111–12.
56   Holt, op. cit., pp. 52, 89.
57   Rough minutes, 7, 11 August 1800, Court of Civil Judicature, NSWSA 2/8147,
     pp. 123, 125, 129.
58   Orders, 4 October 1798, *HRA*, series 1, vol. 2, pp. 358–9; Orders, 8 August 1801,
     HRA, series 1, vol. 3, p. 260; Mann, op. cit., p. 67; Atkinson, 'The Free-Born
     Englishman Transported . . . ', op. cit., pp. 110–12.
59   Orders, 20 March 1797, 6 September 1800, *HRA*, series 1, vol. 2, pp. 76–7, 596;
     Orders, 4 August 1804, *HRA*, series 1, vol. 5, p. 90; Collins, op. cit., vol. 2, pp. 19,
     211.
60   The ticket-of-leave system was foreshadowed in Orders, 3 October 1800 and
     10 February 1801 (*HRA*, series 1, vol. 2, p. 625, and vol. 3, p. 48) and while the lat-
     ter order says 'former tickets' this is probably a reference to Hunter's 'certificates',
     issued as a rule (but only as a rule apparently) to men who had finished their time.
     See Orders, 11 July, 15, 29 October 1796, *HRA*, series 1, vol. 1, pp. 695, 699, 700;
     Orders, 13 January, 15 May 1797, *HRA*, series 1, vol. 2, pp. 72–3, 80; Evidence of
     John Hunter, 28 February 1812, before the House of Commons Select Committee on
     Transportation, op. cit., p. 47; Shaw, op. cit., p. 112.
61   Margaret Steven, *Trade, Tactics and Territory: Britain in the Pacific, 1783–1823*
     (Melbourne 1983), pp. 112–15; Alan Frost, *Convicts and Empire: A Naval Question,
     1776–1811* (Melbourne 1980), pp. 26–8, 121–6.
62   Lord Sydney to Lord George Cavendish, 20 May 1785, Townshend Papers, Beinecke
     Library, Yale University.
63   Edouard A. Stackpole, *Whales and Destiny: The Rivalry between America, France,
     and Britain for Control of the Southern Whale Fishery, 1785–1825* (Boston 1972),
     pp. 71–96.
64   Ibid., pp. 76–9.
65   Samuel Enderby to George Chalmers (Board of Trade), 17 January 1789, quoted
     ibid., p. 147.
66   Stackpole, op. cit., pp. 176–83; Steven, op. cit., pp. 79–80; Dan Byrnes, '"Emptying
     the Hulks": Duncan Campbell and the First Three Fleets to Australia', *Push from the
     Bush*, no. 24 (April 1987), pp. 7–9, 11, 12–15.
67   Governor Phillip's Instructions, 25 April 1787, HRA, series 1, vol. 1, p. 13.
68   Thomas Melville to Samuel Enderby and Sons, 22 November 1791, cited in full in
     John Hunter, *An Historical Journal of the Transactions at Port Jackson and Norfolk
     Island* (London 1793), pp. 557–60, and in Stackpole, op. cit., pp. 396–8.
69   Ibid., pp. 180–3, 398. Phillip's reports (to Lord Grenville, 5 November 1791, to
     Evan Nepean, 18 November 1791, and to the Admiralty, 16, 18 November 1791) do
     not suggest that he thought of the operation as covert: *HRA*, series 1, vol. 1,
     pp. 267–8, 303, 307, 312. See also King to Lord Buckingham, 24 October 1791
     (extract), *HRNSW*, vol. 1, part 2, p. 529; Stackpole, op. cit., pp. 180–1; Steven, op.
     cit., pp. 80–1.
70   Henry Dundas to Phillip, 15 May 1792, and Phillip to Dundas, 4 October 1792,
     HRA, series 1, vol. 1, pp. 354, 380; Stackpole, op. cit., pp. 152, 155; Steven, op. cit.,
     pp. 82–3.

71   Portland to Hunter, 10 April 1799, Hunter to Portland, 25 September 1800, and Orders, 11 November 1799, *HRA*, series 1, vol. 2, pp. 341, 570, 592.
72   Steven, op. cit., pp. 94–5. West says the disposal of convicts was the main reason and Robson gives a variety of explanations, without priority or analysis: John West, *The History of Tasmania* (ed. A. G. L. Shaw) (Sydney 1971; first publ. 1852), p. 30; Lloyd Robson, *A History of Tasmania*, vol. 1 (Melbourne 1983), pp. 32–3.
73   'State of His Majesty's Settlements in New South Wales', 31 December 1801, and King to Portland, 21 May 1802, *HRA*, series 1, vol. 3, pp. 435–6, 490.
74   John Goulden to Portland, 17 August 1801, and William Hiscock, 16 December 1801, CO 201/20, ff. 259, 348; John Williams to John Sullivan, 15 July 1802, CO 201/24, f. 7.
75   William Nichols to [?], 5 August 1802, Willam Fox to Lord Pelham, August 1802, and Edward Box to Hobart 19 October 1802, CO 201/24, ff. 64, 99, 163; Hobart to King, 24 February 1803, *HRA*, series 1, vol. 4, p. 35.
76   Hobart to King, 24 February, 30 November 1803, King to Hobart, 1 March 1804, and editor's note, no. 188, pp. 19, 429, 551–2, 692–3.
77   David Collins to Hobart, 6 August 1804, enclosing William Collins, 'Account of Prospects of Whaling at the Derwent', 4 August 1804, *HRA*, series 3, vol. 1, pp. 275–8.
78   Transport Commissioners to King, 4 February 1802, *HRA*, series 1, vol. 3, pp. 381–2; David Collins to King, 15 May 1804, *HRA*, series 3, vol. 1, p. 239.
79   Hobart to King, 24 June 1803, *HRA*, series 1, vol. 1, pp. 304–5.
80   J. V. Becket, 'The Debate over Farm Sizes in Eighteenth and Nineteenth Century England', *Agricultural History*, vol. 57 (1983), pp. 308–25; John Dwyer, *Virtuous Discourse: Sensibility and Community in Late Eighteenth-Century Scotland* (Edinburgh 1987), pp. 41–2.
81   Fletcher, *Landed Enterprise and Penal Society*, pp. 46–7, 233; Ryan, op. cit., passim.
82   Hainsworth, op. cit., pp. 116–19.
83   Ibid., pp. 63–7.
84   George B. Worgan, *Journal of a First Fleet Surgeon* (Sydney 1978), p. 44.
85   Plummer *v.* Lord, Kable and Underwood, case tried in the Court of Civil Judicature, 26 January 1813, NSWSA 5/2286, cause 216; Eliza Lee Homfray (née Thompson) to John Macarthur, 24 August 1820, ML A2900, pp. 61–4; Statham, 'Making Sense of the Cox & Greenwood Ledger', in Statham, op. cit., p. 221; Hainsworth, op. cit., pp. 149–51; Alan Atkinson, 'Jeremy Bentham and the Rum Rebellion', *Journal of the Royal Australian Historical Society*, vol. 64 (1978), pp. 6–7.

Chapter 11   Vicissitudes of Commonwealth

 1   Walter J. Ong, *Interfaces of the Word: Studies in the Evolution of Consciousness and Culture* (Ithaca, N.Y., 1977), p. 108.
 2   David Collins, *An Account of the English Colony in New South Wales* (ed. Brian H. Fletcher) (Sydney 1975), vol. 1 (first publ. 1798), pp. 22, 363; L. F. Fitzhardinge (ed.), *Sydney's First Four Years* (that is, Watkin Tench, *A Narrative of the Expedition to Botany Bay and A Complete Account of the Settlement at Port Jackson*) (Sydney 1979), p. 59. See also Collins, vol. 1, op. cit., p. 39, 70, 108, 166, 328, 363; Michael Sturma, 'Death and Ritual on the Gallows: Public Executions in the Australian Penal Colonies', *Omega*, vol. 17 (1986–7), pp. 90–6.
 3   Collins, op. cit., vol. 1, p. 408.
 4   *The Ordinary of Newgate his Account*, executions on 4 January 1725, Bodleian Library; 'A.B.', writing in the *Morning Chronicle*, 27 August 1785.

5   *The Ordinary of Newgate his Account*, executions on 9 July 1745, pp. 26–7, 29, Bodleian Library.

6   John Easty, *Memorandum of the Transactions of a Voyage from England to Botany Bay, 1787–1793: A First Fleet Journal* (Sydney 1965), p. 79.

7   Jay Fliegelman, *Declaring Independence: Jefferson, Natural Language, and the Culture of Performance* (Stanford 1993), p. 89.

8   Collins, op. cit., vol. 1, pp. 375, 603.

9   Ibid., p. 375. Chapman had been tried in 1786 for uttering false bill. No record of his connection with this theatre (York Theatre Royal) seems to exist: information kindly supplied by Mr Philip Johnson, of the York City Archives, and Ms Elizabeth Jones, York Theatre Royal.

10   The two playbills from 1800 are in the Mitchell Library, and for the 1796 performance, see W. Farmer Whyte, 'The Australian Stage – A Glimpse of the Past', *Journal of the Royal Australian Historical Society*, vol. 4 (1917), pp. 27–8. Philip Parry had been sentenced to transportation for life at the Old Bailey in April 1796, and arrived by the *Ganges*, and Frances Ferguson had been sentenced to seven years at the Surrey Assizes in March 1797 and arrived by the *Britannia*.

11   *Old Bailey Sessions Papers*, February 1791, pp. 186–9.

12   D.D. Mann, *The Present Picture of New South Wales* (London 1811), p. 54.

13   Fliegelman, op. cit., p. 90; Gillian Russell, 'Theatricality and Military Culture: British Army Camps in the 1770s', *Eighteenth-Century Life*, no. 18 (November 1994), pp. 55–64.

14   Philip Gidley King, 'A Journal of Transactions on Norfolk Island in the Pacific Ocean', 1791–4, CO 201/10, f. 323; King to Henry Dundas, 10 March 1794, *HRNSW*, vol. 2, pp. 140–6.

15   Collins, op. cit., vol. 1, p. 375; Gillen, op. cit., pp. 329–30.

16   Collins, op. cit., vol. 1, p. 44.

17   'Report from the Committee who were appointed to consider the several returns, which have been made to the Order of the House of Commons of the 16th day of December 1778' (Sir Charles Bunbury's committee), *House of Commons Journals*, vol. 37, pp. 379–80.

18   Samuel Marsden to [William Wilberforce?], 4 May 1794, Lambeth Palace Library Arch/P/Moore 22; Hunter to Duke of Portland, 1 February 1800, *HRA*, series 1, vol. 2, p. 448; Phillip to John King, 28 March 1802, and John King to John Sullivan, 30 March 1802, CO 201/23, ff. 163–6; Alan Atkinson, 'Taking Possession: Sydney's First Householders', in Graeme Aplin (ed.), *A Difficult Infant: Sydney before Macquarie* (Sydney 1988), pp. 72–3.

19   Hunter to Portland, 25 May, 7 September 1798, and Portland to Hunter, 5 November 1799, *HRA*, series 1, vol. 2, pp. 150–1, 221–2, 391–2.

20   Newton *v.* Cox, 1, 18 June 1804, and Rowley *v.* Newton, 19 June 1804, Court of Criminal Judicature, NSWSA 2/8148, ff. 621, 629–31; *Sydney Gazette*, 8 July 1804; Mary Newton to Lord Liverpool, 6 March 1810, CO 201/54, f. 24; Joseph Holt, *A Rum Story: The Adventures of Joseph Holt Thirteen Years in New South Wales (1800–12)* (ed. Peter O'Shaughnessy) (Sydney 1988), pp. 74–5.

21   James Mario Matra, memoranda attached to his 'Proposal for Establishing a Settlement in New South Wales', 23 August 1783, *HRNSW*, vol. 1, part 2, p. 7.

22   Ross to Phillip, 22 March 1790, and enclosures, *HRNSW*, vol. 1, part 2, pp. 319–23; Alan Atkinson, 'The Primitive Origins of Parliament', *Push from the Bush*, no. 24 (April 1987), pp. 49–50, 66–7. For the full proceedings of 'the Lieutenant-Governor and Council', see CO 201/9, ff. 3–7.

23   'At a Meeting of the Officers Civil and Military . . . at Government House Sydney on Norfolk Island', 10 March 1798 (signed 22 March), CO 201/18, f. 214.

24   Holt, op. cit., p. 117.

25   'An Officer's Letter', April 1790, *HRNSW*, vol. 2, p. 763; Richard Johnson to Henry
      Fricker, 9 April 1790, in George Mackaness (ed.), *Some Letters of Rev. Richard
      Johnson, B.A., First Chaplain of New South Wales* (Sydney 1954), part 1, p. 28; Paul
      G. Fidlon (ed.), *The Journal of Philip Gidley King: Lieutenant, R.N., 1787–1790*
      (Sydney 1980), pp. 352–3; Collins, op. cit., vol. 1, pp. 85–6; Atkinson, 'The
      Primitive Origins of Parliament', p. 50.

26   Fane Edge and 67 others to King, 29 September 1793, and minutes of a meeting of
      'several settlers and landholders', 22 October 1793, CO 201/9, ff. 247–8, 251–2; Reg
      Wright, *The Forgotten Generation of Norfolk Island and Van Diemens Land* (Sydney
      1986), pp. 19–22.

27   King's regulations for the Settlers Meeting and Higher Meeting, 10 October 1793,
      CO 201/9, ff. 248–50.

28   Minutes of a meeting of 'several settlers and landholders', 22 October 1793, CO
      201/9, ff. 251–2; King, 'A Journal of Transactions on Norfolk Island in the Pacific
      Ocean', 1791–4, CO 201/10, ff. 341–2; King to Joseph Foveaux, 19 December 1800,
      ML A2015, pp. 169–70. The last named letter shows that there was another attempt
      of the same kind, by 'the settlers and landholders', in 1800.

29   Anna Josepha King to John Piper, 24 June 1806, ML A256, p. 359; W.S. Hill-Reid,
      John Grant's Journey: A Convict's Story, 1803–1811 (London 1957), p. 132.

30   J. W. Price, 'A Journal kept on board the Minerva Transport from Ireland to New
      South Wales', 12 Feruary 1800, BL Add. Mss 13,880, f. 80; Mann, op. cit., p. 54. I
      owe the first reference to Rob Jordan.

31   Government and General Orders (hereafter 'Orders'), 14 January 1797, *HRA*, series
      1, vol. 2, p. 73.

32   Orders, 14 April 1797, and Hunter to Duke of Portland, 20 June 1797, *HRA*, series
      1, vol. 2, pp. 23–4, 78.

33   Orders, 18 September 1797, *HRA*, series 1, vol. 2, p. 202.

34   'Remarks and Observations on Norfolk Island by Major Ross', [c. December 1790],
      HRNSW, vol. 1, part 2, p. 419; 'State of the Settlements at Sydney, Parramatta, &c.',
      29 September 1800, *HRA*, series 1, vol. 2, p. 680; 'State of the Settlement on Norfolk
      Island', 13 March 1801, *HRA*, series 1, vol. 3, pp. 70–1.

35   'Expenses of Farming at the Hawkesbury', January 1800, *HRA*, series 1, vol. 2,
      pp. 434–6; Settlers from Parramatta and 'adjacent districts' to Hunter, 9, 25 January
      1800, and Hawkesbury settlers to Hunter, 1 February 1800, *HRA*, series 1, vol. 2,
      pp. 441–6; Original of the document of 25 January, showing seven districts and
      names of 'deputies', CO 201/16, ff. 61–2.

36   Hunter to Hawkesbury settlers, 8 February 1800, *HRA*, series 1, vol. 2, pp. 447, 450.

37   Evan Nepean to Sackville Hamilton, 24 October 1786, in Michael Roe, 'Motives for
      Australian Settlement: A Document', in Ged Martin (ed.), *The Founding of
      Australia: The Argument about Australia's Origins* (Sydney 1978), pp. 54–5.

38   'State of the Settlements at Sydney, Parramatta, &c.', 30 June, 31 December 1799,
      HRA, series 1, vol. 2, pp. 386, 468.

39   Gladys Bryson, *Man and Society: The Scottish Inquiry of the Eighteenth Century*
      (New York 1968), pp. 148–72; John Dwyer, *Virtuous Discourse: Sensibility and
      Community in Late Eighteenth-Century Scotland* (Edinburgh 1987), pp. 38–65. In
      this account of Hunter's ideas, I owe a good deal to Kate Thomas. See Katherine M.
      Thomas, '"Romulus of the Southern Pole [or] Superintendent of Pickpockets"': A
      Biographical Appraisal of John Hunter R.N. (1737–1821)', BA Honours thesis,
      University of New England 1992.

40   Orders, 9 November 1796, *HRA*, series 1, vol. 1, pp. 701–2; Orders, 11 November
      1797, 5 November 1798, *HRA*, series 1, vol. 2, pp. 206, 361. There is no evidence
      of nomination or election in 1799.

41   Orders, 11 April 1797, *HRA*, series 1, vol. 2, p. 78; Atkinson, 'The Primitive Origins
      of Parliament', op. cit., pp. 51–2, 54. See also Orders, 11 January 1797, 6 August

1798, 9 May 1799, and Hunter to Portland, 6 July 1797, and enclosures, *HRA*, series 1, vol. 2, pp. 33–68, 72, 219, 366.

42   Orders, 8, 16 January, 10 June 1799, 'Governor Hunter to the Settlers', 12 June 1799, ibid., pp. 362–3, 374–6, 585; Atkinson, 'The Primitive Origins of Parliament', p. 53.

43   Orders, 2 July 1799, *HRA*, series 1, vol. 2, p. 586.

44   Orders, 5, 26 November 1799, ibid., pp. 591–2, 593.

45   Grose to Henry Dundas, 16 February, 3 September 1793, Dundas to Hunter, 1 July 1794, *HRA*, series 1, vol. 1, pp. 416, 447, 476–7; Collins, op. cit., vol. 1, pp. 224, 241; Sir William Macarthur, Memoranda, n.d., ML A2897, p. 263.

46   William Paterson to Henry Dundas, 15 June 1795, Portland to Hunter, 11 August 1796, Orders, 17 September 1796, and Hunter to Portland, 12 November 1796, ibid., pp. 500, 582, 676–7, 698; Hunter to Portland, 10 July 1799, William Balmain to Hunter, 18 July 1800, and King to John King, 28 September 1800, *HRA*, series 1, vol. 2, pp. 372, 569, 671. Johnston claimed that he had also been Phillip's aide-de-camp: Evidence of George Johnston, 13 April 1812, before the House of Commons Select Committee on Transportation, *Parliamentary Papers*, 1812, II, 341, p. 179.

47   Orders, 17 October 1800, *HRA*, series 1, vol. 2, p. 692.

48   King to William Chinnery, 10 April 1801, Orders, 27 July 1801, and King to Lord Hobart, 9 June 1802, *HRA*, series 1, vol. 3, pp. 88, 260, 650; Orders, 9 October 1802, and King to Hobart, 1 March 1804, with list of unsalaried officers, *HRA*, series 1, vol. 4, pp. 320, 537, 538, 541; Evidence of David Dickenson Mann, in Crossley *v.* Edwards and others, 7 August 1804, NSWSA 2/8148, pp. 655–6. See also editor's commentary, *HRA*, series 1, vol. 4, pp. 690–1.

49   William Balmain, 'Government of New South Wales', 1802, ML A78–3, pp. 61–4.

50   King to Hunter, 6 July 1800, *HRA*, series 1, vol. 2, p. 657; Orders, 24 August 1802, *HRA*, series 1, vol. 3, p. 632. See also King to Portland, 1 March 1802, ibid., p. 399.

51   Jane Austen, *Northanger Abbey* (London 1972; first publ. 1818), pp. 199–200 (and for the period in which the book was written, see Anne Henry Ehrenpreis' introduction, p. 9); Alison Patrick, 'Paper, Posters and People: Official Communication in France, 1789–1794', *Historical Studies*, vol. 18 (1978), p. 23.

52   See, for instance, Joseph Foveaux to King, 10 August 1804, ML A1444, pp. 91–2.

53   The first two such lists, both dated 7 May 1792, are to be found at CO 201/9, ff. 137–8, 147. The practice continued throughout the first period of settlement on Norfolk Island. I am indebted here to Ong, op. cit., pp. 108–9.

54   Hunter to Portland, 25 May 1798, 4 July 1799, *HRA*, series 1, vol. 2, pp. 150, 367–8, 370. The practice was included in the Treasury's instructions to Commissary John Palmer, 1 November 1798, *HRA*, series 1, vol. 3, p. 20.

55   Orders, 9 July, 29 August 1799, *HRA*, series 1, vol. 2, pp. 587–8, 589.

56   King to Portland, 10 March 1801, 1 March 1802, *HRA*, series 1, vol. 3, pp. 8, 399; King to Hobart, 1 March 1804, *HRA*, series 1, vol. 4, p. 470.

57   Orders, 2 October 1800, and 'Instructions to the Commissary', n.d., both enclosed with King to Portland, 28 September 1800, *HRA*, series 1, vol. 2, pp. 623–5, 632–6; Orders, 25, 31 October 1800, 1 June 1801, *HRA*, series 1, vol. 3, pp. 35, 36–7, 254; Orders, 6 February 1804, and King to Hobart, 1 March 1804, *HRA*, series 1, vol. 4, p. 499, 519. See also King to John King, 18 October 1800, and enclosures, ibid., pp. 688–92.

58   Orders, 1 August 1798, *HRA*, series 1, vol. 2, pp. 218–19; Orders, 13 November 1800, *HRA*, series 1, vol. 3, p. 38 (and see also Orders, 10 December 1800, ibid., p. 41). For numbers of clerks, see 'Distribution of free men and male convicts . . . ', July–August 1800, *HRA*, series 1, vol. 2, p. 616, and 'Quarterly Employment', June 1801, *HRA*, series 1, vol. 3, pp. 155–7; and for stationery, see periodical statements of estimates in *HRA*, and account of stationery, 30 December 1802, *HRA*, series 1, vol. 4, pp. 50–1.

59 Noel McLachlan (ed.), *The Memoirs of James Hardy Vaux* (London 1964), p. 101.
60 James Hingston Tuckey, 'A Sketch of the Present State of the Colony of New South Wales', [1804], ML A2001, p. 12.
61 King to Portland, 21 August 1801, *HRA*, series 1, vol. 3, p. 151. See also Theodore J. Lowi, 'Risk and Rights in the History of American Governments', *Daedalus*, vol. 119 (1990), pp. 18–24.
62 Address of farewell to King, October 1796, CO 201/18, f. 139.
63 'Anticipation, or Birthday Ode', and King's notes thereon, n.d., enclosed with King to Hobart, 9 May 1803, *HRA*, series 1, vol. 4, p. 170. Addresses of mere gratitude from the settlers, dated January and March 1803, appear at *HRA*, series 1, vol. 4, pp. 502–3.
64 'Seditious Anonymous Papers, with remarks thereon', enclosed with King to Hobart, ibid., pp. 168–9.

Chapter 12 Varieties of Brotherhood

1   Deposition of Samuel Reddish, [October–November 1794], in connection with the mutiny on the *Surprise*, NSWSA 5/1156, p. 88; James Epstein, 'Understanding the Cap of Liberty: Symbolic Practice and Social Conflict in Early Nineteenth-Century England', *Past and Present*, no. 122 (February 1989), pp. 78–91; J. David Harden, 'Liberty Caps and Liberty Trees', *Past and Present*, no. 146 (February 1995), pp. 66–102.
2   Joseph Holt, *A Rum Story: The Adventures of Joseph Holt Thirteen Years in New South Wales (1800–12)* (ed. Peter O'Shaugnessy), (Sydney 1988), p. 124.
3   Hector St John de Crèvecouer, *Letters from an American Farmer* (London 1912; first publ. 1782), p. 26.
4   Holt, op. cit., p. 124.
5   Peter Linebaugh and Marcus Rediker, 'The Many Headed Hydra: Sailors, Slaves and the Atlantic Working Class in the Eighteenth Century', in Colin Howell and Richard J. Twomey (eds), *Jack Tar in History: Essays in the History of Maritime Life and Labour* (Fredericton, New Brunswick, 1991), pp. 11–36.
6   St John de Crèvecouer, op. cit., pp. 110–12.
7   D. R. Hainsworth, *The Sydney Traders: Simeon Lord and His Contemporaries, 1788–1821* (Sydney 1971), pp. 129, 131; pp. 17, 77–8; Marcus Rediker, *Between the Devil and the Deep Blue Sea: Merchant Seamen, Pirates, and the Anglo-American Maritime World, 1700–1750* (Cambridge 1993), pp. 118–19.
8   Holt, op. cit., pp. 96, 129.
9   Reinhart Koselleck, *Critique and Crisis: Enlightenment and the Pathogenesis of Modern Society* (Oxford 1988), p. 79; Steven C. Bullock, 'A Pure and Sublime System: The Appeal of Post-Revolutionary Freemasonry', *Journal of the Early Republic*, vol. 9 (1989), p. 361.
10 Anon. (1779), quoted Koselleck, op. cit., p. 81; Douglas Smith, 'Freemasonry and the Public in Eighteenth-Century Russia', *Eighteenth-Century Studies*, vol. 29 (1995), p. 37.
11 A. J. B. Milborne, 'Overseas Development and the Military Lodges', in United Grand Lodge of England, *Grand Lodge, 1717–1967* (Oxford 1967), pp. 229–53.
12 Dan Byrnes, 'The Blackheath Connection: London Local History and the Settlement of New South Wales', *Push: A Journal of Early Australian Social History*, no. 28 (1990), pp. 65–71.
13 Adam Weishaupt (1786), quoted Koselleck, op. cit., p. 76.
14 J. R. Clarke, 'The Formation', in United Grand Lodge of England, op. cit., pp. 92–3 (Laurence Dermott [one of the founders of the Ancient tradition], *Ahimon Rezon* [1764], quoted ibid., p. 98); Steven C. Bullock, 'The Ancient and Honorable Society: Freemasonry in America, 1736–1830', PhD thesis, Brown University 1986, p. 108;

Bullock, 'A Pure and Sublime System . . . ', p. 367; Steven C. Bullock, 'The Revolutionary Transformation of American Freemasonry, 1752–1792', *William and Mary Quarterly*, series 3, vol. 47 (1990), pp. 347–69.

15   Robert Freke Gould, *Military Lodges* (London 1900), pp. 53, 157–8; Milborne, op. cit., pp. 261, 263; J. A. Houlding, *Fit for Service: The Training of the British Army, 1715–1795* (Oxford 1981), p. 259; Bullock, 'The Ancient and Honorable Society . . . ', pp. 108, 157–8.

16   Gould, op. cit., pp. 53, 157–8; Bullock, 'The Ancient and Honorable Society . . . ', p. 153; Bullock, 'The Revolutionary Transformation of American Freemasonry, 1752–1792', pp. 366–8.

17   In 1796 three soldiers wrote to the Grand Lodge of Ireland asking for a charter (they apparently received no answer), and in 1803 Sergeant-Major Whittle was central to an effort to form a lodge in Sydney: Karl R. Cramp and George Mackaness, *A History of the United Grand Lodge of New South Wales* (Sydney 1938), vol. 1, p. 7.

18   R. J. Ryan (ed.), *Land Grants, 1788–1809* (Sydney 1981), pp. 49, 54, 305–6.

19   For an example of the death sentence, see court martial of Arthur Cox, 22 April 1807, NSWSA 5/1155, pp. 166–92.

20   Fane Edge and 67 others to King, 29 September 1793, and minutes of a meeting of 'several settlers and landholders', 22 October 1793, CO 201/9, ff. 251–2. The members also planned an annual feast day, St Patrick's day, which was typical of Masonic lodges.

21   Will of the Reverend Peter Edge, 15 July 1782, PROB 11/1100, Public Record Office.

22   Fane Edge to Evan Nepean, 6 November 1786, HO 42/10. I am very grateful to Mrs Colleen Read and Mrs Ila Della, descendants of Fane Edge, for biographical detail. He was married by banns (the method used by the poor) at Weeford, Staffordshire, on 1 July 1788. See also Pamela Statham (ed.), *A Colonial Regiment: New Sources Relating to the New South Wales Corps, 1789–1810* (Canberra 1992), p. 276.

23   Phillip to Evan Nepean, 28 March 1792, *HRA*, series 1, vol. 1, p. 344; Phillip to King, 30 November 1792, ML C187, p. 129; Fane Edge, petition to Hunter, [1798?], *HRNSW*, vol. 3, p. 520.

24   'Progress of Buildings . . . 1793', CO 201/18, f. 173; 'Plan of the Town of Sydney . . . Norfolk Island', 1796, CO 201/18, f. 164; David Collins to King, 17 October 1795, ML C187, p. 303. I refer here to the original French edition of *The Confessions*, part 2. An English translation appeared in 1791, the year of Edge's departure.

25   Joseph Foveaux to King, 16 November 1800, and King to Foveaux, 31 March 1802, ML A2015, pp. 161, 246; Foveaux to King, 18 March 1802, ML A1444, p. 39; Paul Merrill Spurlin, *Rousseau in America, 1760–1809* (Alabama 1969), pp. 108–11; Julie A. Carlson, *In the Theatre of Romanticism: Coleridge, Nationalism, Women* (Cambridge 1994), pp. 136–7.

26   King to Joseph Foveaux, [February 1801?], 14 November 1801, ML A2015, pp. 182–3, 227; Foveaux to King, 12 March 1801, ML A1444, p. 18. Fane Edge died 22 January 1803.

27   Cramp and Mackaness, op. cit., p. 7.

28   Hunter to Duke of Portland, 1 July 1798, and enclosure, *HRA*, series 1, vol. 1, pp. 158–60; James Mitchell to John Palmer, 9 September 1806, NSWSA 2/8136, p. 23; Ryan, op. cit., p. 227.

29   James Mitchell and others to John Piper, 18 December 1807, ML A256, pp. 667–8; Cramp and Mackaness, op. cit., pp. 14–16.

30   *Sydney Gazette*, 9 September 1804. Note, too, the existence in 1806 of the Freemasons Arms, a public house in Parramatta, and presumably a meeting place for local Masons (ibid., 9 March 1806). But this may have been a loyalist, or Orange,

lodge: see J. E. Gallagher, 'The Revolutionary Irish', *Push from the Bush*, no. 19 (April 1985), p. 23.

31   Mollie Gillen, *The Founders of Australia: A Biographical Dictionary of the First Fleet* (Sydney 1989), pp. 423–4.

32   Linda Colley, *Britons: Forging the Nation, 1707–1837* (New Haven 1992), pp. 11–18. For some of the debate over the evolution of Irish nationality, see L. M. Cullen, 'The Hidden Ireland: Re-Assessment of a Concept', *Studia Hibernica*, vol. 9 (1969), pp. 24–6; and for the nation as imagined community, see Benedict Anderson, *Imagined Communities: Reflections on the Origin and Spread of Nationalism* (London 1983). Evidence taken in cases tried by the Judge-Advocate's Bench gives numerous examples of identifiable men and women living together in twos and threes, and see also the early evidence of convict marriages. Among 59 First Fleet men who married, 23 were tried in London or nearby and chose other Londoners. Fourteen First Fleeters were country men who married women from their own or adjacent counties.

33   Marianne Elliott, 'The Origins and Transformation of Early Irish Republicanism', *International Review of Social History*, vol. 23 (1978), pp. 405–6; Thomas Bartlett, 'The End to Moral Economy: The Irish Militia Disturbances of 1793', *Past and Present*, no. 99 (May 1983), pp. 41–64.

34   A. G. L. Shaw, *Convicts and the Colonies: A Study of Penal Transportation from Great Britain and Ireland to Australia and Other Parts of the British Empire* (London 1966), p. 363.

35   'Land and Stock held . . . in 1802', Carol J. Baxter (ed.), *Musters and Lists: New South Wales and Norfolk Island, 1800–1802* (Sydney 1988), pp. 72–86. Of the convict men who came on five Irish ships (1791–7), one in 13.5 appear in the 1802 list, compared with one in 12.4 of the convict men on English ships, also up to 1797.

36   The two Dubliners were Thomas Henderson, or Anderson, and Thomas Doyle, or Daily: 'Land and Stock held . . . in 1802', in Baxter, op. cit., p. 77. For McCarty (or McCarthy) and Dunn (or Dun), see Ryan, op. cit., pp. 122, 141; Baxter, op. cit., p. 81.

37   Complaints of convicts by the *Queen*, n.d., enclosed with John Parker to Philip Stephens, 2 July 1792, ADM 1/2309.

38   Hunter to Portland, 15 February 1798, *HRA*, series 1, vol. 2, p. 129; David Collins, *An Account of the English Colony in New South Wales* (ed. Brian H. Fletcher) (Sydney 1975), vol. 1 (first publ. 1798), p. 160.

39   Hunter to Portland, 15 February 1798, *HRA*, series 1, vol. 2, p. 129; Collins, op. cit., vol. 1, p. 335. See also General Order, 28 October 1802, *HRA*, series 1, vol. 3, p. 691.

40   Miriam Dixson, *The Real Matilda* (Ringwood, Vic., 1994), pp. 163–4 (quotation, from a report of a Select Committee of the House of Commons [1831], p. 163).

41   Hunter to Portland, 15 February 1798, *HRA*, series 1, vol. 2, p. 129; L. F. Fitzhardinge (ed.), *Sydney's First Four Years* (that is, Watkin Tench, *A Narrative of the Expedition to Botany Bay and A Complete Account of the Settlement at Port Jackson*) (Sydney 1979), pp. 243–4, 246; Collins, op. cit., vol. 1, pp. 154–5, 304, 309, 325–6, 335, and vol. 2, pp. 42, 54–5; Gallagher, op cit., p. 21.

42   Hunter to Portland, 15 February 1798, *HRA*, series 1, vol. 2, p. 130.

43   Thomas Bartlett, 'Select Documents XXXVIII: Defenders and Defenderism in 1795', *Irish Historical Studies*, vol. 24 (1985), p. 392. Welsh 'charm papers' incuded a design in which eight lines converged to a centre within a circle, as for a compass. I am very grateful to Sally Hickey for information here.

44   Albert G. Mackey, *The Encyclopaedia of Freemasonry* (New York 1916), p. 518; Nancy J. Curtin, 'The Transformation of the Society of United Irishmen into a Mass-Based Revolutionary Organisation, 1794–6', *Irish Historical Studies*, vol. 24 (1985), p. 471; Bartlett, 'Select Documents . . . ', op. cit., pp. 385, 386, 387, 392.

45   Elliott, 'The Origins and Transformation of Early Irish Republicanism', op. cit.,
     pp. 411, 418; T. J. Dunne, 'The Gaelic Response to Conquest and Colonisation: The
     Evidence of the Poetry', *Studia Hibernica*, vol. 20 (1980), pp. 327–8; Bartlett,
     'Select Documents . . . ', pp. 377–8.
46   Robert Freke Gould, *The History of Freemasonry*, vol. 3 (London 1887), p. 45.
47   Albert G. Mackey, *The Symbolism of Freemasonry* (New York 1869), pp. 111–16;
     Mackey, *Encyclopaedia of Freemasonry*, pp. 634–5; Curtin, op. cit., pp. 464, 476–8;
     Bartlett, 'Select Documents . . . ', op. cit., pp. 387–8, 392–3.
48   Anne-Maree Whitaker, *Unfinished Revolution: United Irishmen in New South Wales,
     1800–810* (Sydney 1994), pp. 23–9.
49   Thomas Bartlett, 'Indiscipline and Disaffection in the Armed Forces in Ireland in the
     1790s', in Patrick J. Corish (ed.), *Radicals, Rebels and Establishments* (*Historical
     Studies*, vol. 15) (Belfast 1985), pp. 115–34.
50   Trial of Edward Dogherty, 5 March 1800, Judge-Advocate's Bench, NSWSA 1/298,
     pp. 152–3; Evidence of Patrick Kennedy, 6 September 1800, *HRA*, series 1, vol. 3,
     p. 581; Holt, op. cit., p. 68; Whitaker, op. cit., pp. 48, 50.
51   Neil McKellar to John Piper, 29 December 1793, ML A256, p. 496; Marianne
     Elliott, 'Ireland and the French Revolution', in H. T. Dickinson (ed.), *Britain and the
     French Revolution, 1789–1815* (London 1989), pp. 86–8. I am grateful to David
     Kent for the second reference.
52   Hunter to Sir Joseph Banks, 30 March 1797, Sir Joseph Banks Correspondence
     (Dawson Transcripts), vol. 10, ff. 77–92, British Museum (Natural History); T. G.
     Parsons, 'Was John Boston's Pig a Political Martyr? The Reaction to Popular
     Radicalism in Early New South Wales', *Journal of the Royal Australian Historical
     Society*, vol. 71 (1985), pp. 163–76.
53   Evidence of James McNally and Roger Gavin, 5 September 1800, and Patrick
     Macanna (Peter McCann), 6 September 1800, *HRA*, series 1, vol. 3, pp. 577, 579–80;
     Letter to King, 15 September 1800, in G. W. Rusden, *Curiosities of Colonization*
     (London 1874), p. 62; Evidence of Roger Grady, 7 September 1800, *HRA*, series 1,
     vol. 2, p. 582; Bartlett, 'Select Documents . . . ', p. 392.
54   Evidence of Henry Grady, [December 1800], NSWSA 5/1156, p. 146; Whitaker, op.
     cit., pp. 66, 134–5; Statham, op. cit., p. 285.
55   Whitaker, op. cit., pp. 50–3.
56   Evidence of Farrell Cuffe, Thomas Davies, Henry Grady and John Welch,
     December 1800, NSWSA 5/1156, pp. 140–1, 142, 143, 144, 146, 154; Whitaker, op.
     cit., pp. 56–8. Gaunt was not a permanent member of either the civil or military staff.
     There is no indication of his Christian name, but in a list dated 1 June 1800 he
     appears as 'Surgeon Asst' on the mainland: 'List of Convicts allowed to Officers . .
     . ', in Baxter, op. cit., p. 88.
57   Evidence of Farrell Cuffe, Michael Murphy and Michael Savage, December 1800,
     NSWSA 5/1156, pp. 138, 140, 149, 150, 151; Gallagher, 'The Revolutionary Irish',
     Push from the Bush, no. 19 (April 1985), pp. 5–6; Whitaker, op. cit., p. 56 (Whitaker
     does not mention John Lees, for whom see evidence of Murphy and Savage, above).
     For relations between convicts and soldiers on Norfolk Island, see King to Grose,
     19 March 1794, ML C187, pp. 190, 191; King to Henry Dundas, 10 March 1794,
     HRNSW, vol. 2, p. 155; Joseph Foveaux to King, 21 November 1802, ML A1444,
     pp. 44–5.
58   Procedings in the trial of Captain Luckyn Betts, 6 July 1802, and Betts to King,
     26 June 1802, *HRA*, series 1, vol. 3, pp. 538, 543, 557.
59   Papers relating to mutiny on the *Marquis Cornwallis*, enclosed with David Collins
     and William Balmain, 30 April 1796, Judge-Advocate's Bench, NSWSA 1/296,
     p. 407; Collins, op. cit., vol. 1, pp. 380–1; Curtin, op. cit., p. 477.

60   Evidence of Henry Grady, December 1800, NSWSA 5/1156, p. 148: William Neate Chapman to his sisters, 13 December 180, 7 January 1801, ML A1974; Whitaker, op. cit., pp. 56–8. See also Dixson, op. cit., pp. 155–72.

61   Evidence of James Harold, 4 September 1800, James McNally, 5 September 1800, and Roger Grady, 7 September 1800, *HRA*, series 1, vol. 3, pp. 576, 577, 582.

62   Extract from depositions of James Butterworth and John Cregmore, March 1802, and from statement of William Maum, 1 September 1804, both in Rusden, op. cit., pp. 67, 87; Whitaker, op. cit., pp. 68–9. See also King to Hobart, 9, 23 November 1802, and William Paterson to King, 18 November 1802, *HRA*, series 1, vol. 3, pp. 698–9, 737, 739–40. For the attempted escapees by the French vessels, see Government and General Orders, 19 November 1802, *HRA*, series 1, vol. 4, p. 327.

63   Maum, in Rusden, op. cit., p. 87; Cramp and Mackaness, op. cit., pp. 2–5, 14; Whitaker, op. cit., pp. 76–8. See also King to William Paterson, 4 October 1802, *HRA*, series 1, vol. 3, pp. 657–61; Bullock, 'The Ancient and Honorable Society . . . ', pp. 17–20.

64   Correspondence between King, Paterson, James Colnett and Alexander Stewart (the last two officrs on the *Glatton*), 3–9 May 1803, ML A1980–2, pp. 85–99; Cramp and Mackaness, op. cit., pp. 6–7.

65   *Sydney Gazette*, 22 May 1803; Cramp and Mackaness, op. cit., pp. 6–13.

66   King to Hobart, 21 August 1804, *HRA*, series 1, vol. 5, p. 142.

67   George Johnston to John Piper, 12 April 1804, ML A256, pp. 325–6.

68   King to Hobart, 12 March 1804, and enclosures, *HRA*, series 1, vol. 4, pp. 563–77; Whitaker, op. cit., pp. 96–106.

69   Ibid, pp. 58, 80–1.

70   Epstein, op. cit., pp. 86–7; Bartlett, 'Select Documents . . . ', pp. 377–8.

71   Thomas Paine, 'The Age of Reason', in his *Political Writings* (ed. Bruce Kuklick) (Cambridge 1989), pp. 235–6; Maurice Margarot, quoted in Rusden, op. cit., pp. 36–7; Steven Blakemore, *Burke and the Fall of Language: The French Revolution as Linguistic Event* (Hanover, N.H., 1988), pp. 77–84.

72   Maurice Margarot, quoted in Rusden, op. cit., pp. 36–7.

73   Trial of Elizabeth Buckner, 14 March 1799, Court of Criminal Judicature, NSWSA X905, f. 115.

74   Portland to Hunter, 3 December 1798, Hunter to Portland, 4 July 1799, and Hunter to King, *HRA*, series 1, vol. 2, pp. 240, 369, 690–1.

75   King to Sir Evan Nepean, 10 March 1801, *HRA*, series 1, vol. 3, p. 75; King to Hobart, 1 March 1804, *HRA*, series 1, vol. 4, p. 459.

76   King to Hobart, 30 October 1802, *HRA*, series 1, vol. 3, p. 583.

77   Journal of Richard Atkins, 20 April 1792, NL MS 4039.

78   Journal of Richard Atkins, 12, 15 December 1792, 27 October, 3 December 1793, 5 April 1794, 12 February 1795; Collins, op. cit., vol. 1, pp. 213–14. Paterson, who was Acting Governor between December 1794 and September 1795, convened two sittings of the Civil Court in July 1795, but they were the only ones between the departure of Phillip and the arrival of Hunter.

79   Sir William Blackstone, *Commentaries on the Laws of England* (London 1809), vol. 1, p. 412; Journal of Richard Atkins, 22 February, 5 April 1794; Arthur N. Gilbert, 'Military and Civilian Justice in Eighteenth-Century England: An Assessment', *Journal of British Studies*, vol. 17 (1978), pp. 41–2; E. E. Steiner, 'Separating the Soldier from the Citizen: Ideology and Criticism of Corporal Punishment in the British Armies, 1790–1815', *Social History*, vol. 8 (1983), pp. 20–4.

80   Trial of Thomas Webb, 19 September 1794, and inquiry into punishments, September 1794, Court of Criminal Judicature, NSWSA 1147A, pp. 387, 391–2.

81   King to John King, 21 August 1801, *HRA*, series 1, vol. 3, p. 246; King to Hobart, 7 August 1803, *HRA*, series 1, vol. 4, p. 354. On 2 May 1792 Atkins quoted at length

in his journal Burke's famous account of Marie-Antoinette ('It is now sixteen or seventeen years since I saw the Queen of France . . . ').

82   John Grant to his mother, 13 July 1804, ML FM4/1141.

83   James Hingston Tuckey, 'A Sketch of the Present State of the Colony of New South Wales', 1804, ML A2001, p. 35. For complaints to the court, see Rough minutes, 7 August 1800, 25 March 1803, Court of Civil Judicature, NSWSA 2/8147, p. 125, and ibid., 25 March 1803, NSWSA 2/8418, p. 430.

84   Tuckey, op. cit., p. 34.

85   Blackstone, op. cit., vol. 1, pp. 441, 443.

86   Fielder *v.* Cummings, 25 July 1795, Rough minutes of the Court of Civil Judicature, NSWSA 2/8147, ff. 59–60. Sir Charles Morgan to King, 4 January 1804, and King's award, 17 February 1804, in George Crossley's appeal from the judgement of the Court of Criminal Judicature, *HRA*, series 1, vol. 4, pp. 453, 582–3.

87   Other cases involving married women include Jane Palmer *v.* William Wilson, 29 December 1800, Rough minutes of the Court of Civil Judicature, NSWSA 2/8147, ff. 312, 316–17, 326–9; and for a discussion of the issue, see Lowry *v.* Harris, 13 August 1801, ibid., NSWSA 2/8148, ff. 447–9.

88   John Grant to his mother and sister, 5 December 1803, 6–17, 21 May, 13 July 1804, ML FM4/1141.

89   Ibid., 28 April 1805.

90   Alan Atkinson, 'Jeremy Bentham and the Rum Rebellion', *Journal of the Royal Australian Historical Society*, vol. 64 (1978), pp. 1–3.

91   Anonymous letter from Sydney, 3 May 1803, excerpt in *Morning Post*, 13 October 1803; King's memorandum, 2 January 1806, *HRA*, series 4, vol. 1, pp. 43–4; George Crossley to King, 2 March 1804, *HRA*, series 1, vol. 4, p. 594. King earlier described his authority in New South Wales as 'the King's Government, established by the Legislature': King to George Johnston, 26 February 1803, ibid., p. 188.

92   George Johnston to John Schank, 8 August 1803, Percy Family Letters and Papers (Alnwick Castle), vol. 61, ff. 141–2.

93   Address of Hawkesbury settlers to William Bligh, September 1806, *HRA*, series 1, vol. 6, p. 569.

94   Enid Campbell, 'Prerogative Rule in New South Wales, 1788–1823', *Journal of the Royal Australian Historical Society*, vol. 50 (1964), pp. 161–91.

Chapter 13   Sydney's Rebellion

1   Government and General Orders (hereafter 'Orders'), 29 September 1795, *HRA*, series 1, vol. 1, p. 678. Bligh described the method of distributing orders in his evidence, 26 February 1812, before the House of Commons Select Committee on Transportation, *Parliamentary Papers*, 1812, II, 341, p. 44.

2   King's proclamation, 22 January 1794, *HRNSW*, vol. 2, pp. 107–8.

3   Noel McLachlan (ed.), *The Memoirs of James Hardy Vaux* (London 1964), p. 104.

4   Maurice Margarot to John King, 1 October 1800, *HRNSW*, vol. 4, pp. 216–17.

5   Joseph Holt, *A Rum Story: The Adventures of Joseph Holt Thirteen Years in New South Wales (1800–12)* (ed. Peter O'Shaughnessy) (Sydney 1988), pp. 63–4. See also John Grant to Sir James Grant of Grant, 30 July 1801, Seafield Muniments GD 248/701/3, Scottish Record Office.

6   Orders, 24 January 1801, *HRA*, series 1, vol. 3, p. 48. See also, 'Order to Settle Public Accounts Quarterly', 14 July 1801, ibid., p. 167.

7   Walter J. Ong, *Orality and Literacy: The Technologizing of the Word* (London 1982), pp. 43–5; Linda Colley, *Britains: Forging the Nation, 1707–1837* (New Haven 1992), pp. 204–36.

8   Lord Sydney to E. M. Despard, [6] February 1788, CO 123/6, ff. 97–9; John Grant, 'Lines written on His Majesty's birthday, 1805', in W. S. Hill-Reid, *John Grant's Journey: A Convict's Story, 1803–1811* (London 1957), p. 213; Holt, op. cit., p. 60.

9   Orders, 26 December 1800, and King to Duke of Portland, 21 August 1801, and 'State of His Majesty's Settlements in New South Wales', 31 December 1801, *HRA*, series 1, vol. 3, pp. 43, 181, 420; Orders, 9 October 1802, and King to Lord Hobart, 9 May 1803, 1 March 1804, *HRA*, series 1, vol. 4, pp. 164, 320, 84–5.

10   Proclamation, 2 April 1802, *HRA*, series 1, vol. 3, pp. 618–19.

11   Enid Campbell, 'Prerogative Rule in New South Wales, 1788–1823', *Journal of the Royal Australian Historical Society*, vol. 50 (1964), pp. 162, 168–70, 181–4; Alan Atkinson, 'The Primitive Origins of Parliament', *Push from the Bush*, no. 24 (April 1987), pp. 61–2.

12   King to William Paterson, 8 September 1800, *HRA*, series 1, vol. 2, p. 543; King to John King, 21 August 1801, *HRA*, series 1, vol. 3, pp. 242–3. See also King to Portland, 29 April, 28 September 1800, King's 'Instructions to the Commissary', enclosed with last-named letter, King to John King, 28 September 1800, Orders, 17 October 1800, and editor's commentary, *HRA*, series 1, vol. 2, pp. 501, 608, 611, 632, 669, 692, 740, 743.

13   Orders, 9 October 1802, *HRA*, series 1, vol. 4, p. 320. See also ibid., pp. 327, 342.

14   George Mackaness (ed.), *Memoirs of George Suttor F.L.S., Banksian Collector (1774–1859)*, (Sydney 1948), p. 41; Holt, op. cit., p. 89.

15   Paul G. Fidlon and R. J. Ryan (eds), *The Journal and Letters of Lt. Ralph Clark, 1787–1792* (Sydney 1981), p. 221.

16   'Anticipation, or Birthday Ode', enclosed with King to Hobart, 9 May 1803, *HRA*, series 1, vol. 4, p. 170; William Maum to Lord Castlereagh, 26 May 1806 and n.d., and 'Mrs King [debtor] to Ferdinand Meurant', bill and receipt, n.d., CO 201/41, ff. 51–6 (copy of the first at *HRNSW*, vol. 6, pp. 76–80); McLachlan, op. cit., p. 114–15. See also Simon Schama, *Citizens: A Chronicle of the French Revolution* (New York 1990), pp. 203–10; Sarah Maza, 'The Diamond Necklace Affair Revisited (1785–1786): The Case of the Missing Queen', in Lynn Hunt (ed.), *Eroticism and the Body Politic* (Baltimore 1991), pp. 63–89.

17   Jane Austen, *Emma* (London 1966; first publ. 1816), p. 95; Jane Austen, *Northanger Abbey* (London 1972; first publ. 1818), p. 58; Colley, op. cit., pp. 237–81; Nancy Armstrong and Leonard Tennenhouse, 'A Novel Nation; or, How to Rethink Modern England as an Emergent Culture', *Modern Language Quarterly*, vol. 54 (1993), pp. 340–1; Julie A. Carlson, *In the Theatre of Romanticism: Coleridge, Nationalism, Women* (Cambridge 1994), pp. 134–75; Anne K. Mellor, 'Joanna Baillie and the Counter-Public Sphere', *Studies in Romanticism*, vol. 13 (1994), p. 561.

18   *Sydney Gazette*, 17 April, 5 June 1803; Lynn Hunt, 'The Many Bodies of Marie Antoinette: Political Pornography and the Problem of the Feminine in the French Revolution', in Hunt, op. cit., pp. 108–30; Dena Goodman, 'Public Sphere and Private Life: Toward a Synthesis of Current Historiographical Approaches to the Old Regime', *History and Theory*, vol. 31 (1992), pp. 16–20.

19   Elizabeth Macarthur to Eliza Kingdon, 7 March 1791, in Sibella Macarthur Onslow (ed.), *Some Early Records of the Macarthurs of Camden* (Sydney 1914), p. 29.

20   Eliza Marsden to Mrs Stokes, 13 December 1794, 13 November 1802, ML A1677–2; Eliza Marsden to John Piper, 15 August 1804, ML C244, p. 5d.

21   John Grant to his mother, 6–17 May 1804, ML FM4/1141. I am much indebted to Mrs Barbara Brockbank for information on Atkins' family.

22   Eliza Marsden to Mrs Stokes, 7 March 1796, and Samuel Marsden to William Wilberforce, [1799], ML A1677–2; Oliver MacDonagh, 'Highbury and Chawton: Social Convergence in *Emma*', *Historical Studies*, vol. 18 (1978), pp. 37–51.

23   Elizabeth Macarthur to Bridget Kingdon, 7 March 1791, 1 September 1799 (incorrectly given as 1795), in Onslow, op. cit., pp. 39, 47; Eliza Marsden to Mrs Stokes, 13 December 1794, ML A1677–2.

24   Ellis Bent to his mother, 4 March 1810, NL MS 195, p. 78; Mackaness, *Memoirs of George Suttor*, op. cit., p. 42.

25   King to Portland, 9 September 1800, and enclosures, *HRA*, series 1, vol. 2, pp. 532–8; King to Hobart, 14 August 1804, *HRA*, series 1, vol. 5, p. 17. See also D. D. Mann, *The Present Picture of New South Wales* (London 1811), pp. 34–5, 57.

26   Elizabeth Paterson to Maria Sophia (Mrs Samuel) Bentham, 7 October 1800, BL Add. Mss. 33543, f. 424. Jeremy Bentham quoted at length from this letter in his 'Panopticon *versus* New South Wales' (1802), in John Bowring (ed.), *The Works of Jeremy Bentham* (New York 1962), vol. 4, pp. 181–2.

27   Samuel Marsden to William Wilberforce, 17 August 1801, ML A1677–2; King to Duke of Portland, 21 August 1801, and Portland to King, 19 June 1801, *HRA*, series 1, vol. 3, pp. 123; Minutes of a meeting of the management committee, 23 August 1802, *HRA*, series 1, vol. 4, p. 97.

28   Rowland Hassall to G. Burder, 8 August 1801, *HRNSW*, vol. 4, p. 447; Elizabeth Marsden to Mrs Stokes, 22 August 1801, ML A1677–2; 'State of His Majesty's Settlements in New South Wales', 31 December 1801, *HRA*, series 1, vol. 3, p. 425; Minutes of a meeting of the management committee, 10 August 1802, *HRA*, series 1, vol. 4, p. 96; Journal of Richard Atkins, [1808], NL MS 4039, p. 212; Samuel Marsden's answers to John Thomas Bigge, Commissioner of Inquiry, 27 December 1820, ML Bonwick Transcripts 8, p. 3392.

29   Michael Flynn, *The Second Fleet: Britain's Grim Convict Armada of 1790* (Sydney 1993), p. 163; R. J. Ryan (ed.), *Land Grants, 1788–1809: A Record of Registered Grants and Leases in New South Wales, Van Diemen's Land and Norfolk Island* (Sydney 1981), p. 300.

30   *Sydney Gazette*, 24 March 1805.

31   King to William Windham, 12 August 1806, *HRA*, series 1, vol. 5, p. 761; *Sydney Gazette*, 7 June 1807; John Harris to Anna Josepha King, 25 October 18076, *HRNSW*, vol. 6, pp. 347, 348.

32   Mary Putland to her sisters, 26 February–15 March 1806, and to Elizabeth Bligh, 10 October 1806, ML safe 1/45, pp. 87, 105, 107; Elizabeth Macarthur to Bridget Kingdon, 29 January 1807, in Onslow, op. cit., p. 137; Journal of Richard Atkins, 27 September 1807, NL MS 4039; 'Adjutant Minchin's Statement', 30 September 1807, *HRA*, series 1, vol. 6, pp. 404–5; Joseph Arnold to his brother, 18 March 1810, ML A1849–2, p. 16; Ellis Bent to J. H. Bent, 2 May 1810, NL MS 195, p. 162; M. H. Ellis, *John Macarthur* (Sydney 1955), pp. 281–2; Lysbeth Cohen, *Elizabeth Macquarie: Her Life and Times* (Sydney 1979), pp. 94–5.

33   Joseph Arnold to his brother, 18 March 1810, ML A1849–2, p. 14; Evidence of Richard Atkins, 23 May 1811, in John Ritchie (ed.), *A Charge of Mutiny: The Court Martial of Lieutenant Colonel George Johnston for Deposing Governor William Bligh in the Rebellion of 26 January 1808* (Canberra 1988), p. 161; Greg Dening, *Mr Bligh's Bad Language: Passion, Power and Theatre on the Bounty* (Cambridge 1993), pp. 55–61 (quotation from Bligh on p. 60).

34   *Sydney Gazette*, 19 May 1805.

35   Sarah Wills to Elizabeth Harding, 1 May 1808, original in the possession of Mr Lawton Wills Cooke and quoted with his kind permission; copy kindly supplied by Mr Terry Wills Cooke.

36   Phillip to Lord Sydney, 9 July 1788, *HRA*, series 1, vol. 1 p. 47; Daniel Southwell to Mrs Southwell, 12 July 1788, *HRNSW*, vol. 2, p. 692; Alan Atkinson, 'Taking Possession: Sydney's First Householders', in Graeme Aplin (ed.), *A Difficult Infant: Sydney before Macquarie* (Sydney 1988), pp. 73–6.

37   'Letter from a Female Convict', 14 November 1788, *HRNSW*, vol. 2, p. 747; J. W. Price, 'A Journal kept on board the Minerva Transport from Ireland to New South Wales', 12 February 1800, BL Add. Mss 13,880, f. 80; Atkinson, 'Taking Possession . . .', op. cit., pp. 76–7.

38   J. F. Campbell, 'The Valley of the Tank Stream', *Journal of the Royal Australian Historical Society*, vol. 10 (1925), p. 80.

39   Ryan, op. cit., pp. 218–36.

40   Collins, op. cit., vol. 1, p. 269, 583; Ryan, op. cit., p. 94, 104; Holt, op. cit., pp. 64–5.

41   Graham Connah, *'Of the Hut I builded': The Archaeology of Australia's History* (Cambridge 1988), pp. 21–36; Alexandro Malaspina, 'Loose Notes on the English Colony of Port Jackson', in Robert J. King (ed.), *The Secret History of the Convict Colony: Alexandro Malaspina's Report on the British Settlement of New South Wales* (Sydney 1990), p. 137.

42   D. R. Hainsworth, *The Sydney Traders: Simeon Lord and His Contemporaries, 1788–1821* (Sydney 1972), caption to picture of Lord's premises between pp. 72–3.

43   See Chapter 10, above, and Hainsworth, *The Sydney Traders*, op. cit.

44   Inhabitants of Sydney, petition to King, n.d., enclosed with King to Hobart, 9 November 1802, *HRA*, series 1, vol. 3, pp. 541; Orders, 9 October 1802, and 'Duties of Civil officers', enclosed with King to Hobart, 1 March 1804, *HRA*, series 1, vol. 4, pp. 320, 680–1; *Sydney Gazette*, 10 June 1804.

45   Rough minutes of the Court of Civil Judicature, 2–15 February 1797, NSWSA 2/8147, pp. 177–84; Collins, op. cit., vol. 1, pp. 36, 409, and vol. 2, pp. 16, 70, 247. Examples of payment by servitude are to be found at 27 August 1796, 3 August 1801, Court of Civil Judicature, NSWSA 2/8147, pp. 173–4, 428; 20 June 1804, ibid., NSWSA 2/8148, p. 645.

46   King to John King, 8 March 1799, *HRA*, series 1, vol. 4, pp. 507–10; Orders, 29 May, 20 June 1801, and King to Hawkesbury petitioners, 23 June 1801, *HRA*, series 1, vol. 3, pp. 136, 253–4, 256–7; D. R. Hainsworth, 'Trade within the Colony', in G. J. Abbott and N. B. Nairn (eds), *Economic Growth of Australia, 1788–1821* (Melbourne 1969), p. 272.

47   King to Hobart, 9 May 1803, *HRA*, series 1, vol. 4, p. 123; Mann, op. cit., p. 70.

48   *Sydney Gazette*, 24 March 1805. In fact, fifteen years before 1805 there had been no European settlement on the Hawkesbury.

49   Ellis Bent to his mother, 4 March 1810, NL MS 195, p. 76; Mann, op. cit., pp. 4–5; *New South Wales Pocket Almanack and Colonial Remembrancer* (Sydney 1806), p. 27. House numbers appear in the evidence given in criminal cases occurring in Parramatta, but very rarely in Sydney.

50   Price, op. cit., f. 80; Atkinson, 'Taking Possession . . .', op. cit., pp. 82–4. There are no population figures for the town itself, but the population of town and district increased from 2163 to 3212 between 1802 and 1804 (ibid.).

51   Orders, 13 November 1800, *HRA*, series 1, vol. 3, p. 38; Orders, 28 June, 5 July 1803, *HRA*, series 1, vol. 4, pp. 342, 343; *New South Wales Pocket Almanack . . .*, p. 41; Atkinson, 'Taking Possession . . .', pp. 81–2.

52   *Sydney Gazette*, 5 June, 3, 10, 31 July, 7 August 1803; King to Hobart, 7 August 1803, and enclosed Orders, 1 July 1803, *HRA*, series 1, vol. 4, pp. 311, 343.

53   Atkinson, 'Taking Possession . . .', op. cit., pp. 81–2, 84.

54   Mann, op. cit., pp. 44, 43, 80; Jane Elliott, 'Was There a Convict Dandy? Convict Consumer Interests in Sydney, 1788–1815', *Australian Historical Studies*, vol. 26 (1995), pp. 373–92.

55   Hainsworth, *The Sydney Traders*, pp. 21–43; Brian H. Fletcher, *Landed Enterprise and Penal Society: A History of Farming and Grazing before 1821* (Sydney 1976), pp. 62–87.

56   Collins, op. cit., vol. 1, p. 605; Mann, op. cit., p. 70. See also the non-commissioned

officers and their wives listed as purchasers from incoming ships, in Hainsworth, *The Sydney Traders*, pp. 231–4.

57   *Sydney Gazette*, 28 October 1804, 28 January 1810; Orders, 25 October 1804, *HRA*, series 1, vol. 5, p. 275.

58   Ryan, op. cit., pp., 184, 190; Lord Bathurst to Lachlan Macquarie, 4 December 1815, *HRA*, series 1, vol. 8, pp. 645–6. Mary Putland also received a grant of 600 acres, and Bligh, after being sworn in, responded with 790 acres for Mrs King (Ryan, op. cit., pp. 179, 181, 186). The grants for King's children and for Mrs Putland are dated 1 January 1806 in Ryan, but since Bligh and his daughter arrived only in August the grants must have been made then.

59   Elizabeth Macarthur to Bridget Kingdon, 29 January 1807, in Onslow, op. cit., p. 137; Bligh to William Windham, 31 October 1807, *HRA*, series 1, vol. 6, pp. 153–4; George Mackaness, *The Life of Vice-Admiral William Bligh, R.N., F.R.S.*, vol. 2 (Sydney 1931), pp. 129–30; George Suttor, in Mackaness, *Memoirs of George Suttor*, op. cit., pp. 44–5; Hainsworth, *The Sydney Traders*, pp. 94–5; Fletcher, op. cit., pp. 110–12.

60   Robert Fitz to William Neate Chapman, 15 October 1807, *HRNSW*, vol. 6, p. 305; Joseph Foveaux to [James Chapman?], 10 September 1808, *HRNSW*, vol. 6, p. 751; Evidence of Anthony Fenn Kemp, 25 May 1811, and of Edward Abbott and David Dickenson Mann, both 30 May 1811, in Ritchie, op. cit., pp. 222, 351, 363, 364.

61   *Sydney Gazette*, 26 July 1807; Bligh to William Windham, 31 October 1807, and Bligh to Lord Castlereagh, 30 June 1808, *HRA*, series 1, vol. 6, pp. 155–6, 525; Atkinson, 'Taking Possession . . . ', p. 85.

62   Evidence of Charles Grimes, 27 May 1811, in Ritchie, op. cit., pp. 276–7; Hainsworth, *The Sydney Traders*, pp. 93–4.

63   'Serjeant-Major Whittle's Statement', 11 April 1808, *HRA*, series 1, vol. 6, p. 404; Robert Fitz to James Chapman, 15 October 1807, and Joseph Foveaux to [James Chapman?], 10 September 1808, *HRNSW*, vol. 6, pp. 305, 751 (the latter reference affirms Bligh's habit of declaring, 'It is all my own'); Evidence of David Dickenson Mann and Thomas Whittle, both 30 May 1811, in Ritchie, op. cit., pp. 364–7, 367–8.

64   George Caley to Sir Joseph Banks, 7 July 1808, Dawson Transcipts, vol. 17, f. 185, British Museum (Natural History); Evidence of Richard Atkins, 23 May 1811, in Ritchie, op. cit., pp. 174–5.

65   Bligh to Banks, 30 October 1792, ML A78–4; Alan Atkinson, 'The British Whigs and the Rum Rebellion', *Journal of the Royal Australian Historical Society*, vol. 66 (1980), pp. 74–5.

66   Bligh's statement of his dealings with Short, 1 April 1806, and accompanying papers, ML A84; Alan Atkinson, 'The Position of John Macarthur and his Family in New South Wales before 1842', MA thesis, University of Sydney 1971, pp. 91–104; Atkinson, 'The British Whigs and the Rum Rebellion', pp. 75–6.

67   Short's defences (there were two courts martial), 10, 14 December 1807, ADM 1/5384; Sir Isaac Coffin to Edward Cooke, 13 December 1807, ADM 1/5384; Elizabeth Bligh to Banks, 14, 25 January 1808, ML A78–5; Elizabeth Bligh to Bligh, 15 February 1808, ML safe 1/45, p. 128.

68   King to Portland, 5 November 1801, and enclosures, *HRA* series 1, vol. 3, pp. 274–320.

69   Robert Farquhar to Hobart, 13 June 1802, Hobart Papers (War Office/Y), Buckinghamshire Record Office.

70   Robert Farquhar to Lord Wellesley, 1 October 1802, and related papers, BL Add. Mss 13622, ff. 5–11; Sir Walter Farquhar to Wellesley, 18 December 1804, ibid., 37283, ff. 280–1; Sir Walter Farquhar to Wellesley, 25 September 1810, ibid., 37292, ff. 103–5; Onslow, op. cit., p. 62.

71   *Coriolanus*, Act I, scene i; James Macarthur's memoir of his father, n.d., in Onslow, op. cit., p. 471.

72 Evidence of John Macarthur, 23 May 1811, in Ritchie, op. cit., pp. 178–9.

73 Mary Putland to Elizabeth Bligh, 10 October 1806, ML safe 1/45, p. 106; Evidence of Charles Walker, 20 May 1811, in Ritchie, op. cit., p. 136.

74 King's memorandum, 2 January 1806, *HRA*, series 4, vol. 1, pp. 43–4; Macarthur's address in Macarthur *v.* Campbell jr, 24 October 1807, *HRA*, series 1, vol. 6, p. 178; Alan Atkinson, 'Jeremy Bentham and the Rum Rebellion', *Journal of the Royal Australian Historical Society*, vol. 64 (1978), pp. 3–4.

75 Evidence of Edmund Griffin at Macarthur's trial, 4 February 1808, Court of Criminal Judicature, *HRA*, series 1, vol. 6, pp. 323–4. Macarthur had five defendants in all, and the cases were heard on 28, 30 October, 4 November 1806 and 3 April 1807, Court of Criminal Judicature, NSWSA 2/8148, pp. 906–23, 959.

76 John Harris to Anna Josepha King, 25 October 1807, *HRNSW*, vol. 6, p. 344; Joseph Foveaux to Lord Castlereagh, 4 September 1808, *HRA*, series 1, vol. 6, p. 629; Macarthur's evidence, 24 May 1811, in Ritchie, op. cit., p. 188. For Gore's influence over the Governor, see evidence of Anthony Fenn Kemp, 25 May 1811, in Ritchie, op. cit., p. 226; J. Pert, 'William Gore, Provost Marshal: The Man and his Office', *Journal of the Royal Australian Historical Society*, vol. 68 (1982), p. 181. For Gore's background, see Lord Harrington to Lord Camden, 19 May 1805, Pratt Mss 023/58, Kent Archives Office. Harrington referred to him as 'one of the nearest relations' of Sir Booth Gore of Lissadell (1744–1804), which could only mean an illegitimate son. The lines of verse are from W. B. Yeats, 'In Memory of Eva Gore-Booth and Con Markiewicz' (1927).

77 Bligh to William Windham, 31 October 1807, *HRA*, series 1, vol. 6, p. 151; William Gore to Lord Castlereagh, 31 October 1807, *HRNSW*, vol. 6, pp. 371–7; Lord *v.* Gore, 29 September 1807, Court of Appeal, NSWSA 2/8136; Journal of Richard Atkins's [23 August 1807?], pp. 211–12, NL MS 4039; Bligh to Banks, 5 November 1807, ML A85; Evidence of Richard Atkins, 23 May, of Anthony Fenn Kemp, 25 May, and of John Blaxland, 30 May 1811, in Ritchie, op. cit., pp. 162–5, 218; Pert, op. cit., p. 183.

78 Journal of Richard Atkins, [23 August 1807?], p. 212, Robert Fitz to James Chapman, 15 October 1807, *HRNSW*, vol. 6, p. 305; Examination of Richard Atkins by committee of rebels, 27–28 January 1808, *HRA*, series 1, vol. 6, pp. 279–80.

79 Apart from Atkins's journal, the only detailed account of the case of Lord *v.* Gore is among the records of the Court of Appeal (appeal dated 29 September 1807), NSWSA 2/8136. The *Sydney Gazette* had ceased publication for lack of paper, and the records of the courts of Civil and Criminal Judicature are all missing for this period, possibly for the same reason.

80 Evidence of various witnesses at the trial of John Macarthur, 2– 6 February 1808, *HRA*, series 1, vol. 6, pp. 294–352 (quotations from pp. 307, 312, 347); Bligh to Lord Minto, 12 August 1808, ML safe 1/45, p. 149; Rowland Hassall to [?], 8 September 1808, ML A859, p. 230; Evidence of John Macarthur, 24 May 1811, in Ritchie, op. cit., pp. 190–4.

81 Evidence of Edward Abbott, 31 May 1811, ibid., pp. 351–2.

82 Evidence of Thomas Whittle, 31 May 1811, ibid., p. 370. For references to Macarthur as the Cromwell of his country, see Edmund Griffin's evidence at John Macarthur's trial before the Court of Criminal Judicature, 4 February 1808, *HRA*, series 1, vol. 6, p. 331; Macarthur to Barron Field, 29 January 1824, ML A2897, p. 89.

83 Whittle's summary record of service appears at WO 25/1070 (list dated 24 June 1806) and WO 25/642 (list dated 16 September 1808). The latter puts his age at 60, but this seems to have been a mistake. He was an out-pensioner 7–16 March 1791, joining the Corps on 17 March: see Out-Pensions Admissions Book 1785–92, 7 March 1791, WO 116/9. For his service as a drummer in the 28th Regiment (pro-

moted corporal June 1775), see WO 12/4416. He was afterwards in the 61st and then briefly a sergeant in Captain Colville's Independent Company.

84 *Sydney Gazette*, 6 July 1806, 22 February 1807; Evidence of Thomas Finnegan, 11 May 1811, in Ritchie, op. cit., pp. 117–18.

85 Statement of Isaac Champion, and untitled paper with Henry Fulton's evidence of the religious opinions of John Macarthur and Thomas Whittle, [both 1811?], WO 72/35.

86 Joseph Foveaux to Macquarie, 27 January 1810, NSWSA 9/2736, p. 50; Statements of William Bremlow (Brumlow, or Bromlow) and of Isaac Champion, [1811?], WO 72/35; Evidence of Bremlow and of Champion, 11 May 1811, in Ritchie, op. cit., pp. 113–16; Pamela Statham (ed.), *A Colonial Regiment: New Sources Relating to the New South Wales Corps, 1789–1810* (Canberra 1992), pp. 258, 262.

87 *Coriolanus*, Act I, scene i.

88 'Sydney Settlers' Address to Governor Bligh', 22 September 1806, *HRA*, series 1, vol. 6, pp. 570–2.

89 Evidence of Anthony Fenn Kemp, 25 May 1811, in Ritchie, op. cit., p. 217.

90 All leaseholders were ordered to bring their deeds to Government House in November 1807: Evidence of David Dickenson Mann, 341 May 1812, Ritchie, op. cit., pp. 364–5. The map, dated 31 October 1806, appears with Bligh to William Windham, 31 October 1806, *HRNSW*, vol. 6, between pp. 366–367.

91 Macarthur's evidence, 24 May 1811, in Ritchie, op. cit., p. 183.

92 George Caley to Banks, 7 July 1808, Dawson Transcripts, vol. 17, f. 187, British Museum (Natural History).

93 Edward Abbott to King, 13 February – 4 April 1808, ML A1976, f. 1211.

94 Statements of John Collinan, or Colonan, and of Thomas Finnegan, or Fenegan, [1811?], WO 72/35.

95 Statements of William Bremlow, and of Thomas Finnegan, ibid.

96 Macarthur's protest at the opening of the Court of Criminal Judicature, 25 January 1808, in Ritchie, op. cit., pp. 465–9.

97 John Palmer, [1811], WO 72/35; 'Memorandums of the Proceedings of the Criminal Court', 25 January 1808, and Atkins to Bligh, 25 January 1808, pp. 440–2, both in Ritchie, op. cit., pp. 432–3; Ellis, op. cit., pp. 332–3.

98 Statement of John Colonan, [1811?], WO 72/35.

99 Statements of William Bremlow, John Mackey and John Gillard, ibid.; Abbott to King, 13 February – 4 April 1808, ML A1976, ff. 121b, 121d; Atkinson, 'Jeremy Bentham and the Rum Rebellion', op. cit., pp. 5–6.

100 Evidence of John Sutherland, James Cox, both 31 May 1811, in Ritchie, op. cit., pp. 374–5, 376–7; Abbott to King, 13 February – 4 April 1808, ML A1976, f. 121m; Rowland Hassall to [?] , 8 September 1808, ML A859, p. 236.

101 Ibid.; Statement of William Bremlow, [1811?], WO 72/35.

102 Ritchie, pp. 220, 236, 267, 354, 403 The letter and signatures are reproduced in facsimile in *HRNSW*, vol. 6, between pp. 434–435.

103 George Suttor's affidavit, 4 June 1808, *HRA*, series 1, vol. 6, p. 549.

104 Statements of [?] Friar and William Hutton, or Hutten, [1811?], WO 72/35. William Gore to Lord Castlereagh, 27 March 1808, and deposition of Michael Marlborough, 11 April 1808 *HRNSW*, vol. 6, pp. 557–8, 575; Statement of William Hutton, [1811?], WO 72/35; Evidence of William Hutton, 11 May 1811, and John Sutherland, 31 May 1811, in Ritchie, op. cit., pp. 117, 373.

105 George Johnston to Bligh, 26 January 1808, ibid., p. 417.

106 Gore to Castlereagh, 27 March 1808, *HRNSW*, vol. 6, p. 559.

107 Robert Townson to Charles Greville, 2 April 1808, BL Add. Mss 42,071, ff. 565–8; Johnston to Castlereagh, 11 April 1808, *HRA*, series 1, vol. 6, p. 219; Rowland Hassall to [?] , 8 September 1808, ML A859; Settlers at Baulkham Hills to Castlereagh, 22 February 1809, *HRA*, series 1, vol. 7, pp. 140, 142; William

Macarthur, 'A few Memoranda respecting the aboriginal Natives', [1835?], ML A2935, p. 173; Atkinson, 'The British Whigs and the Rum Rebellion', pp. 85–6.

108   Bligh's memorandum, 'Sending a Delegate to England', [1808], *HRNSW*, vol. 6. pp. 512–14; Abbott to King, 13 February – 4 April 1808, ML A1976, p. 121g; Bligh to Castlereagh, 30 June 1808, and enclosed copy of an agreement to send John Macarthur to England as delegate, [8 February 1808], *HRA*, series 1, vol. 6, pp. 530–2, 550.

109   Abbott to King, 13 February – 4 April 1808), ML A1976, p. 212m; Robert Townson to Charles Greville, 2 April 1808, BL Add. Mss 42,071, ff. 565–8.

110   Bligh to Sir Edward Pellew, 14 August 1808, ML safe 1/45, p. 169; W. G. C. Kent to J. W. Croker, 19 November 1810, and the evidence of Kent and John Porteous at Kent's court martial, 8–10 January 1811, pp. 12, 14, 18, ADM 1/5412. The proceedings were published as *Minutes of a Court Martial . . . for the Trial of Lieut. W. G. Carlile Kent* (Portsmouth 1811).

111   Bligh to Banks, 5 November 1807, ML safe 1/45, p. 260.

Chapter 14   The Ocean and the Little Fish

1   George, Lord Byron, 'Childe Harold's Pilgrimage', Canto IV, stanza clxxxiii.

2   William Wordsworth, 'The Prelude', Book Third, ll. 61–3.

3   John Keats, 1819, quoted John Beer, 'Literature', in Boris Ford (ed.), *The Romantic Age in Britain (The Cambridge Cultural History*, vol. 6) (Cambridge 1992), p. 85.

4   Stephen C. Behrendt, 'A Possible Corollary Source for *The Gates of Paradise 10*', *Blake: An Illustrated Quarterly*, vol. 28 (1994–5), pp. 92–4.

5   Thomas Fyshe Palmer to [?], 11 September 1795, Shepherd and Ridyard Papers, vol. 10, Manchester College, Oxford.

6   Jeremy Bentham, 'Panopticon; or, The Inspection-House' and 'Tracts on Poor Laws and Pauper Management', in John Bowring (ed.), *The Works of Jeremy Bentham* (New York 1962), vol. 4, pp. 37–172, and vol. 8, pp. 361–439.

7   *Public Advertiser*, 30 September, 10 October, 23 November 1786. For Semple, see also *Public Advertiser*, 8 November 1786.

8   Arthur Jose, 'The "Barrington" Prologue', *Journal of the Royal Australian Historical Society*, vol. 13 (1928), pp. 292–4. The entire Prologue first appeared in the *Annual Register*, 1801, pp. 516–17, and has been attributed to Henry Carter, 'a Gentleman of Leicester'.

9   *Edinburgh Review*, vol. 2 (1803), pp. 33, 36.

10   These appear in a letter which Plummer presented to the Colonial Office (addressed to the new Governor, Lachlan Macquarie, in Macquarie's hand): Plummer to Macquarie, 4 May 1809, *HRA*, series 1, vol. 7, pp. 197–210; Alan Atkinson, 'Jeremy Bentham and the Rum Rebellion', *Journal of the Royal Australian Historical Society*, vol. 64 (1978), pp. 6–8. I would no longer argue that this document was copied nearly verbatim from Macarthur's original, but there can be no doubt that its substance can be attributed to him rather than to Plummer.

11   D. R. Hainsworth, *The Sydney Traders: Simeon Lord and his Contemporaries, 1788–1821* (Sydney 1972), pp. 67–9.

12   Plummer to Macquarie, 4 May 1809, *HRA*, series 1, vol. 7, pp. 204–8.

13   J. H. Tuckey, *An Account of a Voyage to Establish a Colony at Port Phillip in Bass's Strait, on the South Coast of New South Wales, in His Majesty's Ship Calcutta, in the Years 1802–3–4* (London 1805), pp. 187–9.

14   'Freeholders' to William Paterson, 18 April 1808, George Suttor and Andrew McDougall to Robert Campbell, 6 May 1808, and enclosed settlers' address to Paterson, n.d., and settlers to Paterson, 1 May 1808, *HRA*, series 1, vol. 6, pp. 573–7; George Suttor to Bligh, 1 January, 10 February 1809, 'Free Planters and Inhabitants' to Lord Castlereagh, 4 November 1808, Andrew McDougall to Bligh, 22 February

1809, Baulkham Hills settlers to Castlereagh, 22 February 1809, Hawkesbury settlers to Bligh, 17 February 1809, and Hawkesbury settlers to Castlereagh, 17
February 1809, *HRA*, series 1, vol. 7, pp. 131–51; Brian H. Fletcher, 'The
Hawkesbury Settlers and the Rum Rebellion', *Journal of the Royal Australian
Historical Society*, vol. 54 (1968), pp. 229–32; Brian H. Fletcher, *Landed Enterprise
and Penal Society: A History of Farming and Grazing in New South Wales before
1821* (Sydney 1976), pp. 110–12.

15   Baulkham Hills settlers to Castlereagh, 22 February 1809, *HRA*, series 1, vol. 7,
p. 144; Evidence of William Bligh, 24 Febuary 1812, before the House of Commons
Select Committee on Transportation, *Parliamentary Papers*, 1812, II, 341, pp. 35–6,
and see also evidence of John Palmer, 20 March 1812, ibid., p. 61.

16   *Morning Chronicle*, 14, 15 September 1808; *The Times*, 15 September 1808;
Morning Post, 15, 17 September 1808.

17   W. A. Miles to Hugh Elliot, 20 September 1808, National Library of Scotland HE
53; Charles Greville to Sir Joseph Banks, 20 September 1808, ML A78–5.

18   Castlereagh to Lachlan Macquarie, 14 May 1809, and three letters to Bligh, all 15
May 1809, *HRA*, series 1, vol. 7, pp. 81, 86, 88; George Mackaness, *The Life of Vice-
Admiral William Bligh, R.N., F.R.S.* (Sydney 1931), vol. 2, pp. 300–1.   Edward
Cooke, Castlereagh's under-secretary, was said to have told Francis Grose that
Foveaux's only mistake on assuming power in 1808 was his not sending Bligh
straight home: Joseph Foveaux to Macquarie, 10 January 1810, NSWSA 9/2736.

19   Castlereagh to Macquarie, 14 May 1809, ibid., p. 81; Vicary Gibbs and Thomas
Plumer to Castlereagh, 17 November 1809, *HRA*, series 4, vol. 1, pp. 47–8.

20   Duke of Northumberland to George Johnston, 5 July 1811, Percy Family Letters and
Papers (Alnwick Castle), Duke's Letter Book 1809–12, pp. 396–8.

21   Ibid.

22   Edward Macarthur to John Macarthur, 25 October 1808, and John Macarthur to
Elizabeth Macarthur, 14 February 1810, in Sibella Macarthur Onslow (ed.), *Some
Early Records of the Macarthurs of Camden* (Sydney 1914), pp. 175, 191.

23   Lord Liverpool to M. Lewis, 27 October 1810, BL Add. Mss 38,323, ff. 99–100.

24   John Macarthur to Elizabeth Macarthur, 11 November 1810, in Onslow, op. cit., p.
206.

25   George Johnston to Liverpool, 16 November 1810, CO 201/54, ff. 278–9.

26   John Macarthur to Elizabeth Macarthur, 3 May 1819, in Onslow, op. cit., p. 195.

27   M. H. Ellis, *John Macarthur* (Sydney 1955), pp. 396, 401; A. Aspinall,
Correspondence of George Prince of Wales, 1770–1812, vol. 7 (London 1970),
p. 205.   Baird disagreed with the lenity of the sentence, being absent on the day it
was decided: Baird to Macquarie, 30 March 1813, ML A797, pp. 78–9.

28   Charles Manners Sutton's remarks in the House of Commons, 11 March 1811,
Parliamentary Debates, vol. 19, cols. 355, 356; *Dictionary of National Biography*,
vol. 12, pp. 943–4.

29   John Macarthur's address in Macarthur v. Robert Campbell jr, 24 October 1807,
HRA, series 1, vol. 6, p. 178.

30   'Copy of an Agreement', [8 February 1808], *HRA*, series 1, vol. 6, p. 550; Eugene
Charlton Black, *The Association: British Extraparliamentary Political Organization,
1769–93* (Cambridge, Mass., 1963).

31   Bligh to Johnston, 17 February, 25 March 1808, *HRA*, series 1, vol. 6, pp. 254;
Evidence of Richard Atkins, 23 May 1811, in John Ritchie (ed.), *A Charge of
Mutiny: The Court Martial of Lieutenant Colonel George Johnston for Deposing
Governor William Bligh in the Rebellion of 26 January 1808* (Canberra 1988),
pp. 160, 171–2, 174.

32   Atkinson, 'Jeremy Bentham and the Rum Rebellion', p. 9; Macarthur's evidence , 25
May 1811, in Ritchie, op. cit., pp. 214–15.   Bligh himself spoke of 'a civil
Government': ibid., p. 9.

33 Bligh's opening speech and his evidence, 7 May 1811, ibid., pp. 6, 19; Evidence of John Palmer and Francis Oakes, both 10 May 1811, ibid., pp. 76, 82, 91; Hainsworth, op. cit., pp. 52–7; Ross Fitzgerald and Mark Hearn, *Bligh, Macarthur and the Rum Rebellion* (Sydney 1988), pp. 120–1. Macarthur was the only defence witness asked by the prosecution about the barter of spirits, and the question in that case referred to resentment among 'the soldiery': ibid., p. 204.

34 Exchange on 10 May 1811, in Ritchie, op. cit., p. 90.

35 Johnston's speech in defence, 23 May 1811, ibid., p. 148.

36 Compare Johnston's account as to what in the end made him act (Macarthur's arguments or public opinion) in his opening speech, 23 May 1811, and in his closing observations, 5 June 1811, pp. 152, 383–4.

37 Whittle's evidence, 31 May 1811, ibid., pp. 369–71. For the date of the conversation, see 'Serjeant-Major Whittle's Statement', 11 April 1808, *HRA*, series 1, vol. 6, p. 404.

38 Northumberland to Johnston, 10 December 1811, Percy Family Letters and Papers, Letter book 1809–12, pp. 474–6; Johnston's opening speech, 23 May 1811, and Commander-in-Chief's General Orders, 2 July 1811, in Ritchie, op. cit., pp. 134–5, 408–9.

39 Speech of George Holford in the House of Commons, 21 January 1812, *Parliamentary Debates*, vol. 21, cols. 235–8; Speech of Sir Samuel Romilly (moving that a committee be appointed) in the House of Commons, *The Times*, 13 February 1812. Romilly was acquainted, through Northumberland, with Johnston and Macarthur: Northumberland to James Brogden, 4 March 1810, Sperling Correspondence D/DSe3, Essex Record Office; John Macarthur to Elizabeth Macarthur, 21 April 1811, in Onslow, op. cit., p. 218.

40 For Sir Robert Eden, see Bernard C. Steiner, *Life and Administration of Sir Robert Eden* (Johns Hopkins University Studies in Historical and Political Science, series 16, nos 7–9) (Baltimore 1898). George Eden was afterwards first Earl of Auckland.

41 Report of the House of Commons Select Committee on Transportation, 10 July 1812, *Parliamentary Papers*, 1812, II, 341, pp. 7, 8, 14.

42 For these returns, see *HRA*, series 1, vols 1 and 2.

43 'General Statement of the Inhabitants in His Majesty's Settlement, Derwent River, Van Diemen's Land', 28 February 1805, *HRA*, series 3, vol. 1, p. 318; 'Result of General Muster', 1, 5 August 1805, *HRA*, series 1, vol. 5, p. 613. Figures for the mainland in July 1804 are at series 1, vol. 5, p. 40; the proportion then appears as 37 per cent.

44 Bligh's evidence before the House of Commons Select Committee on Transportation, 21, 24 February 1812, pp. 33, 35.

45 Liverpool to Macquarie, 25 June 1810, *HRA*, series 1, vol. 7, p. 337; Report of the House of Commons Select Committee on Transportation, p. 3.

46 Ibid., pp. 10–11.

47 Report, and Bligh's evidence, 24 February 1812, ibid., pp. 13, 36.

48 Report, ibid., p. 12.

49 'Phillip's Views on the Conduct of the Expedition and the Treatment of Convicts', [1787], *HRNSW*, vol. 1, part 2, pp. 51, 52; Trial of John Green, 19 November 1804, Court of Criminal Judicature, NSWSA 5/1149, p. 24.

50 Report of the House of Commons Select Committee on Transportation, p. 119; George Eden to Lord Sidmouth 25 August, 3 September 1812, and Sidmouth to Eden, 30 August 1812, BL Add. Mss. 34,458, ff. 382–4.

51 'A Statement of the Married and Unmarried Women', August 1806, *HRNSW*, vol. 6, p. 162. The list (original ML Mss 18) appears as 'Marsden's Female Muster' in Carol J. Baxter (ed.), *Musters of New South Wales and Norfolk Island, 1805–1806* (Sydney 1989), pp. 146–82. The same distinction was included within a list of landowners apparently compiled in 1807: 'Return of the numbers of acres of land

sown . . . ', [August 1807?], *HRNSW*, vol. 6, pp. 406–9. See also King to Lord Hobart, 1 March 1804, *HRA*, series 1, vol. 4, p. 483.

52 Evidence of James Ives, 3 April 1811, before the House of Commons Select Committee on Laws Relating to Penitentiary Houses, *Parliamentary Papers*, 1810–11, III, 199, pp. 84–5.

53 King to Henry Dundas, 5 October 1795 (and minute thereon), CO 201/18, f. 23; Duke of Portland to Hunter, 11 August 1796, *HRA*, series 1, vol. 1, p. 582.

54 Report of the House of Commons Select Committee on Transportation, p. 14.

55 Lord Bathurst to Macquarie, 23 November 1812, *HRA*, series 1, vol. 7, p. 676.

56 Hobart to King, 24 June 1803, King to John Sullivan, 7 August 1803, and King to Hobart, 15 May 1804, *HRA*, series 1, vol. 4, pp. 304–5, 366–7, 643–7.

57 King to Joseph Foveaux, 20 July 1804, *HRA*, series 1, vol. 5, pp. 26–8; 'Lieutenant-Governor Foveaux's Observations' concerning the Removal of the Settlement at Norfolk Island', 26 March 1805, *HRA*, series 1, vol. 6, pp. 74–6.

58 Ibid., pp. 78–80.

59 William Windham to Bligh, 30 December 1806, *HRA*, series 1, vol. 6, pp. 70–80. I am grateful to Anne-Maree Whitaker for information about Foveaux's connections, which were mainly with the Whigs and the War Office.

60 Bligh to Windham, 31 October 1807, enclosing Bligh to John Piper, 4 September 1807, *HRA*, series 1, vol. 6, pp. 182–7; Piper's order, 17 September 1807, and Piper to Bligh, 21 September 1807, NSWSA 4/1168A, pp. 351–3, 361–3.

61 Evidence of W. G. C. Kent, 30, 31 May 1811, in Ritchie, op. cit., pp. 336, 343–4, 350.

62 Johnston to Piper, 24 May 1808, ML safe 1/51, pp. 133–7; Macarthur to Piper, 24 May 1808, ML A254, p. 137; Robert Nash to Macquarie, 21 May 1810, NSWSA 4/6977A, pp. 43–5; J. E. Calder, 'A Topographical and Historical Sketch', 31 December 1879, in 'Scraps of Tasmanian History' (scrapbook of newspaper cuttings), vol. 3, ML 996C; Michael Flynn, *The Second Fleet: Britain's Grim Convict Armada of 1790* (Sydney 1993), p. 433.

63 For the various totals, see Reg Wright, *The Forgotten Generation of Norfolk Island and Van Diemen's Land* (Sydney 1986), p. 106.

64 Returns of population at the Derwent, 16 October 1806, and at Port Dalrymple, 10 August 1806, *HRA*, series 3, vol. 1, pp. 384, 666. A list of landholders at the Derwent, enclosed with David Collins to Castlereagh, 10 May 1809, is at ibid., pp. 422–3.

65 'A Public Caution', 23 December 1803, Garrison Orders, 3 January 1804, Collins to Hobart, 28 February 1804, and Collins to King, 28 February 1804, 10 March 1804, *HRA*, series 3, vol. 1, pp. 58–9, 82, 88, 217, 264–5; Tuckey, op. cit., pp. 202–3; Mary Nicholls (ed.), *The Diary of the Reverend Robert Knopwood, 1803–1838* (Hobart 1977), pp. 32, 34–5 (12, 31 December 1803).

66 General Orders, 17 April, 27 June 1804, *HRA*, series 3, vol. 1, pp. 267, 271.

67 General Orders, 1 January 1804, ibid., pp. 86–7; Nicholls, op. cit., pp. 34, 37 (29 December 1803, 11 January 1804).

68 Government Orders, 1 June 1804, and Collins to Castlereagh, 31 May 1809, *HRA*, series 3, vol. 1, pp. 269, 426–7; Evidence of Edward Lord before the House of Commons Select Committee on Transportation, 12 June 1812, p. 79.

69 Lists (not all complete) of individuals and claims, ship by ship, are at NSWSA 4/1168A, pp. 355–8, 388–9, and A4110 (formerly ML An 45/2–5), and among the papers of John Piper, at ML A254. Partial copies, taken from the second source, appear in Wright, op. cit., pp. 107–14. It is possible to distinguish 105 families (couples alone, couples with children, and individuals with children), among which there is no evidence of marriage for 66. I am grateful to Trin Truscett for finding records of marriage for couples listed, to which I have added those described as married (presumably by Richard Johnson in 1791, there being no register kept in those cases)

in 'Return of Women not Victualled from the Store, and Their Means of Livelihood', 16 June 1794, CO 201/10, ff. 199–200.

70   List of people by the *Porpoise* and the *Lady Nelson*, NSWSA A4110; R. J. Ryan, *Land Grants, 1788–1809: A Record of Registered Grants and Leases in New South Wales, Van Diemen's Land and Norfolk Island* (Sydney 1981), pp. 90, 95.

71   Collins to Piper, 4 December 1807, ML A254, p. 122; Collins to Foveaux, 23 October 1808, enclosing Robert Knopwood and George Prideaux Harris to Collins, 21 October 1808, *HRA*, series 3, vol. 1, pp. 407, 408.

72   Collins to Castlereagh, 20 April, 1 September 1808, ibid., pp. 400, 404.

73   Collins to Castlereagh, 31 May 1809, *HRA*, series 3, vol. 1, pp. 426–7; J. Macmillan to Robert Brown, 9 June 1809, *HRNSW*, vol. 7, p. 167; Bligh to Castlereagh, 10 June 1809, *HRA*, series 1, vol. 7, p. 125.

74   Diary of James Belbin, University of Tasmania Archives (I am grateful to Mr Bob Broughton, Archivist, for copies of this material); Calder, op. cit., pp. 204, 207–16.

75   Bligh to Castlereagh, 10 June 1809, and enclosed 'Settlers late of Norfolk Island' to Bligh, 21 May 1809, *HRA*, series 1, vol. 7, pp. 125, 127, 159–60; Wright, op. cit., p. 37.

76   Bligh to Castlereagh, 8 July 1809, *HRA*, series 1, vol. 7, p. 161; Deposition of Sergeant James McCauley, 9 August 1809, NSWSA 1152, pp. 297–8.

77   Diary of James Belbin. This was a speech in the trial of Colonel Thomas Picton, late Governor of Trinidad.

78   Lloyd Robson, *A History of Tasmania*, vol. 1: *Van Diemen's Land from the Earliest Times to 1855* (Melbourne 1983), p. 64.

79   Diary of James Belbin; Henry Goulburn to Macquarie, 31 January 1813, enclosing Bligh to Goulburn, 19 December 1812, and Belbin's petition to Lord Bathurst, n.d., *HRA*, series 1, vol. 7, pp. 685–7. For the fare to England, see evidence of James Dowse Harris before the House of Commons Select Committee on Transportation, 28 February 1812, p. 50. Belbin is not said to have had any land requiring compensation, Piper recommending him for a grant nevertheless, but the August 1807 list shows him with 45 acres on Norfolk: 'List of Settlers and Landholders in His Majesty's Settlement in Van Diemen's Land', 2 August 1807, NSWSA 4/1168A, pp. 136–7; List of people by the *City of Edinburgh*, NSWSA A4110.

Chapter 15   The Coming of the Macquaries

1   Elizabeth Macquarie to James Erskine, 13 June 1820, ML Bonwick Transcripts 22, p. 4396.

2   Elizabeth Macquarie to Charles Whalan, 13 February 1831, ML Mss 6/1–2, p. 31.

3   Macquarie's journal, 26 June 1804, ML A770.

4   Ibid., 20 August 1804; Dougal McKellar (a child in Macquarie's time), quoted in J. C. L. Fitzpatrick, *The Good Old Days of the Hawkesbury* (Sydney 1900), pp. 25–6.

5   Macquarie's journal, 26 March 1805, ML A770; Lachlan Macquarie, *Journals of his Tours in New South Wales and Van Diemen's Land, 1810–1822* (Sydney 1956), pp. 7, 51; Macquarie's evidence given to Commissioner Bigge, 4 February 1821, in John Ritchie (ed.), *The Evidence to the Bigge Reports: New South Wales under Governor Macquarie* (Melbourne 1971), vol. 1, p. 202; Elizabeth Henrietta Macquarie's annotation in her copy of James Boswell, *Life of Samuel Johnson* (London 1793), vol. 1, pp. 479–80, ML 928.24/J69/IB1–3.

6   John Ritchie, *Lachlan Macquarie: A Biography* (Melbourne 1986), pp. 93–7, 113–15.

7   Elizabeth Macquarie's diary, 18 June 1809, ML C126, pp. 10–13.

8   Ibid., 31 August – 1 September 1809, pp. 36–8; Jane Austen, *Sense and Sensibility*

(London 1969; first publ. 1811), p. 112.

9   Macquarie to William Paterson, 30 December 1809, ML safe 1/51, p. 164; Paterson to Macquarie, 28, 30 December 1809, NSWSA 9/2736; Journal of Alexander Huey, 31 December 1809, ML B1514; Ellis Bent to his mother, 4 March 1810, NL MS 195, pp. 77–8.

10   *Sydney Gazette*, 7 January 1810; Ellis Bent to his mother, 4 March 1810, NL MS 195, pp. 76–7.

11   *Sydney Gazette*, 7 January 1810. The text is from Samuel, 17: 12.

12   John Macarthur's protest at the opening of the Court of Criminal Judicature, 25 January 1808, in John Ritchie (ed.), *A Charge of Mutiny: The Court Martial of Lieutenant Colonel George Johnston for Deposing Governor William Bligh in the Rebellion of 26 January 1808* (Canberra 1988), p. 469.

13   Bligh to Lord Castlereagh, 30 June 1808, *HRA*, series 1, vol. 6, pp. 534–4; George Caley to Sir Joseph Banks, 7 July 1808, ML A79–1, pp. 180–1. For Reddington, see Peter O'Shaughnessy (ed.), *A Rum Story: The Adventures of Joseph Holt Thirteen Years in New South Wales (1800–12)* (Sydney 1988), p. 101; Alan Atkinson, 'The British Whigs and the Rum Rebellion', *Journal of the Royal Australian Historical Society*, vol. 66 (1980), pp. 85–6; Anne-Maree Whitaker, *Unfinished Revolution: United Irishmen in New South Wales, 1800–1810* (Sydney 1994), pp. 173, 177.

14   *Sydney Gazette*, 9 June 1810; Macquarie's memoranda, 12 August 1810 [unheaded paper; but see *Sydney Gazette*, 18 August 1810], 20 October 1811, ML A772, pp. 25a, 38.

15   *Sydney Gazette*, 24 February, 22 December 1810.

16   Ibid., 22 December 1810, 18 January 1812, (Government and General Orders, 15 December 1810, 11 January 1812, copied for the information of the Secretary of State, *HRA*, series 1, vol. 7, pp. 397–401, 618–22), 19 January 1813. Macquarie's memoranda, 1 January 1811, 1 January 1813, ML A772, pp. 29, 53.

17   Lord correspondence, 27 January – 12 March 1800, enclosed with Macquarie to Lord Castlereagh, 30 April 1810, Macquarie to Lord Liverpool, 27 October 1810, Liverpool to Macquarie, 26 July 1811, and Macquarie to Liverpool, 9 November 1812, *HRA*, series 1, vol. 7, pp. 294–300, 345–6, 364, 536–7, 794, 810.

18   Macquarie to Castlereagh, 8 March , 30 April 1810, ibid., pp. 223–4, 255, 258–9, 272, 276. For the printer, see also Macquarie to Liverpool, 27 October 1810, ibid., p. 347; Evidence of John Palmer, 23 March 1812, before the House of Commons Select Committee on Transportation, *Parliamentary Papers*, 1812, II, 341, p. 63.

19   *Sydney Gazette*, 3 November 1810; Liverpool to Macquarie, 26 July 1811, *HRA*, series 1, vol. 7, pp. 363, 366.

20   Anaïs Nin quoted Sandra M. Gilbert and Susan Gubar, *The Madwoman in the Attic: The Woman Writer and the Nineteenth-Century Literary Imagination* (New Haven 1979), p. 3. Varieties of the Good King appear in Douglas Hay, 'Property, Authority and the Criminal Law', in Douglas Hay, Peter Linebaugh and E. P. Thompson (eds), *Albion's Fatal Tree: Crime and Society in Eighteenth-Century England* (London 1977), pp. 27–8, 39; Pierre Clastres, *Society against the State* (trans. Robert Hurley) (Oxford 1977), esp. pp. 27–8; Patricia Springborg, *Royal Persons: Patriarchal Monarchy and the Feminine Principle* (London 1990).

21   *Sydney Gazette*, 24 February, 31 March, 7 April, 29 December 1810.

22   Ibid., 22 September 1805, 5 March 1809; Testimonial for Charles Whalan by William Paterson and John Piper, 25 March 1810, ML MSS 6/1–2, p. 1; Macquarie's testimonial for Whalan, 12 February 1822, ML DOC 1639; R. J. Ryan (ed.), *Land Grants, 1788–1809: A Record of Registered Grants and Leases in New South Wales, Van Diemen's land and Norfolk Island* (Sydney 1981), pp. 108, 209, 253, 260, 276; Pamela Statham (ed.), *A Colonial Regiment: New Sources Relating to the New South*

Wales Corps, 1789–1810 (Canberra 1992), p. 354.

23   Joseph Arnold to his brother, 18 March 1810, ML A1809–2, p. 8; John Hillas to Walter Spencer-Stanhope, 10 May 1810, Spencer-Stanhope Mss, item 2748, Central Library, Bradford; Holt, op. cit., p. 111. See also George Suttor to Sir Joseph Banks, 12 November 1812, ML A78–3.

24   *Sydney Gazette*, 14 January 1810. But see Ellis Bent to J. H. Bent, 2 May 1910, NL MS 195, pp. 165–8.

25   Elizabeth Macarthur to Eliza Kingdon, March 1816, in Sibella Macarthur Onslow (ed.), *Some Early Records of the Macarthurs of Camden* (Sydney 1914), p. 305; Dougal McKellar (quoting his mother), quoted Fitzpatrick, op. cit., p. 26.

26   Journal of James Mitchell, 1820–3, pp. 52–3, Edinburgh University Library (Australian Joint Copying Project mfm M1677); M. H. *Ellis, Lachlan Macquarie* (Sydney 1958), pp. 4, 129; Ritchie, *Lachlan Macquarie*, op. cit., p. 18.

27   *Sydney Gazette*, 7 January 1810; Ellis, op. cit., p. 43.

28   Macquarie's memoranda, 8 May 1810, ML A772, p. 23; Bligh to Elizabeth Bligh, 11 August 1810, ML safe 1/45, p. 298; 'Grants of Land given by His Excellency Governor Macquarie since January 1st, 1810', enclosed with Macquarie to Liverpool, 18 October 1811, *HRA*, series 1, vol. 7, p. 440.

29   Journal of James Mitchell, pp. 52–3.

30   Macquarie, *Journals of his Tours*, pp. 12, 13, 14, 24, 48, 56, 84–5; Elizabeth Macquarie's notes on Johnson (his comment that 'when a man is tired of London, he is tired of life'), op. cit., vol. 2, p. 566.

31   Macquarie, *Journals of his Tours*, pp. 62–7, 83, 192.

32   Castlereagh to Macquarie, 14´ May 1809, *HRA*, series 1, vol. 7, p. 82; *Sydney Gazette*, 24 February 1810.

33   The three 'concubines' were Hannah Yarmouth (married William Adams, 18 March, Parramatta), Margaret McGuire (married William Murray, 6 May, Parramatta) and Bridget McCarthy (married Joseph Ward, 13 May, Hawkesbury). There were three more during the second half of the year. The conclusions in this paragraph are based on a comparison of the marriage registers with the various lists in Carol J. Baxter (ed.), *Musters of New South Wales and Norfolk Island, 1805–1806* (Sydney 1989).

34   Evidence of Thomas Robson, 2 March 1812, before the House of Commons Select Committee on Transportation, *Parliamentary Papers*, 1812, II, 341, p. 52; and see also the evidence of John Palmer, 20 March 1812, ibid., pp. 60–1. By 'marriage rate' I mean the annual number of recorded marriages. Judging from the fluctuation in numbers Bligh implemented this policy about the beginning of 1807. During 1807 there were 119 marriages throughout the colony.

35   Ellis Bent to his mother, 27 April, 4 March 1810, NL MS 195, pp. 96, 144.

36   Trial of Bridget Brien, reported *Sydney Gazette*, 3 August 1811; Bligh's evidence, 21 Febuary 1812, before the House of Commons Select Committee on Transportation, op. cit., p. 32.

37   Epistle to the Ephesians, 5: 31; Andrew Thompson to J. T. Campbell, 30 January 1810, NSWSA 9/2736; Campbell to Thompson, 3 February 1810, NSWSA 4/3490B.

38   Macquarie, *Journals of his Tours*, p. 34 ; Patricia Grimshaw and others, *Creating a Nation: 1788–1990* (Melbourne 1994), pp. 55–7 (this detail by Marian Quartly). For Partridge and Greenwood, see Mollie Gillen, *The Founders of Australia: A Biographical Dictionary of the First Fleet* (Sydney 1989), p. 150.

39   *Sydney Gazette*, 14 September 1811 (supplement); and for the wife-sale ritual, see S. P. Menefee, *Wives for Sale: An Ethnographic Study of Popular Divorce* (Oxford 1981). This report says that the woman was Malkin's 'lawful wife' but there is no record of any marriage and had she been his wife the magistrates are not likely to have separated them indefinitely. He had arrived in 1801 with a seven-year sentence but he was listed as still a convict in the muster of 1811 and she (judging from her

punishment) was a convict too, so that this was a case of penal discipline.

40   Trial of Michael Cassidy, June 1819, quoted Paula J. Byrne, *Criminal Law and Colonial Subject: New South Wales, 1810–1830* (Cambridge 1993), p. 91. Elizabeth Cassidy appears as a licensed seller of spirits in *Sydney Gazette*, 16 March 1811. There is in fact no record of her marriage.

41   Gwyneth M. Dow, *Samuel Terry, the Botany Bay Rothschild* (Sydney 1974), pp. 48–9, 59.

42   Ellis Bent to J. H. Bent, 9 March 1810, NL MS 195, p. 125.

43   Brian H. Fletcher, *Landed Enterprise and Penal Society: A History of Farming and Grazing in New South Wales before 1821* (Sydney 1976), pp. 121–6, 232.

44   Gavin Souter, *Mosman: A History* (Melbourne 1994), pp. 20–1.

45   Macquarie to John Murray, 15 June 1810, *HRA*, series 3, vol. 1, pp. 439–40; Macquarie to Liverpool, 27 October 1810, 18 October 1811, and Liverpool to Macquarie (enclosing Liverpool to John Murray, 19 May 1812), 19 May 1812, *HRA*, series 1, vol. 7, pp. 344, 382–3, 488, 489–90.

46   'Inhabitants of New Norfolk' to Macquarie, in *Sydney Gazette*, 11 January 1812; Macquarie, *Journals of his Tours*, pp. 58–9.

47   *Sydney Gazette*, 7 July 1810.

48   'A Friend to Civilization' to the editor, ibid., 14, 28 July, 4, 11 August 1810.

49   *Sydney Gazette*, 8 January 1809; David Collins, *An Account of the English Colony in New South Wales* (ed. Brian H. Fletcher) (Sydney 1975), vol. 1 (first publ. 1798), pp. 250–1.

50   'Amicus' to the editor, *Sydney Gazette*, 8 September 1810.

51   *Sydney Gazette*, 19 January 1811.

52   Macquarie, *Journals of his Tours*, pp. 82–3.

53   Macquarie to Bathurst, 8 October 1814 (enclosing William Shelley to Macquarie, 8 April, 20 August 1814, and 'Plan of the Native Institution', 20 August 1814), and Macquarie to Bathurst, 24 March 1815, *HRA*, series 1, vol. 8, pp. 466–7.

54   R. H. W. Reece, 'Feasts and Blankets: The History of Some Early Attempts to Establish Relations with the Aborigines of New South Wales, 1814–1846', *Archaeology and Physical Anthropology in Oceania*, vol. 2 (1967), pp. 191–4; Michael Smithson, 'A Misunderstood Gift: The Annual Issue of Blankets to Aborigines in New South Wales, 1826–48', *Push: A Journal of Early Australian Social History*, no. 30 (1992), pp. 74–5.

55   Elizabeth Macquarie's journal, July 1809, ML C126, p. 31.

56   Macquarie, *Journals of his Tours*, p. 36.

57   Ibid., p. 61–2, 76–8.

58   Ibid., pp. 23, 28, 30, 31, 33, 36, 42, 57, 78.

59   *Sydney Gazette*, 6 October 1810, and for Hyde Park, see also ibid., 5 October 1811.

60   Ibid., 18 August, 6 October, 29 December 1810; Macquarie to Liverpool, 18 October 1811, *HRA*, series 1, vol. 7, pp. 385–6; Byrne, op. cit., p. 68.

61   Foveaux to Castlereagh, 20 February 1809, Macquarie to Castlereagh, 30 April 1810, and Liverpool to Macquarie, 26 July 1811, *HRA*, series 1, vol. 7, pp. 4, 269, 366; Alan Atkinson, 'Taking Possession: Sydney's First Householders', in Graeme Aplin (ed.), *A Difficult Infant: Sydney before Macquarie* (Sydney 1988), pp. 86–7.

62   *Sydney Gazette*, 9 June, 21 July, 29 December 1810. For the Reibeys, see Nance Irvine, *Mary Reibey — Molly Incognita: A Biography of Mary Reibey, 1777 to 1855, and her World* (Sydney 1987).

63   Macquarie to Castlereagh, 30 April 1810, and Macquarie to Liverpool, 27 October 1810, *HRA*, series 1, vol, 7, pp. 264–6, 343; Ellis Bent to his mother, 27 July 1810, NL MS 195, pp. 187–8.

64   *Sydney Gazette*, 19 January 1811; Macquarie to Liverpool, 18 October 1811, *HRA*, series 1, vol. 7, pp. 384–5.

65   James Broadbent, 'Building in the Colony', in James Broadbent and Joy Hughes

(eds), *The Age of Macquarie* (Melbourne 1992), pp. 167–8.

66   Macquarie's memoranda, 9 September 1812, 17 May 1813, ML A772, pp. 46, 59.

67   *Sydney Gazette*, 19 May, 2 June, 21 July, 18, 25 August, 8, 22, 29 September, 20 October 1810; Macquarie's memoranda, 20 September, 15 October 1810, ML A772, p. 27.

68   Quoted Byrne, op. cit., pp. 210–11.

69   *Sydney Gazette*, 1 June 1811.

70   Ibid., 20 October 1810.

71   Byrne, op. cit., pp. 74, 89–94, 163–4.

72   Elizabeth Macquarie's notes on Johnson, op. cit., vol. 1, p. 519, and vol. 3, p. 203.

73   Macquarie to Bathurst, 28 June 1813, *HRA*, series 1, vol. 7, p. 780.

74   Elizabeth Macquarie to Whalan, 18 August 1823, ML MSS 6/1–2, p. 17.

75   Ellis Bent to his mother, 27 April 1810, NL MS 195, p. 138; John Birch to John Piper, 15 August 1815, ML A256, p. 147.

76   Macquarie's memoranda, 4 June 1810, 4 June 1811, ML A772, pp. 24, 32.

77   John Grant to his mother and sister, 21 May 1804, 1 January 1805, ML FM4/1141; Henry Fulton to Elizabeth Bligh, [1809], ML safe 1/45, pp. 276–80.

78   Elizabeth Macarthur to Eliza Kingdon, March 1816, in Onslow, op. cit., p. 305; John Thomas Bigge, *Report of the Commissioner of Inquiry into the State of the Colony of New South Wales* (London 1822), pp. 145, 148; Macquarie, *Journals of his Tours*, p. 163.

79   *Sydney Gazette*, 22 September 1810.

80   Macquarie to Castlereagh, 30 April 1810, and Macquarie to Liverpool, 17 November 1812, *HRA*, series 1, vol. 7, pp. 252, 614–15; A. G. L. Shaw, *Convicts and the Colonies: A Study of Penal Transportation from Great Britain and Ireland to Australia and Other Parts of the British Empire* (London 1966), pp. 100–1; Byrne, op. cit., pp. 38–9.

81   *Sydney Gazette*, 24 July 1810.

82   Ibid., 9 June 1810.

83   Ibid, 2, 16 March 1813; Macquarie to Bathurst, 28 June 1813, *HRA*, series 1, vol. 7, pp. 715–16; McKellar, quoted in Fitzpatrick, op. cit., p. 22; Michael Flynn, *The Second Fleet: Britain's Grim Convict Armada of 1790* (Sydney 1993), pp. 377–9.

84   Bathurst to Macquarie, 23 November 1812, and Macquarie to Bathurst, 28 June 1813, *HRA*, series 1, vol. 7, pp. 674–5, 777–8.

85   Will of Edward Wills, 24 May 1810, copy kindly supplied by Mr Terry Wills Cooke; *Sydney Gazette*, 18 May 1811; Register of Absolute Pardons, NSWSA 4/4486.

Afterword

1   Blaise Pascal, *Pascal's Pensées* (trans. Martin Turnell) (New York 1962), p. 146; William Cowper, 'The Castaway', in Jonathan Raban (ed.), *The Oxford Book of the Sea* (Oxford 1992), p. 166.

2   L. F. Fitzhardinge (ed.), *Sydney's First Four Years* (that is, Watkin Tench, *A Narrative of the Expedition to Botany Bay and A Complete Account of the Settlement at Port Jackson*) (Sydney 1979), p. 252.

3   Janice Barkley, 'Early Boat Building on the Upper Hawkesbury', unpublished research essay, University of New England, 1993, pp. 48–70. I am very grateful to Jan Barkley for a copy of this essay.

4   Macquarie to Henry Goulburn, 21 December 1817, *HRA*, series 1, vol. 9, p. 747.

5   'Merchants, Freeholders, Settlers, and Traders, being the principal Inhabitants of

Sydney' to Macquarie, in *Sydney Gazette*, 18 January 1812.

6   A. G. L. Shaw, *Convicts and the Colonies: A Study of Penal Transportation from Great Britain and Ireland to Australia and Other Parts of the British Empire* (London 1966), pp. 363–7.

7   Macquarie's proclamation, 4 May 1816, *HRA*, series 1, vol. 9, p. 143; R. H. W. Reece, *Aborigines and Colonists: Aborigines and Colonial Society in New South Wales in the 1830s and 1840s* (Sydney 1974), pp. 109–10.

Bibliography

1. Works from the Period and Published Documents

'An Officer', *An Authentic Journal of an Expedition under Commodore Phillips to Botany Bay* (London 1789).

Anon., *A Brief Account of the Causes that have retarded the Progress of the Colony of Georgia, in America* (London 1743).

Bowring, John (ed.), *The Works of Jeremy Bentham* (New York 1962).

Bradley, William, *A Voyage to New South Wales: The Journal of Lieutenant William Bradley RN of HMS Sirius, 1786–1792* (Sydney 1969).

Caley, George, *Reflections on the Colony of New South Wales* (ed. J. E. B. Currey) (Melbourne 1966).

Collins, David, *An Account of the English Colony in New South Wales* (ed. Brian H. Fletcher) (Sydney 1975).

Dampier, William, *Dampier's Voyages* (ed. John Masefield) (London 1906).

Dann, John C. (ed.), *The Nagle Journal: A Diary of the Life of Jacob Nagle, Sailor, from the Year 1775 to 1841* (New York 1988).

Davis, William T. (ed.), *Bradford's History of Plymouth Plantation 1606–1646*, New York 1908.

Defoe, Daniel (writing as Charles Johnson), *A General History of the Robberies and Murders of the most notorious Pyrates, and also Their Policies, Discipline and Government* (London 1724).

Defoe, Daniel, *Robinson Crusoe* (Oxford 1928).

Easty, John, *Memorandum of the Transactions of a Voyage from England to Botany Bay, 1787–1793: A First Fleet Journal* (Sydney 1965).

Fidlon, Paul G. (ed.), *The Journal of Philip Gidley King: Lieutenant, RN, 1787–1790* (Sydney 1980).

Fidlon, Paul G., and R. J. Ryan (eds), *The Journal and Letters of Lt. Ralph Clark, 1787–1792* (Sydney 1981).

Fidlon, Paul G., and R. J. Ryan (eds), *The Journal of Arthur Bowes Smyth: Surgeon, Lady Penrhyn, 1787–1789* (Sydney 1979).

Fielding, Henry, *An Enquiry into the Causes of the Late Increase of Robbers and Related Writings* (ed. Malvin R. Zirker) (Oxford 1988).

Fitzhardinge, L. F. (ed.), *Sydney's First Four Years* (that is, Watkin Tench, *A Narrative of the Expedition to Botany Bay* and *A Complete Account of the Settlement at Port Jackson*) (Sydney 1979).

Grimshaw, Patricia, Susan Janson and Marian Quartly (eds), *Freedom Bound I: Documents on Women in Colonial Australia* (Sydney 1995).

Heney, Helen (ed.), *Dear Fanny: Women's Letters to and from New South Wales, 1788–1857* (Canberra 1985).

Holt, Joseph, *A Rum Story: The Adventures of Joseph Holt Thirteen Years in New South Wales (1800–12)* (ed. Peter O'Shaughnessy) (Sydney 1988).
Hunter, John *An Historical Journal of the Transactions at Port Jackson and Norfolk Island* (London 1793).
Irvine, Nance (ed.), *The Sirius Letters: The Complete Letters of Newton Fowell* (Sydney 1988).
Johnson, Richard, *An Address to the Inabitants of the Colonies established in New South Wales and Norfolk Island* (London 1794).
[Jones, William], *The Principles of Government, in a Dialogue between a Scholar and a Peasant* (London 1782).
Knight, R. J. B., and Alan Frost (eds), *The Journal of Daniel Paine, 1794–1797* (Sydney 1983).
Macarthur Onslow, Sibella (ed.), *Some Early Records of the Macarthurs of Camden* (Sydney 1914).
Mackaness, George (ed.), *Memoirs of George Suttor, F.L.S., Bansian Collector (1774–1859)*, (Sydney 1948).
Mackaness, George (ed.), *Some Letters of Rev. Richard Johnson, BA, First Chaplain of New South Wales* (Sydney 1954).
Macquarie, Lachlan, *Journals of his Tours in New South Wales and Van Diemen's Land, 1810–1822* (Sydney 1956).
Mann, D. D., *The Present Picture of New South Wales* (London 1811).
McLachlan, Noel (ed.), *The Memoirs of James Hardy Vaux* (London 1964).
Minutes of a Court Martial . . . for the Trial of Lieut. W. G. Carlile Kent (Portsmouth 1811).
Nicol, John, *The Life and Adventures of John Nicol, Mariner* (London 1822).
[Oglethorpe, James], *A New and Accurate Account of the Provinces of South-Caroline and Georgia* (London 1733).
Purchas, Samuel, *Hakluytus Posthumus, or Purchas His Pilgrimes* (Glasgow 1906).
Ritchie, John (ed.), *A Charge of Mutiny: The Court Martial of Lieutenant Colonel George Johnston for Deposing Governor William Bligh in the Rebellion of 26 January 1808* (Canberra 1988).
Ritchie, John (ed.), *The Evidence to the Bigge Reports: New South Wales under Governor Macquarie* (Melbourne 1971).
Rusden, G. W., *Curiosities of Colonization* (London 1874).
Sharp, Granville, *An Account of the Constitutional English Polity of Congregational Courts: And More Particularly of the Great Annual Court of the People, called the View of Frankpledge* (London 1786).
Sidney, Algernon, *Discources concerning Government* (London 1704).
Smeathman, Henry, *Plan of a Settlement to be Made Near Sierra Leona, on the Grain Coast of Africa* (London 1786).
St John de Crèvecouer, Hector, *Letters from an American Farmer* (London 1912).
Swift, Jonathan, *Gulliver's Travels* (London 1960).
Tuckey, J. H., *An Account of a Voyage to Establish a Colony at Port Phillip in Bass's Strait, on the South Coast of New South Wales, in His Majesty's Ship Calcutta, in the Years 1802-3-4* (London 1805).
White, John, *Journal of a Voyage to New South Wales* (ed. Alec H. Chisholm) (Sydney 1962).
Worgan, George B., *Journal of a First Fleet Surgeon* (Sydney 1978).

2. Books by Modern Scholars

Aarsleff, Hans, *The Study of Language in England, 1780–1860* (Minneapolis 1983).
Abbott, G. J. and N. B. Nairn (eds), *Economic Growth of Australia, 1788–1821* (Melbourne 1969).
Albion, Robert G., *Forests and Sea Power: The Timber Problem of the Royal Navy, 1652–1862* (Cambridge, Massachusetts, 1926).

Allen, Walter, *The English Novel: From* The Pilgrim's Progress *to* Sons and Lovers (London 1958).

Altick, Richard D., *The English Common Reader: A Social History of the Mass Reading Public, 1800–1900* (Chicago 1957).

Anderson, Benedict, *Imagined Communities: Reflections on the Origin and Spread of Nationalism* (London 1983).

Andrews, Alan E. J. (ed.), *The Devil's Wilderness: George Caley's Journey to Mount Banks, 1804* (Hobart 1984).

Andrews, K. R., N. P. Canny and P. E. H. Hair (eds), *The Westward Enterprise: English Activities in Ireland, the Atlantic, and America, 1480–1650* (Liverpool 1978).

Aplin, Graeme (ed.), *A Difficult Infant: Sydney before Macquarie* (Sydney 1988).

Bagrow, Leo, *History of Cartography* (Chicago 1985).

Bailyn, Bernard, *The Ideological Origins of the American Revolution* (Cambridge, Mass., 1967).

Bailyn, Bernard, *Voyagers to the West: A Passage in the Peopling of America on the Eve of the Revolution* (New York 1986).

Bailyn, Bernard, and Philip D. Morgan (eds), *Strangers within the Realm: Cultural Margins of the First British Empire* (Chapel Hill 1991).

Barker-Benfield, G. J., *The Culture of Sensibility: Sex and Society in Eighteenth-Century Britain* (Chicago 1992).

Barkley, Jan, and Michelle Nichols, *Hawkesbury, 1794–1994: The First 200 Years of the Second Colonisation* (Windsor 1994).

Barrell, John, *The Birth of Pandora and the Division of Knowledge* (London 1992).

Barnard Eldershaw, M., *The Life and Times of Captain John Piper* (Sydney 1973).

Bassett, Marnie, *The Governor's Lady: Mrs Philip Gidley King* (London 1956).

Bateson, Charles, *The Convict Ships* (Glasgow 1959).

Beattie, J. M., *Crime and the Courts in England, 1660–1800* (Oxford 1986).

Bell, Ian A., *Literature and Crime in Augustan England* (London 1991).

Berndt, Ronald M. (ed.), *Australian Aboriginal Anthropology: Modern Studies in the Social Anthropology of the Australian Aborigines* (Nedlands, WA, 1970).

Berndt, Ronald M., and Catherine H. Berndt (eds), *Aboriginal Man in Australia: Essays in Honour of Emeritus Professor A. P. Elkin* (Sydney 1965).

Billias, George A. (ed.), *Law and Authority in Colonial America: Selected Essays* (Barre, Massachusetts, 1965).

Black, Eugene Charlton, *The Association: British Extraparliamentary Political Organization, 1769–93* (Cambridge, Massachusetts, 1963).

Black, Jeremy, and Jeremy Gregory (eds), *Culture, Politics and Society in Britain, 1660–1800* (Manchester 1991).

Blakemore, Steven, *Burke and the Fall of Language: The French Revolution as Linguistic Event* (Hanover, New Hampshire, 1988).

Brewer, John, and John Styles (eds), *An Ungovernable People: The English and their Law in the Seventeenth and Eighteenth Centuries* (London 1983).

Brewer, John, *The Sinews of Power: War, Money and the English State, 1688–1783* (London 1989).

Broadbent, James, and Joy Hughes (eds), *The Age of Macquarie* (Melbourne 1992).

Bryson, Gladys, *Man and Society: The Scottish Inquiry of the Eighteenth Century* (New York 1968).

Butlin, S. J., *Foundations of the Australian Monetary System, 1788–1851* (Sydney 1953).

Byrne, Paula J., *Criminal Law and Colonial Subject: New South Wales, 1810–1830* (Melbourne, 1993).

Canny, Nicholas, and Anthony Pagden (eds), *Colonial Identity in the Atlantic World, 1500–1800* (Princeton 1987).

Carlson, Julie A. *In the Theatre of Romanticism: Coleridge, Nationalism, Women* (Cambridge 1994).

Carter, Paul, *The Road to Botany Bay: An Essay in Spatial History* (London 1987).

Castles, Alex C., *An Australian Legal History* (Sydney 1982).

Cell, Gillian T. (ed.), *Newfoundland Discovered: English Attempts at Colonisation, 1610–1630* (London 1982).

Clark, C. M. H., *A History of Australia* (six volumes, Melbourne 1962–87).

Clark, J. C. D., *English Society, 1688–1832: Ideology, Social Structure and Political Practice during the Ancien Régime* (Cambridge 1985).

Clastres, Pierre, *Society against the State* (trans. Robert Hurley) (Oxford 1977).

Cleverley, John F., *The First Generation: School and Society in Early Australia* (Sydney 1971).

Clune, Frank, *Bound for Botany Bay: Narrative of a Voyage in 1798 Aboard the Death Ship* Hillsborough (Sydney 1964).

Cockburn, J. S. (ed.), *Crime in England, 1550–1800* (London 1977).

Cohen, Lysbeth, *Elizabeth Macquarie: Her Life and Times* (Sydney 1979).

Coleman, D. C., *The British Paper Industry, 1495–1860: A Study in Industrial Growth* (Oxford 1958).

Colley, Linda, *Britons: Forging the Nation, 1707–1837* (New Haven 1992).

Connah, Graham, '*Of the Hut I builded*': The Archaeology of Australia's History (Cambridge 1988).

Corish, Patrick J. (ed.), *Radicals, Rebels and Establishments* (*Historical Studies*, vol. 15) (Belfast 1985).

Cramp, Karl R., and George Mackaness, *A History of the United Grand Lodge of New South Wales* (Sydney 1938).

Dark, Eleanor, *The Timeless Land* (Sydney 1960).

Davidoff, Leonore, *Worlds Between: Historical Perspectives on Gender and Class* (Cambridge 1995).

Dening, Greg, *Mr Bligh's Bad Language: Passion, Power and Theatre on the Bounty* (Cambridge 1993).

Dickinson, H. T. (ed.), *Britain and the French Revolution, 1789–1815* (London 1989).

Dixson, Miriam, *The Real Matilda* (Melbourne 1994).

Dow, Gwyneth M., *Samuel Terry, the Botany Bay Rothschild* (Sydney 1974).

Doyle, J. A., *The English in America: The Puritan Colonies* (London 1887).

Dwyer, John, *Virtuous Discourse: Sensibility and Community in Late Eighteenth-Century Scotland* (Edinburgh 1987).

Ekirch, A. Roger, *Bound for America: The Transportation of British Convicts to the Colonies, 1718–1775* (Oxford 1987).

Ellis, M. H., *John Macarthur* (Sydney 1955).

Ellis, M. H., *Lachlan Macquarie: His Life, Adventures, and Times* (Sydney 1952).

Essays in Colonial History Presented to Charles McLean Andrews by his Students (New Haven 1931).

Fitzgerald, Ross, and Mark Hearn, *Bligh, Macarhur and the Rum Rebellion* (Sydney 1988).

Fitzpatrick, J. C. L., *The Good Old Days of the Hawkesbury* (Sydney 1900).

Flaherty, David H. (ed.), *Essays in the History of Early American Law* (Chapel Hill 1969).

Fletcher, Brian H., *Landed Enterprise and Penal Society: A History of Farming and Grazing in New South Wales before 1821* (Sydney 1976).

Fliegelman, Jay, *Declaring Independence: Jefferson, Natural Language, and the Culture of Performance* (Stanford 1993).

Fliegelman, Jay, *Prodigals and Pilgrims: The American Revolution against Patriarchal Authority* (Cambridge 1982).

Frost, Alan, *Convicts and Empire: A Naval Question* (Melbourne 1980).

Frost, Alan, *Arthur Phillip, 1738–1814: His Voyaging* (Melbourne 1988).

Frost, Alan, *Botany Bay Mirages: Illusions of Australia's Convict Beginnings* (Melbourne 1994).

Fyfe, Christopher, *A History of Sierra Leone* (London 1962).

George, M. Dorothy, *London Life in the Eighteenth Century* (Harmondsworth 1966).

Gibbs, A. M. (ed.), *Masks of Time: Drama and its Contexts* (Canberra 1994).

Gilmore, William J., *Reading Becomes a Necessity of Life: Material and Cultural Life in Rural New England, 1780–1835* (Knoxville, Tennessee, 1989).

Gould, Robert Freke, *Military Lodges* (London 1900).

Gould, Robert Freke, *The History of Freemasonry* (three volumes, London 1884–7).

Green, Martin, *Dreams of Adventure, Deeds of Empire* (London 1980).

Grimshaw, Patricia, and others, *Creating a Nation: 1788–1990* (Melbourne 1994).

Guha, Ranajit, *A Rule of Property for Bengal: An Essay on the Idea of Permanent Settlement* (New Delhi 1981).

Hainsworth, D. R., *The Sydney Traders: Simeon Lord and his Contemporaries, 1788–1921* (Melbourne 1972).

Hardy, John, and Alan Frost (eds), *Studies from Terra Australis to Australia* (Canberra 1989).

Harrison, J. F. C., *The Second Coming: Popular Millenarianism, 1780–1850* (London 1979).

Hay, Douglas, Peter Linebaugh and E. P. Thompson (eds), *Albion's Fatal Tree: Crime and Society in Eighteenth-Century England* (London 1975).

Hill, Christopher, *Change and Continuity in Seventeenth-Century England* (London 1974).

Hill, Christopher, *The World Turned Upside Down: Radical Ideas during the English Revolution* (Harmondsworth 1975).

Hill-Reid, W. S., *John Grant's Journey: A Convict's Story, 1803–1811* (London 1957).

Hirst, J. B., *Convict Society and Its Enemies: A History of Early New South Wales* (Sydney 1983).

Houlding, J. A., *Fit for Service: The Training of the British Army, 1715–1795* (Oxford 1981).

Howell, Colin, and Richard J. Twomey (eds), *Jack Tar in History: Essays in the History of Maritime Life and Labour* (Fredericton, New Brunswick, 1991).

Howson, Gerald, *Thief-Taker General: Jonothan Wild and the Emergence of Crime and Corruption as a Way of Life in Eighteenth-Century England* (New Brunswick, New Jersey, 1985).

Hughes, Robert, *The Fatal Shore: A History of the Transportation of Convicts to Australia, 1787–1868* (London 1987).

Hunt, Lynn (ed.), *Eroticism and the Body Politic* (Baltimore 1991).

Ignatieff, Michael, *A Just Measure of Pain: The Penitentiary in the Industrial Revolution, 1750–1850* (London 1978).

Ignatieff, Michael, *The Needs of Strangers* (London 1994).

Innes, Stephen (ed.), *Work and Labor in Early America* (Chapel Hill 1988).

Irvine, Nance, *Mary Reibey – Molly Incognita: A Biography of Mary Reibey 1777 to 1855, and her World* (Sydney 1987).

Isaac, Rhys, *The Transformation of Virginia, 1740–1790* (Chapel Hill 1982).

Israel, Janice Ruse, 'My Mother Reread Me Tenderley': *The Life of James Ruse* (Sydney 1988).

Jacob, Margaret C., *The Radical Enlightenment: Pantheists, Freemasons and Republicans* (London 1981).

Kenny, Arthur F. (ed.), *Rogues, Vagabonds, and Sturdy Beggars* (Barre, Massachusetts, 1973).

Kerr, Joan, and James Broadbent, *Gothick Taste in the Colony of New South Wales* (Sydney 1980).

Kettner, James H., *The Development of American Citizenship, 1608–1870* (Chapel Hill 1978).

King, Hazel, *Elizabeth Macarthur and Her World* (Sydney 1980).

King, Robert J. (ed.), *The Secret History of the Convict Colony: Alexandro Malaspina's Report on the British Settlement of New South Wales* (Sydney 1990).

Knittle, Walter Allen, *The Early Eighteenth Century Palatine Emigration: A British Government Redemptioner Project to Manufacture Naval Stores* (Philadelphia 1936).

Koselleck, Reinhart, *Critique and Crisis: Enlightenment and the Pathogenesis of Modern Society* (Oxford 1988).

Kumar, Krishan, and Stephen Bann (eds), *Utopias and the Millenium* (London 1993).

Land, Stephen K., *From Signs to Propositions: The Concept of Form in Eighteenth-Century Semantic Theory* (London 1974).

Langford, Paul, *A Polite and Commercial People: England, 1727–1783* (Oxford 1989).

Langford, Paul, *Public Life and the Propertied Englishman, 1689–1798* (Oxford 1991).

Lewis, Michael, *A Social History of the Navy, 1793–1815* (London 1960).

Linebaugh, Peter, *The London Hanged: Crime and Civil Society in the Eighteenth Century* (London 1993).

MacDonagh, Oliver, *The Inspector General: Sir Jeremiah Fitzpatrick and the Politics of Social Reform, 1783–1802* (London 1981).

Macintosh, Neil K., *Richard Johnson, Chaplain to the Colony of New South Wales: His Life and Times, 1755–1827* (Sydney 1978).

Mackaness, George *The Life of Vice-Admiral William Bligh, RN, FRS* (Sydney 1931).

Mackay, David, *A Place of Exile: The European Settlement of New South Wales* (Melbourne 1985).

Malone, Joseph J., *Pine Trees and Politics: The Naval Stores and Forest Policy in Colonial New England, 1691–1775* (London 1964).

Marshall, P. J., and Glyndwr Williams, *The Great Map of Mankind: British Perceptions of the World in the Age of Enlightenment* (London 1982).

Martin, Ged (ed.), *The Founding of Australia: The Argument about Australia's Origins* (Sydney 1978).

Menefee, S. P., *Wives for Sale: An Ethnographic Study of Popular Divorce* (Oxford 1981).

Moore, John H., *The First Fleet Marines, 1786–1792* (St Lucia, Queensland, 1987).

Morphy, Howard, *Ancestral Connections: Art and an Aboriginal System of Knowledge* (Chicago 1991).

Mulvaney, D.J., *Encounters in Place: Outsider and Aboriginal Australians, 1606–1985* (St Lucia 1989).

Neal, David, *The Rule of Law in a Penal Colony: Law and Power in Early New South Wales* (Melbourne, 1991).

Nobbs, Raymond (ed.), *Norfolk Island and its First Settlement, 1788–1814* (Sydney 1988).

Norton, Mary Beth, *Liberty's Daughters: The Revolutionary Experience of American Women, 1750–1800* (Boston 1980).

Oldham, Wilfrid, *Britain's Convicts to the Colonies* (Sydney 1990).

Ong, Walter J., *Orality and Literacy: The Technologizing of the Word* (London 1982).

Ong, Walter J., *Interfaces of the Word: Studies in the Evolution of Consciousness and Culture* (Ithaca, New York, 1977).

Pateman, Carole, *The Sexual Contract* (Cambridge 1988).

Pockley, R. V., *Ancestor Treasure Hunt: The Edward Wills Family and Descendants in Australia, 1797–1976* (Sydney 1976).

Pocock, J. G. A., *Virtue, Commerce, and History: Essays on Political Thought and History, Chiefly in the Eighteenth Century* (Cambridge 1985).

Pocock, J. G. A. (ed.), *The Varieties of British Political Thought, 1500–1800* (Cambridge 1993).

Prior, Mary (ed.), *Women in English Society, 1500–1800* (London 1985).

Rediker, Marcus, *Between the Devil and the Deep Blue Sea: Merchant Seamen, Pirates, and the Anglo–American Maritime World, 1700–1750* (Cambridge 1993).

Reece, Bob (ed.), *Irish Convicts: The Origins of Convicts Transported to Australia* (Dublin 1989).

Reece, R. H. W., *Aborigines and Colonists: Aborigines and Colonial Society in New South Wales in the 1830s and 1840s* (Sydney 1974).

Reynolds, Henry, *The Law of the Land* (Ringwood, Victoria, 1992).

Ringrose, Marjorie, and Adam J. Lerner (eds), *Reimagining the Nation* (Buckingham 1993).

Ritchie, John, *Lachlan Macquarie: A Biography* (Melbourne 1986).

Robbins, Caroline, *The Eighteenth-Century Commonwealthman: Studies in the Transmission, Development and Circumstance of English Liberal Thought from the Restoration of Charles II until the War with the Thirteen Colonies* (Cambridge, Mass. 1959).

Robinson, Portia, *The Women of Botany Bay* (Melbourne 1988).

Robson, Lloyd, *A History of Tasmania, vol. 1: Van Diemen's Land from the Earliest Times to 1855* (two volumes, Melbourne 1983, 1990).

Rollison, David, *The Local Origins of Modern Society: Gloucestershire, 1500–1800* (London 1992).

Rudkin, Olive D., *Thomas Spence and his Connections* (London 1927).

Sahlins, Marshall, *Historical Metaphors and Mythical Realities: Structure in the Early History of the Sandwich Islands Kingdom* (Ann Arbor 1981).

Sahlins, Marshall, *Islands of History* (Chicago 1985).

Saunders, Kay, and Raymond Evans (eds), *Gender Relations in Australia: Domination and Negotiation* (Sydney 1992).

Saye, Albert Berry, *A Constitutional History of Georgia, 1732–1968* (Athens, Georgia, [1971?]).

Sennett, Richard, *The Fall of Public Man* (Cambridge 1977).

Shapiro, Barbara J., *Probability and Certainty in Seventeenth-Century England: A Study of the Relationships between Natural Science, Religion, History, Law, and Literature* (Princeton 1983).

Shaw, A. G. L., *Convicts and the Colonies: A Study of Penal Transportation from Great Britain and Ireland to Australia and Other Parts of the British Empire* (London 1966).

Smith, Olivia, *The Politics of Language, 1791–1819* (Oxford 1984).

Snell, K. D. M., *Annals of the Labouring Poor: Social Change and Agrarian England, 1660–1900* (Cambridge 1987).

Spadafora, David, *The Idea of Progress in Eighteenth-Century Britain* (New Haven 1990).

Stackpole, Edouard A., *Whales and Destiny: The Rivalry between America, France, and Britain for Control of the Southern Whale Fishery, 1785–1825* (Boston 1972).

Statham, Pamela (ed.), *A Colonial Regiment: New Sources Relating to the New South Wales Corps, 1789–1810* (Canberra 1992).

Steele, Ian K., *The English Atlantic 1675–1740: An Exploration of Communication and Community* (New York 1986).

Steven, Margaret, *Merchant Campbell, 1769–1846: A Study in Colonial Trade* (London 1965).

Steven, Margaret, *Trade, Tactics and Territory: Britain in the Pacific, 1783–1823* (Melbourne 1983).

Stone, Lawrence (ed.), *An Imperial State at War: Britain from 1689 to 1815* (London 1994).

Struever, Nancy (ed.), *Language and the History of Thought* (Rochester, New York, 1995).

Swain, Tony, *A Place for Strangers: Towards a History of Australian Aboriginal Being* (Cambridge 1993).

Taylor, Paul S., *Georgia Plan: 1732–1752* (Berkeley 1972).

Thomas, Keith, *Man and the Natural World: Changing Attitudes in England, 1500–1800* (London 1983).

Thompson, E. P., *The Making of the English Working Class* (Harmondsworth 1968).

Thompson, E. P., *Witness against the Beast: William Blake and the Moral Law* (Cambridge 1994).

Tuveson, Ernest Lee, *The Imagination as a Means of Grace: Locke and the Aesthetics of Romanticism* (Berkeley 1960).

United Grand Lodge of England, *Grand Lodge, 1717–1967* (Oxford 1967).

Walker, R. B., *The Newspaper Press in New South Wales, 1803–1920* (Sydney 1976).

Walvin, James, *Black Ivory: A History of British Slavery* (London 1992).
Whitaker, Anne-Maree, *Unfinished Revolution: United Irishmen in New South Wales, 1800–1810* (Sydney 1994).
Wiener, Frederick Bernays, *Civilians under Military Justice: The British Practice since 1689, Especially in North America* (Chicago 1967).
Williams, T. Desmond, *Secret Societies in Ireland* (Dublin 1973).
Wright, Reg, *The Forgotten Generation of Norfolk Island and Van Diemen's Land* (Sydney 1986).
Yarwood, A. T., *Samuel Marsden: The Great Survivor* (Melbourne 1977).

3. Articles in Learned Journals

Armstrong, Nancy, and Leonard Tennenhouse, 'A Novel Nation; or, How to Rethink Modern England as an Emergent Culture', *Modern Language Quarterly*, vol. 54 (1993), pp. 327–44.
Armstrong, Nancy, and Leonard Tennenhouse, 'The Interior Difference: A Brief Genealogy of Dreams, 1650–1717', *Eighteenth-Century Studies*, vol. 23 (1990), pp. 458–78.
Armstrong, Nancy, and Leonard Tennenhouse, 'The American Origins of the English Novel', *American Literary History*, vol. 4 (1992), pp. 386–410.
Atkinson, Alan, 'Jeremy Bentham and the Rum Rebellion', *Journal of the Royal Australian Historical Society*, vol. 64 (1978), pp. 1–13.
Atkinson, Alan, 'The British Whigs and the Rum Rebellion', *Journal of the Royal Australian Historical Society*, vol. 66 (1980), pp. 73–90.
Atkinson, Alan, 'Isaac Transported', *Labour History*, no. 50 (May 1986), pp. 42–53.
Atkinson, Alan, 'The Primitive Origins of Parliament', *Push from the Bush: A Bulletin of Social History*, no. 24 (April 1987), pp. 48–76.
Atkinson, Alan, 'The First Plans for Governing New South Wales, 1786–87', *Australian Historical Studies*, vol. 94 (1990), pp. 22–40.
Atkinson, Alan, 'The Free-Born Englishman Transported: Convict Rights as a Measure of Eighteenth-Century Empire', *Past and Present*, no. 144 (August 1994), pp. 88–115.
Aveling, Marian, 'Imagining New South Wales as a Gendered Society, 1783–1821', *Australian Historical Studies*, vol. 25 (1992).
Bartlett, Thomas, 'Select Documents XXXVIII: Defenders and Defenderism in 1795', *Irish Historical Studies*, vol. 24 (1985), pp. 373–94.
Bartlett, Thomas, 'The End to Moral Economy: The Irish Militia Disturbances of 1793', *Past and Present*, no. 99 (May 1983), pp. 41–64.
Beattie, J. M., 'Scales of Justice: Defense Counsel and the English Criminal Trial in the Eighteenth and Nineteenth Centuries', *Law and History Review*, vol. 9 (1991), pp. 221–67.
Becket, J. V., 'The Debate over Farm Sizes in Eighteenth and Nineteenth Century England', *Agricultural History*, vol. 57 (1983), pp. 308–25.
Bernhard, Virginia, 'Bermuda and Virginia in the Seventeenth Century: A Comparative View', *Journal of Social History*, vol. 19 (1985–6), pp. 57–70.
Billings, Warren S., 'The Cases of Fernando and Elizabeth Key: A Note on the Status of Blacks in Seventeenth-Century Virginia', *William and Mary Quarterly*, series 3, vol. 30 (1973), pp. 467–74.
Blanco, Richard L., 'The Soldier's Friend – Sir Jeremiah Fitzpatrick, Inspector of Health for Land Forces', *Medical History*, vol. 20 (1976), pp. 402–21.
Bolton, G. C., 'William Eden and the Convicts, 1771–1787', *Australian Journal of Politics and History*, vol. 26 (1980), pp. 30–44.
Breen, T. H., '"Baubles of Britain": The American and Consumer Revolutions of the Eighteenth Century', *Past and Present*, no. 119 (May 1988), pp. 73–104.
Brown, Wendy, 'Finding the Man in the State', *Feminist Studies*, vol. 18 (1992), pp. 7–34.

Bullock, Steven C., 'A Pure and Sublime System: The Appeal of Post-Revolutionary Freemasonry', *Journal of the Early Republic*, vol. 9 (1989), pp. 359–73.

Bullock, Steven C., 'The Revolutionary Transformation of American Freemasonry, 1752–1792', *William and Mary Quarterly*, series 3, vol. 47 (1990), pp. 347–69.

Byrnes, Dan, '"Emptying the Hulks": Duncan Campbell and the First Three Fleets to Australia', *Push from the Bush*, no. 24 (April 1987), pp. 2–24.

Byrnes, Dan, 'The Blackheath Connection: London Local History and the Settlement of New South Wales', *Push: A Journal of Early Australian Social History*, no. 28 (1990), pp. 65–71.

Campbell, Enid, 'Prerogative Rule in New South Wales, 1788–1823', *Journal of the Royal Australian Historical Society*, vol. 50 (1964), pp. 161–91.

Clark, Peter, 'Migration in England During the Late Seventeenth and Early Eighteenth Centuries', *Past and Present*, no. 83 (May 1979), pp. 57–90.

Colley, Linda, 'The Politics of Eighteenth-Century British History', *Journal of British Studies*, vol. 25 (1986), pp. 359–79.

Colwill, Elizabeth, 'Just Another *Citoyenne*? Marie-Antoinette on Trial, 1790–1793', *History Workshop*, issue 28 (Autumn 1989), pp. 63–87.

Connell, R. W., 'The Convict Rebellion of 1804', *Melbourne Historical Journal*, vol. 5 (1965), pp. 27–37.

Cullen, L. M., 'The Hidden Ireland: Re-Assessment of a Concept', *Studia Hibernica*, vol. 9 (1969), pp. 7–47.

Cunningham, Hugh, 'The Language of Patriotism, 1750–1914', *History Workshop*, issue 12 (Autumn 1981), pp. 8–33.

Curtin, Nancy J., 'The Transformation of the Society of United Irishmen into a Mass-Based Revolutionary Organisation, 1794–6', *Irish Historical Studies*, vol. 24 (1985), pp. 463–92.

Dawson, Frank Griffiths, 'William Pitt's Settlement at Black River on the Mosquito Shore: A Challenge to Spain in Central America', *Hispanic American Historical Review*, vol. 63 (1983), pp. 677–706.

Dunne, T. J., 'The Gaelic Response to Conquest and Colonisation: The Evidence of the Poetry', *Studia Hibernica*, vol. 20 (1980), pp. 7–30.

Elliott, Jane, 'Was There a Convict Dandy? Convict Consumer Interests in Sydney, 1788–1815', *Australian Historical Studies*, vol. 26 (1995), pp. 373–92.

Elliott, Marianne, 'The Origins and Transformation of Early Irish Republicanism', *International Review of Social History*, vol. 23 (1978), pp. 405–28.

Epstein, James, 'Understanding the Cap of Liberty: Symbolic Practice and Social Conflict in Early Nineteenth-Century England', *Past and Present*, no. 122 (February 1989), pp. 78–91.

Ferguson, J. A., 'The Howes and their Press', *Journal of the Royal Australian Historical Society*, vol. 13 (1928), pp. 344–50.

Fiering, Norman S., 'The Transatlantic Republic of Letters: A Note on the Circulation of Learned Periodicals to Early Eighteenth-Century America', *William and Mary Quarterly*, series 3, vol. 33 (1976), pp. 642–60.

Fletcher, Brian H., 'The Hawkesbury Settlers and the Rum Rebellion', *Journal of the Royal Australian Historical Society*, vol. 54 (1968), pp. 217–37.

Fletcher, Brian, 'Grose, Paterson and the Settlement of the Hawkesbury, 1794–1795', *Journal of the Royal Australian Historical Society*, vol. 51 (1965), pp. 341–9.

Forbes, Thomas R., 'A Study of Old Bailey Sentences between 1729 and 1800', *Guildhall Studies in London History*, vol. 5 (1981), pp. 26–35.

Formigari, Lia, 'Language and Society in the Late Eighteenth Century', *Journal of the History of Ideas*, vol. 35 (1974), pp. 275–92.

Forster, H. C., '"Tyranny Opression and Fraud": Port Jackson, New South Wales, 1792–1794', *Journal of the Royal Australian Historical Society*, vol. 60 (1974), pp. 73–88.

Frost, Alan, '"As it were another America": English Ideas of the First Settlement in New South Wales at the End of the Eighteenth Century', *Eighteenth-Century Studies*, vol. 7 (1973–4), pp. 255–73.

Frost, Alan, 'Botany Bay: An Imperial Venture of the 1780s', *English Historical Review*, vol. 100 (1985), pp. 309–30.

Gallagher, J. E. ,'The Revolutionary Irish', *Push from the Bush*, no. 19 (April 1985), pp. 2–33.

Gilbert, Arthur N., 'Law and Honour among Eighteenth-Century British Army Officers', *Historical Journal*, vol. 19 (1976), pp. 75–87.

Gilbert, Arthur N., 'Military and Civilian Justice in Eighteenth-Century England: An Assessment', *Journal of British Studies*, vol. 17 (1978), pp. 41–65.

Gillen, Mollie, 'The Botany Bay Decision, 1786: Convicts not Empire', *English Historical Review*, vol. 97 (1982), pp. 740–66.

Goodin, Vernon W. E., 'Public Education in New South Wales before 1848', *Journal of the Royal Australian Historical Society*, vol. 36 (1950), in four parts, pp. 1–14, 65–108, 129–75, 177–210.

Goodman, Dena, 'Public Sphere and Private Life: Towards a Synthesis of Current Historiographical Approaches to the Old Regime', *History and Theory*, vol. 31 (1992), pp. 1–20.

Harden, J. David, 'Liberty Caps and Liberty Trees', *Past and Present*, no. 146 (February 1995), pp. 66–102.

Haskell, Thomas L., 'Capitalism and the Origins of the Humanitarian Sensibility', in two parts, *American Historical Review*, vol. 90 (1985), pp. 339–61, 547–66.

Hay, Douglas, 'War, Dearth and Theft in the Eighteenth Century: The Record of the English Courts', *Past and Present*, no. 95 (May 1982), pp. 117–60.

Hentzi, Gary, 'Sublime Moments and Social Authority in *Robinson Crusoe* and *A Journal of the Plague Year*', *Eighteenth-Century Studies*, vol. 26 (1992–3), pp. 419–34.

Hill, Christopher, 'Robinson Crusoe', *History Workshop*, issue 10 (Autumn 1980), pp. 6–24.

Hoppit, Julian, 'Reforming Britain's Weights and Measures, 1660–1824', *English Historical Review*, vol. 108 (1993), pp. 82–104.

Howe, Kerry, 'The Death of Cook: Exercises in Explanation', *Eighteenth-Century Life*, no. 18 (November 1994), pp. 198–211.

Humphries, Jane, 'Enclosures, Common Rights, and Women: The Proletarianization of Families in the Late Eighteenth and Early Nineteenth Centuries', *Journal of Economic History*, vol. 50 (1990), pp. 17–42.

Jose, Arthur, 'The "Barrington" Prologue', *Journal of the Royal Australian Historical Society*, vol. 13 (1928), pp. 292–4.

Kittay, Jeffrey, 'Utterance Unmoored: The Changing Interpretation of the Act of Writing in the European Middle Ages', *Language in Society*, vol. 17 (1988), pp. 209–30.

Koehler, Lyle, 'The Case of the American Jezebels: Anne Hutchinson and Female Agitation during the Years of Antinomian Turmoil, 1636–1640', *William and Mary Quarterly*, series 3, vol. 31 (1974), pp. 55–78.

Kupperman, Karen Ordahl, 'Apathy and Death in Early Jamestown', *Journal of American History*, vol. 66 (1979–80), pp. 24–40.

Laugero, Greg, 'Infrastructures of Enlightenment: Road-making, the Public Sphere, and the Emergence of Literature', *Eighteenth-Century Studies*, vol. 29 (1995), pp. 45–67.

Lloyd, Christopher, 'Cook and Scurvy', *Mariner's Mirror*, vol. 65 (1979), pp. 23–8.

Lowi, Theodore J., 'Risk and Rights in the History of American Governments', *Daedalus*, vol. 119 (1990), pp. 18–24.

MacDonagh, Oliver, 'Highbury and Chawton: Social Convergence in *Emma*', *Historical Studies*, vol. 18 (1978), pp. 37–51.

Marshall, P. J., 'Empire and Authority in the Later Eighteenth Century', *Journal of Imperial and Commonwealth History*. vol. 15 (1987), pp. 105–22.

Martin, Jed, 'Convict Transportation to Newfoundland in 1789', *Acadiensis*, vol. 5 (1975), pp. 84–99.

McGrath, Ann, 'The White Man's Looking Glass: Aboriginal–Colonial Gender Relations at Port Jackson', *Australian Historical Studies*, vol. 24 (1990), pp. 189–206.

Mellor, Anne K., 'Joanna Baillie and the Counter-Public Sphere', *Studies in Romanticism*, vol. 13 (1994), pp. 559–67.

Michals, Teresa, '"That Sole and Despotic Dominion": Slaves, Wives, and Game in Blackston's *Commentaries*', *Eighteenth-Century Studies*, vol. 27 (1993–4), pp. 195–216.

Miller, John, 'Public Opinion in Charles II's England', *History*, vol. 80 (1995), pp. 359–81.

Morgan, Edmund S., 'The First American Boom: Virginia 1618 to 1630', *William and Mary Quarterly*, series 3, vol. 28 (1971), pp. 169–98.

Parsons, T. G., 'Was John Boston's Pig a Political Martyr? The Reaction to Popular Radicalism in Early New South Wales', *Journal of the Royal Australian Historical Society*, vol. 71 (1985), pp. 163–76.

Patrick, Alison, 'Paper, Posters and People: Official Communication in France, 1789–1794', *Historical Studies*, vol. 18 (1978), pp. 1–23.

Penglase, Bethia, '1788: That Illiterate "Freight of Misery"?', *Journal of the Royal Australian Historical Society*, vol. 75 (1989), pp. 99–109.

Pert, J., 'William Gore, Provost Marshal: The Man and his Office', *Journal of the Royal Australian Historical Society*, vol. 68 (1982), pp. 181–92.

Porter, Andrew, 'Religion and Empire: British Experience in the Long Nineteenth Century, 1780–1914', *Journal of Imperial and Commonwealth History*, vol. 20 (1992), pp. 370–90.

Porter, Roy, 'Lay Medical Knowledge in the Eighteenth Century: The Evidence of the *Gentleman's Magazine*', *Medical History*, vol. 29 (1985), pp. 138–68.

Reay, Barry, 'The Context and Meaning of Popular Literacy: Some Evidence from Nineteenth-Century Rural England', *Past and Present*, no. 131 (May 1991), pp. 89–129.

Rediker, Marcus, 'Under the Banner of King Death': The Social World of Anglo-American Pirates, 1716 to 1726', *William and Mary Quarterly*, series 3, vol. 38 (1981), pp. 203–27.

Reece, R. H. W., 'Feasts and Blankets: The History of Early Attempts to Establish Relations with the Aborigines of New South Wales, 1814–1846', *Archaeology and Physical Anthropology in Oceania*, vol. 2 (1967), pp. 190–206.

Robbins, Caroline, 'Algernon Sidney's *Discourses Concerning Government*: Textbook of Revolution', *William and Mary Quarterly*, series 3, vol. 4 (1947), pp. 267–96.

Roberts, Michael, 'Sickles and Scythes: Women's Work and Men's Work at Harvest Time', *History Workshop*, issue 7 (Spring 1979), pp. 3–28.

Schmidt, F. H., 'Sold and Driven: Assignment of Convicts in Eighteenth-Century Virginia', *Push from the Bush*, no. 23 (October 1986), pp. 2–27.

Schofield, Roger, 'Dimensions of Illiteracy, 1750–1850', *Explorations in Economic History*, vol. 10 (1972–3), pp. 437–54.

Sharpe, J. A., '"Last Dying Speeches": Religion, Ideology and Public Execution in Seventeenth–Century England', *Past and Present*, no. 107 (May 1985), pp. 144–67.

Smithson, Michael, 'A Misunderstood Gift: The Annual Issue of Blankets to Aborigines in New South Wales 1826–48', *Push: A Journal of Early Australian Social History*, no. 30 (1992), pp. 73–108.

Statham, Pamela, 'A New Look at the New South Wales Corps, 1790–1810', *Australian Economic History Review*, vol. 30 (1990), pp. 43–63.

Steiner, E. E., 'Separating the Soldier from the Citizen: Ideology and Criticism of Corporal Punishment in the British Armies, 1790–1815', *Social History*, vol. 8 (1983), pp. 19–35.

Steppler, G. A., 'British Military Law, Discipline, and the Conduct of Regimental Courts Martial in the Later Eighteenth Century', *English Historical Review*, vol. 102 (October 1987), pp. 859–86.

Stone, Lawrence, 'Literacy and Education in England, 1640–1900', *Past and Present*, no. 42 (February 1969), pp. 69–139.

Sturma, Michael, 'Death and Ritual on the Gallows: Public Executions in the Australian Penal Colonies', *Omega*, vol. 17 (1986–7), pp. 89–100.

Whyte, W. Farmer, 'The Australian Stage – A Glimpse of the Past', *Journal of the Royal Australian Historical Society*, vol. 4 (1917), pp. 27–46.

Wilson, Kathleen, 'Inventing Revolution: 1688 and Eighteenth-Century Popular Politics', *Journal of British Studies*, vol. 28 (1989), pp. 349–86.

Wilson, Kathleen, 'Citizenship, Empire, and Modernity in the English Provinces, c. 1720–1790', *Eighteenth-Century Studies*, vol. 29 (1995), pp. 69–96.

Zuckerman, Arnold, 'Scurvy and the Ventilation of Ships in the Royal Navy: Samuel Sutton's Contribution', *Eighteenth-Century Studies*, vol. 10 (1976–7), pp. 222–34.

4. Unpublished Research

Atkinson, Alan, 'The Position of John Macarthur and his Family in New South Wales before 1842', MA thesis, Sydney University 1971.

Bullock, Steven C., 'The Ancient and Honorable Society: Freemasonry in America, 1736–1830', PhD thesis, Brown University 1986.

Clarke, C. P. R., 'Gibraltar as a British Possession till 1783', BLitt thesis, Oxford University 1934.

Fletcher, B. H., 'The Development of Small Scale Farming in New South Wales (excluding Norfolk Island) 1787 to 1803', MA thesis, Sydney University 1962.

Jarrett, J. D., 'The Bowood Circle, 1780–1793: Its Ideas and its Influence', BLitt thesis, Oxford University 1955.

McLeish, James, 'British Activities in Yucatan and on the Moskito Shore in the Eighteenth Century', MA thesis, London University 1926.

Roe, Michael, 'New South Wales under Governor King', MA thesis, Melbourne University 1956.

Thomas, Katherine M., '"Romulus of the Southern Pole [or] Superintendent of Pickpockets": A Biographical Appraisal of John Hunter R.N. (1737–1821)', BA Honours thesis, University of New England 1992.

Thompson, Gloria, 'Law and the Courts in New South Wales, 1788–92', research essay, University of New England 1992.

Index